Introduction to

This reprinted edition of Agnes Ja[...] ...glo-Saxon *Charters*, first published by the Cambridge University Press in 1939, forms part of a series of three volumes containing texts and translations, with commentary, of the corpus of surviving vernacular charters from Anglo-Saxon England. Robertson's *Charters* followed Florence Harmer's *Select English Historical Documents of the Ninth and Tenth Centuries* (Cambridge, 1914) and Dorothy Whitelock's *Anglo-Saxon Wills* (Cambridge, 1930). As explained in the introduction to the reprint of Harmer's volume, the series had been conceived by Hector Munro Chadwick, Elrington and Bosworth Professor of Anglo-Saxon in the University of Cambridge (1912–41); and it was not completed until the publication of Harmer's *Anglo-Saxon Writs* (Manchester, 1952), itself reprinted in 1989. A multi-volume edition of the entire corpus of charters – each volume of which presents the charters formerly preserved in the archives of a particular religious house (or group of houses) – is now in progress, published under the auspices of the British Academy–Royal Historical Society Joint Committee on Anglo-Saxon Charters (Oxford, 1973–). The new edition includes charters which have been brought to light in the past fifty years, and incorporates more detailed discussion of each text in its appropriate contexts.

Robertson's *Anglo-Saxon Charters*, here reprinted in its second edition (1956), contains a variety of texts ranging in (apparent) date from the mid-eighth to the end of the eleventh century. It contains examples of all of the recognizable types of document for which the vernacular is known to have been employed in Anglo-Saxon England (apart from the written instructions or notifications known as writs, all of which may be found in Harmer's *Anglo-Saxon Writs*), including royal diplomas, 'private' charters, leases, wills, and records generated by the processes of litigation. Over 70 of the 120 documents (exclusive of the two appendices) are drawn from the archives of three religious houses: Worcester (31), Christ Church Canterbury (22), and the Old Minster, Winchester (18). The rest are drawn from the archives of about 20 other houses, including Bury St Edmunds (7), Rochester (5), Sherborne (5), and Peterborough (4). Several were preserved as records entered on blank spaces or added leaves in gospel-books (Robertson, nos. 24, 62, 71, 78, 80, 84, 88–90, 95–6, 99), or in a *Liber Vitae* (nos. 60, 68 *bis*); about 30 are preserved on single sheets of parchment, written in script judged to be contemporary with the apparent date of the

[i]

text; and the rest as copies entered in cartularies, or in transcripts or printed editions derived from single sheets now lost.

The instruments of government known as royal diplomas, issued in the names of kings (generally at royal assemblies) from the seventh century to the end of the Anglo-Saxon period, granting land and privileges to religious houses or to individuals (ecclesiastical and lay), were composed all but invariably in Latin. The single surviving exception among charters preserved in what would appear to be their original form is a diploma of Berhtwulf, king of the Mercians (840–52), for his thegn Forthred (Harmer, no. 3); but of course there are complications. Royal diplomas in the vernacular are found throughout Robertson's volume (nos. 1–2, 8, 11–13, 23, 25, 30, 38, 45, 48, 50, 82, 85, 95, 118, 120), to which should now be added *StAlb* 1–2. All of them have to be approached with circumspection, and each must be judged in its own archival context. Some are probably English versions of texts drawn up in Latin; others were most likely composed in the vernacular, as part of the process by which certain religious houses provided themselves with a documented past. There is no reason to doubt that some of the transmitted texts may have originated in the tenth or eleventh century. Versions of a purported charter of King Æthelred, in Latin and English, refounding and endowing the church of Canterbury, were entered in a gospel-book at Canterbury in the first half of the eleventh century (Sawyer, no. 914). The question remains whether any such vernacular charters are genuine in this form. Of those in Robertson's volume, the case has been made for a vernacular diploma of King Eadred for his thegn Ælfsige Hunlafing, preserved only in a twelfth-century Peterborough cartulary (no. 30), adding another dimension to the special interest of the small group of mid-tenth century texts known as the 'alliterative' charters, to which it belongs. One should also refer in this connection to the suggestion that the vernacular version of King Edgar's charter for Ely (no. 48) was composed by Ælfric the homilist, which could bring the production of that text back to the late tenth or early eleventh century.

About 40 of the documents in Robertson's volume illustrate the widespread use of the vernacular for recording transactions or agreements which took place at levels below the level which for whatever reason required the production (i.e. the drafting and writing) of a new royal diploma, at a royal assembly, and its ceremonial transfer into the hands of the beneficiary. One imagines that in many cases an estate of bookland passed from one party to another by way of gift, purchase, exchange, or more complex agreement;

and where existing title-deeds would suffice, they would or should in theory have been transferred as part of the transaction. Vernacular records of such transactions appear to have been made, as a matter of course, at the assemblies where the transactions took place, in the presence of witnesses, and set down on single sheets of parchment; but we also find records of the same kind entered, when circumstances allowed, in gospel-books, *libri vitae*, and other special volumes. Several contain particular points of interest. A record of a grant by Ealdorman Æthelstan to Abingdon abbey, set in the context of an assembly at Abingdon, *c*. 930, probably originated some time later, but might reflect knowledge of pre-Conquest ceremonial (no. 22). A transfer of royal diplomas serving as title-deeds appears to lie behind the record of an exchange of lands witnessed by a select few at the court of King Eadwig (no. 31), and one also senses a diploma changing hands behind the record of a purchase of land issued at a shire meeting in Kent (no. 103). A record from the reign of King Edgar incorporates a review of the history of an estate at Ailsworth, Northants., which had been forfeited by a widow and her son for an act of witchcraft (itself punished by drowning at London Bridge); the land had been given by the king to one Ælfsige, the intended victim of the act of witchcraft, whose son Wulfstan exchanged it on a later occasion with Bishop Æthelwold, who gave it to Peterborough abbey (no. 37). We also encounter here some rare records from the distant north (nos. 60, 68). Two documents of much the same date (1014 x 1020), one from the west midlands and the other from east Kent, both drawn up in the form of chirographs, exemplify an early form of prenuptial agreement, and in their similarity appear to represent a class of text which might once have been widespread (nos. 76–7). Of special importance, from the reign of Edward the Confessor, is the record of the endowment by Earl Leofric and his wife Godgifu of the minster at Stow St Mary, Lincolnshire, which affords an unusually detailed view of the arrangements required when providing for the needs of the priests serving a religious house (no. 115).

About 30 of the documents in Robertson's volume are leases of church property to laymen. The majority of these leases are from the archives of the church of Worcester, associated above all with the name of Bishop Oswald (one is reproduced on the cover of this reprint), and as a group have to be set within the context of the even larger number of leases from Worcester drawn up in Latin. The use of both languages in the Worcester leases, without apparent significance of distinction (indeed, with admixture of Latin and English in Robertson, nos. 19, 35, 64), shows how these documents lay somewhere between Latin diplomas and the familiar forms of documentation in the vernacular. The leases also illustrate an aspect of land-holding which was probably more widespread on large ecclesiastical estates, in the tenth and eleventh centuries, than surviving documentation (whether in Latin or the vernacular) would suggest. The Worcester leases, in particular, are renowned for what they reveal about the changing composition of the community from the 960s to the 990s, and for what they represent in terms of the management of the Worcester estates in the tenth and eleventh centuries, symbolized by their preservation in the early eleventh-century cartulary associated with Wulfstan, bishop of Worcester and archbishop of York. They also led to all manner of difficulties in the troublous times which followed.

From the early ninth century onwards, it was evidently a common practice for persons needing to make a will to do so orally, in the presence of the requisite witnesses, and to have the substance of their intentions recorded in writing, for which as a matter of course the vernacular was used. There are five such wills in Robertson, each of which exemplifies a slightly different practice. The will of Æthelnoth, reeve at Eastry in Kent, and his wife Gænburg (no. 3), is extant in what seems to be its original form, on a sheet of parchment which begins with a *copy* of a Latin diploma (805 x 807) granting the land to Æthelnoth in the first place (as it happens, also preserved separately in its original form), and which continues in the same hand with the will of Æthelnoth and his wife (805 x 832). The will of Badanoth Beotting (no. 6), made in the mid-ninth century and extant in its original single-sheet form, is said in the text to have been one of two identical copies of the document, one to be retained by the church to which the reversion of the estate belonged, and the other by his wife and children for their lifetime. The will of Dunn (no. 9), copied in the twelfth-century *Textus Roffensis*, seems to have been preserved up to that point in close association with an earlier Latin diploma which served as Dunn's title-deed for the estate (c. 855); but it is not clear whether it was endorsed on the diploma, or written some time later on a separate strip of parchment. The will of Wulfgar (no. 26) was written, probably in the 930s, on a strip of parchment by a scribe found in another context entering manumissions in a gospel-book at the royal estate at Bedwyn in Wiltshire. The strip has been trimmed very closely along its top edge, as if to separate it from something above; and provisions including a grant of Ham, in Wiltshire, to the Old Minster, Winchester, were added seemingly as an afterthought on the dorse. The estate at Ham passed in time to the Old Minster; and the will, endorsed by a Winchester scribe, came to be stitched to the lower edge of an earlier Latin diploma by which Wulfgar had received the land from King Æthelstan in 931. The will of Æthelwyrd (no. 32) is essentially a statement of arrangements concerning a single estate in Kent, drawn up probably in the 950s, endorsed with a record of an agreement modifying the arrangement in the next generation. The wills of Æthelnoth, Badanoth and Æthelwyrd incorporate lists of witnesses; the wills of Dunn and Wulfgar do not. These five documents, dating from the ninth and from the earlier part of the tenth century, should be set beside the five wills from the same period edited in Harmer's volume (Harmer, nos. 2, 10–11, 20–1); all ten might then be compared as a group with the larger number of wills edited by Whitelock in 1930, which date from the later tenth and eleventh centuries, and which show in their own different ways how practices in the making and publication of wills continued to develop.

Another distinctive set of documents contained in Robertson's volume comprises 14 records generated by processes of litigation (nos. 4–5, 41, 44, 49, 59, 63, 66, 69, 78, 83, 91, 102, 105), complementing the five documents of the same kind found among those edited by Harmer in 1914 (Harmer, nos. 7, 14–15, 18 and 23). Distinctions can and should be made, in such cases, between documents drawn up and submitted as evidence for *use* in impending litigation concerning the estate in question, and documents which represent records of the *outcome* of stages in the legal process. Some of the statements about the history of a particular estate belong with the 'Fonthill Letter' (Harmer, no. 18), and with Queen Eadgifu's declaration about Cooling, Kent (Harmer, no. 23), in the first of these groups. A statement concerning land at Wouldham, Kent (Robertson, no. 41), and a statement concerning Bromley and Fawkham, Kent (no. 59), represent efforts made by bishops of Rochester to recover lands lost in times of trouble; while a claim made on behalf of Archbishop Dunstan to land at Sunbury, Middlesex, and at Send, Surrey (no. 44), preserved at Westminster, and an overtly partisan review of the history of Sandwich, Kent (no. 91), from Christ Church, Canterbury, reflect similar concerns at other houses. The documents which record outcomes of litigation include, as one might expect, several which emanated from shire-meetings. Among them, one of the most interesting is the record of proceedings at a shire-meeting held at Cuckamsley in Berkshire (no. 66): interesting not least for all it reveals about the conduct of litigation in the late tenth century (first at a royal assembly, then at a shire-meeting, to which king sent 'his seal' and others their written declarations), yet no less for its survival in its original form, in this case as the top part of a chirograph (divided by letters which when re-constituted and read alternately would give the legend CIROGRAFVM PLETVM EST), preserved (like the Fonthill Letter) in the archives of the archbishop. A rather different procedure lies behind the record of a shire-meeting held at Aylton in Herefordshire, which was entered in a gospel-book at St Æthelberht's minster at Hereford (no. 78). Analagous records emanating from royal assemblies are rarer than records from shire-meetings, at least in their own right. A record of a case which led to forfeiture of property lies not far behind the information recorded in no. 37 (mentioned above), and records of the same kind were occasionally incorporated in royal diplomas, notably the account of the crimes of Wulfbald (not to mention his widow and son), which led to two judgements in assemblies at London, one before and one after his death (no. 63).

A 'miscellaneous' category, comprising 11 records in Robertson's main series (nos. 24, 39–40, 47, 52, 54, 72, 84, 104, 109–10), and extending naturally from there to include many of the texts in her two appendices, illustrates most effectively how the vernacular was used for a wide variety of other purposes (formal and informal) in connection with lands, rights, customs, and services, as well as for inventories, booklists, and registers of gifts. The cumulative effect, as if it were any surprise, is to reinforce one's appreciation of how writing and record-keeping pervaded English government and society in the ninth, tenth and eleventh centuries, and to suggest how this deep-rooted experience in the use of the written word, whether in Latin or in English, lies not far behind the procedures and products of the Domesday survey. Among these miscellaneous records, we find three of great significance for our understanding of defence against viking invaders: a record for the provision of services for the maintenance of the bridge over the river Medway at Rochester (no. 52), a record for the provision of 'shipmen' from the estates of St Paul's (no. 72), and the 'Burghal Hidage' (Appendix II, no. 1). There are various forms of estate survey, all of interest for the light they cast on aspects of estate management at different religious houses; and for an understanding of the circumstances in which such records were preserved, and in some cases have survived (by the skin of their teeth), one can turn to the remarkable set of notes relating to the management of the estates of Ely abbey in the first half of the eleventh century (Appendix II, no. 9). For more recent editions of the lists of books in Robertson, nos. 39, 104, Appendix I, no. 1, and Appendix II, nos. 2 and 5–7, see Michael Lapidge, 'Surviving booklists from Anglo-Saxon England', *Learning and Literature in Anglo-Saxon England*, ed. M. Lapidge and H. Gneuss (Cambridge, 1985), pp. 33–89.

One should stress finally how records in Latin and records in the vernacular are seen in Robertson's collection to have been manifestations of one and the same culture of 'pragmatic literacy' (signifying the use of the written word for purposes of government and administration) in Anglo-Saxon England. A considerable number of them exemplify the practice of producing documents in two or more copies, to be kept by different parties in the interests of security, and known as chirographs (from the word often found written between the copies of a text on a single sheet of parchment, which was then cut through so that the separate parts could be matched to each other should the need arise). Variations on this practice are attested in certain kinds of Latin document (not including royal diplomas) from the early ninth century, and in vernacular documents from the mid-ninth century, as if they emanated from the same culture; though it was not until the latter part of the tenth century that the use of the chirograph became commonplace, as if in accordance with a code of good practice. Above all, one soon begins to understand from these documents how the Latin diplomas and the vernacular records worked together. For example, three of the vernacular records mentioned above (Robertson, nos. 41, 59, 69) form part of a veritable dossier of documentation reflecting activity at Rochester in the late tenth century, which also includes a will (Whitelock, no. 11) and several royal diplomas (e.g. Sawyer, nos. 671, 864, 885, 893) from the same archive.

A guide to scholarly discussion of each document is provided in the revised and updated version of Peter Sawyer's *Anglo-Saxon Charters: an Annotated List and Bibliography*, available online in the form of the 'Electronic Sawyer' (see below).

SIMON KEYNES
Elrington and Bosworth Professor of Anglo-Saxon
University of Cambridge

CONCORDANCE

In the table below, each document in Robertson's *Anglo-Saxon Charters* is assigned its number in Peter Sawyer's *Anglo-Saxon Charters: a Revised List and Bibliography* (1968), available online in a revised and updated form at www.esawyer.org.uk (the 'Electronic Sawyer'). The number of a charter in the relevant volume of the new edition of the corpus, published under the auspices of the British Academy, is also given where possible.

Abbreviations

Abing	*Charters of Abingdon Abbey*, ed. S. E. Kelly, 2 vols., AS Charters 7–8 (Oxford, 2000–1)
Bath	*Charters of Bath and Wells*, ed. S. E. Kelly, AS Charters 13 (Oxford, 2007)
Burt	*Charters of Burton Abbey*, ed. P. H. Sawyer, AS Charters 2 (London, 1979)
BuryStE	*Charters of Bury St Edmunds*, ed. Katie Lowe and Sarah Foot, AS Charters (forthcoming)
CantCC	*Charters of Christ Church, Canterbury*, ed. Nicholas Brooks and S. E. Kelly, 3 vols., AS Charters (forthcoming)
CantStA	*Charters of St Augustine's Abbey Canterbury*, ed. S. E. Kelly, AS Charters 4 (Oxford, 1995)
LondStP	*Charters of St Paul's, London*, ed. S. E. Kelly, AS Charters 10 (Oxford, 2004)
North	*Charters of Northern Houses*, ed. D. A. Woodman (forthcoming)
Pet	*Charters of Peterborough*, ed. S. E. Kelly, AS Charters 14 (Oxford, 2009)
Roch	*Charters of Rochester*, ed. A. Campbell, AS Charters 1 (London, 1973)
Shaft	*Charters of Shaftesbury Abbey*, ed. S. E. Kelly, AS Charters 5 (Oxford, 1996)
Sherb	*Charters of Sherborne*, ed. M. A. O'Donovan, AS Charters 3 (London, 1988)
StAlb	*Charters of St Albans*, ed. Julia Crick, AS Charters 12 (Oxford, 2007)
WinchNM	*Charters of the New Minster, Winchester*, ed. Sean Miller, AS Charters 9 (Oxford, 2001)
WinchOM	*Charters of the Old Minster, Winchester*, ed. A. R. Rumble (forthcoming)

Robertson	Sawyer	Archive	Summary of content
1	98	Worcester	charter of King Æthelbald for Worcester
2	126	Worcester	charter of King Offa for Worcester
3	1500	CantCC 39a	will of Æthelnoth and his wife Gænburg
4	1432	Worcester	part of a composite record concerning land in Worcs.
5	1437	Worcester	account of an oath taken in settlement of a dispute
6	1510	CantCC 78	will of Badanoth Beotting
7	1440	Pet 9	agreement between Medeshamstede and Wulfred
8	313	WinchOM	charter of King Æthelwulf (decimation)
9	1514	Roch 23	will of Dunn
10	328	CantCC 83	charter of King Æthelberht, endorsement
11	333	Sherb 6	charter of King Æthelberht
12	342	Shaft 6	charter of King Æthelred
13	357	Shaft 7	charter of King Alfred
14	1275	WinchOM	lease of land by Bp Ealhferth
15	1287	WinchOM	lease of land by Bp Denewulf
16	1283	Worcester	lease of land by Bp Wærferth
17	1513	WinchOM	bequest by Ceolwynn to Winchester
18	1281	Worcester	lease of land by Bp Wærferth
19	1280	Worcester	lease of land by Bp Wærferth
20	385	WinchOM	lease of land by King Edward
21	1289	Worcester	grant by Bp Wilfrid to Worcester
22	1208	Abing 28	grant by Æthelstan senator
23	391	Milton	charter of King Æthelstan for Milton
24		Durham	inscription recording gift to St Cuthbert
25	427	WinchOM	charter of King Æthelstan for Winchester
26	1533	WinchOM	will of Wulfgar
27	1509	WinchNM 11	bequest by Alfred to the New Minster
28	1418	WinchNM 14	grant by Æthelnoth to the New Minster
29	1419	WinchNM 16	grant by Eadulf to the New Minster
30	566	Pet 11	charter of King Eadred
31	1292	Abing 76	agreement between Bp Brihthelm and Ab Æthelwold
32	1506	CantCC 121	will of Æthelwyrd
33	693	WinchOM	lease of land by Bp Brihthelm
34	1299	Worcester	lease of land by Bp Oswald
35	1303	Worcester	lease of land by Bp Oswald (Latin and English)
36	1305	Worcester	lease of land by Bp Oswald
37	1377	Pet 17	record of an exchange of land, and of a gift to Peterb.
38	817	WinchOM	charter of King Edgar
39	1448	Pet 29	records of gifts of Bp Æthelwold to Medeshamstead

Robertson	Sawyer	Archive	Summary of content
40		Pet 30	lists of sureties for Peterborough estates
41	1458	Roch 34	account of Abp Dunstan's acquisition of Wouldham
42	1309	Worcester	lease of land by Bp Oswald
43	1310	Worcester	lease of land by Bp Oswald
44	1447	Westminster	account of land at Send and Sudbury
45	806	WinchOM	charter of King Edgar for Winchester
46	1326	Worcester	lease of land by Bp Oswald
47	1452	Exeter	list of sureties for an estate in Devon
48	779	Ely	charter of King Edgar for Ely
49	1449	WinchOM	record of the adjustment of boundaries
50	813	Sherb 10	charter of King Edgar for Sherborne
51	1216	Abing 115	record of Abbot Osgar's acquisition of land in Berks.
52		Rochester	record of services for Rochester bridge
53	1376	WinchOM	record of an exchange of land in Winchester
54	1453	North 6	Abp Oswald's memorandum on estates of York
55	1332	Worcester	lease of land by Abp Oswald
56	1373	Worcester	lease of land by Abp Oswald
57	1374	Worcester	lease of land by Abp Oswald
58	1372	Worcester	lease of land by Abp Oswald
59	1457	Roch 36	statement of Rochester's claim to land at Bromley
60	1660	North 18	record of a grant by Earl Thored to St Cuthbert's
61	1369	Worcester	lease of land by Abp Oswald
62	1455	CantStA 31	agreement between Abbot Wulfric and Ealdred
63	877	WinchNM 31	account of the crimes of Wulfbald and of his widow
64	1363	Worcester	lease of land by Abp Oswald (Latin and English)
65	1362	Worcester	lease of land by Abp Oswald
66	1454	CantCC 133	outcome of litigation at a shire-court of Berks.
67	1366	Worcester	lease of land by Abp Oswald
68	1659	North 19	record of a grant by Earl Northman to St Cuthbert's
68	1661	North 20	record of a grant by Ulfcetel to St Cuthbert's
69	1456	Roch 37	outcome of litigation at a shire-court in Kent
70	1420	WinchNM 32	lease of land by Abbot Ælfsige
71		Ely	record of a grant by Ælfhelm to his goldsmith
72		LondStP 25	note on provision of shipmen from specified estates
73	1219	BuryStE	record of a grant by Ulfcetel to St Edmund's
74	1422	Sherb 14	lease of land by the community at Sherborne
75	1220	CantCC 148	grant of land by Godwine to Leofwine the Red
76	1459	Worcester	record of a marriage agreement
77	1461	CantCC 149	record of a marriage agreement

Robertson	Sawyer	Archive	Summary of content
78	1462	Hereford	outcome of litigation at a shire-court in Herefordshire
79	1421	Worcester	lease of land by the community at Worcester
80	1464	CantCC 162	agreement between Abp Æthelnoth and Toki
81	1423	Worcester	lease of land by Abbot Ælfweard
82	959	CantCC 151a	charter of King Cnut for Christ Church
83	1460	Worcester	outcome of litigation at a shire-court in Worcs.
84		North 7	survey of estates at Sherburn, Otley and Ripon
85	981	CantCC 154	charter of King Cnut for Christ Church
86	1465	CantCC 153	agreement between Eadsige and Christ Church
87	1399	Worcester	lease of land by Bp Brihtheah
88	1222	CantCC 159	record of a grant by Thored
89	1389	CantCC 160	record of a grant by Abp Æthelnoth
90	1466	CantCC 163	agreement between Abp Eadsige and Toki
91	1467	CantCC 164	statement about the history of an estate in Kent
92	1224	BuryStE	agreement between Stigand and his priest Ælfgar
93	1225	BuryStE	record of a grant by Thurkytel to St Edmund's
94	1394	Worcester	lease of land by Bp Lyfing
95	1047	CantCC 181	charter of King Edward for Christ Church
96	1229	CantCC 175	record of a grant by King Cnut and Ælfgifu to Ch.Ch.
97	1468	BuryStE	agreement between Æthelmær and Abbot Ufi
98	1391	WinchOM	agreement between Bp Ælfwine and Osgod
99	1469	Hereford	record of Leofwine's purchase of land from Eadric
100	1470	BuryStE	agreement between Wulfgeat and Bury St Edmunds
101	1471	CantCC 170	agreement between Æthelric and Abp Eadsige
102	1472	CantCC 169	outcome of litigation involving Earl Godwine in Kent
103	1473	CantCC 171	record of Godric's purchase of land
104		BuryStE	composite survey of lands, etc., of Bury St Edmunds
105	1474	Sherb 17	outcome of litigation at a shire-court in Devon
106	1402	WinchOM	lease of land by Bp Stigand and the Old Minster
107	1403	WinchOM	lease of land by Bp Stigand and the Old Minster
108	1400	CantCC 172	record of a grant by Abp Eadsige
109	1555	Bath 24	survey of the estate at Tidenham, Gloucs.
110	359	WinchOM	survey of the estate at Hurstbourne Priors, Hants.
111	1409	Worcester	lease of land by Bp Ealdred
112	1406	Worcester	lease of land by Bp Ealdred
113	1232	Worcester	record of a grant by Earl Leofric and his wife
114	1476	WinchOM	agreement between Wulfweard and OMW
115	1478	Eynsham	record of the endowment of Stow St Mary
116	1234	CantCC 183	agreement between Brihtmær and Abp Stigand

Robertson	Sawyer	Archive	Summary of content
117	1426	*Bath* 23	lease of land by Abbot Ælfwig to Abp Stigand
118	1062	*WinchOM*	charter of King Edward for the Old Minster, Winch.
119		*BuryStE*	agreement with Ordric, cellarer of St Edmund's
120	1032	*Sherb* 22	charter of King Edward (for Horton)
		Appendix I: Post-Conquest Documents	
1		Exeter	gifts of Bishop Leofric to Exeter
2		Durham	lease by Walcher, bp of Durham
3		Peterborough	the 'Northamptonshire Geld Roll'
4		*WinchOM*	dues pertaining to Taunton, Somerset
5		London St P	dues pertaining to Lambourne, Berkshire
6		Worcester	payments by Worcester to King William
		Appendix II: Miscellaneous Documents (undated)	
1			the 'Burghal Hidage'
2		York	inventory of church goods (Sherburn-in-Elmet)
3		Bury St Ed	inventory of farm goods (Bury St Edmunds)
4		Durham	inventory of church goods (Durham)
5		Worcester	list of books (Worcester)
6		Cant St Aug	list of books (Canterbury, St Augustine's)
7		Bury St Ed	list of books (Bury St Edmunds)
8		Bury St Ed	fragment, on funeral arrangements
9		Ely	Ely farming memoranda

CAMBRIDGE STUDIES
IN ENGLISH LEGAL HISTORY

General Editor

H. A. HOLLOND, LL.M.
Vice-Master of Trinity College, Cambridge;
Emeritus Professor of English Law in
the University of Cambridge

ANGLO-SAXON CHARTERS

Edited
with Translation and Notes
by

A. J. ROBERTSON, M.A., Ph.D.

*Reader in English Language, University of Aberdeen;
sometime Pfeiffer Research Fellow of Girton College,
Cambridge*

CAMBRIDGE
AT THE UNIVERSITY PRESS
1956

CAMBRIDGE UNIVERSITY PRESS
Cambridge, New York, Melbourne, Madrid, Cape Town, Singapore,
São Paulo, Delhi, Dubai, Tokyo

Cambridge University Press
The Edinburgh Building, Cambridge CB2 8RU, UK

Published in the United States of America by Cambridge University Press, New York

www.cambridge.org
Information on this title: www.cambridge.org/9780521178327

© Cambridge University Press 1939

This publication is in copyright. Subject to statutory exception
and to the provisions of relevant collective licensing agreements,
no reproduction of any part may take place without the written
permission of Cambridge University Press.

First edition 1939
Second edition 1956
This digitally printed version 2009

A catalogue record for this publication is available from the British Library

ISBN 978-0-521-17832-7 Paperback

Cambridge University Press has no responsibility for the persistence or
accuracy of URLs for external or third-party internet websites referred to in
this publication, and does not guarantee that any content on such websites is,
or will remain, accurate or appropriate.

CONTENTS

	A Note by the former General Editor . . . *page*	xiii
	Preface	xix
	List of Abbreviations	xxvi
I	Remission of dues on two ships	2
II	Grant of land by King Offa to Worcester . .	2
III	The will of Æthelnoth and Gænburg . . .	4
IV	King Ceolwulf and Bromsgrove	6
V	Lawsuit about wood-pasture	8
VI	The will of Badanoth Beotting	10
VII	Agreement between Ceolred, Abbot of Peterborough, and Wulfred	12
VIII	Grant of land by King Æthelwulf to the Old Minster, Winchester	14
IX	Grant in reversion to Rochester	14
X	Summary of a Latin charter	16
XI	Charter of King Æthelbert to Sherborne . .	16
XII	Grant of land by King Æthelred I to Earl Ælfstan	22
XIII	Bequest of King Alfred to Shaftesbury. . .	24
XIV	Lease of land by Ealhferth, Bishop of Winchester	26
XV	Lease of land by Denewulf, Bishop of Winchester	28
XVI	Lease of land by Werfrith, Bishop of Worcester, to Cyneswith	28
XVII	Bequest of Ceolwin to Winchester . . .	30
XVIII	Lease of land by Werfrith, Bishop of Worcester, to Wulfsige	34
XIX	Lease of lands by Werfrith, Bishop of Worcester, to Æthelred and Æthelflæd	34
XX	Lease of land to Denewulf, Bishop of Winchester	38
XXI	Grant of land by Wilfrith, Bishop of Worcester .	42
XXII	Grant of land by Earl Æthelstan to Abingdon .	44

CONTENTS

XXIII	Charter of King Æthelstan to Milton Abbey, Dorset	page 44
XXIV	Grant of a book by King Æthelstan to St Cuthbert's	48
XXV	Grant of lands by King Æthelstan to the Old Minster, Winchester	48
XXVI	The will of Wulfgar	52
XXVII	Grant of land in reversion to the New Minster, Winchester	54
XXVIII	Grant of land to the New Minster, Winchester, by Æthelnoth	54
XXIX	Grant of land to the New Minster and the Nunnery, Winchester	54
XXX	Grant of land by King Edred to Ælfsige Hunlafing	56
XXXI	Exchange of lands between Brihthelm, Bishop of Wells, and Æthelwold, Abbot of Abingdon	58
XXXII	The will of Æthelwyrd	58
XXXIII	Lease of land by Brihthelm, Bishop of Winchester	62
XXXIV	Lease of land by Oswald, Bishop of Worcester, to Æthelm	62
XXXV	Lease of land by Oswald, Bishop of Worcester, to Ælfric	64
XXXVI	Lease of land by Oswald, Bishop of Worcester, to Æthelstan	66
XXXVII	Exchange of lands between Æthelwold, Bishop of Winchester, and Wulfstan Uccea	68
XXXVIII	Renewal of the freedom of Chilcomb by King Edgar	68
XXXIX	The gifts of Bishop Æthelwold to Peterborough	72
XL	List of sureties for Peterborough estates	74
XLI	History of the estate of Wouldham, Kent	84
XLII	Lease of land by Oswald, Bishop of Worcester, to Ælfhild	86

CONTENTS

XLIII	Lease of land by Oswald, Bishop of Worcester, to Eadric	page 88
XLIV	History of the estates of Sunbury and Send .	90
XLV	Renewal of the freedom of Taunton by King Edgar	92
XLVI	Lease of land by Oswald, Bishop of Worcester, to Osulf	96
XLVII	List of sureties for a Devonshire estate . .	98
XLVIII	Charter of King Edgar to Ely	98
XLIX	Adjustment of the boundaries between the monasteries in Winchester	102
L	Grant of land by King Edgar to Sherborne .	104
LI	Purchase of an estate by Osgar, Abbot of Abingdon	106
LII	List of estates liable for work on Rochester Bridge	106
LIII	Exchange of lands between Æthelwold, Bishop of Winchester, and Ælfwine	110
LIV	Statement by Oswald, Archbishop of York, regarding church lands in Northumbria . .	110
LV	Lease of land by Oswald, Archbishop of York and Bishop of Worcester, to Æthelwold . .	114
LVI	Lease of land by Oswald, Archbishop of York and Bishop of Worcester, to Wulfgeat . .	116
LVII	Lease of land by Oswald, Archbishop of York and Bishop of Worcester, to Wulfheah . .	118
LVIII	Lease of land by Oswald, Archbishop of York and Bishop of Worcester, to Wulfgar . .	120
LIX	History of the estates of Bromley and Fawkham, Kent	122
LX	Grant of lands by Earl Thored to St Cuthbert's	124
LXI	Lease of land by Oswald, Archbishop of York and Bishop of Worcester, to Goding . .	124
LXII	Agreement between Wulfric, Abbot of St Augustine's, and Ealdred	128
LXIII	The crimes and forfeitures of Wulfbold . .	128

CONTENTS

LXIV	Lease of land by Oswald, Archbishop of York and Bishop of Worcester, to Beornheah and Brihtstan . . . . *page* 130
LXV	Lease of land by Oswald, Archbishop of York and Bishop of Worcester, to Æthelmær . .	134
LXVI	Record of a lawsuit between Wynflæd and Leofwine	136
LXVII	Lease of land by Oswald, Archbishop of York and Bishop of Worcester, to Eadric . .	138
LXVIII	Two grants of land to St Cuthbert's . .	140
LXIX	Lawsuit about the estate of Snodland, Kent .	140
LXX	Lease of land by the abbot and the community at the New Minster, Winchester, to Wulfmær	142
LXXI	Grant of land by Ælfhelm to his goldsmith .	144
LXXII	List of the contributions of men required for manning a ship	144
LXXIII	Grant of lands by Ulfketel to Bury St Edmunds	146
LXXIV	Lease of land to Edmund the Ætheling by the community at Sherborne	146
LXXV	Grant of swine-pasture in Kent . . .	148
LXXVI	A Worcestershire marriage agreement . .	148
LXXVII	A Kentish marriage agreement . . .	150
LXXVIII	Account of a Herefordshire lawsuit . .	150
LXXIX	Agreement between the community at Worcester and Fulder	154
LXXX	Agreement between Archbishop Æthelnoth and Toki	154
LXXXI	Lease of land by Abbot Ælfweard and the community at Evesham to Æthelmær . .	156
LXXXII	Charter of Cnut to Christchurch, Canterbury	158
LXXXIII	Lawsuit about a Worcestershire estate . .	162
LXXXIV	Types of tenure among church lands in Yorkshire	164
LXXXV	Grant of land by King Cnut to Christchurch, Canterbury	168

CONTENTS

LXXXVI	Grant of lands by Eadsige to Christchurch, Canterbury . . . . *page*	170
LXXXVII	Lease of land by Brihtheah, Bishop of Worcester, to Wulfmær	172
LXXXVIII	Grant of land by Thored to Christchurch, Canterbury	172
LXXXIX	Grant of land by Archbishop Æthelnoth to Christchurch, Canterbury	174
XC	Agreement between Archbishop Eadsige and Toki	174
XCI	Harold Harefoot and Sandwich . . .	174
XCII	Grant in reversion to Bury St Edmunds by Stigand	178
XCIII	Grant of lands by Thurketel to Bury St Edmunds	178
XCIV	Lease of land by Lyfing, Bishop of Worcester, to Æthelric	180
XCV	Charter of Edward the Confessor to Christchurch, Canterbury	180
XCVI	Record of the grant of an estate to Christchurch, Canterbury	182
XCVII	Agreement between Ufi, Abbot of Bury St Edmunds, and Æthelmær . . .	184
XCVIII	Lease of land by Ælfwine, Bishop of Winchester, to Osgod	184
XCIX	Purchase of an estate in Herefordshire . .	186
C	Agreement between the Abbot of Bury St Edmunds and Wulfgeat	186
CI	Agreement between Archbishop Eadsige and Æthelric	188
CII	Agreement between Ælfstan, Abbot of St Augustine's, and the priest Leofwine . .	190
CIII	Purchase of an estate in Kent . . .	192
CIV	Notes with regard to food-rents, charitable gifts, etc. from Bury St Edmunds . .	192

CONTENTS

CV	Agreement between the bishop and community at Sherborne and Care, Toki's son	*page* 200
CVI	Lease of land by Stigand, Bishop of Winchester, to Æthelmær	202
CVII	Lease of land by Stigand, Bishop of Winchester, to Wulfric	202
CVIII	Grant of land by Archbishop Eadsige to St Augustine's	204
CIX	Survey of the manor of Tidenham, Gloucestershire	204
CX	Services and dues rendered at Hurstbourne Priors, Hampshire	206
CXI	Lease of land by Ealdred, Bishop of Worcester, to Wulfgeat	208
CXII	Lease of land by Ealdred, Bishop of Worcester, to Æthelstan the Fat	208
CXIII	Grant of land to Worcester by Leofric, Earl of Mercia, and his wife	210
CXIV	Agreement between the Old Minster, Winchester, and Wulfweard the White	212
CXV	Endowment of Stow St Mary by Earl Leofric and Godgifu	212
CXVI	Grant by Brihtmær of Gracechurch to Christchurch, Canterbury	216
CXVII	Lease of land by the abbot and the community at Bath to Archbishop Stigand	216
CXVIII	Alleged confirmation by Edward the Confessor of a grant by Queen Ælfgifu Emma to the Old Minster, Winchester	218
CXIX	Agreement with Ordric the cellarer at Bury St Edmunds	220
CXX	Charter of Edward the Confessor to Horton Abbey	220

CONTENTS

Appendix I. Post-Conquest Documents

    I The gifts of Bishop Leofric to Exeter   *page* 226

   II Lease of lands by Walcher, Bishop of Durham, to Ealdgyth 230

  III The Northamptonshire Geld Roll 230

  IV Record of the dues pertaining to Taunton . . 236

   V Record of the dues rendered to the church at Lambourn 240

  VI Payments made by the church of Worcester to William I 242

Appendix II. Miscellaneous Documents (undated)

    I The Burghal hidage 246

   II Inventory of church goods at Sherburn-in-Elmet . 248

  III Fragment of an inventory from a Bury St Edmunds MS. 248

  IV Inventory from a Durham MS. 250

   V List of Worcester (?) books 250

  VI List of books from St Augustine's, Canterbury . 250

 VII List of books from a MS. in the Bodleian Library, Oxford 250

VIII Fragment of a will from Bury St Edmunds . . 252

  IX Assignments of property to Thorney Abbey . . 252

Notes 259

Index Nominum 507

Index Locorum 527

Index Rerum 544

A NOTE BY THE FORMER GENERAL EDITOR
ON ANGLO-SAXON DOCUMENTS

In the latter part of the nineteenth century Maitland and other prominent writers on our early social and legal institutions stressed the importance of forming a new *Corpus* of pre-Norman documents based on a re-examination of the manuscript-materials by scholars who were not only trained as philologists, historians, and lawyers, but also practised in modern methods of textual research. Although this project embraced the Latin documents as well as those written in Anglo-Saxon, as yet, however, only vernacular texts have been published in new editions. The *Crawford Collection of Early Charters and Documents* (1895), under the editorship of Napier and Stevenson, has been followed by other collections of Anglo-Saxon documents, chiefly Miss Harmer's *Select English Historical Documents of the Ninth and Tenth Centuries* (1914) and Miss Whitelock's *Anglo-Saxon Wills* (1930). Miss Robertson's *Anglo-Saxon Charters*, which now makes its appearance as the latest contribution to a notable series, will be followed in due course by the publication of a collection of Anglo-Saxon writs, under the editorship of Miss Harmer.

The original indebtedness of scholars to Miss Robertson's skill and learning as an editor of texts through the publication of her *Laws of the Kings of England from Edmund to Henry I* (1925) has now been vastly increased by the gift of her *Anglo-Saxon Charters*. Both by her provision of an accurate and reliable text of many vernacular documents and by the wealth of information which she has embodied in her many notes on the documents Miss Robertson has materially advanced the historical study of pre-Norman times. Nor has the value of her work to all students of early English history been lessened by the inclusion of a few post-Conquest documents written in Anglo-Saxon.

In explanation of the documents in her collection Miss Robertson has made use of other contemporary sources, especially the laws and the Latin charters; and by following this method she has produced fresh and convincing proof of the fact, already well-known to all historians of the pre-Norman age, that the student of documents in Anglo-Saxon must also devote his attention to those in Latin. Not only from the view-point of diplomatic study, but in the labour of searching for historical truth in general, the two groups of documents supplement each other in an amazing, and often unexpected, manner. With the approaching completion of the vernacular part of a modern *Corpus* of Anglo-Saxon documents, the present seems the appropriate time in which to begin the preparation of a new *Codex Diplomaticus* of all the charters and other documents in Latin. Valuable as they are, the collections of Kemble (1839–1848), Thorpe (1865), Earle (1888), and Birch (1885–1893) all require an elaborate revision in compliance with the higher standards of textual criticism and historical accuracy which characterize present-day scholarship. The Latin documents are in fact in need of an editor who will bring to his task the same devotion, skill, and learning which Liebermann spent upon the Anglo-Saxon laws and the Anglo-Norman law-books.

Following the usage of English scholars, Miss Robertson has described as "charters" all the miscellaneous documents which she has collected and edited. From the view-point of the science of diplomatic these documents are, however, of varied character. Most of them are private documents; comparatively few are of royal origin. For the royal documents, and also for many that are private, the Roman term *diploma* may not be inappropriate; for, although this word was adopted by the humanists of the Renaissance as an indication of kingly instruments, its meaning was gradually so extended by the usage of scholars that it came to include most documents of the Middle Ages. Certain of these royal and private diplomas of the Anglo-Saxon age are at the same time "charters", or *cartae*, in the narrower and more technical meaning of that term. In the latter sense the royal charter, or *carta*, begins with a solemn invocation of the Triune God and contains no salutation of mortals; it declares, if it be a royal land-charter, that the King grants, has granted, or will grant, certain land to a certain person; and it ends with the "signatures" and the names of the King and the witnesses. The royal charter in this technical sense, a document confirmed with the sign of Christ's Holy Cross, is to be sharply distinguished from the royal writ, a document which contains no invocation, begins with a salutation, and states in the past tense that the King has made a certain grant to a certain person. Although charters, or *cartae*, in this special and technical sense, are to be found among the vernacular texts in Miss Robertson's collection, a far larger number of these documents are *notitiae*, or purely evidential writings, in contradistinction to *cartae*, which are both the confirmation and the evidence of audible and visible juridical acts. Included among the *notitiae* are "declarations" (*geswutelunga*), chirographs, and entries in Gospel Books. Some of the other documents in the present collection were also written *memoriae causa*. They recount the history of certain estates or of litigation in regard to lands; or they present other facts of interest or importance to men of the time.

Miss Robertson's book not only furnishes material for a study of all these several types of documents from the view-point of diplomatic, but it also enables the reader to estimate the value of the documents as historical evidence by providing him with information on matters other than diplomatic form. Both the date and the nature of the manuscript in which a document appears have significance in the formation of a judgment as to the evidential value of that document. In the case of documents derived from cartularies it is especially important, moreover, to determine the question as to the reliance that can be placed upon the cartularies themselves. The question as to whether a document is genuine or a forgery must always be raised. In the solution of these and many other manuscript-problems concerning the documents in the present collection Miss Robertson's learned notes are indispensable.

For the historical study of the early laws of England these vernacular documents possess special value. Some of them deal with the acts of the King, such as his grants of land, while many others are concerned with the juridical acts of lay and ecclesiastical persons. Some documents are the evidence of contracts and wills; others relate to gifts, exchanges, sales, gages, and leases of land. By throwing light upon the nature of all these legal transactions the documents disclose to us at the same time many of the rules of the unwritten customary law in regard to them. Although this evidence of legal history furnished by Miss Robertson's collection is most valuable, it needs, however, the supplementation to be derived from that larger stock of proof contained in other contemporary sources, such as the laws, the legal tracts, and the vernacular and Latin documents that have been collected and edited by other scholars.

To gain a clear perception of the nature and purport of the miscellaneous documents in Miss Robertson's collection is far from an easy task; it is, in fact, one of great difficulty and complexity requiring infinite patience. That task confronts, however, the historian of any one of the several main aspects of the Anglo-Saxon age who seeks enlightenment in those documents: even the student of dialects is not exempt from the labour. For the special purposes of legal history, which is so closely related to all the other aspects of Anglo-Saxon development, it seems to me essential to study these documents from two points of view, namely, their diplomatic form and their value as materials from which a knowledge of the unwritten customary law of pre-Norman times may be obtained; and, moreover, in respect of both matters the documents in this volume must be studied in their relation to the vernacular and Latin documents in other collections. In the absence of any other connected account of these subject-matters, a short study of Anglo-Saxon documents written as an Introduction to the present collection, but which is far too long for inclusion here, will soon make its appearance as a separate volume in this series of *Studies in English Legal History*. Although this small book, entitled *Anglo-Saxon Documents as Evidence of Legal History*, is in the nature of a companion to Miss Robertson's *Anglo-Saxon Charters*, its scope is much broader; for it deals with many documents not included in her collection. My chief aim has been to reconstruct, on the basis of a study of documentary materials, parts of the unwritten customary law of the Anglo-Saxons in respect of contract and land. In making this preliminary survey of an extensive field of historical research there has been, however, no attempt to do more than draw attention to certain conclusions that have been reached after an examination of only a small part of the entire body of documentary sources. The afore-mentioned historical sketch has in fact been written in the hope that by showing the results to be obtained from such an examination at least a few scholars may be induced to enter upon a far more detailed and critical study of the whole mass of Anglo-Saxon documents as the principal sources of our early social and legal history. Such studies would serve, moreover, a further purpose; for the explanation of many post-Conquest developments in English social and legal structure can come only from the *cartae* and *notitiae* of the Anglo-Saxons. An exact and comprehensive knowledge of the nature and content of these documents, as illumined by the life of the age in which they were written, will in fact enable us to gain a clearer vision of those customary modes of forming contracts and conveying property which persisted long after the Conquest and became an integral part of the medieval common law. In the sphere of diplomatic, contract, and property the Norman age meant adaptation and modification, not destruction; and in the law as administered by the King's justices in Bracton's day, and even in far later times, there were many elements derived from the customary law of the pre-Norman centuries.

Miss Robertson's *Anglo-Saxon Charters*, upon which she has spent so much devoted and painstaking labour, now takes its place in literature as one of the principal source-books for the study of early English history. From the future use of this valuable collection of documents by competent scholars there will come an enrichment of historical writing in regard to the language, the diplomatic, the life, and the law of the pre-Norman age; and in these documents historians will find, moreover, evidence of the origin and early growth of diplomatic forms and of social and legal institutions which played a rôle of even greater importance in later times. The knowledge which they gain from a reading of the charters and other documents in this collection, if supplemented by a study of other contemporary sources, will permit them to grasp with a more enlightened understanding the nature and the meaning of those particular post-Conquest developments which represent a slow transition from Anglo-Saxon times to the later Middle Ages.

H. D. HAZELTINE

May 1939

PREFACE

THIS edition of Anglo-Saxon Charters and other documents has aimed at including every kind of deed and record concerned with the transaction of legal business (apart from writs and manumissions) with the exception of those contained in Miss Harmer's edition of *Select English Historical Documents of the Ninth and Tenth Centuries* (published in 1914) and Miss Whitelock's edition of *Anglo-Saxon Wills* (published in 1930).[1] It opens with two eighth-century charters (which are almost certainly translations of a later date) and has extended beyond the limits of the Anglo-Saxon period in order to include six post-Conquest documents which seemed of special interest. It ends with a small group of undated pieces (chiefly inventories and lists of books) which occur as detached entries in MSS. from various sources. These have been included because of the interest and value of the information which they supply. A document relating to Thorney, the first part of which almost certainly belongs to the tenth century, comes last of all. It was known too late for inclusion earlier in the volume.

All the documents in the present collection (the total number of which is one hundred and thirty-five) have been printed before (with the exception of part of the Thorney document, see pp. 502 f.), and the majority are to be found in Kemble's *Codex Diplomaticus Ævi Saxonici* (1839–1848) and (as far as the end of Edgar's reign) in Birch's *Cartularium Saxonicum* (1885–1893), while a considerable number are included also in Thorpe's *Diplomatarium Anglicum Ævi Saxonici* (1865) and Earle's *Handbook to the Land Charters* (1888). A few which have been brought to light since the publication of these collections and which have appeared in various periodicals (sometimes accompanied by a modern translation and notes) are also included, and I here

---

[1] Only documents in the vernacular are included but the Latin charters have been constantly used for purposes of comparison and are frequently referred to throughout.

acknowledge my great indebtedness to all who have worked before me in the same field.

The text of the documents in the present collection has been taken direct from the MSS. themselves (where such were available). The spelling and punctuation have been preserved throughout, but capital letters have been supplied, where necessary, for proper names. Simple and easily understood abbreviations have been retained and any letters or syllables supplied by expansion have been italicised. Insertions in the MSS. are enclosed within the signs ' ' and emended or supplied readings are given between square brackets. Important variations in MS. readings and in previous editions are given in footnotes.

Twenty-eight of the documents have survived as separate parchments (generally either original or contemporary) and thirteen of these are chirographs (see p. 348). A few, again, are contemporary records of grants or transactions entered in gospel books or works of the kind, but the majority are copies which have been preserved in post-Conquest cartularies. Canterbury Cathedral is well represented by single parchments (the majority of which are now in the British Museum) and by entries in gospel books which formerly belonged to the cathedral. Worcester Cathedral (in spite of the deplorable loss of most of its original documents, some of which survived till the eighteenth century) is represented by a large number of documents drawn for the most part from its valuable eleventh-century cartulary, now in the British Museum. Rochester Cathedral has supplied several interesting records from the twelfth-century cartulary which forms the second part of the *Textus Roffensis*, preserved in the Cathedral Library, while the archives of Winchester Cathedral, Sherborne Abbey and Peterborough Cathedral are likewise represented by copies of documents (not always fully reliable) drawn from twelfth-century cartularies. Abingdon has supplied a few records from the two thirteenth-century MSS. which relate the history of the abbey. Bury St Edmunds is represented by copies of a few pre-Conquest documents from its fourteenth-century registers and by several entries and records of unusual interest from MSS. which at one time formed part of its library. Shaftesbury Abbey supplies two late and corrupt versions of

PREFACE   xxi

ninth-century grants from its mediaeval register (now in the British Museum), while Milton Abbey, Dorset, is represented by the Middle-English version of an early charter derived from a register of the abbey which has now disappeared. The collection likewise includes documents of various dates relating to Ely, Westminster Abbey, St Paul's Cathedral, St Augustine's, Canterbury, the New Minster, Winchester (afterwards the Abbey of Hyde), Bath, Hereford and Exeter, so that very few of the important religious foundations of the south and midlands are wanting. The north of England, however, is only sparsely represented by a few brief entries in two MSS. which formerly belonged to Durham Cathedral (one of them the *Liber Vitae*), by a number of early eleventh-century entries in a MS. of the gospels at York, and by a detached statement concerning church lands in Northumbria, drawn up by Archbishop Oswald and preserved in a MS. now in the British Museum.

In form and content the documents vary enormously. It is noteworthy that comparatively few of them are royal charters. The earliest documents of this type in the collection (Nos. I, II) are probably translations from Latin originals, while the majority are found along with Latin versions to which they are or may be subsidiary (e.g. Nos. XXXVIII, XLV, XLVIII). Very often the Anglo-Saxon versions are simply narrative accounts, more or less summarised, of the grants or transactions recorded in regular charter form in the accompanying Latin versions. Occasionally they supply additional information (e.g. Nos. X, XXIII) and must therefore have been drawn up to some extent independently. In one case (No. VIII) the Anglo-Saxon summary is obviously later than the grant which it records, but in general there is nothing to show conclusively that the two versions are of different date. Some are decidedly suspicious. Alfred's bequest to Shaftesbury (No. XIII) includes privileges of a type not found elsewhere at such an early date, while Edgar's grant of Oborne to Sherborne (No. L) and Cnut's grant of Folkestone to Christchurch, Canterbury (No. LXXXV), both include impossible names in their lists of witnesses. The scarcity of royal grants in the vernacular shows that documents of the kind were usually drawn up in Latin and that only in exceptional cases were they accompanied by an English version. It is possible, however, that where two versions of a charter were in existence, the Anglo-Saxon one was not always included by the mediaeval copyist and that the surviving number of royal charters of this type, therefore, is not entirely representative.

A large proportion of the documents in the collection are leases (generally by bishops), and most numerous of all are the grants of the kind made by Oswald as Bishop of Worcester. The number of these in the vernacular throughout is comparatively small, when compared with the total number which he issued, but many of his Latin grants of the kind contain one or more clauses in English (apart from the boundaries). In many cases these clauses merely express in stereotyped form a blessing on those who uphold the grant and a curse on those who break it, or else they make clear (also in stereotyped form) that, whatever happens, the estates in question must return unforfeited to the holy foundation. Occasionally, however, they give a brief summary of the grant and sometimes supply additional information, as, for example, in the case of a grant of 2 hides at Clifford Chambers where the English summary explains that it consists of '1½ hides of partible land and half a hide on the island' (see p. 299), or in cases where changes in tenure from *lænland* to *bocland* were involved (e.g. K. 617, 651, 679). Sometimes the English clauses may represent later additions to the original grant (perhaps contained in endorsements) which have been incorporated in the charter by the copyist (e.g. B.1240). The system of leasing out church lands for a restricted number of lives had been begun at Worcester by Oswald's predecessors and was continued by his successors, though not to the same extent. It was a fairly common practice at Winchester also, as the present collection shows. The difficulties and losses to which it led at Worcester are narrated by Hemming in the eleventh-century cartulary of the cathedral (see p. 320), and to him is due also the preservation of a remarkable account of the payments extorted by William I from the church of Worcester, which seems to be without parallel elsewhere. It has been included in the present collection (see p. 242).

A certain number of the documents are wills and grants in

PREFACE xxiii

reversion, and these call for no special comment here. It was the common practice for documents of the kind to be in English. Several are records of lawsuits or narratives concerned with the history of estates which had been the subject of dispute or litigation. In many ways these are the most interesting in the collection, for they show the Anglo-Saxon legal system in actual practice. In many ways also they are the most difficult, as the circumstances are not always fully related (presumably because they were generally known at the time that the records were drawn up) and in several cases the course of events is by no means easy to follow. They present many aspects of legal interest and it may be noted in passing here that they bring into prominence a process not mentioned by name in the laws, viz. *talu*, the formal statement of a claim either by the plaintiff or the defendant in a case (once distinguished as the *ontalu* and the *oftalu* respectively), and that they frequently exemplify the importance of the process called *agnung*, the proof that a thing is one's own, and bear out the truth of the assertion that *agnung bið ner ðam ðe hæfð ðonne ðam ðe æftersprecð* (II Æthelred, 9, 4). They are of value also for the incidental information that they give. Few commentaries on the general state of affairs in Æthelred's reign could be more enlightening than the narrative of Wulfbold's crimes (No. LXIII).

Several of the documents in the collection are unique, e.g. the account of 'bridge-work' at Rochester (No. LII) and the specifications for the maintenance and defence of fortifications which follow the Burghal Hidage (Appendix II, No. I). Others again, such as the surveys and accounts of services and dues rendered on certain estates, are valuable for the precise information which they give with regard to particular localities, and supplement the knowledge of social and economic conditions derived from legal treatises.

Very few of the documents seem to be anything but genuine records. Some doubt may be raised by the defiant statement at the end of the account of Harold Harefoot's dealings with Sandwich (No. XCI), *þis is eall soð gelyfe se þe wylle*, and by the animosity shown throughout towards Ælfstan, Abbot of St Augustine's, but the story, though biased, is not necessarily without some foundation in fact. Even in a case such as that of Edgar's grant of Oborne to Sherborne, where the majority of the witnesses cannot possibly agree with the date and seem to have been derived from an earlier grant made by Æthelbert (see p. 349), the possibility of a mistake in the transcription of the charter must be taken into account. Modern instances of accidents of the kind are not wanting. The names of five witnesses who belong by rights to the Anglo-Saxon version of one of Æthelred's charters (K. 715) have been attached by mistake to a writ of Edward the Confessor in the printed copy (K. 847) through the accident that, in the MS. (B.M., Cotton Claudius, A. III), the writ had been entered in the space left at the bottom of the page below Æthelred's charter, while the last five names which belong to the charter are given at the top of the next page. Something of the kind may have happened in the case of Edgar's charter, which seems to have been copied from a gospel book. Charters from the *Codex Wintoniensis* have to be examined with care. The copyist was notoriously careless, especially in the description of witnesses, so that thegns appear in his lists as earls and priests as bishops (the Bishops Tata and Byrnstan 'of unknown sees' are due to an error of his, see p. 289). Mistakes in transcription are easy to make and not always easy to detect or to rectify. An examination of the Sherborne Register, however, has supplied the witnesses of Æthelbert's charter (see pp. 18, 20) who are omitted by Thorpe and Birch and erroneously said to be wanting. It has been suggested elsewhere (see p. 297) that an awkward and apparently meaningless sentence is due to the fact that part of it has been written twice over, but as a rule only a few misprints or misreadings of less importance have been corrected.

The linguistic interest of the documents is considerable. The first ten with one exception (No. VIII) are either Mercian or Kentish and are examples of these dialects in the ninth century. Both dialects are represented also in later documents, e.g. No. XXX, a charter from the Peterborough Register which has characteristic Mercian forms, and No. XXXII, which is a tenth-century will written in Kentish. One document (Appendix II, No. IV) is an excellent example of the Northumbrian dialect.

PREFACE

I gladly take this opportunity of expressing my thanks to all those who have assisted me in preparing this edition. It was undertaken at the suggestion of Professor Chadwick, and I am deeply indebted to him for his unfailing help and encouragement while it was in progress. My thanks are also due to Sir Allen Mawer and to Professor F. M. Stenton for their generous assistance; to Miss Dorothy Whitelock for reading the proofs and making most valuable suggestions; to the Earl of Macclesfield, to Lady Dering of Hamptons, Tonbridge, Kent, to Mr T. FitzRoy Fenwick of Thirlstaine House, Cheltenham, and to Captain Cragg of Threekingham, Lincolnshire, for generously allowing me to examine the MSS. in their possession, and to all those responsible for the facilities afforded me for consulting the MSS. and carrying out my work at the University Library, Cambridge, the British Museum, the Bodleian Library, Oxford, the University Library, Edinburgh, the Library of the Society of Antiquaries of London, Lambeth Palace Library, Canterbury Cathedral, Rochester Cathedral, York Minster, Westminster Abbey and St Paul's Cathedral, Corpus Christi College, Queens' College and Pembroke College, Cambridge, Christ Church, Oriel College and Corpus Christi College, Oxford. Finally I am under a great obligation to Professor H. D. Hazeltine for including this book in his series and for much kind encouragement while I was engaged upon it; to the Syndics of the University Press for undertaking the publication and the staff for the care taken in the printing; to the Council of Girton College for the award of the Pfeiffer Research Fellowship which enabled me to undertake the work, also for a grant in aid of publication, and to the Carnegie Trust for the award of a Research Fellowship and grant which allowed me to extend the original scope of the edition and complete my work upon it.

A. J. R.

May 1939

The MS. and the Facsimile have been used for the text of Nos. LXXVIII and XCIX in the Second Edition.

A. J. R.

June 1956

LIST OF ABBREVIATIONS

Attenborough	Attenborough, *The Laws of the Earliest English Kings*.
B.	Birch, *Cartularium Saxonicum*, quoted by number of document.
Björkman	Björkman, *Nordische Personennamen in England in alt- und frühmittelenglischer Zeit*.
B.T. and B.T., Suppl.	Bosworth and Toller, *Anglo-Saxon Dictionary*, and Supplement.
D.B.	Domesday Book.
Dugdale	Dugdale, *Monasticon Anglicanum*, 1819–1830 edition.
E.	Earle, *A Handbook to the Land Charters and other Saxonic Documents*.
E.D.D.	*English Dialect Dictionary*.
Fl. Wig.	Florence of Worcester.
Foster and Longley	Foster and Longley, *The Lincolnshire Domesday and the Lindsey Survey* (Lincolnshire Record Society Publications, 19).
Haddan and Stubbs	Haddan and Stubbs, *Councils and Ecclesiastical Documents relating to Great Britain and Ireland*.
Harmer	Harmer, *Select English Historical Documents of the Ninth and Tenth Centuries*.
Harmer[2]	Harmer, *Anglo-Saxon Writs*.
K.	Kemble, *Codex Diplomaticus Ævi Saxonici*, quoted by number of document.
Liebermann	Liebermann, *Gesetze der Angelsachsen*.
N.E.D.	*New English Dictionary*.
Pl.N.	Publications of the Place-Name Society.
Robertson	Robertson, *Laws of the Kings of England from Edmund to Henry I*.
R.S.	Rolls Series.
Sax. Chr.	Anglo-Saxon Chronicle. The letters A, B, C, D, E, F refer to the different MSS., see Earle and Plummer, *Two of the Saxon Chronicles Parallel*.
Searle	Searle, *Onomasticon Anglo-Saxonicum*.
T.	Thorpe, *Diplomatarium Anglicum Ævi Saxonici*.
V.C.H.	Victoria County History.
Wallenberg	Wallenberg, *Kentish Place Names* in Uppsala Universitets Årsskrift, 1931.
Whitelock	Whitelock, *Anglo-Saxon Wills*.

ANGLO-SAXON CHARTERS

I. REMISSION OF DUES ON TWO SHIPS

✠ In usses dryhtnes noman hælendes Cristes · ic Æðelbald[1] Myrcna cincg[2] wæs[3] beden from þæm arfullan bisceope Milrede þætt[4] ic him alefde 7 his þæm halegan hirede alle nedbade tuegra sceopa þe þærto limpe'n'de beoð þett[5] ic him forgefe · þa
5 þæm eadgan[6] Petre apostola aldormen in þæm mynstre þeowiað ϸ is geseted in Huicca mægðe · in þære stowe þe mon hateð Weogernacester þære bene swyðe arfulre geðafunge ic wæs syllende for minre sawle læcedome to ðon þætt[4] for minum synnum hi heo geeaðmedden ϸte heo wæren gelomlice þingeras
10 wið drihten swyðe lustfullice þa forgeofende ic him alyfde alle nedbade tuegra sceopa · þa þe þær abædde beoð from þæm nedbaderum in Lundentunes hyðe ond næfre ic ne mine last-weardas ne ða nedbaderas geðristlæcen ϸ heo hit onwenden oððe þon wiðgæn · gif heo ϸ nyllen syn heo þonne amansumade from
15 dælneomencge liceman 7 blodes usses drihtnes hælendes Cristes · 7 from alre neweste geleafulra syn heo asceadene 7 asyndrade nymðe heo hit her mid þingonge bote gebete.

✠ Ic Æþelbald · cincg mine agene sylene trymmende ic[7] heo wrat. Milred bisceop þare halegan rode tacen he heron gefæst-
20 node. Inguwald[8] ƀ geðafiende he hit wrat. Wilfrið ƀ he hit wrat. Alda cinges gefera he hit wrat.

II. GRANT OF LAND BY KING OFFA TO WORCESTER

ÐA ÐA wæron agane fif[9] hundred wintra 7 nigan 7 hund-eahtatig wintra fram Cristes gebyrtide · Offa kyning on þam an and þrittigan geare his kynedomes geuþe ane hide landes æt
25 Bradewassan into þam mynstre on Wigrecestre þam broþran to bryce a on ece swa full 7 swa forð swa he seolf hæfde.

[1] ædel-, He.; aedel-, K.
[2] It seems as if the word *ic* has been erased after *cincg*.   [3] wær, K.
[4] þæti, He., K., E.; þæt, T. A letter, probably *e*, has been erased at the end of this word.
[5] þeti, He., K., E.; þet, T. See preceding note.   [6] eadigan, B.
[7] hic, K.   [8] Ingwuald, K., T.   [9] sif, He.

I. REMISSION OF DUES ON TWO SHIPS

✝ In the name of our Lord, the Saviour Christ, I, Æthelbald, King of Mercia, have been asked by the venerable Bishop Milred to grant remission of all the dues pertaining to two ships to him and his holy community—to make this concession to those who serve the blessed Peter, chief of the apostles, in the monastery which is situated in the province of the Hwicce in the place called Worcester. To this request I have granted my very gracious consent, for the salvation of my soul, upon condition that they would condescend to intercede continually with the Lord for my sins. Very gladly then I have granted them remission of all the dues on two ships which are exacted by the tax-gatherers in the harbour of London; and never shall I or my successors or tax-gatherers presume to change or oppose this. If they will not agree, they shall be excluded from participation in the body and blood of our Lord the Saviour Christ, and they shall be severed and sundered from all the fellowship of the faithful, unless they make amends for it here with intercession.

✠ I, King Æthelbald, have written this, confirming my own gift.

Bishop Milred has affixed here the symbol of the holy cross.
Bishop Ingwald has written this in agreement.
Bishop Wilfrith has written this.
Alda, the king's companion, has written this.

II. GRANT OF LAND BY KING OFFA TO WORCESTER

When 589[1] years had passed since the birth of Christ, King Offa, in the thirty-first year of his reign, granted a hide of land at Broadwas to the monastery at Worcester for the use of the brethren for all time, as fully and completely as he himself held it.

[1] For 789.

4   GRANT OF LAND BY KING OFFA

✠. Ic Offa þurh Cristes gyfe Myrcena kining ðas mine geoue
mid rode tacne gefæstnige. ✠. Ic Aldred Wigracestres under-
cin'in'g þas ylce geoue gefæstnige. ✠ Ic Eadberht bisceop þas
ylce þing gefæstnige. ✠. Ic Berhtun ðis ylce gefæstnige.
5 Ðis syndon ða landgemæra into Bradewassan of Temede
streame in wynna bæce · of wynna bæce in wudumor · of
wudumore in wætan sihtran · of þam wætan sice in ða bakas 7
of þam bacan in ða ealdan dic · of ðære ealdan dic in seges mere ·
7 of seges mere in þæs pulles heafod 7 of ðam heafde to
10 þornbrycge · of ðornbryc[ge][1] in þone pull · 7 æfter þam pulle
in baka brycge of baka brycge in þ̄ wæte sícc · 7 of þam sice in
foxbæce 'of foxbæcæ'[2] in þone wulfseað · of þam seaðe in þa
ealdan stihle · 'of þære stihle'[2] in dodhæma pull · of þam pulle
eft in Temede stream.

III. THE WILL OF ÆTHELNOTH AND GÆNBURG

15 ✠ Æðelnoð se gerefa tó Eastorege 7 Gænburg his wif aræddan
hiora érfe beforan Wulfre'de' arcebiscope 7 Æðelhune his mæsseprioste 7 Esne cyninges[3] ðegne suæ hueðer hiora suæ leng lifes
were foe to londe 7 to alre æhte gif hio bearn hæbbe[4] ðonne[5] foe
ðæt[6] ofer[7] hiora boega dagas to londe 7 to æhte · gif hio ðonne
20 bearn næbbe 7 Wulfred archibiscop[8] lifes sie þonne foe he to
ðæm londe 7 hit forgelde 7 ðæt wiorð gedæle fore hiora gastas
suæ ælmeslice 7 suæ rehtlice suæ he[9] him seolfa on his wisdome
geleornie · 7 ða sprece[10] nænig[11] mon uferran dogor on nænge
oðre halfe oncærrende sie[12] nymne[13] suæ: · þis gewrit hafað[14]:—

25 ✠ Wulfred arc̄ epis̄[15]   ✠ Cuðberht p̄r.   ✠ Gænburg.
✠ Feologeld p̄r ab   ✠ Æðelnoð.   ✠ Esne.
✠ Æðelhun p̄r.

[1] Blurred and illegible.   [2] In the margin.
[3] *erninges*, O'C.   [4] *hehe*, O'C., *hebbe*, K., *haðða*, T.
[5] *þon*, T.   [6] *æt*, O'C., T.; [ð]*æt*, K.
[7] In the margin.   [8] Om. T.   [9] *be*, T.
[10] *this prece*, O'C., *this* [s]*prece*, K., *þas wrece*, T.
[11] *mænig*, T.   [12] *oncær reade si*, T.
[13] *nimne*, O'C., K. ; *mynne*, T.   [14] *wisgewrit. Hafath*, O'C.
[15] T. omits the witnesses.

✠ I, Offa, by the grace of Christ King of Mercia, confirm this my gift with the symbol of the cross.

✠ I, Aldred, Under-king of Worcester, confirm this same gift.

✠ I, Bishop Eadberht, confirm the same thing.

✠ I, Berhthun, confirm the same.

These are the boundaries of Broadwas. From the River Teme to the white(?) brook, from the white(?) brook to the marsh by the wood, from the marsh by the wood to the wet water-course, from the wet water-course to the brooks and from the brooks to the old dyke, from the old dyke to *seges* pond and from *seges* pond to the head of the pool, and from the head to *Thornbridge*, from *Thornbridge* to the pool and along the pool to the bridge over the brooks, from the bridge over the brooks to the wet water-course and from the water-course to *Foxbatch*, from *Foxbatch* to the wolf-pit, from the pit to the old stile, from the stile to the Doddenham pool, from the pool back to the River Teme.

III. THE WILL OF ÆTHELNOTH AND GÆNBURG

✠ Æthelnoth, the reeve at Eastry, and Gænburg his wife have disposed of their inheritance before Archbishop Wulfred and Æthelhun, his priest, and Esne, the king's thegn. Whichever of them lives the longer shall succeed to the estate and to all the property. If they have a child, it shall succeed, after the death of both of them, to the estate and to the property. If, however, they do not have a child and Archbishop Wulfred is alive, he shall succeed to the estate and pay for it and distribute the value on behalf of their souls, as charitably and as justly as he himself can devise in his wisdom. And no-one at a later day shall pervert this agreement in any way from what is contained in this document...

6 THE WILL OF

Þisses¹ londes earan ðrie sulong æt Hægyðe² ðorne · 7 gif hiora oðrum³ oððe bæm suð⁴ fo'r' gelimpe⁵ biscop ðat lond gebycge suæ hie ðonne geweorðe.

IV. KING CEOLWULF AND BROMSGROVE

✝ Ceolulf rex wilnade þæs londes æt Bremesgrefan⁶ to Heaberht
5 bisc̄ 7 to his [higun]⁷ 7 þa sende⁸ he his erendwreocan⁹ to Wulfheard to Intanbeorgum 7 heht þæt he cuome to him 7 [to þæ]m¹⁰ higum¹¹ þa dede he swæ¹² þa hio him to spræcon¹³ se biscop 7 his weotan ymb¹⁴ þæt lond þæt he his him geuþe þæt hio maehten¹⁵ þone freodom begeotan 7 þa wæs he eaðmodlice ondeta þæt he
10 swæ wulde 7 to him wilnende¹⁶ wæs þætte hio him funden suelce londare swelce¹⁷ he mid arum on [b]eon¹⁸ maehte 7 his wic þære on¹⁹ byrig²⁰ on his life · þa sende he monn to þæm ærcebiscope²¹ 7 to Eadberhte 7 to Dynne 7 him heht segcgan þæt he wilnade þæs londes²² æt Intanbeorgan · þa se ærcebiscop
15 7 Eadberht 'hit wæron' erndiende to cyninge þa cuom Dynne to gelærde þone cyninge þæt he his no geþæf wæs þa wæs higen 7 hlaforde lond unbefliten æghuæs 7 sioþþan á oþ his daga ende²³.

¹ *wisses*, O'C. ² *haegesthe*, O'C.; *haegethe*, K.; *Hegyðe*, T.
³ *othru*, O'C., K.; *oðra*, T. ⁴ *baemsuth*, O'C.; *baem siith*, K.
⁵ *forgelimpe*, K., T.
⁶ *Bremergrafan*, MSS. (*a*) and (*c*).
⁷ From MS. (*c*); left blank in MS. (*d*); *hirede*, MS. (*a*).
⁸ The text ends here in MS. (*a*) and is continued on the Middleton leaf.
⁹ *ærendgewrit*, MS. (*b*). ¹⁰ MS. (*d*) has .... *m* in paler ink.
¹¹ *hirede*, MS. (*b*).
¹² -*a* changed to -*æ*; *swa*, MSS. (*b*) and (*c*).
¹³ -*an* changed to -*on*. ¹⁴ *ymbe* changed to *ymb*.
¹⁵ *he mihte*, MS. (*b*); *heo mehtan*, MS. (*c*).
¹⁶ The first part of the word (*wilnen*-) has been written in later.
¹⁷ *suelce* changed to *swe*-. ¹⁸ The MS. has *on..eon*.
¹⁹ *þ. on* has been written in later; *þær on*, MSS. (*b*) and (*c*).
²⁰ The other MSS. add *beon mihte*. ²¹ *erce*- changed to *ærce*-.
²² A space follows.
²³ MS. (*b*) adds *Gode gefultmiendum*.

This estate consists of three ploughlands at Eythorne. And if it happens that one or both of them goes south [on a pilgrimage], the bishop shall buy the estate, as shall then be agreed between them.

IV. KING CEOLWULF AND BROMSGROVE

† King Ceolwulf solicited the estate at Bromsgrove from Bishop Heahberht and the members of his community. The bishop then sent his messenger to Wulfheard at Inkberrow, and told him to come to him and the community. When he did so, the bishop and his advisers spoke to him about the estate—that he should grant it to them, so that they could obtain the freedom; and he humbly agreed to do so, and asked them to find him an estate where he could live honourably and have his dwelling in the manor-house there during his life. Then he (Wulfheard) sent a man to the archbishop and to Eadberht and to Dynne, and told him to say to them that he wanted the estate at Inkberrow. When the archbishop and Eadberht were advocating this to the king, Dynne came and persuaded the king not to consent to it. Then the estate remained quite undisputed in the possession of the community and their lord, and continued so until the end of his days.

V. LAWSUIT ABOUT WOOD-PASTURE

✠ In nomine trino diuino qui est deus benedictus in sæcula amen. Ðy gere þe wæs from Cristes geburde[1] agæn · eahta hund Winter[2] · 7 xxv · 7 æfterre[3] indictio wæs in rime · 7 wæs Beornwulfes rice Mercna cyninges · þa wæs sinodlic[4] gemot on þære
5 meran stowe ðe mon hateþ Clofeshous[5] on þam[6] se siolfa Cyning Biornwulf · 7 his biscopas[7] · 7 his aldormen · 7 alle þa wioton þisse þiode þær gesomnade weron · þa wæs tiolo micel sprec ymb wuduleswe to Suþtune ongægum West on Scirhylte[8] · waldon þa swangerefan þa leswe forður gedrifan 7 þone wudu
10 geþiogan · þonne[9] hit ald geryhta weron · þonne[10] cuæð se biscop · and þara hira[11] wiotan þæt hio him neren maran ondeta þonne[9] hit aræded wæs on Æþelbaldes dæge þrim hunde swina mæst · 7 se biscop 7 ða higen[12] ahten twæde þæs wudu[13] 7 þæs mæstes: · Ða geræhte Wulfred arcebiscop · 7 alle þa wiotan þet
15 se biscop 7 þa higen moston[14] mid aþe gecythan[15] þet hit sua aræden were[16] on Æþelbaldes dage · 7 him mare to ne sohte: · And he þa sona se biscop bewæddade[17] Eadwulfe ðæm aldormen þæs aþes biforan allum þæm wiotum · 7 him mon þone gelædde ymb xxx næhta to þæm biscop-stole æt Wigoerna-Ceastre: · In
20 þa tiid wæs Hama Suangerefa to Suðtune · 7 he ræd[18] ðæt he wæs æt Ceastre · and þone aað gesæh · 7 gesceawade sua hine his aldormon heht Eadwulf · 7 he hine hweþre ne grette · hii sunt nomina et uocabula qui in synodali concilio fuerunt congregati.

25 ✠ Signum manus · Biornwulfi regis Merc.
✠ Wulfred arcepisc̄ · conseñ[19] · hanc condicionem.
✠ Oeðelwald episc̄ conseñ.
30 ✠ Hræðhun episc̄ conseñ.
✠ Heaberht episc̄ conseñ.
✠ Bionna episc̄ conseñ.
✠ Eadwulf episc̄ conseñ.
35 ✠ Wilfred episc̄ conseñ.
✠ Wigðegn episc̄ conseñ.
✠ Alhstan episc̄ conseñ.
✠ Humberht episc̄ conseñ.
✠ Ceolberht episc̄.

✠ Cynred episc̄.
✠ Torthelm prior
✠ Eanmund abb.
✠ Wihtred abb.
✠ Cudwulf abb.
✠ Eanmund abb.
✠ Eaðberht dux
✠ Biornoð dux
✠ Sigred dux
✠ Cuðred dux
✠ Eadwulf dux
✠ Mucel dux
✠ Uhtred dux
✠ Alhheard dux
✠ Bolam ✠ Bynna

✠ Aldred[20] ✠ Wighelm
✠ Heahberht · episc̄.
✠ Eadgar pr̄.
✠ Wigberht pr̄.
✠ Heahstæf pr̄.
✠ Brada pr̄.
✠ Cuðbald pr̄.
✠ Regngar pr̄.
✠ Cuðberht pr̄.
✠ Ecgmund pr̄.
✠ Ecmund pr̄.[21]
✠ Heahferhð diac̄.
✠ Wighelm diac̄.
✠ Erneberht[22] diac̄.

40 Ond[23] alre oðerra priosta butan þissum mæsse-priostum efen LX.

V. LAWSUIT ABOUT WOOD-PASTURE

✠ *In nomine trino divino qui est Deus benedictus in sæcula, Amen.*

In the year 825 which had passed since the birth of Christ, and in the course of the second Indiction, and during the reign of Beornwulf, King of Mercia, a council meeting was held in the famous place called *Clofesho*, and there the said King Beornwulf and his bishops and his earls and all the councillors of this nation were assembled. Then there was a very noteworthy suit about wood-pasture at Sinton, towards the west in *Scirhylte*. The reeves in charge of the swineherds wished to extend the pasture farther, and take in more of the wood than the ancient rights permitted. Then the bishop and the advisers of the community said that they would not admit liability for more than had been appointed in Æthelbald's day, namely mast for 300 swine, and that the bishop and the community should have two-thirds of the wood and of the mast. Then Archbishop Wulfred and all the councillors determined that the bishop and the community might declare on oath that it was so appointed in Æthelbald's time and that they were not trying to obtain more, and the bishop immediately gave security to Earl Eadwulf to furnish the oath before all the councillors, and it was produced in 30 days at the bishop's see at Worcester. At that time Hama was the reeve in charge of the swineherds at Sinton, and he rode until he reached Worcester, and watched and observed the oath, as Earl Eadwulf bade him, but did not challenge it.

Here are the names and designations of those who were assembled at the council meeting...

---

[1] *-byrde*, Smith [2] *wint.*, ibid. [3] *sio æfterre*, ibid.
[4] *sionoðlic*, ibid. [5] *-hoas*, ibid. [6] *ond ðær*, ibid.
[7] *bisc.*, ibid. [8] *scyr-*, ibid. [9] *ðon*, ibid.
[10] *Ðon*, ibid. [11] For *hina*, which is Smith's reading.
[12] *se b. ða tugen*, Smith. [13] *wuda*, ibid.
[14] *-en*, ibid. [15] *-cypan*, ibid. [16] *wære aræden*, ibid.
[17] *-wedd-*, ibid.
[18] *rad*, ibid. [19] *consensi*, Smith throughout.
[20] *Aldran*, Smith. [21] This witness is omitted by Smith.
[22] *Cyne-*, Smith. [23] *Mid*, ibid.

VI. THE WILL OF BADANOTH BEOTTING

✠ IC Badanoð[1] beotting cyðo 7 writan hato hu min willa is ðet min ærfe lond fere ðe Ic et Aeðeluulfe cyninge begæt 7 gebohte mid fullum friodome on æce ærfe æfter minum dege 7 minra ærfewearda ðet is mines wifes 7 minra bearna · ic wille ærist me
5 siolfne[2] Gode allmehtgum[3] forgeofan to ðere stowe æt Cristes cirican 7 min bearn ðę̨r liffest gedoan 7 wiib 7 cild ðæm hlaforde 7 higum 7 ðære stowe befestan ober minne dei to friðe 7 to mundbyrde 7 to hlaforddome on ðæm ðingum[4] ðe him ðearf sie 7 hie brucen londes hiora dei 7 higon gefeormien to minre tide
10 swæ hie soelest ðurhtion megen 7 higon us mid heora godcundum godum swę gemynen swæ us arlic 7 him ælmeslic się 7 ðonne ofer hiora dei wifes 7 cilda. Ic bebeode on Godes noman ðæt mon agefe ðæt lond[5] Inn higum[6] to heora beode him to brucanne on ece ærfe swæ him liofast[7] sie · 7 ic biddo higon for
15 Godes lufe ðæt se monn se higon londes unnen to brucanne ða ilcan wisan leste on swæsendum to minre tide 7 ða godcundan lean minre saule mid gerece swę hit mine ærfenuman ær onstellen · ðonne[8] is min willa ðæt ðissa gewriota sien twa gelice oðer habben higon mid boecum oðer mine ærfeweardas heora
20 dei · ðonne is ðes londes[9] ðe ic higum selle .XVI. gioc ærðe[10] londes 7 medwe[11] all on æce ærfe to brucanne ge minne dei ge[12] æfter swæ to ationne swæ me mest red 7 liofast sie.

✠ Ceolnoð arc̄ episc̄ ðiss writo 7 festnię mid Cristes rode tacne.
✠ Alchhere dux ðiss writo 7 ðeafię.
25 ✠ Bægmund prb ab ðiss writo 7 ðeafię.
✠ Hysenoð pr̄ ðiss writo 7 ðeafię.
✠ Wigmund pr̄.   ✠ Dyddel[13].   ✠ Tile.
✠ Badenoð pr̄.   ✠ Cichus.   ✠ Cyneberht.
✠ Osmund pr̄.   ✠ Sigemund.   ✠ Eðelred.
30 ✠ Suiðberht diac̄   ✠ Eðelwulf.   ✠ Badanoð.

[1] -onoð, Hi.
[2] seolf-, Hi.
[3] -mehtigum, Hi., K.
[4] ding-, Hi.
[5] land, Hi.
[6] nig-, Hi.
[7] leof-, Hi., T., B.
[8] donne, B.
[9] ðæs landes, Hi.
[10] ærðæ, Hi.
[11] An empty space follows.
[12] de ...e, Hi.
[13] Ðydd-, T.

VI. THE WILL OF BADANOTH BEOTTING

✝ I, Badanoth Beotting, declare and order to be put in writing, what I desire to become of my heritable land (which I obtained and bought from King Æthelwulf with full freedom as a perpetual inheritance) after my death and that of my heirs, namely my wife and my children. First of all I desire to dedicate myself to God Almighty at the foundation at Christchurch, and to place my children there, and entrust my wife and children to the lord and to the community and to the foundation after my death, for security and protection and guardianship in the things which they require. And they shall enjoy the estate during their lifetime, and provide the community with a food-rent at my anniversary, as good as they can afford, and the community shall remember us in their divine services, as shall be honourable for us and charitable in them. And after the death of my wife and my children, I enjoin in the name of God that the estate be given to the refectory of the community as a perpetual inheritance, to be used as they think fit. And I entreat the community, for the love of God, that the man to whom the community grants the usufruct of the estate carry out the same arrangements with regard to a feast at my anniversary, as my heirs shall have appointed it, and so obtain the divine reward for my soul.

Further it is my will that there should be two of these documents alike. The community shall keep one with their charters, my heirs shall have the other for their lifetime.

The amount of the estate which I grant to the community is 16 yokes of arable land and meadow, all of it to be enjoyed as a perpetual inheritance during my lifetime, and afterwards to be dealt with in such a way as shall be wisest and best for me...

VII. AGREEMENT BETWEEN CEOLRED, ABBOT OF PETERBOROUGH, AND WULFRED

✠ In nomine patris et filíí et spiritus sċi. Ceolred abb 7 ða higan on Medeshamstede sellað Wulfrede ðet land æt Sempingaham in ðas gerednisse · ðet he hit hębbe 7 bruce sua lange sua he life · 7 anum ærfeuuarde æfter him · 7 elce gere sextig foðra wuda to
5 ðęm ham on Hornan ðæm wuda · 7 tuelf foðer græfan · 7 sex foður gerda. End forðon we him ðis land sellað · ðet he ðes landes fulne friodom bigete · in éce[1] ærfeweardnisse æt Sempingaham · 7 æt Slioforda · 7 bruce þere cirican lafard on Medeshamstede ðes landes æt Slioforda · 7 Wulfred ðes on
10 Sempingaham · 7 he geselle eghwelce gere to Medeshamstede tua tunnan fulle luhtres aloh[2] · 7 tua slegne'a't · 7 sęx hund lafes · 7 ten mittan Węl's'ces aloð · 7 þere cirican laforde geselle eghwelce gere hors 7 ðrittig scillinga · 7 hine ane niht gefeormige · fiftene mitta luhtres aloð .v. mitta welsces aloð fiftene
15 sestras liðes · 7 hi sion symle in allum here life eadmode 7 hearsume · 7 underþeodde · 7 ofer here tuega dęg · þonne agefe hio þet land into þere cirican to Medeshamstede mid freodome · 7 we him þis sellað mid felda 7 mid wuda 7 mid fenne sua þerto belimpeð. Sið heora tuuege dæg agan sie þonne agefe mon
20 tuuenti hida higuum to biodland 7 þere cirican lafe'a'rde[3] .xii. hida land æt Forde 7 æt Cegle · 7 he wes[4] feorm'i'ed tuuege hida landes æt Lęhcotum ·. his erfeweorda sweolcum swelce him ðonne gesibbast were[5] 7 þat were fulfredes cynne[6] ge fre · swa sua þet oðer into þere cirican · Anno uero dominice incarnationis
25 .dºcccº liiº. Indictione .xv. hoc factum est[7].

Her sindan ða naman ðere monna þe þis wreotan 7 festnedan.

Burgred rex. Cęlnoth archeps̄ Tunber'h't ep̄c. Ceored ep̄s. Alchun ep̄c. Berhtred ep̄c Wihtred abb. Werheard ab. Æthelhard dux. Hunberht dux. Aldbert dux. Beornhard dux. Mucel d. Osmund dux.
30 Ælfstan dux. Aldred d. Wenberht dux. Eadulf.

Ic Ceolred abb þas ure selene · mid Cristes rode tacne trymme 7 festnie.

Aldberht p̄po[9] Alcheard pr̄. Eanred pr̄. Wilheard pr̄. Cenferð pr̄. Cyneweald pr̄. Eaduuald pr̄. Egberht diāc. Humberht diāc Aldelm[8].
35 Brynuuald. Tunwulf.

[1] æce, K.,T. [2] aloð, K., T., B. [3] lafarde, K., T.
[4] ðes, K.; þes, T. [5] wære, K., T. [6] The ms. has ful fredescynne.
[7] h. f. est, om. K. [8] Om. K.

VII. AGREEMENT BETWEEN CEOLRED, ABBOT OF PETERBOROUGH, AND WULFRED

✠ *In nomine patris et filii et spiritus sancti.*

Abbot Ceolred and the community at *Medeshamstede* grant to Wulfred the estate at Sempringham on these terms, that he shall hold it and enjoy it as long as he lives, and one heir after him, and every year 60 fothers of wood [shall be given] to the monastery from the wood at Horne, and twelve fothers of brushwood and six fothers of faggots. And we grant him this estate in order that he may enjoy the full freedom of the estate at Sempringham and at Sleaford in perpetuity. And the lord of the church at *Medeshamstede* shall enjoy the estate at Sleaford, and Wulfred that at Sempringham, and every year he shall render to *Medeshamstede* two casks of clear ale and two cattle for slaughter and six hundred loaves and ten *mittan* of Welsh ale; and to the lord of the church he shall render every year a horse and thirty shillings, and supply him with one day's food-rent—fifteen *mittan* of clear ale and five *mittan* of Welsh ale and fifteen sesters of mild ale. And always all their life they shall be humble and obedient and submissive, and after the death of both of them, the estate shall be freely given back to the church at *Medeshamstede*. And we grant him this with the open land, woodland and fen which belong to it. When the lives of both of them are ended, twenty hides shall be given to the community for their refectory, and twelve hides of land at *Forde* and at Cheal to the lord of the church. And Wulfred was supplied with two hides of land at *Lehcotum* for such of his heirs as were most nearly related to him, to be freely granted to Wulfred's kin, as the other was to the church.

This has been done in the year of the incarnation of the Lord 852 and in the fifteenth Indiction.

Here are the names of the men who wrote and confirmed this...

VIII. GRANT OF LAND BY KING ÆTHELWULF TO THE OLD MINSTER, WINCHESTER

In nomine domini et saluatoris nostri Ihesu Christi. Þis gewrit cyð ðæt Æþeluulf cyning geuðe Gode 7 Sc̄e Petre 7 þæm hiwum on Wintacestre on ealdan mynstre twentigra hida landes æt Wænbeorgon ða ða he teoðode gynd eall his cynerice 5 ðone teoðan dæl ealra his landa m[id][1] his witena geþehte into halgun stowun Gode to lofe 7 his sawle to ecre al[y]s[e]d[nesse][1] 7 he bead on Godes ælmihtiges naman 7 on ealra his haligra ðæt na[n cyn]ing[1] ofer his timan ne nan oðer man þis[2] næfre ne[3] awende ac ðæt seo ar æ[fre][1] unbefliten hyrde into þære[4] halgan 10 stowe · 7 gif hit hwa awende þæt he wære on Godes awyrgednesse 7 sc̄e Petres ge on life ge æfter life butan he hit gebette[5] 7 þis wæs gedon ðæs geres ðe wæron agane ehta hund gera 7 feower[6] 7 fifti [g]eara æfter Cristes acynnednesse on þara witena gewitnesse þara naman her beneoðan awritene standað:

15 Æðeluulf[7] rex   ✠ Osric dux   ✠ Ælfred fil regis
Alhstan episc̄   ✠ Wulfhere dux   ✠ Esne miñ
Suiðhun episc̄   ✠ Lullede dux   ✠ Cyneuulf miñ
Æþelbald dux   ✠ Uullaf abb   ✠ Cyneheah miñ
Eanuulf dux   ✠ Uuærferð abb   ✠ Alhstan miñ
20 Æþelberht dux   ✠ Æðered fil reḡ   ✠ Ealdred miñ

IX. GRANT IN REVERSION TO ROCHESTER

✠ IN nomine dñi. Dunn hafað þas boc gesald[8] his wife 7 ðæt land þe þæran gewriten is an Godes est[9] · ðæt hio hæbbe hire dæg 7 his bruce · 7 efter[10] hire dæge[11] · geselle hit on ðæs halgan apostoles naman sc̄e Andreas ðam hirode 'in' mid unnan Godes 25 7 his his[12] ha'l'gena for unc buta[13] 7 ealle uncre eldran butan hi

---

[1] From MS. (b); illegible in the Laing Charter.
[2] *his*, MS. (b).   [3] Om. ibid.   [4] *þore*, B.
[5] *-bætan*, MS. (b).   [6] *feor*, ibid.
[7] ✠ *Ego* is prefixed to all the names in MS. (b).
[8] *-seald*, T.   [9] *æst*, B.   [10] *æf-*, T.
[11] *dæg*, T.   [12] Om. K., T.   [13] *-tu*; K.

VIII. GRANT OF LAND BY KING ÆTHELWULF TO THE OLD MINSTER, WINCHESTER

In nomine domini et salvatoris nostri Jesu Christi.

This document declares that King Æthelwulf granted to God and St Peter and the community at the Old Minster in Winchester 20 hides of land at Wanborough, when, with the consent of his councillors, he granted the tenth part of all his lands throughout all his kingdom to holy foundations for the praise of God and the eternal redemption of his soul; and he commanded in the name of God Almighty and of all his saints, that no king after his time or any other man should ever alter this, but that the property should always belong undisputed to the holy foundation; and if anyone altered it, he should be accursed by God and by St Peter, both during his life and after his death, unless he made amends for it. And this was done in the year after 854 years had passed since the birth of Christ, with the cognisance of the councillors whose names are recorded here below...

IX. GRANT IN REVERSION TO ROCHESTER

✠ *In nomine domini.*

Dunn has given this title-deed and the estate described therein to his wife, with God's goodwill, that she may hold it and enjoy it during her lifetime, and at her death grant it to the community in the name of the holy apostle St Andrew, with the consent of God and his saints, for both of us and all our ancestors, unless

16 GRANT IN REVERSION TO ROCHESTER

hit mit[1] unnan hiredes ofgan to rihtan[2] gafole swa swa hyt hy[3] geðingian magan · butan ælcen bræde · oððe beswice · 7 hy[4] ðonne se hired hit geearnian mid heora godcundnæsse ofer twelf monoð · 7 stande simle mid cwide seo boc on ðæs hiredes handa.

X. SUMMARY OF A LATIN CHARTER

5 ✠ Ðis siondan ðes landes boec et Wassingwellan ðet Eðelbearht cyning Wullafe sealde his ðegne wið oðrum sue miclum lande et Mersaham se cyning sealde 7 gebocade Wullafe fif sulung landes et Wassingwellan[5] wið ðem fif sulungum et Mersaham 7 se cyning dyde ðet land et Mersaham him to folclande ða hie
10 ðem landum iehwerfed hefdan butan ðem merscum 7 butan ðem sealtern et Fefresham 7 butan ðem wioda ðe to ðem sealtern limpð.

XI. CHARTER OF KING ÆTHELBERT TO SHERBORNE

✠ REGNANTE in perpetuum dño nŕo IH̄u xp̄o.

Ricsiendum urum dryhtne hælendun[6] Criste in ecnisse · ðæm
15 hiehstan 7 ðæm untosprecendlican ealra þinga · 7 ealra tida scippende · se þe on manegum ðingum his mihtum setteþ 7[7] waldeð[7]. Eac swylce ðam ure hefenlican[8] 7 þæm unasecgendlican rice · þte he ðisses lifes eadinysse 7 gesælinysse on ænigum þingum ne forlæte · Forþon[9] ic Æþelbreht mid Godes gife
20 Westsaxna kyning witoðlice[10] ic þence 7 me on gemynde is mid þissum eorþlicum ðingum þa ecelican gestreon to begitanne · Sicut Salomon dixit · redemptio animę proprię diuitię · Swa swa Salomon cwæþ · ðæt we sceoldon mid urum spedum urum saulum þa ecen gesælinesse begitan · forþon ic cuþlice mid
25 geðeahte 7 mid geðafonge 7 leafe minre[11] biscepa 7 ældormanna[12]. 7 nohte þon læs minra broðera · Æþelredes 7 Ælfredes · 7 ealra þara selestena witona ures[13] rices · Ic forgyfo[14] for me selfne · 7 for

---

[1] *init*, He.; *mid*, T. [2] *tosihtan*, He. [3] *by*, MS. (*b*), B.; *his*, He., K.
[4] *his*, He., K.; *hi*, T. [5] *Wassinwellan*, B.
[6] *-um*, T., B. [7] Om. T., B. [8] For *upehefenlican*.
[9] *-ðun*, B. [10] *witod-*, T., B. [11] *-ra*, T., B.
[12] *ald-*, T., B. [13] *þæs*, T., B. [14] *-gyfe*, T., B.

with the consent of the community it be obtained at a fair rent, as can be arranged, without any fraud or deceit; and the community shall acquire it by their divine services at the end of twelve months; and the title-deed shall always remain along with the will in the possession of the community.

X. SUMMARY OF A LATIN CHARTER

✠ These are the title-deeds of the estate at Westwell which King Æthelbert gave to Wullaf, his thegn, in return for another estate of the same size at Mersham. The king gave and granted by charter to Wullaf five ploughlands at Westwell in return for the five ploughlands at Mersham; and the king made the estate at Mersham into folkland for himself, when they had exchanged the estates, with the exception of the marshes and the salthouse at Faversham, and the wood which belongs to the salthouse.

XI. CHARTER OF KING ÆTHELBERT TO SHERBORNE

✠ *Regnante in perpetuum domino nostro Jesu Christo.*

Our Lord the Saviour Christ, who rules to all eternity, the most high and ineffable creator of all things and all seasons, he who establishes and governs many things by his power, including the lofty and ineffable kingdom, by no means neglects the happiness and prosperity of this life. For that reason I, Æthelbert, by the grace of God King of Wessex, truly intend and have it in mind to procure the everlasting treasure by means of these earthly things *sicut Salomon dixit, Redemptio animae propriae divitiae,* according to the words of Solomon that by means of our wealth we should obtain everlasting bliss for our souls. For that reason, therefore, with the advice, consent and leave of my bishops and earls and likewise of my brothers Æthelred and Alfred and of all the most distinguished councillors of our realm, I openly grant this freedom on my own

18 CHARTER OF KING ÆTHELBERT

mine þa liofestan lifiende frynd · 7 eac swylce[1] for arwuþnesse[2] Æþelwulfes saule mines fæder · 7 Æþelbaldes mines broþor · soþlice þisne freols · to þære halgan stowe æt Scireburnan ðær[3] Æþelbaldes cyninges lichama hine resteð · þ hit sy fæstlice 7
5 unanwended[4] 7 ecelice gefreod · alra cynelicra 7 alra domlicra[5] þeowdoma · ge ðeoffenges · ge æghwelcre ieðnesse[6] ealles worldlices broces · nymþe fyrde 7 brycge[7] weorces. Gyf[8] hwa þonne sye þ he hine for Godes lufan to þan geeaðmedan wille þ he þas ure gyfe geieacnan[9] wille oððe gemonifældan wille · geiece him
10 ælmihti God eal gód her on worlde · 7 his dagas gesundfulle.

Gyf þanne hwilc man to þan geþristlæce oððe mid deofles searwum to þam beswicen sye þ he þis on ænigum þingum lytlum oððe myclum þence to gebrecanne oððe to onwendanne · wite he þonne þ he þæs riht[10] agieldende sie byforan[11] Cristes ðrym-
15 setle · þonne ealle hefonware[12] 7 eorþware on his andweardnesse beoð onstyrede 7 onhrerede · nymþe he hit ær her on worlde mid ryhte gebete.

Ðis wæs gewriten þæs gære þe wæs agán fram Cristes acennednesse eahta hund wintra 7 feower 7 sixtig · 7 in þam tacencircole
20 þ twelfte gear · ðe dæg[13] wæs septimo kł JaN. Ðis wæs gedon in þam cynelican setle on þære stowe ðe is genæmned Dornwaraceaster · beforan þissum witum geþafigendum þe hære namon her benioþan gewritene 7 gesewene siondon[14].

✠ Ic Æþelbreht cyning mid þære halgan rode tacne þis hét swiþe
25 geornlice getrymman 7 gefæstnian[15].

✠ Ic Alhstan .eps.   ✠ Ic Cyma .miN.   ✠ Ic Æþelwulf .miN.
✠ Ic Eanwulf .dux.   ✠ Ic Beocca .miN.   ✠ Ic Wynsige .miN.
✠ Ic Ælfstan .dux.   ✠ Ic Æþelmod .miN.   ✠ Ic Goda .miN.
✠ Ic Æþelred .fil reg.   ✠ Ic Beorhtnoþ .miN. ✠ Ic Coenwald .miN.
30 ✠ Ic Ælfred .fil reg. ✠ Ic Denegils .miN.   ✠ Ic Æþelric .miN.
✠ Ic Osmund .miN.   ✠ Ic Wulfred .miN.   ✠ Ic Wulfhelm .miN.
✠ Ic Wulfhere .miN.   ✠ Ic Ecgbreht .miN.   ✠ Ic Hunred .miN.
✠ Ic Alhhard .abb.   ✠ Ic Monnel .miN.   ✠ Ic Ecgulf .miN.
✠ Ic Heahmund .pr.   ✠ Ic Eadwulf .miN.   ✠ Ic Ælfhere .miN.
35 ✠ Ic Hwita .ppo's.   ✠ Ic Wistan .miN.

[1] *swylc*, B.   [2] *-wurþ-*, T., B.   [3] *þære*, T., B.
[4] *-awend-*, T., B.   [5] *-lica*, B.   [6] For *unieð-*.
[7] *bryce*, T., B.   [8] *gif*, T., B.   [9] *-nian*, T., B.
[10] Om. T., B.   [11] *be-*, T., B.   [12] *heof-*, T., B.
[13] *deg*, T., B.   [14] *sindon*, T., B.
[15] T. (followed by B.) states erroneously that the other signatures are wanting.

behalf and for my dearest living friends, and likewise in honour of the souls of Æthelwulf, my father, and Æthelbald, my brother, to the holy foundation at Sherborne, where the body of King Æthelbald rests, that it be firmly and immutably and eternally freed from all royal and judicial services, including the arrest of thieves and all the irksomeness of secular labour, with the exception of military service and the construction of bridges. If, further, there is anyone who, for the love of God, will condescend to increase or multiply this our gift, God Almighty shall increase all good things for him here in this world, and make his days prosperous. If, however, any man is so presumptuous or so greatly deceived by the wiles of the devil, as to contemplate breaking or changing this in any particular, small or great, he shall find that he must render account for it before the throne of Christ, when all the dwellers in heaven and earth are moved and agitated in his presence, unless he has duly made amends for it here in this world.

This was written in the year 864 which had passed since the birth of Christ, and in the twelfth Indiction, on December 26. It was done in the royal residence at the place called Dorchester, in the presence and with the consent of these witnesses whose names are written and visible here below...

CHARTER OF KING ÆTHELBERT

Þa æfter þyssum hit gelamp þan ilcan geare þæs þe[1] þis on midne winter wæs gedon · ꝥ Æþelbreht se cining on frigedæg twam[2] nihtum ær estron þisne freols mid his agenre hande unnende mode ufan in[3] þone heah altare alegde æt hám æt
5 Scireburnan · in andweardnesse ealre þære broþorlican gesamnunga ealdra 7 giongra[4] · 7 eac swylce his mægan Æðelredes 7 Ælfredes · 7 his oþræ witona þe þær þa mid him wæron · for hine selfne lifigende · 7 for his twegen broþre þe þæt[5] þa andwearde stodon · 7 for hyra ealra fæder saule Æþelwulfes
10 cyninges · 7 Æþelbaldes cyninges[6] hyra broþor þe his lichama in þære stowe resteð. He þisne freodom on ælmihtiges[7] Godes namon 7 on ealra his halgra fæstlice bebead · þæt hine nán his æfterfylgendra eft ne onwende · ne on anegum dælum læssan ne on maran hine ne oncyrde · ac he swa ecelice forþ þurhwun-
15 edæ[8] · swa lange swa God wolde ꝥ cristen geleafa mid Eongolcynne[9] untosceacen weoxa · Ealra þara worldcundra hefinesse þe her beforan nemde syondon · 7 se hæbbe Godes miltse 7 his halgra · se þe þis mid Gode trymman wille 7 healdon. Gyf þonne hwa sie ꝥ he þis[10] on ænegum dæle wanian þence oððe brecan ·
20 þanne næbbe he naþer ne Godes miltse ne his haligra · nymþe he hit ǽr mid ryhte gebete · þis wæs gedon beforan ðære gewitnesse þe hyro naman her bynyoþan gemearcode standað[11].

  ✠ Ic Æþelbreht .rex.   ✠ Ic Æþelheah .p̄r.   ✠ Ic Herewulf .miN͂
  ✠ Ic Alhstan .ep̄s.   ✠ Ic Oswuulf .p̄r.   ✠ Ic Ærcmund .miN͂
25 ✠ Ic Æþelred .fil reḡ.   ✠ Ic Wistan .p̄r.   ✠ Ic Ceolred .miN͂.
  ✠ Ic Ælfred .fil reḡ.   ✠ Ic Ceolmund .diac̄.   ✠ Ic Burhgred .miN͂.
  ✠ Ic Heahmund .p̄r.   ✠ Ic Luhha .miN͂.   ✠ Ic Wulfric .miN͂.
  ✠ Ic Osmund .miN͂.   ✠ Ic Beorhtwulf .diac̄.   ✠ Ic Cyrred .miN͂.
  ✠ Ic Beorhtmund .miN͂.   ✠ Ic Ceolred .miN͂.   ✠ Ic Æþelwulf .miN͂.
30 ✠ Ic Cyma .miN͂.   ✠ Ic Eanwulf .miN͂.   ✠ Ic Ceolhelm .miN͂.
  ✠ Ic Ecgbreht .miN͂.   ✠ Ic Ealhferþ .miN͂.   ✠ Ic Eadulf .miN͂.
  ✠ Ic Babba .miN͂.   ✠ Ic Ceolwulf .miN͂.   ✠ Ic Ealhstan .miN͂.
  ✠ Ic Mucel .miN͂.   ✠ Ic Cynemund .miN͂.   ✠ Ic Ecgstan .miN͂.
  ✠ Ic Cynelaf .miN͂.   ✠ Ic Ealhstan .miN͂.   ✠ Ic Heorhtric .miN͂.
35 ✠ Ic Torhthelm diac̄ p̄po⁹s.   ✠ Ic Æþelmund .miN͂.   ✠ Ic Ceolheah .miN͂.
  ✠ Ic Burghelm .p̄r.   ✠ Ic Ceofa .miN͂.   ✠ Ic Wulfheah .miN͂.
  ✠ Ic Heoteman .p̄r.   ✠ Ic Duda .miN͂.   ✠ Ic Eardulf .miN͂.
  ✠ Ic Rædnoþ .p̄r.   ✠ Ic Wulfheard .miN͂. ✠ Ic Cuðred .miN͂.

[1] þæsne, T., B.   [2] twa, B.   [3] Om. T., B.
[4] geong-, T., B.   [5] þær, T., B.   [6] 7 Æþ. cyn., om. B.
[7] -an, B.   [8] þurwun-, T., B.   [9] Engol-, T., B.
[10] his, T., B.
[11] T. (followed by B.) states erroneously that the signatures are wanting.

TO SHERBORNE

Then in the same year after this had been done at midwinter it came to pass that King Æthelbert on Friday, two days before Easter, with joyful heart laid this charter of freedom with his own hand upon the high altar at the monastery in Sherborne, in the presence of all the assembled brethren, both old and young, and also of his kinsmen, Æthelred and Alfred, and of his other councillors who were there with him, on behalf of himself, during his lifetime, and for his two brothers, who were standing there present, and for the souls of King Æthelwulf, the father of all of them, and of King Æthelbald, their brother, whose body rests in the foundation. He strictly enjoined, in the name of Almighty God and of all his saints, with regard to this freedom from all the secular burdens named above, that none of his successors should afterwards alter or pervert it in any particular, small or great, but that it should continue to all eternity, as long as it was the will of God that the Christian faith should remain inviolate in England. And he who is willing to confirm and uphold it shall obtain the mercy of God and of his saints. If, however, there is anyone who attempts to diminish or break it in any particular, he shall obtain the mercy neither of God nor of his saints, unless he has duly made amends for it here.

This was done in the presence of the witnesses whose names are recorded here below...

XII. GRANT OF LAND BY KING ÆTHELRED I TO EARL ÆLFSTAN

Regnante imperpetuum domino nostro Ihesu Christo.

Rixiende ure dritte halende Crist · ich Atheldred mid Godes giue Westsaxne king mid leue and eþeafunghe mine ðare seleste [w]iotene[1] · Ich forgiue and selle for me selfne minre saule to 5 alesnesse minne ðam leueste and itreweste alderman Elfstane Alchene idal landes in þare istowe þe is inemned bę Chiselburne fif hide · him to habenne and 'to' brukende on elche halue · þat is þanne þat it bie i·sien fre ⸪ of al ikenelricre · and alderdomelere þinghe an i·witradenne · an of elchene þinghe buten 10 fierde and angieldes. And het it acheliche fre · þurʒwine habbe suelcman suo al se ich it habbe gief donne huelman[2] be segen þat he þis giue · and sale ieche oð manifelde wille i·ache him almiʒti God alle goode here for wolde and his igaste furch · agiue þa ache reste in ðam towarde liue. If þat ilimpe þat oniman þurch 15 deules lore and for þeses middelerdes idle þinghe on onni idale ilitel oþer michel þis ibreke oþer iwanie wite he hine fram alle leaffulle inne þese iworlde asceaden · and he des sel in domes deghe beforen Criste rich agieldende bute he it are her on worlde mid richte ibete.

20 Ðis land is þisen imare · þus ute þinsald arest[3] ⸪ on landscarhlinc ⸪ to Cheselburne þannen · anlang streames · þañ up of streame ⸪ on anne linkes haued þanen ⸪ be suðe ceat[w]anberge[1] · on þanne[4] hlinc · of þanne[4] ihlinche ⸪ on anne castel at swindone uuewearde · of þe castele to burnstowe · þanen up 25 anlang burnstowe þañ ⸪ on anne linkes heued · þanen ⸪ to anne castele[5] of þo icastel ⸪ on þere herepaþ westward op[6] ðe herepað on þat hlincreawe þanen ⸪ on anne crundel to burnstowe on anne cinep on ðan ʒerðe lande[7] nordewarde[8] · þanen ⸪ wið anne crundeles of þi crundele ⸪ on des[9] heges hirnen · 30 þanen eft to herepað of þe ereðe[10] ⸪ on hendune beorch on Deflisch of dune anlang streames · up on streame ⸪ on anne

---

[1] The MS. has þ for p. [2] ·i· oniman is written above. [3] Ærest, K.
[4] ðane, K. [5] castel, B. [6] Sic.
[7] Om. B. [8] norðe-, K. [9] ðes, K.
[10] erepaðe, K.

XII. GRANT OF LAND BY KING ÆTHELRED I TO EARL ÆLFSTAN

Regnante in perpetuum domino nostro Jesu Christo.

In the reign of our Lord the Saviour Christ, I, Æthelred, by the grace of God King of Wessex, with the leave and consent of my most distinguished councillors, give and grant on my own behalf for the redemption of my soul to my very dear and loyal Earl Ælfstan, every part of the estate of five hides in the place called Cheselborne, for him to hold and enjoy on every side. It shall be free from all royal and official burdens, from the payment of fines and from everything except military service and *angild*. And it shall remain free for all time, whoever holds it, just as I myself hold it. If anyone is found who is willing to increase or multiply this gift and grant, God Almighty shall increase all good things for him here in this world and grant his spirit eternal rest in the future life. If it happen that anyone, through the devil's teaching and for the sake of the vain things of this world, break or diminish this in any particular, small or great, he shall find himself cut off from all believers in this world, and he shall render just account of it in the presence of Christ on the Day of Judgment, unless he has duly made amends for it in this world.

The estate is enclosed within(?) these boundaries: first to the dividing ridge at the Cheselborne, thence along the stream, then up from the stream to the head of a ridge, then by the south of *ceatwanberge* to the ridge, from the ridge to a fort at the top of *swindone*, from the fort to the place where the stream runs, then up along the place where the stream runs, then to the head of a ridge, then to a fort, from the fort to the highway, westward up(?) the highway to the line of ridges, thence to a quarry at the place where the stream runs, [then] to a knoll on the north side of the arable land, then towards a quarry, from the quarry to the corner of the hedge, then back to the highway, from the highway to *hendune* tumulus [then] to Dewlish, down along the stream, up from(?) the stream to a furrow [then] to a

24 GRANT OF LAND BY KING ÆTHELRED I

furch on anne stancastel · of þi castele on blieqȝmannes¹ beorg of þa iberge ⁘ on landscare hlinc · and sex made eres be Frume wið Deuliscmad ierð to þise lande². ⁘
Ðises landes freols was iwriten in þare stowe þat is inemned
5 at [w]udegate³ beforen þese wetene þe here namen her beneþen amerkede standen. ⁘

Aþeldred⁴ Rex ✠   Ealferð eꝑc ✠
Heahmund eꝑc 7c ✠ ⁘

XIII. BEQUEST OF KING ALFRED TO SHAFTESBURY

ÐIS is þe quide þat Alured king ian into Sceaftesburi⁵ Gode
10 to loue and seint Marie and alre Godes halegen · mine saule to þearne⁶ on halre tungan ꝥ is an hund hide mid mete and mid manne al so it stant · and mine dochte Agelyue forð mid⁷ þare erie into þan menstre for þanne hie was onbroken ihadod · and mine socne into þan menstre þat ic selue · achte · þat is forsteal ·
15 and hamsocne and mundebreche · and þis sent þare landiname · þe ic þider iunnen habbe · þat is at Dunheued and at Cumtune XL. hide · and at Hanlee · and Gissic xx hide · and at Terente x hide 7 at Ywern .xv. hide · and ffuntemel⁸ xv hiden · and þis is to witnesse Adward mine sune · and Aþered arceb · and
20 Alcheferd bissop and Adelheach b · and Wlfhere alderman and Adwlf Alderman and Cuðred Alderman and Tumbert Abb and Midred⁹ mine þegen and Aþelwulf et Osric and Berthful and Cyma. And loke hwa þeses awande · habbe he Godes curs et Sainte Marien and alle Godes haleges ac on ecnesse. Amen ⁘

¹ *blieque-*, K.   ² *land*, B.
³ The MS. has initial *p* for *þ*.   ⁴ *Aþelred*, B.
⁵ *Shaftes-*, D.   ⁶ For *þearue*.
⁷ *and*, D.   ⁸ *Funt-*, D.
⁹ *Mildred*, B.

stone fort, from the fort to *blieqʒmannes* tumulus, from the tumulus to the dividing ridge. And 6 acres of meadow by the Frome opposite the Dewlish meadow belong to this estate. This land-charter was written in the place called Woodgate in the presence of the councillors whose names are recorded here below...

XIII. BEQUEST OF KING ALFRED TO SHAFTESBURY

This is the bequest which [I,] King Alfred, make unequivocally to Shaftesbury, to the praise of God and St Mary and all the saints of God, for the benefit of my soul, namely a hundred hides as they stand with their produce and their men, and my daughter Æthelgifu to the convent along with the inheritance, since she took the veil on account of bad health; and the [profits of] jurisdiction to the convent, which I myself possessed, namely [the fines for] obstruction and attacks on a man's house and breach of protection. And the estates which I have granted to the foundation are 40 hides at Donhead and Compton, 20 hides at Handley and Gussage, 10 hides at Tarrant, 15 hides at Iwerne and 15 hides at Fontmell.

The witnesses of this are Edward my son and Archbishop Æthelred and Bishop Ealhferth and Bishop Æthelheah and Earl Wulfhere and Earl Eadwulf and Earl Cuthred and Abbot Tunberht and Milred my thegn and Æthelwulf and Osric and Briht[w]ul[f] and Cyma.

If anyone alters this, he shall have the curse of God and St Mary and all the saints of God forever to all eternity. Amen.

XIV. LEASE OF LAND BY EALHFERTH, BISHOP OF WINCHESTER

IN NOMINE DOMINI. Ealhferð Biscéop 7 ða higan on Wintaceastre · habbað gelæneð hiora leófan friond .VIII. hida landes on EASTVNE · ðriora manna deg ðet ís CUÐRED dux 7[1] Wulfriðe his wife 7 ánan
5 man þerto suil him liofost síe him tó hæbbenne 7 to brucénne swa hím sælest síe éghwælces þinges freoh butan brycgeweorce 7 ferde · 7 eahta ciricsceattan 7 mæsseprestes gereohta 7 saulsceattas[2] · 7 hi bebiodað on ælmeahtiges naman · 7 on sc̄es Petres ðes apostoles naman · 7 ón ealra Godes halgona naman · ðæt ðæt
10 land[3] sie laborðe[4] · 7 higan swa géwelde ofer hiora ðriora deg swa hid[5] wæs ðy dege ðe hióe[6] hit hiom sealdan. 7 Ðis is gedon be þara weotena gewitnesse ðe heora naman her beneoðan áwritene standað · 7 mid Cristes rodes getacne gemearcode.

EGO Ælfred Rex.	Ego Tunberð abb.	Ego Milred miñ.
15 EGO Ælferð eр̄c.	Ego Ælfreð[8] pb.	Ego Beorhtnoð miñ.
EGO Ædelheah[7] eр̄c.	Ego Hunsige pb.	Ego Æðelnoð miñ.
EGO Wulfhere Dux.	Ego Cynestan pb.	Ego Dudig miñ.
Ego Æðelstan Dux.	Ego Biornlaf pb.	Ego Heremod miñ.
Ego Eadwulf Dux.	Ego Henulf Diac̄.	Ego Æðelferð miñ.
20 Ego Ordulf Dux.	Ego Ælfstan Diac̄.	Ego Ælfhere miñ.
Ego Elfstan Dux.	Ego Aðeuulf[9] Diac̄.	Ego Wigred miñ.
Ego Cuðred Dux.		

ÐES londes gemero æt EASTVNE · lið óf ycenan in earna bæce æf[10] swa 7lang bæces · útt on ðæt geat æft be þan andheaf-
25 dan od[11] þone midlestan beorg · æft swa on ædeswyrðe eastewearde æft útt on þa roda on heringesleah easteweardne · æft útt on þa furh on smalan dune easte wearde · æft útt on þa furh ðe Wulfred hét · adrífan æft of dune on ða dene swá on ðone mylensteall æt[12] swe of ðem mylenstealle andlang ycenan æft on
30 earna bæce.

[1] Om. B.	[2] -sceott-, B.	[3] lande, K.
[4] -de, K.	[5] hit, K.	[6] higen, K.
[7] Æð-, K., B.	[8] -fred, K.	[9] -wulf, K.
[10] æft, K.	[11] oð, K.	[12] ðæt, K.

XIV. LEASE OF LAND BY EALHFERTH, BISHOP OF WINCHESTER

In nomine domini.

Bishop Ealhferth and the community at Winchester have leased 8 hides of land at Easton for three lives to their dear friend Earl Cuthred and to Wulfthryth, his wife, and to one man of his own choice in addition, to hold and enjoy as may be best for him, free from every burden except the construction of bridges and military service and the payment of eightfold church dues and the priest's dues and burial fees. And they enjoin, in the name of the Almighty and of St Peter the Apostle and in the name of all the saints of God, that this estate shall be as completely subject to the lord and the community after the death of the three of them as it was on the day that they granted it to them. And this is done with the cognisance of the councillors whose names are recorded in writing below and marked with the symbol of the cross of Christ...

The boundary of the estate at Easton extends from the Itchen to the eagles' brook, and then along the brook out to the gate, then by the headlands to the midmost barrow, then to the east of *ædeswyrðe*, then out to the clearing to the east of *heringesleah*, then out to the furrow on the east of the narrow hill, then out to the furrow which Wulfred caused to be made, then from the hill to the valley, then to the site of the mill, then from the site of the mill along the Itchen back to the eagles' brook.

XV. LEASE OF LAND BY DENEWULF, BISHOP OF WINCHESTER

DENEwulf bisceop 7 þa hýwan on Wintanceástre · Ænlænað Ælfrede his deg .XL. hida landes æt Alresforda · æfter þære læna þe Tunbryht bisceop ær alende his yldran 7 agan wés · On ðæt gerað[1] þet he gesylle ælce geáre to hærfestes emnihte · Ðréo pund to gafole · 7 cyresceattas 7 cyresceatweorc · 7 þenne þæs nuð[2] bið his men beon gearúwe ge tó ripe · ge to huntoðe · 7 efter his dege gánge seo ðar[3] umbeflítan ínto sc̄e Petre · þís synt þara wítena hundsetena[4] 7 ðere hina ðe on þære geðafunge wéron.

Ðæt ís Denewulf	And Æðelm cł.	And Ælfsige cł.
bisceop.	And Cynestan cł.	And Wulfhelm cł.
And Tata bisc̄.	And Aðeric cł.	And Wulfsige cł.
And Byrnstan bisc̄.	And Ðruðgar cł.	And Wiglaf cł.
And Wighelm Diac̄.	And Wulfric cł.	And Wulfred miñ.
And Æþelstan cler̄.	And Winsige cł.	And Beornulf miñ.
And Eadwulf cł.	And Wulfred cł.	And Winstan miñ.
And Ælfstan cł.	And Beorhtsige cł.	And Aðulf miñ.
And Wulfstan cł.		

XVI. LEASE OF LAND BY WERFRITH, BISHOP OF WORCESTER, TO CYNESWITH

✠ In usses Dryhtnes noman hælendes Cristes · ic Uuerfriþ biscop mid alles ðæs heoredes leafe on Weogornaceastre ge gunges ge aldes selle Cyneswiþe mire[5] megan ðreora hida lond on Alhmundingtune ðaes fif hida ðe higen me gebocedan aer on ðreora monna dæg. Nu gewrite ic hit eft hire mid hina leafe ðaet ðreora hida lond on ðreora monna daeg 7 heo hæbbe ða wuduraeddenne in ðæm wuda ðe ða ceorlas brucaþ · 7 ec ic hire lete to ðaet ceorla graf to sundran: · 7 elles ðæt twega hida lond 7 ða ceorlas 7 se Alhmunding snaed here into Preosdabyrig ða hwile hit unagaen seo. Ond Cyneswið hit to nængum oþrum men ne lete ða hwile hit unagæn se butun to hire bearna sumum swa hweolcum swa heo ðonne wille gif heo lifigen · gif heo ðonne ne

[1] -rad, K.
[2] neod, K.; nud, B.
[3] ar, K.
[4] hand-, K.
[5] minre, K.

XV. LEASE OF LAND BY DENEWULF, BISHOP OF WINCHESTER

Bishop Denewulf and the community at Winchester lease to Alfred for his lifetime 40 hides of land at Alresford, in accordance with the lease which Bishop Tunbriht had granted to his parents and which had run out, on condition that he renders every year at the autumnal equinox three pounds as rent, and church dues, and [does] the work connected with church dues; and when the need arises, his men shall be ready both for harvesting and hunting; and after his death the property shall pass undisputed to St Peter's.

These are the signatures of the councillors and of the members of the community who gave their consent, namely...

XVI. LEASE OF LAND BY WERFRITH, BISHOP OF WORCESTER, TO CYNESWITH

✠ In the name of our Lord the Saviour Christ, I, Bishop Werfrith, with the permission of all the community at Worcester, both young and old, grant to Cyneswith, my kinswoman, three of the five hides of land at Elmstone which the community formerly granted me by charter for three lives. Now subsequently, with the permission of the community, I make over to her the three hides of land for three lives, and she shall have the right of cutting timber in the wood which the peasants enjoy; and likewise I let to her separately the peasants' copse. And the remaining two hides of land and the peasants and the Elmstone wood shall belong to Prestbury, as long as the lease of the land runs. And Cyneswith shall not leave it to anyone, while the lease runs, except one of her children—whichever she pleases—

30 LEASE OF LAND BY WERFRITH

lifigen · lete hit to sweolcum hire mega swelce hit hire to geearnigan wille. Ond ic Uuerfrið biscop biddu 7 halsigu ðæt ðis ðreora hida lond 7 ec ðæt twega ðonne hit agæn seo ðæt hit se agefen into Clife to ðæm biscoprice butan eghweolcum wiðer-
5 cwide. Ond ec ic Uuerfriþ biscop 7 all higen halsigaþ usse æterfylgend[1] ðæt heora nænig ðas gefe gewonige aer hit swa agæn se swa hit on ðissum gewrite stondeþ · 7 all higen eodan to minum bure on Weogornaceastre 7 me saldan heora hondsetene ðisse geraednesse · ðara noman her beneoþan awriten stondaþ ·
10 7 heo hit haebben eghwæs to freon butun agefen elce gere ðreo mittan hwætes to ciricsceatte to Clife[2]: ·

✠ Werfriþ Episc.   ✠ Berhþelm.   ✠ Heahred.
✠ Cynhel[3] abb.   ✠ Cynah.   ✠ Wulfgar.
✠ Werfrið pre.   ✠ Eamberht.   ✠ Eardwulf.
15 ✠ Ecfriþ pr.   ✠ Wullaf.   ✠ Cynelaf.
✠ Wighard.   ✠ Cynhelm.   ✠ Wigfriþ.
✠ Berhþelm.   ✠ Cenfriþ.   ✠ Wulfric.
✠ Eardwulf.   ✠ Cynhelm.   ✠ Ceolhelm.
✠ Wulfred.

XVII. BEQUEST OF CEOLWIN TO WINCHESTER

20 CEOLWIN[4] cyð on ðis gewríte þæt hi an ðæs · landes æt AWELTVNE · ðara xv. hida ðæ hire hlaford hire læfde 7 him man ón agene æht gereahte · on ÆlfrEDES cynges gewithnesse[5] ðenne an hio his ðæm híwum to Wintanceástre æfter hire dége into hære beddarn æt ðam bisceopstole mid swelcan yrfe swelcan
25 hi ðenne to gehagað on ða gerað ðe hi gemunen hi 7 Osmodes saulæ swa him rihtlic 7 cynlic þince to his gemunde dege ðæt beoð seofan nihtan ær gangdagan 7 hio he bebot[6] on Godæs naman 7 sc̄e Petres ðet ða híwan hit næfre útt ne syllan of hira bæddern wið nanan feo buton hi hit wið oðre lande sullan ðæ hím gehændre
30 beo[7] 7 behefre 7 hiwan habbað hire behaton ðet hi finden ðet

---
[1] æfter-, K.
[2] Between the body of the charter and the signatures Smith inserts *Inferiori parte hujus cartæ sunt semilitteræ hujus vocis, viz. Cyrographum*: ·
[3] Cynehel, B.   [4] -wen, K.
[5] -wiðn-, K.; -witn-, T.   [6] hebot, B.
[7] heo, B.

if they survive. If they do not survive, she shall leave it to whichever of her kinsmen is willing to earn it from her. And I, Bishop Werfrith, beg and beseech that these three hides of land and likewise the two hides, when the lease has run out, be given back to Cleeve for the bishopric without any controversy. And likewise I, Bishop Werfrith, and all the community entreat our successors that none of them diminish this grant before the lease has run, as it is recorded in this document. And all the members of the community went to my room in Worcester and gave me their signature to this agreement. Their names are recorded in writing below. And she shall hold it free in every respect, except for rendering every year three *mittan* of wheat as church dues to Cleeve...

XVII. BEQUEST OF CEOLWIN TO WINCHESTER

Ceolwin declares in this document that she grants the estate of 15 hides at Alton, which her lord left her and which was made over to him as his own property with the cognisance of King Alfred, to the community at Winchester after her death for their refectory at the episcopal see, with such stock as is fitting at the time, on condition that they remember her and Osmod's soul, as seems right and fitting to them, on his commemoration day which is seven days before the Rogation Days. And she commands, in the name of God and of St Peter, that the community shall never give it away from their refectory for money, unless they give it in return for another estate which is nearer and more convenient for them. And the community has promised her to

32 BEQUEST OF CEOLWIN

Wulfstan hire broðor sunu hæbbe an hiwissce ægefæles[1] landæs
ða wíle ðe hæ libbe.
Aweltunæ metæ[2].

ÐES londes gemæro sindon to Aweltune Ærest of þam west-
5 mæstan æwylle angerihta[3] upp to ðam ealdan hærepaðe[4] be
westan wodnes beorge þonne ón ænne stan æt ceorlacumbes
heafoð[5] þonne on ænne stán on woncumb neopeweardne ís
ufeweard hol · þonne ofer randune to þæm ealdan díc on æfen
þær liggeþ on oþre healfe an lytel crundol þonne on þane
10 gemænan garan beúton þæm díc of[6] þæt eft geð inna þet read
geát þonne on anne[7] micelne stán æt þera hlinca eastheafdum
þonon on oþerne micelne stán on þam wege middan on þære
denæ bytnan þe ligged[8] útt on woddes geat þonne on ænne
crundol of[9] þam suðhlíðe niopeweardum þonne up ofer þa dune
15 ón ænne þórn stent inne of[9] þem díc be eastan ciceling wege ·
þonne andlang þes[10] hlinces óf moxes dune on þane ealdan walweg
to wearcingwege[11] niopeweardan ón þone díc þonon on wicleáge
þonon on anes hlinces heafod on Beorhtnoðes gemære · þonon
on gerihto to ruwan hlince · þonne 7lang þæs hlinces to heaþo-
20 brihtting leáge niopoweardre þonne ón anne ealdne holne weg
andlang þæs sledes to ewelforda þonne andlang þæs broces[12] eft
to þæm æwelle. Fram moxes dune suðeweardre on þa díc þonne
andlang díc ꝥ wið eastan cealfa mære · þonne óf þære díc on
þone midmæstan scrippan[13] þonne on þawæres leáge ufeweárde ·
25 þonne andlang rode on þone litlan garan middeweardne þonan
andlang gewyrpes to herpoðe · þonne to þære dice hyrnan þonne
andlang díc to creodan hylle þonne to herpoðe ongean þa xv.
æceras þonne óf þæm andlang hærpaðes to tesan mede · 7 se
heðfeld eal gemæne.

[1] -fæl-, T. [2] This heading is omitted by K. and T.
[3] -tra, B. [4] here-, T. [5] -od, K.
[6] For oð. [7] ænne, K. [8] -eð, K.
[9] For on. [10] þæs, T. [11] weascing-, K., T.
[12] K. and T. have [be ðam ealden eadenne] after broces.
[13] The reading might be either scrippan (cf. K., T., B.) or scriwwan as p
and ƿ are very difficult to distinguish between in the MS.

arrange that Wulfstan, her brother's son, shall have a hide of rent-free land as long as he lives.

The boundaries of Alton.

These are the boundaries of the estate at Alton, first from the westernmost spring straight up to the old highway to the west of Woden's barrow, then to a stone at the head of 'peasants' combe', then to a stone in the bottom of *woncumb* which is hollow at the top, then over *randune* to the old dyke, level with which on the other side there lies a little quarry, then to the common 'gore' beyond the dyke until it comes back through the red gate, then to a large stone at the eastern headlands of the ridges, thence to another large stone in the middle of the road at the bottom of the valley which runs out to Woden's gate, then to a quarry at the foot of the southern slope, then up over the hill to a thornbush which stands on the inside of the dyke to the east of the *ciceling* road, then along the ridge from *moxes* hill to the old *walweg* [leading] to the bottom of the *wearcingwege*, [then] to the dyke, thence to the meadow by the dairy farm, then to the head of a ridge in Brihtnoth's boundary, then straight on to the rough ridge, then along the ridge to the bottom of 'Heathobriht's clearing', then to an old hollow road, along the valley to the ford by the spring, then along the brook back to the spring.

From the south of *moxes* hill to the dyke, then along the dyke towards the east of the calves' pond, then from the dyke to the midmost *scrippan*, then to the upper side of *pawæres* clearing, then along the clearing to the middle of the little 'gore', then along the bank (?) to the highway, then to the corner of the dyke, then along the dyke to Creoda's hill, then to the highway opposite the 15 acres, then from them along the highway to Tawsmead; and the unenclosed heath [is held] entirely in common.

XVIII. LEASE OF LAND BY WERFRITH, BISHOP OF WORCESTER, TO WULFSIGE

Rixiendum on ecnisse ussum drihtne hælende Criste seðe all ðing gemetegað ge on heofenum ge on eorðan þæs inflæscnisse ðy gere þe agen wæs DCCCC wintra 7 IIII winter 7 ðy .VII. gebongere · Ic Uuerfrid bisco'p' mid mines arweorðan heorodes
5 geðafuncga 7 leafe on Weogernaceastre sylle Wulfsige minum gerefan wið his holdum mægene 7 eadmodre hernesse anes hides lond on Easttune swa swa Herred hit hæfde on ðreora monna dæg 7 all ðæt Innlond beligeð án dic utane 7 þonne ofer ðreora monna dęg agefe monn eft[1] ðaet lond butan elcon wiðer-
10 cwide Innto Weogernaceastre 7 ðis seondan ðara monna noman ðe ðæt geðafedon 7 mid Cristes rode tacne gefæstnedon

✠ Uuerfrið biscop	✠ Cynað diacon	✠ Cynehelm
✠ Cynehelm abb	✠ Berhthelm	✠ Uulfric
✠ Uuerfrið prs	✠ Wigheard	✠ Cenfrið
15 ✠ Eadmund prs	✠ Monn	✠ Hwituc
✠ Berhtmund prs	✠ Earduulf	✠ Cynelaf
✠ Tidbald prs	✠ Uullaf	✠ Ceolhelm
✠ Hildefrið prs	✠ Berhthelm	✠ Uullaf
✠ Ecfrið prs	✠ Heahred	✠ Ealhmund[2]
20 ✠ Eaduulf prs	✠ Cynelaf	✠ Earduulf
✠ Wiglaf prs	✠ Uulfred	✠ Uulfgar
✠ Oslac diacon		

XIX. LEASE OF LANDS BY WERFRITH, BISHOP OF WORCESTER, TO ÆTHELRED AND ÆTHELFLÆD

EÐEREDES GERĘDNESSE 7 EÐELFLEDE WIÐ WERFRIÐ B̃[3]:—

25 OMNIBUS NAMQUE SAPIENTIBUS NOTVM AC MANIFESTVM CONstat[4] · quod dicta hominum uel facta pro multiplicibus criminum perturbationibus[5] et cogitationum uaga-

---
[1] aft, B.   [2] Ealmund, B.
[3] This heading is not found in MS. (b), which has Lænhaga 7 landlæn Æþerede 7 Æþelflæde in the left margin.
[4] The first line ends at CON- in MS. (a).
[5] multiplici erumnarum perturbatione, MS. (b).

XVIII. LEASE OF LAND BY WERFRITH, BISHOP OF WORCESTER, TO WULFSIGE

In the everlasting reign of our Lord the Saviour Christ who governs all things both in heaven and on earth, and in the year 904 of his incarnation, and the seventh Indiction, I, Bishop Werfrith, with the permission and leave of my honourable community in Worcester, grant to Wulfsige, my reeve, for his loyal efficiency and humble obedience, one hide of land at Aston as Herred held it, for three lives—and all the demesne land is surrounded by a dyke outside—and then after three lives the estate shall be given back without any controversy to Worcester. And these are the names of the men who permitted it and confirmed it with the symbol of the cross of Christ...

XIX. LEASE OF LANDS BY WERFRITH, BISHOP OF WORCESTER, TO ÆTHELRED AND ÆTHELFLÆD

The agreement of Æthelred and Æthelflæd with Bishop Werfrith.

It is known and manifest to all the wise that the words and deeds of men frequently slip from the memory, through the manifold agitations caused by wicked deeds, and as the result

36 LEASE OF LANDS BY WERFRITH

tionibus[1] frequenter ex memoria recedunt nisi litterarum apicibus et custodię cautela scripturarum reseruentur et ad memoriam reuocentur. Quamobrem anno dominicę incarnationis DCCCC. IIII. indictione .I. has ob memoriam posteritatis litteras scribere
5 iussimus. Þæt is þonne ꝥ Werfrið b 7 se hired[2] æt Wigraceastre[3] syllað 7 gewritað Æþelrede 7 Æþelflæde heora hlafordum þonæ hagan binnan byri æt Wigraceastre[3] · se is fram þære ea sylfre bi þæm norðwalle eastwardes .XXVIII. roda lang · 7 þonon suþwardes .XX. IIII. roda brad · 7 eft þonon westwardes on
10 Sæferne .XIX. roda long · 7 eac hi syllað him ꝥ medwe land bewestaN Sæferne on efen þone hagan · andlang þæs bisceopes dic[4] of þære ea ꝥ hit cymð west ut on ꝥ mór dic[5] · 7 swa norð ꝥ hit cymð[6] ut on efen ꝥ gelad · 7 swa estwardes ꝥ hit cymð eft wiðneoþan ꝥ gelad on Sæferne. Eac hi syllað him Beferburnan[7] ·
15 7 eac þærto .LX. æcera earðlondes besuþan Beferburnan · 7 oþre .LX. benorðan · 7 ec swyþe rumedlice .XII. æceras þærto fulgodes[8] mædlandes · 7 eall hi syllað þiss heom mid[9] milde mode · 7 wilniað him to ꝥ hi sýn eigðer ge hlafordes freond ge þara hina · ge þære cyrcan · 7 hig his wyllað alning hieom
20 toearnien dæges 7 nihtes mid heora godcundnesse · swa hi betst magoN · 7 hi hit habban á ge binnan byrig ge butan unbesacen wið ælce hand þa hwyle þe hi lifgean · 7 gif Ælfw̄ leng sy · þonne sy hit[10] swa unbesacen þa hwıle þe heo lifige · 7 ofer heora þreora dæig · agefe hit mon eft þære circean hlaforde · swa gegodad
25 swa hit þonne sy · for heora þreora sawle · buton ælcum[11] geflite · gif God wile ꝥ hig hit godian motan. Augentibus et custodientibus retributio ęternę beatitudinis augeatur in cęlo · minuentes et frangentes sempiterna increpatione redarguantur · nisi prius digna satisfactione emendauerint · þas gerædnesse eall se hired
30 ge iunge ge ealde mid[12] Cristes rode tacne gefæstnodon · 7 þara

---

[1] -ione, MS. (b).   [2] seo heoredden, ibid.   [3] Weogernaceastre, ibid.
[4] þære bisceopes dice, ibid.   [5] ón dic, ibid.
[6] ꝥ hit cymð, om. ibid.   [7] be Beferburnan þa ludading wic, ibid.
[8] fúlgodes, ibid.; Fulgodes, B.   [9] hiora, MS. (b).
[10] sy hit hvre, ibid.   [11] [æg]hwelcum, ibid.   [12] into, B.

TO ÆTHELRED AND ÆTHELFLÆD 37

of wandering thoughts, unless they are preserved and recalled to mind in the form of words and by the precaution of entrusting them to writing. For this reason, in the year of the incarnation of our Lord 904 and in the first Indiction, we have ordered this document to be written for the sake of the memory of posterity, namely that Bishop Werfrith and the community at Worcester give and grant by charter to Æthelred and Æthelflæd, their lords, the messuage within the town wall at Worcester which is 28 rods in length from the river itself along the north wall eastwards and thence southwards 24 rods in breadth and then westwards to the Severn 19 rods in length. And likewise they grant them the meadow-land west of the Severn, on a level with the messuage, [extending] west along the bishop's dyke from the river, until it comes out at the moor-dyke, and then north until it comes out on a level with the water-course, and then eastwards until it comes back below the water-course to the Severn.

They likewise grant them Barbourne, and in addition 60 acres of arable land south of Barbourne and another 60 acres to the north, and likewise, very generously, 12 acres of very good meadow-land in addition; and they graciously grant them this, and desire of them their friendship both towards their lord and towards the community and towards the church, and desire to earn it from them always, day and night, by their divine services, as best they can. And Æthelred and Æthelflæd shall hold it for all time, both within the town wall and without, uncontested by anyone as long as they live. And if Ælfwyn survives them, it shall similarly remain uncontested as long as she lives; and after the death of the three of them, it shall be given back without dispute to the lord of the church for the souls of the three of them, endowed as it is then, if it be God's will that they may endow it.

To those who increase and uphold this shall be added the reward of eternal bliss in heaven. Those who diminish and break it shall be confounded by eternal punishment, unless they have made due amends.

All the community, both young and old, have confirmed this agreement with the symbol of the cross of Christ, and twelve of

38   LEASE OF LANDS BY WERFRITH

.XII. noman her standað awritene bæftan[1] · 7 eac þara freonda noman þe we us to gewitnesse curon[2].

✠ Æþelred aldorman 7 Æþelflæd Myrcna hlafordas mid us hit geWRITON.
5 ✠ Ego Werfrið eps propria manu consensi et corroboro[3].
✠ Ego Kinelm abb.[4]   ✠ Bernhelm.   ✠ Aldred.
✠ Ego Ecgfrið pbr   ✠ Eardwulfus.   ✠ Æþelfrið ealdor-
   consensi.   ✠ Wlfred.   mann.
✠ Ego Wiglaf pbr.   ✠ Ceolhelm.   ✠ Ælfred.
10 ✠ Ego Oslac pbr.   ✠ Wllaf.   ✠ Ælfstan.
✠ Ego Cinað dia-   ✠ Alhmund.   ✠ Eadric.
   conus.   ✠ Edgar b.   ✠ Wlfhun.

✠ Æþeredes gerædnesse[5] 7 Æþelflæde wið Werfrið b 7 wiþ þone hired on WegernaceaSTER.

XX. LEASE OF LAND TO DENEWULF, BISHOP OF WINCHESTER

15 IN NOMINE DÑI.

EADWARD cyning 7 þa hiwan in Wintanceastre lætað to Dænewulfe bisceópe twentig hida landes be Ticceburnan swa géirfað swa hít nu stent þreóra manna deg æfter his dege swilcum frand to tolætenne swilce hím leofost boð[6] on þa gerad þe man 20 gemynd[7] æfter his dege to þære halgan stowe dó in Wíntanceastre swa swa hé þænne finde þæt hít mæðlic síe 7 aberendlíc be þæs landes meðe ælce geáre to þære edmeltide · þæt mon geselle twelf seoxtres beóras 7 twelf geswettes wilisc ealoð · 7 twentig ambra hluttor ealoð · 7 tu hund greates hlafes 7 þridde 25 smales[8] · 7 tu hrieðeru oþer sealt oþer ferse[9] · 7 six weðeras 7 feower 7[10] swin 7 feor fliccu 7 twentig cysa · gyf hít on lencten gebyrige ꝥ þæ þonne þære flæscun geweorð on fisce gestriene buton ꝥ þis forgenge síe · gíf hit þænne sie se ðe þæt land hæbbe · ꝥ he þis his geagenes þances tuwa forgymeleasie buton hít

[1] be æftan, MS. (b).   [2] gecuron, ibid.
[3] Illegible in MS. (b); subscripsi He.
[4] Cynhelm diac. et abb. subscripsi, MS. (b).   [5] -nis, ibid.
[6] beoð, K.   [7] [his] gem., T.   [8] smalles, K.
[9] fersc, K., T.   [10] Om. K., T.

TO ÆTHELRED AND ÆTHELFLÆD 39

their names are recorded hereafter in writing, and likewise the names of the friends whom we selected as witnesses...

✠ The agreement of Æthelred and Æthelflæd with Bishop Werfrith and the community at Worcester.

XX. LEASE OF LAND TO DENEWULF, BISHOP OF WINCHESTER

In nomine domini.

King Edward and the community at Winchester lease to Bishop Denewulf for three lives 20 hides of land at Tichborne, stocked as they now are, to be leased after his death to a friend of his own choice, on condition that after his (Denewulf's) death, his commemoration shall be celebrated at the holy foundation in Winchester, as shall be found at the time to be fitting and possible in view of the condition of the estate. Every year, as the time recurs, there shall be rendered 12 sesters of beer and 12 of sweet Welsh ale and 20 ambers of clear ale and 200 large loaves and another hundred of small loaves and 2 oxen—one salt, the other fresh—and 6 wethers and 4 swine and 4 flitches of bacon and 20 cheeses. If it occurs in Lent, then the value of the meat shall be taken in fish, unless this is impracticable. If it happens, however, that he who holds the estate neglects this twice of his own free will, unless it arise through stress caused by a raid, then I pray the community for the love of God...to take possession of the estate and celebrate my commemoration according to the regulations which pertain to it, as they are set

40 LEASE OF LAND TO DENEWULF

hæres[1] unæmetta sie þonne bid hic hiwan for Godæs lufan (to tidsongum min gemund dón · þonne bebeodað hie on Godes ælmihtiges naman 7 on sc̄es Petres 7 on sc̄es Paules)[2] þæt hi fon to þan lande 7 min gemund þær on þam gerihtum þæ þartó[3]
5 bælimpað arerad[4] be þam ilcan þe hít her bufan gecweden ís · buton þæt hi for Godes lufan to tidsangam[5] min gémund dón. Þonne bebeodad[4] hie on Godes ælmihtiges naman 7 on sc̄es Petres 7 on sc̄es Paules þæ hit hiera yrfe is ꝧ hit swa umbesæccen gange into þære Cyrican swa hit þa on dæg wes þa hit man hím
10 to læt · 7 his[6] gewrit was awriten on Wintanceastre on þara witena gewitnesse þe hiera naman hær bæniþan awriten standad[4].

Þæt is génemned EADWARD cyning.

And Plegmund arceb.	And Beornulf m̄.	And Wulfsige cł.
And Friðestan bisc̄.	And Æþelstan cł	And Winsige cł.
15 And Osulf Dux.	And Eaduf[9] cł	And Wulfsige cł.
And Deormod miñ.	And Ælfstan cł.	And Wilaf cł.
And Tata pb	And Æþelweard cł.	And Wulfstan cł.
And Beornstan pb	And Wulfhelm cł	And Æðehelm[10] cł.
And Æþelstan pb	And Wulfstan cł.	And Cynestan cł.
20 And Ælfstan pb	And Wulfric cł.	And Heremod cł.
And Ealhstan pb	And Winsige cł.	And Ðrudgar[11] cł.
And Wulfric pb	And Beorhtsige cł.	And Æðric cł.
And Æþelbyrth[7] pb	And Ælfsige cł.	And Ælfred cł.
And Yðelbeard pb	And Eadulf cł.	And Vffa cł.
25 And Wigelm[8] Diac̄		

ÐÍS synt ða gemæro to TICCEBVRNAN erest[12] on ellen forð þanon on þone miclan hlinc ðonne on æpphangran easteweardne · ðanón on hormæres wudu middeweardne · þanon on gerihte to scealdæmeres hamme · þonon on mælanbeorh middeweardne
30 þonne þær to wuda on þone heal andlang weges utt to hig leáge · þanón norh 7 west innan þone heal þanon 7lang leage · þonne 7lang weges to torscagan þanon 7lang weges upp on gandran dune andlang weges to readan anstigan · þanon 7lang weges on ceaforleáge þanon on þone miclan hlinc þanon on cuþænes ford

---

[1] T. suggests that *hæres* may be an error for *hærfestes*.
[2] The passage put within brackets in the text has been omitted in the translation, see p. 297.   [3] *þær-*, T.
[4] *-að*, K.   [5] *-um*, T.   [6] *ðis*, K.; *þis*, T.
[7] *-ht*, K.   [8] *-helm*, K., B.   [9] *-ulf*, K., T.
[10] *Æðelh-*, T.   [11] *Ðruð-*, K.   [12] *Ær-*, K., T.

LEASE OF LAND TO DENEWULF

out above, unless, for the love of God, they celebrate my commemoration at their services. And now they enjoin, in the name of God Almighty and of St Peter and of St Paul, whose property it is, that it shall pass uncontested into the possession of the church, as it was on the day when it was leased to him.

This document was written at Winchester with the cognisance of the councillors whose names are recorded below in writing...

These are the boundaries at Tichborne, first to the elder-tree ford, then to the large ridge, then to the east side of the hanging wood of aspens, then to the middle of *hormæres* wood, then straight to the enclosure by the shallow pond, then to the middle of Milbarrow, then as far as the hollow in the wood, along the road out to the hay meadow, then north and west into the hollow, then along the clearing, then along the road to 'Torshaw', then along the road up on to Gander Down, along the road to the red path, then along the road to 'beetle' clearing, then to the large ridge, then to the north of *cupænes* ford, then

42 LEASE OF LAND TO DENEWULF

norþeweardne þanon on tornageat · þanon útt þurh[1] beaddes scagan to áclea andlang weges útt tó felda þanon be wyrtwalan on langan leáge norþewearde þanon to hindsceata þanón on ostercumb norþeweardne þanón to mænanleáge · þanon on oster-
5 cumb suðewearðne[2] þanon 7lang weges on wines[3] heafod · þonne[4] 7lang weges útt on ellen ford.

XXI. GRANT OF LAND BY WILFRITH, BISHOP OF WORCESTER

Disponente regi regum cuncta[5] cæli[6] secreta necnon quæ sub cæli culmine apud homines notantur miro ordine gubernante cujus incarnationis humanæ anno DCCCCXXII indictione x hæc
10 donatio quæ in ista cartula saxonicis sermonibus apparet confirmata ac[7] donata erat.

In usses dryhtnes noman hælendes Cristes · Ic Wilfrið biscop cyðu minum æfterfylgendum ðæt ic sylle sumne dæl londes æt Clifforda higen to hiora biode æt Weogernaceastre on ece
15 erfeweardnesse mid monnum 7 mid allum þæm nytnessum ge on fixnoðum ge on medwum ðe ðærto belympað on ðæt gerad þ min gemynd for Gode mid him þy fæstlicor sio 7 hio ælce gere of ðæm londe ec be sumum dælæ gemyndgien[8] ða tide mines forðsiðes mid ðæm nytnessum ðe hio on ðæm londe
20 begeten · 7 nu we halgsiað[9] ðurh Godes mildhiortnesse alle ure æfterfylgend godcundra hada 7 weorldcundra þ þios ure sylene staðulfæstlice[10] ðurhwunian mote 7 gif ænges hades mon sio ure æfterfylgendra swa wemne wircað þ ðæs ure sylene on ængum wisum gewemman[11] oððe gewanian wille wite he hine riht agel-
25 dendne[12] beforan Gode in[13] ðæm forhtigendlican domes dæge

[1] þurð, K.; þurþ, T., B.   [2] -dne, K.
[3] pines, K.   [4] ðanon, K.
[5] cunta, B.   [6] coeli, Hi.
[7] The original reading was et corrected to ac.
[8] The final n has been added later.
[9] The original reading was halsigeað or halgigeað corrected later; halgiað, Hi.; halsiað, K.
[10] staþulf festlice, Hi.
[11] -in, Hi., K.
[12] The original reading was agelde bidne corrected later.
[13] on, Hi.

to the turnstile, then out through *beaddes* copse to the oak clearing, along the road out to the open country, then along the foot to the north side of the long clearing, then to the *hindsceata*, then to the north side of Eastercombe, then to the clearing held in common, then to the south side of Eastercombe, then along the road to Wine's headland, then along the road out to the elder-tree ford.

XXI. GRANT OF LAND BY WILFRITH, BISHOP OF WORCESTER

In the year 922 of the incarnation of the King of kings, who governs all the secret things of heaven and likewise controls in marvellous order those which are recorded among men under the dome of heaven, and in the tenth Indiction, this grant which appears in this charter in the Saxon speech was confirmed and given.

In the name of our Lord the Saviour Christ, I, Bishop Wilfrith, inform my successors that I grant a certain piece of land at Clifford to the refectory of the community at Worcester, as a perpetual inheritance, with its men and with all the profits from fisheries and meadows which belong to it, on condition that the remembrance of me in the sight of God be the more steadfastly observed among them. And every year also, by means of the estate, they shall commemorate to a certain extent the anniversary of my death with the profits which they obtain from the estate. And now we entreat all our successors, both ecclesiastics and laymen, by the mercy of God, that this our gift may steadfastly endure, and if there be a man of any rank among our successors who acts so vilely as to impair or diminish this our grant in any way, he shall find that he must render account for it before God on the terrible Day of Judgment,

44 GRANT OF LAND BY WILFRITH

butan he hit ær Gode 7 monnum wyrðlice gebete · þisses londes siond twa hida binnan ðissum gemærum ærust up of Sture suð onlong dic[es][1] on ðone herpað onlong herpaðes to Westtunniga gemære swa onlong gemæres norð ꝥ in Afene up onlong Afene
5 eft on Sture in ða[2] dic.

XXII. GRANT OF LAND BY EARL ÆTHELSTAN TO ABINGDON

Æðelstan ealdorman geboce[3] þis land of Uffentune into sc̄e MARIE stowe to Abbendone · be þes kinges deige Æðelstanes · 7 ꝥ wes be Winsies[4] biscopes gewittnysse of Bearrucscire · 7 Wulfhem arcebiscop · 7 Rodward biscop · 7 manega oþra ægþer
10 ge biscopas · 7 abbodes · 7 þeinas · þe þer gegaderod wæron · ꝥer þes tun be þyssan gemæran geled wes into sc̄a MARIA are into Abbendune · 7 se arcebiscop Wulfhem 7 ealla þa biscopes · 7 abbodes þe þer gesomnode wæron amansumeden fram Criste · 7 fram eallum Cristes gemænnes · 7 fram eallam[5] cristendome ·
15 þe æfre þas gife undyde · oððe þis land gelytlede · on læsu oððe on gemæru · beo he ascyred · 7 gesceofen into helle grunde · aa buten ende · 7 cwæþ eall ꝥ folc þe þer embstod · sy hyt swa · amen · amen.

XXIII. CHARTER OF KING ÆTHELSTAN TO MILTON ABBEY, DORSET

In Godes name[6] · ich Aþelstan[7] God gyuing[8] kyng welding eal[9]
20 Brytone · mid alle mine wytene · 7 alle biscope of þan kinedome of Engelonde · gelad by þe pricingge of ðe Haly Goste · grantye and confirmye by ðisse minre chartre · for me and for þe kingges of Engelonde ðæt comeþ æfter me ene and euere ich · tille Gode and sainta Marian · and sainte Michaele · sainte Sampsone · and
25 sainte Branwaladre xxvi. hyde londes æt Muleburne · mid ðan

---

[1] From Hi.; the original reading in Harl. MS. was *dic* with two letters added later.   [2] *ea*, Hi.   [3] *-bocade*, MS. (*b*).
[4] *Wynries*, ibid.   [5] *-um*, ibid.   [6] *-es*, K.
[7] *Æðel-*, K.   [8] *giuing*, B.   [9] Om. B.

unless he has duly made amends for it both to God and men.

There are two hides of this land within the following boundaries. First up from the Stour south along the dyke to the highway, along the highway to the Weston boundary, then along the boundary north as far as the Avon, up along the Avon back to the Stour to the dyke.

XXII. GRANT OF LAND BY EARL ÆTHELSTAN TO ABINGDON

Earl Æthelstan has granted by charter this estate of Uffington to St Mary's foundation at Abingdon in the time of King Æthelstan, and this was done with the cognisance of Wynsige, Bishop of Berkshire, and Archbishop Wulfhelm and Bishop Hrothward and many others, both bishops and abbots and thegns, who were assembled there, when the manor within the stated boundaries was handed over to the possession of St Mary's at Abingdon. And Archbishop Wulfhelm and all the bishops and abbots who were there assembled excommunicated from Christ and from all the fellowship of Christ and from the whole of Christendom anyone who should ever undo this grant or reduce this estate in pasture or in boundary. He shall be cut off and hurled into the abyss of hell for ever without end. And all the people who stood by said, 'So be it, Amen, Amen.'

XXIII. CHARTER OF KING ÆTHELSTAN TO MILTON ABBEY, DORSET

In the name of God, I, Æthelstan, by the grace of God King ruling the whole of Britain, along with all my councillors and all the bishops of the kingdom of England, led by the instigation of the Holy Ghost, grant and confirm by this my charter for myself and for the kings of England who come after me, one and all, to God and St Mary and St Michael and St Sampson and St Branwalader 26 hides of land at Milborne with every-

46 CHARTER OF KING ÆTHELSTAN

þ ðereto liþ · and fif æt Wonlonde · and þreo atte Fromemouþe · atte yle ðan ye to on see · and on on londe þ is to seggende[1] æt Ore · and þreo at Clyve mid ðare mede þ þereto liþ · and þreo and on half at Liscombe · and on at[2] Burdalueston · and on at
5 Litele Pudele · and fiue at[3] Cattesstoke · and vi. at Comptone · and to at Widecome · and v. at Osmyntone · 7 vi. at Holewertþe[4] · þ is alles seuene and sixty hyden into Middeltone[5] · and anne were on Auene at Twynham · and al þ water binne staþe of Waimouþe · and half strym on ðan Waymouþe out on see · and
10 twelf acres to þan were 7 ðan werhurde · and þreo ðegne on Suþsexan · and salterne by were · and xxx. hyden on Sidemyntone · to fosterland · and to at Chelmyntone · and six at Hylfelde · 7 x. hyde at Ercecombe · to tymberlonde ∴ And ich wolle þ al ðis myn almeslonde mid al ðan þ ðereto liþ · and freo beo in alle
15 ðinge · and freo custumes · þ is for mine saule helpe and for ðe helpe of here saulen þ tofore me were and after me comen schulle kynges of Engelonde ðan minster to fore gesed of Middeltone in rigte clene almesse wulle 7 grantye þ hit beon al so freo in alle ðinge mid ðan þ ðerto liþ in eche stede in Englonde in myne
20 cynedome alswa myn ogen ore ∴ And ich stedeuastliche hote · and bebeode in Gode almigties hege name · Fader and Son and Holy Gost · þ ðis min wille and gifte · and of ðis writ fastnynge ungewemmed beo and ungewered · and ungewendelich ðe hwile þ Christendom dureþ in ðis gelonde Englisckan ∴ Oure Lourd
25 God almigtig and alle his halgen al ðe ylc ho so hit beo þ ðis my dede in oðere wise hit byturne[6] · oþer gewanye · oþer ho þ euere beo · be hey Judan feyre Christes traytour on helle wytte pynende 7 on echenysse ∴ And þ ðis sond beo and stedeuast euere boute ende · ich ðe foresedene kyng Adelstan[7] ðis gewritene
30 bocleof habbe gemerked mid Cristes holy rode tokne ✠ and min ogen honde mid ðisse gewitnesse of alle mine gewytene þ herafter gewriten beo gefunden · 7 mid mine biscopes ∴

✠ Ego Wolfhelmus, Dorobernensis ecclesiæ archiepiscopus testimonium perhibeo, et cum signo agiæ crucis hoc donum et hanc senten-

[1] *leggende*, K., B. [2] *æt*, K.
[3] *æt*, B. [4] *-werðe*, K.
[5] *Middle-*, K. [6] *bu-*, K.
[7] *Æðel-*, K.

TO MILTON ABBEY, DORSET

thing pertaining to them, and 5 at Woolland, and 3 at the mouth of the Frome on the island...—two at sea and one on land, that is to say at Ower—and 3 at Clyffe with the meadow belonging to it, and 3½ at Lyscombe, and 1 at Burleston, and 1 at Little Puddle, and 5 at Cattistock, and 6 at Compton [Abbas], and 2 at Whitcombe, and 5 at Osmington, and 6 at Holworth, making altogether 67 hides to be attached to Milton, and a weir on the Avon at Twyneham, and all the water within the shore of Weymouth, and half the river at Weymouth out to sea, and 12 acres for the weir and the keeper of the weir, and 3 thegns in Sussex and a salthouse by the weir, and 30 hides at Sydling as land to supply food, and 2 at Chalmington and 6 at Hillfield and 10 hides at *Ercecombe* as land to supply timber.

And I desire that all this land given by me in charity, with all that pertains to it, shall be free in every way and free from customary dues—this land that, for the benefit of my soul and the souls of those who were kings of England before me and those who shall come after me, I bequeath and grant in pure and lawful alms to the aforesaid monastery of Milton, shall be as free in everything, with all that belongs to it, in every place in my kingdom of England, as my own property. And I steadfastly command and enjoin in the most high name of God Almighty, Father, Son and Holy Ghost, that this my bequest and gift and the ratification of this document shall remain unviolated and unimpaired and unalterable as long as Christianity endures in this English land. Our Lord God Almighty and all his saints...all those, whoever they be, who distort or diminish this my deed—whoever they be—shall be the companions of Judas, the betrayer of Christ, enduring punishment for all time in the torment of hell.

And in order that this shall remain firm and steadfast for ever without end, I, the aforesaid King Æthelstan, have marked this written page with the symbol of Christ's holy cross with my own hand, with the cognisance of all my councillors who are recorded hereafter in writing, and with my bishops...

48 CHARTER OF KING ÆTHELSTAN

tiam prædictam confirmavi. ✠ Ego Atheldredus[1], Londoniensis urbis episcopus consensi et subscripsi. ✠ Ego Cenwaldus episcopus consensi et subscripsi. ✠ Ego Alfredus[2] episcopus consensi et subscripsi. ✠ Ego Caynan episcopus consensi et subscripsi. ✠ Ego Egwynus episcopus consensi et subscripsi. ✠ Ego Radulphus episcopus consensi et subscripsi. ✠ Ego Brinstanus episcopus consensi et subscripsi. ✠ Ego Alla episcopus consensi et subscripsi. ✠ Ego Offerdus[3] princeps consensi et subscripsi. ✠ Ego Alfledus[4] minister domini regis consensi et subscripsi. ✠ Ego Athelmundus[5] minister consensi et subscripsi.

✠ Acta est hæc nostra donatio et concessio ac præsentis nostræ cartæ confirmatio anno ab incarnatione Domini DCCCXLIII · in villa regali quæ dicitur Doracestria[6] secunda die Paschæ Domini.

XXIV. GRANT OF A BOOK BY KING ÆTHELSTAN TO ST CUTHBERT'S

In nomine dñi nṙi Ihū Xp̄i. Ic Æþelstan cyning selle þas boc into sĉo Cuðberhte · 7 bebeode on Godes noman · 7 on þæs halgan weres · þæt hio næfre nan monn of þisse stowe · mid nanum facne ne reaflace ne afirre ne nane þara geofona þe ic to þisse stowe gedoo. Gif þonne hwelc monn to þæm dyrstig beo · þæt he þisses hwæt breoce oððe wende · beo he scyldig wiþ God 7 wiþ menn · 7 dæl neomende Iudases hletes Scariothes, 7 on Domes dæge þæs egeslican cwides to geheranne 7 to onfone · discedite a me maledicti in ignem æternum et reliq.

XXV. GRANT OF LANDS BY KING ÆTHELSTAN TO THE OLD MINSTER, WINCHESTER

MID Godæs gifæ Ic ÆÞELSTAN Ongolsaxna cyning 7 brytænwalda eallæs ðyses Iglandæs þurh Godæs sælene · and ealra hís halegra ðas land æcelice sælle into sĉe TRinitatan þam hiwum to hira beodlandæ 7 to hregltalæ · Đæt is ðonnæ æt ENEDforda .xxx. hida · and æt Ceolbaldinctuna .x. hidæ · 7 æt

---
[1] Æðelredus, K.　　[2] Æl-, K.　　[3] Osferdus, K.
[4] Ælfredus, K.　　[5] Æðel-, K.　　[6] Dorca-, K.

✠ This our gift and grant and the ratification of this present charter were carried out in the year of the incarnation of the Lord 843, in the royal manor called Dorchester, on the second day of Easter.

XXIV. GRANT OF A BOOK BY KING ÆTHELSTAN TO ST CUTHBERT'S

In nomine domini nostri Jesu Christi.

I, King Æthelstan, give this book to St Cuthbert's and enjoin in the name of God and of the holy saint, that no one remove it from this foundation by any fraud or robbery, or any of the gifts which I bestow upon this foundation. If, however, anyone is so presumptuous as to violate or change this in any particular, he shall incur the wrath both of God and of men, and shall participate in the fate of Judas Iscariot, and on the Day of Judgment shall hear and receive the dread sentence, 'Depart from me, ye accursed, into everlasting fire, etc.'

XXV. GRANT OF LANDS BY KING ÆTHELSTAN TO THE OLD MINSTER, WINCHESTER

I, Æthelstan, King of England by the grace of God, and ruler of all this island by the favour of God and of all his saints, grant these estates for all time to the community at the Holy Trinity to supply them with food and clothing, namely 30 hides at Enford and 10 hides at Chilbolton and 10 hides at Ashmans-

50 GRANT OF LANDS BY KING ÆTHELSTAN

Æscmeresweorðæ[1] .x. hida · 7 ic wulla ðæt þas land durhwunién[2] on æcelecum freodomæ fróm æghwelcum eorðlecum ðeowdomæ butan firdæ 7 festæn[3] gewæorcæ 7 brycggewæórce. And ic bebeodæ on Godæs ælmihtiges naman ðæt nauðær næ síe to ðon
5 geðurstig[4] · ne cyning næ bisceop ne nanes hades man · þæt þas minæ gife onwændæ oððæ gewaníe. And íc wille ðet þa híwan ælce gere gefermien for mæ hie selfæ ðríe dagas · tó omnium sanctorum. And á hwilæ ðæ cristendom síe fullicæ mid hira godcundnessæ for me síen. And gif hwa ðas minæ gife écan
10 willæ iecæ God his on hæfæna rice. And gif hit hwa þonne waníge · þæt he hit næfre næ gebæte ær ætforan Cristes drymsetle[5] · nymðæ he hít mid weorðelicre dedbote gébæte. And ic wille ðæt ealra hira beodland þæ mine magas ðydær sealdon béon on ðam ylcan freodomæ. And se ðæt sæ bisceop á þæ ðær
15 þonne sie him do hira fullan fostær butan híra beodlandum of his bisceophamum. Þis wæs gesæt on þam cynelicun hamæ æt Fromæ ón .xvii. kł. Januaríí · Indic⁹tio[6] .vii. þu gere þe wæs ágangen from Cristes ácennednesse .dccccxxxiiii. wintra · on þissæ gewitnessæ ðæ hira naman hærón áwritenæ sint.

20 ÆÐELSTAN Ongolsaxna cyning and brytenwalda ealles þyses iglandæs þurh Godæs gifæ þis gesætte and gefestnedæ[7] mid Cristæs rodætacnæ.

Huwal Vndercyning.	Tidhelm bisceop.	Wullaf[9] miñ.
Wulfhelm Arce-	Cynæsige bisceop.	Wulfmær miñ.
25 bisceop.	Wulfhelm bisceop.	Ælfheah miñ.
Wulfstan Arce-	Ælfræd bisceop.	Ælfric miñ.
bisceop.	Alfwald[8] ealdorman.	Wulfric miñ.
Þeodred bisceop.	Æþelstan miÑ.	Wulfnod[10] miñ.
Wulfhun bisceop.	ODDA miÑ.	Æþelstan miñ.
30 Ælfheah bisceop.	Æþelstan miÑ.	Eadric miñ.
ODA bisceop.	Wulfhelm miÑ.	Aðelwald[11] miñ.
Ælfred bisceop.	Ælfhære miÑ.	Wigar miñ.
Ælfheah bisceop.	Ælfheah miÑ.	Wulfric miñ.
Æðelgar bisceop.	Wulsige miÑ.	Ælfsige miñ.
35 Burhric bisceop.	Wulfgar miÑ.	Ælfsige miñ.
Cenwald bisceop.	Æðelmund miñ.	Ælfhære miñ.
Ælla bisceop.	Wulfgar miñ.	Æþelgerð[12] miÑ.
Wunsige bisceop.		

[1] -mæres-, K. [2] ðurh-, K. [3] fæst-, K.
[4] ged-, K. [5] ðrym-, B.; ðrymsetlæ, K. [6] -ione, K.
[7] -fæst-, K., B. [8] Ælf-, K. [9] -lfl-, K.
[10] -oð, K. [11] Æð-, K. [12] -gerd, K.

TO THE OLD MINSTER, WINCHESTER

worth. And I desire that these estates shall enjoy perpetual freedom from every secular service, except military service and the construction of fortifications and bridges. And I enjoin, in the name of God Almighty, that no one—king or bishop or man of any rank—be so presumptuous as to alter or diminish this my gift. And I desire that the community provide a three days' feast for themselves for my sake every year at All Saints'. And always as long as Christianity endures, they shall wholeheartedly intercede for me at their divine services. And if anyone desires to increase this my gift, God shall increase his [reward] in the kingdom of heaven. And if anyone on the other hand diminishes it, he shall never atone for it until before the throne of Christ, unless he make amends for it with due reparation. And I desire that all the estates which my kinsmen have given them for their refectory shall enjoy the same freedom. And the bishop who is there at the time shall always furnish them with their full supply of food from his episcopal estates, apart from those appropriated to their refectory.

This meeting took place at the royal manor at Frome on December 16 in the year 934 after the birth of Christ and in the seventh Indiction, with the cognisance of those whose names are written here...

XXVI. THE WILL OF WULFGAR

✠ Ic Wulfgar an[1] þæs landes æt Collingaburnan ofer minne dæg Æffan hiere dæg 7 heo tilige uncer begea[2] sawla þearfe gemænelice ðæron · 7 feormige þrie dagas þa Godes þeowas þær min lic reste ʻon þone gemynddæg' 7 selle þam mæssepreoste
5 fif peningas 7 þara oþra ælcum twegen 7 ofer hiere dæg to Winteceastre þam niwan hierede for mine[3] sawle to habbenne 7 to brucenne 7 na of þam mynstre to sellanne · 7 ic an þæs landes æt Ingepenne ofer minne dæg Æffan to brucenne 7 to bewitanne 7 þæt heo hæbbe ælce gere to þam tune ealra gear-
10 wæstma þa þrie dælas 7 þone feorþan to Cynetanbyrig þam Godes þeowum for mine[3] sawle 7 for mines fæder 7 for mines ieldran fæder · þonne ofer hiere dæg into Cynetanbyrig to þære halgan stowe for Wulfgares sawle þe ic hit in selle 7 for Wulfrices 7 for Wulfheres þe hit ærest begeat to habbenne 7 to brucenne
15 7 næfre ut to sellanne ↙ Þonne an ic þæs landes æt Cræft ofer minne dæg Wynsige 7 Ælfsige 7 ealles þæs[4] þe ic þæron begite 7 ic an þæs landes æt Denforda ofer minne dæg Æþelstane 7 Cynestane gif hie me oþ þ on ryht gehieraþ ↙ 7 ic an þæs landes æt Butermere ofer minne dæg Byrhtsige twegea[5] hida 7 Ceol-
20 stanes sunum anes gif hie me oð ðæt on ryht gehieraþ ↙ 7 ic cweþe on wordum be Æscmere on minum geongum magum swelce me betst gehieraþ ↙
    7 ic wille þ Æffe feormige of þæm þrim dælum æt Ingepenne þa Godes þeowas æt Cynetanbyrig þrie dagas on twelf monþum
25 ænne dæg for me operne for minne fæder þriddan for minne ieldran fæder · 7 ic an þæs landes æt Hamme Æffan ofer minne dæg 7 heo tilige þæron uncer begea sawla þearfe 7 feormige[6] þrie dagas þa Godes þeowas þær min lic reste on Eastron 7 ofer hiere dæg into Wʻiʼnteceastre to þæm ealdan hierede to sče
30 Trinitate · to hæbbenne 7 to brucenne 7 næfre ut to sellanne ↙

Endorsed in a contemporary hand:
    Her swutelaþ þ Wulfgar geuþe Hamme into ealdan mynstre æfter Æffan dæge hys wifes.

[1] *Wulfgaran an*, Addit. MS.   [2] *beara*, ibid.
[3] *minre*, ibid.   [4] *þæs landæs*, ibid.   [5] *-en*, K., T.
[6] *for minre*, Addit. MS.

XXVI. THE WILL OF WULFGAR

✠ I, Wulfgar, grant the estate at Collingbourne after my death to Æffe for her lifetime, and she shall provide for the needs of both our souls in common by means of it, and on the commemoration day she shall provide the servants of God, where my body rests, with a three days' food-rent, and give the priest five pence and each of the others twopence, and after her death [it shall pass] to the new community at Winchester, on behalf of my soul, to be held and enjoyed and never given away from the Minster. And I grant the estate at Inkpen after my death to Æffe to enjoy and take care of, and every year at the manor she shall have three parts of all the crops for the year, and the fourth part [shall go] to the servants of God at Kintbury, on behalf of my soul and my father's and my grandfather's; then after her death [it shall pass] to the holy foundation at Kintbury to be held and enjoyed and never given away, for the soul of Wulfgar who gives it, and for Wulfric's, and for Wulfhere's who first acquired it.

I likewise grant the estate at *Cræft*, and all that I acquire there, to Wynsige and Ælfsige after my death, and I grant the estate at Denford, after my death, to Æthelstan and Cynestan, if they show me due obedience until then. And I grant two hides of the estate at Buttermere, after my death, to Brihtsige and one to Ceolstan's sons, if they show me due obedience until then. And I shall verbally bequeath *Æscmere* to such of my young kinsmen as obey me best.

And I desire that from the three parts at Inkpen Æffe shall provide the servants of God at Kintbury with a three days' food-rent in the twelve months, one day for me, the second for my father, and the third for my grandfather. And I grant the estate at Ham to Æffe after my death, and she shall supply the needs of both our souls by means of it, and at Easter provide with a three days' food-rent the servants of God, where my body rests, and after her death [it shall pass] to the old community of the Holy Trinity at Winchester, to be held and enjoyed and never to be given away.

Endorsed:

Here it is declared that Wulfgar has granted Ham to the Old Minster after the death of Æffe his wife.

XXVII. GRANT OF LAND IN REVERSION TO THE NEW MINSTER, WINCHESTER

Ic Ælfreod ðein an þæs [landes][1] æt Stanham ofer minne dæge minan wifan [to hire][1] dægi 7 ofer hiere dæg on niwan minister on Winceacester uncer begea sawla[2] þearfe swa freolre[3] swa cing Æthelstan minan leofan leord ge me gegifan · 7 nanan manan
5 hit on enig oþer wænde[4] gif[5] þonne ic heafan gifan foran ic hit self on noþer wænde gifan 7 nanan on niwan minister on Winceacester hit ut sillan on enig wænde 7 si habban on æcnisse 7 sind gewritan gewitenesse 7 hiera handa setene.

✠ Aelstan cynig[6].   ✠ Ælfyn biscop.   ✠ Odda ðeyn.
10 ✠ Ælfryc ðeyn.   ✠ Eadric ðeyn.   ✠ Wihtgar ðeyn.

XXVIII. GRANT OF LAND TO THE NEW MINSTER, WINCHESTER, BY ÆTHELNOTH

Ic Æthelnoð sacerd an þes landes æt Basyngum mid ealra þæra landes þæt me cining Edmund sealde into niwan ministre on Wintanceacestre m[i]nra sawla þearfe æc to fremdon 7 mæge ut to seallan · mid ealra freogdom þæt me cining Edmund giefan
15 habban. Gewitenesse ✠ Eadred cining[7] · ✠ Æthelgar biscop̄ · ✠ 7 Ælfric biscop̄ · ✠ 7 menigfeald oþæra manna.

XXIX. GRANT OF LAND TO THE NEW MINSTER AND THE NUNNERY, WINCHESTER

7 Ic Eadulf mæsse preost of þyses[8] stowan æt Leahtford an on niwan ministre on Wintanceaster fifan stowan on Leahtford þær min lic[9] to rest aftir minan dægan 7 oðara fifan stowan æt
20 Leahtford on nunan ministre on Wintanceaster eal swa freoge swa Eadred c[i]ning me gifan habbaþ 7 is gewritan on cining Eadredes gewrite 7 seo wæron gewitenesse is foran alisnesse of minra sawle.

[1] Not in MS.   [2] *sayla*, Edwards.   [3] *swa freolre*, om. B.
[4] *wæne*, B.   [5] Sic, MS.; *gifan*, Edwards.
[6] *cying*, Edwards.   [7] *cuning*, ibid.
[8] Edwards adds [*tyn*].   [9] The MS. adds *minan licoman*.

XXVII. GRANT OF LAND IN REVERSION TO THE NEW MINSTER, WINCHESTER

I, the thegn Alfred, grant the [estate] at Stoneham after my death to my wife for her lifetime, and after her death to the New Minster at Winchester, for the benefit of the souls of both of us, as freely as King Æthelstan, my dear lord, granted it to me; and no one shall give it in any other way than I have given it, because I myself shall give it in no other way. And no one at the New Minster in Winchester shall alienate it in any way. And they shall hold it in perpetuity, and the witnesses and their signatures are recorded...

XXVIII. GRANT OF LAND TO THE NEW MINSTER, WINCHESTER, BY ÆTHELNOTH

I, the priest Æthelnoth, grant the estate at Basing with all the lands that King Edmund has given me to the New Minster at Winchester for the benefit of my soul, with the right of giving it to strangers or kinsmen [and] with all the freedom which King Edmund has given me.

Witnesses: ✠ King Edred, Bishop Æthelgar and Bishop Ælfric and numerous other men.

XXIX. GRANT OF LAND TO THE NEW MINSTER AND THE NUNNERY, WINCHESTER

I, the priest Eadulf, grant five of these hides at Leckford to the New Minster at Winchester, where my body shall rest after my death, and the other five hides at Leckford to the Nunnery at Winchester, as freely as King Edred has granted them to me and as is written in King Edred's charter. And these were the witnesses [that this] is for the salvation of my soul.

XXX. GRANT OF LAND BY KING EDRED TO ÆLFSIGE HUNLAFING

En onomatis[1] cyrion[2] doxa · Al wisdom ge for Gode ge for werolde is gestaðelad[3] on þæm hefonlican goldhorde almæhtiges Godes per Ihm Xp̄m cooperante gratia spiritus sc̄i. He hafað geweorðad mid cynedome Angulseaxna Eadred cyning 7 casere
5 totius Brittannię[4] Deo gratias · for ðem weolegað 7 árað gehadade 7 læwede þa ðe mid rihte magon geærnian · þet mæg to soðe seggan ðes þegn Ælfsige Hunlafing be þere geagnunga þisses landes fif hida æt Æþelwoldingtune elces þinges to freon him 7 his erfeweardum · buton burhbote bryggeweorces · 7 ferdnǫðes ·
10 geþencend londagende · Ciricsceat · saulsceat · 7 teogeðunga. Þus trymeð 7 streongað se forespecena kyng mid Cristes rode tacne 7 his weotena hondsetena his geofa écelice to habbene 7 to syllene micclum þingum 7 medmiclum to belimpendum. Eadred cyng þy teogeðan gere þes ðe he gehalgad wes gesette þas hand-
15 setene. Anno dn̄icę incarnationis .DCCCCLV.

Oda ærcabiscup · Wulstan p̄sul · Ælfsie biscup · Wulfsie pontifex · Oscetel antistes · Cynsige biscup · Osulf p̄sul · Koeuuald[5] monachus · Wulfelm pont̚ · Berhtsige biscup · Berhthelm p̄sul · Ælfuuold ant̚ · Ędgęfu euax · Eadwi æþeling · 7 Eadgar · Morcant regł · 7 Owen ·
20 Syferð 7 Iacob · Eadmund dux · 7 Ęþelmund.

Þes landes[6] is into Æþelwoldingtúne .v. hida · 7 þis synd þa landgemæru · On Earninga stræte æt þam stapelan · 7 þonne norþ æfter strate[7] to þere dic · On Ceastertuninga gemærie 7langes þere dic in on þa ea to healfan strame · 7 ðonne eft
25 andlanges þere eá to goldege · 7 þonne of goldege to ofertuninga gemęre · 7 þonne suð be þen Æfden 7lang þere mære to fægran broce · 7 þonne up 7lang ðes broces to þere smalan ryðige · 7 ðonne suð efter þem riðige to þem mære · 7 swa suðrihte to þem litle lawe · 7 þonne get suðrihte on þa lytlan þyrnan · 7 of þere

[1] -os, K., B.   [2] -iou, B.
[3] The MS. has gestaḷð- with a dot under the l showing that the scribe meant to delete it.
[4] Britann-, K.   [5] Koenuuald, K.
[6] K. does not give the boundaries.   [7] stræte, B.

XXX. GRANT OF LAND BY KING EDRED TO ÆLFSIGE HUNLAFING

In the name of the Lord be glory (?).

All wisdom, both spiritual and secular, is laid up in the heavenly treasury of Almighty God *per Jesum Christum cooperante gratia spiritus sancti*. He has endowed with a kingdom Edred, King of the Anglo-Saxons and Emperor of the whole of Britain *Deo gratias*, wherefore he enriches and honours men, both ecclesiastic and lay, who can justly deserve it. The truth of this can be acknowledged by the thegn Ælfsige Hunlafing through his acquisition of the estate of 5 hides at Alwalton for himself and his heirs, free from every burden except the repair of fortifications, the building of bridges and military service (?); a prudent landowner [will also make himself responsible for] church dues, burial fees and tithes. The aforesaid king confirms and ratifies his gift with the symbol of the cross of Christ and the signatures of his councillors, to be held for all time and granted along with the things both great and small belonging to it.

King Edred in the tenth year after he was consecrated attached this signature, in the year of the incarnation of the Lord 955...

The estate at Alwalton consists of 5 hides and these are the boundaries: the posts on Ermine Street, then north along the street to the dyke as far as the Chesterton boundary, along the dyke to the river mid-stream, and then back along the river to 'gold island', and then from 'gold island' to the Orton boundary, and then south by the headlands (?) along the boundary to the fair brook, and then up along the brook to the narrow streamlet, and then south along the streamlet to the boundary, and so due south to the little hill, and then still due south to the little

GRANT OF LAND BY KING EDRED

þyrnan westrihte to þem coppedan þonne¹ eft on earninga stræte. Eadred cyning biddeð 7 halsað on þere halgan þrinnesse noman Dei patris et filii et spiritus sċi þet nan man þurh diofles searucræft geðristlece² his cynelican gefe on woh gewonian · gif
5 hit hwa do gewrecen hit dioflu on helle witan butan he hit ær gebete for Gode and for weorlde swa him riht wisie. Pax x͞pi nobiscum Amen.

XXXI. EXCHANGE OF LANDS BETWEEN BRIHTHELM, BISHOP OF WELLS, AND ÆTHELWOLD, ABBOT OF ABINGDON

Ðis is seo gerædnes ðe Byrhtelm Biscop and Aþeluuold abb hæfdon ymbe hira landgehwerf · þæt is þonne þe se biscop
10 gesealde þa hida æt Cenintune into þære cyricean æt Abbend to ecan yrfe 7 se abbud gesealde þ seofontyne hyda³ æt Crydanbrigce þan biscope to ecenesse ge on life ge efter life · 7 hi eac ealra ðinga gehwyrfdon ge on cucan ceape ge on oðeorn⁴ swa swa hi betwehs him geræddon 7 ðis wæs Eadwiges leaf cyninges
15 7 ðis syndon ða gewitnessa Ælfgifu⁵ þæs cininges wif 7 Æþelgifu þæs cyninges wifes modur · Ælfsige biscop · Osulf biscop · Coenwald biscop · Byrhtnoð ealdorman · Ælfheah cyninges discðen · Eadric his brodur.

XXXII. THE WILL OF ÆTHELWYRD

✠ Ðis is Æðelwyrdæs⁶ cwide mid geðæhte Odan ærcebisscopæs⁷
20 7 ðæs hioredæs æt Cristæs cirican þ is ðonne þ Æðelwyrd bruce ðæs landæs on Geocham · his dæg on freodome be Godes leafe 7 be ðæs ærcebisscopæs⁸ 7 be ðæs heoredæs ðonne yftær his dæge Eadric gif he libbe his dæg wið ðon gofole ðe hit gecwedæn⁹ is ðæt sint .v. pund 7 ælce gære æne dæg feorme In hiowum þ
25 is ðonne .XL. sæstra ealað .LX. hlafa weðær 7 flicce 7 an hriðres

---

¹ Sic MS., þorne, B.   ² -lice, K., B.
³ hida, R.S.   ⁴ oðrum, K.
⁵ Ælgifu, R.S.   ⁶ -es, B.
⁷ -biscop-, Lye, K., T.   ⁸ -biscop-, K., T.
⁹ -cwæden, K., T.

thornbush, and from the thornbush due west to the pollarded [? thorn], then back to Ermine Street.

King Edred prays and entreats in the name of the holy Trinity *Dei patris et filii et spiritus sancti*, that no one through the wiles of the devil presume wrongfully to diminish his royal gift. If anyone does so, the devils in the torment of hell shall avenge it, unless he has made amends for it in the eyes both of God and of men, as justice directs him. *Pax Christi nobiscum.* Amen.

XXXI. EXCHANGE OF LANDS BETWEEN BRIHTHELM, BISHOP OF WELLS, AND ÆTHELWOLD, ABBOT OF ABINGDON

This is the agreement which Bishop Brihthelm and Abbot Æthelwold have made about their exchange of lands, namely, that the bishop should give the hides at Kennington as a perpetual inheritance to the church at Abingdon, and the abbot should give the seventeen hides at Creedy Bridge to the bishop in perpetuity, [to be held] during his life and [disposed of] at his death. And they have likewise exchanged everything, both livestock and other things, as they agreed between themselves. And this has been done with King Edwy's permission, and these are the witnesses: Ælfgifu, the king's wife, Æthelgifu, the king's wife's mother, Bishop Ælfsige, Bishop Osulf, Bishop Cenwald, Earl Brihtnoth, Ælfheah, the king's seneschal, Eadric, his brother.

XXXII. THE WILL OF ÆTHELWYRD

✠ This is Æthelwyrd's will, with the advice of Archbishop Oda and the community at Christchurch, namely that Æthelwyrd shall enjoy the estate at Ickham in freedom during his lifetime, with the leave of God and of the archbishop and of the community, then after his death Eadric, if he is alive, for his lifetime, at the rent stated, namely five pounds and one day's food-rent to the community every year, to consist of 40 sesters of ale, 60 loaves, a wether sheep, a flitch of bacon and an ox's haunch,

THE WILL OF ÆTHELWYRD

læuw .II. cesas .IIII. hæn fugulas 7 v. pænningas to beðe 7 ðis sio gelæst to sce Michaelæs tide 7 bio he ælces wites wyrðe 7 gif hwilc forwyrht man hiowan gesæce bio se ðingað[1] swa hit medlic sia[2] be ðæs geltes meðe: ⸍ Gif hit ðonne gebærige ðæt
5 Æðelwyrd læng libbe ðone[3] Eadric ðonne fo Æðelgifu[4] to wið ðan ilcan gofole ðe hit hær beufan gecwedæn[5] is hire dæg: gif hit þonne geberige ðæt Æðelwyrd læng libbe ðone[3] Eadric oððe Æðelgifu[4] 7 he ða unætnessa gebidan[6] scel ágefe[7] man land '7 boc'[8] in yfter his dæge In mid him selfum for hine 7
10 for ða[9] ðe him · land fram com: ⸍

Ðisæs is Odá ærcebisscop gewita 7 Byrhtere · mæsse · pre Cænwig · mæs · pr Wealdred · mæs · pre · Sigefreð · diac · Osweald · diac · Freðegod · diac · Sigered · diac · Heared · diac · Sired · pr · Byrhtmund · Eadsige[10] · Eadelm Byrhtsige Æðelm · Byrhtsige Byrhtwig Liofric
15 Sielm Wulfred Cænric Eadweard: ⸍

Ðisæs · wes · gewita · Eadelm · abbod æt sce Agustine[11] · 7 Byrhtsige · diac · Æorlebyrht[12] · mæs · pre · Roðin · mæs · pre Bærhtram · mæs · Beornmund · pre · 7 ða · III°. Ælfstanas · Æðelweald · Eadmund · Wenelm · Cynsige · Eadric · Liofing Eadsige Wulfelm Sigefreð Liofric
20 Liofstan Eadstan Eadmund: ⸍ ...stan[13] · cynges[14] ðægen · Byrhtric · Wyhtgar[15] · Wulfstan · 7 ða .III°. geferscipas Innanburwara[16] 7 útanburhwara 7 micle mættan: ⸍

Endorsed:

[Ðis i]s[17] seo gered'n'æs þe Eadric hæfð wið ðane hired to
25 Cristes cirican þ is ðonne ðæt Eadric gesealde ðan[18] hirede to gerisenum .v. pund twa ðæm ældæstum 7 ðreo eallum hirede an þ gerad þ he hebbe land mid fullre unnan ælde 7 gegeðe mid eallæn[19] ðan netwyrðan ðingum lessan 7 maran ðe to ðæm lande belimppað unbesprecæn wið æghwyl'c'ne lifes man.

[1] -ad, Lye, K., T.
[2] sio, Lye, K., T.
[3] ðonne, Lye, K., T.
[4] -gyfu, K., T.
[5] -cwædæn, K., T.
[6] abidan, K., T.
[7] agefe, Lye, K., T.
[8] 7 boc, om. Lye, K., T.
[9] ðam, K., T.
[10] An erasure follows.
[11] Aug-, K., T.
[12] Eorle-, Lye, K., T.
[13] A corner of the MS. has been torn off.
[14] cyninges, K., T.
[15] Wiht-, K., T.
[16] -burh-, Lye, T.
[17] [Ðeos is], K., T.
[18] ðam, K., T.
[19] -an, Lye, K., T.

THE WILL OF ÆTHELWYRD

2 cheeses, 4 hens and 5 pence......and this shall be rendered at Michaelmas; and he shall be entitled to every fine; and if any malefactor betake himself to the community, his case shall be settled, as is fitting, in proportion to the crime. If it happen, however, that Æthelwyrd live longer than Eadric, then Æthelgifu shall succeed to the estate for her lifetime for the same rent as is stated above. If it happen, however, that Æthelwyrd live longer than Eadric or Æthelgifu, and he must then suffer afflictions, both the estate and the title-deed after his death shall be delivered up along with himself on his own behalf and for the benefit of those from whom he received the estate.

Endorsed:

This is the agreement that Eadric has [made] with the community at Christchurch, namely that Eadric should give five pounds as a gift to the community—two to the senior members and three to the whole community—on condition that he should hold the estate with the full consent of old and young, with everything needful, both small and great, belonging to it, uncontested by any living man.

XXXIII. LEASE OF LAND BY BRIHTHELM, BISHOP OF WINCHESTER

Byrhtelm bisceop 7 eall se hired on Wintanceastre on ealdum mynstre lætað þæt land æt Cenelmestune to Apulfe mid geþafunge EadGARES cyninges · 7 ealra þara witena gewithnesse[1] þæ heora naman hær bufan standað · swylce eác ægþeres hiredes
5 ge preosta gé nunnena hær on túne gehwylces weorces frig butan þæs cericlican weorces þe seo boc belycð 7 þæs woruldweorces þe a eal folc weorcean sceal twegra manna deg æfter him · þonne beode íc on Godes naman 7 on sc̄e Petres 7 on ealra hís haligra þæt nan mán swa geðurstig ne seo · þæ hit leng óf þære cyrican
10 do · gíf hit þonne hwa do þæt he síe ascáden fram Gode 7 fram eallum his gecorenun butan hé hit[2] medomlíce gebæte ær hís ænde.

XXXIV. LEASE OF LAND BY OSWALD, BISHOP OF WORCESTER, TO ÆTHELM

Æþelmodestreow Æþelme 7 Ælfstane 7 Wulfrice[3].

⁂ Ic Oswald þurh Godes gyfe[4] bisceop mid geþafunge 7 leafe
15 Eadgares Angulcyniges 7 Ælferes Myrcna heretogan 7 þæs heoredes æt Weogernaceastre landes sumne dæl ꝥ i[5] þridde hid þe fram cuðum mannum Æþelmodestreow is gehaten sumum men þam is Æþelm nama mid eallum þingum þe þærto belimpað · freolice his dæg forgeaf 7 æfter his dæge 'anum' yrfewear-
20 dum 7 æfter heora forðsiðe to þære halgan stowe into Weogernaceastre þam bisceope to brice. Sit autem terra ista libera omni regi nisi ęcclesiastici censi. Ðonne is ealles þæs landes þridde healf hid þe Oswald bisceop bocað Æþelme · mid his hlafordes leafe þriora manna dæg on þa gerad wyrce ꝥ he wyrce ꝥ ꝥ land
25 si unforwor'h't into þære halgan stowe. Anno dominicę

---

[1] -witn-, K.
[2] butan hé hit is repeated in the MS.
[3] This is entered in the right margin; om. K.
[4] gefe, He., K.   [5] Sic.

XXXIII. LEASE OF LAND BY BRIHTHELM, BISHOP OF WINCHESTER

Bishop Brihthelm and all the community at the Old Minster in Winchester, with the permission of King Edgar and the cognisance of all the councillors whose names are recorded above, and likewise of each of the communities both of priests and nuns here in the town, lease the estate at Kilmeston to Athulf and for two lives after him, free from every service except the service of the church, which the charter specifies, and the secular service which must be performed by the whole nation. And now I enjoin, in the name of God and of St Peter and all his saints, that no one be so presumptuous as to keep it longer from the church. If, however, anyone does so, he shall be separated from God and from all his elect, unless he duly make amends for it before his death.

XXXIV. LEASE OF LAND BY OSWALD, BISHOP OF WORCESTER, TO ÆTHELM

Elmestree, to Æthelm and Ælfstan and Wulfric.

⁊ I, Oswald, bishop through the grace of God, with the consent and leave of Edgar, King of England, and Ælfhere, Earl of Mercia, and the community at Worcester have freely granted a certain piece of land, namely $2\frac{1}{2}$ hides, called by those familiar with it Elmestree, to a certain man whose name is Æthelm, with all the things which belong to it, for his lifetime, and after his death to [two] heirs, and after their death to the holy foundation at Worcester for the use of the bishop. And that estate shall be free from everything except church dues.

The whole of the estate, therefore, is $2\frac{1}{2}$ hides which Bishop Oswald grants by charter to Æthelm, with his lord's leave, for three lives, on condition that whatever he does, the estate shall return unforfeited to the holy foundation.

incarnationis .DCCCCLXII. Scripta[1] · hæc carta his testib*us* consentientib*us* quo*rum* inferius nomina notantur.

✠ Ego Wulfric prb.   ✠ Ego Eadgar diāc.   ✠ Ego Cyneþen cl.
✠ Ego Ælfric prbt.   ✠ Ego Wulfhun · cl.   ✠ Ego Byrhstan cl.
5 ✠ Ego Ælfred cl.

XXXV. LEASE OF LAND BY OSWALD, BISHOP OF WORCESTER, TO ÆLFRIC

Æt Coddanhrycce · Ælfrice · 7 Æþelsie[2].

☩ Ego Osuuald ergo xp̄i krismate præsul iudicatus dominicæ · Incarnationis anno .DCCCCLXIII annuente regi Anglorum · EADGARO · ÆLFEREque Merciorum comite nec non *et*
10 familiae Wiogornensis ecclesiae · quandam ruris particulam unam uidelic*et* mansam in loco qui celebri a solicolis nuncupatur æt Coddanhrycce uocabulo cuidam ministro meo nomine · Ælfric · perpe*t*ua largitus sum hereditate *et* post uite suæ terminum duobus tantum heredibus immunem derelinquat quibus de-
15 functis ecclesiae dei in Uuigornaceastre[3] restituatur.

On þæt gerad þe he ælce geare of þam lande geerige twegen æceras 7 þæron his circsceat gesawe 7 þæt eft[4] geripe 7 in gebringe · 7 ic an him ælce geare on minum wudu[5] .XII. foþre wudas butan ceape. Ðis sindan þa landgemæru to Coddan-
20 hrycge[6] · ærest up on Temedan andlang biscopes[7] gemæres norðrihte on ætincweg of ætincwege[8] in Coddanhrycges bece andlang beces to bricgeburnan fordes þanan andlang stræte þæt hit cymeð beneoþan obantreow þanan suðrihte andlang þære hegeræwe[9] in rixuc andlang rixuc on hihtes gehæg þanan
25 suðrihte in þa stræte andlang stræte ꝥ in bregnesford up andlang temedan ꝥæt eft on biscopes[7] gemære. Scripta est hęc carta is testibus consentientibus quorum inferius nomina notantur.

✠ Ego Wulfric prbt.   ✠ Ego Cynestan clr.   ✠ Ego Æþelstan cirward.
✠ Ego Ælfric pbr.   ✠ Ego Cyneðegn clr.
30 ✠ Ego Eadgar diac.   ✠ Ego Wynstan clr.   ✠ Ego Æþelwold clr.
✠ Ego Ælfred clr.   ✠ Ego Eadwine clr.
✠ Ego Wulfun clr.   ✠ Ego Byrhstan clr.   ✠ Ego Wulfeah clr.
✠ Ego Cynesige clr.   ✠ Ego Wulfgar clr.

[1] *est* has been omitted.   [2] K. omits the heading.   [3] *Uuiog-*, He.
[4] *æft*, He., B.   [5] *wuda*, K.   [6] *-brycge*, He.
[7] *-ceopes*, He.   [8] *-weg*, He.   [9] *bege-*, He.

BISHOP OF WORCESTER, TO ÆTHELM 65

In the year of the incarnation of our Lord 962 this charter was written with the consent of those witnesses whose names are recorded below...

XXXV. LEASE OF LAND BY OSWALD, BISHOP OF WORCESTER, TO ÆLFRIC

Cotheridge, to Ælfric and Æthelsige.

☧ I, Oswald, ordained bishop by the chrism of Christ, in the year of the incarnation of our Lord 963, with the consent of Edgar, King of England, and Ælfhere, Earl of Mercia, and likewise the community of the church of Worcester, have granted to one of my thegns, named Ælfric, a certain piece of land as a perpetual inheritance, namely 1 hide in the place which by those familiar with it is called by the well-known name of Cotheridge, and after the end of his life he shall leave it unburdened to two heirs at most, after whose death it shall be restored to the church of God at Worcester. The condition is that every year he shall plough two acres of the land and sow [the grain for] his church dues there, and afterwards reap it and bring it in. And I grant him every year 12 fothers of wood in my wood without payment.

Here are the boundaries of the estate at Cotheridge. First up to the Teme, along the bishop's boundary due north to the *Atchen* road, from the *Atchen* road to the Cotheridge Brook, along the brook to the Bridge Bourne ford, along the made way until it comes below *Obantreow*, thence due south along the hedgerow to the *Rixuc*, along the *Rixuc* to *Hiht's* enclosure (?), thence due south to the made way, then along the made way to Bransford, thereafter up along the Teme back to the bishop's boundary.

This charter has been written with the consent of those witnesses whose names are recorded below...

Ic Ælfric cyþe minan leofan[1] hlaforde þæt ic ón Æþelsige minan suna þæs landes þe ic to þe[2] gearnode æfter minan dæge to habbanne his dæg 7 æfter his dæge to syllanne þæm þe him leofast seo 7 þæt sio on þa spere hand.

XXXVI. LEASE OF LAND BY OSWALD, BISHOP OF WORCESTER, TO ÆTHELSTAN

✠ Mid type 7 mid geþafunge Eadgares cynenges 7 Ælfheres Merna[3] ealdermannes 7 þæs[4] heorodes æt Wiogornaceastre ic OSwald þurh þa rumgiflan Godes cyste to biscope gehadod sumne dæl landes ꝥ synd .III. hida æt Þorndune Æþelstane minum þegne his dæg freoh ælces weoruldcundes þeowetes geuþe buton þreom þingum an is circsceat 7 ꝥ he mid eallum cræfte twuga on geare æne to mæþe[5] 7 oþre siðe to ripe[6] 7 æfter his dæge twam mannum swylce him gecwemest sy 7 æfter heora forðsiþe þam biscope to bryce into Wiogurnaceastre. Ðis synd þa landgemæra to Þordune[7] ondlong amman broces ꝥ hit sticað in pidelan ondlong pidelan ꝥ hit cymð to oredeshamme of oredeshamme on deorelmes dic of deorelmes dic on incsetena gemære of incsetena gemære in þa stræt of þære stræte in þornhæma[8] dic of þære dic in ꝥ sic of þam sice ꝥ hit sticað in ammam broc · 7 XII. æceras[9] on incsetena lande 7 seo wudung on gemænan grafe to Þordune[7]. Ðonne is ealles þæs landes .III. hida þe Oswald bisceop bocað Æþelstane his ðegne on þa gerad wyrce ꝥ he wyrce ꝥ ꝥ land seo unforworht into þære halgan stowe.

Anno dominicae incarnationis .DCCCC. LXIII. scriptum est · Hec carta his testibus consentientibus quorum inferius nomina notantur.

✠ Ego Wulfric prbt	✠ Ego Wulfgar clr	✠ Ego Æþelstan clr
✠ Ego Ælfric prbt	✠ Ego Brihstan clr	✠ Ego Cyneþeng clr
✠ Ego Eadgar prbt	✠ Ego Wulfhun clr	✠ Ego Wynstan clr
✠ Ego Ælfred clr	✠ Ego Eadwine clr	✠ Ego Wulfheh clr
✠ Ego Cynestan clr	✠ Ego Cynesige clr	

[1] *leofe*, B.
[2] Om. B.
[3] Sic for *Mercna*.
[4] Sic for *þæs*.
[5] *ænetom æþe*, MS., He.
[6] *riþe*, B.
[7] *Ðorndune*, K.
[8] *Þorahæma*, H.
[9] *æcras*, He.

I, Ælfric, inform my dear lord that I grant the estate which I have acquired from you to Æthelsige, my son, after my death, to hold during his lifetime, and at his death to grant to whomsoever he pleases, as long as it remains on the male side.

XXXVI. LEASE OF LAND BY OSWALD, BISHOP OF WORCESTER, TO ÆTHELSTAN

✝ With the consent and permission of King Edgar and Ælfhere, Earl of Mercia, and the community at Worcester, I, Oswald, ordained as bishop by the bountiful goodness of God, have granted a certain piece of land, namely 3 hides at Thorne, to my thegn Æthelstan for his lifetime, free from every secular service except for three things, one is church dues and that he [work] with all his might twice a year, once at haymaking and the other time at harvest. And after his death [it shall pass] to the two men who please him best, and after their death to Worcester for the use of the bishop.

These are the boundaries at Thorne, along the *Amman* brook till it runs into the Piddle, along the Piddle till it comes to *Oredeshamme*, from *Oredeshamme* to Deorhelm's dyke, from Deorhelm's dyke to the Inkberrow boundary, from the Inkberrow boundary to the made way, from the made way to the Thorne people's dyke, from the dyke to the watercourse, from the watercourse till it runs into the *Amman* brook. And 12 acres of the Inkberrow land and the right of cutting wood in the common copse shall belong to Thorne.

The whole amount of land, therefore, is 3 hides which Bishop Oswald grants by charter to his thegn Æthelstan, on condition that whatever he does, the estate shall return unforfeited to the holy foundation.

In the year 963 of the incarnation of our Lord this charter was written with the consent of the witnesses whose names are recorded below...

XXXVII. EXCHANGE OF LANDS BETWEEN ÆTHELWOLD, BISHOP OF WINCHESTER, AND WULFSTAN UCCEA

Her sutelað[1] on þyssum gewrite þet[2] Aþelwold[3] bisceop 7 Wulstan[4] Úccea hwyrfdon landa on Eadgares cyninge's' 7 on his witena gewytnesse. Se bisceop sealde Wulstane[5] þet[2] land[6] æt Hwessingatune · 7 Wulstan[5] sealde him þet[2] land æt Jaceslea 7 æt Ægeleswurðe · þa sealde Se bisceop þet[2] land æt Jaceslea into Þornige 7 þet[2] æt Ægeleswyrðe[7] into Buruh · 7 ꝥ land æt Ægeleswyrðe headde an wyduwe 7 hire sune[8] ær forwyrt forþanþe hi drifon serne stacan on Ælsie[9] Wulfstanes feder[10] 7 ꝥ werð æreafe 7 man teh ꝥ morð forð of hire inclifan · þa nam man ꝥ wif 7 adrencte hi æt Lundene brigce 7 hire sune ætberst 7 werð utlah 7 ꝥ land eode þam kynge to handa 7 se kyng hit forgeaf þa Ælfsige 7 Wulstan[5] Uccea his sunu hit sealde eft Adeluuolde[11] bisceope swa swa hit her bufan sægð.

XXXVIII. RENEWAL OF THE FREEDOM OF CHILCOMB BY KING EDGAR

HER is geswutelod on þisum gewrite · hu Aþelwold bisceop begeat æt his leofan cynehlaforde Eadgare cyninge[12] þæt he mid geþeahte his witana[13] geniwode · Ciltancumbes freols þære halgan þrynnesse 7 sce Petre 7 sce Paule into Wintanceastre · þan hirede on ealdan mynstre · ealswa his yldran hit ær gefreodon; ærest Cynegils cyning 7 his sunu Cynewald cyning · þe on angynne cristendomes hit sealdan · ealswa hit lið on ælche healfe þæs portes into þære halgan stowe · 7 syððan ealle heora æftergengen[14] · þæt wæs Egcbirt cynincg · and Aþulf cyning · 7 Ælfred cynincg · 7 Eadweard cynincg · 7 he geuðe þæt man þæt land on eallum

---

[1] *swut-*, K., T., B.   [2] *ðæt*, K.   [3] *Æþel-*, K.
[4] *Wulf-*, K., T.   [5] *Wulf-*, K.   [6] *lond*, K.
[7] *Ægelles-*, K., T.   [8] *sunu*, K.   [9] *Alsie*, T.
[10] *fæder*, K.   [11] *Æðel-*, K.
[12] A letter has been erased after the final *e*.
[13] *r* has been written above later between the *w* and the *i*.
[14] The final *-en* has been written on an erasure.

XXXVII. EXCHANGE OF LANDS BETWEEN ÆTHELWOLD, BISHOP OF WINCHESTER, AND WULFSTAN UCCEA

Here it is declared in this document that Bishop Æthelwold and Wulfstan Uccea have exchanged lands with the cognisance of King Edgar and his councillors. The bishop gave Wulfstan the estate at Washington, and Wulfstan gave him the estate at Yaxley and at Ailsworth. Then the bishop gave the estate at Yaxley to Thorney, and that at Ailsworth to Peterborough. The estate at Ailsworth had been forfeited by a widow and her son, because they drove an iron pin into Ælfsige, Wulfstan's father, and it was discovered, and the deadly image was dragged out of her room. Then the woman was taken and drowned at London Bridge, but her son escaped and became an outlaw, and the estate passed to the king, and the king then granted it to Ælfsige, and Wulfstan Uccea, his son, gave it afterwards to Bishop Æthelwold, as is related above.

XXXVIII. RENEWAL OF THE FREEDOM OF CHILCOMB BY KING EDGAR

Here it is declared in this document how Bishop Æthelwold procured from his dear lord, King Edgar, with the advice of his councillors, the renewal of the freedom of Chilcomb on behalf of the community at the Old Minster of the Holy Trinity and St Peter and St Paul in Winchester, just as his ancestors had freed it—first King Cynegils and his son King Cynewalh who, when Christianity first began, granted it, as it lies on each side of the town, to the holy foundation, and afterwards all their successors, namely King Egbert and King Æthelwulf and King Alfred and King Edward. And he granted that the estate should

70 RENEWAL OF THE FREEDOM OF

þingon for ane hide werode · swa swa his yldran hit ær gesetton 7 gefreodon · wære þær mare[1] landes · wære þær læsse · 7 he bead on Godes naman þæt naðer ne þære stowe bisceop ne nanes bisceopes æftergenga þæt lánd[1] næfre of þære stowe
5 geutode · ne hit nanan portmen[2] wið nanan sceatte ne wið ceape gesealde · 7 he bead þurh[3] Godes ælmichtiges myclan mægenþrymm þæt nan[1] his bearna ne nan heora æftergengcana þæt menster æfre leng mid preostan gesette · ac þæt hit efre mid munecan stode · swa swa he hit mid Godes ælmilhtiges fultume
10 gesette · þa þa he hit þa modigan preostas for heora mandædon þanan út adrefde · 7 þerinne munecas gelogode þæt hi Godes þeowedom æfter sc̄e Benedictes tæcinge · 7 dæghwamlice to Gode cleopodon for ealles cristenes folces alidsednesse. Ealles þæs landes is an hund hida · ac þa godan cynegas 7 þa wisan ælc
15 æfter oþran ꝥ ylce land swa gefreodon Gode to lofe 7 his þeowan to brycen 7 to fostorlande · ꝥ hit man æfre on ende for ane hide werian sceolde. Se þe þysne freols healdan wille · God ælmihtig hine gehealde her 7 on ecnesse. Gif hwa þonne[4] þurh ænige dyrstignesse oððe þurh deofles lare þisne freols abrecan wille ·
20 oððe þas gesetednesse on oðer awendan durre · Se he awyrged mid eallan þan awyrgednessan þe synd áwritene on eallan halgan bocan · 7 sy he ascyred fram ures drichtnes[5] gemanan 7 ealra hís halgana · 7 sy hé gebunden þa hwile þe he libbe on þisam life mid þan ylcan bendan þe God ælmihtig þyrh[6] hine sylfne
25 betæchte his halgan apostolan Petre 7 Paule · 7 æfter hís awyrgedan forðsiðe ligge[7] he efre on healle grundleasan pytte · 7 byrne he on þan ecan fyre mid deofle 7 his englan a butan ælcan ende · butan he hit ær his forðsiðe gebete. AMEN.

[1] In this word original *o* has been changed later to *a*.
[2] The first part of the word seems to have been *word* changed later to *port*.
[3] In this word final *c* has been changed later to *h*.
[4] *freols* has been added later in the margin after *þonne*.
[5] *-enes*, B.
[6] Final *c* has been changed later to *h*.
[7] Final *-ge* has been written on an erasure.

be assessed for all purposes at one hide, as his ancestors had established and freed it, whether there was more land or less, and he enjoined, in the name of God, that neither the bishop of the foundation nor any successor of the bishop should ever alienate the estate from the foundation, or grant it for money or for kind to any townsman. And he enjoined, by the great majesty of God Almighty, that none of his children or any of their successors should ever again put priests in the monastery, but that it should be occupied for all time by monks, as he had furnished it with the help of Almighty God, when he drove out from it the proud priests for their evil deeds and placed monks there to serve God, according to the teaching of St Benedict, and daily intercede with God for the redemption of all Christian people.

The amount of the estate is altogether 100 hides, but the good and wise kings, one after the other, freed it, to the praise of God and for the use and sustenance of his servants, so that for all time it should be assessed at one hide.

If anyone is willing to uphold this freedom, God Almighty shall uphold him here and to all eternity. If, however, anyone through any presumption or through the instigation of the devil, attempts to violate this freedom or dares to alter what is here established, he shall be accursed with all the curses which are written in all the holy books, and cut off from the fellowship of our Lord and of all his saints, and bound as long as he lives in this life with the very bonds which God Almighty, by his own power, entrusted to his holy apostles, Peter and Paul, and after his accursed death he shall lie for ever in the bottomless pit of hell, and burn in the everlasting fire with the devil and his angels for ever without end, unless he make amends for it before his death. Amen.

XXXIX. THE GIFTS OF BISHOP ÆTHELWOLD TO PETERBOROUGH

Þis synd þa madmas þe Adeluuold bisceop sealde into þam mynstre þe is Medeshamstede gehaten Gode to loue 7 sce͂ PETRE · his saule to alysednesse · ꝥ is þonne an Cristes boc mid sylure berenod · 7 .III. rode eac mid sylure berenode .II.
5 sylurene candelsticcan · 7 .II. ouergylde · 7 .I. sylurene storcille · 7 .I. æren · 7 .I. sylurene waterfet · 7 .II. sylurene bellen · 7 .IIII. silurene[1] calices .IIII. patenan [2] · 7 syluren pipe · 7 .VI. masse hacelan · 7 .IIII. cæppan · 7 .I. roc · 7 .VIII. stolan · emfela 'h'andlina · 7 .XI. subumbrale · 7 .II. pistolclaþas · 7 .III. cor-
10 porale · 7 .III. offrincsceatas [3] · 7 .XVIIII. albæn · 7 .IIII. pælles · 7 .II. linenweb to albæn · 7 .II. blace rẹgl cẹsternisce · 7 VI. uuahryft · 7 .VIIII. setreil · 7 .X. hangiende bellan .VII. handbellan · 7 .IIII. bedreaf · 7 .VI. hornas .IIII. gerenode · 7 .VIII. sylfrene cuppan · 7 .II. gegylde weofodsceatas.
15 And antwentig is þara boca þe Adeluuold biscop gesealde into Burch · ꝥ is þonne Beda in Marcum · Liber miraculorum · Expositio Hebreorum nominum · Prouisio futurarum rerum · Augustinus de achademicis · Vita sc͂i Felicis metrice · Sinonima Isidori · Vita Eustachii · Descidia Parisiace polis · Medicinalis ·
20 De duodecim abusiuis · Sermo super quosdam psalmos · Commentum cantica canticorum · De eucharistia · Commentum Martiani · Alchimi[4] · Auiti[5] · Liber differentiarum · Cilicius[6] Ciprianus · De litteris[7] Grecorum · Liber bestiarum.

Her is geswitelung hwet landum wes þe Adeluuold biscop
25 betehte his dryhtene into Medeshamstede þa he hit mid munecum gesette · þat is þonne ærest Medeshamstede · 7 ta berewican þa þarto heren · 7 Anlafestun · 7 þam berewican þarto.

Þonne 'is æt' Farresheafde .XVI. weorcwurðe[8] men · 7 .VIII. iunge men · 7 Witlesmere[9] 'h'alfendel. Þonne is Vndelum 7 to
30 berewicum þarto gebyreð · Þonne is Keteiringan.

Þonne sind þa fennas[10] þe he bohte 'æt Æalsige 7 æ[t][11] Vfige'

[1] *syl-*, B. [2] *-eran*, B. [3] *-sceatt-*, B.
[4] *Alchuini*, B. [5] *Aum*, D. [6] *-cus*, D.
[7] *liter-*, D. [8] *weorce-*, D. [9] *-mære*, D.
[10] *-es*, D. [11] The MS. has æ; *Ævfige*, D.

XXXIX. THE GIFTS OF BISHOP ÆTHELWOLD TO PETERBOROUGH

These are the treasures which Bishop Æthelwold gave to the monastery which is called *Medeshamstede* to the praise of God and St Peter, for the redemption of his soul, namely a gospel book adorned with silver, and 3 crosses likewise adorned with silver, 2 silver candlesticks and 2 covered with gold, and 1 silver censer and 1 made of brass and 1 silver water vessel and 2 silver bells and 4 silver chalices, 4 patens and a silver tube and 6 chasubles and 4 copes and 1 upper garment and 8 stoles, the same number of maniples and 11 subuculas and 2 epistle vestments and 3 corporals and 3 offertory cloths and 19 albs and 4 cloaks and 2 webs of linen for albs and 2 black robes......and 6 wall curtains and 9 seat covers and 10 hanging bells, 7 hand bells and 4 bed covers and 6 horns—4 of them decorated—and 8 silver cups and 2 gilded altar-cloths.

And the number of books is twenty-one which Bishop Æthelwold gave to Peterborough, namely *Beda in Marcum, Liber Miraculorum, Expositio Hebreorum Nominum, Provisio Futurarum Rerum, Augustinus: De Academicis, Vita Sancti Felicis* in verse, *Synonyma Isidori, Vita Eustachii, Descidia Parisiace polis, Medicinalis, De Duodecim Abusivis, Sermo super quosdam Psalmos, Commentum Cantica Canticorum, De Eucharistia, Commentum Martiani, Commentum Alchimi Aviti, Liber Differentiarum, Caecilius Ciprianus, De Litteris Grecorum, Liber Bestiarum.*

Here is the declaration of what the estates were which Bishop Æthelwold granted to his Lord at *Medeshamstede*, when he supplied it with monks, namely first *Medeshamstede* and the berewicks which belong to it, and *Anlafestun* and the berewicks pertaining to it; then at Farcet 16 able-bodied men and 8 young men, and half of Whittlesey Mere; then Oundle and the berewicks which belong to it; then Kettering; then the many fens at *Well* which he bought from Ælfsige and from Ufi for 13 ores.

From the two hundreds which owe suit to Norman Cross 350 acres of seed and 23 acres of clean wheat were given as tithes to *Medeshamstede*. From the two hundreds out on the

74 THE GIFTS OF BISHOP ÆTHELWOLD

manige æt Wellan · mid XIII. oran. Of þam twam hundredum þe secæð into Normannescros man ageaf to tioðunge into Medeshamstede feorð healf hund æcere sed · 7 .XXIII. æcera clenes wetes. Of þam twam undredum[1] ute o'n' þam nesse þe
5 Medeshamstede onstent man ageaf of six tunan[2] swa man ær simle dide tioþunge æt ælcere sylh an foðer cornes þe eahte þreues cornes on weron.
Þonne letan þa tioþunge of þan .XXIIII. tunan man ageald to mynstre twa hund æcera sæd 7 .III.
10 Of Macuseige fourtene æcer sed tioþunge.
Of Æsctune tioþunge healf fourtende æcer sed · 7 .V. georde sed.
Of Nunnetune .VI. æcer sed · 7 .V. giorde sed tiþunge.
Of þan oþren Macuseige · to tioþunge .VIIII. æcer sed.
15 Of Æstune to tiþunge · healf .XVIII. æcer sed · 7 .XIIII. giorde sed · 7 .III. roda sed. Of Pilesgete tioþunge .VI. æcer sed.
Þis is Þ erfgewrit æt Geaceslea · þryttene wepmen weorcewyrþe · 7 .V. wimmen · 7 æhta geonge men · 7 .XVI. oxan · fal'd're þere · 7 .III. hund scepa 7 .V. scep · 7 .XXX. swina · 7
20 hundteongig fliccena 7 eal þa smean ðe[3] þerto gebyriað · 7 .XXX. forþer cornes · 7 hundehtetig æcera[4] gesawen · 7 an egþwirf · 7 .VI. bidenfate · 7 .II. cuflas · 7 · þry trogas · 7 lead 7 trefet · 7 .IX. winterstellas · 7 .I. fedelsswin.
Þa Ætheluuine aldorman 7 Ealdulf biscop sealdan Æthestane
25 7 Alfwolde for[5] Iacesle 7 Faresheued þone latostan pęnig for þan lande into Burch · þa weron þer feste'r'men · Frana · 7 Æthelsige · þes ealdormannes eam · 7 Osferð Fryðegistes sune · 7 Ælfnoð Badan sunu · 7 Sumerlyda preost.

XL. LIST OF SURETIES FOR PETERBOROUGH ESTATES

Þis synd þa festermen þe Osferð swade beard funde · Adeluuolde
30 bisc̄ · 7 Eadulfe ab 7 Sumerlydan preoste þe þane feste nam æt þan land æt Wyrmingtune · an is Hudeman æt Asencircan · oðer is Ælfuuard æt Dentune .III. is Sumerlyde æt Stoce .IIII. is Oðul

---

[1] *hund-*, B. [2] *-am*, D. [3] The MS. has *þas meanðe*.
[4] *-ere*, D. [5] *far*, D.

promontory on which *Medeshamstede* stands tithes were rendered from six manors, as had always been done, in the ratio of a fother of corn containing 8 thraves for every plough.

Then......from the 24 manors 203 acres of seed were rendered to the monastery.

From Maxey 14 acres of seed as tithes.

From Ashton 13½ acres and 5 quarter-acres of seed as tithes.

From Nunton 6 acres of seed and 5 quarter-acres of seed as tithes.

From the other Maxey 9 acres of seed as tithes.

From Ashton 17½ acres of seed and 14 quarter-acres and 3 roods of seed as tithes. From Pilsgate 6 acres of seed as tithes.

This is the inventory of the stock at Yaxley: 13 able-bodied men and 5 women and 8 young men and 16 oxen, a stalled ox and 305 sheep and 30 swine and 100 flitches of bacon and all the delicacies that belong to them, and 30 fothers of corn and 80 acres sown and 1 harrow (?) and 6 barrels and 2 tubs and 3 troughs and a cauldron and a trivet and 9 year-old stallions and 1 fat pig.

When Earl Æthelwine and Bishop Ealdulf gave Æthelstan and Ælfwold the final penny for the estates at Yaxley and Farcet on behalf of Peterborough, the sureties were Frana and Æthelsige, the earl's uncle, and Osferth, Frithegist's son, and Ælfnoth, Bada's son, and Sumerlida the priest.

XL. LIST OF SURETIES FOR PETERBOROUGH ESTATES

These are the sureties whom Osferth *Swade* Beard found for Bishop Æthelwold and Abbot Ealdulf and Sumerlida the priest, who took the security for the estate at Warmington, the first is Hudeman of Achurch, the second is Ælfweard of Denton, the third is Sumerlida of Stoke, the fourth is Othulf of Barnwell,

76 SURETIES FOR PETERBOROUGH ESTATES

æt Byrnewilla .v. is Fastulf æt Finnesthorpe .vi. is Steigncytel æt Lullingtune .vii. is Ogga æt Suthwycan · viii. is Þurfeorð æt Wermingtune · viiii. is Cytel is broðer .x. is Oswið æt Æthelingtune · xi. is Osmund æt Catteswyrðe .xii. is Cytel
5 Clacces sune æt Wermingtune .xiii. is Sumerlyda preost þe þane feste nam.

Þis sind þa festermen þe Osferð 7 Þúr funden Adeluuolde .b. 7 Ælfrice cylde · 7 Ealdulfe ab. on æhte hundred gemote æt Wylmesforda for hiora magas æt þan lande æt Beringafelde · an
10 is Osferð himself .ii. Ealhstan æt Isslepe .iii. Wulnoð Strices sune .iiii. is Sumerlyda æt Stoce .v. is Ætheric þes langa.

Þis synd þa festermen þe Friðolf 7 his broðra fundel Ældulfe ab æt þat lande æt Waltune · þat is hundehtetig æcera wudes 7 feldes · þonne is þer borhhand Frena 7 Wulnoð Clacces sune ·
15 7 Ætlebrant æt Pilesgeate · 7 Cnut 7 Styrcyr on Uptune · 7 Boia on Mylatune · 7 Drabba 'h'is broðor. Þa Ealdulf ab bohte þane toft æt Godinge on Waltune þa was him boroh · Vlf 7 Eincund 7 Grim on Castre. Þa Elfric ealdorman bohte þat land æt Leobrantestune æt Frenan on ealles heres gemote on Hamtone
20 þe wes him eal se here boruhhand clenes lande's'.

Þis synd þa festermen þa Osgar funde Ealdulfe ab þa he bohte þat land æt Macusie an Frena .ii. is Vlf Doddes sune .iii. is Osbern .iiii. is Hundulf .v. is Boia on Myletune .vi. Wiulf Sunta sune .vii. Eadric on Þorp .viii. Grim his broðor .ix. Brenting.
25 Four 7 tuentig æcere is þes wudes · 7 .iixx. hęredlandes buton oðrum gemęnum þe Ealdulf ab gebohte æt Cyneferðe 7 wes Vlf Doddes sune borhhand · 7 Eadric on Þorp · 7 Eincund · 7 Orm · 7 he bohte æt Orme .xii. æceras 7 was Vlf borhhand 7 Eincund · 7 siððon eal wepentac · 7 æt Hungife .xx. æcera · 7 wes Eadric
30 litle borhhand · 7 Fastolf preost · 7 Orm. Þis sint þa festermen þe Osgot funde Ealdulfe ab æt þet lande æt Castre · þe he geald

SURETIES FOR PETERBOROUGH ESTATES

the fifth is Fastulf of *Finnesthorpe*, the sixth is Steigncytel of Luddington, the seventh is Ogga of Southwick, the eighth is Thurferth of Warmington, the ninth is Cytel his brother, the tenth is Oswi[g] of Elton, the eleventh is Osmund of Catworth, the twelfth is Cytel, son of Clac of Warmington, the thirteenth is Sumerlida the priest, who took the security.

These are the sureties whom Osferth and Thur found for Bishop Æthelwold and Ælfric *cild* and Abbot Ealdulf at a meeting of 8 hundreds at Wansford, on behalf of their kinsmen, with regard to the estate at Benefield, the first is Osferth himself, the second Ealhstan of Islip, the third Wulfnoth, Stric's son, the fourth is Sumerlida of Stoke, the fifth is Ætheric the Long.

These are the sureties whom Frithulf and his brothers found for Abbot Ealdulf with regard to the estate at Walton, which consists of 80 acres of woodland and open country. The sureties are Frena and Wulfnoth, Clac's son, and Ætlebrant of Pilsgate and Cnut and Styrcyr of Upton and Boia of Milton and Drabba his brother. When Abbot Ealdulf bought the homestead from Goding of Walton, his sureties were Ulf and Eincund and Grim of Castor. When Earl Ælfric bought the estate at *Leobrantestune* from Frena at a meeting of the whole host at Northampton, the whole host was security on his behalf that the estate was unburdened.

These are the sureties whom Osgar found for Abbot Ealdulf, when he bought the estate at Maxey, the first is Frena, the second is Ulf, Dodd's son, the third is Osbern, the fourth is Hundulf, the fifth is Boia of Milton, the sixth Wigulf, Sunte's son, the seventh Eadric of Thorpe, the eighth Grim his brother, the ninth Brenting.

There are 24 acres of woodland and 22 of arable land, apart from the other land held in common, which Abbot Ealdulf bought from Cyneferth, and Ulf, Dodd's son, was security, and Eadric of Thorpe and Eincund and Orm; and he bought 12 acres from Orm, and Ulf was security, and Eincund and then all the wapentake, and 20 acres from Hungifu, and Eadric the Small was security and Fastulf the priest and Orm.

These are the sureties whom Osgot found for Abbot Ealdulf on behalf of the estate at Castor, which he paid over to him for

78 SURETIES FOR PETERBOROUGH ESTATES

him for þam utlage þe he Styrcyr ofslogh Oggod · 7 .II. suna · Oswi preost · Grim · Boia · 7 Drabba · Ethestan on Optune · 7 Clac · 7 Styrcyr · þet is 'an' toft · 7 fourtig æcere herdelandes 7 mædwe. Þes landes æt Wiðeringige is þe Mannel sealde Adeluuolde .b. an hide buton anes oxangang · þonne sint festermen · Gyreweard · Gyrping · Þurwold on Macusige 7 Steigncytel · þonne sealde Clac ane hide · buton anes oxangang · þonne sint festermen · Oggod on Castre · Vlf Doddes suna · Þurwold æt Hylpestune · Clac on Castre · þonne æt Vfige
10 festermen · Vlf eorles suna · 7 Cytelbearn · 7 Osferð Fryðgistes suna · 7 Clac æt Byrnewillan. Þe Eðered sealde Adeluuolde · b synd festermen · Vlf Doddes suna · Þurwold æt Hylpestune · Clac on Castre · Þurhlac ferðeng.

Ealdulf ab bohte þa mylne æt Esctune mid twam pundum æt
15 Martine · 7 him sin festermen · Frena · 7 Sygeferð · 7 Osferð.

Her ges'w'uteleð þæt Ealdulf ab gebohte ane hyde landes on Esctune æt Ealfuuolde on þere .III. hundred gewytnesse æt Wyðreðe crosse · 7 him sin festermen · 7 him festermen Osferð Fryðegystes suna · 7 Byrcsige Warmundes suna · 7 Sumerlyda
20 preost · 7 Hudeman æt Asecyrcan. Þa Ethelwine ealdorman 7 E̹aldulf ab sealdon E̹thestane 7 Ealfuuolde þane latestan penign · æt þam lande æt Burh þa weren þer festermen Frena 7 Eþelsige þes ealdormannes eam · 7 Osforð Fryðegystes suna · 7 Ealfnoð Badan suna · 7 Sumerlyda preost. Þes landes is .xx. æcera wudes
25 an feldes butan þere leswe þe þer to gebyrið þe Ealdulf ab gebohte æt Osgode on Badingtune on þære twegera hundreda gewitnesse æt Dicon · 7 him sind festermen · Þurlac · 7 Herulf · 7 Etlebrant · 7 Hundulf. Ealdulf ab 7 Alfuuold Bohton oðer healfe hyde æt Swifte mid ehta pundun · þonne synd festermen ·
30 Frena · 7 Vlf eorles suna · 7 Osferð Fryðegistes suna · 7 Hudeman · 7 Sumerlyda · on þeræ þreora hundred gewytnesse into Undelum.

Þis synd þa festermen þe Wulfgeat 7 Gyrping fundon þam ab Æddulfe þa hi þat lande guldun æt Macusige for ðan útlage

SURETIES FOR PETERBOROUGH ESTATES 79

the outlawry he had incurred through slaying Styrcyr, Oggod and his two sons, Oswig the priest, Grim, Boia, Drabba, Æthelstan of Upton, Clac and Styrcyr. It consists of a homestead and 40 acres of arable land and meadow.

The estate at Wittering which Mannel gave to Bishop Æthelwold consists of one hide less an oxgang. These are the sureties, Gyreweard, Gyrping, Thurwold of Maxey and Steigncytel. Then Clac gave a hide less an oxgang. These are the sureties, Oggod of Castor, Ulf, Dodd's son, Thurwold of Helpston, Clac of Castor. The sureties for Ufi were Ulf, *Eorl's* son, and Cytelbearn and Osferth, Frithegist's son, and Clac of Barnwell. The sureties for what Æthelred gave to Bishop Æthelwold are Ulf, Dodd's son, Thurwold of Helpston, Clac of Castor, Thurlac Farthing.

Abbot Ealdulf bought the mill at Ashton from Martin for two pounds, and his sureties are Frena and Sigeferth and Osferth.

Here it is declared that Abbot Ealdulf bought a hide of land at Ashton from Ælfwold, with the cognisance of the three hundreds at *Wyðreðe* cross, and his sureties are Osferth, Frithegist's son, and Brihtsige, Warmund's son, and Sumerlida the priest and Hudeman of Achurch.

When Earl Æthelwine and Abbot Ealdulf gave Æthelstan and Ælfwold the final penny for the estate at Peterborough, the sureties were Frena and Æthelsige, the earl's uncle, and Osferth, Frithegist's son, and Ælfnoth, Bada's son, and Sumerlida the priest.

The estate consists of 20 acres of woodland and open country, apart from the pasture which pertains to it, that Abbot Ealdulf bought from Osgod of Bainton with the cognisance of the two hundreds at the Dykes, and his sureties are Thurlac and Herulf and Ætlebrant and Hundulf. Abbot Ealdulf and Ælfwold bought 1½ hides from Swift for 8 pounds. These are the sureties, Frena and Ulf, *Eorl's* son, and Osferth, Frithegist's son, and Hudeman and Sumerlida, with the cognisance of the three hundreds attached to Oundle.

These are the sureties whom Wulfgeat and Gyrping found for Abbot Ealdulf, when they paid over the estate at Maxey for the

80 SURETIES FOR PETERBOROUGH ESTATES

þa he on Wulnoðe wor'h'te · þonne is an Hundulf oðer is Ulf Doddes sune .III. Þurlac .IIII. Sigar .v. Þurold on Macesige. Þes landes is under eal .IX 7 XX. gedale.

On þissum gewrite cyð hwet þa festermen synd þes landes
5 ceapes þe Adeluuold .b. gebohte æt mislicum mannum ut on Wiðeringa eige ærest on Gyrewerde .XXIIII. æcera 7 þerto god gebotl · 7 him man sealde wið .XII. mancusas goldes · 7 .VIII. oran mære wites feos · 7 him weron festermen · Frena · 7 Sigeferð · 7 Oggod · þa bohte man æt Mannele 7 æt 'h'is wife .LX. æcera
10 mid þrim pundum 7 mid anum ýre · 7 him weron festermen Þurlac · 7 Oggod. Þa bohte man æt Tuce 7 æt hire sune Clacce .LX. æcera ælc mid .x. penegum · 7 hire weron festermen Gunna 7 Hundulf 7 Saxa 7 Þurferð. 7 æt þan .xx. æcera þa man bohte æt Vfige ælne mid .XX. penegun · 7 mid
15 .VIII. penegun · 7 him weron festermen Tunna his feder 7 Vlf · 7 Osulfe 7 æt is modur Aswige man bohte .LX. æcera elcne mid .x. penegun[1] · 7 him weron festermen Wulgar 7 Eadric 7 Osferð 7 Styrcyr 7 Ætlebrant.

Þonne bohte man æt Wulnoðe metere Oxanege · þonne on
20 Oxanige is ametenes wudes 7 feldes 7 medwe .XXV. æcera 7 wiðutan þan ige sixti sticca landes þet is ámeten to .XXX. æcerum · 7 on wude þe þridde treow · þer wiðutan 7 him man sealde wið Oxanige 7 wið ðan þer utan .XXV. mancussa goldes · 7 him weron festermen Gyreweard · 7 Æthelnoð Ætþelferðes sune greatan ·
25 7 Wulnoðes agen sune. Þonne is geseald wið Wyðeringaige 7 Oxanige .xv. pund. Þis synd þa festermen þere þreore hyda æt Þeorp þe Adeluuold .b. gebohte æt Sygeferðe mid .XVI. pundun · þet is þonne ærest Frena 7 Ælsige 7 Ælfnoð Badan sune · 7 Osferð Friðegistes sune · 7 Hudeman · 7 Oggod · 7
30 Ælfuuard · 7 Gyreweard · 7 Maneboia · 7 þis was gedon æt Wylmesforda. Þis synd þa festermen þe Herulf Adan sune funde Aldulfe ab 7 Goduine Ælfsies sune þa hi þat land bohton æt Badingtune · þat is Æthestan Catlan sune · 7 Leofsie Þurlaces sune · 7 Tufes on Hylpestune 7 Æðestan on Uptune · 7 Osulf

[1] -um, B.

SURETIES FOR PETERBOROUGH ESTATES

outlawry which he pronounced on Wulfnoth, the first is Hundulf, the second is Ulf, Dodd's son, the third Thurlac, the fourth Sigar, the fifth Thurwold of Maxey. The estate consists altogether of 29 portions.

In this document it is declared who are the sureties for the purchase of land which Bishop Æthelwold made from various men out at Wittering; first of all 24 acres from Gyreweard, and a good dwelling-house in addition, and it was given him for 12 mancuses of gold and 8 ores of pure white money, and his sureties were Frena and Sigeferth and Oggod. Then 60 acres were bought from Mannel and his wife for 3 pounds and one ore, and his sureties were Thurlac and Oggod. Then from Tuce and her son Clac 60 acres were bought for 10 pence each, and her sureties were Gunna and Hundulf and Saxa and Thurferth. And for the 20 acres which were bought from Ufi for 28 pence each, the sureties were Tunna his father, and Ulf and Osulf, and from his mother Aswig 60 acres were bought for 10 pence each, and the sureties were Wulfgar and Eadric and Osferth and Styrcyr and Ætlebrant.

Then from Wulfnoth the painter was bought Oxney. The amount of woodland and open country and meadow at Oxney is 25 acres by measure, and outside the island 60 pieces of land which amount to 30 acres, and in the wood outside every third tree. And for Oxney and what lay outside were given 25 mancuses of gold, and his sureties were Gyreweard and Æthelnoth, son of Æthelferth the Stout, and Wulfnoth's own son. For Wittering and for Oxney 15 pounds were paid.

These are the sureties for the three hides at Thorpe which Bishop Æthelwold bought from Sigeferth for 16 pounds, namely first Frena and Ælfsige and Ælfnoth, Bada's son, and Osferth, Frithegist's son, and Hudeman and Oggod and Ælfweard and Gyreweard and Maneboia, and this was done at Wansford.

These are the sureties whom Herulf, Ada's son, found for Abbot Ealdulf and Godwine, Ælfsige's son, when they bought the estate at Bainton, namely Æthelstan, Catla's son, and Leofsige, Thurlac's son, and Tufes of Helpston, and Æthelstan of Upton and Osulf of Castor and Osferth, Oggod's son, and at the west end Ælfweard of Denton and Sumerlida the priest and

82 SURETIES FOR PETERBOROUGH ESTATES

on Castre · 7 Osferð Oggodes sune · 7 on þam westende Ælfuuard on Dentune · 7 Sumerlyda preost · 7 Oswi on Æðelingtune · 7 Þurferð Rolfes sune · 7 Cytel is broðer · 7 Sumer æt Stoce · 7 Osulf Hudemannes sune · 7 þis wes gedon æt Vndelum on þere
5 .VIII. hundreda gewytnesse. Þis synd þa festermen þe Æincund funde Ældulfe ab æt þan lande æt Anlafestune þe he æt him bohte · þet is Eadric on Torp · 7 Eðestan Catlan sune 7 Tufes on Beornican · 7 Tufes on Hylpestune · 7 Leofsie Þurlaces sune · 7 Grymkytel · 7 Vlf his agen broðor · 7 þerto twa hun-
10 dreda. Þis synd þa borhhanda þe Swuste 7 hire dohter funden Ældulfe ab æt oðre ælfe hyde æt Lundingtune on þere .VIII. hundred gewytnesse æt Vndelum þet wes Goduine Ælfsies sune · 7 Ælfnoð æt Creast · 7 Sumerlyda preost · 7 Sumerlyda æt Stoce · 7 Osulf Hudemannes sune · 7 Adeluuold Fryðegistes
15 sune · 7 Leofsie Alhstanes sune æt Hyslepe · 7 Þurforð Rolfes sune · 7 Cytel his broðor · 7 Oswi on Æilintune · 7 þer to ealle þa .VIII. hundreda into Undelum. Þis synd þa Wynemannes lafe æt Randan funde Ældulfe ab æt are hyðe[1] æt We'r'mingtune þet is hyre agan sune an 7 hyre þreo gebroðre · Osulf 7 Fastolf
20 7 Beorneh · 7 Adeluuold Fryðegistes sune · 7 Sumerlyda preost · 7 Sumerlyda æt Stoces · 7 Þurferð Rolfes sune 7 Cytel his broðor · 7 Oswi on Æþelingtune · 7 Ęduuine Ędrices sune · 7 Ęlfuueard on Dentune. Þis is seo swutelung þe Ælfweard on Dentune wroðte wið Ealdulf ab þa he him þat land agæf æt
25 Wermingtune þe he on woh genumen hæfde · þet is Frena · 7 Osferð Fryðegystes sune · 7 Adeluuold his broðor · 7 Sumerlyda preost · 7 Osulf Hudemannes sune · 7 on his wedde gesealde þet land æt Wermingtune æfter his dæg into sc̄e PETRE for his saule on hyra gewytnesse.

[1] *hyde*, B.

SURETIES FOR PETERBOROUGH ESTATES 83

Oswig of Elton and Thurferth, Rolf's son, and Cytel his brother, and Sumer[lida] of Stoke and Osulf, Hudeman's son, and this was done at Oundle with the cognisance of the 8 hundreds.

These are the sureties whom Eincund found for Abbot Ealdulf for the estate at *Anlafestune* which he bought from him, namely Eadric of Thorpe and Æthelstan, Catla's son, and Tufes of Barnack and Tufes of Helpston and Leofsige, Thurlac's son, and Grimketel and Ulf, his own brother, and 2 hundreds in addition.

These are the sureties whom Swuste and her daughter found for Abbot Ealdulf for the 1½ hides at Lutton, with the cognisance of the 8 hundreds at Oundle, namely Godwine, Ælfsige's son, and Ælfnoth of *Creast* and Sumerlida the priest and Sumerlida of Stoke and Osulf, Hudeman's son, and Æthelwold, Frithegist's son, and Leofsige, son of Ealhstan of Islip, and Thurferth, Rolf's son, and Cytel his brother and Oswig of Elton, and in addition the 8 hundreds attached to Oundle.

These are [the sureties] whom the widow of Wineman of Raunds found for Abbot Ealdulf for the one hide at Warmington, namely first her own son and her three brothers—Osulf and Fastulf and Beornheah—and Æthelwold, Frithegist's son, and Sumerlida the priest and Sumerlida of Stoke and Thurferth, Rolf's son, and Cytel his brother and Oswig of Elton and Edwin, Eadric's son, and Ælfweard of Denton.

This is the declaration [of the agreement] which Ælfweard of Denton made with Abbot Ealdulf when he gave up to him the estate at Warmington which he had wrongfully taken, [and produced sureties], namely Frena and Osferth, Frithegist's son, and Æthelwold his brother and Sumerlida the priest and Osulf, Hudeman's son; and on his security granted the estate at Warmington with their cognisance to St Peter's after his death on behalf of his soul.

XLI. HISTORY OF THE ESTATE OF WOULDHAM, KENT

✠ Þus wæron ða seox sulung æt Wuldaham sce Andrea geseald into Hrofesceastre · Æðelbryht cinc hit gebocode þam apłe on ece yrfe · 7 betæhte hit ðam biscope Eardulfe to bewitenne · 7 his æftergæncan · ða betweonan þam wearð hit ute · 7 hæfdon hit
5 cynegas oð Eadmund cinc · ða gebohte hit Ælfstan[1] Heahstaninc æt ðæm cince mid hundtwelftigan mancesan goldes · 7 ðrittigan pundan · 7 ðæt him sealde mæst eal Ælfeh his sunu · æfter Eadmunde cincge ða gebocode hit Eadred cinc Ælfstane on ece yrfe · þa æfter Ælfstanes dæge wæs Ælfeh his sunu his yrfewærd
10 7 þ he beleac[2] on halre tungon · 7 ofteah Ælfrice his breðer landes 7 æhta butan he hwæt æt him geearnode · ða for ðære broðorsibbe geuðe he him · Earhiðes · 7 Cræganes · 7 Ænesfordes · 7 Wuldahames his dæg · ða oferbad Ælfeh ðæne broðor 7 feng to his læne · þa hæfde Ælfric suna Eadric hatte 7 Ælfeh nænne ·
15 ða geuðe Ælfeh þam Eadrice · Earhiðes · 7 Cræganes · 7 Wuldahames · 7 hæfde himsylf Ænesford · þa gewat Eadric ær Ælfeh cwideleas · 7 Ælfeh feng to his læne · ða hæfde Eadric lafe 7 nan bearn · þa geuþe Ælfeh hire hire morgengife · æt Cræganes · 7 stod Earhið · 7 Wuldaham · 7 Lytlanbroc on his læne · ða him eft
20 geðuhte ða nam he his feorme on Wuldaham · 7 on ðam oþran wolde ac hine geyflade · 7 he ða sænde to ðam arcebiscope Dunstane · 7 he com to Scylfe to him · 7 he cwæþ his cwide beforan him · 7 he sette ænne cwide to Cristes cyrican · 7 oðerne to sce Andrea · 7 ðañ[3] ðriddan sealde his lafe · ða bræc syððan
25 Leofsunu ðurh þ wif ðe he nam Eadrices lafe ðæne cwide · 7 herewade þæs arcebiscopes gewitnesse · rad ða innon ða land mid þam wife butan witena dome · þa man þ ðam biscope cyðde[4] · ða gelædde se biscop ahnunga ealles Ælfehes cwides to Earhiðe

[1] *Æfstan*, Text. Roff.   [2] *leac*, ibid.
[3] *ðane*, ibid.   [4] *ciðde*, ibid.

XLI. HISTORY OF THE ESTATE OF WOULDHAM, KENT

✠ The six ploughlands at Wouldham were given to St Andrew's at Rochester as follows. King Æthelbert granted the estate by charter to the Apostle as a perpetual inheritance, and entrusted it to the guardianship of Bishop Eardwulf and his successors. Then in the course of time it was alienated, and kings up to King Edmund held it. Then Ælfstan, Heahstan's son, bought it from the king for 120 mancuses of gold and 30 pounds [of silver], and nearly all that sum was given him by his son Ælfheah. After King Edmund King Edred granted it by charter to Ælfstan as a perpetual inheritance. Then after Ælfstan's death Ælfheah, his son, was his heir, and that he plainly established and refused his brother Ælfric both land and possessions, except for what he acquired from him. Then because of their relationship as brothers, he granted him Erith and Cray and Eynsford and Wouldham for life. Then Ælfheah survived his brother and resumed possession of the estates which he had leased to him. Now Ælfric had a son called Eadric, but Ælfheah had none. Ælfheah, therefore, granted to Eadric Erith and Cray and Wouldham, but kept Eynsford himself. Then Eadric died before Ælfheah, intestate, and Ælfheah resumed possession of the estates which he had leased to him. Eadric left a widow but no children. Ælfheah granted her Cray, which had been her marriage gift, while Erith, Wouldham and Littlebrook remained on lease from him. Later, in his own good time, he collected his food-rent from Wouldham, and intended to do the same from the others, but he was taken ill. He sent then to Archbishop Dunstan, and he came to him at Shelve, and Ælfheah declared his will before him, and appointed one copy [to be sent to] Christchurch and another to St Andrew's and the third he gave to his widow. Afterwards, however, Leofsunu, on the strength of having married Eadric's widow, broke the terms of the will and set at nought the Archbishop's testimony, and with his wife took possession of the estates without the authority of the council. When the [Arch]bishop was informed of this, he proved possession of the whole of Ælfheah's bequest at Erith, in the presence

on gewitnesse Ælfstanes biscopes on Lundene · 7 ealles þæs
hiredes 7 ðæs æt Cristes cyrican · 7 ðæs biscopes Ælfstanes an
Hrofesceastre · 7 Wulfsies pre'o'stes þæs scirigmannes · 7 Bryht-
waldes on Mæreweorðe · 7 ealra East Cantwarena · 7 West
5 Cantwarena 7 hit wæs gecnæwe on Suþ Seaxan · 7 on West
Seaxan 7 on Middel Seaxan · 7 on East Seaxan · þ̄ se arcebiscop
mid his selfes aðe geahnode Gode · 7 sc̄e Andrea mid þam bocan
on Cristes rode[1] ða land þe Leofsunu him toteah 7 ðæne aþ nam
Wulfsige se scirigman ðá hé nólde to ðæs cinges handa · 7 þær
10 wæs god eaca ten hundan mannan ðe þane að sealdan.

XLII. LEASE OF LAND BY OSWALD, BISHOP OF WORCESTER, TO ÆLFHILD

Hindehlyp · Ælfild 7 Cynelm · 7 Æþelgerd[2].

[Ic][3] Oswald bisceop þurh Godes giefe mid geþafunge 7 leafe
[Ea]dgares[3] Angulcyningces 7 Ælfheres Mercna heretogan 7
þæs heorodes on Wiogornaceastre landes sumne dæl þ̄ synd
15 .III. hida þe fram cuþum mannum Hindehlep ís gehaten sumum
wife þære[4] is noma Ælfild for Godes lufon 7 for uncre sibbe mid
eallum þingum þe þærto belimpað freolice hiere dæg forgieaf[5]
7 æfter hiere dæge twam yrfeweardum 7 æfter heora forðsiþe to
þære halgan stowe into Wiogornaceastre þam biscope to bryce
20 si hit ælces þinges freoh[6] butan ferdfare 7 walgeworc[7] 7 brycge-
worc 7 circanlade þis wæs gedon ymbe nigon hund wintra 7 seox
7 seoxtig þæs þe drihtnes gebyrdtide wæs · on þy seofoþan geare
þæs þe Oswald bisceop tó folgaðe feng. Sc̄a Maria · 7 sc̄s
Michahel · cum sc̄o Petro 7 eallum Godes halgum gemiltien[8]
25 þis haldendum · gif hwa buton gewrihtum[9] hit abrecan wille
God hine to rihtere bote gecerre · amen.

Her ís seo hondseten Oswaldes biscopes.

✠ Ego Wulfric prbt   ✠ Ego Wulfhun cl   ✠ Ego Ælfgar cl
✠ Ego Eadgar prbt   ✠ Ego Ælfstan cler   ✠ Ego Vfic cl
30 ✠ Ego Æþelstan   ✠ Ego Byrhstan cl.   ✠ Ego Wulfheh cl
    prbt   ✠ Ego Wulfgar cl   ✠ Ego Leofwine cl
✠ Ego Ælfred cl

as witnesses of Ælfstan, Bishop of London, and all the community and that at Christchurch, and of Ælfstan, Bishop of Rochester, and the sheriff, Wulfsige the priest, and Brihtwold of Mereworth, and all the men of East Kent and West Kent; and it was known in Sussex and Wessex and Middlesex and Essex that the Archbishop with his own oath had secured possession of the estates, which Leofsunu had usurped, on behalf of God and St Andrew, with the title-deeds on the cross of Christ. And Wulfsige the sheriff, as the king's representative, accepted the oath when Leofsunu refused it. And there were in addition a good thousand men who gave the oath.

XLII. LEASE OF LAND BY OSWALD, BISHOP OF WORCESTER, TO ÆLFHILD

Hindlip, to Ælfhild and Cynelm and Æthelgeard.

I, Oswald, bishop through the grace of God, with the permission and leave of Edgar, King of England, and Ælfhere, Earl of Mercia, and the community at Worcester, have freely granted a certain piece of land, namely 3 hides, called by those familiar with it Hindlip, to a certain woman whose name is Ælfhild, for the love of God and the relationship between us, with everything belonging to it, for her lifetime, and after her death to two heirs, and after their death to the holy foundation at Worcester for the use of the bishop. And it shall be free from every burden except military service and the construction of walls and bridges and carrying service for the church.

This was done in the year 966 after the birth of our Lord, in the seventh year after Bishop Oswald succeeded to office. May St Mary and St Michael, with St Peter and all the saints of God, be merciful towards those who observe this. If anyone, without due cause, attempts to break it, may God turn him to due amendment. Amen...

---

[1] *hrode*, Text. Roff. [2] This is entered in the right margin; om. K.
[3] A fragment has been cut off the page.
[4] *þær*, He.
[5] *forgæaf*, He., K., which may possibly be the MS. reading.
[6] *freo*, He. [7] *-weorc*, B.
[8] *-miltsien*, K. [9] *geriht-*, K.

XLIII. LEASE OF LAND BY OSWALD, BISHOP OF WORCESTER, TO EADRIC

[Æ]t Eanulfestune [Ea]drice 7 Wulfrune[1].

✝ Albuscente[2] hac[3] consentiente · EADGARO · basileo · Aelfhere · que Merciorum[4] · Ego Oswold · largiflua dei clementia antistites[5] · Quandam rusculi partem .iii. silicet[6] mansas tribus
5 tamen in locis diuisam cui uocabulum est · æt Eanulfestune · oþer healf hid 7 æt Uferan Strætforda on þære gesyndredan hide þone oþerne æcer 7 æt Fachanleage þone þriddan æcer feldlandes · 7 healfne þone wudu on easthealfe þæs weges 7 þone æt þære eorðbyrig · 7 on easthealfe[7] Afene eahta æceras mædwa 7
10 forne gean biccenclife .xii. æceras mædwa 7 þreo æcras benorðan Afene[8] to myllnstealle · EADRICO · meo compatri · æternaliter concessi · et post uitę suę terminum duorum[9] derelinquat cleronomo[10] eorumque uitę finito curriculo ad usum primatis in Wiogornaceastre redeat immunis. Þonne is ealles þæs landes
15 þreo hida þe Oswald biscop bocað Eadrice his þegne on þa gerad wyrce ƥ he wyrce ƥ ƥ land seo unforworht into þære halgan stowe twe'g'ra monna dæg æfter him. Anno dominicae incarnationis DCCCC.LXVI. Scripta est hec carta his testibus consentientibus quorum inferius nomina notantur.

20 ✠ Ego OSwald eps. hanc consentientionem[11] signo crucis xpi confirmo.
✠ Ego Wulfric prbt   ✠ Ego Brihstan prbt   ✠ Ego Eadward clr
✠ Ego Eadgar prbt   ✠ Ego Wulfgar clr   ✠ Ego Tuna clr
✠ Ego Wistan prbt   ✠ Ego Ælfstan clr   ✠ Ego Wulfhæh clr
✠ Ego Æþelstan prbt   ✠ Ego Eadwine clr   ✠ Ego Leofwine clr
25 ✠ Ego Ælfred prbt   ✠ Ego Ælfgar clr   ✠ Ego Wenstan clr
✠ Ego Wulfhun prbt   ✠ Ego Ufic clr   ✠ Ego Wulfnoð clr.

---

[1] This is entered in the left margin; om. K.
[2] *Allubescente*, He., K.
[3] *ac*, K.
[4] *M. duce*, K.
[5] Sic; *antistes*, He., K., B.
[6] Sic; *scil-*, He., K., B.
[7] *-healf*, He.
[8] *æfene*, He.
[9] *duobus*, K.
[10] *-onomis*, K.
[11] Sic; *concessionem*, K., B.

XLIII. LEASE OF LAND BY OSWALD, BISHOP OF WORCESTER, TO EADRIC

Alveston, to Eadric and Wulfrun.

☩ With the approval and consent of King Edgar and of Ælfhere of the Mercians, I, Oswald, bishop by the bountiful goodness of God, have granted for all time to Eadric, my fellow sponsor, a certain piece of land, namely 3 hides, divided between three places—1½ hides at the place called Alveston, and every other acre in the divided hide at Upper Stratford, and every third acre of open land at *Fachanleah*, and half the wood on the east side of the road, and that at the earthwork, and 8 acres of meadow on the east side of the Avon, and 12 acres of meadow opposite *Biccenclif*, and 3 acres north of the Avon as a site for a mill. And at the end of his life he shall leave it to two heirs, and when the course of their life is ended, it shall return intact for the use of the Bishop of Worcester.

The total amount of land, therefore, is 3 hides which Bishop Oswald grants by charter to Eadric, his thegn, on condition that whatever he does, the estate shall return unforfeited to the holy foundation at the end of two lives after his.

In the year of the incarnation of the Lord 966 this charter was written with the consent of the witnesses whose names are recorded below...

XLIV. HISTORY OF THE ESTATES OF SUNBURY AND SEND

Sé fruma wæs ꝥ mon forstælænne wimman · æt Iecesleá[1] Ælfsige Byrhsiges suna · Þurwif hatte sé wimman. Þa befeng Ælfsige þone mann æt Wulfstane Wulfgares fæder[2] · þá tymde Wulfstan hine tó Æþelstane æt Sunnanbyrg · þa cende hé tem · 7³ let þone
5 forberstan · 7³ forbeh þone andagan[4] · æfter þam bæd Ælfsige ǽgiftes hís mannes · 7 hé hine ágef[5] 7 forgeald hím mid twam pundum · þá bæd Byrhferð ealdormann Æþelstan hys[6] wer · for þam tembyrste · þá cwæð[7] Æðelstan ꝥ he næfde him tó syllanne[8] · þá cleopode[9] Eadweard Æðelstanes broðor · 7 cwæð[10] · íc · hæbbe
10 Sunnanburges bóc ðe uncre yldran me læfdon · læt me ꝥ land tó handa íc agife þinne wér ðam cynge · þá cwæð Æðelstan ꝥ him leofre wære ꝥ hit tó fyre oððe flode gewurde · þonne he hit æfre gebide · ða cwæð Eadweard hit ís wyrse ꝥ uncer naðor hit næbbe · þa wæs ꝥ[11] swa · 7 forbead Byrhferð ꝥ land Æðelstane ·
15 7 he óf ferde 7 gebeh under Wulfgare ǽt Norðhealum · binnan ðam wendun gewyrda · 7 gewat Eadræd[12] cyng · 7[13] feng Eadwig tó rice · 7 wende Æðelstan hine eft intó Sunnanbyrg · ungebetra þinga · þa geahsode ꝥ Eadwig cyng[13] · 7 gesealde ꝥ land Byrnrice · 7 hé feng tó · 7 wearp[14] Æðelstan út · gemang þam getidde ꝥ
20 Myrce gecuran Eadgar tó cynge[15] · 7 him anweald[16] gesealdan[17] ealra cynerihta · þa gesohte Æðelstan Eadgar cyng 7 bæd domes · þá ǽtdemdon him Myrcna[18] witan land buton hé hís wer agulde þam cynge swa he oðrum ǽr sceolde · þa næfde he hwanon · ne he hit Eadwearde his breðer geðafian nolde · þa
25 gesealde sé cyng · 7 gebecte[19] ꝥ land Æðelstan'e' ealdormenn · tó hæbbenne · 7 tó syllanne for life · 7 for legere þam him leofost wære · æfter þam getidde ꝥ Ecgferð gebohte bóc 7 land ǽt Æðelstane ealdormenn · ón cynges gewitnesse · 7 hís witena swa

[1] Icc-, K., E.; Ices-, T.
[2] fad-, K., E.
[5] ágif, K., E.
[8] -ane, K., E.
[11] ðá, K., E.
[14] wearf, K., E.
[17] -on, T.
[3] Om. K., E.
[6] his, T.
[9] -ade, T.
[12] -red, K., E.
[15] cyng, T.
[18] Myrena, K.
[4] -en, K., E.
[7] cwæð, K.
[10] cwæd, B.
[13] 7......cyng, om. T.
[16] -weold, T.
[19] -bette, T., B.

XLIV. HISTORY OF THE ESTATES OF SUNBURY AND SEND

The beginning [of this case] was that a woman was stolen at Yaxley from Ælfsige, Brihtsige's son. The woman's name was Thurwif. Then Ælfsige attached the woman in the possession of Wulfstan, Wulfgar's father. Then Wulfstan vouched Æthelstan of Sunbury to warranty for her. Then Æthelstan declared that he would carry on the process; but he let it go by default, and failed to appear on the appointed day. After that Ælfsige asked for the return of the woman, and Æthelstan gave her up and paid him two pounds as compensation. Then Earl Brihtferth asked Æthelstan for his wergeld, because of the failure of the vouching. Then Æthelstan said that he had nothing to give him. Then Edward, Æthelstan's brother, spoke up and said, 'I have the title-deeds of Sunbury which our parents left me; give me possession of the estate and I will pay your wergeld to the king.' Then Æthelstan said that he would rather that it perished by fire or flood than suffer that. Then Edward said, 'It would be worse for neither of us to have it.' But that was what happened. Brihtferth forbade Æthelstan to hold the estate, and he left it and put himself under Wulfgar of *Norðhealum*.

In the meantime fortune changed and King Edred died, and Edwy succeeded to the kingdom. Then Æthelstan went back to Sunbury without making amends. When King Edwy heard of it, he gave the estate to Beornric, who took possession of it and ejected Æthelstan. In the meantime it happened that the Mercians chose Edgar as king, and gave him control of all the royal prerogatives. Then Æthelstan betook himself to King Edgar and asked for judgment. Then the Mercian council decreed that he should lose the estate, unless he paid his wergeld to the [present] king, as he should have done to the other one. Then he had nothing with which to pay, nor would he allow his brother Edward to do so. Then the king gave the estate and confirmed it by charter to Earl Æthelstan, to be held and granted, during his lifetime or at his death, to anyone he pleased.

92 HISTORY OF THE ESTATES OF

hís gemedo wæron · hæfde 7 breac oð hís ende · þá betæhte
Ecgferð on halre tungan · land 7 bóc ón cynges gewitnesse
Dunstane arcebisceope tó mundgenne hís lafe · 7 his bearne[1] ·
þa hé geendod wæs þa rad sé bisceop tó þam cynge myngude
5 þære munde 7 his gewitnesse · þa cwæð sé cyng him tó andsware
mine witan habbað ǽtrecð[2] Ecgferðe ealle hís are · þurh Þ[3]
swyrd þe him ón hype hangode þá hé adranc · nam þa sé cyng
ða are þe he ahte .xx. hyda[4] ǽt Sendan .x. ǽt Sunnanbyrg · 7
forgef Ælfhege ealdormenn[5] · þa bead[6] sé bisceop his wér þam
10 cynge · þa cwæð sé cyng · Þ mihte beon geboden him wið
clænum legere · ac íc hæbbe ealle þa spæce tó Ælfhege læten.
Þæs ón syxtan gere gebohte sé arcebisceop ǽt Ælfhege ealdormenn · Þ land ǽt Sendan · mid .xc. pundum · 7 æt Sunnanbyrg
mid .cc. mancussan goldes · únbecwedene · 7 únforbodene wið
15 ælcne mann[7] tó þære dægtide · 7 he him swa þa land geagnian
derr · swa him sé sealde ðe tó syllenne[8] ahte · 7 hi þam sé cyng
sealde · swa hí[9] hím hís witan[10] gerehton.

XLV. RENEWAL OF THE FREEDOM OF TAUNTON BY KING EDGAR

HER ys geswutelod on þysum gewrite hu EADgar cyning mid
geþeahte his witena geniwode Tantunes freols þære halgan
20 þrynnesse 7 sc̄e Petre 7 sc̄e Paule into Wintanceastre to þam
biscopstole ealswa Eadweard cyning hit ær[11] gefreode 7 geuþe Þ
ægþer ge twelfhynde men ge twyhynde weron on þam Godes
hame þara ylcan gerihta wyrþe þe his agene men sindon on his
agenum cynehamum · 7 man ealle spæca 7 gerihtu on Þ ylce
25 gemet gefe[12] to Godes handa þe man to his agenre drifh[13] 7 þes
tunes ciyping[14] 7 seó ínnúng þara portgerihta gange into þere
halgan stowe ealswa heo ær[15] dyde on myra vldrena[16] dagon 7

[1] -na, T.
[2] ætreeð, K., E.; ætre, T.
[3] ðæt, K., E.
[4] hida, T.
[5] earld-, K., E.
[6] beod, B.
[7] man, T.
[8] -ene, K., E.
[9] he, K., E.
[10] wihtan, B.
[11] her, (b), om. B.
[12] drife, (b).
[13] drifð, (b).
[14] cyp-, (b), K.
[15] her, (b).
[16] yld-, (b), K., B.

After that it happened that Ecgferth bought both the estate and the title-deeds from Earl Æthelstan with the cognisance of the king and his councillors, as was his good pleasure, and held and enjoyed it till the end of his life. Then Ecgferth unequivocally committed both the estate and the title-deeds, with the cognisance of the king, to Archbishop Dunstan, in order that he might act as guardian to his widow and child. When he was dead, the [Arch]bishop rode to the king and reminded him of the guardianship and of his cognisance. Then the king said to him in answer, 'My councillors have declared all Ecgferth's property forfeit, by the sword that hung on his hip when he was drowned.' Then the king took possession of the property which he owned—20 hides at Send and 10 at Sunbury—and gave it to Earl Ælfheah. Then the [Arch]bishop offered his wergeld to the king. Then the king said, 'That might be offered to obtain a consecrated grave for him, but I have left the whole case to Ælfheah.'

Six years afterwards the Archbishop bought from Earl Ælfheah the estate at Send for 90 pounds and that at Sunbury for 200 mancuses of gold, uncontested and unopposed by anyone at the time, and he is thus emboldened to claim ownership of the estates, since he who had the power of granting them and to whom the king had granted them, as his councillors directed, gave them to him.

XLV. RENEWAL OF THE FREEDOM OF TAUNTON BY KING EDGAR

Here it is declared in this document how King Edgar, with the advice of his councillors, renewed the freedom of Taunton for the episcopal see of the Holy Trinity and St Peter and St Paul at Winchester, exactly as King Edward had freed it, and granted that both noblemen and commoners on the manor of God should be entitled to the same dues as his own men are on his own royal manors. And all [the proceeds of] lawsuits and all dues shall be given for the benefit of the church in the same proportion as they are exacted on his own behalf, and the trading dues of the town and the receipt of the market dues shall go to the holy foundation, as they used to do in the days of my ancestors, and

94 RENEWAL OF FREEDOM OF TAUNTON

Ælfeage biscope gehafod[1] wæs 7 gewylcvm þara þe þes landes breac. Se þe þisne freols geycean wille geyce God his gesynta to langsumun life her 7 on ecnesse. Gif hwa þonne þurh gedyrstignesse 7 deofles oþþe his lima lare þysne freols abrecan
5 wille oþþe on oþer awendan buton he hit ær his fordsiþe gebete[2] sy he mid awurgednesse ascyred[3] fram ures drithnes gemanan 7 ealra his halgena 7 on helle susle ecelice getintragod mid Iudan þe Cristes lewa wes. Ðonne gesealde AÐELwold biscop his cynehlaforde twa und mancussa goldes 7 anne sylfrene lefel on
10 fif pundum wiþe niwunge[4] þyses freolses 7 Ælfþryde his gebeddan healf hund mancussa goldes wiþ richtes ærendes fultume 7 ær wænon[5] wiþ[6] freolse gesealt on Eadwardes dege cinges · syxtig hide landes[7] .x. æt Crawancumbe · 7 .x. æt Cumbtune · 7 æt Bananwille .xx. 7 .xx. æt Scealdeburnan stoce ·
15 7 eft Eadward cyning gesealde þ land æt Cumbtune · 7 æt Bananwille þan hiwon æt Ceodre wiþ þan lande æt Carintune. Þis wes gedon æt Ceodre on þere halgan easter tide · þy geare[8] weron agangene .DCCCC. geara 7 eahta 7 hundseofontig fram Cristes acynnednesse · 7 þe teoþan geáre his cynelican anwealdes
20 on gewitnesse þara witena þe hiora noman herwiþ neoþan awritene syndon.

Ego EADGAR Anglorum basileus hoc priuilegium in honore reuerende Trinitati atque consubstantialis unitatis crucis signo deuotissime confirmaui.

25   Ego DVNSTAN archiep̄s confirmaui.   Ego Ælfþryþ regina.
   Ego OSCYTEL archiep̄s consensi.   Ego Æþestan dux.
   Ego AÐELWOLD ep̄s corroboraui.   Ego Ælfhere dux.
   Ego ÆLFSTAN ep̄s consolidaui.   Ego Elfheah dux.
   Ego BYRHTELM ep̄s consensi.   Ego Ordgar dux.
30   Ego OSWOLD ep̄s corroboraui.   Ego Æþelwine dux.
   Ego ALFWOLD ep̄s consolidaui[9].   Ego Byrthnoð dux.
   Ego OSVLF ep̄s consensi[10].   Ego Oslac dux.
   Ego WYNSIGE ep̄s corroboraui[11].   Ego Eadulf dux.
   Ego Ælfric abb.   Ego Eanulf miñ.
35   Ego Osgar abb.   Ego Ælfwine miñ.
   Ego Elfstan abb.   Ego Æþelweard miñ.
   Ego Æscwig abb.   Ego Wulfstan miñ.
   Ego Æþelgar abb.   Ego Byrtferð miñ.
   Ego Cynewerd abb.   Ego Oswerd miñ.
40   Ego Þyrcytel abb.   Ego Osulf miñ.
   Ego Ælfheah abb.   Ego Elfwerd miñ.
   Ego Ealdred abb.   Ego Eþelweard miñ.

RENEWAL OF FREEDOM OF TAUNTON 95

as was allowed to Bishop Ælfheah and each of those who enjoyed the estate.

If anyone is willing to increase this freedom, God shall increase his well-being during a long life here and throughout eternity. If anyone, however, through presumption and the teaching of the devil or his servants, attempts to violate or to change this freedom, he shall be cut off with curses from the fellowship of our Lord and of all his saints, and tortured eternally in the torment of hell with Judas who was the betrayer of Christ, unless he has made amends for it before his death.

Then Bishop Æthelwold gave to his royal lord 200 mancuses of gold and a silver cup worth five pounds in return for the renewal of this freedom, and to Ælfthryth, his wife, 50 mancuses of gold, in return for her help in his just mission; and formerly in the time of King Edward 60 hides of land were given for the freedom—10 at Crowcombe and 10 at Compton and 20 at Banwell and 20 at Stoke near Shalbourn. And afterwards King Edward gave the estates at Compton and at Banwell to the community at Cheddar, in return for the estate at Carhampton.

This was done at Cheddar at the holy Easter season in the year when 978 years had passed since the birth of Christ, and in the tenth year of his royal authority, with the cognisance of the councillors whose names are recorded here below.

I, Edgar, King of England, have confirmed this privilege with the utmost devotion, in honour of the holy Trinity and the consubstantial Unity, with the symbol of the cross...

---

[1] -þafod, (b).
[2] a gebete, (b).
[3] 7 ascyred, (b), B.
[4] wið geniw-, (b); wið edniw-, K.
[5] wæron, K.; weron, (b), B.
[6] wiðam, (b).
[7] Om. B.
[8] þa instead of þy geare, (b).
[9] consignaui, (b), cosignavi, B.
[10] consolidaui, (b), -avi, B.
[11] adquieui, (b), -evi, B.

XLVI. LEASE OF LAND BY OSWALD, BISHOP OF WORCESTER, TO OSULF

✠[1] Ic Oswold bisceop þurh Godes gefe mid geþafunge 7 leafe Eadgares Angulkynincges 7 Ælfheres Mercna heretogan 7 þæs hieredes on Wiogerneceastre landes sumne dæl þæt sint · ·[2] hida on twuam tunum þe fram cuþum mannum Teottingctun 7
5 Ælfsigestun sint gehatenne sumum cnihte þæm is Osulf nama for Godes lufan 7 for uncre sibbe[3] mid eallum þingum tofreon þe þærto belimpað his dæg forgeaf 7 æfter his dæge twam erf'e'weardum þæt beo his bearn swilc lengest mote gief him þæt giefeþe bið æfter þara bearna dæge fo Eadleofu to his
10 gebedde hire dæg æfter hire dæge becweþe hire broþrum twam swilc hire leofest sy æfter hieora dæge eft into þære halgan stowe. Sy hit ælces þinges freoh butan ferdfare 7 walgeweorc 7 brygcgeweorc þis wæs godon ymbe nigon hund wintra 7 nigon 7 seoxtig þæs þe drihtnes gebyrdtide wæs · on þy nigoþan geare þæs þe
15 Oswold bisceop to folgaþe fengc. Sc̄a Maria 7 sc̄s Michahel cum sc̄o Petro 7 eallum Godes halgum gemiltsien þis healdendum gief hwa buton gewyrhtum hit awendan wille God adilgie his noman of lifes bocum 7 habbe him gemæne wið hine on þam ytemestan dæge þysses lifes butan he to rihtere bote gecerre.

20 ✠ Her is seo hondseten Oswoldes bisceopes 7 unna þæs hierdes on Wiogernaceastre.

✠ Wulfric mæsse-   ✠ Ælfred clerc[5]   ✠ Ælfgar cł
    preost[4].   ✠ Wulfhun clerc   ✠ Eadward cł
✠ Eadgar mæsse-   ✠ Brihstan clerc   ✠ Tuna cł
25   preost[4].   ✠ Wulfgar clerc   ✠ Ufic cł
✠ Æþelstan mæsse-   ✠ Cynsige cł   ✠ Wulfheah cł
    preost[4].   ✠ Ælfstan cł   ✠ Leofwine cł
✠ Wistan mæsse-   ✠ Eadwine cł   ✠ Wulfnoð cł
    preost[4].

---

[1] MS. (b) has a marginal note [Te]ottinctun · 7 Ælfsi[ge]stun Osulfe · 7 Leo-[fa]n · 7 Wihtgare.
[2] Blank also in MS. (b).   [3] symbe, ibid.
[4] prōt, ibid.   [5] cł throughout, ibid.

XLVI. LEASE OF LAND BY OSWALD, BISHOP OF WORCESTER, TO OSULF

✠ I, Oswald, bishop by the grace of God, with the permission and leave of Edgar, King of England, and Ælfhere, Earl of Mercia, and the community at Worcester, have freely granted for life a certain piece of land, namely...hides in two manors which are called by those familiar with them Teddington and Alstone, with everything belonging to them, to a certain *cniht* whose name is Osulf, for the love of God and the relationship between us, and after his death to two heirs, namely whichever of his children survives longest, if that is granted to him. After the death of his children, his wife Eadlifu shall succeed for her lifetime. After her death she shall bequeath it to whichever two of her brothers she pleases. After their death it shall revert to the holy foundation. It shall be free from every burden except military service and the construction of walls and bridges.

This was done 969 years after the birth of the Lord, in the ninth year after Bishop Oswald succeeded to office. May St Mary and St Michael, with St Peter and all the saints of God, be merciful to those who uphold this. If anyone, without due cause, attempts to change it, God shall blot out his name from the books of life, and he shall have to account for it to him on the last day of this life, unless he set about making due amendment...

XLVII. LIST OF SURETIES FOR A DEVONSHIRE ESTATE

Ðis synt þa men þe synt anburge betwinon Eadgyfe abbedysse[1] 7 Leofrice abbode æt þam[2] lande · æt Sto'c'tune Wulfsige EDwig · 7 Cytel · 7 Denisc · 7 Godwine · 7 Hunwine · 7 Sweta[3] · 7 Edwig boga · 7 Brun p̄. ꝥ se abbod · hit hębbe his dæg 7 æfter
5 his dæg into mynstre.

XLVIII. CHARTER OF KING EDGAR TO ELY

God ęf[4] ælmihtigum rixiende ðe ræt 7 gewissað[5] eallum gesceaftum þurh his agenne wisdom · 7 he ealra cininga cynedom gewylt · Ic EADGAR cining eac þurh his gife ofer Engla þeode · nu up aræred 7 he hæfð nu gewyld to minum anwealde Scottas 7
10 Cumbras · 7 eac[6] swylce Bryttas · 7 eall ꝥ ðis igland him on innan hæfð[7] ꝥ ic nu on sibbe gesitte minne[8] cynestol hohful embe ꝥ hu ic his lof arære ðe læs ðe his lof alicge to swyðe nu on urum timan þurh ure asolcennysse · ac ic wille nu þurh Godes wissunge þa forlætenan mynstru on minum anwealde gehwær
15 mid munecum gesettan[9] · 7 eac mid mynecenum 7 Godes lof geédniwian ðe ær wæs forlæten Criste wissiendum ðe cwæð ꝥ he wolde wunian mid us oð þissere geendunge[10] · 7 þa munecas libban heora lif æfter regole þæs halgan Benedictes us to þingunge ꝥ we þone hælænd[11] habban us glædne · 7 he us gewissige
20 7 urne eard gehealde 7 æfter geendunge ꝥ éce lif us forgife; Nu is me on mode æfter mynegungum Atheluuoldes biscopes þe me oft manode ꝥ ic wille góódian[12] ðurh Godes silfes fultum · ꝥ mynster on Elig mid agenum freodome 7 sinderlicum wurðmynte[13] · 7 siððan mid æhtum þam to bigleofan þe we gelogiað
25 þær to Godes ðeowdome þe ðær simble wunion. Seo stow wæs gehalgod íu[14] fram ealdum dagum þam halgan Petre to wyrð-

---

[1] -esse, B. [2] þa, Davidson. [3] Speta, ibid.
[4] Only the most important of the variant readings are noted.
[5] -ad, B. [6] ealc, B.
[7] hærð, Addit. MS. [8] on minne, K., T.
[9] municunige settan, B. [10] þ. worulde geend-, K., T.
[11] hælend, K., T.; helænd, B. [12] gegoodian, K., T.
[13] þurð-, B. [14] in, K.

XLVII. LIST OF SURETIES FOR A DEVONSHIRE ESTATE

These are the men who are sureties between Abbess Eadgifu and Abbot Leofric for the estate at Stoke [Canon], Wulfsige, Edwy and Cytel and Denisc and Godwine and Hunwine and Sweta and Edwy *boga* and the priest Brun, that the abbot shall have it for his lifetime, and after his death [it shall pass] to the minster.

XLVIII. CHARTER OF KING EDGAR TO ELY

In the reign of God Almighty, who counsels and directs all creatures by his own wisdom and controls the kingdoms of all kings, I, Edgar, [have been] exalted as king over the English nation by his grace, and he has now reduced beneath my sway Scots and Cumbrians and likewise Britons and all that this island contains, so that now I occupy my throne in peace, and am anxiously taking thought how to promote his worship, lest it fall away too greatly in our time through our sluggishness. I desire now, with the guidance of God, to fill the deserted monasteries everywhere in my dominion with monks and also with nuns, and with the guidance of Christ, who said that he would dwell with us till the end of this world, to renew the worship of God which has been neglected. And the monks shall live their life according to the rule of the holy St Benedict to intercede for us, that the Saviour may be propitious towards us, and that he may guide us and uphold our country, and after the end grant us eternal life.

Now as the result of the frequent admonitions of Bishop Æthelwold, I have it in mind to endow, with the help of God, the monastery at Ely with its own freedom and special honour, and afterwards with possessions for the sustenance of those whom we place there for the service of God, and who shall continually dwell there. The foundation was consecrated in days of old in honour of the holy Peter, chief of the apostles, and it

100 CHARTER OF KING EDGAR TO ELY

mynte ðæra apostola yldost · 7 heo wæs geglengd þurh Godes sylfes wundra þe gelome wurdon æt Atheldrythe byrgene þæs halgan mædenes þe ðær gehal lið oð þis on eall hwittre ðryh of marmstane geworht[1] · be hyre we rædað hu heo her on liue wæs
5 7 hu heo Gode ðeowode on godre[2] drohtnunge · 7 be hyre geendunge · 7 hu heo up adon wæs ansund of hyre byrgene swa swa Beda awrat Engla þeodæ lareow on his larbocum. Nu wæs se halga stede ýuele forlæten mid læssan ðeowdome þonne us gelicode nu on urum timan · 7 eac[3] wæs gehwyrfed þam cyninge
10 to handa ic cweðe be me sylfum · ac Atheluuold bisceop þe his min rædbora 7 soð Godes freond · sealde me to gehwærfe þone ham Heartingas · on sixtigum hidum wið þam mynster lande þe lið into Helig · 7 ic þa geeacnode into Elig[4] mynstre[5] þas ðry hamas ðe þus sind gehatene · Meldeburna · Earningaford[6] ·
15 Norðwold · 7 he þær rihte mid minum ræde 7 fultume mid munecum gesette þæt mynster æfter regole · 7 him ealdor gesette us eallum ful cuðne Brihtnoð gehaten · þæt he under him þane halgan regol for Gode geforðade æfter mynsterlicum þeawe; Ða gelicode me þ he hit swa gelogode mid Godes þeowum Gode to
20 lofe · 7 ic þa geeacnode[7] to þære ærran sylene tyn þusenda[8] elfixa ælce geare þam munecum þe me for fyrdinge gefyrndagum aras binnan þam[9] iggoðe of þam folce æt Wyllan · 7 ealla þa socna eac ofer þ fennland into þam twam hundredum him to scrudfultume · 7 on east Englan æt Wichlawan · eac ealle þa
25 socna ofer fif hundredum · 7 ofer ealle þa land gelice þa socna þe into þam mynstre nu synd begytene[10] · oððe ða þe him gyt becumað þurh Cristes foresceawunge · oððe þurh ceap · oððe[11] þurh gife · habban hi æfre on eallum þa socne[12] · 7 þone feorðan pening on folclicre steore into Grantanbricge be minre unnan ·
30 7 gif ænig mann þiss awendan wylle þonne gange eall seo socn þe to anre niht feorme gebyreð into þære stowe · 7 beo þis priuilegium þ is sindorlice wyrðmynt · oððe agen freodom into

[1] -wroht, B.
[2] on godre, om. Addit. MS.
[3] uc, ibid.; ac, B.
[4] Helig, Addit. MS.
[5] mynster, B.
[6] Earm-, K.; -iga-, B.
[7] ge ac-, B.
[8] -de, B.
[9] Om. Addit. MS., K.
[10] betytene, B.; a tear in the MS. makes the third letter doubtful but part of the tail is left and Addit. MS. has begyt-.
[11] oðð, B.
[12] socng, Addit. MS.

was embellished by the miracles of God himself which frequently took place at the tomb of Etheldreda, the holy maiden, who lies there uncorrupted until this day in a pure white tomb made of marble. Of her we read how she passed her life here and how she served God by her excellent mode of life, and of her death, and how she was taken up unblemished from her tomb, as Bede, the teacher of the English, has written in his books. In our time the holy place was sadly neglected, with less service than pleased us, and it had also passed into the king's possession—I speak of myself—but Bishop Æthelwold, who is my adviser and the true friend of God, gave me in exchange the manor of Harting, consisting of 60 hides, in return for the monastic land belonging to Ely, and I added to the monastery at Ely the three manors which are called Melbourn, Armingford and Northwold; and he straightway, with my advice and help, filled the monastery with monks observing a rule, and appointed a superior over them, named Brithnoth, well known to all of us, to promote under him the holy rule in the sight of God according to monastic custom. I was pleased that he filled it in this way with the servants of God, to the praise of God, and I added to the earlier gift 10,000 eels yearly for the monks, which accrued to me in days of old, in place of military service within the isle, from the people at *Well*, and likewise, to provide them with clothing, all the jurisdiction over the fenlands included in the two hundreds, and at *Wicklow* in East Anglia likewise all the jurisdiction over five hundreds, and similarly the jurisdiction over all the lands which are now assigned to the monastery, or which shall come to it yet by the providence of Christ or by purchase or by grant—they shall have jurisdiction over all of them for all time—and the fourth penny of the public penalties paid at Cambridge, by my grant. And if any man attempts to alter this, then all [the proceeds of] the jurisdiction pertaining to one day's food-rent shall pass to the foundation. And this privilege, that is this special honour or peculiar freedom belonging

102 CHARTER OF KING EDGAR TO ELY

þære stowe mid eallum þisum ðingum Gode geoffrod mid urum góodum willan · Gode æfre frig 7 Godes halgum for minre sawle 7 minra yldrena us to alysednesse[1] · swa þæt nan þæra cyninga ðe cumað æfter me oððe ealdorman · oððe oðer ríca mid ænigum
5 riccetere oððe unrihte þiss ne awende odde[2] gewanige be þam þe he[3] nelle habban Godes awyrgednysse 7 his halgena · 7 minne · 7 minra yldrena þe þas ðing fore synd gefreode on ecum freote on ecnysse. AMHN.

XLIX. ADJUSTMENT OF THE BOUNDARIES BETWEEN THE MONASTERIES IN WINCHESTER

HER is geswitulod on ðysum gewrite hú Eadgar cining mid
10 rymette gedihligean het þa mynstra on Wintancestræ[4] syþþan he hi ðurh Godes gyfe to munuclife gedyde · 7 þet asmeagan het ꝥ nan ðera mynstera þær binnan þurh þet rymet wid oðrum sace næfde · ac gif oðres mynstres ár 'on' oðres mynstres rymette lege ꝥ þes mynstres ealdor ðe to þam rymette fenge ofeode þæs oðres
15 mynstres are mid swilcum þingum swylce ðam hirede ðæ[5] þa are ahte gecweme wære · for ðy ðonne Aþelwold[6] bisceop on þes[7] cinges gewitnesse 7 ealles þæs hiredes his bisceopstoles gesealde twa gegrynd butan svð[8] geate into niwan mynstre ongén ðes mynstres mylne ðe stod on ðam rymette ðe se cing het
20 gerymen into ealdan mynstre · 7 se abbod Æþelgar mid geðeahte ures cynelafordes 7 þes bysceopes[9] Aþelwoldes[6] 7 ealles þæs hiredes þa ylcan mylne þe se bisceop seolde 7 oðre þæ hi ær ahtun binnan þære byrig to sibbe 7 to sóme gesealde into nunnan mynstre · 7 Eadgyfe abbedesse þæs cinges dohter betehte ongen
25 ðone weterscype þe he into niwan mynstre[10] be ðes cinges leafan

[1] *alyssed-*, B.   [2] *oððe*, Addit. MS., K., T.   [3] Om. Addit. MS.
[4] *-ceast-*, T.   [5] *ðe*, K.   [6] *Æðel-*, K.
[7] *þæs*, B.   [8] *Suð*, K.; *Syð*, T.   [9] *bisc-*, B.
[10] *min-*, B.

to the foundation, along with all these things, shall be offered to God with our goodwill, [to remain] free for all time for God and the saints of God, for the redemption of my own soul and the souls of my ancestors, in such wise that none of the kings who come after me, and no earl or other powerful man shall alter or diminish this with any arrogance or injustice without incurring the malediction of God and his saints and mine and my ancestors', before whom these things are freed in perpetual freedom for all time. Amen.

XLIX. ADJUSTMENT OF THE BOUNDARIES BETWEEN THE MONASTERIES IN WINCHESTER

Here it is declared in this document how King Edgar caused the monasteries in Winchester to have their privacy secured for them by means of a space, after he had made them adopt the monastic life, by the grace of God, and ordered it to be devised so that none of the monasteries involved should have any quarrel with any other, because of the spacing, but if the property of one monastery lay within the space assigned to another, then the superior of the monastery which took possession of the space should acquire the property of the other monastery by such exchange as might be agreeable to the community which owned the property. For that reason, therefore, Bishop Æthelwold, with the cognisance of the king and of all the community attached to his episcopal see, has granted two plots of ground outside the south gate to the New Minster, in exchange for the mill belonging to that minster which stood in the space which the king ordered to be assigned to the Old Minster, and Abbot Æthelgar, with the advice of our royal lord and of Bishop Æthelwold and of all the community, has granted the aforesaid mill, which the bishop gave him, and another which they already possessed within the town to the Nunnery, for the sake of peace and concord, and has assigned it to the Abbess Eadgifu, the king's daughter, in exchange for the watercourse which he has diverted to the New Minster with the king's leave, and which formerly

104 ADJUSTMENT OF BOUNDARIES BETWEEN

geteah · 7 ær ðes nunhiredes wes · 7 him se tige sume mylne adilgade · 7 he gesealde þam cinge hundtwelftig mancæs reades goldes to ðance beforan Ælfdryðe[1] ðære hlæfdian 7 beforan þam bisceopan Aðelwolde[2] wið þam lande ðæ seo éa ón yrnð · fram 5 ðam norðwealle to þæs mynstres suðwealle an lencge · 7 twegræ metgyrda[3] brad ðer ꝥ wæter ærest infylð · 7 þær ꝥ land unbradest is þer hit sceol beon eahtatyne fota brad · ðyses ic geann Æþelgare abbode · 7 þam hirede into niwan mynstre for his gecwemre gehyrsumnesse á on ecnesse · 7 ic halsige ælc ðara ðe 10 eftær[4] me cynerices wealde þurh ða halgan ðrynnesse þet hyra nan nǽ úndo þet[5] ic to ðam haligum mynstrum binnan þære byrig gedon hebbe[6]. Se þe ðis þonne awendan wylle ðe ic to sibbe 7 to gesehtnesse betweoh þam mynstre [g]eradigod[7] hæbbe odðe[8] þara ðinga þe on þissan þrim cyrogafum[9] ðe on ðissum 15 þrym mynstrum to swytelungum gesette syndon · awende hine sé eca drihten fram heofenan rice · 7 su[10] his wunung æfter his forðsiðe on helle wite mid þam ðe symle on ælcre ungeþwærnesse blissiað butan he hit ær his forðsiðe gebete.

L. GRANT OF LAND BY KING EDGAR TO SHERBORNE

IN nomine dñi IHU xpi · Ic EADGAR cing cyðe on þisse bec 20 ꝥ is Cristes boc ꝥ ic habba þa fif hyda æt Womburnan agifen Gode 7 Sca MARIA for me sylfne 7 for mine yldran ðe þar restat æt Scireburnan[11] · Aðelbold cing · 7 Æthelbyrht cing · 7 ðis ic habbe idón for ure ealra saule lufon · to ecre reste. Gif hwa beo swa dyrtig[12] ꝥ þis abrece oððe awenden wylle ꞉́ þas 25 mine gife 7 sylene mid ænegum uncræfte þære stowe atbredan þence oððe wille ꞉́ wite he on domes dæge riht to agildanne beoforan Gode 7 eallum his halgum nymþe · bute he hit ær her

---

[1] -ðryðe, K.
[2] Æðel-, K.
[3] twegræm et gyrda, B.
[4] æfter, K.
[5] ðæt, K.
[6] hæbbe, K., B.
[7] The first letter seems to be p; B. takes it as þ.
[8] oððe, K., T., B.
[9] -graf-, K., T.
[10] sii, K., T., B.
[11] Scirb-, B.
[12] For dyrstig.

THE MONASTERIES IN WINCHESTER 105

belonged to the community of nuns—and the diverting [of the water] destroyed a mill of his—and he has given the king 120 mancuses of red gold in acknowledgment, before the Lady Ælfthryth and Bishop Æthelwold, in return for the land through which the water runs, extending lengthwise from the north wall to the south wall of the monastery, and 2 rods in breadth where the water first flows in, and where the land is narrowest it must be 18 feet in breadth.

This I grant to Abbot Æthelgar for his pleasing obedience and to the community at the New Minster in perpetuity, and I entreat by the holy Trinity, that none of those who rule the kingdom after me undo what I have done to the holy monasteries within the town. If anyone, however, attempts to alter what I have arranged between the monasteries for the sake of peace and concord, or any of the things in these three chirographs, which are placed as evidence in these three monasteries the eternal Lord shall remove him from the kingdom of heaven, and his dwelling after his death shall be in the torment of hell with those who always rejoice in every discord, unless he make amends before his death.

L. GRANT OF LAND BY KING EDGAR TO SHERBORNE

In nomine domini Jesu Christi.

I, King Edgar, declare in this book, which is a gospel book, that I have granted 5 hides at Oborne to God and St Mary for myself and my ancestors, King Æthelbald and King Æthelbert, who rest there at Sherborne; and this I have done for love of the souls of all of us, to obtain eternal rest. If anyone is so presumptuous as to infringe or attempt to alter this—if he contemplates or attempts to take away this my gift and grant by any evil practice from the foundation—he shall find that justice must be rendered on the Day of Judgment before God and all his saints, unless he has made amends in this world.

GRANT OF LAND TO SHERBORNE

on worolde gebete · Ic EADGAR cyning mid þara halgan rode tacn ðis hate swiþe geornlice getrymman[1] 7 gefæstnian.

✠ Dunstan archieps Cantwarubyri.
5 ✠ Wulsin eps.
✠ Alfstan eps.
✠ Eanwulf .dux.
✠ Ælfstan .dux.
✠ Alhhard .abb.
10 ✠ Heahmund .pr̄.
✠ Huita .p̄poš
✠ Osmund .miñ

✠ Wulfhere .m̄.
✠ Cyma .m̄.
✠ Wulfred .m̄.
✠ Ecgbreht .m̄.
✠ Monnel .m̄.
✠ Eadwulf .m̄.
✠ Wistan .m̄.
✠ Æþelwulf .m̄.
✠ Wynsige .m̄.
✠ Goda .m̄.

✠ Coenwald .m̄.
✠ Wulfhelm .m̄.
✠ Beocca .m̄.
✠ Æþelmod .m̄.
✠ Beorhnoð[2] .m̄.
✠ Hunred .m̄.
✠ Ecgulf .m̄.
✠ Æþelric .m̄.
✠ Ælfhere .m̄.

LI. PURCHASE OF AN ESTATE BY OSGAR, ABBOT OF ABINGDON

Ælfheah[3] ealdorman becwæð Ælfhere ealdormenn[4] .xx. hida 'æt' Kingestune · ða abæd Osgar abbud æt Ælfhere ealdormenn ·
15 ꝥ he moste ofgan ꝥ land æt him mid sceatte · ða tiþode se ealdorman him · And se abbod sealde him ða · an hund mancosa goldes · ða wes ofer eastron micel gemot æt Aþelwarabirig · 7 hit wes gesitolad ðar þam hlafardingan þa ðæron weron · þæt wes Adelwold bisceof · 7 Ælfstan bisceop · 7 Æthelgar ab̄b. 7 Ead-
20 wine · 7 Ælfric cild · 7 Ælfric Sirafes sunu · 7 Brihtric his broðor · 7 swiðæ manega oðra ðegenas · And þis wes gedon on micelre gewitnesse · 7 þysses gewrites geclofan nam se ealdorman Ælfhere to swytelunga.

LII. LIST OF ESTATES LIABLE FOR WORK ON ROCHESTER BRIDGE

Þis is þære bricce geweorc on Hroucæstre.

25 Her syndon genamad þa land þe man hi of scæl weorcan · ærest þære burge biscop fehð[5] on þone earm to wercene þa land peran · 7 þreo gyrda to þillianæ[6] · 7 .III. sylla to lyccanne ·

---

[1] *-mnian*, B.
[2] *Beornoth*, B.
[3] *-hea*, R.S.
[4] *-men*, ibid.
[5] *fæhð*, Lambarde, He. Only the most important variant readings are given.
[6] *-anne*, L.; *-ianne*, He.

GRANT OF LAND TO SHERBORNE

I, King Edgar, with the symbol of the holy cross enjoin that this shall be very earnestly established and confirmed...

LI. PURCHASE OF AN ESTATE BY OSGAR, ABBOT OF ABINGDON

Earl Ælfheah bequeathed 20 hides at Kingston to Earl Ælfhere. Then Abbot Osgar asked Earl Ælfhere whether he might obtain the estate from him by purchase. The earl agreed, and the abbot gave him 100 mancuses of gold. Then after Easter there was a great meeting at Alderbury, and the sale was declared to the lords who were there, namely Bishop Æthelwold and Bishop Ælfstan and Abbot Æthelgar and Edwin and Ælfric *cild* and Ælfric, Siraf's son, and Brihtric his brother, and very many other thegns. And this was done with a great number of witnesses and Earl Ælfhere took the counterpart of this document as proof.

LII. LIST OF ESTATES LIABLE FOR WORK ON ROCHESTER BRIDGE

This is the work for the bridge at Rochester.

Here are named the estates which must supply the labour for it. First the bishop of the city undertakes to construct the landpiers at the [eastern] extremity, and to provide planks for 3 poles

108 LIST OF ESTATES LIABLE FOR WORK

Þ is of Borcstealle · 7 of Cucclestane · 7 of Frinondesbyrig · 7 of Stoce · Þanne seo oðer[1] per gebyrað to Gyllingeham · 7 to Cætham · 7 an gyrd to þillanne[2] · 7 III sylla to leccanne. Þonne seo þridde per gebyrað eft þam biscope · 7 þridde healf gyrd to
5 þillianne[3] · 7 III. sylla to leccenne · of Heallingan · 7 of Trotescliue · 7 of Meallingan · 7 of Fliote · 7 of Stane · 7 of Pinindene[4] · 7 of Falchenham. Þonne is se[5] feorðe þe[6] per[7] þæs cinges · 7 fiorðe healf gyrd to þillanne[8] · 7 sylla .III. to leccanne · of Ægelesforda · 7 of ellan þam læþe þe þær toliþ[9] · 7 of Ufanhylle · 7 of
10 Aclea · 7 of þam smalanlande · 7 of Cusintune · 7 of Dudeslande · 7 of Gisleardeslande · 7 of Wuldeham 7 of Burhham · 7 of Æcclesse[10] · 7 of Horstede · 7 of Fearnlege · 7 of Cærstane[11] · 7 of Cealce · 7 of Hennhyste[12] · 7 of Ædune. Þonne is sy[5] fifte per þæs arcebiscope[13] to Wroteham · 7 to Mægþanstane · 7 to
15 Woþringabyran[14] · 7 to Netlestede · 7 to þam twam Peccham · 7 to Hæselholte · 7 to Mæranwyrþe · 7 to Lillanburnan · 7 to Swanatune · 7 to Offaham · 7 to Dictune · 7 to Westerham · 7 IIII. gyrda to þyllanne · 7 III. selle to leccanne; Þonne is syo syoxte per to Holinganburnan · 7 to eallan þam læþe · 7 IIII.
20 gyrda to þelliene · 7 III.[15] sylla to leccenne. Þonne is syo syoueþe · 7 syo eahteþe per to Howaran lande to wyrcenne · 7 fifte healf gyrd to þillanne · 7 VI. sylla to lyccanne. Þonne is syo nigaþa per þæs arcebiscopes · Þ is syo landper æt þam west ænde · to Flyote · 7 to his Cliue · 7 to Hehham · 7 to Denetune · 7 to
25 Melantune · 7 to Hludesdune · 7 to Meapeham · 7 to Snodilande · 7 to Berlingan · 7 to Peadleswyrþe · 7 ealla þa dænewaru · 7 IIII. gyrdu to þilianne · 7 þryo sylle to leccanne.

[1] oþres, L., He.
[2] -ianne, L., He., B.
[3] -anne, L.
[4] Pundene, L., He.
[5] seo, L., He.
[6] Om. L., He.
[7] þær, L., He.
[8] -ane, He.; -ianne, B.
[9] þerto liþ, L., He.
[10] A blank of nearly a line follows.
[11] Ter-, L., He.
[12] Henhyste, L.; -hystæ, B.
[13] -es, L., He.
[14] Wohringa-, B.
[15] IIII, L., He., B.

and put 3 beams in position; and this is due from Borstall, Cuxton, Frindsbury and Stoke.

Then the second pier belongs to Gillingham and to Chatham, and to provide planks for 1 pole and put 3 beams in position.

The third pier again belongs to the bishop, and to provide planks for $2\frac{1}{2}$ poles and put 3 beams in position. [This is due] from Halling and from Trottiscliffe and from Malling and from Fleet and from Stone and from Pinden and from Fawkham.

The fourth pier is the king's, and to provide planks for $3\frac{1}{2}$ poles and put 3 beams in position. [This is due] from Aylesford and from all the lathe dependent upon it, and from Overhill and from Oakley and from the strip of land and from Cossington and from *Dudesland* and from *Gisleardesland* and from Wouldham and from Burham and from Eccles and from Horsted and from Farleigh and from Teston and from Chalk and from Henhurst and from Haven [Street].

The fifth pier is the archbishop's [and belongs] to Wrotham and to Maidstone and to Wateringbury and to Nettlestead and to the two Peckhams and to Hadlow and to Mereworth and to Leybourne and to Swanton and to Offham and to Ditton and to Westerham, and to provide planks for 4 poles and put 3 beams in position.

The sixth pier belongs to Hollingbourn and to all the lathe, and to provide planks for 4 poles and put 3 beams in position.

The work for the seventh and eighth piers is due from the Hoo people's land, and to provide planks for $4\frac{1}{2}$ poles and put 6 beams in position.

The ninth pier is the archbishop's—that is the land-pier at the west end—[and belongs] to Fleet and to Bishop's Cliffe and to Higham and to Denton and to Milton and to Luddesdown and to Meopham and to Snodland and to Birling and to Paddlesworth and all the people in the valley, and to provide planks for 4 poles and put 3 beams in position.

LIII. EXCHANGE OF LANDS BETWEEN ÆTHELWOLD, BISHOP OF WINCHESTER, AND ÆLFWINE

Her sweotelað hu Aðelwold[1] biscop 7 se hired on Winceastre on ealdan mynstre be Eadwardes cyninges leafe gehwyrfdon landa wið Ælfwine Ælfsiges sunu 7 Æðelhilde · þæt is ðonne þet se biscop 7 se hired him sealdon .xii. hida landes æt Mordune þe
5 his yldran heora æftergengan to ði betehtan þet hi ælce geare of ðan lande geformædon forða þe þa are gestrynden 7 Ælfsige his agen fæder þet ylcæn land æft ðem hyrde on ealdan mynstre þær eal his forðfædren rest forða feormæ betehte · 7 he him on þæt ylcan gera þær togeanes gesealde binnan Wintanceastre
10 twegra æcera gewirde landes 7 ðene stream þe ðærto ligð binnan ðæm rymette þe se biscop mid wealle into ðem mynstre befangan hæfð to ðan ealdan portwealle · 7 þa boc þærto agæf ðe Ælfred cining his yldran gebocode · ðonne wes ðises gehwerfes to gewitnesse Eadward cining 7 Aþelwold biscop 7
15 Æþælmær ealdorman 7 Æþelgar abbod 7 Æðelhild 7 ða ðry hyredas on ealdan mynstre 7 on niwan mynstre 7 on nunnan mynstre 7 seo burhwaru on Winceastre. Þonne synt ðyses gehwerfes .iiii. gewrytu to geswitulunge · an is mid Ælfwine · oðer in ealdan mynstre · þridde on niwan mynstre · feorðe on
20 nunnan mynstre.

LIV. STATEMENT BY OSWALD, ARCHBISHOP OF YORK, REGARDING CHURCH LANDS IN NORTHUMBRIA

Ðis swutelunge[2] gedihte Oswald arceb 7 awritan het;
Þis syndon þa tunas þe syndan adon of Ottanlege · an ys Haddincham · oþer ys Hyllicleg[3] · þridde Mensinctun · feoþe healf Burhleg fifte Gislicleh sixfe[4] Scefinc · seofeþe Middeltun
25 ehtaþe[5] Dentun healf ix. Timmel[6] .x. Lindeleh .xi. Stanburne[7]

[1] Æ-, K.
[3] Hill-, B.
[5] æhtoþe, B.
[7] -burhe, B.

[2] Ðas swit-, B.
[4] -te, MS. (b), B.
[6] Tunmel, MS. (b), B.

LIII. EXCHANGE OF LANDS BETWEEN ÆTHELWOLD, BISHOP OF WINCHESTER, AND ÆLFWINE

Here it is declared how Bishop Æthelwold and the community at the Old Minster in Winchester have exchanged lands with Ælfwine, the son of Ælfsige and Æthelhild, with King Edward's leave. The bishop and the community have given him 12 hides of land at Moredon which his ancestors bestowed upon their successors, on condition that they paid a food-rent every year from the estate on behalf of those who acquired the property, and Ælfsige, his own father, afterwards bestowed this same estate upon the community at the Old Minster, where all his forefathers lie, because of the food-rent. Ælfwine in the same year has given them in return land amounting to 2 acres within Winchester, and the stream adjacent to it within the space extending to the old town-wall, which the bishop has enclosed with a wall for the monastery, and has granted them in addition the charter which King Alfred drew up for his ancestors.

The witnesses of this exchange were King Edward and Bishop Æthelwold and Earl Æthelmær and Abbot Æthelgar and Æthelhild and the three communities at the Old Minster, the New Minster and the Nunnery, and the citizens of Winchester. There are also four documents as evidence of this exchange; one is in the possession of Ælfwine, the second at the Old Minster, the third at the New Minster, the fourth at the Nunnery.

LIV. STATEMENT BY OSWALD, ARCHBISHOP OF YORK, REGARDING CHURCH LANDS IN NORTHUMBRIA

Archbishop Oswald drew up this declaration and had it written down.

These are the manors which have been taken away from Otley: the first is Addingham, the second is Ilkley, the third Menston, the fourth half of Burley, the fifth Guiseley, the sixth Chevin, the seventh Middleton, the eighth half of Denton, the

.XII. Becwudu .XIII. Byllinctun[1] healf · þas tunas sindan[2] adon of Rypum .I. ys Heawic oþer Heawic .III. Ansætleh .IIII. Stanleh an[3] hid .V. Helperby .VI. æt Myðtune[4] · Of Popeltune twa hida · þis is genumen of Scirebunnan[5] · Ceoredesholm healf · 7 Cawudu healf 7 Gisferþ[es]dæll hyrðe[6] æfre into Scirebunnan[5] · 7 healfe socne þe gebyreþ into Scireburnan · þis syndan þa land þe Oscytel[7] yrcebiscop begeat on Norþhymbralande mid his feo 7 him mon geald for unrihtan hæmede · an ys Æffeltune[8] he gebohte mid .XXIIII. pundun · æt Deor[w]ulfe[9] · Yferingaham he gebohte mid feower 7 feowertigun pundun æt fæge Osulfes fæder · 7 þ̄ land æt Neoweboldan he gebohte mid hundtwelftigun [ge]mancsun[10] reades[11] goldes æt Eadgare cyn[ing]eþ[12] 7 æt Heolperbi him wæs gegolden for unrihtan hæmede wæron twegen gebroþra hæfdon[13] an wif · 7 into Heolperby hyrð Mytun twa dæl 7 Wibustan socn · 7 Þurulfestun[14] · 7 Ioletun[15] · 7 Þorp · 7 æt Scyteby he gebohte mid .XX. pundun · 7 þreo hida æt Bracenan[16] he gebohte æt Eadgare cinge 7 he hit him gebocode into sc̄e Iohanne · 'Ic Oswold arceb swutelige þ̄'[17] ealle þas land þe 'se' yrcebiscop Oscytel begeat on Norþhymbralande 7 min hlaford forgeaf hi me 'into sc̄e Pe[tre]'[18] þa he[19] wæs æt Snotingaham · þas oþre land þe her elles onstandaþ ⁖ ealle ic hy[20]......
...... þa wæs sc̄e Peter bereafod... syððan[21] · wrece God swa he wille[22].

[1] byll-, MS. (b); hyll-, B. The first letter is very faint and difficult to read.
[2] synd-, B.   [3] ten, MS. (b), B.
[4] Nyð-, MS. (b), B.   [5] -burn-, B.
[6] dælhhyrde, MS. (b).   [7] Us-, B.
[8] Æppel-, MS. (b), B.
[9] MS. (b); a letter has been erased in MS. (a).
[10] gemanc-, MS. (b).   [11] reod-, B.
[12] Not clearly legible; MS. (b) and B. have cyn...eþ̄.
[13] -an, B.   [14] -tune, B.
[15] toletun, B.   [16] Drac-, MS. (b).
[17] Ic...þ̄ has been inserted above the line in later handwriting; MS. (b) has i' Oswold arceð swuteligaþ; B. has 7 ic Oswold arcebiscop switelige þ̄.
[18] In the margin in later handwriting.
[19] An erasure follows; MS. (b) has þa he...wæs.
[20] Only a few letters here and there of what follows are legible; MS. (b) has ic hy hæf...oð þerað incom; B. has ealle ðe hy hæf...oðþe rað in com.
[21] sydd-, B.
[22] wrece...wille, in later handwriting; MS. (b) has bereafod, then an illegible word of apparently three letters, then syððan sece god swa he wille.

CHURCH LANDS IN NORTHUMBRIA

ninth Timble, the tenth Lindley, the eleventh Stainburn, the twelfth Beckwith, the thirteenth half of *Byllinctun*.

These manors have been taken away from Ripon: the first is Hewick, the second Hewick, the third *Ansætleh*, the fourth one hide at Stainley, the fifth Helperby, the sixth Myton. Two hides from Poppleton.

This has been taken from Sherburn: half of *Ceoredesholm*—and half of Cawood and *Gisferþesdæll* still belong to Sherburn—and half the soke which belongs to Sherburn.

These are the estates which Archbishop Oscytel obtained in Northumbria with his money, or which were given him because of an illicit union. One is Appleton which he bought from Deorwulf for 24 pounds, Everingham which he bought for 44 pounds from Osulf's father, now dead(?), and the estate at Newbald which he bought for 120 mancuses of red gold from King Edgar; and Helperby was given him because of an illicit union—there were two brothers who had one wife—and to Helperby belong two parts of Myton and the soke of Wide Open, and Tholthorpe and Youlton and Thorpe. And he bought Skidby for 20 pounds, and he bought 3 hides at Bracken from King Edgar who granted it to him by charter for St John's.

I, Archbishop Oswald, declare that all these estates which Archbishop Oscytel obtained in Northumbria, and which my lord granted to me for St Pe[ter's] when he was at Nottingham, [and] these other estates which are entered here besides, all of them I...... Then St Peter's was afterwards robbed [of them], may God avenge it as he will.

LV. LEASE OF LAND BY OSWALD, ARCHBISHOP OF YORK AND BISHOP OF WORCESTER, TO ÆTHELWOLD

[Wulf]ringctun [Æþelw]old[1].

✠ Ic Osuuold arcebisceop þurh Godes giefe[2] mid geþafunge · 7 leafe EADWARDES Angulcyninges 7 Ælfheres Mercna heretogan 7 þæs heorodes on Weogornaceastre landes sumne dæl ƥ
5 synd .II. hida buton .LX. æcran ƥ hæft se arcebisceop genumen into Cymesige to his hame him to hwætelande þe fram cuþum mannum Wulfringctun[3] is gehaten sumum cnihte þæm is noma Æþelwold mid allum þingum þe þarto[4] belimpað freolice his dæge forgeaf 7 æfter his dæge twam yrfweardum 7 æfter heora
10 forðsiþe to þære halgan stowe into Wiogornaceastre þæm bisceope to bryce · sie hit ælces þinges freoh[5] buto[6] ferdfare 7 walgeworc · 7 brygcgeweorc 7 cyrcanlade. Þis wæs gedón ymbe .VIIII. hund wintra 7 VII 7 hundseofantig þæs þæ drihtnes gebyrdtide wæs.
Sca Maria 7 scs Michahel cum sco Petro 7 allum Godes halgum
15 gemiltsien þis haldendum · gief hwa buton gewrihtum hit abrecan wylle God hine to rihtere bote gecyrre · amen. Her is seo hondseten.

Æþelwold is se forma man.
20 ✠ Oswold arcebysceop.
✠ Ego Winsige prbt
✠ Ego Wulfric prbt
✠ Ego Wulfeah prbt
25 ✠ Ego Eadgar prbt
✠ Ego Æþelstan prbt
✠ Ego Ælfsige prbt

✠ Ego Eadweard prbt
✠ Ego Ælfgar diac
✠ Ego Godingc diac
✠ Ego Leofstan diac
✠ Ego Æþelsige diac
✠ Ego Wulfweard diac
✠ Ego Cyneþegn cl
✠ Ego Wulfhuni[7] cl
✠ Ego Wulfgar cl

✠ Ego Brihstan cl
✠ Ego Leofwine cl
✠ Ego Cynestan cl
✠ Wynstan cl
✠ Eadwine cl
✠ Ælfstan cl
✠ Ælfnoð cl
✠ Æþelwold cl
✠ Wulfnoð cl
✠ Æþric cl
cl[8]

[1] This is entered in the left margin; om. K.
[2] *gief*, He.   [3] *-ringe-*, He.
[5] *freo*, He.   [6] Sic; *buton*, K.
[8] No name has been entered.
[4] *þær-*, He.; *ðær-*, K.
[7] *-hum*, He.; *-hun*, K.

LV. LEASE OF LAND BY OSWALD, ARCHBISHOP OF YORK AND BISHOP OF WORCESTER, TO ÆTHELWOLD

Wolverton, to Æthelwold.

✠ I, Oswald, archbishop by the grace of God, with the permission and leave of Edward, King of England, and Ælfhere, Earl of Mercia, and the community at Worcester, have freely granted a certain piece of land, called by those familiar with it Wolverton, consisting of 2 hides less 60 acres, which the archbishop has attached as wheat-growing land to his manor at Kempsey, to a certain *cniht*, whose name is Æthelwold, with everything belonging to it, for his lifetime, and after his death to two heirs, and after their death to the holy foundation at Worcester for the use of the bishop. It shall be free from everything except military service and the construction of walls and bridges and carrying service for the church.

This was done in the year 977 after the birth of the Lord. May St Mary and St Michael, with St Peter and all the saints of God, have mercy on those who uphold this. If anyone, without due cause, attempts to break it, may God turn him to due amendment. Amen.

Here are the signatures...

LVI. LEASE OF LAND BY OSWALD, ARCHBISHOP OF YORK AND BISHOP OF WORCESTER, TO WULFGEAT

Æt Hymeltune · Wulfgete · 7 Wulfmære[1].

⁊ Ic Osuuold þurh Godes giefe arcebisceop mid geþafunge 7 leafe Eadwardes Angulcyninges 7 Ælfheres Mercna heretogan 7 þæs hiredes æt Wiogernaceastre landes sumne dæl þæt is an 5 hid æt Hymeltune sumum cnihte þam is Wulfgeat noma mid eallum þingum þe þærto belimpað freolice his dæge forgeaf 7 æfter his dæge twæm yrfweardum 7 æfter hiera forðsiþe to þære halgan stowe into Wiogernaceastre þæm biscope to bryce. Sit autem terra ista libera omni regi nisi ecclesiastici[2] censi. Sca 10 Maria 7 scs Michahel cum sco Petro 7 eallum Godes halgum gemiltsien þis haldendum · gief hwa buton gewrihtum hit abrecan wille hæbbe him wið God gemæne on þam ytemestan dæge þisses lifes buton he ær to dædbote gecyrre. Þis is þære are hide landgemæru æt Hymeltune ꝥ is ærest æt egcbrihtingc- 15 þirne ufeweardre of þære þyrne ondlond[3] þære hægce ꝥ on scipene lea of scipene lea ꝥ on efene lea þæt to mægdenne brigce of þære brigce ondlong[4] hegce þæt to hryancrofte ondlong þæs croftes heafodlondes ꝥ to þæm oþran heafodlonde of þæm heafodlonde þæt to bercrofte of þæm crofte þæt[5] eft to hegc- 20 brihtigncþyrne ufeweardre · þonne gebirað se fifta æcer þære dalmædue to þære hide. Þis is þæs wuda gemære þe to þære hide gebyreð ꝥ is ærest æt ceastergeate to ceasterwege ondlong ceasterweges to middelwege of middelwege þæt eft to ceastergeate of þæm geate to longan leage of longan leage ondlong þære 25 díc to deorleage to þæm hriþige ondlong hriþies to dúnhæmstedes æcergearde ondlong þæs æcergeardes to longan æcre[6] ondlong þæs æceres[6] to þæm midlestan wícwege ondlong þæs weges þæt eft to ceastergeate. Wulfgeat wæs se forma man 7 Wulfmær is þe oðer þe hit nu on honda stant.
30 Her is seo hondseten.

✠ Ego Oswold archiepis.	✠ Ego Eadweard prbt	✠ Ego Brihstan cł
✠ Ego Wynsige prbt	✠ Ego Ælfgar diac̄	✠ Ego Wulfgar cł
✠ Ego Wulfric prbt	✠ Ego Æþelsige diac̄	✠ Ego Cynestan cł
35 ✠ Ego Wulfheah prbt	✠ Ego Godingc diac̄	✠ Ego Eadwine cł
✠ Ego Ælfsige prbt	✠ Ego Leofstan diac̄	✠ Ego Wynstan cł
✠ Ego Æþelstan prbt	✠ Ego Leofwine cler	✠ Ego Ælfnoð cł
✠ Ego Eadgar prbt	✠ Ego Kyneþegn cł	✠ Ego Wulnoð cł
	✠ Ego Wulfhun cł	✠ Ego Wulfweard cł
		✠ Ego Æþeric cł

LVI. LEASE OF LAND BY OSWALD, ARCHBISHOP OF YORK AND BISHOP OF WORCESTER, TO WULFGEAT

Himbleton, to Wulfgeat and Wulfmær.

⚓ I, Oswald, archbishop by the grace of God, with the permission and leave of Edward, King of England, and Ælfhere, Earl of Mercia, and the community at Worcester, have freely granted a certain piece of land, namely 1 hide at Himbleton to a certain *cniht*, whose name is Wulfgeat, with everything belonging to it, for his lifetime, and after his death to two heirs, and after their death to the holy foundation at Worcester for the use of the bishop. The estate, moreover, shall be free from every burden except church dues. May St Mary and St Michael, with St Peter and all the saints of God, have mercy on those who uphold this. If anyone, without due cause, attempts to break it, he shall have to answer for it to God on the last day of this life, unless he has set about making amends.

Here are the boundaries of the one hide at Himbleton, namely first beginning at the upper side of 'Ecgbriht's thornbush', from the thornbush along the hedge to the clearing with the cattle-shed, from the clearing with the cattle-shed to the level clearing, then to 'Maiden's Bridge', from the bridge along the hedge to the rye-growing croft, along the headland of the croft to the other headland, from that headland to the barley-growing croft, from the croft back to the upper side of 'Ecgbriht's thornbush'. The fifth acre of the partible meadow also belongs to the hide.

Here is the boundary of the wood that belongs to the hide, namely first from the Worcester gate to the Worcester road, along the Worcester road to the middle road, from the middle road back to the Worcester gate, from the gate to the long clearing, from the long clearing along the dyke to the deer park, [and so] to the brook, along the brook to the Dunhampstead cultivated enclosure, along the cultivated enclosure to the long field, along the field to the midmost Droitwich road, along the road back to the Worcester gate.

Wulfgeat was the first man and Wulfmær is the second in whose possession it now is.

Here are the signatures...

---

[1] This is entered in the margin; om. K.   [2] *eccleastici*, He.; *aeccles-*, K.
[3] Sic; *-long*, K.   [4] *on long*, He.   [5] *þat*, He.; *ðat*, K.   [6] *æt-*, He.

LVII. LEASE OF LAND BY OSWALD, ARCHBISHOP OF YORK AND BISHOP OF WORCESTER, TO WULFHEAH

Æt Genanofre Wulfege Godwine Ælfrice[1].

✠ Ic Osuuald þurh Godes giefe arcebisceop mid geþafunge Eadwardes Angulcyninges · 7 Ælfheres Mercna heretogan 7 þæs heorodes æt Wygernaceastre landes sumne dæl þæt is an gyrd
5 æt Genenófre mon cweð sumum preoste þam is Wulfheah noma mid allum þingum þe þærto belimpað freolice his dæge forgeaf 7 æfter his dæg twam yrfweardum 7 æfter heora forðsiðe to þære halgan stowe into Wiogerneceastre þæm biscope[2] to bryce. Eac we writað him þone graf þærto. Þis syndon þæ gemæru þe to
10 þæm grafe gebyriaþ · Ærest of þam clife in norðwearden stodleage[3] þæt swa eastriht in þone æcergeard[4] ondlong geardes þæt in lipperdes gemære ondlong gemæres þæt in steorfanhalh ondlong ofre þæt in þone croft of þæm crofte neoþewearde eft up in þone holan weg of þæm wege in Wulfgares gemære ondlong
15 gemæres ꝥ eft on ꝥ clif besuþan þæm suðmestan holan wege. Sit autem terra ista libera omni regi nisi ecclesiastici censi. Sc̄a Maria 7 sc̄s Michahel cum sc̄o Petro 7 allum Godes halgum gemiltsien þis haldendum · gief hwa butan gewrihtum hit abrecan wylle hæbbe him wið God gemæne on þam ytemestan
20 dæge þisses lifes buton he ær to dædbote gecyrre. Þis is seo hondseten.

✠ Osuuold arcebisceop.	✠ Ego Ælfgar diac̄	✠ Ego Kynestan cl̄
✠ Ego Wynsige prb̄t	✠ Ego Godingc diac̄	✠ Ego Brihstan cl̄
25 ✠ Ego Wulfric prb̄t	✠ Ego Leofstan diac̄	✠ Ego Eadwine cl̄
✠ Ego Æþelstan prb̄t	✠ Ego Æþelsige diac̄	✠ Ego Wynstan cl̄
	✠ Ego Wulfweard diac̄	✠ Ego Ælfstan cl̄
✠ Ego Ælfsige prb̄t		✠ Ego Æþelwold cl̄
✠ Ego Eadgar prb̄t	✠ Ego Kyneþegn cl̄	✠ Ego Ælfnoð cl̄
30 ✠ Ego Wistan prb̄t	✠ Ego Leofwine cl̄	✠ Ego Æþeric cl̄
✠ Ego Eadward prb̄t	✠ Ego Wulfgar cl̄	✠ Ego Ufic cl̄
	✠ Ego Wulfhun cl̄	

[1] This is entered in the margin.
[3] -leag, He.
[2] -ceope, He.
[4] acer-, He.

LVII. LEASE OF LAND BY OSWALD, ARCHBISHOP OF YORK AND BISHOP OF WORCESTER, TO WULFHEAH

Genanofer, to Wulfheah, Godwine and Ælfric.

☩ I, Oswald, archbishop by the grace of God, with the permission of Edward, King of England, and Ælfhere, Earl of Mercia, and the community at Worcester, have freely granted a certain piece of land, namely a yardland at the place called *Genanofer*, to a certain cleric named Wulfheah, for his lifetime, with everything belonging to it, and after his death to two heirs, and after their death to the holy foundation at Worcester for the use of the bishop. We likewise assign to him the copse in addition.

Here are the boundaries of the copse, first from the cliff on the north side of the clearing for the stud of horses, then due eastwards to the cultivated enclosure, along the enclosure to the Leopard boundary, along the boundary to *Steorfanhalh*, along the bank to the croft, from the bottom of the croft back to the hollow track, from the track to Wulfgar's boundary, along the boundary back to the cliff south of the southmost hollow track.

The estate shall be free from everything except church dues. May St Mary and St Michael, with St Peter and all the saints of God, have mercy upon all those who uphold this. If anyone, without due cause, attempts to break it, he shall have to answer for it to God on the last day of this life, unless he has set about making amends.

Here are the signatures...

LVIII. LEASE OF LAND BY OSWALD, ARCHBISHOP OF YORK AND BISHOP OF WORCESTER, TO WULFGAR

Æt Witlea Wulfgare[1].

✠ Ic Osuuald þurh Godes giefe arcebisceop mid geþafunge 7 leafe EADWARDES · Angulcyningæs 7 Ælfheres Mercna heretogan 7 þæs heorodes æt Wygerneceastre landes sumne dǽl þæt is án híd æt Witlea sumum preoste þam is Wulfgar noma mid allum þingum þe þarto belimpað freolice hís dæge forgeaf 7 æfter his dæge twam yrfweardum 7 æfter hieora forðsiþe to þære halgan stowe into Wiogornaceastre þæm biscope to bryce. Sit autem terra ista libera omni regi nisi ecclesiastici censi. Sc̄a Maria 7 Sc̄S Michahel cum sc̄o Petro 7 allum 'Godes' halgum gemiltsien þis haldendum gief hwa buton gewrihtum hit abrecan wille hæbbe him wið God gemæne on þam ytemestan dæge þisses lifes buton he ær[2] to dædbote gecyrre. Þis sindon þæs landes gemæra þe gebyriað into þære westmestan hide æt Witleage feldlondes 7 wudulandes swa hit todæled[3] is of ðrym gemæran westrihte on þa díc andlang dices on kyllan hrigc of kyllan hrigce on sylweg andlang weges on þa hæþihtan leage 7 swa on þæt fule sloh of þæm sló ofer buttingc[4] graf on eccles bróc andlang broces on doferic[5].

✠ Her is 'sio' hondseten Oswald arceb̄.
✠ Wynsige prb̄t ✠ Kyneþeg clr ✠ Brihstan clr
✠ Wulfric prb̄t ✠ Leofwine clr ✠ Eadwine clr
✠ Wulfheah prb̄t ✠ Wulfhun clr ✠ Wynstan clr
✠ Æþelstan prb̄t ✠ Kynestan clr ✠ Ælfstan clr
✠ Ælfgar diac̄ ✠ Ælfsige prb̄t ✠ Æþelwold clr
✠ Godinc diac̄ ✠ Eadgar prb̄t ✠ Ælfnoð clr
✠ Leofstan diac̄ ✠ Wistan prb̄t ✠ Ufic clr
✠ Æþelsige diac̄ ✠ Eadward prb̄t ✠ Æþeric clr
✠ Wulfward diac̄

[1] Om. K. [2] ar, He.
[3] -diel-, He. [4] -ge, He.
[5] ond oferic, He.

LVIII. LEASE OF LAND BY OSWALD, ARCHBISHOP OF YORK AND BISHOP OF WORCESTER, TO WULFGAR

Witley, to Wulfgar.

☩ I, Oswald, archbishop by the grace of God, with the permission and leave of Edward, King of England, Ælfhere, Earl of Mercia, and the community at Worcester, have freely granted a certain piece of land, namely 1 hide at Witley, to a certain cleric whose name is Wulfgar, for his lifetime, with everything belonging to it, and after his death to two heirs, and after their death to the holy foundation at Worcester for the use of the bishop. The estate shall be free from everything except church dues. May St Mary and St Michael, with St Peter and all the saints of God, have mercy on those who uphold this. If anyone, without due cause, attempts to break it, he shall have to answer for it to God on the last day of this life, unless he has set about making amends.

Here are the boundaries of the estate which apply to the westernmost hide at Witley, divided as it is into open land and woodland, from the three boundaries due west to the dyke, along the dyke to 'Cylla's ridge', from 'Cylla's ridge' to the muddy track, along the track to the heath-grown clearing, and so to the dirty bog, from the bog over 'Butta's copse' to *Eccles* brook, along the brook to the *Doferic*.

Here are the signatures...

LIX. HISTORY OF THE ESTATES OF BROMLEY AND FAWKHAM, KENT

Þus wæron ða land · æt Bromleage · 7 æt Fealcnaham · þam cinge Eadgare gereht · on Lundenbyrig · ðurh Snodinglandes landbec · ða þa preostas forstælon þam biscope on Hrofesceastre[1] · 7 gesealdan heo Ælfrice Æscwynne sunu · wið feo dearnunga · 5 7 heo Æscwyn Ælfrices modor sealde heo ær ðiderin · ða geacsode se biscop þ ða becc[2] forstolene wæron · bǽd þara boca ða geornlice · under ðam þa gewátt Ælfric · 7 he bæd ða lafe syððan · oð man gerehte on cinges ðeningmanna gemote ðære stowe 7 ðam biscope ða forstolenan bécc Snodiglandes[3] · 7 bote æt ðære 10 ðyfðe · þ wæs on Lundene · þær wæs se cing Eadgar · 7 se arcebiscop Dunstan · 7 Aðelwold[4] biscop · 7 Ælfstan biscop · 7 oðer Ælfstan · 7 Ælfere ealdorman · 7 fela cynges witena · 7 man agǽf ðá íntó ðære stowe ðam biscope ða bécc · ða stod ðara wydewan[5] áre · on ðæs cinges handa · ða wolde Wulfstan se gerefa niman 5 þa are to[6] ðæs cinges handa · Bromleah · 7 Fealcnaham · ða gesohte seo wydewe ða halgan stowe · 7 ðane biscop · 7 agæf ðam cinge Bromleages boc · 7 Fealcnahames · 7 se byscop gebohte ða bécc 7 ða land æt ðam cinge on Godeshylle · mid fiftigan mancesan[7] goldes · 7 hundteontigan · 7 ðrittigum[8] 20 pundum · þurh forespræce · 7 costnunge · into scę Andrea[9] · siððan ða lefde se biscop ðare wydewan · ðara lande bryces · under ðam ða gewatt[10] se cing. Ongan ða syððan Byrhtric ðare wydewan mæg · 7 heo to ðam genedde þ hy brucan ðara landa on reaflace · gesohtan[11] ða ðane ealdorman Eadwine · 7 þ folc ðe 25 wæs Godes anspreca · 7 geneddan ðane biscop be ealre[12] his are agiftes ðara boca · ne moste he beon þara ðreora nanes wyrðe ðe eallum[13] leodscipe geseald wæs on wedde · Tale · ne teames · ne ahnunga.

Þis is seo gewitnesse ðæs ceapes · Eadgar cing · 7 Dunstan 30 arceƀ · 7 Oswald arceƀ · 7 Aðelwold .ƀ. Æðelgar .ƀ. 7 Æscwi .ƀ.

[1] *Hrofec.*, T.
[2] *bec*, K.; *bece*, B.
[3] *-ing-*, T.
[4] *Æð-*, K., B.
[5] *-eran*, K.
[6] *on*, T.
[7] *-ess-*, T.
[8] *-egam*, K.
[9] *-reæ*, T.
[10] *-wat*, T.
[11] *7 ges.*, T.
[12] *al-*, T.
[13] *ðe [be] eallum*, K.

LIX. HISTORY OF THE ESTATES OF BROMLEY AND FAWKHAM, KENT

The estates at Bromley and at Fawkham were assigned to King Edgar at London, because of the title-deeds of Snodland which the priests stole from the Bishop of Rochester, and secretly gave for money to Ælfric, Æscwyn's son. It was Æscwyn, Ælfric's mother, who had given them to the foundation. When the bishop discovered that the title-deeds had been stolen, he earnestly demanded the deeds. In the meantime Ælfric died, and he demanded them from the widow, until at a meeting of the king's thegns, the stolen deeds of Snodland were assigned to the foundation and to the bishop, and compensation for the theft. This was at London, and there were present King Edgar and Archbishop Dunstan and Bishop Æthelwold and Bishop Ælfstan and the other Ælfstan and Earl Ælfhere and many of the king's councillors, and the deeds were given to the bishop for the foundation. The widow's property was forfeited to the king. When the reeve Wulfstan was about to take possession of the property—Bromley and Fawkham—on the king's behalf, the widow betook herself to the holy foundation and to the bishop, and gave up to the king the title-deeds of Bromley and Fawkham, and the bishop procured the deeds and the estates from the king at Gadshill (?) on behalf of St Andrew's by means of argument and persuasion for 15 mancuses of gold and 130 pounds [of silver]. Afterwards the bishop allowed the widow the usufruct of the estates.

In the meantime the king died. Then Brihtric, the widow's kinsman, took action and compelled her [to agree] that they should take violent possession of the estates. They applied then to Earl Edwin and the section of the public which was the adversary of God, and compelled the bishop to give up the title-deeds, under pain of losing all his property, nor could he obtain permission to offer any of the three [modes of proof], formally granted to the whole population, namely statement of his claim, vouching to warranty or declaration of his ownership.

These are the witnesses of the purchase: King Edgar and Archbishop Dunstan and Archbishop Oswald and Bishop

7 Ælfstan .b. 7 oðer Ælfstan .b. 7 Sideman .b. 7 ðæs cinges modor Ælfðryð · 7 Osgar .ab. 7 Ælfere ealdorman · 7 Wulfstan on Dælham · 7 Ælfric · on Ebbesham · 7 seo duguð folces on westan Cænt · þær þæt land · 7 þæt læð tolið.

LX. GRANT OF LANDS BY EARL THORED TO ST CUTHBERT'S

5 Her is gemearcod hu manega hyda landes Þureð eorl betæht hafað[1] into sc̄e Cuðberhtes stowe. Nu is æryst[2] on Smiþatune twa hyda landes · and on Creic twa hyda · and on Suþtune anre hyde · þæt he afað ðam[3] halegan 'were' to lofe and to weorðmynde gegyfen[4] á to ęcean life · and se þe þyses ofteo hæbbe hit
10 wiþ Gód gemæne and wið ðone halgan[5] wer[6] · ær oððe siþor.

LXI. LEASE OF LAND BY OSWALD, ARCHBISHOP OF YORK AND BISHOP OF WORCESTER, TO GODING

Æt Bradingccotan Godingce 7 æt Genenof[re][7].

✠ Ic Osuuald þur Godes giefe arcebisceop mid geþafunge 7 leafe Æþelredes Angulcyningces 7 Ælfrices aldermannes 7 þæs heorodes æt Wygerneceastre landes sumne dæl þæt syndon .III.
15 hida æt Bradingccotan 7 an gyrd æt Genenofre mon cweð sumum preoste þam is · GODINGC · noma mid allum þingum þe þarto belimpað freolice his dæg forgeaf 7 æfter his dæge twam yrfweardum þæm þe he sylf wille 7 æfter heora forðsiðe to þære hal[g]an stowe into Wygerneceastre þæm biscope to bryce · 7
20 þærto Ic him sylle .VII. æcras mædue on þæm homme þe gebyrað into Tidbrihtingctune feorþe halfne[8] on anum stede 7 feorðe halfne án oþrum stede alswa hit to gedale[9] gebyrað. Eac

---

[1] -eð, Surtees Soc.   [2] -est, ibid.
[3] ðæm, ibid.   [4] -an, ibid., B.
[5] An e has been erased between the l and the g.
[6] þer, Surtees Soc.
[7] This is entered in the margin; om. K.
[8] hælfne, He., K., which may be the MS. reading.
[9] The reading may be gedæle.

Æthelwold and Bishop Æthelgar and Bishop Æscwig and Bishop Ælfstan and the other Bishop Ælfstan and Bishop Sideman and Ælfthryth, the king's mother, and Abbot Osgar and Earl Ælfhere and Wulfstan of Dalham and Ælfric of Epsom and the leading people in West Kent, where the land and the lathe are situated.

LX. GRANT OF LANDS BY EARL THORED TO ST CUTHBERT'S

Here it is recorded how many hides of land Earl Thored has assigned to St Cuthbert's foundation. First of all he has given 2 hides of land at Smeaton and 2 hides at Crayke and 1 hide at Sutton, to the praise and honour of the holy saint for all time. He who withholds this shall have to account for it to God and to the holy saint, sooner or later.

LXI. LEASE OF LAND BY OSWALD, ARCHBISHOP OF YORK AND BISHOP OF WORCESTER, TO GODING

Bredicot and *Genenofer*, to Goding.

☩ I, Oswald, archbishop by the grace of God, with the consent and leave of Æthelred, King of England, and Earl Ælfric and the community at Worcester, have freely granted a certain piece of land, namely 3 hides at Bredicot and a yardland at the place called *Genenofer*, to a certain cleric whose name is Goding, with everything pertaining thereto for his lifetime, and after his death to two heirs of his own choice, and after their death to the holy foundation at Worcester for the use of the bishop. And I grant him in addition 7 acres of meadow in the river pasture belonging to Tibberton—$3\frac{1}{2}$ acres in one place and $3\frac{1}{2}$ acres in another, as it may fittingly be divided. We convey to him likewise the

126 LEASE OF LAND BY OSWALD TO GODING

we writað him þone hagan þe he hæfð beforan þæm gete · 7 twam yrfweardum æfter his dæge.

Þis sindon þæra[1] þreora hida landgemæru to Bradingccotan þæt is þonne ærest of calawan hylle on foreweardan þære aldan
5 díc · andlang þære aldan díc · to þære mære stowe · of þære mære stowe þæt in þa díc andlang þære díc ꝥ to þære saltstræte swa west ofer þære stræte in þa hegestowe to Spæchæme[2] gemære of Spǽchæme[2] gemære be westan oxnaleage be þæm hliþe of oxna leage norð in þa hegestowe andlang þære hegestowe to
10 þæm fulan slo · of þæm fulan slo in þa díc · of þære díc to wynne mæduan be þære stræt andlang stræte þæt to þæm lytlan hylle of þæm hylle þæt swa be þæm .IIII. þornan of þæm þornan be þæm heafdon to þæm þornihtan heafodlonde of þæm heafodlonde to þære hegestowe · andlang þære hegestowe to Huni-
15 burnan[3] · andlang Huniburnan[3] to þære díc of þære díc to þæm lytlan slo · of þæm slo to þære aldan díc · andlang þære díc to þæm hæþe foreweardan swa suð andlang þære lytlan díc ꝥ þonne westweard ofer þone hæð to þæm lytlan grafe · of þæm grafe suðweard beastan[4] þæm wulfseaðe andlang þære stige þæt eft
20 to calawan hylle to þære díc foreweardan. Sit autem terra illa libera ab omni secularis rei neg[o]tio preter pontis *et* arcis restaurationem *et* contra hostes expeditionem. Sca Maria 7 scs Michahel cu*m* sco Petro 7 allum Godes halgum gemiltien[5] þis halde[n]dum · gief hwa butan gewrihtum hit abrecan wille hæbbe
25 him wid God gemæne on þam ytemestan d[æg] þisses lifes buton he ær to dædbote gecyrre.

✠ Ðis is seo hondseten.

✠[6] Oswold arce-
bisceop.
30 ✠ Ego Æþelstan
prbt
✠ Ego Ælfsige prbt
✠ Ego Eadgar prbt
✠ Ego Wistan prbt

✠ Ego Æþelsige prbt
✠ Ego Leofstan diac
✠ Ego Æþeric diac
✠ Ego Wulfward diac
✠ Ego Æþelstan prbt

✠ Ego Kyneþeng clr
✠ Ego Wulfgar clr
✠ Ego Osuui[7] clr
✠ Ego Leofwine clr
✠ Ego Wulfric clr
✠ Ego Wulnoð clr
✠ Ego Wulfwine clr

---

[1] *þiera*, He., which may be the MS. reading.
[2] *Swæchæme*, He., K.
[3] *Humburnan*, He., K.
[4] *be eastan*, K.
[5] *-miltsien*, K.
[6] K. supplies *Ego*.
[7] *Osuin*, He.

LEASE OF LAND BY OSWALD TO GODING

messuage which he has before the gate, and to two heirs after his death.

These are the boundaries of the 3 hides at Bredicot, namely first from the bare hill in front of the old dyke, along the old dyke to the famous (?) site, from the famous (?) site back to the dyke, along the dyke as far as the saltway, then west over the saltway to the hedged enclosure at the Spetchley boundary, from the Spetchley boundary along the slope to the west of the oxen's pasture, from the oxen's pasture north to the hedged enclosure, along the hedged enclosure to the dirty bog, from the dirty bog to the dyke, from the dyke to the white (?) meadow by the made way, along the made way to the little hill, then from the hill past the four thornbushes, from the thornbushes along the headlands to the thorny headland, from the headland to the hedged enclosure, along the hedged enclosure to the Honey Bourne, along the Honey Bourne to the dyke, from the dyke to the little bog, from the bog to the old dyke, along the dyke to the foreside of the heath, then south along the little dyke, then westward over the heath to the little grove, from the grove southward to the east of the wolfpit, thereafter along the path back to the bare hill in front of the dyke.

This estate, moreover, shall be free from every duty of a secular nature except the repair of bridges and fortifications and military service against enemies. May St Mary and St Michael, with St Peter and all the saints of God, have mercy on those who uphold this. If anyone, without due cause, attempts to break it, he shall have to account for it to God on the last day of this life, unless he has set about making amends.

Here are the signatures...

LXII. AGREEMENT BETWEEN WULFRIC, ABBOT OF ST AUGUSTINE'S, AND EALDRED

✠ In nomine dñi nŕi[1] Ihū Xp̄i. Her swutelað on þisum gewrite hu Wulfric abb · 7 Ealdred Lifinges sunu þæs ðegnes wæron sammæle ymbe ꝥ land æt Clife · þæt he gebéh for Godes ege 7 for sc̄s Augustinus · 7 for hys[2] freonda mynegunge · mid lande 5 intó sc̄e Augustine · 7 ælce geare sylð[3] on sc̄s Augustinus mæssedæg .i. p̄d tó geswutelunga · 7 æfter hys[2] dæge[4] gange ꝥ land into sc̄e Augustine · swá gewerud swa hyt[2] þonne byð; þises ys[2] tó gewitnesse sé hired æt sc̄e Augustine 7 sé æt Xp̄es cyrcean · 7 Lifing his fæder[5] · 7 Síweard · 7 Síred his broðor · 7 Wulfstan 10 æt Sealtwuda · 7 oðer Wulfstan; 7 þis sý gedón for Siferð[6] · 7 for his ofsprincg to hyra sawle ðearfe á butan ende; amen.

LXIII. THE CRIMES AND FORFEITURES OF WULFBOLD

Þis sind þa forwyrhto þe Wulfbold hine wyþ his hlaford forworhte · þæt is ærest þa his fædor wæs forfæren þa ferd he to his steopmoder land 7 nam þær eal ꝥ he þær funde inne 7 ute 15 læsse 7 mare. Þa send se cyng him to 7 bead him þæt he agefe ꝥ[7] reaflac ða forset[8] he ꝥ þa getæhte mon þan cyng his wer 7 se cing him send eftsoma[9] to 7 bead him ꝥ[10] ilce þa forset[8] he ꝥ þa getæhte eft oþre siðe þam cingi[11] his wer · ufonan ꝥ þa ferde he to 7 gerad his mæges land Byrhtmæres æt Burnan þa send se 20 cing him to 7 bead him ꝥ he hit rymde ꝥ land þa forsæt he ꝥ þa getæhte mon þam cynge his wer þriddan siðe 7 se cyng sende him þa gyt to 7 bead him of þa forsæt he ꝥ þa getæhte mon þam cynge his wer feorðan siðe þa ꝥ micel gemote[12] wæs æt Lundene þā wæs Æþelwine ealdorman þaru[13] 7 ealle þæs cyngis wito[n][14] 25 þa getæhton ealle ꝥ[10] witan þe þær wæron ge gehadode ge læwide

[1] Om. Hi.   [2] Hi. has *i* for *y*.   [3] *syld*, Hi.; *gyld*, K.
[4] *dege*, Hi.   [5] *fader*, Hi.   [6] *Siwerð*, Hi.
[7] *þæ*, Edwards.   [8] *-sæt*, ibid.   [9] *-sona*, ibid.
[10] *þa*, ibid.   [11] *cinge*, ibid.   [12] *-mot*, ibid.
[13] *þar*, ibid.   [14] The MS. reading seems to be *witoai*.

LXII. AGREEMENT BETWEEN WULFRIC, ABBOT OF ST AUGUSTINE'S, AND EALDRED

✠ *In nomine domini nostri Jesu Christi.*

Here it is declared in this document how Abbot Wulfric and Ealdred, son of the thegn Lyfing, came to an agreement about the estate at Cliffe. Through the fear of God and St Augustine and by the advice of his friends he commended himself and the estate to St Augustine's, and every year on St Augustine's day he shall give a pound in token, and after his death the estate shall pass to St Augustine's, furnished as it is at the time.

The witnesses of this are the community at St Augustine's and that at Christchurch, and Lyfing, his father, and Siweard and his brother Sired and Wulfstan of Saltwood and the other Wulfstan. And this is done forever without end on behalf of the souls of Siferth and his children. Amen.

LXIII. THE CRIMES AND FORFEITURES OF WULFBOLD

These are the crimes by which Wulfbold ruined himself with his lord, namely first, when his father had died, he went to his stepmother's estate and took everything that he could find there, inside and out, small and great. Then the king sent to him and commanded him to give up what he had seized, but he paid no attention and his wergeld was assigned to the king. And the king sent to him again and repeated his command, but he paid no attention to it and for the second time his wergeld was assigned to the king. Over and above this he went and took possession of the estate belonging to his kinsman, Brihtmær of Bourne. Then the king sent to him and commanded him to give up the estate, but he paid no attention and his wergeld was assigned to the king for the third time. The king sent to him once again and commanded him to leave the estate, but he paid no attention and his wergeld was assigned to the king for the fourth time. Then the great meeting was held at London; Earl Æthelwine was there and all the king's councillors. Then all the councillors

130 CRIMES AND FORFEITURES OF WULFBOLD

þam cynge ealle Wulboldes ære 7 hine silfne to þam þe se cynge wolde swa to life swa to deaþe 7 he hæfne ealle[1] þis ungebet oþe[2] he forþferd[3] eft þa he þæs[4] forþfaran ufenan eal þis þa ferd[3] his laf to mid hyre cilde 7 ofsloh Eadmær[5] þæs cyngis þegen Wulf-
5 boldis faderan sune 7 his fiftyne geferan on þan land æt Burnan þe he on reaflace ongen þæne cynyng hefde[6] 7 þa Æþelgare arcebisceop hæfde þæne miclan sinoþ an Lundene þa getæhte man þam cinge hine 7 ealle his are · þis sind þa men þa wæron æt þære tæcinge[7] · Æþelgar arcebiscop 7 Oswold arcebiscop 7
10 Ælfstan biscop of Londone 7 Sigeric biscop 7 Ælfstan bisceop on Hrofeceastre 7 Ordbyrht bisceop Ælfeah[8] bisceop 7 Aþulf bisceop 7 Aþelwine ealdorman 7 Byrhnoþ ealdorman 7 Aþelweard ealdorman 7 Alfric ealdorman Þeodred eorl 7 Eadulf abbod 7 Byrnoþe abbod 7 Germanus abbod 7 Wlfsige abbod 7
15 Leofric abbod of Miclanige 7 Leofric abbod of Eaxcestre 7 Ælfhun abbod 7 Ælfelm 7 Wlfeah 7 Wulfric Wulfrune suni 7 Stir Wulfes suni 7 Nafena 7 Norwina[n][9] his broðor 7 Leofwine Leoftætan suni 7 Leofsige æt Mordune 7 Bonda 7 Ælfhelm polga 7 Aþelwold 7 Leofric 7 Sigeward on Cent
20 7 Leofsunn 7 Aþelwold þes greta 7 Ælfgar se Hunitunisca 7 Wulsegat[10] 7 Æþelmer 7 Æþelric 7 Æþelnoðe Wiftanes suni 7 Leofwine Æþulfes suni 7 Sigebrht[11] 7 Leofstan on Suþseaxan.

LXIV. LEASE OF LAND BY OSWALD, ARCHBISHOP OF YORK AND BISHOP OF WORCESTER, TO BEORNHEAH AND BRIHTSTAN

[M]ortun · Beornege · [7] Byrhstane[12].

✝ Disponente regi regum cuncta caeli secreta necnon quę sub
25 cęli culmine aput homines mutantur miro ordine gubernante cuius incarnationis humanę anno .DCCCC.XC. Indictione .III. haec

---

[1] *hæfde eall*, Edwards.
[2] *oþþ*, ibid.
[3] *-ferde*, ibid.
[4] *þær*, ibid.
[5] *-mer*, ibid.
[6] *hæfde*, ibid.
[7] *tœtinge*, ibid.
[8] *-heah*, ibid.
[9] The MS. reading seems to be *-winaai*.
[10] *-gar*, Edwards.
[11] *-briht*, ibid.
[12] In the margin; om. MS. (*b*), K.

CRIMES AND FORFEITURES OF WULFBOLD

who were there, both ecclesiastics and laymen, assigned the whole of Wulfbold's property to the king, and himself likewise to be disposed of as the king desired, either to remain alive or to be condemned to death. And he had made no amends for all this up to the time of his death. And after he was dead, over and above all this, his widow along with her son went and slew Eadmær the king's thegn, Wulfbold's uncle's son, and his fifteen companions on the estate at Bourne which he had held by seizure despite the king. And then Archbishop Æthelgar had the great synod at London, and he himself and all his property were assigned to the king.

These are the men who took part in the decision: Archbishop Æthelgar and Archbishop Oswald and Ælfstan, Bishop of London, and Bishop Sigeric and Ælfstan, Bishop of Rochester, and Bishop Ordbriht, Bishop Ælfheah and Bishop Athulf and Earl Æthelwine and Earl Brihtnoth and Earl Æthelweard and Earl Ælfric and Earl Thored(?) and Abbot Eadulf and Abbot Brihtnoth and Abbot Germanus and Abbot Wulfsige and Leofric, Abbot of Michelney, and Leofric, Abbot of Exeter, and Abbot Ælfhun and Ælfhelm and Wulfheah and Wulfric, Wulfrun's son, and Stir, Wulf's son, and Nafena and Northwine his brother and Leofwine, Leoftæta's son, and Leofsige of Morden and Bonda and Ælfhelm Polga and Æthelwold and Leofric and Siweard of Kent and Leofsunu and Æthelwold the Stout and Ælfgar, the Honiton man, and Wulfgeat and Æthelmær and Æthelric and Æthelnoth, Wi[s]tan's son, and Leofwine, Athulf's son, and Sigebriht and Leofstan of Sussex.

LXIV. LEASE OF LAND BY OSWALD, ARCHBISHOP OF YORK AND BISHOP OF WORCESTER, TO BEORNHEAH AND BRIHTSTAN

Moreton, to Beornheah and Brihtstan.

✢ In the year 990 of the human incarnation of the King of kings who governs all the secret things of heaven and likewise controls in marvellous order those which change among men

LEASE OF LAND BY OSWALD

donatio quę in ista cartula saxonicis sermonibus appar*et* confirmata *et* donata erat. In usses drihtnes noman · hælendes Cristes. Ic Oswald ercebisceop cyþu þæt seo heorædden æt Wiogurnacestre ge ealdde ge iunge me þafedan[1] ꝥ ic moste
5 gebocian twa hida landes[2] on Mortune on þreora monna dæg minum twam getreowum mannum Beorhnæge 7 Byrhstane twæm gebroþrum 7 se eldra hæbbe þa þreo æceras 7 se iungra þone feorðan ge innor ge utter swa to þam lande gebyrige ꝥ mon nemneð oðre naman Uppþrop · 7 we ealle halsigað[3] on Godes
10 naman ꝥ hio nænig mann þæs ne bereafige þa hwile þe hieo[4] lifien 7 ofer heora dæg cerre to þæs honda þe heo unnen[5] 7 hit seo þonne þæm agen æg'h'wæs to brucenne to freon twegra manna[6] dæg butan þæm circsceatte 7 ic cyðe ꝥ ða gebroþ'r'a twegen me gesealdon .iiii. pund licwyrðes feos wið fullan unnan. Et
15 nunc obsecramus[7] *per* mis*eri*cordia*m* dei qui est *pro*prius *et* uerus d*omi*n*u*s omnium terraru*m* quę ad ęcclesi*am* dei p*er*tinent *et* p*er* amorem[8] sc̄ae Marię in[9] cuius nomine consecratu*m* est monasteriu*m* in Wiogurnaceastre in quo seruire debemus · ut hæc nostra largitia siue[10] consentio inuiolata[11] p*er*manere queat · *et* si
20 quis de n*os*tris successoribus hoc in aliquo foedare temptauerit *et* n*os*trę fraternę congregationis licentiam disrumpere sciat se rationem redditurum in tremendo examinis die nisi prius satisfaciendo emend*et*. Ðis syndan þara broþra naman þe þas sylene geþafedan 7 gesealdan[12] 7 mid Cristes rode tacne gefæstnodon.

25 ✠ Oswald arce-
   bisceop.
   ✠ Æþelstan prim*us*
   ✠ Ælfsige prbt
   ✠ Eadgar prbt[13]
30 ✠ Wistan prbt

   ✠ Æþelsige prbt
   ✠ Æþelstan prbt
   ✠ Godingc diāc
   ✠ Leofstan diāc
   ✠ Wulfweard[14] diāc
   ✠ Æþelric diāc

   ✠ Cyneþegn clr
   ✠ Wulfgar clr
   ✠ Leofwine clr[15]
   ✠ Wulfric cler
   ✠ Wulfnoð clr
   ✠ Wulfwine clr

---

[1] *geþafedon*, MS. (*b*); *-an*, Hi. [2] *twega hida lond*, MS. (*b*), Hi.
[3] *we alle halle halsiað*, MS. (*b*), Hi. [4] *þa hw. þ[æs]*, MS. (*b*); *þa hw.þes*, Hi.
[5] *betst unnen*, MS. (*b*), Hi. [6] *mannum*, MS. (*b*), Hi.
[7] *o[mnes ora]mus*, MS. (*b*). [8] *pro amore*, ibid.
[9] Om. MS. (*b*), Hi. [10] *suę*, MS. (*b*).
[11] MS. (*b*) has a lacuna after *consentio*, then *ut*, with *ta* written above it later, *permanere*, etc.
[12] 7 *gesealdan*, om. MS. (*b*). [13] *Ea pr*, ibid.
[14] *-hard*, ibid. [15] *moñ*, MS. (*b*), Hi.

under the dome of heaven, and in the third Indiction, this gift which appears in this charter in Saxon words was granted and confirmed.

In the name of our Lord the Saviour Christ I, Archbishop Oswald, make known that [the members of] the community at Worcester, both old and young, have given me permission to grant by charter 2 hides of land at Moreton for three lives to my two loyal servants, Beornheah and Brihtstan, two brothers, and the elder shall always have 3 acres and the younger the fourth, both central and outlying, as pertains to the estate, the other name of which is *Upthorp*. And all of us implore in the name of God that no one deprive them of this estate as long as they live, and after their death it shall pass into the possession of the man to whom they grant it, and it shall be their own to enjoy freely in every respect for two lives except for church dues. And I declare that the two brothers have given me 4 pounds of sterling money in return for this unrestricted grant.

And now we entreat by the mercy of God who is the one true lord of all the lands which belong to the church of God, and by the love of St Mary, in whose name the monastery at Worcester, in which it is our duty to serve, has been consecrated, that this our grant or agreement shall remain inviolate, and if any of our successors attempts to distort this in any way and to disregard the ratification of our brotherly community, he shall find that he shall have to answer for it on the terrible Judgment Day, unless he has already atoned for it by making amends.

These are the names of the brothers who have permitted and made this gift, and have confirmed it with the symbol of the cross of Christ...

LXV. LEASE OF LAND BY OSWALD, ARCHBISHOP OF YORK AND BISHOP OF WORCESTER, TO ÆTHELMÆR

Æt Cumtune Æþelmære[1].

✠ In usses drihtnes noman hælendes[2] Cristes[2]. Ic Oswald arcebisceop mid geþafunge 7 leafe þæs arwurðan hyredes on Wiogernaceastre ge iunges ge ealdes gebocige sumne dæl landes minan holdan 7 getriowan men þæm is Æþelmær nama[3] on twam stowum twega hida landes on þreora manna dæg ane hide on Cumtune on his hamstealle 7 healf þone wudu þærto 7 oþre on Mersce for his eadmodre hyrsumnysse 7 for his licweorðan feo ꝥ is twa pund merehwites seolfres · 7 xxx. euwna mid hiora lambum · 7 IIII. oxan 7 twa cy 7 an hors ꝥ is þæt[4] hæbbe 7 wel bruce his dǽg 7 æfter his dæge twam erfeweardan[5] þam þe him leofest sy 7 him to geearnian wylle 7 hio hit hæbben tofrion ælces þinges butan wealgeworce 7 brygcgeweorce 7 ferdsocne; þis synd þære anre hide landgemæru on Mersce[6] ærest of Æþestanes gemære to þam wylle on Biles hamme þoñ út to þam middel ge[m]are[7] · þis wæs gedon þy geare þe wæs agan fram Cristes gebyrdtide nigon hund wintra 7 hundnigontig wintra on þara broðra gewitnysse þe hiora naman her beneoðan awritene[8] standað.

✠ Ic Oswald arcebisceop mid Cristes rode tacne þas sylene gefæstnode.

✠[9] Æþelstan primus.
✠ Ælfsige prbt.
✠ Eadgar prbt.
✠ Wistan prbt.
✠ Æþelsige prbt.
✠ Æþelstan prbt.

✠ Godingc diāc.
✠ Leofstan diāc.
✠ Wulfweard diāc.
✠ Æþelric diāc.
✠ Cyneþen cl.

✠ Wulfgar cl.
✠ Leofwine moñ.
✠ Wulfric cl.
✠ Wulfnoð cl.
✠ Wulfwine cl.

✠ 7 Ic gean him þæs worðiges æt Brynes hamme þe Æþelm ahte 7 þæs croftes þærto be eastan þære stræte on ꝥ ilce gerad þe þis oðer is.

[1] K. omits the heading.
[2] Om., MS. (a).
[3] hatte, ibid.
[4] þæt he, ibid.
[5] erfn[uman], ibid.
[6] -ste, He.
[7] geare, MS. (b); gema..., MS. (a); gemare, K.
[8] Om., MS. (a).
[9] All the names found in the Middleton fragment are preceded by Ic.

LXV. LEASE OF LAND BY OSWALD, ARCHBISHOP OF YORK AND BISHOP OF WORCESTER, TO ÆTHELMÆR

Compton, to Æthelmær.

✠ In the name of our Lord the Saviour Christ, I, Archbishop Oswald, with the consent and leave of the honourable community at Worcester, both young and old, grant by charter for three lives a certain piece of land to my faithful and loyal servant whose name is Æthelmær, namely 2 hides in two places—one hide at his homestead in Compton and half the wood in addition, and the other at Marsh—because of his humble obedience and in return for his sterling money, namely two pounds of pure white silver, and 30 ewes with their lambs and 4 oxen and 2 cows and a horse; and he shall hold it and enjoy it during his lifetime, and after his death [it shall pass] to the two heirs who please him best and are willing to earn it from him, and they shall hold it free from every obligation except the construction of walls and bridges and military service.

These are the boundaries of the one hide at Marsh, first from Æthelstan's boundary to the well in Bilsham, then out to the middle boundary.

This was done in the year 990 after the birth of Christ, with the cognisance of the brothers whose names are written below...

✠ And I grant him the homestead at Bryne's enclosure, which Æthelm owned, and the croft in addition to the east of the highway, on the same conditions as the other.

LXVI. RECORD OF A LAWSUIT BETWEEN WYNFLÆD AND LEOFWINE

✠ Her cyþ on þysum gewrite hu Wynflæd gelædde hyre gewitnesse æt Wulfamere beforan Æþelrede cyninge · ꝥ wæs þonne Sigeric arcebiscop · 7 Ordbyrht biscop · 7 Ælfric ealderman 7 Ælfþryþ þæs cyninges modor · ꝥ hi wæron ealle to gewitnesse
5 þæt Ælfric sealde Wynflæde ꝥ land æt Hacceburnan · 7 æt Bradanfelda ongean ꝥ land æt Deccet · þa sende se cyning þær rihte be þam arcebiscope · 7 be þam þe þær mid him to gewitnesse wæron to Leofwine 7 cyþdon him þis · þa nolde he butan hit man sceote to scirgemote[1] · þa dyde man swa · þa sende se cyning
10 be Æluere abbude his insegel to þam gemote æt Cwicelmeshlæwe 7 grette ealle þa witan þe þær gesomnode wæron · ꝥ wæs[2] Æþelsige biscop · 7 Æs'c'wig biscop · 7 Ælfric abbud · 7 eal sio scir 7 bæd 7 het ꝥ hi scioldon Wynflæde 7 Leofwine swa rihtlice geseman swa him æfre rihtlicost þuhte · 7 Sigeric arcebiscop
15 sende his swutelunga þærto · 7 Ordbyrht biscop his · þa getæhte man Wynflæde ꝥ hio moste hit hyre geahnian · þa gelædde hio þa ahnunga mid Ælfþryþe fultume þæs cyninges modor · ꝥ is þonne ærest Wulfgar abbud · 7 Wulfstan priost · 7 Æfic þara æþelinga discsten · 7 Eadwine · 7 Eadelm · 7 Ælfelm · 7 Ælfwine · 7
20 Ælfweard · 7 Eadwold · 7 Eadric · 7 Ælfgar · 7 Eadgyfu[3] abbudisse · 7 Liofrun abbudisse · 7 Æþelhild · 7 Eadgyfu æt Leofecanoran[4] · 7 hyre swustor · 7 hyre dohtor · 7 Ælfgy[fu 7 hyr]e[5] dohtor · 7 Wulfwyn · 7 Æþelgyfu · 7 Ælfwaru · 7 Ælfgyfu · 7 Æþelflæd · 7 menig god þegen · 7 god wif þe we ealle atellan ne
25 magon ꝥ [þær][6] forþcom[7] eal se fulla[8] ge on werum ge on wifum. Þa cwædon þa witan þe þær wæron ꝥ betere wære ꝥ man þene aþ aweg lete þonne hine man sealde · forþan þær syþþan nar freondscype nære · 7 man wolde biddan þæs reaflaces ꝥ he hit sciolde agyfan 7 forgyldan · 7 þam cyninge his wer · þa let he

---

[1] *scire-*, T.   [2] *wære*, T.
[3] *-gifu*, T.   [4] *-tan*, T.
[5] There is a hole in the MS. K. reads *Ælfgyf*[*u hyr*]*e* but there is room for more.
[6] The lower portions of the letters are visible below the hole. K. reads [*wære*].   [7] *cõm*, K., T.
[8] K. and T. supply *aþ* after *fulla* which comes at the end of a line.

LXVI. RECORD OF A LAWSUIT BETWEEN WYNFLÆD AND LEOFWINE

✠ Here it is stated in this document how Wynflæd produced her witnesses at Woolmer before King Æthelred, namely Archbishop Sigeric and Bishop Ordbriht and Earl Ælfric and Ælfthryth, the king's mother, all of whom bore witness that Ælfric gave Wynflæd the estates at Hagbourne and at Bradfield in return for the estate at Datchet. Then the king sent straightway to Leofwine by the archbishop and those who had acted as witnesses along with him, and informed him of this, but he would not [agree], unless the matter were referred to a shire-meeting. This was done. The king sent his seal to the meeting at Cuckamsley by Abbot Ælfhere, and greeted all the councillors who were assembled there, namely Bishop Æthelsige and Bishop Æscwig and Abbot Ælfric and the whole shire, and prayed and commanded them to settle the case between Wynflæd and Leofwine as justly as they could; and Archbishop Sigeric sent his declaration to the meeting and Bishop Ordbriht his. Then Wynflæd was informed that she might prove her ownership of the estate, and she adduced proof of her ownership with the help of Ælfthryth, the king's mother, her supporters being first Abbot Wulfgar and Wulfstan the priest and Æfic, the Æthelings' seneschal, and Edwin and Eadhelm and Ælfhelm and Ælfwine and Ælfweard and Eadwold and Eadric and Ælfgar and the Abbess Eadgifu and the Abbess Leofrun and Æthelhild and Eadgifu of Lewknor and her sister and her daughter and Ælfgi[fu and her] daughter and Wulfwyn and Æthelgifu and Ælfwaru and Ælfgifu and Æthelflæd and many a good thegn and good woman, all of whom we cannot enumerate, so that the full number was produced, including both men and women. Then the councillors who were there declared that it would be better for the oath to be dispensed with rather than sworn, because thereafter friendship would be at an end [between them], and he (Leofwine) would be asked to return what he had seized and pay compensation and his wergeld to the king. Then he dispensed with the oath, and handed over the estate uncontested

138 RECORD OF A LAWSUIT BETWEEN

þone aþ aweg · 7 sealde Æþelsige biscope unbesacen land on hand þ he þanon forð syþþan þæron ne spræce · þa tæhte man hyre þ hio sciolde bringan his fæder gold 7 siolfor eal þ hio hæfde · þa dyde hio swa hio dorste hyre aþe gebiorgan · þa næs
5 he þagyt on þam gehealden butan hio sceolde swerian þ his æhta þær ealle wæron · þa cwæþ hio þ hio ne mihte hyre dæles ne he his · 7 þyses wæs Ælfgar þæs cyninges gerefa to gewitnesse · 7 Byrhtric · 7 Leofric æt Hwitecyrcan · 7 menig god man toeacan him.

LXVII. LEASE OF LAND BY OSWALD, ARCHBISHOP OF YORK AND BISHOP OF WORCESTER, TO EADRIC

10 On Tætlinctune 7 æt Neoweboldan Eadrice[1].

† In usses drih't'nes noman hælendes Cristes. Ic OSWALD arcebiscop mid geþafunge 7 leafe · þæs arwyrðan hiredes on Wiogernaceastre ge iunges ge aldes gebocie sumne dæl landes minum holdan 7 getriowan þegne þæm is Eadric noma on twam
15 stowum þriora hida landes on twera monna dæg twa on Tætlintune 7 ane æt Nioweboldan[2] 7 þ inlond þærto · þe Leofinc[3] hædde · for his eadmodre hersumnesse · þ is þ he hæbbe 7 wel bruce his dæg 7 æfter his dæg anum erfewarde þæm þe him leofest se 7 him to gearnian wille 7 he hit hæbbe tofrion ælces
20 þingces butan geweorce[4] 7 bry'c'ggeworce 7 ferdsocne. Þis wæs gedon þu[5] geare þe agán wæs 'fron' Cristes gebyrdtide[6] nigon hund wintra 7 an 7 hundnigonti wintra on þara broðra gewitnesse þe hiora naman her beneoðan awritene standað.

✠ Ic OSWALD ercebiscop mid Cristes rode tacne þas sylene
25 gefestnade.

✠ Ego Æþelstan primus
✠ Ego Ælfsige prbt
✠ Eadgar prbt
30 ✠ Ego Æþelsige prbt
✠ Ego Godingc diac

✠ Ego Wistan prbt
✠ Ego Æþelstan prbt
✠ Ego Leofstan diac
✠ Ego Æþelric diac
✠ Ego Cyneþeng[7]
✠ Ego Wulfgar clr

✠ Ego Leofwine clr
✠ Ego Wulfric clr
✠ Ego Wulfnoð clr
✠ Ego Wulfwine clr
✠ Ego Godwine clr

[1] K. omits the heading.
[4] For *wealgeweorce*.
[7] K. adds *clericus*.

[2] *Mowe-*, He.
[5] *ðy*, K.

[3] *Leofric*, K.
[6] *-byrð-*, K.

to Bishop Æthelsige, [affirming] that henceforth he would make no further claim to it. Then Wynflæd was directed to produce all his father's gold and silver that she had. Then she did [as little] as she dared to protect her oath. Then he was still not satisfied with it, unless she should swear that all his property was there. She said that she could not [do so] for her part nor he for his. And the witnesses of this were Ælfgar, the king's reeve, and Brihtric and Leofric of Whitchurch and many good men in addition to them.

LXVII. LEASE OF LAND BY OSWALD, ARCHBISHOP OF YORK AND BISHOP OF WORCESTER, TO EADRIC

Talton and Newbold, to Eadric.

✝ In the name of our Lord the Saviour Christ, I, Archbishop Oswald, with the consent and leave of the honourable community at Worcester, both young and old, grant by charter for two lives a certain piece of land to my loyal and faithful thegn whose name is Eadric for his humble obedience, [namely] 3 hides in two places—2 at Talton and 1 at Newbold—and the demesne land in addition which Lyfing had. And he shall hold it and make good use of it during his life, and after his death [leave it] to [the] one heir who is most agreeable to him and who is willing to earn it from him, and he shall hold it free from every obligation except the construction [of walls] and bridges and military service.

This was done in the year 991 after the birth of Christ, with the brothers as witnesses whose names are written below...

LXVIII. TWO GRANTS OF LAND TO ST CUTHBERT'S

Her syleð Norðman eorl into sce Cuðberhte Ediscum 7 eall[1] ꝥ ðær into hyreð · 7 ðone feorðan æcer æt Feregenne[2].

7 ic Ulfcytel Osulfes sunu sylle Norðtun mid mete 7 mid mannan into sce Cuðberhte · 7 all ꝥ ðer[3] into hyreð mið[4] sace
5 7 mið socne 7 se ðe þis awende sy he ascyred from Godes dæle[5] 7 from eallum haligdome.

LXIX. LAWSUIT ABOUT THE ESTATE OF SNODLAND, KENT

☧ Her cyð on ðysum[6] gewrite · hu Godwine biscop on Hrofeceastre · 7 Leofwine Ælfeages sunu wurðon[7] gesybsumode ymbe ꝥ land æt Snoddinglande[8] · on Cantwarabyrig.
10 Þa ða se biscop Godwine com to ðam biscopstole þurh hæse his cynehlafordes Æðelredes[9] cynges æfter Ælfstanes forðsiþe ƀ. þa gemetæ[10] he on ðam mynstre þa ylcan[11] swutelunga þe his foregenga hæfde · 7 þærmid on ꝥ land spæc · ongan ða to specenne on ðæt[12] land · 7 elles for Godes ege ne dorste · oððæt seo
15 spræc wearð þam cynge cuð. Þa ða[9] him seo talu cuð wæs · þa sende[13] he gewrit 7 his insegl to þam arcebisceope[14] Ælfrice · 7 bead him ꝥ he 7 hys þegenas on East Cent · 7 on West Cent · hy onriht gesemdon · be ontale · 7[9] be oftale. Þa ꝥ wæs ꝥ se bisceop Godwine com to Cantwarabyrig to ðam arcebiscope · þa com
20 ðider se scyresman[11] Leofric · 7 mid him Ælfun[15] abƀ · 7 þegenas[16] ægþer ge oft[17] East Cent ge of West Cent · eal seo duguð · 7 hy ðær þa spæce[18] swa lange handledon · syððon se bisceop his swutelunge ge'e'owod hæfde · oþ hy ealle bædon þone biscop eaðmodlice · ꝥ he geunnan scolde[19] ꝥ he moste mid
25 bletsunga[20] þæs landes brucan æt Snoddinglande his dæg · 7 se

[1] eale, B.
[2] Fore-, Surtees Soc.
[3] ðær, B.
[4] mid, K.
[5] dæde, Surtees Soc.
[6] -ss-, Hi.
[7] wurd-, K., T.
[8] -ung-, Hi.
[9] Om. Hi.
[10] -mæte, Hi.; -mætæ, T.
[11] Hi. has i for y.
[12] þat, T.
[13] send, Hi.
[14] -cope, Hi.
[15] Al-, Hi.
[16] -es, Hi.
[17] of, Hi., K., T.
[18] spræce, Hi.
[19] sceolde, T.
[20] blæt-, Hi.

LXVIII. TWO GRANTS OF LAND TO ST CUTHBERT'S

Earl Northman here grants to St Cuthbert's Escomb and all that belongs to it, and the fourth acre at Ferryhill.

And I, Ulfketel, Osulf's son, grant Norton to St Cuthbert's with its produce and its men and all that belongs to it and with rights of jurisdiction. He who alters this shall be cut off from any part in God and from all holy things.

LXIX. LAWSUIT ABOUT THE ESTATE OF SNODLAND, KENT

⁊ Here it is stated in this document how Godwine, Bishop of Rochester, and Leofwine, Ælfheah's son, were reconciled at Canterbury about the estate at Snodland.

When Bishop Godwine succeeded to the episcopal see, by the command of his royal lord King Æthelred, after the death of Bishop Ælfstan, he found in the cathedral the very deeds which his predecessor had had and with which he laid claim to the estate. Then he set about laying claim to the estate—and durst not do otherwise for the fear of God—until the suit became known to the king. When the claim was known to him, he sent a letter and his seal to Archbishop Ælfric, and gave orders that he and his thegns in East Kent and West Kent should settle the dispute between them justly, weighing both claim and counter-claim.

The next stage was that Bishop Godwine came to Canterbury to the Archbishop, and thither came [also] Leofric the sheriff and with him Abbot Ælfhun and the thegns both of East Kent and West Kent—all the leading men—and there they dealt with the suit, after the bishop had produced his evidence, until finally they humbly prayed the bishop to allow Leofwine to enjoy the estate at Snodland with his blessing during his lifetime. And the bishop granted this to the gratification of all the

142   LAWSUIT ABOUT THE ESTATE

biscop[1] þa þæs[2] getiðode on ealra þæra witena þanc þe þær[3]
gesomnode wæran · 7 he behet þæs truwan ꝥ land æfter his dæge
unbesacen eode eft into þære stowe þe hit ut alæned wæs[4] · 7
ageaf þa swutelunga þe he to þam lande hæfde þe ær of þære
5 stowe geutod wæs · 7 þa hagan ealle þe he bewestan þære cyrcan
hæfde into þære halgan stowe · 7 þises loces ærendracan wæran ·
Ælfun abbod 7 Wulfric abbod · 7 Leofric sciresman · 7 Siweard ·
7 Wulfstan æt Sealtwuda · 7 Ælfelm[5] Ordelmes sunu. Þonne is
her[6] seo gewitnes[7] þe æt þisum loce wæs · ꝥ is ærest se arcebiscop
10 Ælfric · 7 se biscop Goduuine · 7 Wulfric abb. 7 Ælfun abb ·
7 Ælfnoð æt Orpedingtune · 7 se hired æt Cristes cyrcan · 7 se
hired æt sc̄e Augustine · 7 so[8] burhwaru on Cantwarebyrig · 7
Leofric sciresman · 7 Lifing[9] æt Meallingan · 7 Siweard · 7 Sired
his broðor · 7 Leostan[10] æt Mærseham · 7 Godwine Wulfeages
15 sunu · 7 Wulstan[11] æt Sealtwuda · 7 Wulstan[11] iunga[12] · 7 Leoswine[13]
æt Dictune · 7 Leofric Ealdredes sunu · 7[14] Goda Wulfsiges
sunu · 7 Ælfelm[15] Ordelmes sunu · 7 Sidewine æt Pealleswyrðe[16] ·
7 Wærelm · 7 Æþelred portgerefa on byrig 7 Guðwold. Gif
hwa þis ðence to awendenne · 7 þas[17] foreword to abrecenne ·
20 awende him God fram his ansyne on þam miclan dome · swa ꝥ
he si ascyred[18] fram heofenarices[19] myrhðe[20] · 7 sy eallum
deoflum betæht into helle. AMEN.

LXX. LEASE OF LAND BY THE ABBOT AND
THE COMMUNITY AT THE NEW MINSTER,
WINCHESTER, TO WULFMÆR

In nomine domini. Her swytelað on þisym gewryte hu Ælfsige
abbod 7 se hired on niwan mynstre[21] alendan Wlfmære an hide
25 landes æt Bertune his dæg 7 his wifes on þæt gerad ꝥ syo hid
7 oðer hid æt Dregtune gangan into ðam mynistre swa gewered

[1] -ceop, T.   [2] wæs, Hi.   [3] þæs, Hi.
[4] was, Hi., T.   [5] -ælm, Hi.   [6] here, Hi.
[7] -nesse, Hi.   [8] seo, K., T.   [9] -nig, Hi.
[10] -fstan, Hi., K., T.   [11] -fstan, K., T.   [12] lunga, Hi.
[13] Leof-, Hi., K., T.   [14] Hi. omits the next two witnesses.
[15] -helm, T.   [16] Weales-, Hi., T.; Wealles-, K.
[17] þes, Hi.   [18] Hi. has i for y.   [19] heofenes-, Hi.
[20] Hi. ends here.   [21] min-, Edwards.

councillors who were there assembled, and Leofwine gave his solemn assurance that after his death the estate should revert uncontested to the foundation from which it was leased, and gave up the deeds relating to the estate which he had and which had been alienated from the foundation, and all the messuages which he had west of the church to the holy foundation. And the negotiators of this settlement were Abbot Ælfhun and Abbot Wulfric and Leofric the sheriff and Siweard and Wulfstan of Saltwood and Ælfhelm, Ordhelm's son. And these are the witnesses who were present at this settlement, namely first Archbishop Ælfric and Bishop Godwine and Abbot Wulfric and Abbot Ælfhun and Ælfnoth of Orpington and the community at Christchurch and the community at St Augustine's and the citizens of Canterbury and Leofric the sheriff and Lyfing of Malling and Siweard and Sired his brother and Leofstan of Mersham and Godwine, Wulfheah's son, and Wulfstan of Saltwood and Wulfstan the Young and Leo[f]wine of Ditton and Leofric, Ealdred's son, and Goda, Wulfsige's son, and Ælfhelm, Ordelm's son, and Sidewine of Paddlesworth and Wærelm and Æthelred, the reeve of Canterbury, and Guthwold.

If anyone attempts to alter this or break this agreement, God shall avert his countenance from him at the great Judgment, so that he shall be cut off from the bliss of the kingdom of heaven and delivered over to all the devils in hell. Amen.

LXX. LEASE OF LAND BY THE ABBOT AND THE COMMUNITY AT THE NEW MINSTER, WINCHESTER, TO WULFMÆR

In nomine domini.

Here it is declared in this document how Abbot Ælfsige and the community at the New Minster have leased a hide of land at Barton to Wulfmær for his lifetime and his wife's, on condition that this hide and another hide at Drayton shall pass to the

LEASE OF LAND TO WULFMÆR

swa hy beon ofer hyra dæg 7 þisra twegra hida landgemæra sind on ðæra bec ðe Drægtune uton be lið 7 his[1] is gedon be Æðelredes cininges unnan[2] 7 gewitnesse 7 Ælfrices arcebisceopes 7 Ælfheges bisceopes 7 Ælfrices ealdermannes[3] 7 Æðelmæres 7
5 Ordulfes 7 Sulgeates 7 Æðelrices 7 Æðelweardes 7 þara þreora hireda on ealdan ministre 7 on nywan[4] ministre 7 on nunan ministre 7 his[1] is on þ gerad gedon þ Wlfmære sy freond 7 hold into ðem mynstre on ælcere stowe ægðer ge for Gode ge for worulde.

LXXI. GRANT OF LAND BY ÆLFHELM TO HIS GOLDSMITH

10 ✠ Her is on þysse Crystes bec siu geswytelung þære healfre hyde æt Pottune þe Ælfhelm Leofsige sealde hys goldsmiþe on lyfe 7 æfter lyfe to atenne swa hym leofæst sy; þonne wæron þas to gewitnesse þe heron geswyteliað · Ælfhelm his hlaford · Byrhtnoþ abbod 7 Ælfgar munuc 7 Ælfhelm se gunge 7 his twegen sunu ·
15 Æþelhric 7 Alfwold[5] 7 Wulfmær þæs bisceopes broþar 7 Ælmær cild 7 Leofric æt Holewelle 7 his sunu Godric 7 Æþelric æt Hernicwelle 7 Ælfsige preost 7 his sunu 7 Osferþ preost.

LXXII. LIST OF THE CONTRIBUTIONS OF MEN REQUIRED FOR MANNING A SHIP

[S]cipmen[6]. Of Ticc .iiii. Of Tillingaham .ii. Of Dunmæwan · 7 of Tollesfuntan .i. Of Næsingstoce · 7 of Neosdune .iiii.
20 Of Hinawicun · 7 of Tollandune .ii. Of Gnutungadune · 7 of Bræmbelege .i. Of Þottanheale .i. Of Clopham .ii. Of Bærnun · 7 of Ceswican .i. Of Drægtune .i. Of Caddandune .i. Of Sandune .i. Of Ceaddingtune .i. Of Fullanhamme .v. Of Forþtune .iii. Of Stybbanhyþe · 7 of Gislandune .ii. Of
25 Orseaþun .i. Of Ligeandune .i. of Seopinglande · 7 of þam westrum Orseaþum .i. Of Bylcham .i. Of Coppanforda 7 Holande .i. Of Suðmynster .v. Of Claccingtune .ii. Of Hæþlege · 7 of Codanham .i.:—

[1] *þis*, Edwards.   [2] *cunuges minan*, ibid.   [3] -*dor*-, ibid.
[4] *niw*-, ibid.   [5] *Ælf*-, K.
[6] A space has been left for the initial capital.

LEASE OF LAND TO WULFMÆR 145

minster, stocked as they are, after their death. And the boundaries of these two hides are in the charter which gives the limits of Drayton. And this has been done with the consent and cognisance of King Æthelred and Archbishop Ælfric and Bishop Ælfheah and Earl Ælfric and Æthelmær and Ordulf and [W]ulfgeat and Æthelric and Æthelweard and the three communities at the Old Minster and the New Minster and the Nunnery; and it is done on condition that Wulfmær be loyal and friendly towards the minster in every place, in matters both religious and secular.

LXXI. GRANT OF LAND BY ÆLFHELM TO HIS GOLDSMITH

✠ Here in this gospel book is the declaration relating to the half hide at Potton which Ælfhelm gave to Leofsige, his goldsmith, to dispose of during his life and at his death as pleased him best. The witnesses of this were those who appear in this document: Ælfhelm his lord, Abbot Brihtnoth and the monk Ælfgar and Ælfhelm the young and his two sons—Æthelric and Ælfwold—and Wulfmær, the bishop's brother, and Ælfmær *cild* and Leofric of Holwell and his son Godric and Æthelric of *Hernicwelle* and the priest Ælfsige and his son and the priest Osferth.

LXXII. LIST OF THE CONTRIBUTIONS OF MEN REQUIRED FOR MANNING A SHIP

Seamen: from St Osyth 4, from Tillingham 2, from Dunmow and from Tolleshunt 1, from Navestock and from Neasden 4, from Wickham St Paul's and from *Tollandune* 2, from *Gnutungadune* and from Bromley 1, from Tottenham 1, from Clapham 2, from Barnes and from Chiswick 1, from Drayton 1, from Caddington 1, from Sandon 1, from *Ceaddingtune* 1, from Fulham 5, from *Forþtune* 3, from Stepney and from Islington 2, from Orsett 1, from Leyton 1, from Shopland and from the western Orsett 1, from Belchamp [St Paul] 1, from Copford and Holland 1, from Southminster 5, from Clacton 2, from Hadleigh and from Coddenham 1.

LXXIII. GRANT OF LANDS BY ULFKETEL TO BURY ST EDMUNDS

[H]Er[1] switeleþ on þis write ihu þat Vlfketel God vthe and sc̄e Eadmunde · þat ís þat lond at Rikinghale 7 al þat þerto hireð[2] · and þat[3] lond at Rucham · and þat lond at Wlpet · and þat lond at Hildericlea · and þat[4] at Redfaresþorpe · also so[5] it stonden 5 mid mete and mid manne and mid Sake and Sokne also ic it aihte. Se þe þis awende ⁏ God almíhtín aWende his ansene on domesday from him buten he it er her þe rathere bete.

LXXIV. LEASE OF LAND TO EDMUND THE ÆTHELING BY THE COMMUNITY AT SHERBORNE

Her swutelaþ on þisum[6] gewrite þ Eadmund æþeling bæd þone hyred[7] æt Scireburnan þ he moste ofgan þ land æt Holancumbe; 10 ða ne dorste se hyred hym þæs wyrnan · ac cwæþon[8] þ hy þæs wel uðon · gyf se cing 7 se bisceop þe heora ealdor wæs þæs geuðon. Ða gewærþ[9] hym · 7 se æþeling 7 se prafost 7 þa yldostan munecas comon to þam cinge 7 him fore cyddon 7 his leafe bædon · 7 þ ærende abead Wulfstan archebisceop. Ða 15 cwæð se cing þ he nolde þæt þ land mid ealle ut aseald wære · ac þ hi elles swilce foreword worhton þæt þ land eft into þære halgan stowe agifen wære to þam fyrste þe hym ealle gewurde. Ða gewearþ hi þæt se Æþeling sealde þam hyrede .xx. punda wið þam lande ælswa[10] hit stod mid mete 7 mid mannon 7 mid 20 ællon þingon · 7 bruce[11] his dæg · 7 ofer his dæg eode þ land eft into ðære halgan stowe mid mete 7 mid mannon[12] 7 mid eallum þingum swa swa hit ðonne wære. Ðises wæs to gewitnesse Wulfstan archebisceop · 7 Lyfing ƀ · 7 Æþelric ƀ · 7 Æþelsie ƀ · 7 Eadric ealdorman · 7 Æðelmer[13] ealdorman · 7 Æþelfand 25 Æþelmeres[14] suna[15] · 7 Leofsuna abbud æt Cernel · 7 Ælfget

---

[1] A space has been left for the initial capital. [2] byreð, Addit. MS.
[3] al þat, ibid. [4] þat lond, ibid. [5] Om. ibid.
[6] ðys-, K. [7] hir-, T. [8] -don, K.
[9] -werþ, T. [10] al-, K. [11] brice, K.
[12] -un, K., T. [13] -mær, K., T. [14] -mær-, T.
[15] sunu, K.

LXXIII. GRANT OF LANDS BY ULFKETEL TO BURY ST EDMUNDS

Here it is declared in this document that Ulfketel has granted to God and St Edmund the estate at Rickinghall and all that belongs to it, and the estate at Rougham and the estate at Woolpit and the estate at Hinderclay and that at *Redfaresthorpe*, as they stand with their produce and their men and with rights of jurisdiction, as he has owned them. If anyone alters this, God Almighty shall avert his countenance from him on the Day of Judgment, unless he has made amends for it here as quickly as possible.

LXXIV. LEASE OF LAND TO EDMUND THE ÆTHELING BY THE COMMUNITY AT SHERBORNE

Here it is declared in this document that Edmund the Ætheling asked the community at Sherborne for permission to hold the estate at Holcombe. The community did not dare refuse him this [request], but said that they would certainly grant it, if the king and the bishop who was their superior gave their consent. Then they came to an agreement, and the Ætheling and the prior and the chief monks came to the king and informed him of the matter, and asked his consent, and Archbishop Wulfstan acted as spokesman. Then the king said that he did not wish the estate to be given away completely, but that on the contrary they should make such an arrangement that it should be given back to the holy foundation at a time agreed upon by all of them. Then it was agreed that the Ætheling should give the community 20 pounds for the estate as it stood with its produce and its men and everything, and should enjoy it during his lifetime, and after his death it should revert to the holy foundation with its produce and its men and everything as it then was.

The witnesses of this were Archbishop Wulfstan and Bishop Lyfing and Bishop Æthelric and Bishop Æthelsige and Earl Eadric and Earl Æthelmær and Æthelfand, Æthelmær's son, and Leofsunu, Abbot of Cerne, and Ælfgeat, Hength's son, and

LEASE OF LAND TO EDMUND

Hengþes suna[1] · 7 Siwærd[2] · 7 Brihtric reada · 7 ealle þa ildostan ðægnas on Dorsæton · 7 Ealdwine p̄[3] · 7 Wulfric p̄[3] · 7 Lofwine[4] æþelinges discþen · 7 Ælfget 7 Ælwerd[5] his cnihtas · 7 ealle þe geoþre hiredmen.

LXXV. GRANT OF SWINE-PASTURE IN KENT

✠ Her swutelað on ðysan gewrite ꝥ Godwine geánn Leofwine readan ðæs dænnes æt Swiðrædingdænne on éce yrfe · to habbanne 7 to sellanne on dæge 7 æfter dæge ðam ðe him leofost sy · æt þon sceatte ðe Leofsunu him geldan scolde · ꝥ is feowertig penega 7 twa pund 7 eahta ambra cornes. Nu ánn Leofwine þæs dænnes ðon ðe Boctun to handa gegá æfter his dæge. Nu is þyses to gewittnesse · Lyfingc[6] bisceop · 7 Ælfmær abbud · 7 se hired æt Cristescyrcean · 7 se híred æt scē Augustíne · 7 Síred · 7 Ælfsige cild · 7 Æþelric[7] · 7 manig oþer god man binnan byrig 7 bútaN.

LXXVI. A WORCESTERSHIRE MARRIAGE AGREEMENT

✠ Her swutelað on ðysum gewrite ymbe ða forwerda ðe Wulfric 7 se arcebisceop geworhtan ða he begeat ðæs arceb. swuster him to wife · ꝥ is ðæt he behet hyre ꝥ land æt Ealretune 7 æt Ribbedforda hire dæg · 7 he behet hire ꝥ land æt Cnihtewican · ꝥ he wolde hit hire begytan ðreora manna dæg æt ðam hirede on Wincelcumbe · 7 sealde hyre ꝥ land æt Eanulfintune to gyfene 7 to syllenne ðam ðe hire leofest wære on dæge 7 æfter dæge · ðær hire leofest wære · 7 behet hire .L. mances goldes · 7 xxx. manna · 7 xxx. horsa. Nu wæs ðyses to gewitnesse Wulfstan arceb · 7 Leofwine ealdorman · 7 Aeþelstan bisc · 7 Aelfword abb · 7 Brihteh munuc · 7 manig god man toeacan heom · ægðer ge gehadode ge leawede · ꝥ ðas forewerda ðus geworhte wæran. Nu syndon to ðysum forwordan twa gewrita · oþer mid ðam arceb · on Wigereceastre · 7 oþer mid Aeþelstane bisc · on Herforda[8].

[1] *sunu*, K., T.   [2] -*werd*, T.   [3] *p̄r*, T.   [4] *Leof-*, T.
[5] *Ælf-*, K.   [6] -*inge*, K.   [7] *Æðel*[*uu*]*ine*, K.
[8] Smith adds: *Ad imam Pag. vox* (*cyrographum*) *dimidiata.*

Siweard and Brihtric the Red and all the chief thegns of Dorset and Ealdwine the priest and Wulfric the priest and Leofwine, the Ætheling's seneschal, and Ælfgeat and Ælfweard, his *cnihtas*, and all the other members of his household.

LXXV. GRANT OF SWINE-PASTURE IN KENT

✠ Here it is declared in this document that Godwine grants to Leofwine the Red the swine-pasture at Surrenden as a perpetual inheritance, to hold during his lifetime and to grant at his death to whomsoever he pleases, at the price which Leofsunu had to pay him, namely two pounds and forty pence and eight ambers of corn. Now Leofwine grants the pasture to whoever acquires possession of Boughton after his death.

The witnesses of this are Bishop Lyfing and Abbot Ælfmær and the community at Christchurch and the community at St Augustine's and Sired and Ælfsige *cild* and Æthelric and many another good man within the city and outside it.

LXXVI. A WORCESTERSHIRE MARRIAGE AGREEMENT

✠ Here in this document is stated the agreement which Wulfric and the archbishop made when he obtained the archbishop's sister as his wife, namely he promised her the estates at Orleton and Ribbesford for her lifetime, and promised her that he would obtain the estate at Knightwick for her for three lives from the community at Winchcombe, and gave her the estate at Alton to grant and bestow upon whomsoever she pleased during her lifetime or at her death, as she preferred, and promised her 50 mancuses of gold and 30 men and 30 horses.

The witnesses that this agreement was made as stated were Archbishop Wulfstan and Earl Leofwine and Bishop Æthelstan and Abbot Ælfweard and the monk Brihtheah and many good men in addition to them, both ecclesiastics and laymen. There are two copies of this agreement, one in the possession of the archbishop at Worcester and the other in the possession of Bishop Æthelstan at Hereford.

LXXVII. A KENTISH MARRIAGE AGREEMENT

Her swutelaþ on þysan gewrite þa foreward þe Godwine worhte wið Byrhtric þa he his dohter awogode, ꝥ is ærest ꝥ he gæf hire anes pundes gewihta goldes wið þonne[1] þe heo his spæce underfenge, 7 he geuþe hire þæs landes æt Stræte mid eallan þon þe 5 þærto herð, 7 on Burwaramersce oðer healf hund æcera, 7 þærto þrittig oxna, 7 twentig cuna, 7 tyn hors · 7 tyn ðeowmen[2]. Ðis wæs gespecen æt Cincgestune beforan Cnute cincge on Lyfinges arcebiscopes gewitnesse, 7 on þæs hiredes æt Cristescircan, 7 Ælfmeres abbodes, 7 þæs hiredes æt S. Augustine, 7 Æþelwines 10 sciregerefan, 7 Siredes ealdan, 7 Godwines Wulfeages sunu[3], 7 Ælfsige cild, 7 Eadmer æt Burham, 7 Godwine Wulfstanes sunu, 7 Kar[4] þæs cincges cniht, 7 þa man ꝥ mædan fette æt Byrhtlingan, þa eode þyses ealles on borh Ælfgar Syredes sunu, 7 Frerþ preost on Folcestane 7 of Doferan Leofwine preost, 7 15 Wulfsige preost, 7 Eadræd Eadelmes sunu, 7 Leofwine Wærelmes sunu, 7 Cenwold rust, 7 Leofwine Godwines sunu æt Hortune, 7 Leofwine se reade, 7 Godwine Eadgeofe sunu, 7 Leofsunu his broðer: 7 swa hwæðer heora læng libbe fo to eallan ætan[5] ge on ðam lande þe ic heom gæf ge o[6] ælcon þingan. Ðyssa þinga is 20 gecnæwe ælc dohtig man on Kænt, 7 on Suþsexan[7] on ðegenan 7 on ceorlan, 7 þyssa gewrita synd ðreo · an[8] is æt Cristescyrcan, oðer æt S. Augustine, ꝥ[9] þridde hæfð Byrhtric self.

LXXVIII. ACCOUNT OF A HEREFORDSHIRE LAWSUIT

Her swutelað on þissum gewrite · ꝥ an scirgemot sæt æt Ægelnoðes stane be Cnutes dæge cinges þær sæton Æþelstan ƀ 25 7 Ranig ealdorman · 7 Edwine þæs ealdormannes[10] 7 Leofwine Wulsiges sunu · 7 Þurcill hwita 7 Tofig pruda com þær

---

[1] ðone, K.; þon, T.; ðon, E.
[2] þeowinen, T.
[3] suna, T.
[4] Sic; Kar[l], K., T., E.
[5] Sic; æ[h]tan, K., T., E.
[6] Sic; o[n], K., T., E.
[7] Sud-, E.
[8] æn, T.
[9] and, K., E.; 7, T.
[10] Probably sunu should be supplied.

LXXVII. A KENTISH MARRIAGE AGREEMENT

Here is declared in this document the agreement which Godwine made with Brihtric when he wooed his daughter. In the first place he gave her a pound's weight of gold, to induce her to accept his suit, and he granted her the estate at Street with all that belongs to it, and 150 acres at Burmarsh and in addition 30 oxen and 20 cows and 10 horses and 10 slaves.

This agreement was made at Kingston before King Cnut, with the cognisance of Archbishop Lyfing and the community at Christchurch, and Abbot Ælfmær and the community at St Augustine's, and the sheriff Æthelwine and Sired the old and Godwine, Wulfheah's son, and Ælfsige *cild* and Eadmær of Burham and Godwine, Wulfstan's son, and Car[l], the king's *cniht*. And when the maiden was brought from Brightling Ælfgar, Sired's son, and Frerth, the priest of Folkestone, and the priests Leofwine and Wulfsige from Dover, and Edred, Eadhelm's son, and Leofwine, Wærhelm's son, and Cenwold *rust* and Leofwine, son of Godwine of Horton, and Leofwine the Red and Godwine, Eadgifu's son, and Leofsunu his brother acted as security for all this. And whichever of them lives the longer shall succeed to all the property both in land and everything else which I have given them. Every trustworthy man in Kent and Sussex, whether thegn or commoner, is cognisant of these terms.

There are three of these documents; one is at Christchurch, another at St Augustine's, and Brihtric himself has the third.

LXXVIII. ACCOUNT OF A HEREFORDSHIRE LAWSUIT

Here it is declared in this document that a shire-meeting sat at Aylton in King Cnut's time. There were present Bishop Æthelstan and Earl Ranig and Edwin, the Earl's [son], and Leofwine, Wulfsige's son, and Thurkil the White; and Tofi the Proud

ACCOUNT OF A

on þæs cinges ærende · 7 þær wæs Bryning scirgerefa · 7
Ægelgeard æt Frome · 7 Leofwine æt Frome · 7 Godric æt
Stoce 7 ealle þa þegnas on Herefordscire · þa com þær farende
to þam gemote · Edwine Enneawnes[1] sunu 7 spæc þær on his
5 agene modor æfter sumon dæle landes · þ̄ wæs Weolintun 7
Crydes læh · þa acsode se bisceop hwa sceolde andswerian for
his moder · þa 7sweorode Þurcil hwita 7 sæde þ̄ he sceolde
gif he ða talu cuðe · þa he ða talu na ne cuðe þa sceawode
man þreo þegnas of þam gemote þær[2] ðær heo wæs · 7 þ̄ wæs
10 æt Fæliglæ · þ̄ wæs Leofwine æt Frome · 7 Ægelsig þe reada ·
7 Wynsige[3] scægðman · 7 þa ða heo to hire comon þa acsodon
heo hwylce talu heo hæfde · ymbe þa land þe hire sunu æfter
spæc · þa sæde heo þ̄ heo nan land næfde þe him aht to ge-
byrede · 7 gebealh heo swiðe eorlice wið hire sunu[4] · 7 gecleopode
15 ða Leofflæde hire magan to hire · Þurcilles wif · 7 beforan
heom to hire þus cwæð her sit Leoffled min mage þe ic geann
ægðer ge mines landes ge mines goldes ge rægles ge reafes ge
ealles þæs ðe ic ah æfter minon dæge · 7 heo syððan to ðam
þegnon cwæð · doð þegnlice 7 wel · abeodað mine ærende to
20 ðam gemote beforan eallon þam godan mannum 7 cyðaþ heom
hwæm ic mines landes geunnen hæbbe · 7 ealre minre æhte ·
7 minon agenan suna · næfre nan þingc · 7 biddað heom eallum
beon þisses to gewitnesse · 7 heo ða swæ dydon · ridon to ðam
gemote · 7 cyddon eallon þam godan mannum hwæt heo on
25 heom geled hæfde · þa astod Þurcyll hwita up on þam gemote
7 bæd ealle þa ðegnas syllan his wife þa land clæne þe hire
mage hire geuðe · 7 heo swa dydon · 7 Þurcyll rad ða to sc̄e
Æðelberhtes mynstre be ealles þæs folces leafe 7 gewitnesse
7 let settan on ane Cristes boc.

---

[1] *Eanwene*, K.
[2] [*ða sceoldon ridan*] *ðær*, K.
[3] *Winsig*, K., T.
[4] *suna*, K.

came there on the king's business, and Bryning the sheriff was present, and Æthelgeard of Frome and Leofwine of Frome and Godric of Stoke and all the thegns of Herefordshire. Then Edwin, *Enneawnes* son, came travelling to the meeting and sued his own mother for a certain piece of land, namely Wellington and Cradley. Then the bishop asked whose business it was to answer for his mother, and Thurkil the White replied that it was his business to do so, if he knew the claim. As he did not know the claim, three thegns were chosen from the meeting [to ride] to the place where she was, namely at Fawley, and these were Leofwine of Frome and Æthelsige the Red and Winsige the seaman, and when they came to her they asked her what claim she had to the lands for which her son was suing her. Then she said that she had no land that in any way belonged to him, and was strongly incensed against her son, and summoned to her her kinswoman, Leofflæd, Thurkil's wife, and in front of them said to her as follows: 'Here sits Leofflæd, my kinswoman, to whom, after my death, I grant my land and my gold, my clothing and my raiment and all that I possess.' And then she said to the thegns: 'Act rightly and like thegns; announce my message to the meeting before all the worthy men, and tell them to whom I have granted my land and all my property, and not a thing to my own son, and ask them all to be witnesses of this.' And they did so; they rode to the meeting and informed all the worthy men of the charge that she had laid upon them. Then Thurkil the White stood up in the meeting and asked all the thegns to give his wife the lands unreservedly which her kinswoman had granted her, and they did so. Then Thurkil rode to St Æthelbert's minster, with the consent and cognisance of the whole assembly, and had it recorded in a gospel book.

LXXIX. AGREEMENT BETWEEN THE COMMUNITY AT WORCESTER AND FULDER

✠ Her swutelað on [þissum gewrite] ymb¹ þa foreward þe wæron geworhte betwux þam hirede on Wihgeraceastre · 7 Fuldre · ꝥ is ꝥ he hæbbe ꝥ land æt Ludintune .III. gear ⸱⸍ for þam ðreom pundum þe he lænde · 7 þone · bryce þe on þam lande beo .III. 5 gear · 7 binnon þrym gearum · agife ꝥ land þam hirede · mid² swa myclum swa se hired him on hand sette · ꝥ synd .XII. þeowe men · 7 .II. gesylhðe oxan · 7 .I. hund sceapa · 7 half hundred foðra cornes. And seðe þas foreward tobreke ne³ gewurðe hit him næfre forgifen · ac beo 'he' fordemed into helle wite · 7 þær 10 mid deofle wunige oð to domes dæge.

LXXX. AGREEMENT BETWEEN ARCHBISHOP ÆTHELNOTH AND TOKI

✠ Her swuteliað on ðisse Cristes bec Æþelnoðes arceb forword 7 Tokiges embe ꝥ land æt Healtune · ꝥ wæs ꝥ Tokig com to Hrisbeorgan to ðam arceb syþþan Æðelflæd his wif forðfaren wæs · 7 cydde him Wulfnoðes cwyde ꝥ he ꝥ land becweden 15 hæfde into Xp̄s cyrcean æfter his dæge 7 his wifes · 7 bæd þone arceb ꝥ he ꝥ land habban moste his dæg · 7 æfter his dæge ꝥ hit lage into Xp̄s cyrcean mid eallum þingum þe he þæron getilian mihte unbesacen · 7 cwæð ꝥ he wolde þam b þances kepan 7 his mannum · 7 se arceb him þæs tiðude · 7 sæde ꝥ he 20 riht wið hine gedon hæfde ꝥ he sylf him for ðam cwyde secgean wolde · þeh he hit ær ful georne wiste · 7 ðises wæs to gewitnysse Æþelstan æt Bleddehlæwe · 7 Leofwine his sunu · 7 Leofric æt Eaningadene · 7 feala oðra godra cnihta · þeh we hi ealle ne nemnon · 7 eall ðæs arcebiscopes hired · ge gehadude ge læwede.

[1] The MS. has *swutelað on ymb*; *swutelaðon*, K., T.
[2] *into*, K.   [3] *he*, K., T.

LXXIX. AGREEMENT BETWEEN THE COMMUNITY AT WORCESTER AND FULDER

☩ Here is stated in [this document] the agreement made between the community at Worcester and Fulder, namely that he should hold the estate at Luddington for three years in return for the three pounds which he lent, and should have the usufruct of the estate for three years, and by the end of three years should return the estate to the community with the full equipment supplied him by the community, namely 12 slaves and 2 teams of oxen and 100 sheep and 50 fothers of corn. And if anyone breaks this agreement, he shall never be forgiven, but shall be condemned to the torment of hell, and shall dwell there with the devil until Doomsday.

LXXX. AGREEMENT BETWEEN ARCHBISHOP ÆTHELNOTH AND TOKI

☩ Here is declared in this gospel book the agreement made by Archbishop Æthelnoth and Toki with regard to the estate at Halton. It happened as follows, that Toki came to the archbishop at Risborough, after Æthelflæd his wife was dead, and informed him of Wulfnoth's will—that he had bequeathed the estate to Christchurch after his own and his wife's death—and asked the archbishop that he might have the estate during his lifetime, and after his death it should pass to Christchurch uncontested with everything that he could produce upon it; and he said that he would be very grateful to the bishop and his men [for this concession]. And the archbishop granted him his request, and said that he had acted justly towards him in voluntarily speaking to him himself about the will, although he (the archbishop) was already perfectly familiar with its terms. And the witnesses of this were Æthelstan of Bledlow and Leofwine his son and Leofric of *Eaningadene* and many other good *cnihtas*, although we do not name them all, and all the archbishop's household, both ecclesiastics and laymen.

LXXXI. LEASE OF LAND BY ABBOT ÆLFWEARD AND THE COMMUNITY AT EVESHAM TO ÆTHELMÆR

Ðis syndon þa foreword þe Ælfwerd abb 7 se hired on Eoueshamme worhtan wið Æðelmær þa ða hi him ƀ land sealdon æt Norðtune · wiþ .III. pundon þreora manna dæg · ƀ syndon .III. hida to inware · 7 oðer healf to utware swa swa he hit gebohte
5 þa ða hit weste læg · æt Hacune 7 æt Leofrice · 7 æt ealre scire · ƀ is ƀ we hit unnon him on Godes est · 7 on Sca Marian · 7 on þæs halgan weres S...[1] Egwines · þe hit into þam mynstre beget · 7 gange ægðer ge cyricsceat ge teoðunge into þam halgan mynstre swa he mycele þearfe ah · ƀ hi don · 7 toll 7 team sy
10 agifen into þam mynstre butan he hit geearnian mæge to þam ðe þæñ ah mynstres geweald · 7 æfter þreora manna dæge gange ƀ land in mid .I. men · 7 mid .VI. oxan · 7 mid .XX. sceapum · 7 mid .XX. æcerum gesawenes cornes.

7 þyssa gewrita synd .III. an lið on Wigracestre æt Sca Marian
15 mynstre · 7 oðer lið on Eofeshamme · 7 þridde hæfð Æðelmer. Se þe þis gehealde gehealde hine God · 7 se ðe hit awende oððe gelytlige · gelytlige God his mede on þam toweardum life · butan he hit ær his ende þe deoppor gebete · 7 þis wæs gedon be þyssa witena gewytnessæ þe herwið nyðan awritene standað · ƀ is ærest
20 Ælfgeofu seo hlæfdie þe þæs mynstres walt ·

7 Wulfstan arce- biscop.	7 Leofsige abb.	7 Leofric · 7 Eadwine.
7 Leofsige biscop.	7 Afa abb.	7 Byrhtteg munuc.
7 Byrhtwold biscop.	7 Hacun eorl.	7 Byrhtwine · 7 Ælf-
25 7 Ælfsige abb.	7 Eglaf eorl.	sige m̄.[2]
7 Ælfwerd abb.	7 Leofwine ealdor- man.	

[1] Illegible because of a stain on the MS.
[2] 7 Ælfsige m̄. is written at the side in much smaller handwriting.

LXXXI. LEASE OF LAND BY ABBOT ÆLFWEARD AND THE COMMUNITY AT EVESHAM TO ÆTHELMÆR

These are the terms which Abbot Ælfweard and the community at Evesham have made with Æthelmær when they granted him for 3 pounds the estate at Norton for three lives—it consists of 3 hides for home service and 1½ hides for national service—just as he bought it, when it was lying waste, from Hakon and Leofric and the whole shire. And we grant it to him with the blessing of God and St Mary and of the holy man St Ecgwine who acquired it for the monastery. And both church dues and tithes shall go to the holy monastery, as he has much need [to see] that they do, and [payments for] toll and vouching to warranty shall be rendered to the monastery, unless he can acquire them from whoever is in control of the monastery at the time. And after three lives the estate shall pass to the monastery with 1 man and 6 oxen and 20 sheep and 20 acres of sown corn.

And there are three of these documents. One is at St Mary's monastery in Worcester, and one is at Evesham, and Æthelmær has the third. May God uphold him who upholds this, and if anyone alters or curtails it, God shall curtail his reward in the future life, unless he make amends for it before his death as fully as possible.

This was done with the cognisance of the councillors whose names are herewith recorded below, namely first the Lady Ælfgifu, who governs the monastery...

LXXXII. CHARTER OF CNUT TO CHRISTCHURCH, CANTERBURY

✠ On ðas hegestes Godes · 7 ures hlauordes hælendes xp̄es naman · ure halige 7 ure rihtwise fæderes mid soðre gefæstnunge · 7 mid gelomrædre menunge us gemenegið þ̄ we ðone ælmihti God ðe we luuiað[1] 7 we onbeleuað mid inweardre[2] gelustful-
5 nesse ure heorten 7 mid geornfulnesse godre wurke unatirendlice ondræden 7 luuian · Forði ðe he scel geldan edlean ealre[3] ure weorke on domesdæge æfter æghwilces mannes earnunge · 7 forði mid ðam[4] hehlicastan gewinne ures modes swinke we him to gefolgienne þeahðe we gesæmde beon mid ðare berdene ðás[5]
10 deadlices liues · 7 ðare gewitendre æhte þises middaneardes beon awémde · þeahhwædere[6] we magen gebecgen ða éce meden ðas heouenlices liues mid þam riosenden welan; 7 forði ic CNVT ðurh Godes geue Ænglelandes kining 7 ealre ðare eglande þe ðærto licgeð · legge upan xp̄es weoued inne[7] Cantwareberig[8]
15 mines heouodes kinehelm mid minen agenen hánden to ðas ilcen menstres freme · 7 ic ánn þam ilikan menstre to ðare munece bigleoue ða hæuene on Sandwic 7 ealle ða lændinge 7 þa gehrihte[9] of ðam ilkan wætere of ægder[10] healue ðas streames age land seðe hit age · fram Pipernæsse to Mærcesfleote · swa þ̄
20 ðonne hit bið full flód 7 þ̄ scip bið aflote · swa feorr swa mæg an taperæx beon geworpen ut of ðam scipe up on þ̄ land þa gereflanges of xp̄es circean underfon ða gerihte. Ne næfre nan man an anes kennes wisan næfð nænne anweald[11] on þare ilicere[12] hæue'ne' butan ða munekes of xp̄es circean · 7 heore is þ̄ scip
25 7 si[13] ouerfæreld þare hæuene · 7 si[13] tolne of ealle scipen bi þas ðe hit beo 7 cume ðanon þe hit cume þe to þare ilicare[12] hæuene æt Sandwic cumð · 7 gif aht is in ðare micelre sǽ wiðutan ðare hæuene swa micel swa seo sǽ heo mæst wiðteohð 7 git anes mannes længe[14] þe healt ænne[15] spreot on his hand 7 strecð hine
30 swa feor swa he mæg aræcen into ðare[16] sǽ þ̄ is ðare muneke ·

[1] luf-, T.　　　　[2] -weordre, T.　　　　[3] alre, T.
[4] þan, T.　　　　[5] ðæs, K., T.　　　　[6] -hwæð-, K., T.
[7] in, T.　　　　　[8] -byrig, K.　　　　　[9] gerihte, T.
[10] -ðer, K., T.　　[11] -wæld, T.　　　　　[12] ilik-, K.
[13] se, K., T.　　　[14] lenge, T.　　　　　[15] anne, T.
[16] ðere, T.

LXXXII. CHARTER OF CNUT TO CHRISTCHURCH, CANTERBURY

✠ In the name of the most high God and of our Lord the Saviour Christ. Our holy and our righteous fathers with true insistence and with frequent admonition remind us that we should dread and love untiringly with inward joyfulness of heart and with zeal in good works the Almighty God whom we love and believe in. Since he shall requite all our works on the Day of Judgment, according to each man's deserts, let us strive with the utmost endeavour of our hearts to follow him. Although we are laden with the burden of this mortal life and defiled with the transitory possessions of this world, yet we may purchase the eternal reward of the heavenly life with these crumbling riches, and therefore I, Cnut, by the grace of God King of England and of all the adjacent islands, lay the royal crown from my head with my own hands upon the altar of Christ in Canterbury for the benefit of the said monastery, and I grant to the said monastery for the support of the monks the haven at Sandwich and all the landing places and the water dues from both sides of the river from Pepperness to *Mærcesfleote*, whoever owns the land, in such wise that when it is high tide and a ship is afloat, the officers of Christchurch shall receive the dues from as far inland as can be reached by a small axe thrown from the ship. And no one shall ever in any kind of way have any control in the said haven except the monks of Christchurch, and theirs shall be the ship and the ferrying across the haven and the toll of every ship that comes to the said haven at Sandwich, whatever it be and wherever it come from. And if there is anything in the open sea outside the haven, the rights of the monks shall extend as far as the utmost limit to which the sea recedes and the length of a man in addition who holds a pole in his hand and stretches it as far as he can reach into the sea, and half of all that is found

CHARTER OF CNUT

7 eal þ ðe of ðas healue þare middelsæ wurð gefunden 7 to
Sandwic gebroht · bi hit scrud · bi hit net · oððe wæpne · oððe
isen · gold oððe seoluer þ healue dæl sceal beon[1] ðare muneke ·
7 þ oðer dæl scel beliuan þam ðe hit findæð · 7 gif ænig oðer
5 gewrit heoneforð wurð forðgebroht þe beo heortoforen gemaked
þe on æniges kinnes wisen beo geðuht þissere ure gefæstnunge
to wiðcweðene þ gewrit beo geworpen musen to gnagene oððe
on fere to forbærnenne · 7 se ðe hit forðbrængð beo swilces hades
swilc he beo bio he gehealden for æscegeswap · 7 mid ealre ðare
10 unwurðreste scame beo he gescænt 7 of eallan þan mannen[2] ðe
ðær gehænde beoð mid ane mode wurðe[3] he gescuned[4] · 7 seo
strange gefæstnunge þi's'sere landboc æfrema heoneforð beo
gestranged · 7 ægder[5] mid ðas[6] ælmihtiges[7] Godes ealderdome
7 mire[8] · 7 ealre minre ðegene gefæstnunge togænes ealre þare
15 wiðcweðendre smæigunge on ecnesse staðelfæst 7 unawægendlic
mid ðurhwuniende rihte beo gefæstned · 7 gif ænig is þ gewilnað
oððe to brekene oððe to gelitligene mid toðundene modignesse
þas ure gefæstnunge ʒ́ wite he hine selfne amansumod fram
Gode 7 fram eallen[2] his halgan · butan he toforan ðam deaðe mid
20 wurðe behriwsunge gebete þ he unrihtwislice forgelte. Ðeos
landboc wæs gewriten on ðan þusende 7 ðri 7 twentehte gære
fram ures hlauordes hælendes x̄p̄es akennednesse · mid ðare
geðwærunge þissere manne þe here naman heræfter beoð gewritene[9]

25 ✠ Ic CNVT se kining of Ænglelande þas gefæstnunge of ðisen
gewrite unawendedlice gefæstni.
✠ Ic Ægelnoð[10] erceb of Cantwareberig þas sundergeoue mid þam
halige tacne getremde.
✠ Ic Ælfric se erceb of Euerwic ðas ilces[11] kinges godne wille mid
30 ðam halege[12] rode tacne gefæstni.
✠ Ic Ælfwine[13] se b of Lundene geðwærðe.
✠ Ic Ælfwine[14] b of Wincæstre[15] gæf geðwærunge.
✠ Ic Brihwald b Coruiniensis ęcclę geðwærde.
✠ Ic Ægelric b of Dorsætscire gefæstnede.
35 ✠ Ic Ælmer b.   ✠ Ic Wulnoð abb.   ✠ Ic Ægelric .m̄.
✠ Ic Godwine b.   ✠ Ic Godwine eorl.   ✠ Ic Ælfwine .m̄.
✠ Ic Brihtwine b.   ✠ Ic Ægelaf eorl.   ✠ Ic Brihtric .m̄.
✠ Ic Æðelstan b.   ✠ Ic Ðrim eorl.   ✠ Ic Leofric .m̄.
✠ Ic Ælmær abb.   ✠ Ic Yric eorl.   ✠ Ic Siræd .m̄.
40 ✠ Ic Brihtmær abb.   ✠ Ic Ðord minister.   ✠ Ic Godwine .m̄.
✠ Ic Brihtwine[16] abb.   ✠ Ic Agemund .m̄.   ✠ Ic Eadmær .m̄.

TO CHRISTCHURCH, CANTERBURY 161

on this side of the 'middle sea' and brought to Sandwich, whether it be clothes or nets or weapons, iron, gold, or silver, shall fall to the monks and the other half shall be left to those who find it. And if any other document is henceforth produced which was made heretofore and which in any kind of way seems to gainsay what is here established, that document shall be cast to mice to gnaw or into the fire to be burned, and he who produces it, whatever his rank, shall be regarded as the sweepings of ashes and confounded with the most ignominious shame and with one accord shunned by all the men who are nearby. And what is firmly established by this charter shall be enforced for all time henceforth, and with the authority of Almighty God and with mine and with the ratification of all my thegns it shall be established with lasting justice, steadfast and immovable forever against all attempts to gainsay it. And if there is anyone who attempts with swollen pride either to violate or to diminish what we here establish, he shall find himself accursed by God and by all his saints, unless before his death he make amends with due repentance for the sin that he has unrighteously committed.

This charter was written in the year 1023 after the birth of our Lord, the Saviour Christ, with the consent of the men whose names are recorded hereafter...

---

[1] *bion*, K., T.
[2] *-an*, T.
[3] *wurð*, T.
[4] *-scunned*, T.
[5] *-ðer*, K., T.
[6] *ðæs*, K., T.
[7] *Al-*, T.
[8] *minre*, T.
[9] T. omits the witnesses.
[10] *Æðel-*, K.
[11] *ilk-*, K.
[12] *-egen*, K.
[13] For *Ælfwig*.
[14] For *Ælfsige*.
[15] *Winccest-*, K.
[16] For *Brihtwig*.

LXXXIII. LAWSUIT ABOUT A WORCESTERSHIRE ESTATE

✠ Her swutelað on ðissum gewrite [þæt]¹ Æþelstan bisceop gebohte æt Leofrice æt Blacewellan fif hide landes · æt Intebyrgan be Æþelredes cynges leafe · 7 be Ælfeges arcebisceopes gewitnesse · 7 be Wulfstanes Arcebisceopes 7 be ealra þæra
5 witena þe ða on Englalande lifes wæron · mid ten pundan reodes goldes · 7 hwites seolfres · unforboden 7 unbesacan · to geofene 7 to syllanne · ær dæge 7 æfter dæge · sibban oððe fremdan þær him leofost wære; 7 Se cyng het þone arcebisceop Wulfstan þærto boc settan · 7 Æþelstane bisceope · boc 7 land betæcan
10 unnendere heortan; Þa æfter þysan manegum gearum · soc Wulfstan 7 his sunu Wulfric on sum þæt land · þa ferde se bisceop to sciregemote to Wigeranceastre 7 draf þær his spræce · þa sealde Leofwine ealdor[m]an 7 Hacu[n]² 7 Leofric · 7 eal seo scir his land clæne þa he hit unforbodan 7 unbesacan bohte³ 7
15 settan dæg to þæt man to ðam lande scolde faran · 7 þa ilcan þe him ær landgemære læddon hit⁴ e....an⁵ · 7 cwædan gif ða landgemære ealswa wæron swa man heo on fruman lædde · þæt se bisceop þæt land fulriht⁶ ahte · þa com se bisceop þærto 7 se þe him land sealde 7 þa þe⁷ him ær⁸ [to gewit]nesse⁹ wæron ·
20 7 com Wulfstan 7 his sunu 7 þa þe hyra geferan wæron · 7 heo ealle þa þa landgemære geridan eal swa heo man on fruman þam bisceope lædde · 7 heo ealle cwædan þe [þær æt]¹⁰ wæron þæt se bisceop fulriht þæt land ahte · þa se þær geanwyrde¹¹ wæs þe him land sealde. Spæcon ða Leofrices freond · 7 Wulfstanes
25 freond · þæt hit betere wære þ heora seht togæ......de¹² þonne hy ænige [sa]ce¹³ hym betweonan heoldan ⸴ worhtan¹⁴ þa hyra seht · þæt wæs þ[æ]t Leofric sealde Wulfstane 7 his suna · an

---

¹ There are two holes in the MS. hence the lacunae.
² *Hacc..*, Hi., K.   ³ *behæt*, Hi., K.   ⁴ *hatt*, T.
⁵ Not more than about four letters seem to be missing; Hi. and K. have E[þelst]an.
⁶ *fulrihte*, Hi., K., T.   ⁷ *he*, Hi., K.   ⁸ Om. Hi., K.
⁹ *to [wit]nesse*, Hi., K.; *[to wit]nesse*, T., Bond.
¹⁰ *[hyre]*, Hi.; *[ðær]*, K., T.
¹¹ *þam getenwyrde*, Bond; *þar geanwyrde þæs*, T.
¹² *togæd[dre dy]de*, Hi.; *togæd[dre wur]de*, K.; *togæ[dere wur]de*, T.
¹³ *sace*, Hi., K.; *[spæ]ce*, Bond.   ¹⁴ *sohtan*, Hi., K., T.; *forletan* Bond.

LXXXIII. LAWSUIT ABOUT A WORCESTERSHIRE ESTATE

✠ Here it is declared in this document that Bishop Æthelstan bought 5 hides of land at Inkberrow from Leofric of Blackwell with King Æthelred's leave and the cognisance of Archbishop Ælfheah and Archbishop Wulfstan and all the councillors who were alive at the time in England, for 10 pounds of red gold and white silver, unopposed and uncontested, to give and grant them before or at his death to kinsmen or strangers, whichever he preferred. And the king commanded Archbishop Wulfstan to draw up a charter to this effect, and gladly entrust both charter and land to Bishop Æthelstan. Then many years after this Wulfstan and his son Wulfric brought a claim against part of the estate. The bishop thereupon went to the shire-meeting at Worcester and urged his suit there. Then Earl Leofwine and Hakon and Leofric and all the shire granted him his estate without reservation, as he had bought it unopposed and uncontested, and appointed a day for going to the estate, and the same people who had traced the boundaries for him [should do so again], and they said that if the boundaries were the same as when they were first traced, the bishop was the rightful owner of the estate. Then the bishop and the man who sold him the estate and those who had been his witnesses came to the appointed place, and Wulfstan and his son and their companions came, and they all rode round the boundaries, as they had been first traced for the bishop, and all who were there said that the bishop was the rightful owner of the estate, and the man who sold him the land acknowledged it to be so. Then both Leofric's friends and Wulfstan's said that it would be better for them to come to an agreement than to keep up any quarrel between them. Thereupon they made their agreement as follows, that Leofric should give Wulfstan and his son a pound and take an

164 LAWSUIT ABOUT A

pund · 7 twegra þegna að 7 wære himsylf þridde · þæt he [on
þ]am¹ ilcan wolde beon gehealden gif seo spæc to Leofrice eode
s[wa s]wa heo þa wæs to Wulfstane gega[n] · þis wæs ur[e] ealra
seht; Wulfstan 7 his sunu² sealdon þa þæt land clæne Leofrice ·
5 7 Leofric 7 [W]u[lfs]tan · 7 Wulfric · þam bisceope clæne land
7 unbesacan · ær dæge 7 æfter to gyfanne þær him leofost wære;
Her swutelað seo gewitnes 7 se borh³ þe þær æt wæron · þæt
wæs ærest se bisceop 7 Le[ofric]⁴ · 7 Wulfstan · 7 Brihtwine ·
7 Cynsig⁵ · 7 Wynstan · 7 Ægelwig munuc · 7 Ælwine mæsse-
10 preost · 7 Ælmær mæssepreost · 7 Wulfric mæssepreost · 7
Cyneword æt Pebbewurðy · 7 Ælewig⁶ ....nham⁷ · 7
Eadwig his mæg · 7 Wulfri[c] æt Cloddesheale · 7 Sæword æt
Uptuny · 7 Wulfric æt Bynningtune · 7 Wulfsig Madding · 7
mænig god cniht toeacan þysan; Nu syndan þissa gewrita þreo ·
15 an on Wigernaceastre æt SCA Marian þær⁸ þæt land toherð ·
7 oðer on Hereforda æt Sce Æþelbrihte · 7 þridde a mid þam
þe þæt land on hande⁹ stande; God ælmihtig þone gehealde þe
þis wille rihtlice healdan · 7 gif ænig man þonne seo þe þis
awendan wille · God ælmihtig · 7 SCA MARIA · 7 ealle his
20 leofan halgan þæne aniðerige ægþær ge her on life ge þær¹⁰ he
længast wunian sceal · buton he hit þe deoppor ær geb[e]te swa
bisceop him tæce.

LXXXIV. TYPES OF TENURE AMONG CHURCH LANDS IN YORKSHIRE

Ðis is seo socn into Scyreburna mid folcrihte · twa dæl of Cauda ·
7 Wicstow eal · 7 ufer Soleby eal · 7 twa oxnagang on Fleaxlege ·
25 7 healf Bernlege · 7 eal Breiðetun butan healf plogesland · 7 eall
Byrne · 7 eall Burhtun butan healf plogesland · 7 eall Gæiteford ·
7 eall twegen Þorpas · 7 twa Hyrst eal · 7 twa Haðelsǽ eall · 7 fif
oxnagang on þriddan Haðelsǽ · 7 healf Byrcene · 7 eall Suðtun ·
7 eall Byrum¹¹ 7 Breiðetun eal · 7 Broðertun eall · 7 eall Faren-

---

¹ he ðam, Hi., K.; he [þ]am, Bond, T. ² suna, Hi., K.
³ boch, K. ⁴ L[eofric]e, Hi., K. ⁵ -sige, T.
⁶ -sig, Hi., K. ⁷ [æt] Sec[can]ham, Hi., K.; [æt Secca]nham, T.
⁸ þæs, Hi., Bond. ⁹ haade, Hi. ¹⁰ þær þær, Hi., K.
¹¹ Byrnum, Stevenson.

oath along with two thegns that he would have been satisfied with the same, if the case had turned out for him as it had for Wulfstan. This was the agreement made by all of us. Wulfstan and his son thereupon gave the estate without reservation to Leofric, and Leofric and Wulfstan and Wulfric gave it without reservation or controversy to the bishop to be granted before or at his death to whomsoever he pleased.

Here are declared the witnesses and sureties who were present, namely first the bishop, and Leofric and Wulfstan and Brihtwine and Cynesige and Wynstan and the monk Æthelwig and the priest Ælfwine and the priest Æthelmær and the priest Wulfric and Cyneweard of Pebworth and Æthelwig of [Fecka]nham (?) and Edwy his kinsman and Wulfric of Cladswell and Siweard of Upton and Wulfric of *Bynningtune* and Wulfsige Madding and many a good *cniht* besides these.

There are three of these documents; one is at St Mary's in Worcester to which the estate belongs, and the second at St Æthelbert's in Hereford, and the third shall remain with those in whose possession the estate is. May God Almighty uphold him who is willing to observe this duly, and if there is anyone who attempts to alter this, God Almighty and St Mary and all his beloved saints shall abase him both here in this life and there where he must longest dwell, unless he has made amends as fully as possible, as the bishop directs him.

LXXXIV. TYPES OF TENURE AMONG CHURCH LANDS IN YORKSHIRE

This is the soke which belongs to Sherburn in accordance with public law: two-thirds of Cawood and the whole of Wistow and the whole of Upper Selby and two oxgangs in Flaxley and half of Barlow and the whole of Brayton, except half a ploughland, and the whole of Burn and the whole of Burton, except half a ploughland, and the whole of Gateforth and the whole of the two Thorpes and the whole of the two Hirsts and the whole of the two Haddleseys and five oxgangs in the third Haddlesey and half of Birkin and the whole of Sutton and the whole of Byrom and the whole of Brayton and the whole of Brotherton and the

burne · butan healf þridde plogesland · 7 twa plogesland on Ledesham · 7 an on Niwan Þorp · 7 eall Miclafeld · 7 eall Hyllum · 7 eall Fristun · 7 eal¹ Lundby · 7 eall Styfetun · 7 eall Myleford · 7 eall Fenntún · butan healf plogesland · 7 twa
5 plogesland 7 fif oxnagang on Barcestune · 7 eall Luteringtun · 7 eall Hehferðehegðe · 7² eall Hudelestun;; On Scireburnan toecan þam inlande syndan .IIII. hida weorclandes · 7 on Luteringatune .III. hida 7 on Barcestune .I. hid · 7 fif oxnagang · 7 of Styfingtune tune þreora oxnagang.
10 7 on Wicstowe twegea oxnagang · 7 on Cawuda twa dæl þæs landes is agenland into Scireburnan · 7 Fentun is læn oðer healf plogesland; INto Ottanleage .IIII. plogaland · 7 on Bægeltune .II. On Hafecesweorðe .II. On oðeran Hafecesweorðe .II. On Dentune
15 .II. on Timbel oðer healf plogesland. On Ectune healf plogesland · þis is unbesacen agenland; 7 þærto eacan hyrað þas socnland³. Into Ottanleage. On Ottanleage .II. ploh · 7 on Bældune .II. 7 on Hafecesweorðe .II. 7 on 'o'ðeran Hafecesweorðe .II. On Scefinge .I. On Mensingtune .III. On Burh-
20 leage .VI. On Meðeltune .III. On Yllicleage syx oxnagang. On Dentune .II. ploh. On Cliftune .I. On Biceratune .III. On Fearnleage .IIII. On Ectune oðer healf. On Pofle .III. On Lindeleage .III.
Æt Rypum ærest milegemet on ælce healfe · 7 Biscoptun is
25 in on þam .II. hida · 7 Carlewic .V. hida · 7 healf Munecatun his agenland feorðe healf hide · 7 healf Mercingatun · þridde healf hide. On Herelesho healf hid. On Stodlege .III. hida. On Suðtune oþer healf hide. On Nunnewic .III. hida. On Þorntune .II. hida;
30 7 þys synd weste land. An is Sallege. Oðer is Grantelege · þridde is Efestun · 7 feorðe is Wifeleshealh · 7 .V. is healf Cnearresweorð; Þonne syndan þis preostaland · on Westwic .IIII. hida. On Norð Staulege .IIII. On Gyðingdale .I. hide. On Mercingtune ·
35 þreo oxnagang. On Munecatune þreo oxnagang. On Hotune .II. oxnagang;

¹ eall, Stevenson. ² Om. ibid.
³ -lande, ibid.

CHURCH LANDS IN YORKSHIRE 167

whole of Fairburn, except 2½ ploughlands, and two ploughlands in Ledsham and one in Newthorpe and the whole of Micklefield and the whole of Hillam and the whole of Fryston and the whole of Lumby and the whole of Steeton and the whole of Milford and the whole of Fenton, except half a ploughland, and two ploughlands and five oxgangs in Barkston and the whole of Lotherton and the whole of *Hehferðehegðe* and the whole of Huddleston.

At Sherburn in addition to the demesne land there are four hides of 'service land', and three hides at Lotherton, and one hide and five oxgangs at Barkston, and three oxgangs of the manor of Steeton.

And two oxgangs at Wistow and two-thirds of the land at Cawood is land held in absolute possession belonging to Sherburn, and 1½ ploughlands at Fenton are held on lease.

To Otley [belong] four ploughlands and at Baildon two, at Hawksworth two, at the other Hawksworth two, at Denton two, at Timble 1½ ploughlands, at *Ectune* half a ploughland—this is incontestably land held in absolute possession. And these soke-lands in addition belong to Otley—at Otley two ploughlands and at Baildon two and at Hawksworth two and at the other Hawksworth two, at Chevin one, at Menston three, at Burley six, at Middleton three, at Ilkley six oxgangs, at Denton two ploughlands, at Clifton one, at *Biceratune* three, at Farnley four, at *Ectune* 1½, at Poole three, at Lindley three.

At Ripon first a mile's space on each side. And Bishopton is included in the two hides, and five hides at *Carlewic*, and the half of Monkton is land held in absolute possession—3½ hides—and half of Markington—2½ hides—half a hide at How Hill, at Studley three hides, at Sutton 1½ hides, at Nunwick three hides, at Thornton two hides.

And these lands are waste: the first is Sawley, the second Grantley, the third Eaveston, the fourth Wilsill, the fifth is half of *Cnearresweorð*.

The following are the priests' lands: four hides at Westwick, four at North Stainley, one hide at Givendale, three oxgangs at Markington, three oxgangs at Monkton, two oxgangs at Hutton.

168 TYPES OF TENURE AMONG

Ðis syndan socnland into Rypum. On Gypingadeal .VIII. hida · 7 ofer eall Munecatun .VII. hida · 7 on Eastwic .II. hida. On Mercingatune þridde healfe hide · 7 on Herelesho · þridde healfe hide · 7 on Suðtune · oðer healf hide. On nyrran Stanlege
5 .v. hida · 7 on Norð Stanlege .I. hide · 7 on Nunnewic .I. hide · 7 on Heawic .v. hida · 7 on Sleaningaforda .II. hida;

LXXXV. GRANT OF LAND BY KING CNUT TO CHRISTCHURCH, CANTERBURY

Her geswutelað on þisum gewrite þ Cnut kynig læt þ land æt Folkenstane into Cristes cyrcean on Cantwarabirig þa Eadsi his preost gecyrde þiderin to munuce · to þam forewearde þ Eadsi
10 munuc hit habbe his lyfes timan for his gehyrsumnisse þe he him wel gehyrde. And he hit ne mæg naðor ne gyfen ne syllan · ne forspekan · ne forspillan ut of þam halgan mynstre. Ac æfter his dæge ga þ land þam hyrede on hand þe þonne Criste þeniað innan þam mynstre[1] · mid sake 7 mid socne 7 mid eallon þam
15 þingon þe þær fyrmest tolæg · forþamþe his witan him sædan þ hit hwilon ær læg þiderin on Æðelstanes dæge kyninges 7 on Odan arceb · 7 hit wearð syððan ut gedon mid mycelan unrihte. Nu geuðe he þis land into Cristes cyrcean his sawle to ecere alysednisse. And gyf ænig[2] sy swa dyrstig ongæn God þ þis
20 awændan wille awænde hine God ælmihtig fram heofene[rice]s myrcðe into helle grunde buton[3] he ær his ænde hit þe deopper gebete. Ðis wæs gedon innon Suðrie on Kyngestune · on þone halgan dæg pentecosten. And þises wæs to gewitnesse Ælfgyua Imma seo hlæfdige · 7 Ægelnoð arcebiscop · 7 Ælfwi'ne'[4] b on
25 Lundene · 7 Ælfsi b on Winceastre · 7 Ægelric b on Suðsexan · 7 Ælmær abbud æt sce Augustine 7 Wulnoð abb æt Westminstre 7 Ælfwine abb æt Niwan Mynstre · 7 Wulfsi abb æt Certesige[5]. And Ulf eorl 7 Eglaf[6] eorl 7 Lyfwine[7] eorl 7 Harold eorl · 7 Yric eorl · 7 Þored steallara 7 Agamund · 7 Osgod Clapa 7 Tofig ·

[1] þam halgan m., Cott. Vit.
[2] ænig man, ibid.
[3] buton ðas, ibid.
[4] Ælfwi, ibid.
[5] uortesige, D.; Portes-, K.
[6] -lað, Cott. Vit.
[7] Leofric, ibid.

CHURCH LANDS IN YORKSHIRE 169

These are the soke-lands which belong to Ripon: eight hides at Givendale and seven hides throughout the whole of Monkton and two hides at Eastwick, 2½ hides at Markington, 2½ hides at How Hill and at Sutton 1½ hides, at Nearer Stainley five hides, at North Stainley one hide and at Nunwick one hide and at Hewick five hides and at Sleningford two hides.

LXXXV. GRANT OF LAND BY KING CNUT TO CHRISTCHURCH, CANTERBURY

Here it is declared in this document that King Cnut conceded the estate at Folkestone to Christchurch, Canterbury, when his priest Eadsige became a monk there, on condition that the monk Eadsige should hold it during his lifetime for the obedience which he duly showed him. And he cannot alienate it from the holy monastery by gift or sale or loss in a lawsuit or forfeiture, but after his death the estate shall pass into the possession of the community which at that time is serving Christ within the monastery, with jurisdiction and with all the things which it most fully possessed, because his councillors told him that it formerly belonged to Christchurch in the time of King Æthelstan and Archbishop Oda, and was afterwards alienated from it with great injustice. He has now granted this estate to Christchurch for the eternal salvation of his soul, and if anyone is so presumptuous towards God as to desire to alter this, God Almighty shall remove him from the bliss of heaven to the abyss of hell, unless before his death he make amends as fully as possible.

This was done at Kingston in Surrey on the holy day of Pentecost, and the witnesses were the Lady Ælfgifu Emma and Archbishop Æthelnoth and Ælfwi[g], Bishop of London, and Ælfsige, Bishop of Winchester, and Æthelric, Bishop of Sussex, and Ælfmær, Abbot of St Augustine's, and Wulfnoth, Abbot of Westminster, and Ælfwine, Abbot of the New Minster, and Wulfsige, Abbot of Chertsey, and Earl Ulf and Earl Eglaf and Earl Leofwine and Earl Harold and Earl Eric and Thored the Staller and Agemund and Osgod Clapa and Tofi and Æthelwine

170   GRANT OF LAND BY KING CNUT

7 Ægelwine Ælfhelmes sunu · 7 Siword æt Cilleham · 7 Ægelric bigga 7 Ælfword 'se'[1] Kæntisca 7 Eadmer æt Burhham · 7 ealle þæs kynges rædgyfan gehaðode 7 læwede þe þær gesamnod wæron. And þissera gewrita synd þreo an is innon Cristes
5 cyrcean · 7 oðer æt sc̄e Augustine · 7 þ̄[2] þridde is inne mid þæs kynges haligdome.

LXXXVI. GRANT OF LANDS BY EADSIGE TO CHRISTCHURCH, CANTERBURY

✠ Her swutelaþ on þysan gewrite hu Cnut cyng[3] 7 Ælfgifu seo hlæfdige geuþan Eadsige heora preost[4] ða he gecyrde to munece þ̄ he moste ateon þ̄ land æt Apoldre swa him sylfan leofast
10 wære. Þa sealde he hit into Cristes-cyrican þ̄[5] Godes ðeowum for his sawle, 7 he hit gebohte þ̄ æt þam Hirede his dæg 7 Ædwines[6] mid feower pundan[7], on þ̄ forwyrd þ̄ man gelyste[8] ælce geare into Cristes-cirican[9] .iii. wæga cyses[10] of þam lande, 7 þreo gebind æles, 7 æfter his dæg 7 Ædwines[6] gange þ̄ lande[11] into
15 Cristes-cirican[9], mid mete 7 mid mannan[7] eal swa hit þænne gegodod sy for Eadsiges sawle, 7 he gebohte þ̄ land æt Werhornan æt ðam Hirede his dage[12] 7 Eadwines eac mid feower pundan, ðænne gað[12] þ̄ land forð mid þam oþran æfter his dæge 7 Edwines[6] into Cristes-cirican[9] mid ðære tilþe þe þar þænne
20 on si[13], 7 þ̄ land on his dæg æt Berwican ðe he geearnode æt his hlaford[14] Cnute cynge, 7 he geunn eac þæs landes æt Orpedingtune on his dæge for his sawle into Cristes-cyrican ðam Godes ðeowum to scrudland, ðe he gebohte mid hundeahtigan[7] marcan hwites seolfres be hustinges gewihte, 7 he geun eac ðæs landes
25 æt Palstre 7 æt Wihtriceshamme æfter his dæge 7 Edwines[6] forð mid ðam oðrum ðam Godes ðeowum to fostorlande[15] for his sawle. Ðises cwides he geunn ðam Hirede to þam forwyrdan þ̄ hi æfre hine wel healdan, 7 him holde beon on life 7 æfter life,

[1] Om. Cott. Vit. [2] ðe, ibid. [3] cyncg, K., T.
[4] preoste, K., T. [5] ðam, K., T. [6] Ead-, K., T.
[7] -um, K., T. [8] -læste, K., T. [9] cyr-, K., T.
[10] cæs-, K., T. [11] land, K., T. [12] K., T. have æ for a.
[13] sy, K., T. [14] -orde, K., T. [15] foster-, T.

Ælfhelm's son and Siweard of Chilham and Æthelric Bigga and Ælfweard the Kentishman and Eadmær of Burham and all the king's councillors, both ecclesiastics and laymen, who were assembled there.

There are three of these documents. One is at Christchurch, the second at St Augustine's and the third is in the king's sanctuary.

LXXXVI. GRANT OF LANDS BY EADSIGE TO CHRISTCHURCH, CANTERBURY

✠ Here it is declared in this document how King Cnut and the Lady Ælfgifu granted permission to Eadsige their priest, when he became a monk, to dispose of the estate at Appledore as pleased him best. Then he gave it to Christchurch to the servants of God on behalf of his soul, and bought it back from the community for his own lifetime and Edwin's for four pounds, on condition that every year 3 weys of cheese and 3 binds of eels shall be rendered to Christchurch from the estate; and after his death and Edwin's the estate shall pass to Christchurch on behalf of Eadsige's soul, with its produce and its men exactly as it is stocked at the time. And he bought the estate at Warehorne from the community for his lifetime and Edwin's for four pounds also, and that estate shall pass to Christchurch along with the other after his death and Edwin's with the produce which is on it at the time, and during his lifetime [he grants] the estate at Berwick which he acquired from his lord King Cnut. And he likewise grants to Christchurch during his lifetime, on behalf of his soul, the estate at Orpington which he bought for 80 marks of white silver by the standard of the husting, to provide clothing for the servants of God, and he grants likewise the estates at Palster and at Wittersham after his death and Edwin's along with the others on behalf of his soul, to provide food for the servants of God.

He grants this bequest to the community on condition that they always give him staunch support and are loyal to him during his life and after his death. And if by any folly they break this

7 gif hi mid ænegan unrede[1] wið hine ðas forwyrd tobrecan[2], þænne[3] stande hit on his agenan gewealde hu he siþþan his agen ateon wille. Ðises is to gewitnesse Cnut cyng, 7 Ælfgifu[4] seo hlædige[5], 7 Æðelnoð Arceb. 7 Ælfstan Abb. 7 se Hired æt S. Augustine, 7 Brihtric geounga[6] 7 Æþelric bigenga, 7 Þorð Þurkilles[7] nefa, 7 Tofi, 7 Ælfwine preost, 7 Eadwold preost, 7 ealle ðæs cynges rædesmen, 7 þissa gewrita synda[8] .III. an is æt Cristes cyrican, 7 an æt S. Augustine, 7 an hæfð Eadsige mid him sylfan.

LXXXVII. LEASE OF LAND BY BRIHTHEAH, BISHOP OF WORCESTER, TO WULFMÆR

✠ In nomine dñi. Ic Byrhteh .b. mid Godes geðeahte 7 þæs arwyrðan hiredes on Wigernaceastre · 7 on ealre þæra ðegena gewitnysse into Glæaweceastrescire ic cyþe þ ic gean Wulmære minum cnihte twegra hida landes in Easttune for his godra gearnunge swa ful 7 swa forð swa he hit hæfde under Leofsige .b. 7 under me syðþan hæbbe he 7 wel bruce þreora manna dæg to rihtere geyrsumnysse · into ðære halgan stowe to Wigernaceastre butan he hit forwyrce. Ðæs is to gewitnysse se hired on Wigraceastre 7 on Glæaweceastre · 7 on Eofeshom · 7 on Prescoran.

LXXXVIII. GRANT OF LAND BY THORED TO CHRISTCHURCH, CANTERBURY

✠ Ic Þored geann þ land æt Horslege þam hirede æt X̄p̄es cyrcean for mine sawle swa full 7 swa forð swa ic sylf hit ahte.

[1] -ræde, K., T. [2] -en, K., T. [3] ðonne, K., T.
[4] -gyfu, K., T. [5] hlæfdige, K., T. [6] geonga, K., T.
[7] -cylles, K., T. [8] syndon, K., T.

agreement with him, it shall be in his own power to decide how he will then dispose of his property.

The witnesses of this are King Cnut and the Lady Ælfgifu and Archbishop Æthelnoth and Abbot Ælfstan and the community at St Augustine's and Brihtric the Young and Æthelric Bigga and Thored, Thurkil's nephew, and Tofi and the priest Ælfwine and the priest Eadwold and all the king's councillors.

There are three of these documents. One is at Christchurch and one at St Augustine's and Eadsige has one in his own possession.

LXXXVII. LEASE OF LAND BY BRIHTHEAH, BISHOP OF WORCESTER, TO WULFMÆR

In nomine domini.

I, Bishop Brihtheah, by the direction of God and the honourable community at Worcester, and with the cognisance of all the thegns of Gloucestershire, declare that I grant to Wulfmær, my *cniht*, two hides of land at [Cold] Aston, for his excellent deserts, as fully and completely as he held them under Bishop Leofsige. And he [and his heirs] shall henceforth hold them and make good use of them under me for three lives, in return for due obedience to the holy foundation at Worcester, unless he forfeit it.

The witnesses of this are the communities at Worcester and at Gloucester and at Evesham and at Pershore.

LXXXVIII. GRANT OF LAND BY THORED TO CHRISTCHURCH, CANTERBURY

✠ I, Thored, grant the estate at Horsley to the community at Christchurch for the sake of my soul, as fully and completely as I myself owned it.

LXXXIX. GRANT OF LAND BY ARCHBISHOP ÆTHELNOTH TO CHRISTCHURCH, CANTERBURY

✠ Ic Æþelnoð Xp̄es cyrcean arceb gebohte þ̄ land æt Godmæresham æt Sirede eorle mid twam 7 hundseofontigan marcan hwites seolfres be gewihte · 7 geaf hit on minon halan life into Xp̄es cyrcean þan hirede to bigleofan into heora beod-
5 derne for mine sawle · 7 se þe þis wille awendan · awende hine Crist fram heofenan rices myrhðe into helle wite.

XC. AGREEMENT BETWEEN ARCHBISHOP EADSIGE AND TOKI

✠ Eadsige arceb cyþ on ðisse Cristes bec þ̄ Tokig sende to me to Hrisbeorgan his twegen cnihtas oðor hatte Sexa oðor Leofwine · 7 bæd me þ̄ þa forword moston standan þe Æðelnoð arceb
10 7 he geworht hæfdon ymbe þ̄ land æt Healtune þ̄ he his bruce his dæg[1] · 7 eode æfter his dæge into Xp̄s cyricean 7 ic him[2] ðæs tiðude on manegra godra manna gewitnysse 7 ealles mines hiredes ge gehadudra ge læwedra.

XCI. HAROLD HAREFOOT AND SANDWICH

Her kyþ on þison gewrite þ̄ Harold king · let beridan Sandwic
15 of Xp̄es cyrcean him sylfan to handa · 7 hæfde hit him wel neh twelf monað · 7 twegen hæri'n'gc[3] timan swa þeah fullice · eall ongean Godes willan · 7 agen ealra þara halgena þe restað innon Xp̄es cyrcean swa swa hit him syððan sorhlice þær æfter agiode · 7 amanc þisan[4] siþan[5] siðe[6] wearð Ælfstan abb. æt[7] sc̄e A. 7
20 begeat mid his smehwrencan · 7 mid his golde 7 seolfre eall dyrnun'c'ga[8] æt Steorran þe þa wæs þæs kinges rædesmann[9] þ̄ him gewearð se þridda penig[10] of þære tolne on Sandwic þa

[1] *dag*, Addit. MS. [2] *hi*, ibid. [3] *-igc*, D.
[4] Sic. [5] Om. K. [6] Om. T.
[7] *et*, D. [8] *-unga*, D., K., T. [9] *-man*, T.
[10] *pæn-*, T.

LXXXIX. GRANT OF LAND BY ARCHBISHOP ÆTHELNOTH TO CHRISTCHURCH, CANTERBURY

✠ I, Æthelnoth, Archbishop of Christchurch, have bought the estate at Godmersham from Earl Sired for 72 marks of pure silver by weight, and while alive and well have given it, for the sake of my soul, to the refectory at Christchurch for the support of the community. And if anyone attempts to alter this, Christ shall remove him from the bliss of the kingdom of heaven into the torment of hell.

XC. AGREEMENT BETWEEN ARCHBISHOP EADSIGE AND TOKI

✠ [I], Archbishop Eadsige, state in this gospel book that Toki sent to me at Risborough his two *cnihtas*, one of whom was called Sexa, the other Leofwine, and asked me that the agreement might remain in force which Archbishop Æthelnoth and he had made with regard to the estate at Halton, namely that he should enjoy it during his lifetime, and after his death it should pass to Christchurch. And I granted them this with the cognisance of many trustworthy men and of all my household, both ecclesiastics and laymen.

XCI. HAROLD HAREFOOT AND SANDWICH

Here it is made known in this document that King Harold had Sandwich taken from Christchurch for his own use, and kept it himself for about a year, and at any rate for two whole herring-seasons, entirely against the will of God and of all the saints who rest within Christchurch, with grievous consequences for himself thereafter. At the time of these happenings (?) Ælfstan was Abbot of St Augustine's, and by means of his crafty devices and his gold and silver he acquired for himself quite secretly from Steorra, who was the king's steward at the time, the receipt of the third penny of the toll at Sandwich. Then Archbishop Eadsige,

gerædde Eadsige arceƀ þa he þis wiste · 7 eall se hired æt X̄p̄es cyrc⁹ betweonan heom ꝥ man sende Ælfgar munuc[1] of X̄p̄es cyrc⁹ to Harolde kingce · 7 wæs se king þa binnan Oxanaforde[2] swyþe geseocled · swa ꝥ he læg orwene[3] his lifes · þa wæs
5 Lyfingc[4] ƀ of Defenanscire · mid þam kincge · 7 Þancred munuc mid him · þa com Cristes cyrc⁹ sand to þam ƀ · 7 he forð[5] þa to þam kincge · 7 Ælfgar munuc mid him · 7 Oswerd[6] æt Hergerdesham · 7 Þancred · 7 sædon þam kinge · ꝥ he hæfde swyðe agylt[7] wið Crist ꝥ he æfre sceolde niman ænig þing · of
10 X̄p̄es cyrc⁹ þe his foragengceon dydon þiderinn[8] · sædon þam kinge þa embe Sandwic ꝥ hit wæs him to handa geriden · þa læg se king 7 asweartode eall · mid þare sage · 7 swor syþþan under God ælmihtine 7 under ealle halgan[9] þarto ꝥ hit næfre næs · na his réd na his dæd · ꝥ man sceolde æfre Sandwic don ut of X̄p̄es
15 cyrc⁹. Þa wæs soðlice gesyne · ꝥ hit wæs oðra manna geþeaht næs na Haroldes kinges · 7 soðlice Ælfstanes abbodes ræd wæs mid þam mannan þe hit of X̄p̄es cyrc⁹ ut geræddon[10] · þa sende Harold king Ælfgar munuc agen to þam arceƀ Eadsige · 7 to eallon X̄p̄es cyrc⁹ munecan · 7 grette hig ealle Godes gretincge
20 7 his · 7 het 'ꝥ' hig sceoldan habban Sandwic into X̄p̄es cyrc⁹ · swa full · 7 swa forð[5] swa hig hit æfre hæfdon on ænies kinges dæge · ge on gafole · ge on streame · ge on strande · ge on witun[11] · ge on eallon þam þingan þe hit æfre ænig king fyr'm'est hæfde ætforan him · þa Ælfstan aƀƀ · þis ofaxode þa com he to Eadsige
25 arceƀ · 7 bæd hine fultumes to þam hirode[12] embe þone · þriddan penig · 7 hi begen[13] þa to eallon gebroþran 7 bædon þone hired ꝥ Ælfstan aƀƀ moste beon þæs þriddan peniges wurðe of þære tolne · 7 gyfan þam hirede .x. p̄d. ac hy forwyrndon[13] heom ealle togædere endemes · ꝥ he hit na sceolde næfre gebidan · 7 wæs
30 þeah Eadsige arceƀ swiðor his fultum þonne þæs hiredes · 7 þa he ne mihte na forð hermid þa gyrnde he ꝥ he moste macian fornan[14] gen Mildryþe æker ænne[15] hwerf wið þone[16] wodan to werianne · ac eall se hired him forwyrnde þæs forð út mid ealle ·

[1] mon-, D. [2] Oxna-, T. [3] -wenæ, K.
[4] -inge, D. [5] ford, D. [6] -perd, D.
[7] agylte, D. [8] -mu, D. [9] -gar, D.
[10] ge rieddon, D. [11] -an, D. [12] -ede, D.
[13] begen ... forwyrndon, om. D. [14] foran, T.
[15] tenne, D. [16] þon, T.

HAROLD HAREFOOT AND SANDWICH

when he knew this, and all the community at Christchurch decided among themselves to send Ælfgar, a monk of Christchurch, to King Harold. The king at the time was lying in Oxford very ill and despairing of his life, and Lyfing, Bishop of Devonshire, and the monk Thancred were with him. Then the messenger from Christchurch came to the bishop, who forthwith went to the king, accompanied by the monk Ælfgar and Osweard of Harrietsham and Thancred, and they said to the king that he had greatly sinned against Christ in taking anything from Christchurch which his predecessors had assigned to it. Then they spoke to the king about the seizure of Sandwich for his own use. The king lay and grew black as they spoke, and swore thereafter by God Almighty and by all the saints that it was neither by direction nor deed of his that Sandwich had been taken from Christchurch. Then it was plainly evident that it had been planned by other men and not by King Harold, and as a matter of fact Abbot Ælfstan had supported the men who had advised taking it from Christchurch. Then King Harold sent the monk Ælfgar back to Archbishop Eadsige and to all the monks of Christchurch, and greeted them all in God's name and his own, and gave orders that they should hold Sandwich for Christchurch as fully and completely as they had ever done in any king's day, with rent, water[-dues], shore-[dues], fines and everything, as fully as any king had ever held it before him. When Abbot Ælfstan learned of this, he came to Archbishop Eadsige and asked for his support in approaching the community about the third penny. Then they both approached all the brothers, and asked the community that Abbot Ælfstan might be entitled to the third penny of the toll and give the community ten pounds, but all of them together without exception refused to grant him any such thing, even although Archbishop Eadsige supported him rather than the community. And when he could make nothing of this, he asked for permission to make a wharf opposite 'Mildred's field' as a protection

7 se arceb Eadsige let hit eall to heora agene ræde · þa gewearð se abb Ælfstan æt · mid micelan fultume · 7 let delfon æt Hyppeles fleote an mycel gedelf · 7 wolde þ scipryne sceolde þærinne licgean eall swa hig dydon on Sandwic · ac him na speow nan
5 þingc þæron · forþam he swingð eall on idel þe swincð ongean Xp̄es willan · 7 se abb let hit eall þus · 7 se hired fengc to heora agenan · on Godes gewitnesse 7 sc̄a Marian 7 ealra þara halgena þe restað innan Xp̄es cyrcean · 7 æt sc̄e Augustine · þis is eall soð gelyfe se þe wylle · na gebad Ælfstan abb næfre on nanan
10 oþre wisan þone þriddan penig of Sandwic. Godes bletsung si mid us eallon a on ecnysse. Amen.

XCII. GRANT IN REVERSION TO BURY ST EDMUNDS BY STIGAND

[H]Er[1] suyteleþ on þise wrtte[2] wilke forwarde Stigand and Alger[3] his *pr*est Wrouhten þo he let him þat lond to hande[4] at Playford · þat is þat Alger[3] prest habbe þat lond his day · and ouer his
15 day ⸫ fonge Stigand þerto gif he leng libbe · and ouer here boþere day ⸫ go þat lond into seynt Eadmu*n*de mid mete and mid manne and mid alle þinge so it þanne tyled beth · buten alken gentale · and he it ne may neyþer ne forsegen ne forwerken · þis aren .II.[5] witnesse · Alfric[3] bisscop · 7 Vui[6] Abbot · 7 al se hird
20 binnen seynt Eadmundes biri · and Stigand an'd' Aelfwine Wluardes sune · 7 Alfric[3] Withgares sune · 7 Eadric and Ordger[7] · 7 Lemmer and manie oþere · þise wrtte[8] sinden tua · on is binnen seynt Eadmu*n*des biri · 7 oþer hauið Stigand.

XCIII. GRANT OF LANDS BY THURKETEL TO BURY ST EDMUNDS

Þis sendan þa land þe Þurkytel gean Gode 7 sc̄e Marian 7 sc̄e
25 Eadmunde þ is þ land æt Culeforde þ his agen wæs swa hit stænt mid mete 7 mid mannu*m* 7 mid sake 7 mid socne 7 eal þ land æt Wridewellan · 7 þ land æt Gyxeweorðe swa hit stent mid mete 7 mid mannum.

---

[1] A space has been left for the initial capital. [2] *writte*, K.
[3] *Æl-*, K. [4] *honda*, K. [5] *to*, K.
[6] *Wi*, K. [7] *-gar*, K. [8] *write*, K.

against the tide (?), but the whole community absolutely and unanimously refused his request, and the archbishop left it entirely to them to decide. Then Abbot Ælfstan came on the scene with a great company and had a trench dug at Ebbsfleet, with the intention of providing a channel for ships such as they had at Sandwich, but it was an utter failure, for he who labours against the will of Christ labours in vain. Then the abbot let the matter drop, and the community took possession of what was theirs, in the sight of God and of St Mary and of all the saints who rest within Christchurch and at St Augustine's. This is all true, believe it who will. Abbot Ælfstan never in any other way tried to obtain the third penny from Sandwich. May the blessing of God be with us all for evermore. Amen.

XCII. GRANT IN REVERSION TO BURY ST EDMUNDS BY STIGAND

Here is declared in this document the agreement that Stigand and Ælfgar his priest have made when he let him the estate at Playford, namely that Ælfgar the priest should hold the estate for his lifetime, and after his death Stigand should resume possession of it, if he survived. And after the death of both of them it shall pass without controversy to St Edmunds with its produce and its men and everything as it is then supplied. And he can neither lose it by a lawsuit nor forfeit it.

Two of the witnesses of this are Bishop Ælfric and Abbot Ufi, also all the community at Bury St Edmunds, and Stigand and Ælfwine, Wulfweard's son, and Ælfric, Wihtgar's son, and Eadric and Ordgar and Leofmær and many others. There are two of these documents; one is at Bury St Edmunds and Stigand has the other.

XCIII. GRANT OF LANDS BY THURKETEL TO BURY ST EDMUNDS

These are the estates which Thurketel grants to God and St Mary and St Edmund, namely the estate at Culford, which was his own, as it stands with its produce and its men and with rights of jurisdiction, and the whole of the estate at Wordwell, and the estate at Ixworth as it stands with its produce and its men.

XCIV. LEASE OF LAND BY LYFING, BISHOP OF WORCESTER, TO ÆTHELRIC

☩ In ures drihtnes naman hælendes Cristes ic LEOFINC bisceop mid þafunge 7 leafe HEARÐACNUTES cynges 7 þæs arwurþan hiredes æt Wigornaceastre ge iunges ge ealdes gebocige sumne dæl landes minan holdan 7 getreowan þegene þam is
5 ÆGELRIC nama .II. 'hida' æt EADMUNDDescótan hæbbe he 7 wel bruce · for his eadmodre gehersumnysse 7 for his licwurðan sceatte · þæt is þæt he hit hæbbe 7 well bruce his dæg · 7 æfter his dæge twam erfewardum þanðe him leofest sy · 7 him betst to geearnian wylle · 7 he hit hæbbe to freon ælces
10 þinges butan wallgeweorce 7 brygcgeweorce 7 ferdsocne. God ælmihtig þone gehealde · þe þas ure sylena 7 ure gerædnyssa healdan wylle on ælce healfe · gif ænig þonne sy uppahofen 7 inblawen on þa oferhyda þære geættredan deofles lare · 7 wylle þas ure sylena gewemman oððe gewonian on ænigum þingum ·
15 wite he hine amansumadne mid Annaníam 7 Saphíram on ece forwyrd · butan he hit her ǽr wurðlice gebete Gode 7 mannum. Ðis wæs gedon þy geare þe wæs agan fram Cristes gebyrtide an þusend wintra 7 twa 7 XLII. wintra. Ðis is seo gewitnes · ꝥ is Hearþacnut cyng 7 Ælfgeofu his modor · 7 LYFING .b. 7 eall
20 se hired on Wigraceastre · 7 Ælfward .b. 7 se hired on Eofeshomme · 7 Godwine abbod 7 se hired on Wincelcumbe · 7 Leofric .eorl. 7 ealle þa þegenas on Wigraceastrescire · ge englisce ge denisce.

XCV. CHARTER OF EDWARD THE CONFESSOR TO CHRISTCHURCH, CANTERBURY

✠ Ic Eadwerd cyng 7 Englalandes wealdend under Criste þan
25 heofenlican cyninge geann þæs landes æt Certham into X̄pes cyrcean for mine sawle þan hirede to fosterlande þe þærinne Gode þeowað · 7 ic eom þæs[1] mynstres mund 7 upheald · 7 nelle geþafian þæt ænig mann geútige ænig þara landa þe mid rihte into þan halgan mynstre gebyrige[2] · 7 ic wille þæt ælc þara landa

[1] þær, D.   [2] -byrað, K.

XCIV. LEASE OF LAND BY LYFING, BISHOP OF WORCESTER, TO ÆTHELRIC

☩ In the name of our Lord the Saviour Christ, I, Bishop Lyfing, with the permission and leave of King Hardacnut and the honourable community at Worcester, both young and old, grant by charter a certain piece of land to my loyal and faithful thegn whose name is Æthelric. He shall hold and make good use of two hides at Armscott, because of his humble obedience and in return for his sterling money, that is, he shall have the estate and make good use of it during his lifetime, and at his death [leave it] to the two heirs who please him best and are willing to earn it from him most deservedly. He shall hold it free from every obligation except the construction of walls and bridges and military service.

May God Almighty uphold him who is willing to uphold these our gifts and our enactments in every particular. If anyone, however, is uplifted and inflated with the arrogance of the devil's poisoned teaching and attempts to impair or diminish in any way these our gifts, he shall find himself cast out with Ananias and Sapphira to everlasting perdition, unless he has duly made amends for it here both to God and to men.

This was done in the year 1042 after the birth of Christ.

The witnesses of this are King Hardacnut and Ælfgifu, his mother, and Bishop Lyfing and all the community at Worcester, and Bishop Ælfweard and the community at Evesham, and Abbot Godwine and the community at Winchcombe, and Earl Leofric and all the thegns in Worcestershire, both English and Danish.

XCV. CHARTER OF EDWARD THE CONFESSOR TO CHRISTCHURCH, CANTERBURY

✝ I, Edward, King and ruler of England under Christ, the heavenly king, grant, for the sake of my soul, the estate at Chartham to Christchurch to supply food for the community which serves God therein. And I am the guardian and upholder of the monastery and will not permit any man to alienate any of the lands which by right belong to the holy

182 CHARTER OF EDWARD THE CONFESSOR

þe on mines fæder dæge læg into Xp̄es cyrcean · wære hit kynges gife wære hit bisceopes · wære hit eorles · wære hit þegenas[1] · eall ic wille þæt ælces ma'n'nes gife stande · 7 ic nelle geþafian þ̄ ænig mann þis awende · 7 gif ænig mann si swa dyrstig · oþþe
5 þærto geþwærlæce þæt ænig þara lande þe lið into Xp̄es cyrcean þanon geútige[2] · si he Iudas gefera þe Crist belæwade · 7 þe þisne cwyde æfre awende · þe ic mid minre agenre hand on þissere Xp̄es béc Xp̄e betæhte on uppan Xp̄es weofod · drihten fordo hine á on ecnesse. Amen.
10 Ðis synd þara landa[3] nama · Sandwic · Eastryge · Tænet · Edesham · Ieoccham[4] · Certaham · Godmæresham · Wytt · East Cert · 7 oþer Cert · Berwica · Werhornas · Apuldra · Merseham · Orpedingtun · Preostatun · Meapaham · Culingas · Frinningaham[5] · Holingaburnan[6] ·
15 Fernlege[7] · Peccham.
On Suðsexan · Pæccingas · Wudutun[8]. On Suðrian · Wealawurð · Mersetham · Ceigham · Horslege; On Estsexan · Suðcyrcean · Middeltun[9] · Lællingc · Boccing.
On Eastenglum · Hæðleh[10] · Illaleh; Innon Buccinghamscire
20 be Cilternes[11] efese · Hrysebyrgan.
Innon Oxenafordscire · Niwantun · Brutuwylle.

XCVI. RECORD OF THE GRANT OF AN ESTATE TO CHRISTCHURCH, CANTERBURY

✠ Ic Ælfgyfu seo hlæfdige Eadweardes cyninges modor geærndede æt Cnute cyninge minum hlaforde þæt land æt Niwantune 7 þæt þærto hyrð into Xp̄es cyrcean þa Ælfric se þegen hit hæfde
25 forworht þan cyninge to handan · 7 se cyning hit geaf þa into Xp̄es cyrcean þan hirede to fosterlande for uncre beigra sawle.

[1] -es, K.   [2] ge atige, D.   [3] landu, D.
[4] Leocc-, D. The blanks in the text represent erasures in the MS.
[5] -ingu-, D.   [6] -am, D.   [7] -legc, D.
[8] Pudutnn, D.   [9] -tan, D.   [10] Hæd-, D.
[11] eilt-, D.

monastery. And it is my will with regard to each of the estates which in my father's day belonged to Christchurch, were it the gift of a king or a bishop or an earl or a thegn—it is my will that every man's gift shall remain in force. And I will not permit any man to alter this; and if any man is so presumptuous or agrees to this, that any of the estates which belong to Christchurch should be alienated, he shall be the companion of Judas who betrayed Christ. And if anyone ever alters this bequest, which with my own hand on this gospel book I have dedicated to Christ on the altar of Christ, the Lord shall destroy him forever to all eternity. Amen.

These are the names of the estates: Sandwich, Eastry, Thanet, Adisham, Ickham, ... Chartham, ... Godmersham, ... Westwell, East Chart and the other Chart, Berwick, Warehorne, Appledore, Mersham, Orpington, ... Preston, ... Meopham, Cooling, Farningham, Hollingbourn, Farleigh, ... Peckham. In Sussex Patching, Wootton. In Surrey Walworth, Merstham, Cheam, Horsley. In Essex Southchurch, Milton, Lawling, ... Bocking. In East Anglia Hadleigh, Eleigh. In Buckinghamshire, at the edge of the Chilterns, Risborough. In Oxfordshire Newington, Brightwell.

XCVI. RECORD OF THE GRANT OF AN ESTATE TO CHRISTCHURCH, CANTERBURY

✠ I, the Lady Ælfgifu, mother of King Edward, acquired from King Cnut my lord the estate at Newington and all that belongs to it on behalf of Christchurch, when the thegn Ælfric had forfeited it to the king. And the king then granted it to Christchurch to provide food for the community, on behalf of the souls of both of us.

XCVII. AGREEMENT BETWEEN UFI, ABBOT OF BURY ST EDMUNDS, AND ÆTHELMÆR

[H]Er[1] SWiteleþ on þís Write þe forwarde þat Ailmer þe biscopes brother hauede Wrouht With Vuí Abbot and Wið alle þen hird bínnen seynt Eadmundes birí · ymbe þat litle lond at Swanetone and þat halue lond at Hildoluestone · þat ís þat he
5 selde hem on marc goldes to þe forwarde þat he habbe þat lond hís day · and ouer hís day ∶′ go þo londes eft ongeyn ínto sc̄e Eadmunde · and þat halfe lond forþmide · míd mete and míd manne and alle þínge buten alken gentale. Ðise sínden þe mannes names þe to Witnesse sínden þises · þat ís Stigande
10 bisscop and Vuí Abbot and Lefstan þe dean and al se hired bínnen seynt Eadmundes birí And Lefsi Abbot 7 al se hird bínnen Ely · And Alfsy Abbot at sc̄e Benedc̄e 7 al se hird þerbínnen · 7 Alfwíne 7 Alfríc and Edríc and Godwíne 7 Fredegist 7 Vlf aet Welle · 7 Scule Leofwoldes sune · and Godwíne at
15 Críngelforð 7 Eadwíne Vlfketeles sune · þise Write sínden tua on ís bínnen seynt Eadmundes bírí and oþer haued Aylmer hymself.

XCVIII. LEASE OF LAND BY ÆLFWINE, BISHOP OF WINCHESTER, TO OSGOD

HER cyð on þysum gewrite þa forewearde þe Ælfwine bysceop[2] 7 se hyred on ealdan mynstre worton wið Osgoð[3] þa hy letan
20 him to ꝥ land æt EADBVRGEbyrig · wið þan lande æt Wroccesheale þe he binnan Wiht hæfde · ꝥ wæs ꝥ Osgod bruce þæs landes æt EADBVRGEbyrig his deg · 7 hæfter[4] his dege ga · ꝥ land eft into ealdan mynstre mid mæte 7 mid mannum 7 mid eallum þingan swá swá hit stande eall swá hy hít hím ær to handa
25 leton. Þyses is to gewitnesse · EADWEARD · cingc · 7 Ælfgyfu seo hlefdige · 7 EADSIGE arceb. 7 Ælfric archebisceop · 7 Brihtwold ƀ. 7 Lyfincg ƀ. 7 Duduc ƀ. 7 Æþestan[5] ƀ. 7 Eadnod[6] .ƀ. 7 Ælfwerð[7] .ƀ. 7 Grimcytel ƀ. 7 Godwine eorl · 7 Leofric

---

[1] A space has been left for the initial capital.
[2] bisc-, K. [3] -god, K. [4] æfter, K.
[5] -lst-, K. [6] -noð, K. [7] -werd, K.

XCVII. AGREEMENT BETWEEN UFI, ABBOT OF BURY ST EDMUNDS, AND ÆTHELMÆR

Here is declared in this document the agreement that Æthelmær, the bishop's brother, has made with Abbot Ufi and all the community at Bury St Edmunds about the little estate at Swanton and the half estate at Hindolveston, namely he has given them a mark of gold on condition that he should hold the estate during his lifetime, and after his death the estates, including the half estate, shall revert without any controversy to St Edmunds with their produce and their men and everything.

These are the names of the men who are witnesses of this, namely Bishop Stigand and Abbot Ufi and Leofstan, the dean, and all the community at Bury St Edmunds, and Abbot Leofsige and all the community at Ely, and Abbot Ælfsige at St Benedict's and all the community there, and Ælfwine and Ælfric and Eadric and Godwine and Frithegist and Ulf of *Welle* and Scule, Leofwold's son, and Godwine of Cringleford and Edwin, Ulfketel's son.

There are two of these documents. One is at Bury St Edmunds and Æthelmær himself has the other.

XCVIII. LEASE OF LAND BY ÆLFWINE, BISHOP OF WINCHESTER, TO OSGOD

Here is stated in this document the agreement which Bishop Ælfwine and the community at the Old Minster made with Osgod when they let to him the estate at Adderbury in return for the estate which he held at Wroxall in the Isle of Wight, namely that Osgod should enjoy the estate at Adderbury during his lifetime, and after his death it should return to the Old Minster with its produce and its men and everything as it stands, just as it was when they let it to him.

The witnesses of this are King Edward and the Lady Ælfgifu and Archbishop Eadsige and Archbishop Ælfric and Bishop Brihtwold and Bishop Lyfing and Bishop Duduc and Bishop Æthelstan and Bishop Eadnoth and Bishop Ælfweard and Bishop Grimketel and Earl Godwine and Earl Leofric and Earl Siweard

186 LEASE OF LAND BY ÆLFWINE

eorl · 7 Siwerd eorl · 7 Swegen eorl · 7[1] Ordgar · 7 Odda · 7 Ælfgar · 7 þærtóeacan manig god mann ægðær[2] ge hadode ge léwede þe heora naman ne magon beon hǽr on ealle ámearcóde. Þyssa gewrita syndon þreo · án ís on ealdan mynstre · oþer ís mid þæs bisceopes landbocan · þridde hæfð Osgod.

XCIX. PURCHASE OF AN ESTATE IN HEREFORDSHIRE

Her swutelað on þissum gewrite þ Leofwine Leofflæde broðor hæfð geboht healfe hide landes æt Mælueshylle · æt Edrice[3] his mæge Ufices suna · mid healfe marce goldes · 7 mid ane punde seolfres 7 twegen oran · æfre in his cynn · to fane 7 to syllanne 10 þam þe him æfre leofost beo · On Swegnes eorles gewitnesse · 7 Æþelstanes bisceopes · 7 Þurceles hwitan · 7 Ulfceteles scirgerefan · 7 ealra þara þegna on Herefordscire 7 þara twegra hireda · æt sc̄e Æþelberhtes mynstre 7 sc̄e Guðlaces.

C. AGREEMENT BETWEEN THE ABBOT OF BURY ST EDMUNDS AND WULFGEAT

[H]Er[4] Switeleþ on þise wríte þe forwarde þe Wlfgeat and his 15 wif wrouhten with þan Abbot on sc̄e Eadmundes birí 7 alle þe hirde · þat ís þat he nímen[5] þat lond at Gyselíngham to þe forwarde þat þat ilke lond go ínto sc̄o Eadmunde[6] after Aelfwínes[7] day and hís wíues · and þat lond at ffakenham so ful and so forth so Wlgeat it oh ·⸍ go ít into seynt Eadm̄ after here boþere day 20 buten alken gentale · þise wríte sínden þre on hauið Wlfgeat hímself · oþer ís ín[8] seynt Eadmundes birí · þride hauid Stigand bisscop.

[1] Om. K. [2] -er, K.
[3] Ead-, K.
[4] A space has been left for the initial capital.
[5] unnen, K.
[6] Seinte Edmundes kyrke, MS. (b).
[7] Athelwynes, ibid.
[8] into, ibid.

and Earl Swegn and Ordgar and Odda and Ælfgar and in addition many good men, both ecclesiastics and laymen, whose names cannot all be recorded here.

There are three of these documents. One is at the Old Minster, the second is with the bishop's land-charters, Osgod has the third.

XCIX. PURCHASE OF AN ESTATE IN HEREFORDSHIRE

Here it is declared in this document that Leofwine, Leofflæd's brother, has bought half a hide of land at Mansell from Eadric his kinsman, Ufic's son, for half a mark of gold and a pound of silver and two ores, to be retained (?) for all time within his kin, and to be bestowed upon whomsoever he prefers.

[This has been done] with the cognisance of Earl Swegn and Bishop Æthelstan and Thurkil the White and Ulfketel the sheriff and all the thegns of Hereford and the two communities at St Æthelbert's monastery and at St Guthlac's.

C. AGREEMENT BETWEEN THE ABBOT OF BURY ST EDMUNDS AND WULFGEAT

Here is declared in this document the agreement that Wulfgeat and his wife have made with the abbot and all the community at Bury St Edmunds, namely that they shall take the estate at Gislingham, on condition that it shall pass to St Edmunds after the death of Ælfwine and his wife. And the estate at Fakenham, as fully and completely as Wulfgeat possesses it, shall pass without any controversy to St Edmunds after the death of both of them.

There are three of these documents. Wulfgeat himself has one, the second is at Bury St Edmunds, Bishop Stigand has the third.

CI. AGREEMENT BETWEEN ARCHBISHOP EADSIGE AND ÆTHELRIC

✠ Her swutelað on þisum gewrite embe þa forewyrd þe Ægelric worhte wið Eadsige arcebisceop æt þam lande æt Cert · þe Ceolnoð arcebisceop gebohte æt Hæleþan þam þegene mid his agenan sceatte · 7 Aþelulf[1] cing hit gebocode Ceolnoþe arce-
5 bisceope on ece yrfe · þis synd þænne þa forewyrd ꝥ Ægelric hæbbe ꝥ land æt Cert his dæg · 7 æfter his dæge ga þænne ꝥ land þam arcebisceope Eadsige on hand · swa gegodod swa heom bam gerisan mage · 7 syððan heora begra dæg agan si · Ægelrices 7 þæs arcebisceopes Eadsiges · þænne ga þis foresprecene land
10 into X̄p̄es cyricean mid mete 7 mid mannan eal swa hit stande · for Ægelrices sawle · 7 for Eadsiges arcebisceopes · þam Godes þeowan to fostre · 7 to scrude · þe þærinne Godes lof dreogan sceolan dæges 7 nihtes · 7 Ægelric gifð þa landboc þe þærto gebyreð on his life Criste · 7 þam hirede[2] him to ecere ælmessan ·
15 7 bruce Ægelric · 7 Esbearn his sunu þara oðra landa heora twegra dæg to þam ilcan forewyrdan þe Ægelnoð arcebisceop 7 Ægelric ær geworhtan · ꝥ is Stuting · 7 Melentun · 7 se haga binnan port þe Ægelric himsylfan getimbrod hæfde · 7 æfter heora twegra dæge fo se arcebisceop Eadsige þærto · gyf he leng
20 libbe þænne hi · oððe loc hwa his æftergencga þænne beo · butan sum heora freonda þa land furþor on þæs arcebisceopes gemede ofgan mage · to rihtan gafole · oððe to oþran forewyrdan · swa hit man þænne findan mage wið þone arcebisceop þe þanne libbe · 7 þises is to gewitnesse Eadweard cyncg · 7 Ælfgyfu seo
25 hlæfdige · 7 Ælfwine ƀ · 7 Stigand ƀ · 7 Godwine ƀ · 7 Godric decanus · 7 eal se hired æt Cristes cyricean · 7 Wulfric abbud · 7 eal se hired æt s̄c̄e Augustine · 7 Ælfwine abbud · 7 Siweard abbud · 7 Wulfnoð abb · 7 Godwine eorl · 7 Leofric eorl · 7 Atsur roda · 7 Ælfstan steallære · 7 Eadmær æt Burhham · 7
30 Godric æt Burnan · 7 Ælfwine se reada · 7 mænig man þærtoeacan ge gehadude ge læwede · binnan burgan 7 butan · 7 gif ænig

---

[1] *Æþel-*, T.   [2] *hired*, E.

CI. AGREEMENT BETWEEN ARCHBISHOP EADSIGE AND ÆTHELRIC

✠ Here is declared in this document the agreement which Æthelric has made with Archbishop Eadsige about the estate at Chart which Archbishop Ceolnoth bought from the thegn Hæletha with his own money, and which King Æthelwulf granted by charter to Archbishop Ceolnoth as a perpetual inheritance. These are the arrangements, that Æthelric shall have the estate at Chart for his lifetime, and after his death it shall pass into the possession of Archbishop Eadsige with such endowment as may suit them both, and after the life of both of them—Æthelric and Archbishop Eadsige—is over, the aforementioned estate shall pass to Christchurch with its produce and its men exactly as it stands, on behalf of the souls of Æthelric and Archbishop Eadsige, to provide food and clothing for the servants of God whose duty it is to celebrate the praise of God therein day and night. And Æthelric presents the title-deeds of this estate during his lifetime to Christ and the community as a perpetual charitable gift. And Æthelric and his son Esbearn shall enjoy their other estates, namely Stowting and Milton and the messuage in the town which Æthelric himself had built, during the lifetime of both of them, in accordance with the arrangements which Archbishop Æthelnoth and Æthelric had made. And after the death of both of them Archbishop Eadsige shall take possession of them, if he lives longer than they, or whoever is his successor at the time, unless one of their friends can continue to hold the estates, agreeably to the archbishop, at a fair rent or in accordance with such other arrangements as may be devised at the time with the existing archbishop.

The witnesses of this are King Edward and the Lady Ælfgifu and Bishop Ælfwine and Bishop Stigand and Bishop Godwine and Godric the dean and all the community at Christchurch and Abbot Wulfric and all the community at St Augustine's and Abbot Ælfwine and Abbot Siweard and Abbot Wulfnoth and Earl Godwine and Earl Leofric and Atsur the Red and Ælfstan the Staller and Eadmær of Burham and Godric of Bourne and Ælfwine the Red and many men in addition, both ecclesiastics and laymen, within the city and without.

190 AGREEMENT BETWEEN

man on uferan dagan gehadud oððe læwede þisne cwyde wille awendan · awende hine God ælmihtig hrædlice of þisan lænan life into helle wite · 7 þær a wunige mid eallan þam deoflan þe seo laðlice wunung betæht is · buton he þe deoppor hit gebete 5 ær his ende · wið Crist sylfne 7 wið þone hired. Nu synd þissa gewrita þreo · an is innan Cristes cyricean · 7 oþer æt sc̄e Augustine · 7 þ̃ þridde hæfð Ægelric mid him sylfan.

CII. AGREEMENT BETWEEN ÆLFSTAN, ABBOT OF ST AUGUSTINE'S, AND THE PRIEST LEOFWINE

✠ Her swutelað on þisum gewrite [þa forew]eard[1] þe Godwine eorl worhte betweonan Ælfstane abb 7 þam hirede æt sc̄e 10 Augustine 7 Leofwine preoste embe sc̄a Myl[dryþe a]re[2] · þ̃ is ðæt Leofwine cænde þ̃ he bohte þa are æt Cnute cinincge · 7 se abb cænde þ̃ Cnut cing gelogode þa halig . . . . . . e þ[3]. . .ra eama wergeld wæs into sc̄e Augustine una[wen]dedlice · þam Godes ðyowan bi to libbanne ða hwile . . . . nu is þis[4] se seht þe God-15 wine eorl worhte betweonan þæm [ab]b[5] [7] þam hirede æt sc̄e Augustine · 7 Leo[fw]ine preoste . . . . . .an[6] Leofwine preoste .II. suling landes an æt Lang[a]dune[7] 7 oþer æt Gildinge 7 .v. pund penega æt[3] . . . . .es[8] mæssan[8] · 7 healf to midlængtene · on ful . . . . . . 7 æfter[9] his dæge ga land 7 feoh into sc̄e Augustine 20 mid[3] . . . .ā[3] 7 magum 7[3] . . . geborenan mæn · si abb se ðe si · nu is þises [to gewitnesse] Eadsi arceb · 7 Siword b · 7 Godwine eorl þe ðone seh[t worhte 7] se hired æt[10] Cristesciricean · 7 se hired æt Sc̄e Augustine · nu [sin]d[11] þisse gewrite þreo · an is æt Cristes cyricean · 7 oþer æt Sc̄e Augustine · 7 þridde hæfð 25 Leofwine preost.

---

[1] The MS. is badly stained in two places (a large stain towards the left and a smaller one on the right) hence the illegible parts.
[2] *sancta*......*ne*, K.; *sancte*......*ne*, O.S. transcript.
[3] Om. K., O.S.   [4] *nu is þis*, om. K., O.S.
[5] *arcebisceop*, K.   [6] *man*, K.; *unnan*, O.S.
[7] *Langtune*, K.   [8] *elmæssan*, K.
[9] *7 æfter*, om. K., O.S.   [10] *on*, K.; om. O.S.
[11] [*Nu si*]*nd*, K.; om. O.S.

If any man in days to come, ecclesiastic or layman, attempts to alter this bequest, God Almighty shall remove him speedily from this transitory life to the torment of hell, and there he shall dwell forever with all the devils to whom the loathsome dwelling is assigned, unless before his death he make amends as fully as possible to Christ and to the community.

There are three of these documents. One is at Christchurch, the second at St Augustine's, and the third is in the possession of Æthelric himself.

CII. AGREEMENT BETWEEN ÆLFSTAN, ABBOT OF ST AUGUSTINE'S, AND THE PRIEST LEOFWINE

✠ Here is declared in this document the agreement that Earl Godwine has made between Abbot Ælfstan and the community at St Augustine's and the priest Leofwine about St Mildred's property (?). Leofwine declared that he bought the property from King Cnut, and the abbot declared that King Cnut placed the holy [body in the monastery and that her] uncles' wergeld passed unalterably to St Augustine's for the servants of God to live by as long as .... Now this is the settlement that Earl Godwine has made between the Abbot and the community at St Augustine's and the priest Leofwine, [namely that they should grant] to the priest Leofwine two ploughlands, one at Langdon and the other at Ileden, and 5 pounds of pennies at ......mas and half at mid-Lent ...... and after his death both the money and the estate shall pass to St Augustine's with its men (?) and women and every (?) human being then born, whoever happens to be abbot.

The witnesses of this are Archbishop Eadsige and Bishop Siweard and Earl Godwine, who made the settlement, and the community at Christchurch and the community at St Augustine's. There are three of these documents. One is at Christchurch, the second at St Augustine's and the priest Leofwine has the third.

CIII. PURCHASE OF AN ESTATE IN KENT

✠ Her swutelað on þisum gewrite hu Godric æt Burnan[1] begeat þ land æt Offaham þ is ðonne þ he sealde Eadgyuan his sweostor an marc goldes 7 XIII. p̄d. 7 LXIII. pen̄. on geceapodne ceap to gyfanne 7 to syllanne[2] on dæge 7 æfter dæge þam þe him leofust
5 sy. Þes ceap wæs geceapod on Wii[3] ætforan ealra scyre. Þises is to gewitnesse Eadsige arceb. 7 Siward b. 7 Godric decanus · 7 eall se hired æt Cristes cyricean · 7 Wulfric abb 7 se hired æt[4] sc̄e Augustine · 7 Ægelric bygga · 7 Þurgar Ælfgares sunu · 7 Eadric Ælfrices sunu · 7 Osweard æt Hergeardesham · 7 Leof-
10 wine preost 7 Godric portgerefa[5] · 7 Wulfsige þæs cynges gerefa · 7 manig god mann[6] þarto. Nu synd þissa gewrita þreo an is æt Cristes cyricean · 7 oþer æt sc̄e Augustine · 7 þridde hæfð Godric mid him.

CIV. NOTES WITH REGARD TO FOOD-RENTS, CHARITABLE GIFTS, ETC. FROM BURY ST EDMUNDS

hic instat[7]
Her stent ða forwarde ðe Æþeric worhte wið ðan abbode on
15 Nīwentune · þ is .III. sceppe mealtes 7 healf sceppe hwæte · án slægryðer .v. scep .x. fliccen · 7 .x. hund hlafe · þ sceal beon gære · on pridie NON*AS* Septembris · Leofstan abb[8] doð to þis fermfultum · an sceppe malt · 7 .III. hund hlafe · 7 .VI. fliccen · 7 oþer .VI. to fyllincge · into þan ealdan fyrme · 7 .X. cesen · 7
20 eallswa mycel Brihtric p̄r · 7 eallswa mycel Leofstan buton .X. cesen wane · 7 Đurstan syflincge to III hund lafe · 7 twegen oran into kycene · 7 Brihtric .XVI. pen̄.
On Elsingtun-hundred ah Sc̄e Eadmund XXVII. manslot. On Spelhoge hundred .XLV. manslot. On Ín hundred .X. manslot.
25 On Fuwelege hundred healf eh't'eþe manslot. On Ærnehogo hundred .XXV. manslot. On Clencware hundred healf ehteþe manslot. On Lynware hundred .V. manslot. Fram Aþolfes

---

[1] -nam, Madox.   [2] -ane, ibid.   [3] wu, ibid.
[4] et, ibid.   [5] -geresa, ibid.   [6] man, T.
[7] This is in smaller handwriting.   [8] abbode, Douglas.

CIII. PURCHASE OF AN ESTATE IN KENT

✠ Here it is declared in this document how Godric of Bourne acquired the estate at Offham. The transaction was as follows: he gave his sister Eadgifu a mark of gold and 13 pounds [of silver] and 63 pence to complete the purchase, so that he might have the right of giving and granting it during his lifetime and at his death to whomsoever he preferred. This purchase has been completed at Wye before the whole shire, and the witnesses are Archbishop Eadsige and Bishop Siweard and Godric the dean and all the community at Christchurch, and Abbot Wulfric and the community at St Augustine's, and Æthelric Bigga and Thurgar, Ælfgar's son, and Eadric, Ælfric's son, and Osweard of Harrietsham and Leofwine the priest and Godric the town reeve and Wulfsige the king's reeve and many good men in addition.

There are three of these documents. One is at Christchurch and the second at St Augustine's and the third is in Godric's possession.

CIV. NOTES WITH REGARD TO FOOD-RENTS, CHARITABLE GIFTS, ETC. FROM BURY ST EDMUNDS

Here is stated the agreement that Ætheric has made with the abbot at Newton, namely 3 bushels of malt and half a bushel of wheat, one ox for slaughtering, 5 sheep, 10 flitches of bacon and 1000 loaves, to be ready on September 4. Abbot Leofstan adds this additional contribution to the old food-rent—1 bushel of malt and 300 loaves and 6 flitches of bacon and another 6 to complete it, and 10 cheeses, and Brihtric the prior (?) the same amount, and Leofstan the same amount, except for the 10 cheeses, and Thurstan relish for 300 loaves, and 2 ores to the kitchen, and Brihtric 16 pence.

In Islington Hundred St Edmund has 27 single holdings. In Spellow Hundred 45 single holdings. In *In* Hundred 10 single holdings. In *Fuwelege* Hundred 7½ single holdings. In *Ærnehogo* Hundred 25 single holdings. In Clenchwarton Hundred 7½ single holdings. In Lynn Hundred 5 single holdings. From Athulf's

194 NOTES ON FOOD-RENTS, ETC.

suðtun · to álde Walbec · Fram Watlingetune norð into sæ · ah Sc̃e Eadmund landes dæle · mid his landemacan.

Ures drihtnes hælendes Cristes freo náma á on ecnyssa sy gewurþod þe ængla wuldorheap him sylfum to wyrðscipe ge-
5 gearawode · 7 eac manna wynsumlic wlita · æfter his agenan anlicnessan gehywlæhte · syllende heom genihtsumlice geofa heofonas 7 eorþan · swa he nu dagum Breotanrices fægran iglandes · Eadwearde cyncge sealde 7 geuþe · ealswa he æror geara his magum dyde · ðæra wæs sum æþel 7 wurðful Sc̃e
10 Eadmund gehaten · 7 se mid Criste sylfum nu eardað on heofonum.

Betæhte nu cincg se goda Eadward 7 se wurðfulla his mæges mynstere on Bædericeswyrðe Leofstan abbode þ he bewiste þ þæt þær wære inne 7 ute · 7 he þa þær þus mycel funde .x. bec
15 inne ðæra circean .IIII. Cristes bec 7 I mæsseboc 7 I pistelboc · 7 .I. salter · 7 .I. god spellboc · 7 .I. capitularia · 7 Sc̃e Eadmundes uita. In madmhus .XII. mæssehácelan · 7 nigon cantercæppa 7 .IIII. roccas · 7 .VII. stolan · 7 .XXXIII. pella · 7 .IX. weofodsceatas · 7 .XV. superumerale gerenode · 7 .XXV. alba · 7 .VII.
20 setrægl · 7 .XIII. wahrægl · 7 .III. rygcrægl · 7 .II. scufrægl · 7 .V. calices · 7 .III. offringclaþas · 7 .VII. corporale · 7 .II. storscylle · 7 .III. marmarstan gesmiðede · 7 .IIII. scrinan · 7 .XIIII. rodan. Blakere hæfð .I. winter rædingboc. Brihtric hæfð I mæssereaf calix 7 disc 7 .I. mæsseboc · 7 winter rædingboc · 7 sumerboc.
25 Siuerð hæfð an mæssereaf · 7 an mæsseboc · 7 Leofstan an handboc. Æþeric an mæsseboc · 7 capitularia. Đurstan an psalter. Oskytel hæfð an mæssereaf · 7 an mæsseboc 7 an Ad te leuaui. On Sc̃e Eadmundes byrig beoð .XVI. hida eorðes landes .VI. hida into þæra byrig 7 þa .X. hida manna earningaland. On
30 Wirlingaweorðe lið anes monðes ferme mid þan berwica · Saham. On Pallegrafe anes monðes ferme mid Þorpa. On Redgrafe anes monðes ferma. On Ricyncgahale anes monðes ferma mid Stoca 7 Brocaforde. On Byrtune anes monðes ferma. On Ruhham · anes monðes ferma. On Elmeswella anes monðes

'Sutton' to the old 'Walbeck', from Watlington north to the sea St Edmund has a share of the land with his neighbours.

May the noble name of our Lord the Saviour Christ be honoured for ever to all eternity. He formed the glorious company of angels for his own honour, and likewise fashioned the winsome countenance of men after his own image, bestowing abundantly upon them the gifts of heaven and earth. In these days he has given and granted to King Edward the fair island of Britain, as he did of yore to his kinsmen, one of whom was by name the noble and honourable St Edmund, who now dwells in heaven with Christ himself.

The good and honourable King Edward has now entrusted his kinsman's monastery at Bedericesworth to Abbot Leofstan to take charge of everything there, both inside and out, and he has found this much there, namely 10 books inside the church, consisting of 4 gospel books and 1 missal and 1 epistle book and 1 psalter and 1 good book of homilies and 1 capitulary and the Life of St Edmund. In the treasure house [he has found] 12 chasubles and 9 cantor's copes and 4 vestments and 7 stoles and 33 cloaks and 9 altar cloths and 15 ornamented superhumerals and 25 albs and 7 seat covers and 13 wall curtains and 3 dorsals and 2 movable curtains and 5 chalices and 3 offertory cloths and 7 corporals and 2 censers and 3 marble stones bound with metal and 4 chests and 14 crosses. Blacere has 1 winter lectionary. Brihtric has 1 mass vestment, a chalice and a paten, 1 missal and a winter lectionary and a summer book. Siferth has one mass vestment and one missal and Leofstan one manual; Ætheric one missal and a capitulary; Thurstan one psalter. Oscytel has one mass vestment and one missal and one *Ad te levavi*.

At Bury St Edmunds there are 16 hides of arable land— 6 hides in demesne and the [remaining] 10 hides held by men in return for services.

Worlingworth supplies a month's food-rent along with the berewick of Soham; Palgrave a month's food-rent along with Thorpe; Redgrave a month's food-rent; Rickinghall a month's food-rent along with Stoke and Brockford; Barton a month's food-rent; Rougham a month's food-rent; Elmswell a month's

196 NOTES ON FOOD-RENTS, ETC.

ferma · mid Wulpettas 7 Grotene. On Koccefelda anes monðes ferma mid Ceorlesweorðe. On Hwipstede anes monðes ferma · mid Bradefeldæ. On Horningasearðe anes monðes ferma · mid Rysebi. On Lecforde anes monðes ferma · mid Hyrningcwylle.
5 On Runcgetune anes monðes ferma · mid Culeforde 7 mid Fornham. Her syndon .xxx. boca · ealre on Leofstanes abbodes hafona · butan mynsterbec.
On Paccenham anes monðes ferma mid Stantune[1].
10 hic instat conscriptum quid inuentum fuerit apud Eggemere postquam Her[2] onstent gewriten hwæt man funde æt Eggemere syððan Cole eam dimisit hoc est seofene boues et ahte uaccę et fower pascuales Cole hit let. Ðæt is .VII. oxen · 7 .VIII. cy · 7 .IIII. feldhryuituli et equi uiles et quinquies uiginti oues et fiftene oues inte
15 þera · 7 .II. stottas · 7 .V. scora scæp · 7 .XV. scæp under ealde et et octies uiginti agri seminati et an bacun et an porcus et fower 7 iunge ·7 .VIII. score æcere gesawen 7 .I. flicce 7 .I. swin 7 twenti casei.
7 .XXIIII. cesen.
20   Her[3] stant gewriten hwæt Baldwine abb.ᵗ hæfð geunnen[4] his
                                       twegra
gebroþra to caritatem þ is .II. mylnegafel æt Lacforde · hælf pund æt þ án 7 XII. 'or' æt þ oþer · þ hea'l'f pund we sculan habban æt natiuitatem scæ Mariæ · 7 'ða' VI. 'or' æt 'Sc̄e'[5] Dionisius messę 7 VI. 'or' æt 'Sc̄e'[6] Nicholaus · 7 þær sculan eac
25 .II. fætte swyn up arisan to smolte · oððe .III. oran.
Ðis is seo caritas þe Baldwine abb hæfð geunnen[4] his gebroðrum for Eadwardes sawle þæs godan kynges · þ is healf pund æt his geargemynde to fisce · to þan forewardan þ hi hine þæs þe oftor gemunon on heora gebedreddene · 7 healf pund to þan
30 timan ealswa ic hider com to mynstre .XIIII. k. Sep⁹ · 7 stande þis pund æfre on Godes est 7 on Sc̄e Eadmundes cume her to se þe cume · to minon geargemynde · þis feoh sceal arisan of Ixewyrðe þe lið into Pakenhame. Æt[7] Vuiges gearimynd abbes we sculan habben half pund to fisce · 7 feowerti · p[8] · to mede ·
35 7 .II. mett hwæte · 7 þ sceal risen of Lecforde.

---

[1] The first handwriting continues as far as this which is the final entry on f. 107 b.
[2] This paragraph, which is the first on f. 108, may be by the first hand. The interlinear Latin translation may be by the same hand as the Latin on f. 108 b.

food-rent along with Woolpit and Groton; Cockfield a month's food-rent along with Chelsworth; Whepstead a month's food-rent along with Bradfield; Horringer a month's food-rent along with Risby; Lackford a month's food-rent along with Herringswell; Runcton a month's food-rent along with Culford and Fornham.

There are 30 books here, all in Abbot Leofstan's possession, apart from the monastery books.

Pakenham [supplies] one month's food-rent along with Stanton.

Here is recorded what was found at Egmere after Cole left it, namely 7 oxen and 8 cows and 4 grazing bullocks and 2 inferior horses and 115 sheep, including both full-grown and young ones, and 160 acres sown and 1 flitch of bacon and 1 pig and 24 cheeses.

Here is recorded what Abbot Baldwin has granted to his brethren as a charitable gift, namely the rent of two mills at Lackford, half a pound from the one and 12 ores from the other. We shall have the half pound at the Nativity of St Mary and 6 ores at the festival of St Dionysius and 6 ores at [the festival of] St Nicholas, and 2 fat pigs shall likewise be produced to supply lard, or else 3 ores.

This is the charitable gift which Abbot Baldwin has granted to his brethren for the soul of Edward, the good king, namely half a pound to supply fish at his anniversary, on condition that they remember him the oftener in their prayers, and half a pound on the anniversary of my coming here to the monastery, i.e. August 19. And this pound shall continue to be given at my anniversary by the grace of God and St Edmund, whosoever succeeds here. The money shall be due from Ixworth which belongs to Pakenham. At Abbot Ufi's anniversary we shall have half a pound for fish and 40 pence for mead and 2 measures of wheat, and that shall be due from Lackford.

---

[3] This paragraph and the one which follows are in rather smaller handwriting than what precedes.
[4] *-an*, Douglas.   [5] Entered later in the margin.
[6] Entered later above the line.
[7] This entry, which is the last on f. 108, is in a different hand, perhaps identical with that of the Latin which follows.
[8] *pund*, Douglas.

NOTES ON FOOD-RENTS, ETC.

Ad[1] anniuersarium diem depositionis regis Willi constituit donnus abbas Balduuinus ut nobis eodem die ad pitantiam dentur quoque anno .x. solidi · et in die obitus reginę eiusdem · scilicet Mahtildę tantundem idem .x. sol ex[2] debito perpetuo adaugere nobis censuit. Et ut certitudo sit unde hec pecunia scilicet .xx. solidi debeant omni anno reddi ad opus fratrum · ipsemet donnus abbas in pleno capitulo coram omnibus confirmauit quod de manerio 'Werkentune'[3] quod ipse rex .W. pro anima reginę prefatę dedit Sc̄o Eadmundo solueretur ⁄ dignum scilicet iudicans ut fratribus 'in' illorum anniuersariis in uictu aliquid melius fiat · quorum mentionem ante deum ipsi in orationibus suis frequenter et ut ita dicam sine intermissione celebrare non trepidant.

Ad anniuersarium depositionis diem regis Æduuardi constituit idem supradictus abbas fratribus suis .x. solidos ad pitantiam · ut deuotius · eius animę memoriam habeant.

Constituo etiam ego Balduuinus abbas in perpetuum tenendum quicunque post me ueniat abbas .x. sol. ad diem anniuersarium mei aduentus abbatia mihi data · hoc est .xiiii. kalendas SEPTEMBRIS · Isti .xx. sol. debent dari de Ixeuuorde · quę pertinet ad Pakenham.

Ad anniuersarium Vulj abbatis debent fratres habere .x sol ad pitantiam · et .iii. sol et iiii. deñ. ad medonem · et ii. mensuras frumenti. Et hec dantur de Lacforde.

Hanc caritatem constituit abbas .B. ad natiuitatem Sc̄e MARIE · scilicet .x. sol. et .viii. sol. ad festum Sc̄i Dionisii · et or .iiii. sol ad festum sc̄i Nicholai · et super hęc .ii. porcos pingues · or aut .iiii. sol ad saginam. Istud totum dabitur de duobus molendinis de Lacforde · quorum .i. reddit .x. sol · et alterum .xvi. sol.

Ðis[4] is Sc̄e Eadmundes ferme on Byrtune .iiii. met maltes under masc 7 grut · halmet hwæte · an[5] ryðer · 7 ii. swin .iiii. ges .xx. hennen. Of Ruham ealswa mycel · 7 of Redgraue ealswa

---
[1] The Latin paragraphs which follow have been entered on f. 108 b in a different and later handwriting.
[2] et, Douglas.   [3] In the margin; Werketone, Douglas.
[4] This begins on f. 109 and is in a different handwriting from any which precedes.
[5] An oblong, which may have contained a word, has been cut out of the page before an.

At the anniversary of the burial of King William the Lord Abbot Baldwin has appointed that every year on the same day 10 shillings shall be given to us as a charitable gift, and on the day of the death of his queen, namely Matilda, he has decreed that the same amount, namely 10 shillings, shall be paid to us in addition as a perpetual obligation. And in order that it may be established whence this money, namely 20 shillings, shall be paid every year for the use of the brethren, the same Lord Abbot has decreed in full chapter in the presence of all, that it should be paid from the manor of Warkton which the said King William gave to St Edmund for the soul of the aforesaid queen, since he (the abbot) judges it proper that the brethren should enjoy something better as food on the anniversaries of those whose names they do not hesitate to repeat in their prayers before God frequently and, so to say, without intermission.

At the anniversary of the burial of King Edward the same above-mentioned abbot has appointed 10 shillings as a charitable gift for his brethren, that they may remember his soul with the greater devotion.

I, Abbot Baldwin, likewise appoint for perpetual observation, whoever comes after me as abbot, that 10 shillings be given on my behalf on the anniversary of my coming as abbot, namely on August 19. These 20 shillings shall be given from Ixworth which belongs to Pakenham.

On the anniversary of Abbot Ufi the brethren shall have 10 shillings as a charitable gift, and 3 shillings and 4 pence for mead and 2 measures of wheat. And these shall be given from Lackford.

This is the charitable gift which Abbot Baldwin has appointed for the Nativity of St Mary, namely 10 shillings, and 8 shillings at the festival of St Dionysius and 4 shillings at the festival of St Nicholas, and in addition 2 fat pigs or 4 shillings for lard. The whole of this shall be given from two mills at Lackford, of which one shall render 10 shillings and the other 16 shillings.

This is St Edmund's food-rent from Barton, namely 4 measures of malt, including both mash and grist, half a measure of wheat, one bullock, 2 pigs, 4 geese, 20 hens. From Rougham the same amount, and from Redgrave the same. From Pakenham and

200 NOTES ON FOOD-RENTS, ETC.

Of Pakenham 7 of Stantune ealswa mycel. Of Elmeswelle 7 of Wulpet 7 of Grotene ealswa. Of Herningwelle 7 of Cunegestune ealswa mycel Of Palegraue 7 of Ðorpe ealswa mycel. Of Horningeseorðe 7 of Risby ealswa micel. Of Kokefelde 7 of 5 Ceorleswurðe ealswa micel. Of Hwepstede 7 of Bradefelde ealswa mycel. Of Wyrlingwurðe 7 of Saham ealswa mycel. Of Rungetune · 7 of Culeforde 7 of Fornham ealswa mycel. On Brokeforde 7 of Rikingehale · ealswa mycel. Of Tifteshale .i. met maltes under masc 7 grut[1] 7 .i. lepene hwæte · 7 feorðendæl 10 an ryðer 7 an half swin 7 an gos 7 .v. hennen.

CV. AGREEMENT BETWEEN THE BISHOP AND COMMUNITY AT SHERBORNE AND CARE, TOKI'S SON

Her cyð on þisum[2] gewrite hu þa forword wæron geworhte on Excestre ætforan Godwine eorle[3] 7 ætforan ealra[4] scire betwyx Alfwolde bisceope 7 þam hirede æt Scireburnan 7 Care Tokies suna æt þam lande æt Holacumbe · þ wæs þ hi wurdon sehte 15 þæt þa gebroðra eallæ geodon[5] of þam lande butan anum · se is[6] Ulf gehatan[7] þe hyt becweden wæs · þ he hyt hæbbe his dæg · 7 ofer his dæg gá þæt land swa swa hit stent mid mete 7 mid mannum unbesacun 7 unbefliten into þam halgan mynstre to Scireburnan. Þyses is to gewitnesse Godwine eorl · 7 Alfwold 20 bisceop on Dorsæton · 7 Lyfing b be norðan · 7 Ælfwine abb on Bucfæsten · 7 Sihtric abb on Tæfingstoce · 7 Odda · 7 Ælfric his broðor · 7 Ordgar 7 his twegen gebroðra · Ælfgær 7 Escbern · 7 Dodda cild · 7 Alon · 7 Æþelmær Cola sunu · 7 Osmær · 7 Leofwine æt Exon · 7 Ælfweard Alfwoldes sunu · 7 Wiking 7 25 Ælfgær æt Mynheafdon · 7 Wulfweard æt Winesham · 7 Hunewine Héca sunu · 7 Ælfwig æt Hægdune · 7 Godman preost · 7 Lutsige on Wiht; · 7 se þe þis awendan wylle oþþe ætbredan þænce[8] þære[9] halgan stowe ⸴ si he awend fram Gode on

[1] An erasure follows.   [2] ðys-, K.   [3] eorl, T.
[4] -re, K., T.   [5] geeodon, K., T.   [6] his, T.
[7] -en, K.   [8] ðæna, K.   [9] ðone, K.

from Stanton the same amount. From Elmswell and from Woolpit and from Groton the same. From Herringswell and from Coney Weston the same amount. From Palgrave and from Thorpe the same amount. From Horringer and from Risby the same amount. From Cockfield and from Chelsworth the same amount. From Whepstead and from Bradfield the same amount. From Worlingworth and from Soham the same amount. From Runcton and from Culford and from Fornham the same amount. From Brockford and from Rickinghall the same amount. From Tivetshall 1 measure of malt, including mash and grist, and 1 *lepene* of wheat and the quarter of a bullock and half a pig and one goose and 5 hens.

CV. AGREEMENT BETWEEN THE BISHOP AND COMMUNITY AT SHERBORNE AND CARE, TOKI'S SON

Here it is announced in this document how arrangements were made at Exeter before Earl Godwine and the whole shire between Bishop Ælfwold and the community at Sherborne and Care, Toki's son, with regard to the estate at Holcombe. They agreed that all the brothers should leave the estate except one, called Ulf, to whom it was bequeathed, and that he should have it for his lifetime, and after his death the estate should pass as it stands with its produce and its men, uncontested and undisputed, to the holy monastery at Sherborne.

The witnesses of this are Earl Godwine and Ælfwold, Bishop of Dorset, and Lyfing, Bishop to the north, and Ælfwine, Abbot of Buckfast, and Sihtric, Abbot of Tavistock, and Odda and Ælfric his brother, and Ordgar and his two brothers, Ælfgar and Esbearn, and Dodda *cild* and Alon and Æthelmær, Cola's son, and Osmær and Leofwine of Exe and Ælfweard, Ælfwold's son, and Wiking and Ælfgar of Minehead and Wulfweard of Winsham and Hunewine, Heca's son, and Ælfwig of Haydon and Godman the priest and Lutsige of Wight.

And if anyone attempts to alter this or intends to take it away from the holy foundation, he shall be cast out by God and by

202 AGREEMENT BETWEEN SHERBORNE

domesdæg 7 fram eallum his halgum · 7 si he besenct on middan
þam weallendan bryne helle wites mid Iudan Cristes læwan á
ecelice fordemed · butan[1] he hit her ær þe deoppor gebete; ·
Þyssera gewrita syndon twá · án ys æt Scireburnan · 7 þæt oþer
5 æt Cridiantúne · sprecaþ buta[2] án:—

CVI. LEASE OF LAND BY STIGAND, BISHOP OF WINCHESTER, TO ÆÞELMÆR

HER swytelað on þissum gewritæ þæt Stigand Bisceop · And
sæ hiræð on ealdan mynstræ lætan to Æþælmære[3] ane hidæ
landæs æt Spæresholte hís dæg and Sæmannes dæg his suna
wyð swylcan sceattæ swylcæ[4] he hit þa findon mihte. Þyses ís
10 to gewitnæssæ Stigand bisceop · And sæ hireð on ealdan mynstræ
and Ælfwinæ abbod · and sæ hireð on níwan mynstræ · And
eallæ scyrþægenas on Hamtunsciræ. Þissa gewrita syndan twa
an ís on ealdan mynstræ · and oþær hæfð Æþelmær.

CVII. LEASE OF LAND BY STIGAND, BISHOP OF WINCHESTER, TO WULFRIC

HER swytelað on þissum gewrite þa foreweard þæ[5] Stigand
15 bisceop 7 se hired on ealdan mynstre worhtan wið Wulfric þa
ða hy letan him to þa twa hida landes æt AWeltune[6] 7 ane gyrde ·
7 æt Peattanigge þreo gyrda · 7 þa mæde þa gebyrað to ðam
gereflande 7 twegra getymæna[7] læse[7] · 7 tyn cúna forð[8] mið[9] þas
hlafordes · 7 his sceapa læse æfter þæs hlafordes his deg[10] 7 anes
20 mannes deg æfter him swylce hæ best geunne wið swylcan
sceatte swylce he hít þa findæ mihte. Þises is to gewitnesse
Stigand b · 7 Godwine eorl · 7 se hired ón ealdan mynstre · 7
Ælfwine abb · 7 se hired on niwan mynstre and ealle scirþegenas
on Hamtunscire. Þissa gewrita syndan þreo an ís on ealdan
25 mynstre · and oþer is on Wiltune · and þridde æfed Wlfric.

[1] *buton* changed to *-an*; *-on*, K., T.   [2] *butu*, K.
[3] *-mæræ*, K.   [4] *-ce*, K.   [5] *þe*, B.
[6] *Apel-*, K.   [7] *gecy mænalæse*, K.   [8] *ford*, B.
[9] *mid*, K.   [10] *dæg*, B.

all his saints on the Day of Judgment and plunged into the midst of the surging fiery torment of hell, damned for ever with Judas, the betrayer of Christ, unless he has made amends for it here as fully as possible.

There are two of these documents. One is at Sherborne and the other at Crediton. Both say the same.

CVI. LEASE OF LAND BY STIGAND, BISHOP OF WINCHESTER, TO ÆTHELMÆR

Here it is declared in this document that Bishop Stigand and the community at the Old Minster have let a hide of land at Sparsholt to Æthelmær for his lifetime and that of his son Sæman, for as much money as he could furnish at the time.

The witnesses of this are Bishop Stigand and the community at the Old Minster, and Abbot Ælfwine and the community at the New Minster, and all the thegns in Hampshire.

There are two of these documents. One is at the Old Minster and Æthelmær has the other.

CVII. LEASE OF LAND BY STIGAND, BISHOP OF WINCHESTER, TO WULFRIC

Here is declared in this document the agreement that Bishop Stigand and the community at the Old Minster have made with Wulfric, when they let to him for his lifetime, and that of [the] one man after him to whom he most willingly grants it, the two hides of land and one yardland at Alton and three yardlands at Patney, and the meadow belonging to the 'reeveland', and pasture for two teams and ten cows along with the lord's, and pasture for his sheep after the lord's, in return for as much money as he could furnish at the time.

The witnesses of this are Bishop Stigand and Earl Godwine and the community at the Old Minster, and Abbot Ælfwine and the community at the New Minster, and all the thegns in Hampshire.

There are three of these documents. One is at the Old Minster, and the second at Wilton, and Wulfric has the third.

CVIII. GRANT OF LAND BY ARCHBISHOP EADSIGE TO ST AUGUSTINE'S

✠ Her swutelað on þisum gewrite þ Eadsi arcebisceop hæfð geunnan Gode 7 sc̄e Augustine .v. æcera landes butan reada gatan · 7 þa mæda wiðutan Wiwergatan þe þarto lið · unawendedlice for his sawle · on þa forwyrd ðæt þa gebroðra him beon holde 5 on heora gebedum · ægþer ge on life · ge æfter life swa hy him behatan habbað. Nu is ðises to gewitnesse Godwine b on Rofeceastra · 7 Godwine b æt sc̄e Martine · 7 Godric decanus 7 eall se hired æt X̄p̄es cyrcean · 7 Leofwine preost · 7 eall se hired on Doferan · 7 Ægelric bicga · 7 Esbearn · 7 Ægelwine 10 Ælfelmes sunu · 7 Þurgar · 7 Eadric æt Æþelham · 7 Eadwine þæs arceb broðor · 7 Ælfwine se reada · 7 Godric æt Burnan · 7 Ælfred · 7 his broðor Gyldewine · 7 seo burwara eall on Cantwarabyrig · 7 þarto manig god mann · ægðer ge binnan byrig ge buton. Nu synd ðissa gewrita twa · an is æt X̄p̄es cyrcean · oþer 15 æt sc̄e Augustine.

CIX. SURVEY OF THE MANOR OF TIDENHAM, GLOUCESTERSHIRE

ON Dyddanhamme synd .xxx. hida .ix. inlandes · 7 .xxi. hida gesettes landes. To Stræt synd .xii. hida .xxvii. gyrda gafollandes · 7 on Sæuerne .xxx. cytweras. To Middeltune .v. hida .xiiii. gyrda gafollandes .xiiii. cytweras on Sæuerne · 7 .ii. hæc- 20 weras on Wæge. To Cingestune .v. hida sind .xiii. gyrda gafollandes · 7 .i. hida bufan dic þ is nu eac gafolland · 7 þ utan hamme is gyt sum inland · Sum hit is þan[1] scipwealan to gafole gesett. To Cyngestune on Sæuerne .xxi. cytwera · 7 on Wæge .xii. To Bispestune[2] Synd .iii. hida · 7 .xv. cytweras · on Wæge. On 25 Landcawet synd .iii. hida · 7 .ii. hæcweras on Wæge · 7 .ix. cytweras. Ofer eall þ land gebyrað at[3] gyrde .xii. pæneḡ. 7 .iiii. ælmespeneḡ. Æt ælcum were þe binnan þam .xxx. hidan

[1] þam, B.   [2] Biscopes-, K., E.   [3] æt, K., E.

CVIII. GRANT OF LAND BY ARCHBISHOP EADSIGE TO ST AUGUSTINE'S

✠ Here it is declared in this document that Archbishop Eadsige has granted to God and St Augustine, unalterably on behalf of his soul, 5 acres of land outside Ridingate and the meadow outside Worth Gate which belongs to it, on condition that the brethren shall be loyal to him in their prayers, both during his life and after his death, as they have promised him.

The witnesses of this are Godwine, Bishop of Rochester, and Godwine, Bishop of St Martin's, and Godric the dean and all the community at Christchurch, and the priest Leofwine and all the community at Dover, and Æthelric Bigga and Esbearn and Æthelwine, Ælfhelm's son, and Thurgar and Eadric of Elham and Edwin, the Archbishop's brother, and Ælfwine the Red and Godric of Bourne and Alfred and his brother Goldwine and all the citizens of Canterbury and many good men in addition, both within the city and without.

There are two of these documents. One is at Christchurch and the other at St Augustine's.

CIX. SURVEY OF THE MANOR OF TIDENHAM, GLOUCESTERSHIRE

In Tidenham there are 30 hides, [made up of] 9 hides of demesne land and 21 hides of land occupied [by tenants]. At Stroat there are 12 hides, [including] 27 yardlands of rent-paying land and 30 basket weirs on the Severn. At Milton 5 hides, [including] 14 yardlands of rent-paying land, 14 basket weirs on the Severn and 2 hackle weirs on the Wye. At *Kingston* there are 5 hides, [including] 13 yardlands of rent-paying land, and 1 hide above the dyke is now rent-paying land also, and what there is outside the enclosed land is still partly in demesne, partly let for rent to the Welsh sailors. At *Kingston* there are 21 basket weirs on the Severn and 12 on the Wye. At Bishton there are 3 hides and 15 basket weirs on the Wye. In Landcaut there are 3 hides and 2 hackle weirs on the Wye and 9 basket weirs.

Throughout the whole estate 12 pence is due from every yardland and 4 pence as alms. At every weir within the 30 hides

SURVEY OF THE MANOR OF

is · gebyreð æfre se oðer fisc þam landhlaforde · 7 ælc seldsynde fisc þe weordlic[1] byð · styria · 7 mereswyn · healic oðer sæfisc · 7 nah man nænne fisc wið feo to syllanne þone[2] hlaford on land byð ær man hine him gecyðe. Of Dyddanhamme gebyreð micel
5 weorcræden[3]. Se geneat sceal wyrcan swa on lande · swa of lande · swa[4] hweðer swa him man byt · 7 ridan · 7 auerian · 7 lade lædan · drafe drifan · 7 fela oðra ðinga don · Se gebur sceal his riht don · he sceal erian healfne æcer · to wiceworce · 7 ræcan sylf þ sæd on hlafordes berne · gehalne to cyrcscette sahweþere[5]
10 of his agenum berne to werbolde .XL. mæra oððe an foþer gyrda · oððe .VIII. geocu byld .III. ebban tyne · æcertyninge .XV. gyrda · oððe diche · V tyne · 7 dicie .I. gyrde burhheges · ripe oðer healfne æcer · mawe healfne · on oþran weorcan wyrce · a be weorces mæþe · Sylle .VI. penneḡ[6] ofer Estre ·
15 healfne sester hunies · to hlafmæssan .VI. systres mealtes · to Martines mæsse an cliwen godes nett gernes. On ðam sylfum lande stent se ðe .VII. swyn hæbbe þ he sylle .III. 7 swa forð a þ teoþe · 7 ðæs naþulæs mæstenrædene þonne mæsten beo.

CX. SERVICES AND DUES RENDERED AT HURSTBOURNE PRIORS, HAMPSHIRE

HER synd gewriten þa gerihta þæ ða ceorlas sculan dón to
20 Hysseburnan. Ærest æt hilcan hiwisce feorwerti[7] penega tó herfestes emnihte · 7 VI. ciricmittan eálað · 7 III. sesðlar hlafhwetes · 7 III. æceras géerian on heora agenre hwile 7 mid heora agenan sæda gerawan[8] 7 on hyra agenre wile on bærene gebringan · 7 ðreo púnd gauolbærer[9] 7 heafne[10] æcer gauolmæde on
25 hiora agienre hwile 7 þæt on hreace gebringan · 7 IIII. foðera aclofenas gauolwyda · to scidhræce on hiora agenre hwile · 7 XVI. gyrda gauoltininga eác[11] 7[12] hiora ágenre wile · 7 to easran[13] twó ewe mid twam lamban · 7 we[14] two geong sceap tó eala[15] sceapan · 7 hi sculan waxan sceáp 7 sciran on hiora agenre hwile ·
30 7 ælce wucan wircen ðæt hi man háte butan ðrim · and[16] to middan wintra oðeru to easran[13] · ðridde to ganddagan[17].

[1] weorð-, K., E.	[2] ðonne, K., E.	[3] -æn, B., Hunt.
[4] Om. K., E.	[5] sa hweþere, K., E., B.	[6] penegas, K., E.
[7] Sic.	[8] -sawan, K.	[9] -bæres, K.
[10] healf-, K.	[11] Om. K.	[12] on, K.
[13] eastran, K.	[14] we [talað], K.	[15] Sic; eald, K.
[16] an, K.	[17] Sic; gang-, K.	

every alternate fish belongs to the lord of the manor and every rare fish which is of value—sturgeon or porpoise, herring or sea fish; and no one has the right of selling any fish for money, when the lord is on the estate, without informing him about it.

From Tidenham much labour is due. The *geneat* must labour either on the estate or off the estate, whichever he is bidden, and ride and furnish carrying service and supply transport and drive herds and do many other things. The *gebur* must do what is due from him—he must plough half an acre as week work and himself fetch the seed from his lord's barn, a whole one, however, for church dues, [supplied with seed] from his own barn. For weir-building [he must supply] 40 larger rods (?) or a fother of small rods, or he shall build 8 yokes for 3 ebb tides, supply 15 poles of field-fencing or dig 5, fence and dig 1 pole of the manor-house hedge, reap an acre and a half and mow half an acre and work at other kinds of work, always in proportion to the work.

He shall give 6 pence after Easter [and] half a sester of honey, at Lammas six sesters of malt, at Martinmas a ball of good net yarn. On the same estate it is the rule that he who has 7 swine shall give 3 and thereafter always the tenth, and in spite of this [pay] for the right of having mast when there is mast.

CX. SERVICES AND DUES RENDERED AT HURSTBOURNE PRIORS, HAMPSHIRE

Here are recorded the dues which the peasants must render at Hurstbourne. First from every hide [they must render] 40 pence at the autumnal equinox, and 6 church *mittan* of ale and 3 sesters of wheat for bread, and [they must] plough 3 acres in their own time and sow them with their own seed and bring it to the barn in their own time, and [give] 3 pounds of barley as rent, and [mow] half an acre of meadow as rent in their own time, and make it into a rick, and [supply] 4 fothers of split wood as rent, made into a stack in their own time, and [supply] 16 poles of fencing as rent, likewise in their own time, and at Easter [they shall give] two ewes with two lambs—and we [reckon] two young sheep to a full-grown sheep—and they must wash the sheep and shear them in their own time, and work as they are bidden every week except three—one at midwinter, the second at Easter, the third at the Rogation Days.

CXI. LEASE OF LAND BY EALDRED, BISHOP OF WORCESTER, TO WULFGEAT

✠ Her swutelað on ðissum gewrite · þ Ealdred b · hæfþ geunnen Wulfgeate sumne dæl landes · þ is oþer healf hid on ðam tune ðe Dicford is genamad · to habbanne 7 to brucane ðreora manna dæg · 7 æfter hyr[1] dæge · gange ðæt land eft agean to ðam ðe se
5 wylle ðe ðonne bisceoprices wealde on Wigeraceastre 7 hig syn æfre underþeodde · 7 gehersume · 7 ðam hlafordscipe folhgien ðe ðonne bisceop beo · 7 gif hig ænigne frambyge don[2] ðolian ðære are · 7 ðisses is to gewitnysse eall se hired on Wigeraceastre · 7 se hired on Eofeshamme · 7 se hired on Persceoran · 7 Leofric
10 eorl · 7 Odda eorl · 7 Aelfric his broðor · 7 Berhtric Ælfgares sunu · 7 Owine · 7 Wagan · 7 Aeglric ðæs b. broþor · 7 Ceolmær · 7 Atsur · 7 Esebearn[3] · 7 Ordwig · 7 Aeþestan fætta · 7 Aelfward æt Langadune · 7 ealle ða yldestan ðegnas on Wigeraceastrescire denisce 7 englisce · 7 hredde he ða oðra healfe hida
15 for are ðreora manna dæg to cinges banne: ·

CXII. LEASE OF LAND BY EALDRED, BISHOP OF WORCESTER, TO ÆTHELSTAN THE FAT

IN NOMINE DNI. Her swutelað on ðissum gewrite · þæt Ealdred .b. hæfð geunnen Æþestane fættan sumne dæl landes þ synd twa hida · mid þam þe he ær hæfde · 7 mid þam hrofleasan lande · 7 he hig[4] eac wérige for twa hida to þam forewear-
20 dum · þ he hit hæbbe 7 well bruce his dæg · 7 æfter his dæge twam yrfeweardum · þam þe him betst to gearnian wylle · 7 þiss land is on þam tune þe fram cuðum mannum · Hylle is gehaten · 7 æfter þissera þreora manna forþfore · gange þæt land eft into Wigeraceastre to þam þingan þe se wylle · þe þonne bisceopes[5]

---

[1] *hys*, K. [2] *fram bygedon*, Smith; *frambygedon*, K.
[3] *Ece-*, K. [4] Om. Harley MS.
[5] For *bisceoprices*.

CXI. LEASE OF LAND BY EALDRED, BISHOP OF WORCESTER, TO WULFGEAT

✠ Here it is declared in this document that Bishop Ealdred has granted to Wulfgeat a certain piece of land, namely 1½ hides in the manor called Ditchford, to be held and enjoyed for three lives, and after their time the estate shall return once more to the disposal of him who is in control of the bishopric of Worcester at the time. And they shall always be submissive and obedient and acknowledge the lordship of whoever is bishop at the time, and if they are guilty of any defection, they shall forfeit the property.

The witnesses of this are all the community at Worcester and the community at Evesham and the community at Pershore and Earl Leofric and Earl Odda and Ælfric his brother and Brihtric, Ælfgar's son, and Owine and Wagen and Æthelric, the bishop's brother, and Ceolmær and Atser and Esbearn and Ordwig and Æthelstan the Fat and Ælfweard of Longdon and all the leading thegns in Worcestershire, both Danish and English.

And at the king's summons the holder shall discharge the obligations on these 1½ hides at the rate of one, for three lives.

CXII. LEASE OF LAND BY EALDRED, BISHOP OF WORCESTER, TO ÆTHELSTAN THE FAT

In nomine domini.

Here it is declared in this document that Bishop Ealdred has granted to Æthelstan the Fat a certain piece of land, namely 2 hides along with what he had before and with the uninhabited land—and he shall discharge the obligations upon them at the rate of 2 hides—on these terms, that he hold it and make good use of it during his lifetime, and after his death [it shall pass] to the two heirs who are most willing to earn it from him. This land is in the manor which by men familiar with it is called Hill. And after the death of these three men the estate shall return to Worcester without any controversy, [to be used] for any purpose desired by him who at the time is in control of the bishopric.

wealde · butan ælcan wiþercwyde · 7 þiss wæs gedon be Eadwardes cynges leafe · 7 be his fullan unnan · 7 þisses is to gewitnysse eall se hired on Wigeraceastre · 7 Manni abb. 7 se hired on Eofeshamme · 7 Ælfric abb. 7 se hired on Persceoran · 7
5 Leofric eorl · 7 Odda · 7 Ælfric his broþor · 7 Byrhtric Ælfgares sunu · 7 Æglric þæs .b. broþer · 7 Leofric · 7 Owine · 7 Wagan[1] · 7 Atsur · 7 Ceolmær · 7 Ordwig · 7 Wulfric · 7 Ælfric æt Cumbrintune[2] · 7 Godric finc · 7 Berhtwine · 7 Cola · 7 ealle þa þegnas on Wigeraceastrescire · denisce 7 englisce · 7 sy þiss land
10 ælces þinges freols · butan weallgeweorce · 7 brygcgeweorce · 7 ferosocne[3] · 7 ciricsceatte. God ælmihtig þone gehealde þe þiss gehealde · 7 se þe hit awende · oððe on ænigum þingum gewanige · hæbbe him wiþ[4] God sylfne gemæne · butan he geswice · 7 to rihte gecerre.

CXIII. GRANT OF LAND TO WORCESTER BY LEOFRIC, EARL OF MERCIA, AND HIS WIFE

15 ⚜ HER SWVTELAÐ ON ÐISSVM GEWRITE Þ Leofric eorl 7 his gebedda habbað geunnen twa land for Godes lufan 7 for hyra sawle[5] into þære halgan stowe sca Marian mynstre æt Wi'h'graceastre þam gebroðran[6] to bryce inn[7] to[7] heora beodderne þe þær dæighwamlice Gode þeowiað · to þam forewear-
20 dan · þ þa gebroðra beon þingiende for uncrum saulum þæt synd .v. hida landes æt Wulfweardiglea · 7 twa æt Blaca'wyllan' 7 ænne hagan on porte þæt hit sig æfre into heora beodderne freols 7 hit nan man ne geutige · 7 gyf ænig sy þe hit mid ænigan þingan · geecean wylle oððe godian God ælmihtig him geunne gesundfull
25 lif 7 ece mede · 7 gyf ænig þonne sy up áhafen 7 swa swiðe gredig þissere worulde þ[8] þas ure sylena geutian wylle · hæbbe he her on ðisse life Godes curs 7 sca Marian 7 sce Oswaldes 7 eal[ra][9] gehadedra manna · 7 sy he amansumod on domes dæige toforan drihtnes cneowan fram Gode 7 fram eallan his halgan 7 mid
30 Iudan 7 his geferan æfre on éce wite cwylmed · butan he geswice 7 to rihte gecyrre · 7 wit synd þisra landa hald 7 mund into þam halgan mynstre þa hwile þe uncker[10] lif bið.

[1] *Pagan*, Harley MS.   [2] *Tymbrin-*, ibid.   [3] For *ferd-*; *forð-*, ibid.
[4] *þæt wið*, ibid.   [5] *saule*, K.   [6] *-am*, He.; *-um*, K.
[7] *into*, He., K.   [8] *and*, K.
[9] The last two letters are illegible.   [10] *unker*, He., K.

This was done by King Edward's leave and with his full consent. And the witnesses of this are all the community at Worcester, and Abbot Manni and the community at Evesham, and Abbot Ælfric and the community at Pershore, and Earl Leofric and Odda and Ælfric his brother and Brihtric, Ælfgar's son, and Æthelric, the bishop's brother, and Leofric and Owine and Wagen and Atser and Ceolmær and Ordwig and Wulfric and Ælfric of Comberton and Godric Finch and Brihtwine and Cola, and all the thegns in Worcestershire, both Danish and English.

This estate shall be free from every burden except the construction of walls and bridges and military service and church dues. May God Almighty uphold him who upholds this, and he who alters it or diminishes it in any particular shall have to account for it to God himself, unless he desists and turns to a proper mode of conduct.

CXIII. GRANT OF LAND TO WORCESTER BY LEOFRIC, EARL OF MERCIA, AND HIS WIFE

☧ Here it is declared in this document that Earl Leofric and his wife have granted two estates, for the love of God and the sake of their souls, to the refectory of the holy foundation, the monastery of St Mary at Worcester, for the use of the brethren who daily serve God therein, on condition that they intercede for our souls. Our gift comprises five hides of land at Wolverley and two at Blackwell and a messuage in the town, and it shall freely belong to their refectory for all time, and no one shall alienate it. And if there is anyone who desires to augment or endow it in any way, God Almighty shall grant him a prosperous life and eternal reward; and if, on the other hand, anyone is puffed up and so greatly covetous of earthly things that he desires to alienate this our gift, he shall have the curse of God and St Mary and St Oswald and all men in holy orders here in this life, and he shall be excommunicated on the Judgment Day in the presence of the Lord by God and by all his saints, and tormented for all time in everlasting punishment along with Judas and his companions, unless he desist and turn to a proper mode of conduct. And both of us shall be the protectors and guardians of these estates, on behalf of the holy monastery, as long as our life lasts.

CXIV. AGREEMENT BETWEEN THE OLD MINSTER, WINCHESTER, AND WULFWEARD THE WHITE

HER swytelað on þisum gewritæ þæt Ælfgifu seo hlefdige bæcweð .v. hida æt[1] Heilincigæ into ealdan mynstræ. And heo bæcwæð Wulfweardæ hwitan .v. hida of þam ilcan landæ his dæg. And æftær his dæge ga þa .v. hida into ealdan mynstræ ·
5 þus seo hlæfdige hit bæcwed[2] Wulfweardæ. Þa wes Wulfweard gyrnenðæ[3] þæt hæ mostæ ofgan his deg þa .v. hida þæ wæron into mynstre bæcweðene. And sæ bisceop Stigandæ and sæ hiræd on ealdan mynstræ him þæs gætiþodon wið scylcon[4] gersumen swylce hi þa sehtæ[5] wæron. Nú wæron þus heora fore-
10 wæarð þæt Wulfweard hebbæ þa .v. hida his dæg · And æftær his dæge ga þa .v. hida into ealdan mynstræ · And þa oþræ .v. hida forð mið[6] þæ seo hlæfdige him bæcwæð · mid mæte 7 mid mannum 7 mid eallum þingum swa hit þonnæ stænt butan ælcon geantalæ. Ðises ís to witnæssæ Stigandæ bisceop · and
15 Harold eorl · And sæ hired on ealdan mynstræ · And Ælfwine abb. And sæ hired on niwan mynstræ · And Leofing stæallære · And Raulf stæallære · And Æscar steallære · And Eadsige scirgeræfa · And Wulfric æt Wernæforda · And Ælfwine · And Ælfweard · And Cupping · And eallæ scirþegnas on Hamtun-
20 sciræ · Þissæ gewrita syndon .iii. an is on ealdan mynstræ · And þæt oþær ís on niwan mynstre · And þæt þridde heafð Wulfwearð.

CXV. ENDOWMENT OF STOW ST MARY BY EARL LEOFRIC AND GODGIFU

[H]er[7] swutelað on þisan gewrite hu þa forewearde geworhte syndon · þe · Wlwig .b. 7 Leofric eorl · 7 Godgife þæs eorles wif
25 geworhtan ymbe ꝥ mynster æt Sc̄e MARIAN stowe · ꝥ is ærost ꝥ hig bædan þone bisceop ꝥ hig mostan ꝥ mynster godian · 7

---

[1] *at*, K. [2] *-cweð*, K. [3] *-dæ*, K., T., B.
[4] *swylc-*, T.; *scwlc-*, B. [5] *sehtte*, B.
[6] *mid*, K. [7] The initial letter is in pencil.

CXIV. AGREEMENT BETWEEN THE OLD MINSTER, WINCHESTER, AND WULFWEARD THE WHITE

Here it is declared in this document that the Lady Ælfgifu bequeathed 5 hides at Hayling to the Old Minster, and she bequeathed 5 hides of the same estate to Wulfweard the White for his lifetime, and after his death these 5 hides were to go to the Old Minster; these were the terms of the Lady's bequest to Wulfweard. Then Wulfweard asked that he might be allowed to hold, during his lifetime, the 5 hides which had been bequeathed to the Minster, and Bishop Stigand and the community at the Old Minster granted him this in return for the payment of such a sum as they agreed upon at the time. The arrangements made were as follows, that Wulfweard should have the 5 hides during his lifetime, and after his death they should pass to the Old Minster along with the other 5 hides which the Lady bequeathed to him, with their produce and their men and with everything as the estate stood at the time, without any controversy.

The witnesses of this are Bishop Stigand and Earl Harold and the community at the Old Minster and Abbot Ælfwine and the community at the New Minster and Lyfing the Staller and Raulf the Staller and Esgar the Staller and Eadsige the sheriff and Wulfric of Warnford and Ælfwine and Ælfweard and Cupping and all the thegns in Hampshire.

There are three of these documents. One is at the Old Minster and the second is at the New Minster and Wulfweard has the third.

CXV. ENDOWMENT OF STOW ST MARY BY EARL LEOFRIC AND GODGIFU

Here it is declared in this document how arrangements have been made between Bishop Wulfwig and Earl Leofric and Godgifu, the earl's wife, with regard to the monastery at Stow St Mary. In the first place they asked the bishop for permission to endow the monastery and assign lands to it with his

214 ENDOWMENT OF STOW ST MARY

land þiderinn tolecge[1] · be his fullre leafe · þa tyðede heom se bisceop · 7 wæs swyðe bliðe ꝥ he ænigne fultum hæfde þæt him þærto fylstan wolde. Nu habbað hig hit gesett mid preostan · 7 willað þær habban þeowdom eallswa man hæfð on Paulesbyrig
5 binnan Lundene · 7 þa land þe hig þiderinn lecgeað[2] beon þa þam gebroðran þe þær binnan beoð to fodnoðe · 7 to scrude · 7 Se .ƀ. habbe into his feorme ælc þæra þinga þe Æðeric .ƀ. 7 Ædnoð .ƀ. hefdan ætforan him of ðam þe mid rihte gebyrað ìntó his bisceoprice · ꝥ is þa twegen deles ælc þæra þinga þe
10 kymð into ðam mynstre · 7 þa preostas habban þone þriddan dæl · forutan þam twam mærsan[3]. Ðonne habbe se .ƀ. eall ꝥ þær tokymð · ehta dagas to ðære ærre · Sc̄e Maria mæssan[4] · 7 ehta dagas · to ðære æftsan[5] · Sc̄a Marian mærsan[3] · butan þam mete anum · þonne habban þa preostas þone þriddan dæl · of ðam
15 mete þe þær tokymð[6] · 7 þa land þe Se .ƀ. 7 se eorl · 7 Godgife · 7 Gode menn þidernn geunnað[7] · beon þa æffre[8] into ðæra halgan stowe · þam gebroðran to neode · 7 ꝥ mynster to godianne · ꝥ nan .ƀ. þe æfter him kymð þærof nane feorme ne crafige · Butan of ðam þe him mid rihte togebyrað into his .ƀ. rice ·
20 eallswa oðre bisceopas ær ætforan him hæfdon · 7 þis is gedon be · Eadweardes cynges fullra leafe · 7 on his gewitnesse · 7 on Eadgyðe his gebeddan · 7 on Stigandes arcebes · 7 on Kynsiges arcebes · 7 on Heremannes ƀes · 7 ón Dodika · ƀes · 7 ón Leofrices · ƀes · 7 ón Ealdredes · ƀes · 7 ón Heka · ƀes · 7 ón Ægel-
25 mæres · ƀes · 7 ón Alfwoldes · ƀes · 7 ón Willelmes · ƀes · 7 ón Leofwines · ƀes · 7 ón Sigweardes eorles · 7 ón Haroldes eorles · 7 ón Raulfes eorles · 7 ón Ælfgares eorles · 7 ón Manniges abƀ · 7 ón Ælfwines abƀ · 7 ón Leofsiges abƀ · 7 on Leofrices abƀ · 7 ón oðres Leofsiges abƀ · 7 ón Brihtmæres abƀ · 7 ón Esgeres
30 stealres · 7 ón Raulfes steallres · 7 ón Lifinges steallres · 7 ón eallra þæs kynges huscarlan · 7 ón his mæssepreostan · 7 ón Þurgodes lagen · 7 on Sigferðes · 7 on Godrices · 7 ón Owines · 7 ón Sigrices · 7 ón eallra þara burhware gewitnesse ón Lincolne ·

---

[1] *lande þider into lecge*, D.; *þ. innto l.*, Salter.
[2] *þider inlecgeað*, D.; *þ. innl.*, Salter.   [3] Sic.
[4] Sic; *Sanctæ Marian mærsan*, D.; *Sancte Marian mæssan*, with note that MS. has *mærsan*, Salter.   [5] Sic; *æfstan*, D.
[6] *þærto k.*, D., Salter.   [7] Sic; *þider ungeunnað*, D., Salter.
[8] Sic; *æffne*, Salter.

BY EARL LEOFRIC AND GODGIFU

full consent, and the bishop granted their request, and was very glad to have any assistance for that purpose. Now they have furnished it with priests and desire that divine service should be celebrated there as it is at St Paul's in London. And the lands which they assign to it shall provide food and clothing for the brethren who are therein. And the bishop shall have as food-rent for himself everything which Bishop Æthelric and Bishop Eadnoth had before him and which by rights belongs to his bishopric, namely two-thirds of everything that comes into the monastery, and the priests shall have the remaining third except at the two festivals. The bishop, however, shall have everything that accrues to it for eight days at the earlier festival of St Mary, and for eight days at the later festival of St Mary, except for food alone. The priests, however, shall have the third part of the food which accrues to it. And the lands which the bishop and the earl and Godgifu and good men grant to it shall remain for all time in the possession of the holy foundation for the needs of the brethren and the endowment of the monastery, so that no bishop who succeeds him shall demand any food-rent from it except what by rights belongs to his bishopric, as other bishops had before him.

This is done with King Edward's full consent and with his cognisance and that of his wife Eadgyth and of Archbishop Stigand and of Archbishop Cynesige and of Bishop Hereman and of Bishop Duduc and of Bishop Leofric and of Bishop Ealdred and of Bishop Heca and of Bishop Æthelmær and of Bishop Ælfwold and of Bishop William and of Bishop Leofwine and of Earl Siweard and of Earl Harold and of Earl Raulf and of Earl Ælfgar and of Abbot Manni and of Abbot Ælfwine and of Abbot Leofsige and of Abbot Leofric and of the other Abbot Leofsige and of Abbot Brihtmær and of Esgar the Staller and of Raulf the Staller and of Lyfing the Staller and of all the king's household officers and chaplains and of Thurgod *lagen* and of **Siferth** and of Godric and of Owine and of Siric, and with the

216 ENDOWMENT OF STOW ST MARY

7 ón eallra þæra manna þe seceað gearmarkett to Stowe · 7 se
ðe ða geferædene mid gode geéce · God ælmihtig geece his
lifdagas her on life · 7 ón þam toweardan life þ he mote wununga
habban mid Godes gecoranan · 7 se ðe hig tódræfe · 7 þa land
5 ut of ðære halgan stowe geutige · adrefed wurðe he fram Gode ·
7 fram Sc̄a Marian · 7 fram eallan his halgan o ðam[1] myclan
domes dæge. Nu syndon þisse gewrita · þreo · an is mid þæs
kyngces[2] haligdome · 7 oðer is mid Leofrice eorle · 7 þ þridde
is mid þam be. on ða halgan stowe.

CXVI. GRANT BY BRIHTMÆR OF GRACECHURCH TO CHRISTCHURCH, CANTERBURY

10 Hyer[3] suotelen on þísen ywrite embe þo vorewerde þe Brithmer
at Gerschereche wroȝte with Stigant archebiscop · and with
Godric þane den · and with alle þan[4] hird at Xp̄es chereche at
Cantwarberi · þet is þanne þet he vþe Xp̄e ínto Xp̄es chereche
þane homstal þet he on set · and alre haleȝene cheriche efter his
15 daȝe · and efter Eadgefan his ybedden · and efter his childrene
daȝe · Edmeres and Eþelwínes swo hi hít alþerbest ygodeden ·
vor hire saule · alesednesse · and swo þet se hired sholde witen ·
þet se þeudom[5] ne adeswen · þe ínto þare cheriche belímpcht[6]
ne[6] ne[6] atfalle al be þan · þe si chereche were ygoded. Hierto
20 byeth[7] · ywitnesse Lyefstan portireue and biscop · and Eylwíne
stikehare · and manye oþre[8] · þeyne[8] binne burȝ an[9] bute.

CXVII. LEASE OF LAND BY THE ABBOT AND THE COMMUNITY AT BATH TO ARCHBISHOP STIGAND

HER swutelað on þisum gewrite þ Ælfwig abbud and eall seo
geferræden on Baðan · hæfð gelæten to Stigande archeb .xxx.
hyda landes æt Dyddanhamme[10] his dæg[11] · wið .x. marcan goldes ·

---

[1] *on ða*, D.; *oð an*, Salter.   [2] *kynges*, D., Salter.   [3] *Her*, T.
[4] *þem*, T.   [5] *þendom*, K., T.
[6] *belimpeht*, T.; *belimpehe nene*, MS. (*b*); *belimpe hene ne*, K.
byreð, T.   [8] *oþre þar þeyne*, MS. (*b*), T.; *o. ðas þ.*, K.
[9] *and*, K., T.   [10] *-en-*, K., E.   [11] *dæge*, K., E.

cognisance of all the citizens of Lincoln and of all the men who attend the yearly market at Stow. And if anyone increases [the property of] the community with benefactions, God Almighty shall increase the days of his life here in this life, and in the future life he shall be allowed to have his dwelling with God's elect. And if anyone expels them and alienates the lands from the holy foundation, he shall be rejected by God and St Mary and all his saints on the great Judgment Day.

There are three of these documents. One is in the king's sanctuary, the second is in Earl Leofric's possession, and the third is in the possession of the bishop at the holy foundation.

CXVI. GRANT BY BRIHTMÆR OF GRACECHURCH TO CHRISTCHURCH, CANTERBURY

Here is declared in this document the agreement which Brihtmær of Gracechurch has made with Archbishop Stigand and with Godric the dean and with all the community at Christchurch, Canterbury. He has granted to Christ, to be held by Christchurch after his death and that of Eadgifu his wife and after the death of his children, Eadmær and Æthelwine, the homestead which he occupies and the church of All Hallows with all the endowments which they have bestowed upon it, for the redemption of their souls, on these terms, that the community shall see to it that the service which belongs to the church neither ceases (?) nor falls off in view of the endowments of the church.

The witnesses of this are Leofstan the town reeve and Bishop [William] and Æthelwine *Stikehare* and many other thegns both within the city and without.

CXVII. LEASE OF LAND BY THE ABBOT AND THE COMMUNITY AT BATH TO ARCHBISHOP STIGAND

Here it is declared in this document that Abbot Ælfwig and all the community at Bath have let 30 hides of land at Tidenham to Archbishop Stigand for his lifetime in return for 10 marks of

218 LEASE OF LAND BY ABBOT OF BATH

and wið .xx. pundon seolfres · 7 æfter hys¹ dæge ga hyt eft into
þam halegan mynstre · mid mete · 7 mid mannu*m* · swa full 7
swa forð swa hyt² þænne byþ · 7 .I. marc goldes toeacan · 7
.VI. merswun³ · 7 .XXX. þusenda hæringys⁴ · ælce eare. Þisys⁵
5 ys to gewittnysse · Eadweard ciningc⁶ · 7 Eadgyð seo hlæfdige ·
7 Ealdryd⁷ archeb · 7 Hereman .b. 7 Gisa .b. 7 Harold eorl · 7
Tosstig eorl · 7 Æþelnoð abb. 7 Ægylwig⁸ abb · 7 Ægylsige
abb · 7 Ordric abb · 7 Esegar steallere · 7 Roulf steall*ere* · 7
Bondig steall*ere* · 7 manega oþre gode menn þe heora naman
10 her awritene ne syndon · 7 gyf ænig mann si swa dyrstig þ wylle
þis⁹ awendan si he amansumod fram Criste · 7 fram sca Marian
7 fram sce Petre · þam halegan apłe · 7 fram eallum Cristes
halegum æfre on æcnysse · buton he hyt eft þe raþor gebete.

CXVIII. ALLEGED CONFIRMATION BY EDWARD THE CONFESSOR OF A GRANT BY QUEEN ÆLFGIFU EMMA TO THE OLD MINSTER, WINCHESTER

✠ On God ælmihtiges nama 7 ealra his halgan · ic Eadward
15 kincg luuelice an þa elmessan 'þæ' Elfgyuu Ymme min moder
geúþe him aforeworda 7 ealla his halgan into Ealdan mynstre of
þan tunæ þe hatte Weregrauæ mid saka 7 mid socne 7 mid
eallan witan · and on eallon þingon eallswa fri eallswa hit stod
hyre syluan fyrmest on handan · for Æþelredes kinges mines
20 fæderes saule an Hardacnudes mines broþer an ealra þara kinge
þe tefore me wæron oþþe æfter me cumeð to þise rice. Nu ic
bidde of Godes healua an ealra his halga and of mine · þet
ealswa hi willað habban del on þære ylkan elmesse · ealswa hi
fæstlice healdan aþan þet hy seo stedefest into þam halige stowe.
25 And lochwa þis willæ awændan · awænde hine God fram him ·
and fram þan ecæ life. ✠ Ego Stigand*us* arc̄ consensi. Ego
Ealdred arc̄ consensi. Ego Hæreman eb̄s consensi. Ego Ræimballd cancell consensi. Ego Godwine dux consensi.

¹ *his*, K., E., B.   ² *hit*, K., E., B.   ³ *-swin*, K., T., E.
⁴ *-yng-*, K., E.   ⁵ *Ðis*, K., E.; *Þis*, B., Hunt.
⁶ *-cg*, K., E.   ⁷ *-uyd*, B.   ⁸ *-el-*, K., E.
⁹ Om. Hunt.

gold and 20 pounds of silver, and after his death it shall revert to the holy monastery with its produce and its men, entirely and completely as it is then, and in addition 1 mark of gold and 6 porpoises and 30,000 herrings [shall be given] annually.

The witnesses of this are King Edward and the Lady Eadgyth and Archbishop Ealdred and Bishop Hereman and Bishop Gisa and Earl Harold and Earl Tostig and Abbot Æthelnoth and Abbot Æthelwig and Abbot Æthelsige and Abbot Ordric and Esgar the Staller and Raulf the Staller and Bondig the Staller and many other worthy men whose names are not recorded here.

And if anyone is so presumptuous as to attempt to alter this, he shall be accursed by Christ and by St Mary and by St Peter, the holy apostle, and by all the saints of Christ for ever to all eternity, unless he make amends for it thereafter as quickly as possible.

CXVIII. ALLEGED CONFIRMATION BY EDWARD THE CONFESSOR OF A GRANT BY QUEEN ÆLFGIFU EMMA TO THE OLD MINSTER, WINCHESTER

✠ In the name of Almighty God and of all his saints, I, King Edward, gladly allow the charitable gift which Ælfgifu Emma, my mother, granted in the first place, for him and for all his saints, to the Old Minster from the manor which is called Wargrave, with jurisdiction and [the receipt of] all the fines and complete freedom in every respect as when she herself most fully owned it. [And this I do] for the souls of King Æthelred, my father, and of Hardacnut, my brother, and of all the kings who were before me or who shall succeed to this kingdom after me. Now I pray on behalf of God and of all his saints and on my own, that as they desire to have a share in this same charitable gift, they will steadfastly maintain their oaths of loyalty to the holy foundation. And if anyone attempts to alter this, God shall remove him from himself and from the eternal life...

CXIX. AGREEMENT WITH ORDRIC THE CELLARER AT BURY ST EDMUNDS

[Þ]is[1] forward was makid wid[2] Ordric hordere[3] · þat es þat aelc man ín sce Eadmundes Byri husfast on his owe land sal gifen to þe halegenes Bideripe þe hordor on pení at Petermasse on gínnínge heruest. An sea þat[4] sit on oderes land sea sceal gifen oan halpení for þat he aalle scolden sceren þe halegenes corn. Fram þis sceal naefre no maen be scyr buton sce Eademundes þewes 7 sea cnytes[5] ...... and þe[6] preostes ínne[7] þeo[8] síngen at þo wyuedes[9] God seonde heore frieond þe worden sce Eadmund.

CXX. CHARTER OF EDWARD THE CONFESSOR TO HORTON ABBEY

REGNANTE in perpetuum dño nřo IHu Xp̄o. [R]ixiendum[10] urum drihtne hælendum[11] Criste on ecnysse ðam heahstan 7 þan untosprecen'd'lican ealra þinga 7 ealra tida scyppend[12] · se þe manegum þingum his mihtum setteð 7 wealdeþ · Eac swylce[13] þam upahafenlican 7 þam unasecgendlican ríce ꝥ[14] ðe[14] he þises[15] lifes eadignysse[16] 7 gesælignesse nænigum[17] þingum ne forlæte; forþan ic Eadwerd Englalandes cyngc mid Godes gyfe 7 mid minra witena geþeahte 7 ræde ic forgyfe þisne freols into þære haligan[18] stowe æt Hortune Gode to lofe 7 Sca MARIAN to wurðmynte ðe seo stowe ys fore gehalgod · 7 me on gemende

---

[1] A space has been left for the initial letter.
[2] Om. MS. (c).
[3] Written on an erasure in paler ink with a note in the margin in a later hand, *Hordere .i. cellerario ut thesaurario*. [4] *þe*, MS. (a).
[5] *7 sea cnytes agen* has been written into a blank in the text in paler ink with what looks like *nnre* or *nure* in the margin. MS. (a) leaves a blank while MS. (c) has *7 sea cnyteʒ a sen nure*; *agen nure*, K.; *agenn ure*, T.; *agen mire*, Hervey.   [6] *seo*, MS. (a).   [7] *ine*, K.
[8] *ðes*, K.   [9] *co windes*, MS. (a); *wyne des*, Hervey.
[10] A space has been left for the capital letter. It was probably meant to be ornamental although it does not come at the beginning of a line.
[11] *-un*, K.   [12] *-ende*, K.   [13] *swilce*, T.
[14] *ðætte*, K.   [15] *ðisses*, K.   [16] *-gysse*, T.
[17] *ænig-*, K.   [18] *halgan*, K.

CXIX. AGREEMENT WITH ORDRIC THE CELLARER AT BURY ST EDMUNDS

This agreement has been made with Ordric the cellarer, namely that every man in Bury St Edmunds occupying a house on his own land shall give the cellarer a penny on St Peter's Day at the beginning of harvest, when summoned to the saint's reaping. And he who occupies another man's land shall give a halfpenny, because all of them ought to cut the saint's corn. From this no man shall ever be exempt except St Edmund's servants and the *cnihtas*...and the priests within the monastery who sing at the altars. God shall be the friend of those who honour St Edmund.

CXX. CHARTER OF EDWARD THE CONFESSOR TO HORTON ABBEY

Regnante in perpetuum domino nostro Jesu Christo.

Our Lord the Saviour Christ who rules to all eternity, most high and ineffable, the creator of all things and all seasons, he who establishes and governs many things by his power, including the lofty and marvellous kingdom, by no means neglects the happiness and prosperity of this life. For that reason I, Edward, King of England, grant this liberty, by the grace of God and with the support and advice of my councillors, to the holy foundation at Horton, to the praise of God and the honour of St Mary, to whom the place is dedicated, for it is in my mind to obtain the everlasting treasure by means of these earthly

222 CHARTER OF EDWARD THE CONFESSOR

ys mid þisum eorðlicum þingum þa ecanlican gestreon to be-
gytende · sicut Salomon dixit · Redemptio animę proprię
diuitię · Swa swa Salomon cwæð · ꝥ we sceoldon mid urum
spedum urum sawlum[1] þa ecan gesælignysse[2] begytan · forþan
5 ic cuðlice mid geþeahte geþafunge 7 leafe ealra minra biscope
7 eorla 7 butan ðan ealra minra selostra witena · ic forgef þisne
freols for mine agene sawle 7 for mire[3] leofostra frenda · ꝥ eall
ꝥ land þe lið into þan haligan mynstre æt Hortune · ꝥ hyt[4] sy
fæstlice 7 unawendedlice[5] á ecelice gefreod ealra cynelicra 7
10 ealdordomlicra þeowdoma · ge þeoffengces[6] ge æghwylcere[7]
uneaðnesse ealles woroldlices broces · buton fyrdsocne 7 burhgeweorce 7 bricggeweorce[8]. Gif[9] hwa þanne si ꝥ he hine for Godes
lufon to þam[10] geeadmedan wylle[11] ꝥ he þas mine gyfe geycan
wylle oððe gemenigfyldan ·́ geyce him ælmihtig God eall god
15 her on worolde · 7 his dagas gesundfullie[12]. Gif ðonne hwylc
mann to þam geþristlæce oððe mid deofles searwum to þam
beswicen sy—ꝥ he þis on ænegum[13] þingum lytlum[14] oððe
mycelum þence to abrecende oððe to awendenda[15] wite he
þonne ꝥ he þæs riht agyldende[16] sy[17] beforan Cristes þrymsettle ·
20 þonne ealle heofonwara 7 eorðwara on his andwerdnysse beoð
onstyred 7 onhrerede buton he hyt ær her on worolde mid rihte
gebete. Ðis wæs gewriten on þam geare þe wæs agan fram
Cristes acennednysse · an þusend geara 7 án 7 sixtig geara · 7 an
þam tacncircule ꝥ seofanteoþe gear. Ic Eadwerd cyngc mid
25 þære halgan Cristes rode tacne þis het swiþe geornlice getrymman 7 gefæstnian þisne freodóm on ælmihtiges Godes naman ·
7 on ealra his halgena. Ic fæstlice bebeode · ꝥ hine nænig minra
æfterfyligendra[18] eft ne onwende ne on nænigum dælum læssum
ne on marum hyne ne onwyrdon[19] · ac þes[20] freols á ecelice forð
30 þurhwunige swa lange swa God wylle ꝥ cristen geleafa mid
Angelcynne untosceacan wurþe[21] · ealra þæra woroldcundra[22]
hefignyssa þe her beforan genemnede syndon · 7 se hæbbe[23]...

[1] *saul-*, K. [2] *-nesse*, K. [3] *mine*, T.
[4] *hit*, K., T. [5] *unanw.*, K. [6] *-ges*, K.
[7] *-cre*, K. [8] *brygge-*, K., T. [9] *gyf*, K.
[10] *þan*, K., T. [11] *wille*, K. [12] *-fulie*, K.
[13] *æneum*, K. [14] *lyttl-*, K. [15] *-de*, T.
[16] *agyeld-*, K. [17] *sye*, K. [18] *-fylg-*, T.
[19] *-myrd-*, T. [20] *þeos*, T. [21] T. ends here.
[22] *-uld-*, K.
[23] This is the last word at the bottom of f. 29 b; f. 30 is missing.

things, *sicut Salomon dixit: Redemptio animae propriae divitiae*, according to the saying of Solomon that by means of our wealth we should obtain everlasting bliss for our souls. For that reason, therefore, with the advice, consent and leave of my bishops and earls and in addition of all my most distinguished councillors, I have granted this freedom, for the sake of my own soul and those of my dearest friends, namely that all the land that belongs to the holy monastery at Horton shall be firmly and immutably freed for all time from all royal and official services, including the arrest of thieves and all the irksomeness of secular labour, with the exception of military service and the construction of fortifications and bridges. If by chance it happen that anyone will condescend, for the love of God, to increase or multiply this my gift, the Almighty God shall increase his possessions here in this world and make his days prosperous. If, however, any man is so presumptuous or so greatly deceived by the wiles of the devil as to contemplate breaking or changing this in any particular, small or great, he shall find that he must render account for it before the throne of Christ, when all the dwellers of heaven and earth are moved and agitated in his presence, unless he has duly made amends for it here in this world. This was written in the year 1061 after the birth of Christ and in the seventeenth year of the lunar cycle.

I, King Edward, with the sign of the holy cross of Christ have commanded this liberty to be very earnestly confirmed and established in the name of Almighty God and of all his saints. I strictly enjoin that none of my successors afterwards change it or hinder it in any particular, small or great, but this freedom from all the secular burdens named above shall continue to all eternity as long as it is the will of God that the Christian faith shall remain inviolate in England...

APPENDIX I

POST-CONQUEST DOCUMENTS

I. THE GIFTS OF BISHOP LEOFRIC TO EXETER

Her[1] swutelað on þissere Xp̄es[2] bec hwæt Leofric .b. hæfð gedon innto sc̄e Petres minstre on Exanceastre · þær his bisceopstol is · þ is þ he hæfð geinnod þ ær geutod wæs þurh Godes fultum 7 þurh his foresþræce · 7 þurh his gærsuma · þ is ærost þ land æt
5 Culmstoke · 7 þ land æt Brancescumbe · 7 æt Sealtcumbe · 7 þ land æt Sc̄e Maria circean · 7 þ land æt Stofordtune · 7 æt Spearcanwille · 7 þ land æt Morceshille · 7 Sidefullan hiwisc · 7 þ land æt Brihtricesstane · '7 þ land æt Toppeshamme þeahþe Harold hit mid unlage utnam' · 7 þ land æt Stoce · 7 þ land æt
10 Sydebirig · 7 þ land æt Niwantune · 7 æt Norðtune.'7 þ land æt Clist[3] þe Wid hæfde'. Ðonne ys þis se eaca on landum þe he hæfð of his agenum þ mynster mid gegodod · for his hlaforda sawlum 7 for his agenre · þam Godes þeowum to bigleofan þe for heora sawlum þingian sceolon · þ ys ærost þ land æt Bem-
15 tune · 7 æt Esttune · 7 æt Ceommenige · 7 þ land æt Doflisc · 7 æt Holacumbe · 7 æt Suþwuda · 7 he ne funde þa he to þam mynstre feng nan mare landes þe ðider ynn gewylde wære · þonne twa hida landes æt Ide · 7 þæron næs orfcynnes nan mare buton · vii.[4] hruðeru. Ðonne ys þis[2] seo oncnawennis[5] þe he
20 hæfð God mid gecnawen 7 sc̄m Petrum into þam halgan mynstre on circlicum madmum · þ is þ he hæfð þider ynn gedon .ii. ƀ roda · 7 .ii. mycele gebonede roda · butan[6] oðrum 'litlum' silfrenum swurrodum · 7 .ii.[7] mycele Xp̄es bec gebonede · 7 .iii. gebonede scrin · 7 .i. geboned altare · 7 .v. silfrene caliceas ·
25 7 .iiii. corporales · 7 .i. silfren pipe · 7 .v. fulle mæssereaf · 7 .ii. dalmatica · 7 .iii. pistelroccas · 7 iiii. subd'i'acones handlin · 7 .iii. cantercæppa · 7 .iii. canterstafas · 7 v. pællene weofod-sceatas · 7 vii. oferbrædelsas · 7 .ii. tæppedu · '7 .iii. bera scin' · 7 vii. setlhrægel · 7 iii. ricghrægel · 7 .ii. wahreft · 7 .vi. mæsene
30 sceala · 7 .ii. gebonede hnæppas · 7 .iiii. hornas · 7 .ii. mycele gebonede candelsticcan · 7 .vi. læssan candelsticcan gebonede · 7 .i. silfren storcylle mid silfrenum storsticcan · 7 .viii. læflas ·

---

[1] Only the most important variant readings in the Exeter Book and Harley 258 are noted.   [2] Om. Ex. Bk.   [3] *Clift*, Harl.
[4] vi., Ex. Bk.   [5] -*cnap*-, Harl.
[6] .ii. has been entered above the line in the Ex. Bk.   [7] Om. Harl.

I. THE GIFTS OF BISHOP LEOFRIC TO EXETER

Here is declared in this gospel book what Bishop Leofric has bestowed upon St Peter's Minster at Exeter where his episcopal see is. With the help of God and by means of his advocacy and his treasure he has restored what had been alienated, namely first the estate at Culmstock, and the estates at Branscombe and at Salcombe, and the estate at St Mary Church, and the estates at Staverton and at Sparkwell, and the estate at Marshall and St Sidwell's holding, and the estate at 'Brightston', and the estate at Topsham, although Harold unjustly took it away, and the estate at Stoke [Canon], and the estate at Sidbury, and the estates at Newton [St Cyres] and at Norton, and the estate at Clyst that Wid had. These are further the additional estates with which he has endowed the minster from his own [possessions], on behalf of the souls of his lords and of his own, for the maintenance of the servants of God whose duty it is to intercede for their souls, namely first the estates at Bampton and at Aston and at Chimney, and the estates at Dawlish and at Holcombe and at Southwood, and when he took over the minster the only land he found under its control was an estate of 2 hides at Ide, and the only livestock on it was 7 bullocks. This is further the acknowledgment that he has made to God and to St Peter in the shape of church treasures for the holy minster, namely he has bestowed upon it 2 episcopal crosses and 2 large ornamented crosses, besides other little silver neck crosses, and 2 large ornamented gospel books and 3 ornamented reliquaries and 1 ornamented altar and 5 silver chalices and 4 corporals and 1 silver tube and 5 complete mass vestments and 2 dalmatics and 3 epistle vestments and 4 sub-deacon's maniples and 3 cantor's copes and 3 cantor's staffs and 5 altar cloths of costly stuff and 7 [altar] covers and 2 carpets and 3 bear-skins and 7 seat covers and 3 dorsals and 2 wall hangings and 6 *mæsene* vessels and 2 ornamented bowls and 4 horns and 2 large ornamented candlesticks and 6 smaller ornamented candlesticks and 1 silver censer with a silver incense spoon and 8 basins and

228 THE GIFTS OF BISHOP LEOFRIC

7 .II. guðfana · 7 .'I'. merc · 7 .VI. midreca · 7 .I. firdwæn · 7 .I. cyste · 7 þær næron ær buton .VII. upphangene bella · 7 nu þær[1] sind .XVI. upphangene · 7 XII. handbella · 7 .II. fulle mæssebec · 7 .I. collectaneum · 7 .II. pistelbec 7 .II. fulle sangbec · 7 .I. nihtsang · 7 .I. adteleuaui · 7 .I. tropere · 7 .II. salteras · 7 se þriddan saltere[2] swa man singð on Rome · 7 .II. ymneras · 7 .I. deorwyrðe bletsingboc · 7 .III. oðre · 7 .I. englisc Xp̄es boc[3] · 7 II. sumerrædingbec · 7 .I. winterræding boc · 7 regula canonicorum · 7 martyrlogium · 7 .I. canon on leden · 7 .I.[2] scriftboc on englisc · 7 .I. full spelboc wintres 7 sumeres · 7 Boeties boc on englisc · 7 .I. mycel englisc boc be gehwilcum þingum on leoðwisan geworht · 7 he ne funde on þam mynstre þa he tofeng boca na ma buton ane capitularie · 7 .I. forealdodne nihtsang · 7 .I. pistelboc · 7 .II. forealdode rædingbec swiðe wake · 7 .I. wac mæssereaf. ⁊ þus fela leden boca he beget innto þam mynstre · liber pastoralis · 7 liber dialogorum · 7 libri .IIII. prophetarum · 7 liber Boetii de consolatione[4] · 7 isagoge Porphirii[5] · 7 .I. passionalis · 7 liber Prosperi · 7 liber Prudentii psicomachie · 7 liber[2] Prudentii ymnorum · 7 liber[2] Prudentii de martyribus[6] 7 liber Ezechielis prophetę · 7 cantica canticorum · 7 liber Isaie prophetę onsundron · 7 liber Isidori ethimolagiarum[7] · 7 passiones apostolorum · 7 expositio Bede super euuangelium Lucę · 7 expositio Bede super apocalipsin · 7 expositio Bede super VII. epistolas canonicas · 7 liber Isidori de nouo et ueteri testamento · 7 liber Isidori de miraculis Xp̄i · 7 liber Oserii 7 liber Machabeorum · 7 liber Persii · 7 Sedulies boc · 7 liber Aratoris · 7 diadema monachorum[8] · 7 glose Statii · 7 liber officialis Amalarii. ⁊ ofer his dæg he ann his capellam þider binnan forð mid him silfum · on eallum þam þingum þe he silf dide mid Godes ðeninge · on þ gerad þ þa Godes þeowas þe þær binnan beoð æfre his sawle gemunon · mid heora gebedum 7 mæssesangum ·

---

[1] þa, Harl. [2] Om. Ex. Bk.
[3] þeos englisce cristes boc, ibid.
[4] Followed by liber officialis Amalarii, ibid.
[5] This is followed by an erasure. The Ex. Bk. adds de dialectica in a later hand.
[6] The Ex. Bk. adds on anre bec in later handwriting on an erasure.
[7] At this point in the Ex. Bk. come the remaining two books of Isidore.
[8] Instead of this work the Ex. Bk. has liber de sanctis patribus entered in a later hand.

TO EXETER

2 standards and 1 banner and 6 boxes and 1 military wagon and 1 chest, and there had been only 7 hanging bells and now there are 16 hanging bells and 12 hand-bells and 2 complete missals and 1 collectarium and 2 epistle books and 2 complete choral books and 1 nocturnale and 1 *Ad te levavi* and 1 book of tropes and 2 psalters and a third as they sing it at Rome and 2 hymnbooks and 1 valuable benedictional and 3 others and 1 English gospel book and 2 summer lectionaries and 1 winter lectionary and the *Regula Canonicorum* and a martyrology and 1 book of the Canon Law in Latin and 1 penitential in English and 1 complete book of homilies for winter and summer and Boethius' book in English and 1 large English book about various things composed in verse; and at his accession the only books he found in the minster were 1 capitulary and 1 worn-out nocturnale and 1 epistle book and 2 very poor worn-out lectionaries and 1 poor mass vestment. And he acquired the following Latin books for the minster, the *Liber Pastoralis* and the *Liber Dialogorum* and the books of the four prophets and Boethius' book *De Consolatione* and the *Isagoge* of Porphyrius and 1 *Passionalis* and Prosper's book and the *Psychomachia* of Prudentius and the *Liber Hymnorum* of Prudentius and Prudentius' *De Martyribus* and the book of the prophet Ezekiel and the *Cantica Canticorum* and the book of the prophet Isaiah separately and the *Etymologiae* of Isidore and the *Passiones Apostolorum* and Bede's *Expositio super Evangelium Lucae* and Bede's *Expositio super Apocalipsin* and Bede's *Expositio super* VII. *epistolas canonicas* and Isidore's book *De Novo et Veteri Testamento* and Isidore's book *De Miraculis Christi* and the book of Oserius and the *Liber Machabeorum* and Persius' book and Sedulius' book and Arator's book and the *Diadema Monachorum* and the glosses of Statius and the *Liber Officialis* of Amalarius.

And after his death he grants his *capella* to the minster along with himself, as far as concerns all the things with which he himself performed the service of God, on condition that the servants of God who are therein continually in their prayers and

THE GIFTS OF BISHOP LEOFRIC

to Xp̄e · 7 to Sc̄e Petre · 7 to eallum þam halgum þe ꝥ halige minster is fore gehalgod · ꝥ his sawle beo Gode þe anfengre · 7 se þe ðas[1] gyfu 7 þisne unnan wille Gode 7 Sc̄e Petre ætbredan · si him heofena rice ætbroden · 7 si he ecelice geniðerod into helle wíte.

II. LEASE OF LANDS BY WALCHER, BISHOP OF DURHAM, TO EALDGYTH

Walchear b. 7 eal Sc̄e Cuðberhtes hyred Sealdan Ealdgyðe ꝥ lánd æt Ðornhlawa to þyse male ꝥ is þus ꝥ gyf heo hit forlæteð beo hit æt deadum oððe æt cwicvm swa swa hyre þearfe sy · ꝥ mala is VIII. exen · 7 XII. cyg · 7 IIII. menn · 7 eac hé lænde hyre ꝥ land æt Windegatum ealle ða hwile þe hyre þearf byð.

III. THE NORTHAMPTONSHIRE GELD ROLL

Ðis is into Suttunes hundred þat is an hundred hida · swa hit wæs on Æduuardes deige kynges · 7 þerof is gewered an 7 tuenti hide 7 twadel an hide 7 fourti hide inland · 7 .x. hide þes kynges ahhen ferme land · 7 VIII. 7 .xx. hide weste 7 þriddel an hide. Þis is into Werdunes hundret ꝥ is an hundret hida swa hit was on Eadwardes dege kynges 7 þerof is gewered .xvIII. hide buton are gearde · 7 .xL. hide inland · 7 .I. 7 xL. hide weste · 7 .I. gearde.

Þis is into Klegele hundred ꝥ is an hundred hide swa it wes on Ędv⁹ dege kynges 7 þerof is gewered .xvIII. hide 7 fourti hide inland 7 .II. 7 xL. hide weste.

Þis is into Grauesende hundred ꝥ is an hundred hide swa it wes on Eadw⁹ dege kynges · 7 þerof is gewered .xvIII. hide 7 .I. alfhide 7 .v. 7 .xxx. inland · 7 .v. hidæ þes kynges agen ferme land 7 .I. 7 xL. hide weste · 7 .I. healf hide. Þis is into Eadboldes-stowe hundred ꝥ is an hundred hida swa it wes on Eadw⁹ dege kynges 7 þerof is gewered .III. 7 xx.[2] hida · 7 .I. healf hide 7 .v. 7 xL. hide inland · 7 v. hide þes kynges · 7 xxvI. hide weste 7 .I. healf hide.

[1] þar, Harl.   [2] A third 'x' has been erased.

in their services commend his soul to Christ and to St Peter and to all the saints to whom the holy minster is dedicated, that his soul may be the more acceptable to God.

If anyone attempts to deprive God and St Peter of this gift and this grant, he shall be deprived of the kingdom of heaven and condemned for ever to the torment of hell.

II. LEASE OF LANDS BY WALCHER, BISHOP OF DURHAM, TO EALDGYTH

Bishop Walcher and all the community at St Cuthbert's have granted to Ealdgyth the estate at Thornley on these terms, namely that if she leaves it, whether at her death or during her life, as the necessity may arise, the terms shall be [the payment of] 8 oxen and 12 cows and 4 men. And he has likewise lent her the estate at Wingate for as long as she requires it.

III. THE NORTHAMPTONSHIRE GELD ROLL

To Sutton Hundred belong 100 hides, as was the case in King Edward's time, and of these 21 hides and two-thirds of a hide have paid geld and 40 hides are in demesne and 10 hides are the king's own food-rent land and 28 hides and one-third of a hide are waste.

To Warden Hundred belong 100 hides, as was the case in King Edward's time, and of these 18 hides less one yardland have paid geld and 40 hides are in demesne and 41 hides and 1 yardland are waste.

To Cleyley Hundred belong 100 hides, as was the case in King Edward's time, and of these 18 hides have paid geld and 40 hides are in demesne and 42 hides are waste.

To *Gravesende* Hundred belong 100 hides, as was the case in King Edward's time, and of these 18 hides and half a hide have paid geld and 35 hides are in demesne and 5 hides are the king's own food-rent land and 41 hides and half a hide are waste.

To *Eadboldesstowe* Hundred belong 100 hides, as was the case in King Edward's time, and of these 23 hides and half a hide have paid geld and 45 hides are in demesne and 5 hides are the king's and 26 hides and half a hide are waste.

232 THE NORTHAMPTONSHIRE GELD ROLL

Þis is into Egelweardesle hundred · ꝥ is an hundred hide swa hit wes on Eadwardas dege kynges · 7 þerof is gewered .xvi. hide 7 .i. healf hide · 7 xl. hide inland · 7 æt Nortune seueðe healf hide ne com nan peni of · ꝥ ah Osmund þes kynges writere · 7
5 seuen · 7 xxx. weste.

Þis is into Uoxle hundred ꝥ is an hundred hida ealswa hit was on Eadw⁹ dege kynges 7 þerof is gewered .xvi. hide 7 xxx. hide inland · 7 .i. 7 .xx. hide þes kynges ahhen[1] land 7 .iii. 7 xxx. hide weste.
10 Þis is into Uyceste hundred · ꝥ is an hundred hida · swa hit wes on Ędw⁹ dege kynges 7 þerof is gewered .xviiii.[2] hide · 7 xl. hide inland · 7 .xx. hide þes kynges ahhen land · 7 .i. 7 .xx. hida weste.

Þis is into Hocheshlawa hundred ꝥ is .ii. 7 .lx. hida þus hit
15 was on Ędw⁹ dege kynges · 7 þerof is gewered .viii. hida 7 xv hida inland · 7 viiii. 7 xxx. hida weste.

Þis is into Wilebroce hundred .ii. 7 lx. hida þus hit wes on Ędw⁹ dege kynges · 7 þerof his[3] gewered .vii. hida 7 .xi. hida inland 7 .xiii. hida weste þis is into ꝥ healfe hundred 7 ꝥ healfe
20 hundred eal unwered ꝥ heah se kyng.

Þis is into þas twa hundred to Uptunegrene fif syðe twenti hida 7 nigeða healf hida þus it was on Eadw⁹ dege kynges · 7 þer is gewered fifti hida 7 .vii. 7 .xx. hida inland 7 .viiii.[4] 7 xx. hida weste 7 .i. healf hida · 7 of .v. siðe .xx. hidæ is þridde healf hide
25 unwered 7 ꝥ heah Ricard engaigne.

Þis is into Nauereslund twa hundred .viii. 'syðe' twenti hide þus hit wes on Eadw⁹ dege kynges 7 þus micel is gewered into þas twa hundred · ꝥ is .viiii. 7 .xx. hida 7 .i. hida · 7 viiii. 7 fifti hida inland 7 twelfta healf hide westa[5] 7 of þas .viii. syða twenti
30 hida is .viii. hida unwered · 7 ꝥ eah si læfdi þes kynges wif.

Þis is into Nęresforda hundred .ii. 7 lx. hida þus hit wes on Ędw⁹ dege kyng⁹ 7 þus micel is gewered xv. hida · 7 .xiiii. hida inland 7 .iii. 7 xxx. hida westa.

---

[1] *-an*, Ellis.   [2] xviii, ibid.
[3] Sic with a dot below the *h* to show that the scribe meant it to be erased.
[4] viii, Ellis.   [5] *westæ*, ibid.

THE NORTHAMPTONSHIRE GELD ROLL

To *Egelweardesle* Hundred belong 100 hides, as was the case in King Edward's time, and of these 16 hides and half a hide have paid geld and 40 hides are in demesne and from 6½ hides at Norton not a penny has been received—Osmund, the king's secretary, owns that estate—and 37 hides are waste.

To Foxley Hundred belong 100 hides, as was the case in King Edward's time, and of these 16 hides have paid geld and 30 hides are in demesne and 21 hides are the king's own land and 33 hides are waste.

To Towcester Hundred belong 100 hides, as was the case in King Edward's time, and of these 19 hides have paid geld and 40 hides are in demesne and 20 hides are the king's own land and 21 hides are waste.

To Huxloe Hundred belong 62 hides, as was the case in King Edward's time, and of these 8 hides have paid geld and 15 hides are in demesne and 39 hides are waste.

To Willybrook Hundred belong 62 hides, as was the case in King Edward's time, and of these 7 hides have paid geld and 11 hides are in demesne and 13 hides are waste. All this belongs to half the hundred and the king owns the half hundred which has paid no geld.

To the double hundred of Upton Green belong 108½ hides, as was the case in King Edward's time, and of these 50 hides have paid geld and 27 hides are in demesne and 29 hides and half a hide are waste, and of the 100 hides 2½ hides have not paid geld, and that estate is owned by Richard Engayne.

To the double hundred of *Navereslund* belong 160 hides, as was the case in King Edward's time, and the amount of land belonging to this double hundred which has paid geld is 29 hides and 1 hide and 59 hides are in demesne and 11½ hides are waste, and of these 160 hides 8 hides have not paid geld, and that estate is owned by the Lady, the King's wife.

To Navisford Hundred belong 62 hides, as was the case in King Edward's time, and the land which has paid geld amounts to 15 hides and 14 hides are in demesne and 33 hides are waste.

234 THE NORTHAMPTONSHIRE GELD ROLL

Þis is into Pocabroc hundred .II. 7 LX. hida þus it was on Edw⁹ dege kyng⁹ 7 þer 'is' .x. hida wered 7 .xx. hida inland · 7 .II. 7 xxx hida westa.

Þis is into ðet oþer healfe hundred into Neowbotlegraue þ is 5 oðer healf hundred hida þer is inne fif 7 feorwerti¹ hida buton an healf gearde wane sea² land 7 gewered 7 þer is healf hundred hide 7 .II. 7 xx. hide inland 7 .III. 7 .xxx. hida 7 .I. healf gerde westa 7 þus hit wes on Edw⁹ dege king⁹.

Þis is þ oðer healfe hundred into Gildesburh · 7 þer is inne 10 oðer healf hundred hida · 7 þer is .xvi. hida sett 7 gewered · 7 þer is healf hundred hida 7 xviii. hide inland · 7 þer is healf hundred hida 7 .xvi. westa · 7 þus hit wes on Eaduuard dege kynges.

Þis is into Spelhoh hundred four syðe twenti hida 7 .x. hida · 15 7 þer is twenti hida 7 .I. alf hida sett 7 gewered · 7 fif 7 .xx. hida byrigland 7 into Habintune .x. hida · Ricardes land ne com nan peni of 7 into Multune .vi. hida Willmes land ne com nan peni of 7 .viii. 7 xx. hida weste · 7 an healf .ħ.

Þis is into Hwiccleslea west hundred þ syndon foursyðe xx. 20 hida · 7 þus hit wes on Edw⁹ dege kyng⁹ · 7 þerof is gewered .x. hida 7 fourti hit inland 7 .xxx. hida weste.

Þis is into Hwicceslea east hundred þ sindon foursyðe .xx. hide ealswa hit was on Edw⁹ dæge kyng⁹ 7 þerof is xv. hide wered · 7 þer is four 7 .xxx. hide inland 7 .I. 7 xxx. hide weste.

25 Þis is into Stotfalde hundred þ is an hundred hide swa hit wes on Edw⁹ dæge kyng⁹ 7 þer is gewered of .viiii. hide 7 .I. healf gerde · 7 þer is fourti hide inland · 7 fifti hide weste 7 ferðe healf gerde.

Þis is into Stoce hundred þ is fourti hida · swa hit weron on 30 Edw⁹ dæge kyng⁹ · 7 þerof his gewered eahtetende healf hide · 7 ælleofte healf hide · inland · 7 .xii. hide weste.

Þis is into oðer healfe hundred into Hehhám þ is oðer healf hundred hide swa hit wes on Edw⁹ dæge³ kyng⁹ 7 þerof is gewered fifti hide buton an alf hide 7 four 7 fourti hide inland 35 7 six 7 fifti hide weste · 7 .x. hida mare þ lið into Anforðesho⁴.

Þis is into Maleslę hundred þ is foursiðe .xx. hida · 7 þerof is wered .xii. hide · 7 þer is .xxx. hide inland 7 þer is .xxx. hide weste · 7 þer is .viii. hide unwered þ ah se kyng.

[1] Sic. [2] For *sett*? [3] *deege*, Ellis. [4] *-ford-*, ibid.

THE NORTHAMPTONSHIRE GELD ROLL 235

To Polebrook Hundred belong 62 hides, as was the case in King Edward's time, and of these 10 hides have paid geld and 20 hides are in demesne and 32 hides are waste.

To the hundred and a half attached to Nobottlegrove belong 150 hides of which 45 hides less half a yardland are occupied (?) and have paid geld and 72 hides are in demesne and 33 hides and half a yardland are waste, and it was the same in King Edward's time.

There is a hundred and a half attached to Guilsborough, and it consists of 150 hides, and of these 16 are occupied and have paid geld, and there are 68 hides in demesne and 66 hides waste, and it was the same in King Edward's time.

To Spelhoe Hundred belong 90 hides, and of these 20 hides and half a hide are occupied and have paid geld and 25 hides are borough-land, and from 10 hides belonging to Abington—Richard's land—not a penny has been received, and from 6 hides belonging to Moulton—William's land—not a penny has been received, and 28 hides and half a hide are waste.

To Witchley West Hundred belong 80 hides, and it was the same in King Edward's time, and of these 10 hides have paid geld and 40 hides are in demesne and 30 hides are waste.

To Witchley East Hundred belong 80 hides, as was the case in King Edward's time, and of these 15 hides have paid geld and there are 34 hides in demesne and 31 hides waste.

To *Stotfalde* Hundred belong 100 hides, as was the case in King Edward's time, and of these 9 hides and half a yardland have paid geld and there are 40 hides in demesne and 50 hides and 3½ yardlands waste.

To Stoke Hundred belong 40 hides, as they did in King Edward's time, and of these 17½ hides have paid geld and 10½ hides are in demesne and 12 hides are waste.

To the hundred and a half attached to Higham belong 150 hides, as was the case in King Edward's time, and of these 50 hides less half a hide have paid geld and 44 hides are in demesne and 56 hides are waste and 10 hides in addition belong to Hamfordshoe.

To Mawsley Hundred belong 80 hides, and of these 12 hides have paid geld and there are 30 hides in demesne and 30 hides waste, and 8 hides which have not paid geld are owned by the king.

236 THE NORTHAMPTONSHIRE GELD ROLL

Þis is into Corebi[1] hundred þ is .VII. 7 XL. hide swa hit wes on Ędw⁹ dæge kyng⁹ 7 þerof is gewered .VIII. healf hide 7 .XII. healf hide inland · 7 þer is .XII. hide 7 .I. gerde þes kynges fermeland[2] weste 7 unwered · 7 .V. hide unwered þa .III. hide eah þe ðe Scotte kyng · 7 oþer healf hide eah þy læfedi[3] 7 Vrs .I. healf hide · 7 XI. hide weste buton ane gerde.

Þis is into Roðewelle hundred þ is .LX. hida þus hit wes on Ędw⁹ dæge kyng⁹ · 7 þerof[4] is .X. hide wered · 7 .XX. hida inland · 7 .XV. hide unwered þa seuen hide 7 .I. healf hide eah ðe kyng 7 seuen hide 7 .I. healf hide eah ðes kynges wif 7 Rodbertes wif heorles 7 Willelm enganie.

Þis is into Anduerðeshoh hundred þ is .IIII. siða twenti hida · 7 .X. hida þus hit was on Ędw⁹ dæge kyn⁹ 7 þerof is gewered .V. 7 XX. hide inland 7 .IX. 7 XXX. hide weste.

Þis is into Ordlingbære hundred .IIII. syðe twenti hide þus hit wes[5] on Edw⁹ dæge kyn⁹ · 7 þerof his gewered .VIIII. 7 XX. hide 7 .I. healf hide 7 .IIII. 7 .XX. hide 7 .I. healf hide inland 7 .V. hide unwered þ eah Willelm enganie 7 Witeget preost · 7 .I. 7 XX. hide weste.

Þis is into þ oðer healfe hundred into Wimereslea þ is oðer healf hundred hida swa hit wes on Ędw⁹ dæges kyn⁹ 7 þerof is wered .I. 7 XL. hide 7 .III. syðe twenti hide inland 7 .VIIII. 7 .XL. hide weste.

IV. RECORD OF THE DUES PERTAINING TO TAUNTON

HER swutelad[6] on þisum gewrite hwylce gerihta langon into TANTVNE on þam timan þe EADWERD cing wes cucu 7 dead · þæt ís ærest of þam lande æt Nigonhidon seo mann redden into TANTVNE · cirhsceattas · 7 burhgerihtu · heorðpenegas · 7 hundred penegas · 7 teoþung · of ælcere hide eahta penegas · hamsocn · 7 forsteall · griþbrice · 7 handfangenþeof · aþ · 7 ordel · fyrdwíte · 7 eall swa oft swa him ma[7] bude to gemote he come ofþe[8] hine man badode. Dunna wes þæs biscopes mann to þam

---

[1] *Cop-*, Ellis. [2] *-de*, ibid. [3] *-eth*, ibid.
[4] *-eof*, ibid. [5] *wæs*, ibid. [6] *-að*, K.; *-ulað*, T.
[7] Sic; *man*, K. [8] For *oþþe* ?

To Corby Hundred belong 47 hides, as was the case in King Edward's time, and of these 7½ hides have paid geld and 11½ hides are in demesne and there are 12 hides and 1 yardland of the king's food-rent land which are waste and have not paid geld and 5 hides have not paid geld—of these the Scottish king owns 3 hides and the Lady 1½ hides and Urs half a hide—and 11 hides less a yardland are waste.

To Rothwell Hundred belong 60 hides, as was the case in King Edward's time, and of these 10 hides have paid geld and 20 hides are in demesne and 15 hides have not paid geld—the king owns 7 hides and half a hide and the king's wife and Earl Robert's wife and William Engayne own 7 hides and half a hide.

To Hamfordshoe Hundred belong 90 hides, as was the case in King Edward's time, and of these 25 hides have paid geld [and 26 hides are] in demesne and 39 hides are waste.

To Orlingbury Hundred belong 80 hides, as was the case in King Edward's time, and of these 29 hides and half a hide have paid geld and 24 hides and half a hide are in demesne and 5 hides, owned by William Engayne and Witeget the priest, have not paid geld, and 21 hides are waste.

To the hundred and a half belonging to Wymersley belong 150 hides, as was the case in King Edward's time, and of these 41 hides have paid geld and 60 hides are in demesne and 49 hides are waste.

IV. RECORD OF THE DUES PERTAINING TO TAUNTON

Here are set forth in this document the dues which pertained to Taunton on the day when King Edward died, namely first from the estate at Nynehead the tenants rendered to Taunton church dues and borough dues, hearth pence and hundred pence and a tithe of eightpence from every hide, [payments for] attacks on a man's house and obstruction, breach of the peace and thieves caught in the act, oath and ordeal and the fine for the neglect of military service, and each tenant had to come to the [court] meeting as often as he was summoned or else distraint was made upon him. On the day when King Edward died Dunna was the

238 RECORD OF THE DUES

timan þe Eadward cing wæs cucu 7 dead of þam lande æt Acón · 7 of Taálande · 7 of twam Cedenon · 7 he geaf to gerihton .v. circsceattas · 7 heorðpenegas · 7 hundredpenegas · hamsocne · 7 forsteall · griðbrice · 7 handfangenne[1] þeof · aþ · 7 ordel · 7 5 þriwa secan gemot · on .XII. monþum · 7 of Eaforde þa ilcan gerihtu. And Ealdreð[2] wæs þæs biscopes mann · of þam lande æt Hele · 7 dyde þe ilcan gerihta þæ ma[3] dyde of Nigonhidon. And of þam fif hidon æt Baggabeorgan .III. circsceattas · 7 burgerihta · heorðpenegas · 7 hundredpenegas · 7 handfangene 10 þeof aþ · 7 ordel · hamsocn · 7 forsteall · griðbrice · 7 þreo motlæþu ungeboden · on .XII. monþum. Of Lidigerde .I. circsceatt · 7 eall þe geilcan gerihta þe ma[3] dyde of Baggabeorge. Of Hylle .I. circsceatt · 7 burhgerihtu · heorðpenegas · 7 hundreðpenegas[4] · hamsocne · 7 forðsteall[5] · griðbrice · 7 handfangene þeof · aþ · 15 7 ordel · 7 .III. gemót on geare buton he hít gebicge oþþe gebidde. Of þære oþre healfre hide · æt twam Holaforda .II. circsceattas · 7 eall þæ geylcan gerihta þe ma[3] deð of Cedon[6]. Ðises ys gewítnes · Gisa bisceop · 7 Ælfsie abb · 7 Wulgeat abb · 7 · Ælfnod · mynsterprauost · 7 Wulfwerd wita · 7 Godwine Eadwies sunu · 20 7 Ælmer þæs abbodes broþor · 7 Ælgelric[7] æt Healswege[8] · 7 Heardinc · Eadnoðes sunu · 7 Garmund · 7 Ælfric tigel · 7 Ordgar se wite · 7 · Ælfwerd Leofsunes sunu · 7 · Brichtric se calewa · 7 Dodda æt Curi · 7 Ælmer werl[9] · 7 Sæwold æt Iliacum · 7 Wulfric æt Pauleshele · 7 Ealdred æt Sulfhere · 7 Wulger æt 25 Hiwerc 7 Æilwine wunge[10].

[1] -ene, K.   [2] -red, K.   [3] man, K.
[4] -red-, K.   [5] forst-, T.   [6] Cedenon, K., T.
[7] Æg-, K.   [8] Healf-, K., T.   [9] yerl, K.
[10] yunge, K.

bishop's tenant of the estates at Oake and Tolland and the two Cheddons, and he gave as dues 5 measures of church dues and hearth pence and hundred pence, [payments for] attacks on a man's house and obstruction, breach of the peace and thieves caught in the act, oath and ordeal, and had to attend the court three times in the twelve months. And the same dues [were rendered] from Ford. Ealdred was the bishop's tenant of the estate at Hele, and rendered the same dues as were rendered from Nynehead. And from the five hides at Bagborough [were rendered] 3 measures of church dues and borough dues, hearth pence and hundred pence and [payments for] thieves caught in the act, oath and ordeal, attacks on a man's house and obstruction and breach of the peace, and attendance [was demanded] at three court meetings in the twelve months without summons. From Lydeard 1 measure of church dues [was paid] and exactly the same dues as were rendered from Bagborough. From Hillfarrance 1 measure of church dues [was paid] and borough dues, hearth pence and hundred pence, [payments for] attacks on a man's house and obstruction, breach of the peace and thieves caught in the act, oath and ordeal, and [the tenant had to attend] three courts in the year, unless he obtained exemption by payment or petition. From the 1½ hides at the two Holfords [are demanded] 2 measures of church dues and exactly the same dues as are rendered from Cheddon.

The witnesses of this are Bishop Gisa and Abbot Ælfsige and Abbot Wulfgeat and Ælfnoth, prior of the monastery, and Wulfweard the White and Godwine, Edwy's son, and Ælfmær, the abbot's brother, and Æthelric of Halsway and Hearding, Eadnoth's son, and Garmund and Ælfric *tigel* and Ordgar the White and Ælfweard, Leofsunu's son, and Brihtric the Bald and Dodda of Curry and Ælfmær *werl* and Sæwold of *Iliacum* and Wulfric of Poleshill and Ealdred of Monksilver and Wulfgar of Ludhewish (?) and Æthelwine *wunge*.

V. RECORD OF THE DUES RENDERED TO THE CHURCH AT LAMBOURN

Þis syndan þa gerichte þe liccaþ into þam minstre on Lambourne · þæt is an hyde landes sker 7[1] sacleas sake 7 · sokne tol · 7 · team · 7 · þanne teoþeu[2] æker on þæs kynges lande · 7 tuwegen scriftækeres on hærfeste 7 þat teoþe lamb · 7 · þat teoþe fearh · 7 · on Michaeles meassan ane wæge cyses an on Martines meassan twegeu sester corues · 7 au swyn 7 · on eastrian .xv. panigas to elefen 7 · þas preostes tyn eoxene[3] · 7 · twa[4] ky ⁒ mid[5] þæs kinges · 7 · his gielde hryþere mid þære hæman 7 · þæs preostes scyp ⁒ forþ æfter þas kynges ealre next swa þæt heo ne mængen togædre 7 · feowerti swyne æuer freo ⁒ on wude *and* on feolde *and* ælce dæge on hors berinde · oðþe twegen men ⁒ of þæes kynges wude to dæes preostes fyre *and* þæs preostes twa horis · mid þær gerefan · 7 · of ælcere hide geneatlandes · on vp . hæme toune *and* on byrihæme tune oenne æker to teoþunge oðþe an hundred sceafa on hærueste *and* ælc geneat ænne sester cornes to syricsceatte *and* bunan Cobbaudoune[6] ⁒ twelf pænigas æt ælcere hida on Martines meassan to cyricsceatte *and* ælc gebur æt Eastbury ⁒ aune sester cornes to cyricsceatte · 7 · of þan þegenlande upe tun twegen ækeres to teoþunge · 7 · twegen sester cornes to cyricsceatte · 7 · on Bokhamtoune · R · twegen akeres to teoþunge · 7 twegen sester cornes to cyricsceatte · 7 · of Eadwardes twegen akeres to teoþunge · 7 · of Eastbury twegen akeres to teoþunge · 7 ænne cyricsceat. Se þe þis benime þan minstre æt Lambourne · 7 · þan preoste Cristes cours habbe he · 7 · Sca̅ Maria · 7 · Sc̄e Michaeles 7 Sc̄us Petrus · 7 · Sc̄us Nicholaus · 7 · ealra Cristes halgena · þis is bitealð · be þæs kinges hase innan þare scire · 7 · innan þan hundred on Lambourne · þars to is gewitnesse · Croc p⁹[7] · 7 Heardyng p⁹ · 7 · [W]erman[8] p⁹ · 7 · Wattear p⁹ · 7 · Þeodric p⁹ · 7 · Wealtear diacon · 7 · Anffriȝ · 7 · Rauf ou ƀ · 7 · Oda · 7 · Wikyng ou Traue[9] 7 · Ægelwine on Minbiry · 7 · Cafi 7 · Ealfric lif⁹[10] · 7 · Ealri km⁹[11] · 7 · Ælfwine ƀ.

---

[1] Footman omits the A.S. symbol for *and* throughout.
[2] *u* is frequently written for *n* in the MS. copy of this document.
[3] *eoþene*, Footman.   [4] *swa*, ibid.

V. RECORD OF THE DUES RENDERED TO THE CHURCH AT LAMBOURN

These are the dues which belong to the church at Lambourn, namely 1 hide of land free and quit, jurisdiction, toll and vouching to warranty, and the tenth acre in the king's land, and two... acres at harvest, and the tenth lamb and the tenth young pig, and at Michaelmas a wey of cheese, and at Martinmas two sesters of corn and 1 pig, and at Easter 15 pence......, and pasture for the priest's 10 oxen and 2 cows along with the king's, and for his...bullocks........, and for the priest's sheep next after the king's so that they do not mix together, and free pasture for 40 pigs in wood and open country, and every day 1 horse or 2 men carrying wood from the king's wood for the priest's fire, and pasture for the priest's two horses along with the reeve's. And from every hide of *geneat*-land in Up Lambourn and in Lambourn itself 1 acre as tithes or 100 sheaves at harvest, and every *geneat* a sester of corn as church dues, and 12 pence from every hide above Coppington as church dues at Martinmas, and every *gebur* at Eastbury 1 sester of corn as church dues, and from the thegn-land on the manor 2 acres as tithes and 2 sesters of corn as church dues, and from R[alph]'s estate at Bockhampton 2 acres as tithes and 2 sesters of corn as church dues, and from Edward's [estate at Bockhampton] 2 acres as tithes, and from Eastbury 2 acres as tithes and 1 measure of church dues.

He who takes this away from the church at Lambourn and from the priest shall have the curse of Christ and St Mary and St Michael and St Peter and St Nicholas and all the saints of Christ. This has been made known by the king's command within the parish and within the hundred of Lambourn, and the witnesses are the priests Croc, Hearding, Werman, Walter and Theodric, and the deacon Walter, and Anfrith and Ralph of Bockhampton and Oda and Wiking of *Traue* and Æthelwine of Membury and Cafi and Ælfric *lif*[9] and Ælfric *km*[9] and Ælfwine *b*.

---

[5] Footman has *Kynud* instead of *ky ᛬́ mid*.   [6] *Cowau-*, Footman.
[7] Footman has *þ* for *p*[9] throughout.   [8] The MS. has *per-*.
[9] The MS. has *outraue* or *-craue*.   [10] The reading might be *lis*[9].
[11] The reading might be *kin*[9]. Footman has [*Kur*].

VI. PAYMENTS MADE BY THE CHURCH OF WORCESTER TO WILLIAM I

Ðis mycel is gegolden of þære cyricean .W. cyninge syððan he þis land ahte wiðutan þam hídgelde þe nan man wiðutan Gode anum atellan ne mæg ·;· Ðæt is ærest of þam æscene þe is oðre namon hrygilebúc gecleopad .x. pund · 7 of þam .xv. hrodan
5 .vi. marc · 7 of þam oðran æscene · 7 of þam hlæfle · 7 of þære crucan · 7 of þam hnæpfe .xi. 'marc'; 7 of þære hlangan scrine .viii. pund · 7 of þam .iii. hornan .iii. marc · 7 of þam candelstæfe .x. pund · 7 of þære hæcce .xxxiii. 'marca' · 7 þærtoeakan .xl. marca · 7 sixte half marc goldes ·;·

VI. PAYMENTS MADE BY THE CHURCH OF WORCESTER TO WILLIAM I

This much has been paid by the church to King William, since he owned this land, apart from the tax on every hide which no one but God alone can reckon, namely first for the vessel which is called by another name the 'incense bowl' 10 pounds, and for the fifteen crosses 6 marks, and for the other vessel and for the cup and for the jar and for the bowl 11 marks, and for the long chest 8 pounds, and for the 3 horns 3 marks, and for the candlestick 10 pounds, and for the crosier 33 marks, and in addition to all this 45½ marks of gold.

APPENDIX II
MISCELLANEOUS DOCUMENTS (UNDATED)

I. THE BURGHAL HIDAGE

Þreo hund hida hyrð to Eorpeburnan[1] · 7 xxiiii. hida to[2] Hæstingaceastre hyrþ .v. hund[3] hida 7 to Læwe hyrþ twelf [hund][4] hida · 7 to Burham[5] hyrþ seofan hund hida · 7 xx. hida to Cisseceastre[6] hyrþ .xv. hund hida · þonne hyrþ to Port-
5 ceastre[7] .v. hund hida · 7 oþer healf hund hida hyrþ[8] to Hamtune · 7 to Wintaceastre hyrþ feower 7 twentig hund hida · 7 to Wiltune hyrþ feowertine hund hida · 7 to [T]issanbyrig[9] hyrþ .v. hund hida[10] · 7 to Tweoneam hyrþ .v. hund hida butan .xxx. hidan[11] 7 to Werham hyrþ .xv.i. hund hida 7 to Brydian
10 hyrþ eahta hund hida butan feowertigan hidan · 7 to Eaxanceastre hyrþ feower 7 xxx. hida 7 .vii. hund hida · 7 to Halganwille hyrþ þreo hund hida · 7 to Hlidan hyrþ oþer healf hund hida butan .x. hidan · 7 to Pilletune hyrþ feower hund hida butan .xl. hidan · 7 to Weced hyrð .v. hund hida · 7 xiii. hida · 7 to
15 Axanbrycge hyrþ feower hund hida · 7 to Lengen hyrþ .c. hida 7 to Langport hyrð .vi. hund hida · 7 to Baðan hyrð tyn hund hida · 7 twelf hund[12] hida hyrð to Mealdmesbyring · 7 to Crecgelade hyrþ .xiiii.[13] hund hida · 7 xv. hund[14] hida to Oxnaforda 7 to Wælingforda hyrð xxiiii. hund hida · 7 xvi hund hida hyrð
20 to Buccingahamme[15] · 7 to Sceaftesige hyrð .x. hund hida · 7 .vi. hund[16] hida hyrþ to Escingum · 7 to Suþriganaweorce hyrþ eahtatyne hund hida.

To anes æceres bræde on wealstillinge 7 to þære wære gebirigeað .xvi. hida gif ælc hid byþ be anum men gemannod þonne
25 mæg man gesettan ælce gyrde mid feower mannum þon gebyred[17] to twentigan gyrdan on wealstillinge · hundeahtatig[18] hida · 7 to þam furlange gebirgeað oþer healf hund hida · 7 x hida be þam ilcan getæle þe ic her bebufan tealde · to twam furlangum gehyrað[19] xx. hida · 7 þreo hund hida · to þrim furlangum hund-
30 eahtatig hida 7 cccc hida þonne gebyrigeað to .iiii. furlangum

---

[1] *Heoreweburan*, Lib. Rub., C.C.C.; *Heorepeburan*, Cott. Cl.
[2] 7 *at*, Cott. Cl., C.C.C., Or.; Hastings and Lewes are om. in Lib. Rub.
[3] 15 (for 1500), Cott. Cl.; 5 (for 500), C.C.C., Or.
[4] 1300, Cott. Cl., C.C.C., Or.
[5] Burpham is omitted in the other mss.
[6] Om. Cott. Cl.

I. THE BURGHAL HIDAGE

To *Eorpeburnan* belong 324 hides, to Hastings belong 500 hides, and to Lewes belong 1200 hides, and to Burpham belong 720 hides, to Chichester belong 1500 hides. Then to Portchester belong 500 hides, and 150 hides belong to Southampton, and to Winchester belong 2400 hides, and to Wilton belong 1400 hides, and to Tisbury belong 500 hides, and to Twyneham belong 500 hides less 30 hides, and to Wareham belong 1600 hides, and to Bridport [or Bredy] belong 800 hides less 40 hides, and to Exeter belong 734 hides, and to Halwell belong 300 hides, and to Lidford belong 150 hides less 10 hides, and to Pilton belong 400 hides less 40 hides, and to Watchet belong 513 hides, and to Axbridge belong 400 hides, and to Lyng belong 100 hides, and to Langport belong 600 hides, and to Bath belong 1000 hides, and 1200 hides belong to Malmesbury, and to Cricklade belong 1400 hides, and 1500 hides to Oxford, and to Wallingford belong 2400 hides, and 1600 hides belong to Buckingham, and to *Sceaftesige* belong 1000 hides, and 600 hides belong to Eashing, and to Southwark belong 1800 hides.

For the maintenance (?) and defence of an acre's breadth of wall 16 hides are required. If every hide is represented by 1 man, then every pole of wall can be manned by 4 men. Then for the maintenance of 20 poles of wall 80 hides are required, and for a furlong 160 hides are required by the same reckoning as I have stated above. For 2 furlongs 320 hides are required; for 3 furlongs 480 hides. Then for 4 furlongs 640 hides are required.

---

[7] Cott. Cl. has *Đonne his to P. DCL. hid to H.* 7 *to W. hirað* xxiiii^c. *hidas*; C.C.C. has *to P. D* (an erasure) *hid · to H.* 'C. 7 .L.' (entered above the line); Or. has the same without the erasure and with *C* 7 *L* in the text.
[8] Om. Lib. Rub.   [9] *c-*, MS.
[10] The other MSS. have 700 hides and include Shaftesbury with the same assessment.
[11] The other MSS. have 'less 40 hides' (which rightly applies to Bredy) and omit Wareham and Bredy.
[12] The other MSS. have 2200.   [13] The other MSS. have 1500.
[14] The other MSS. have 1300.
[15] The other MSS. give Buckingham the same assessment as *Sceaftesige*.
[16] The other MSS. have 500.   [17] *Đonne gebyreð*, Hi.
[18] *-eahta*, Hi.   [19] *gebyrað*, Hi.

248   THE BURGHAL HIDAGE

.XL hida 7 .VI. hund hida · to fif furlangum gebyreð ymbganges eahta hund hida on wealstillinge · to six furlangum gebyreð sixtig hida · 7 nigan hund hida · to VII. furlangum .XX. hida 7 XI hund hida · to eahta furlangum ymbeganges wealstillinge 5 hundeahtatig hida · 7 XII. hund hida · to¹ nigan furlangum .XL. hida 7 XIIII. hund hida · to X furlangum gebyreþ XVI. hund hida · to XI furlangum gebyreþ .LX. hida · 7 XVII hund hida · to XII. furlangum ymbeganges wealstillige gebyreð .XX. hida · 7 nigantyn hund hida · gif se ymbegang mara biþ · þon mæg man eaþe þone 10 ofereacan geþencan of þisse tale for þon ealning to anum furlange gebyreð sixtig manna · 7 .C. þonne biþ ælc gyrd mid feower mannum geset.

II. INVENTORY OF CHURCH GOODS AT SHERBURN-IN-ELMET

Þis syndon þa cyrican madmas on Scirburnan · ꝥ² synd twa Xp̄es bec · 7 II. rodan · 7 I. aspiciens · 7 I. adteleuaui · 7 II. pis-
15 tolbec 7 I. mæsseboc · 7 I. ymener · 7 I. salter · 7 .I. calic · 7 .I. disc · · 7 twa mæssereaf · 7 III. mæssehakelan · 7 II. weouedsceatas · 7 II. ouerbrædels · 7 IIII. handbellan · 7 VI. hangende bellan³.

III. FRAGMENT OF AN INVENTORY FROM A BURY ST EDMUNDS MS.

[x]l weorcwyrðra⁴ manna .XVIII. oxana ·
20   [7] xxxvi faldhriþera⁵ hundteontig swina 7 .VI.
[7 hu]ndnigontig sceapa · sifon hund flicca ·
...nhund ceasa .VII. systras⁶ huniges · oþar⁷
[he]alf hund foþra cornes⁸ .CCC. æcera asawen.

---

¹ Hickes omits the statistics for 9 and 10 furlongs.
² Thær, Raine, B.   ³ bollan, B.
⁴ weon wvnðna, James.   ⁵ faldhiu þena, ibid.
⁶ svstnas, ibid.   ⁷ oþan, ibid.
⁸ foþna connes, ibid.

For the maintenance of a circuit of 5 furlongs of wall 800 hides are required. For 6 furlongs 960 hides are required; for 7 furlongs 1120 hides; for the maintenance of a circuit of 8 furlongs 1280 hides; for 9 furlongs 1440 hides; for 10 furlongs 1600 hides are required; for 11 furlongs 1760 hides are required. For the maintenance of a circuit of 12 furlongs of wall 1920 hides are required. If the circuit is greater, the additional amount can easily be deduced from this account, for 160 men are always required for 1 furlong, then every pole of wall is manned by 4 men.

II. INVENTORY OF CHURCH GOODS AT SHERBURN-IN-ELMET

The following are the church treasures at Sherburn, namely 2 gospel books and 2 crosses and 1 *Aspiciens* and 1 *Ad te levavi* and 2 epistle books and 1 missal and 1 hymn-book and 1 psalter and 1 chalice and 1 paten and 2 mass vestments and 3 chasubles and 2 altar cloths and 2 [altar] covers and 4 hand-bells and 6 hanging bells.

III. FRAGMENT OF AN INVENTORY FROM A BURY ST EDMUNDS MS.

... 40 able-bodied men, 18 oxen [and] 36 stalled oxen, 100 swine and 96 sheep, 700 flitches of bacon, ... hundred cheeses, 7 sesters of honey, 150 fothers of corn, 300 acres sown.

IV. INVENTORY FROM A DURHAM MS.

Tea · calices · 7 sex · disces · 7 twœgentig · bleod · 7 feower · steapas · 7 · án bælt · 7 · án · hana · 7 · ðrea · condel · stafas · 7 · fíf · tene · cuppa · 7 · fíftene · bleda · 7 · nion · leoda · 7 án · cetel · 7 · fíf calices · 7 feawer · discas · 7 sex · tene · hornas · 5 gerínade · 7 ðrea · ún. rinade.

V. LIST OF WORCESTER (?) BOOKS

.i. .ii. .iii.
Ðeo englissce passionale · 7 .II. englissce dialogas · 7 Oddan
.iiii. .vi.
boc · 7 þe 'englisca' martirlogium · 7 .II. englisce · salteras · 7 .II. pastorales · englisce · 7 þe englisca regol · 7 Barontus.

VI. LIST OF BOOKS FROM ST AUGUSTINE'S, CANTERBURY

Þis syndon ðá[1] bec þe Æþestanes[2] wæran · de natura rerum · 10 Persius · de arte metrica · Donatum 'minorem' · Excerptiones de metrica arte · Apocalipsin · Donatum maiórem · Alchuinum · Glossam super Catonem · libellum de grammatica arte · 'quę sic incipit' terra quę pars ⸝ Sedulium[3] · ∴ 7[4] .I. gerím · wæs[5] Alfwoldes preostes · Glossa super Donatum · Dialogorum.

VII. LIST OF BOOKS FROM A MS. IN THE BODLEIAN LIBRARY, OXFORD

15 Þas bocas haueð Salomon prst · þ is þe codspel traht · 7 þe martyrliua[6] · ...7 þe æglisce saltere 7 þe cranc · 7 ðe tropere 7 Wulfmer cild · þe atteleuaui · 7 pistelari[6] · ...7 ðe imnere · 7 ðe capitelari[7]...7 þe spelboc · 7 Sigar prst · þe leceboc · 7 Blakehad boc · 7 Æilmer ðe grete sater · 7 ðe litle tropere forbeande · 7 ðe 20 'do'natum. .xv. bocas.
Ealfric · Æilwine · Godric · 7 Bealdewuine abb · 7 Freoden · 7 Hu[8]... · 7 Ðuregisel.

[1] ðea, James. [2] æþel-, ibid. [3] An erasure follows.
[4] Om. James. [5] þæs, ibid.
[6] An erasure follows in which the words 7 þe can be distinguished.
[7] An erasure follows. [8] There is a tear in the MS.

IV. INVENTORY FROM A DURHAM MS.

Ten chalices and six patens and twenty bowls and four cups and a girdle and a cock (?) and three candlesticks and fifteen cups and fifteen bowls and nine cauldrons and one kettle and five chalices and four patens and sixteen ornamented horns and three without ornament.

V. LIST OF WORCESTER (?) BOOKS

(1) The English Passional and (2) two English Dialogues and (3) Odda's Book and (4) the English Martyrology and (5) and (6) two English Psalters and two Pastorals in English and the English Rule and Barontus.

VI. LIST OF BOOKS FROM ST AUGUSTINE'S, CANTERBURY

These are the books which belonged to Æthelstan: *De Natura Rerum*, Persius, *De Arte Metrica*, Donatus *minor*, Excerpts from *De Metrica Arte*, the Apocalypse, Donatus *major*, Alcuin, a gloss on Cato, a treatise *De Grammatica Arte* which begins thus, 'Terra quae pars', Sedulius ∴ and 1 calendar belonged to the priest Ælfwold, a gloss on Donatus, the Dialogues.

VII. LIST OF BOOKS FROM A MS. IN THE BODLEIAN LIBRARY, OXFORD

The priest Solomon has these books, namely the gospel exposition and the Martyrology...and the English psalter and the chronicle and the book of tropes, and Wulfmær *cild* has the *Ad te levavi* and the epistolar...and the hymn-book and the capitulary...and the book of homilies, and the priest Sigar has the book on medicine and the book of the Black Order (?), and Æthelmær has the great psalter and the little book of tropes......and the Donatus. Fifteen books altogether.

Ælfric, Æthelwine, Godric and Abbot Baldwin and Freoden and Hu... and Thurgisl.

VIII. FRAGMENT OF A WILL FROM BURY ST EDMUNDS

... 7 twælf oræn · under · p̄restæs 7 dæacnæs[1] 7 clǣrcæs 7 fyf oræ · at his þruth 7 an 7 twænti peniges at his hoferbredles 7 seuen · peniges · at hale 7 twa ore 7 an ære · at bræad 7 hoþær hæræ · at an flychca 7 at an buch 7 seuæn 7 twænti peniges · at wax[2];.
5 7 fyf oræ · at te fyrræ[3] · ærflæ · at malt 7 at hældyggæ[4] 7 twa 7 fæouhærti peniges · at bræad[5] 7 seuentene peniges · at an swin 7 twa ore · an reþær 7 an æræ þræ buces 7 VIII. pe. an cese · 7 þræ peniges · at fysc 7 fæouer pæniges[6] · at milch.
(7 fyf ora)[7] 7 half twælf ere · at te hoþær · hærflæ · 7 Hafslæin[8]
10 half marc 7 an mentel 7 Swædæ · twa ore 7 at Swægildæ · twa ore 7 Alfnoþ · prest · twa marc · Wægen 7 his sune I. marc. Wægen ✠ ✠

IX. ASSIGNMENTS OF PROPERTY TO THORNEY ABBEY

Ðys sĕnd[9] þa þing þ[e man] gedon hæfþ to Ðornige · [ær]est man bohte twa ðusend hæringes myd .xl. penegun; 7 þ[onne (?)]
15 to beansæde .xl. pene[ga]; fif oran Æþelferþe æt Niwantune æt hys men; twegen or[an wæ]ron to scipe 7 to net[tum] to Fearresheafde; 7 wyþ þrim gegrindum æt Þiutforda man [sealde ... o]ran 7 xii. penegas; [7 a]nne wifman .v. orena wyrþe to Stangrunde; 7 iii. ege[ðan þr]eora[10] orena wyrþe · [an] man
20 sealde to Niwantune · oþer to Geaceslea · þridde to Stan[grunde 7] xv. penegas wyþ bean[sæ]de to Geaceslea · 7 to oþrum scipe to Witlesmere 7 wið ne[ttum ... p]eniga · 7 nigon ora[n w]ið anum mæder werde to Huntandune · an scip twegra or[ena wyrþ m]an sealde fram Elig [to W]itlesige þ̄ ís þonne ealles
25 feorðe healf pund butun þritti[gun p̄] · þonne dyde man æf[te]r

[1] dæc-, James.   [2] pax, ibid.   [3] tesyrræe, ibid.
[4] heel-, ibid.   [5] bræd, Förster.   [6] pen-, James.
[7] The brackets are mine as I do not think that the first three words are meant to be included, see Notes.
[8] hofslæm, James; Hafslæm, Förster.
[9] Sic.   [10] feora, Skeat.

VIII. FRAGMENT OF A WILL FROM BURY ST EDMUNDS

...and 12 ores among the priests and deacons and clerics and 5 ores for his coffin and 21 pence for his pall and 7 pence for ale and 2 ores, and 1 ore for bread and another ore for a flitch of bacon and for a buck and 27 pence for wax.

And 5 ores for the first funeral feast for malt and for fuel and 42 pence for bread and 17 pence for a pig and 2 ores [for] a bullock and 1 ore [for] three bucks and 8 pence [for] a cheese and 3 pence for fish and 4 pence for milk.

And 11½ ores for the second funeral feast, and *Hafslæin* half a mark and a cloak and *Swædæ* 2 ores, and for *Swægildæ* 2 ores and Ælfnoth the priest 2 marks. Wægen and his son 1 mark. Wægen ✠ ✠

IX. ASSIGNMENTS OF PROPERTY TO THORNEY ABBEY

These are the things which have been supplied to Thorney. First of all 2000 herrings were bought for 40 pence and then 40 pence [went] for bean-seed; 5 ores [went] to Æthelferth of Newton for his man; 2 ores were for a ship and nets at Farcet; and for three plots of ground at Thetford ... ores and 12 pence were given; and a woman worth 5 ores to Stanground; and three harrows worth 3 ores—one was given to Newton, the second to Yaxley and the third to Stanground—and 15 pence for bean-seed at Yaxley and ... pence for another ship and nets at Whittlesey Mere, and 9 ores for a ...... at Huntingdon. One ship worth 2 ores was given from Ely to Whittlesey Mere. This amounts altogether to three and a half pounds less 30 pence.

Then after that 80 swine and the swineherd were transferred

ðæm hundeahtatig swyna 7 þone swan fra*m* Middeltune......
ne; þa `ge'eah`ta'de man¹ þa [swi]n to oðran healfan punde 7
þone swan to healfan punde; ...... 7 .xii. wænas myd h[un]d-
eahtigu*n* penegun; 7 .iiii. scipa myd eahta oran ælc myd .ii.
5 o[ran an man] dyde to Niwantune · [oþ]er to Geaceslea þridde to
Stangrunde feorðe to Witles[mere 7 man] sealde Ælfnoþe tyn
[ma]ncusas goldes to mylenoxan to Huntadune 7 Ælfsige
munuce ...... c² on fif mancesun · [go]ldes 7 Swetan an pund
to mylenoxan to Geaceslea 7 to ...... `x. pund' 7 butan þæ*m* se
10 abbu[d s]ealde Ælfsige munuce to fyrþrunge to Þorniges are
[... manc]usa goldes; `7 v. orena w[æron] to þry*m* mylnun to
isene [t]wegra orena wyrþ to Huntandune · twegra [to G]eaceslea
· [7 anes] to St[angrun]de'³ ϸ is þo[nne] ealles geseald of Elig to
Ðornige butun hyra scrudfeo þe ...... lste; on golde 7 on s[eol-
15 fre] syxtena punda wyrþ butun feowertigu*m* penegun⁴   þæs
þe asme...... 7 marun;* ⁵þonne s[iþ]þan `ofer þa .x.vi pund'
man sealde fra*m* Hæþfelda xxx. ealdra swyna · ælce [t]o .vi
pænegu*n* ofer ...; 7 man sealde wyþ þan `æt þæm' smyþe fif
mancusas gold ...... 7 .. dware⁶; 7 man [sea]lde Cynesiges
20 swystor mylen ... [Blun]tesha*m* geh..ht (?) to ...... de (?)⁷; 7
ane dægan [to] Lindune to þiuwan; ✠

7 butan þisu*m* eallu*m* [ϸ her]on (?) gewriten is ma... sealde
ærest se bisceop þriu pund to Geaceslea to fyrþrunge 7 [þa] man
sealde þriu punda wyrþ goldes · þa na*m* man þærof an pund to
25 scrude oþer to Fear[resheafde t]o dycynge · þæt þr[idd]e to
fyrþrunge to Geaceslea; 7 man sealde Ælfsige munece .lx.
m[ancusa]s 7 fif pænega ge[ri]hta to Geaceslea to fyrþrunga.
nenien · briht⁸

✠ Æt⁹ byryg .xlvii. ealdra swina · 7 .cc. geongra bu[tun] ðrim¹⁰;
30 æt Stræthaᵐ .xx. sugen[a] æt¹¹   .xx. sugena · 7 .l. hogga; æt
Horningesige .xviii. [eal]de swyn · 7 .xl. hogga; æt ...... e · 7

---

¹ *þætt eah,ᵗᵃ deman*, Skeat.   ² Or possibly -*e*.
³ This sentence has been entered above the line in smaller handwriting and projects into the margin, part of which has been cut off.
⁴ There is a small hole at this point.
⁵ The second handwriting begins here.   ⁶ *eadware*, Skeat.
⁷ This sentence is very difficult to read as an attempt seems to have been made to erase it.
⁸ These two words occupy the last line of column 1 of the Queens'

from Milton......; the swine were valued at one and a half pounds and the swineherd at half a pound; ...... and 12 wagons [were obtained] for 80 pence; and 4 ships at 2 ores each for 8 ores—one was given to Newton, the second to Yaxley, the third to Stanground, the fourth to Whittlesey Mere. And 10 mancuses of gold were given to Ælfnoth for mill-oxen at Huntingdon, and ...... worth 5 mancuses of gold to the monk Ælfsige, and a pound for mill-oxen at Yaxley and at ...... to Sweta; 10 pounds. And apart from this the abbot gave the monk Ælfsige ... mancuses of gold for the improvement of the property belonging to Thorney. And 5 ores were for iron for three mills—2 ores worth for Huntingdon and 2 for Yaxley and 1 for Stanground. The value of the total amount given by Ely to Thorney (apart from the money for their clothes which ......) is 16 pounds in gold and silver less 40 pence...............

Then later, over and above these 16 pounds, 30 full-grown swine—each over ... worth 6 pence (?)—were given from Hatfield; and in return (?) 5 mancuses of gold were given for the smith............; and a mill at Bluntisham (?) was given to Cynesige's sister ......; and a dairymaid to Linton (?) as a slave.✠

And apart from all this which is recorded here ... the bishop in the first instance gave 3 pounds for improvements at Yaxley and then 3 pounds worth of gold was given. Then one pound of this was taken for clothes, the second for digging at Farcet (?), the third for improvements at Yaxley. And dues (?) amounting to 60 mancuses and 5 pence were given to the monk Ælfsige for improvements at Yaxley.

✠ At [St Etheldreda's] *burh* 47 full-grown swine and 200 young ones all but three; at Stretham 20 sows, at ...... 20 sows and 50 hogs; at Horningsea 18 full-grown swine and 40 hogs;

College fragments. The second is in different handwriting and they seem to have no connection with what precedes. They are probably merely scribblings.
[9] The remaining entries are on the verso of the leaf. The handwriting changes again and to begin with is small and neat.
[10] *ðrun*, Skeat.
[11] The rest of the line (the first of column 4 of the Queens' College fragments) is blank.

256 ASSIGNMENTS OF PROPERTY

.xliiij hogga; æt Hafucestune .xxx. ealdra swyna · 7 .c. hogga butun .i.; æ[t M]eldeburnan .xxiij. suge[na]; Of þære heorde þe Alfwold heold æt Hæðfelda .xiij. sige · 7 .lxxxiij [ge]ongra swina; 7 Ælfnoð [of] þære oþre heorde .xiiij. sige · 7 lx hogga[1];
5 Of þæm feo þe Æþelflæd sealde man sealde to sceap[um (?)] to Bromdune .lx. p̄; 7 ea......e .lx. p̄; iii. oran Leofrice æt Strætham æt his corne; x. 'p̄'. ufan · æt hi[s....]nde; 7 .x. p̄ þæm sceaph[yrd]e; healf pund · þæm abb; healf pund Byryhtmære 7 Wulfrice; 7 ... oran · æt .i. wife æt Stræ[tham 7] æt
10 twam (?) werum þærto; 7 .iii. mancusas hyringmannum[2]; Þa man betæhte Ælfnoðe þone folgað æt Hæðfel[da] þa wæs þær .xl. oxana · ......[3] þrydde healf hund sceapa .xlvii. gata · 7 xv. cealfra .cc. [swin]a (?) butun .x; xliii. flicca ......[3];

Þis[4] is þæs fænnes hyre æt Fordham [7] æt Hyllingyge þe[5]...
15 get (?) Eadgares sunu 7 æt Wulfsie þ̄ sent .iiii. ðusend · of ðæ[m e]ast (?) fenne .ii. ðuse[nd...]pole xx snasa. Of tynadwere (?) 7 of forwerde x [sna]sa. Of soþan éa 7 g (?)......xx. snasa. Of ladwere .i. þusend. Of burhwere [... ð]usend. Of mudecan[wer]e .. wewer (?) 7 of ðæm ....[3] þusend. Of
20 sceld......xiiii snasa. Of h......were oðer healf [hund(?)][3]. Of wratwere (?) ii. ðusend. Of bulingge ... snasa. Of batlin[6] [.... ð]usend. Of brade sealde .xx. snasa. Of Wulfgaringwere x [sn]asa. Of heamuces (?)[7]...... Of norþwere[8] xx [sna]sa. Of Osgoding (?) .i. ðusend. Of p......were[9] .ii.
25 ðusend. Of ...... .i. ðusend. [Þi]s synd xxvi ðusend 7 xi. sticcan.

[1] There is a space of about a line between this paragraph and the next.
[2] There is a space of about 3 lines between this paragraph and the next in which has been scribbled *abb. healf. manus tue fecer...*
[3] Illegible.
[4] The fourth handwriting, which is much larger and rougher, begins here. Unfortunately this is the most badly faded part of the MS. and the names in particular are very difficult to read.
[5] Part of a letter, which may be *r, m* or *n*, follows immediately.
[6] *bacling-*, Skeat.
[7] *beansædes* (?), ibid. The initial letter may be *b*.
[8] *-west*, ibid.
[9] *wene*, ibid.

at .... and 44 hogs; at Hauxton 30 full-grown swine and 100 hogs all but one; at Melbourn 23 sows; from the herd of which Ælfwold had charge at Hatfield 13 sows (?) and 83 young swine, and Ælfnoth from the other herd 14 sows and 60 hogs.

Of the money which Æthelflæd gave 60 pence was given to Brandon for sheep and 60 pence to ......; 3 ores to Leofric of Stretham for his corn and 10 pence over and above for his ......, and 10 pence to the shepherd; half a pound to the abbot; half a pound to Brihtmær and Wulfric; and ... ores for one woman at Stretham and for two weirs (?) in addition; and 3 mancuses to the hired men (?).

When Ælfnoth was entrusted with his office at Hatfield there were 40 oxen there ...... 250 sheep, 47 goats and 15 calves, 200 swine all but 10, 43 flitches of bacon.

This is the rent of the fen at Fordham and at Hilgay [which is obtained (?) from] ... Edgar's son and from Wulfsige, namely 4000 [eels]. From the east (?) fen 2000, from ...*pole* 20 'sticks' [of eels]. From the fenced weir and from in front of it (?) 10 'sticks'. From the true watercourse and ...... 20 'sticks'. From the lode weir 1000 eels. From the *burh* weir ... thousand. From *mudecan* weir ...... and from the ...... thousand. From *sceld*...... 14 'sticks'. From ...... weir 150. From *wrat* weir 2000. From *bulingge* ... 'sticks'. From *batlin* .... thousand. From *brade* 20 'sticks' were given. From Wulfgar's weir 10 'sticks'. From *heamuces* ...... From the north weir 20 'sticks'. From Osgod's 1000. From ...... weir 2000. From ...... 1000. The total amount is 26,000 and 11 'sticks'.

NOTES

I

MS. British Museum, Cotton Tiberius A. XIII, f. 20, generally called Hemming's cartulary. This MS., which was written towards the end of the eleventh century, contains copies of a large number of Worcester documents, followed by an account by a certain monk named Hemming of how the collection came to be made. Many of the leaves are badly stained and the edges considerably worn so that parts of the marginal notes have disappeared.

EDITIONS. Hearne, *Hemingi Chartularium Ecclesiae Wigorniensis*, I, p. 45.
K. 95.
T. p. 28.
E. p. 41.
B. 171.

DATE. Between 743 and 745, see notes on Bishop Milred and Bishop Ingwald below.

LANGUAGE. No Latin version of this grant has survived, but it is so long before the employment of English in other documents of the kind that it is almost certainly a translation from a Latin original. It is noteworthy that the non-West Saxon forms are all late Mercian, and I owe to Professor Chadwick the suggestion that the translation may have been made in the time of Bishop Werfrith, who assisted King Alfred in his literary work and at his suggestion translated the Dialogues of Gregory into English (Asser, *Life of King Alfred*, ed. Stevenson, c. 77).

p. 2, ll. 1 f. *Æðelbald Myrcna cincg*. Æthelbald was King of Mercia from 716 to 757.

l. 2. *Milrede*. Fl. Wig. records the death of Wilfrith, Bishop of Worcester, and the appointment of Milred in 743. Simeon of Durham (R.S. II, p. 39) records the death of a bishop of Worcester, without mentioning his name, in 745, to which year he attributes also the death of Wilfred II, Bishop of York. The death of the latter is assigned to the year 744 in the Saxon Chronicle, followed by Fl. Wig. The Continuation of Bede, which records the death of *Uilfrid episcopus* in 745, refers most probably to Wilfred of York. There is no mention of the death of Wilfrith of Worcester or the appointment of Milred in the Saxon Chronicle. The fact that the present grant is attested by a Bishop Wilfrith, as well as by Milred, suggests that the latter was appointed to the see of Worcester before the death of his predecessor. Fl. Wig., the best authority for Worcester affairs, makes no mention of such a fact, but the evidence of Simeon of Durham might be taken to corroborate that of the present grant. It is most unlikely that the witness in the present instance is Wilfred of York. He was succeeded by Egbert in 732 and probably retired to Ripon, although it is only known for certain that he was buried there after his death. It was a subject of bitter controversy later between Canterbury and York as to whether the bones translated from Ripon to Canterbury were those of Wilfred II or of his more distinguished and saintly predecessor Wilfred I, see William of Malmesbury, *Gesta Pontificum*, R.S. p. 245; *Historians of the Church of York*, ed. Raine, R.S. pp. xliii–xlviii.

ll. 3 f. *nedbade tuegra sceopa*. Payments of toll. The rates charged at London on ships and cargoes of various kinds at the end of the tenth century are set out in IV Æthelred. Instances of the remission of toll granted to Kentish foundations (Minster, Rochester, Reculver) at specified places by Æthelbald and later kings are found in B. 149, 150, 152, 173, 177, 188, 189.

l. 6. *Huicca mægðe*. The territory of the Hwicce, which formed the diocese of Worcester, included Gloucestershire, Worcestershire and part of Warwickshire.

l. 20. *Inguwald b*. Ingwald, Bishop of London, died in 745.

l. 21. *Alda cinges gefera*. A member of the king's household or retinue. He does not seem to appear elsewhere.

II

MS. British Museum, Cotton Tiberius A. XIII, f. 148. See p. 259.
EDITIONS. Hearne, *Hemingi Chartularium* etc., II, p. 329.
K. 154; boundaries, III, p. 386.
B. 233.

LANGUAGE. In the cartulary this grant is given first in Latin followed by the Anglo-Saxon version headed *De eadem re*. The translation is obviously of much later date than the original grant. It may have undergone a certain amount of modification in the course of transcription but retains traces of the Mercian dialect, e.g. in *geoue* and *-cestre(s)*, and the proper names are Mercian in form. It should probably be assigned also to the time of Bishop Werfrith, see p. 259.

DATE. In the Latin version the grant is dated 786, in the thirty-second year of Offa's reign. These figures must have been wrongly transcribed, see following note.

l. 23. *Offa kyning*. Offa was King of Mercia from 757 to 796. The year 789 is described as the thirty-first of his reign in one other charter (B. 256) and it would seem, therefore, that his coronation did not take place until 758. If so, it must have been early in the year, as a charter dated 12 April 790 (B. 259) is attributed to the thirty-third year of his reign.

l. 25. *Bradewassan.* Broadwas, Worcestershire. This estate was held by the church of Worcester in 1086 as part of the manor of Hallow (D.B. I, f. 173 b; V.C.H. *Worc.* I, p. 295).

p. 4, ll. 2 f. *Aldred Wigracestres undercining.* Ealdred was the last survivor of three brothers who appear in the charters from about 757 (B. 183) onwards as hereditary rulers of the Hwicce (subject to Offa) and benefactors of the church of Worcester. This is his last appearance.

l. 3. *Eadberht bisceop.* This is the last appearance of Eadberht, Bishop of London, in the charters. His successor Edgar signs two grants of the same year (B. 255, 257).

l. 4. *Berhtun.* The signature *Borthunus* is attached to a grant of Offa dated 784 (B. 244) but the name does not seem to appear elsewhere.

l. 5. *ða landgemæra.* For the boundaries worked out in detail see Grundy, *The Saxon Charters of Worcestershire* (reprinted from the *Transactions of the Birmingham Archaeological Society*, Vols. LII and LIII), pp. 37–40.

l. 6. *wynna bæce.* This is probably the unnamed brook which at the present day forms the boundary between the parishes of Broadwas and Cotheridge. It is mentioned again in the bounds of the area dependent upon Wick Episcopi (B. 219) which begin *of Temede gemyðan andlang Temede in wynnabæces gemyðan* and proceed point by point the same as those given here as far as *Thornbridge.* I am indebted to Professor Chadwick for the suggestion that the descriptive adj. may be derived from the Welsh *gwyn*, 'white'.

in wudumor. The reading of B. 219 is *in wuda mor*, interpreted by Grundy as 'the swampy ground of the wood'. The form in the present survey might mean 'the moor (or swampy ground) by the wood'.

l. 7. *in wætan sihtran* (*sice*, B. 219). The adj. 'wet' is probably to be interpreted in the sense of 'marshy'.

ða bakas. The word *bæc* is used of an intermittent stream.

l. 8. *in seges* (*secges*, B. 219) *mere.* The genitival form suggests that *seges* (*secges*) is a proper name, cf. *secges bearu*, now *Sedgeberrow*, Pl.N. *Worc.* p. 164. Grundy interprets it, however, as 'the pond where sedge grows'. He points out that a neighbouring copse in Wichenford parish is called at the present day Sledgemoor Coppice.

l. 10. *in pone pull.* B. 219 reads here *in kadera pull, of kadera pulle in beka brycge* and then leaves the Broadwas boundary altogether. Grundy notes the occurrence of the name Poolfield in the north-west corner of the parish.

ll. 11 f. *in foxbæce.* Grundy notes the survival of the field names Fox Batch and Far Fox Batch in a little valley running eastwards from Doddenham over the western boundary of Broadwas.

l. 12. *wulfseað*, i.e. a pit in which wolves were trapped, see Pl.N. *Worc.* p. 392.

l. 13. *dodhæma pull*, literally 'pool of the men of Doddenham'. For the formation *Dodhæma*, see Pl.N. *Worc.* p. 46, s.v. Doddenham.

III

MS. British Museum, Stowe Charters, No. 8, a contemporary parchment.

FACSIMILE. *Ordnance Survey Facsimiles*, Part III, No. 8.

EDITIONS. O'Conor, *Bibliotheca MS. Stowensis*, II, p. 125.
K. 191, from O'Conor with emendations.
T. p. 462.
B. 318.

DATE. Æthelnoth received Eythorne from Cuthred, King of Kent, and his bequest of the estate is preceded on the same parchment by Cuthred's grant (in Latin), of which another contemporary copy also exists (B.M. Cotton Augustus, II, 100). The grant of Eythorne must have been made between 805, when Wulfred became Archbishop of Canterbury, and 807, the year of Cuthred's death. His bequest is written in the same handwriting as the grant and was probably drawn up at the same time or soon afterwards. The dialect is Kentish.

l. 15. *se gerefa*. In the Latin grant Cuthred describes Æthelnoth as *praefectus meus* from which it would seem that he was in charge of the royal estate at Eastry. This estate is mentioned in another charter (B. 380) as *terra regis quae pertinet ad Eastræge*. The name Eastry was likewise applied to a district (cf. *in regione Easterege*, B. 332), for which the royal estate probably acted as administrative centre (see Chadwick, *Anglo-Saxon Institutions*, pp. 251–254).

l. 16. *Wulfre˙de' arcebiscope*. Wulfred was appointed Archbishop of Canterbury in 805 and received his pallium in the following year. He signs a charter of 805 as *electus* (B. 321). His signature occurs for the last time in a charter dated 1 September 831 (B. 400).

ll. 16 f. *Æðelhune his mæsseprioste*. Æthelhun attests three grants made by Archbishop Wulfred to Christchurch, Canterbury (B. 332, 380, 381), and his signature is attached to two other Kentish documents of later date, B. 412 (see also Harmer, No. II) and B. 439 (dated 842). He appears as a witness on the archbishop's behalf in a lawsuit (B. 378, where he is described as *presbiter propositusque*).

l. 17. *Esne cyninges ðegne*. Kentish charters of 801 and 805 (B. 303, 319) are witnessed by a man of this name, while a third document dated 809 (B. 328) is witnessed by two men of the name, one of whom is described as *comes*.

l. 20. *lifes sie*. A charter, dated 824, records the grant of 5 ploughlands at Eythorne and Langdon to Christchurch by Archbishop Wulfred in exchange for certain other estates (B. 381). It would seem, therefore, that he fell heir to Æthelnoth's estate as provided by the will. Eythorne is not mentioned in D.B.

l. 21. *hit forgelde*. Æthelnoth received Eythorne on the payment of 3000 pence.

NOTES

l. 23. *ða sprece.* A verbal agreement.
l. 25. *Cuðberht pr̄.* His signature occurs also in 803 (B. 312) and 813 (B. 342).
l. 26. *Feologeld pr̄ ab.* Feologeld witnesses Kentish charters from 803 (B. 312) to 825 (B. 384). On the death of Wulfred he was appointed Archbishop of Canterbury but survived for less than three months (Sax. Chr. 929 F, for 932).

p. 6, l. 2. *suð fo`r´*, i.e. a journey south, a pilgrimage to Rome. One of the regulations of an Exeter guild is *æt supfore ælc mon V. pening* (T., p. 614). For two instances of the sale of estates by owners who wished to betake themselves to Rome, see B. 537, 640.

IV

MSS. (*a*) British Museum, Cotton Nero E. I, Part II, f. 182 *b*, and (*b*) a single leaf among Lord Middleton's MSS. (see W. H. Stevenson's *Report on Lord Middleton's MSS.* published by the Historical Manuscripts Commission, 1911, pp. 197 ff.). The Middleton leaf along with ff. 181–184 of the Cotton Nero MS. are relics of an early Worcester cartulary which dated from the end of the tenth or the beginning of the eleventh century. The Middleton leaf originally came between ff. 182 and 183 of the Cotton Nero MS., so that the first seventeen words of the present record occupy the last two lines of f. 182 *b* of the latter and the rest is found on the Middleton leaf. This cartulary (the earliest known in England) reproduces the original charters less fully and exactly than the later one (Cotton Tiberius A. XIII), so that the versions given by the latter are generally to be preferred.

(*c*) British Museum, Cotton Tiberius A. XIII, f. 9. See p. 259.

(*d*) British Museum, Harley 4660, f. 6 *b*. This MS. contains a list of ninety-two Worcester charters followed by copies in full of fifteen. The list is one drawn up by Dugdale in 1643, and first published by Hickes, *Institutiones Grammaticae* etc., Part II, pp. 169 ff. The documents given in full were still extant when Hickes was Dean of Worcester (a list of them was first published in his *Institutiones* etc., Part II, p. 171) and they were first printed in his *Thesaurus*, I, pp. 139–141, 142, 169–176. Wanley, who gives a new list of them in the *Thesaurus*, II, p. 300 (prepared from the printed copies) states that by that time the originals had disappeared.

EDITIONS. Hickes, *Thesaurus*, I, p. 172 f.
Dugdale, *Monasticon*, I, p. 588 (from Hickes).
Hearne, *Hemingi Chartularium* etc., I, p. 21.
K. 183.
T. p. 47.
E. p. 69.
B. 308.
Stevenson, *op. cit.* pp. 206 f.

The present text is from the copy in MS. Harley 4660 which regularly retains the early Mercian forms of the original.

DATE. 822–823, see notes on Ceolwulf and Bishop Heahberht. The transaction recorded in this document is somewhat difficult to follow without some knowledge of the previous history of the estates involved. Inkberrow (along with Bradley) had been bequeathed to Worcester by Hemele and Duda but was claimed by Wulfheard, son of Cussa. The dispute between him and Bishop Heathored was settled in 789, when it was agreed that Wulfheard should hold the estate during his lifetime, and after his death it should pass to Worcester (B. 256). This agreement was confirmed by Bishop Deneberht in 803, and the account of the present transaction was entered as an endorsement on the document (now lost) which contained these two agreements (see Hickes, *Thesaurus*, I, pp. 171 ff.). It records Wulfheard's last attempt to gain absolute possession of Inkberrow, and it is evident from the last line that it was drawn up considerably later than the events which it describes.

The history of Bromsgrove is more obscure. It was part of the inheritance of Æthelric, son of Æthelmund, and in the disposition of his property made in 804, to take effect after his death, he bequeathed it to a certain Werfrith with reversion to the church of Worcester (B. 313 f.). It would seem that in the interval between 804 and the date of the present transaction it had actually come into the possession of the church of Worcester and been granted (on terms unknown) to Wulfheard. There is no record of Æthelric's death, but a certain amount of indirect evidence suggests that it took place before that of his mother, Ceolburh, Abbess of Berkeley, to whom, in the disposition referred to above, he bequeathed estates at Westbury and Stoke in Gloucestershire, with reversion to Worcester. His mother died in 807, and in 824 a dispute between Berkeley and Worcester for possession of Westbury was settled in favour of the latter (B. 379). The claim put forward by Berkeley is difficult to understand, unless Ceolburh had actually been in possession of the estate before her death, and in that case her son must have predeceased her.

It is natural to suppose that Ceolwulf's request for Bromsgrove was accompanied by some kind of grant on his part to Worcester, and it would seem from the little that is said with regard to the transaction that it was a grant of freedom. The only reference to any concession of the kind on the part of Ceolwulf occurs in a late list of benefactors of the church (Dugdale, I, p. 608), where it is said that during the episcopate of Deneberht he freed the estates of Ripple, Stratford and Daylesford as his predecessors had done. Deneberht was succeeded as bishop by Heahberht in 822, the year after Ceolwulf became king, and it is possible, therefore, that negotiations begun under Deneberht were completed under his successor. The evidence, however, is too slight and inconclusive for any certainty in the matter, and the two transactions may be quite distinct. The interesting fact is that a grant

NOTES 265

of freedom was traditionally ascribed to Ceolwulf, and that the present document seems to refer to a concession of the kind, although unfortunately no indication is given either of its application or its extent.

l. 4. *Ceolulf rex.* Ceolwulf I, King of Mercia from 821 to 823. *Bremesgrefan.* See above. This estate apparently passed entirely from the church of Worcester. It was held by Earl Edwin in the time of King Edward but passed into the king's hands at the Conquest (D.B. I, f. 172; V.C.H. *Worc.* I, p. 285).

ll. 4 f. *Heaberht bisc̄.* Heahberht became Bishop of Worcester in 822 and according to Fl. Wig. died in 848. The signature *Alchhun* attached to B. 448, dated 845, however, is probably that of his successor.

l. 5. *þa sende he.* I take this to refer to the bishop in view of what follows.

l. 8. *ymb þæt lond.* Apparently Bromsgrove is meant, although there is nothing to show that it was ever in Wulfheard's possession. On the other hand if Inkberrow is meant, Wulfheard's homeless condition without it can be understood, but in that case his humble agreement to the bishop's request must be regarded, from what follows, as entirely false. His part in the proceedings is obscure.

l. 9. *þone freodom,* i.e. freedom from taxation or services or both. It seems as if the account of the transaction given here is not the full one but merely a summarised version of interest in so far as it concerns Inkberrow.

l. 12. *þære on byrig.* For an instance of *burg* used in the sense of a manor-house, see *Rectitudines,* cap. 2. For the post-Conquest use of *bury* in the sense of manor-house, see *Chief Elements in English Place-Names* (English Place-Name Society, I, Part 2), p. 11, and for an example in Worcestershire see *Sagebury Farm,* Pl.N. *Worc.* p. 285.

þa sende he. I take this to refer to Wulfheard.

ll. 12 f. *þæm ærcebiscope.* Wulfred, Archbishop of Canterbury, see p. 262.

l. 13. *Eadberhte.* Probably the Eadberht who signs as *dux* up to 825, see p. 268.

Dynne. The signature Dynne *dux* occurs about half a dozen times between 805 (B. 322) and 816 (B. 357).

l. 15. '*hit wæron' erndiende,* see B.T., *Suppl.* p. 18, s.v. *ærendian,* I *a.*

l. 16. *gelærde.* It seems as if the conjunction 7 has dropped out before this verb. The reading is the same, however, in all the extant copies.

ll. 17 f. *oþ his daga ende.* I understand this to mean that Wulfheard lived peaceably at Inkberrow until the end of his life, and never again made any attempt to dispute the proprietary rights of the bishop and the community.

V

No MS. copy of this document has survived, see below.

EDITIONS. (a) Hickes, *Dissertatio Epistolaris*, p. 80, in *Thesaurus*, I, from a charter in the Somers collection, see (b).

(b) Smith, *Beda: Historiæ Ecclesiasticæ* etc., Appendix, p. 768. In this appendix (pp. 764-782) are found copies of twenty-four Worcester documents which were at one time in the possession of Lord Somers (1651-1716), Lord Chancellor under William III. This collection perished in a fire at Lincoln's Inn in 1752.

K. 219, from (b).
T. p. 70, from (b).
Haddan and Stubbs, III, p. 604, from K.
E. p. 285, from (b).
B. 386, from (b).
Essays in Anglo-Saxon Law, Appendix, No. 11, from K.

The text is from (a).

DATE. The year 825 falls in the third Indiction and it would seem at first sight, therefore, as if xxv had been copied by mistake for xxiv. The presence of Wilfred, Bishop of Dunwich, among the witnesses, however, shows that the dispute rightly belongs to the later year.

p. 8, ll. 3 f. *Beornwulfes rice.* Beornwulf was King of Mercia from 823 to 825.

l. 4. *sinodlic gemot.* It appears from the list of names at the end of the document that the meeting was one of the general council. It seems, however, to have been presided over by the archbishop.

l. 5. *Clofeshous.* The locality of this celebrated place is uncertain. It has been identified with Cliffe-at-Hoo near Rochester (see Plummer, II, pp. 69 f.) but this seems like guesswork from the similarity of the two names. Other places suggested at various times include Abingdon, Tewkesbury, the neighbourhood of London and a spot where four ways join in the hamlet of West Row and the parish of Mildenhall, Suffolk (see M. R. James, *Suffolk and Norfolk*, p. 4). For the ending -*ho*, A.S. *hoh*, used in place-names of a projecting piece of ground (not necessarily of any great height), see *Chief Elements in English Place-Names*, p. 38.

Meetings, presided over by the King of Mercia or the Archbishop of Canterbury or both, are recorded at *Clofesho* at various dates between 716 (Haddan and Stubbs, III, p. 300) and 825, the year which saw the downfall of Mercian supremacy in Kent. It seems probable, therefore, that *Clofesho* was somewhere within the bounds either of Kent or E. Mercia. It must have been easily accessible from Canterbury.

l. 8. *Suptune.* This is identified with Sinton in Grimley (Pl.N. *Worc.* p. 128). The phrase *on Scirhylte* which follows can be more easily connected with Sinton Leigh, as a *scirhyltgeat* appears somewhere in that region as one of the landmarks in the boundaries of Powick

(B. 1282), and the modern Sherrards Green in the same vicinity may be derived from a similar form (Pl.N. *Worc.* p. 212). It is possible, however, that the *scirhylt* (the 'bright' or perhaps the 'boundary' wood) at one time extended much farther north and so came partly at least within the bounds of the Worcester lands. The early history of the Abbey of Pershore (the owner at a later date of Powick, Leigh and the adjacent lands) is too obscure to admit of any argument from its non-appearance in the present dispute.

l. 9. *þa swangerefan.* This official does not seem to be mentioned elsewhere. He was apparently under the authority of the earl and, as his name implies, acted as superintendent of (presumably) the royal swineherds. Interesting details with regard to the swineherds on a private estate are given in the *Rectitudines*, caps. 6 and 7.

l. 10. *geþiogan.* See B.T. p. 455, s.v. *geþicgan.*

l. 14. *Wulfred arcebiscop.* See p. 262.

l. 16. *on Æþelbaldes dage.* See p. 259.

l. 17. *Eadwulfe ðæm aldormen,* i.e. the chief representative of civil authority in the county to whom, apparently, the *swangerefan* were answerable. Two earls of this name attest *Clofesho* documents of 824 and 825 (B. 378, 384), but one only signs B. 379 (dated 824) and 387 (dated 825). The name appears for the last time with the title *dux* in 831 (B. 400).

l. 20. *Hama.* Not apparently mentioned elsewhere.

l. 21. *Ceastre.* Worcester.

l. 22. *he hine hwepre ne grette.* See B.T., *Suppl.* p. 486, s.v. *gretan,* v (1) *b.*

l. 25. *Cynred.* Bishop of Selsey. His signature appears for the first time in 824 (B. 378 f.) and for the last in 839 (B. 421).

Aldred. An *Aldred thelonius* signs in 824 (B. 379), while two men of the name witness B. 384 and B. 452 (844–845). One only appears in B. 400, 416, 429.

Wighelm. This witness was present at *Clofesho* in 824 (B. 379).

l. 26. *Torhthelm.* Torhthelm signs B. 384 as prior. The name without the title is attached to a document of 814 (B. 348).

l. 27. *Eanmund abb.* Two abbots of this name (one of whom is described as *presbiter abbas,* the other as *abbas*) attest two other *Clofesho* documents dated 824 and 825 respectively (B. 378, 384). Two grants made by Berhtwulf to Abbot Eanmund and the monastery of Bredon are extant (B. 434, 454) but there seems to be no clue to the identity of the other abbot of the name. The signature *Eanmund abbas* is found from 816 (B. 356) to 848 (B. 454). A grant to Worcester dated 851 (B. 462), in which it also appears, is very suspicious.

Heahberht · episc. etc. The names which follow in the third column are those of the members of the community at Worcester who took the oath along with Bishop Heahberht.

l. 28. *Wihtred abb.* This signature occurs in Mercian charters from 816 (B. 356 f.) to 852 (see p. 12, l. 28).

l. 29. *Oeðelwald.* Bishop of Lichfield, 818-830.
Cudwulf abb. This signature is found from 814 (B. 343) to 825 (cf. B. 384). Is he the Cuthwulf who became Bishop of Hereford?
l. 30. *Hræðhun.* The signature of Hræthhun, Bishop of Leicester, appears for the first time in 816 (B. 356) and for the last in 841 (B. 432, note). His predecessor signs for the last time in 814 (B. 343, 350 f.) and his successor for the first time in 841 (B. 434 f.).
l. 31. *Eaðberht dux.* Eadberht is a regular witness from 809 (B. 328) to 825 and his name appears also in B. 462 (see p. 267).
l. 32. *Heaberht.* Bishop of Worcester, see p. 265.
Biornoð dux. Biornoth signs as *dux* from 798 (B. 289) to 825 (cf. B. 384).
l. 33. *Bionna.* Bishop of Hereford. He signs as bishop elect in 824 (B. 378) and his name appears for the last time in 825 (cf. B. 384, another *Clofesho* document).
Sigred dux. This signature is found between 814 (B. 343) and 848 (B. 454). It occurs also in B. 462 (see p. 267).
l. 34. *Eadwulf.* Bishop of Lindsey. He signs as bishop elect in 796 (B. 277 ff.). In 836 he signs along with Eadwulf, Bishop of Hereford (B. 416). His successor Brihtred signs in 839 (B. 421).
Cuðred dux. This witness appears also in B. 378, 384. The name occurs earlier (B. 340) with the title *pessessor* and again in B. 364 with the title *pedisequus.*
l. 35. *Wilfred.* Bishop of Dunwich. He signs B. 384 as bishop elect and appears for the last time in 845 (B. 448).
Eadwulf dux. See p. 267.
l. 36. *Wigðegn.* Bishop of Winchester. He appears for the first time in a reliable document in 814 (B. 343). His predecessor Ealhmund signs for the last time in 805 (B. 321 f.) and it seems probable that the *Wignoth* of a doubtful Winchcombe charter of 811 (B. 338) is a mistake for *Wigthegn.* His death is recorded in the Saxon Chronicle in 833 (for 836).
Mucel dux. This signature is found from 814 (B. 343) onwards. In 836 (B. 416) a second man of the same name and title appears as a witness. They sign together for the last time (with the title *princeps*) in 848 (B. 454). The signature of the younger Mucel continues until 866 (B. 513).
l. 37. *Alhstan.* Bishop of Sherborne. He is probably represented by the signature *Alfstanus electus* of 824 (B. 377). He died in 867 (Sax. Chr., Fl. Wig.).
Uhtred dux. This witness was present at *Clofesho* in the previous year (B. 378 f.). He does not appear again.
l. 38. *Humberht.* Bishop of Elmham. His signature appears for the first time in 824 (B. 379).
Alhheard dux. His signature is found from 814 (B. 343) to 825 (cf. B. 384).
l. 39. *Ceolberht.* Bishop of London. His signature appears for the first time in 824 (B. 378 f.) and for the last in 845 (B. 448).

NOTES 269

Bolam. Probably identical with the Bola who signs two *Clofesho* documents of 824 and one other of 825 (B. 378 f., 384). In two of these he is called *pedis(s)ecus*.

Bynna. The king's brother, who also witnesses B. 379, 384.

l. 40. *priosta...mæsse-priostum.* See p. 364

VI

MS. British Museum, Cotton Augustus, II, 42, a contemporary parchment.

FACSIMILE. Bond, *Facsimiles of Ancient Charters in the British Museum,* Part II, No. 25.

EDITIONS. Hickes, *Dissertatio Epistolaris,* p. 54, in *Thesaurus,* I.
K. 238.
T. p. 476.
B. 417.

DATE. An endorsement in a fourteenth-century hand dates this bequest 837, but this date cannot be accepted in view of the fact that the Badenoth who signs here as *presbiter* signs three charters of 838 as *diaconus* (B. 419, 421, 426). It is almost certain, likewise, that the Badanoth Beotting of the present document is the Badanoth to whom King Æthelwulf granted a certain amount of land in the vicinity of Canterbury in 845 (B. 449), see below. His will was probably drawn up at the same time or soon afterwards. The dialect is Kentish.

p. 10, l. 1. *Badanoð beotting.* King Æthelwulf in the grant referred to above describes Badanoth as *apparitor meus*.

l. 2. *min ærfe lond.* The land granted by King Æthelwulf was to be held as a perpetual inheritance with full right of disposal.

gebohte. Fifteen mancuses of gold were given by Badanoth to King Æthelwulf.

ll. 4 f. *me siolfne...forgeofan.* There are numerous examples of the admission of laymen to confraternity by monastic communities (see Harmer, pp. 71 f.), but the phrase used here suggests that Badanoth desired to become an inmate of the monastery.

l. 6. *liffest gedoan.* See B.T., *Suppl.* p. 617, s.v. *liffæst,* III. No other instance of the phrase is recorded.

ðæm hlaforde, i.e. probably the Archbishop of Canterbury who occupied the place of abbot in the cathedral monastery.

ll. 20 f. .XVI. *gioc ærðe londes 7 medwe.* The ordinary land measure employed in Kent was the *sulung,* which represented the amount of land which could be ploughed by a team of oxen in a year. The smaller measure called *geoc,* i.e. 'yoke', represented a quarter of a *sulung*.

The estate granted by Æthelwulf to Badanoth is described as *villam unam ab orientale parte muris Doroverniæ civitatis* [Canterbury] .X.VIIIIque *jugera hoc est* .VI. *jugera ubi nominatur et Uuihtbaldes hlawe 7 in australe parte puplice strate altera* .VI. 7 *in australe occidentaleque puplice strate ubi appellatur uueoweraget in confinioque Deoring londes* .VII. *jugero seu etiam tria prata......una ab orienti fluminis qui dicitur Stur quæ appellatur Aling med · altera quæ nominatur longan med* 7 *jacit be norðan hege · tertia in media urbanorum pratorum.*

With the *Uueoweraget* mentioned here should be compared the *Wiwarawic* of B. 496. The first element in each case is derived from the place name Wye (see Chadwick, *Anglo-Saxon Institutions*, p. 249). The gate appears in a later charter as *Wiwergatan*, see p. 204, l. 3, and was afterwards known as the Worth Gate.

With the *urbanorum pratorum* should be compared the *burgwaramedum* of B. 497 and the *burhwarefelda* of p. 377. The reference is to the meadows and open country attached to Canterbury.

l. 23. *Ceolnoð arc̄ episc̄.* Ceolnoth was Archbishop of Canterbury from 833 to 870.

l. 24. *Alchhere dux.* Æthelwulf's grant to Badanoth is said to have been made at the request of Earl Ealhhere. His signature occurs for the first time with the title *dux* in 841 (B. 437), and he received two grants of land in Kent in 850 (B. 459 f.). In 851 he took part with King Æthelstan of Kent in defeating the Danes at Sandwich. In 853 he was killed in another battle against the Danes (Sax. Chr. 853 A, 852 E).

l. 25. *Bægmund prb̄ ab̄.* Bægmund's signature is found with the title *diaconus* in 824 (B. 381), *presbiter* in 825 (B. 384) and *presbiter abbas* in 838 and 839 (B. 421, 426), as well as in a charter (B. 380) of uncertain date.

l. 26. *Hysenoð pr̄.* His signature is found in Kentish charters from 838 (B. 421) to 844 (B. 445), as well as in B. 380 (see above) and B. 538, which is attributed to Æthelwulf but dated 874.

l. 27. *Wigmund pr̄.* His signature occurs in Kentish charters from 835 (B. 412; H. rmer, No. 11) to 844 (B. 445), also in B. 380 (see above).

Dyddel. His signature is attached also to B. 406, which is dated 831 in an endorsement but probably belongs to the period 863–867, and he is possibly identical with the *Duddel* who signs B. 445. The name is a diminutive, see Redin, *Uncompounded Personal Names in Old English*[1], p. 140.

Tile. This name does not seem to be recorded elsewhere at the time.

l. 28. *Badenoð pr̄.* His signature with the title *diaconus* is found in B. 380, 412 as well as in the three charters of 838 (see p. 269). It does not occur elsewhere with the title *presbiter*.

Cichus. He signs three other Kentish charters, B. 380, 426 (dated 839) and 445. For the name see Redin, *op. cit.* p. 28.

Cyneberht. He signs Kentish charters of 822, 823 and 831 (B. 370, 373, 400).

l. 29. *Osmund pr̄.* Osmund signs Kentish charters, the date of which is certain, from 825 (B. 384) to 839 (B. 426).

---

[1] *Uppsala Univ. Årsskrift*, 1919.

NOTES 271

Sigemund. He signs three other Kentish charters, B. 406, 445 and 496 (dated 858).

Eðelred. Æthelred signs King Æthelwulf's grant to Badanoth as well as four earlier Kentish charters of the years 839 to 844 (B. 426, 437, 439, 445).

l. 30. *Suiðberht diac.* Swithberht signs a Kentish document of 843–863 with this title (B. 405; Harmer, No. IV) and his name with the title *presbiter* is attached also to B. 406.

Eðelwulf. Æthelwulf signs another Kentish charter, B. 395.

Badanoð. Probably the testator.

VII

MS. The Society of Antiquaries of London, MS. 60, f. 46. This is a twelfth-century cartulary of the Abbey of Peterborough.

EDITIONS. K. 267.
T. p., 104.
B. 464.

A summary of this grant is entered in the Saxon Chronicle, s.a. 852 E. The dialect is Mercian.

p. 12, l. 1. *Ceolred abb.* Ceolred's name occurs between those of Beonna and Hedda in the list of the abbots of Peterborough given by Hugo Candidus in his twelfth-century history of the abbey (ed. Sparke, *Historiae Anglicanae Scriptores Varii,* p. 13). The signature of the former is not found after 805 (B. 318) and it may have been he who became Bishop of Hereford in 824 (see Stubbs, *Archaeological Journal,* XVIII, 1861, p. 206). Ceolred's signature is attached to a suspicious Crowland charter dated 806 (B. 325) and an abbot of the name also signs in 841 (B. 432, 434–436). Hedda's name appears (as *Hebba*) in a Crowland charter (B. 461) with the impossible date 851, but he is mentioned in the Saxon Chronicle, s.a. 963 E, as Abbot of Peterborough at the time of its destruction by the Danes.

l. 2. *Medeshamstede.* Afterwards called the Abbey of St Peter at *Burh* (see Sax. Chr. 963 E), then Peterborough.

Wulfrede. The name Wulfred is attached to two Mercian charters, B. 450 (dated 845) and B. 452 (which should be dated 844–845, see Harmer, p. 81).

Sempingaham. Sempringham, Lincolnshire. An estate there was bequeathed to St Benedict's at Ramsey by a certain Ulf sometime between 1066 and 1068 but his will never took effect. In 1086 Alfred of Lincoln was holding Sempringham in succession to Morcar who is entered as the owner in the time of King Edward of several of the estates mentioned in Ulf's will (see Whitelock, pp. 208 f.).

l. 4. *foðra.* See B.T., *Suppl.* p. 259, s.v. *foþer,* III, 'a wagon load', used of grain, wood etc. The word 'fother' is still employed with reference to lead and denotes a quantity equivalent to 19½ cwt., see N.E.D.

ll. 4 f. *to ðęm ham.* The translation follows the summary in the Saxon Chronicle which reads 7 *he scolde gife ilca gear into þe minstre sixtiga foðra wuda* etc.

l. 5. *on hornan ðæm wuda.* Horne, Rutland. I am indebted to Professor Stenton for this identification.
græfan. See B.T., *Suppl.* p. 483, s.v. *græfe*; Napier and Stevenson, *Crawford Charters*, p. 61.

l. 8. *Slioforda.* Sleaford, Lincolnshire. According to D.B. no land was held by the Abbey of Peterborough either at Sempringham or Sleaford in 1066 or later.

l. 11. *slegne`a't.* This compound does not occur elsewhere, but cf. *slægryðer*, p. 192, l. 16.

l. 12. *ten mittan Węl`s'ces aloð.* According to one account the *mitta* contained two ambers (see Harmer, p. 2, ll. 2 f.). It was used as a measure of salt as late as the fifteenth century, see N.E.D. s.v. *mit.* The earliest mention of Welsh ale is in Ine, 70, 1. It is frequently recommended in potions for the relief of various illnesses and diseases, see Cockayne, *Leechdoms* etc., R.S. II, pp. 78, 120, 136.

þere cirican laforde. He is not mentioned in the Saxon Chronicle as the recipient of any part of the payment due.

ll. 13 f. *gefeormige* etc. It is curious that only ale is specified.

ll. 14 f. *fiftene sestras liðes.* The capacity of the sester, which was used both as a liquid and as a dry measure, is uncertain and seems to have varied both during the Anglo-Saxon period and later (see Harmer, p. 79). In 1043, during a time of famine, the price of a sester of wheat rose to the unprecedented height of 60 pence (Sax. Chr. E). Henry of Huntingdon, rightly or wrongly, interprets the sester of this passage as a horseload (see Plummer, II, p. 224).

For another reference to mild ale see B. 273.

l. 15. *hi sion symle* etc., i.e. Wulfred and his successor.

l. 19. *Sið.* The use of *sið* as a conjunction is very unusual, see B.T. p. 878, s.v., III.

l. 21. *Forde.* Unidentified.
Cegle. Cheal in Gosberton, Lincolnshire.

l. 22. *Lęhcotum.* An estate called *Cotum* was bequeathed by Ulf (see p. 271) to his mother, and is identified by Miss Whitelock as Keelby Cotes or Nun Coton (D.B. *Chelebi ul Cotes*) which in 1086 was held by Drew de Beuere in succession to a certain Rolf. Great Cotes, Bradley (D.B. *Cotes*), was held in 1086 by Alfred of Lincoln in succession to Morcar (see Foster and Longley, p. 124). It is possible that one or other of these is represented by the *Lęhcotum* of the present document.

l. 23. *fulfredes cynne.* I have taken this as equivalent to *Wulfredes cynne,* cf. T. p. 105.

l. 27. *Burgred rex.* Burgred was King of Mercia from 852 (see Plummer, II, p. 78) till his expulsion by the Danes in 874 (Sax. Chr.). His wife Æthelswith was the daughter of Æthelwulf, King of Wessex, and sister of King Alfred.

NOTES

Cęlnoth archeƥs. See p. 270.

Tunber`h't eƥc. Bishop of Lichfield. He appears for the first time as a witness on 8 November 845 (B. 448, an original charter) and for the last in 857 (B. 492).

Ceored eƥs. Bishop of Leicester. He makes his first appearance in a grant dated 844, probably for 843 (B. 443), and his last in 872 (B. 535).

ll. 27 f. *Alchun eƥc.* Alhhun became Bishop of Worcester sometime between Christmas 844, when his predecessor Heahberht was still alive (B. 450, see Harmer, p. 81), and 8 November 845, when he appears as a witness (B. 448). He signs till 872 (B. 535), the year of his death (Fl. Wig.).

l. 28. *Berhtred eƥc.* Bishop of Lindsey. He signs for the first time in 839 (B. 421) and for the last in 872 (B. 535).

Wihtred aƀƀ. See p. 267.

Werheard aƀ. An abbot of this name signs Kentish charters from about 835 (B. 412, see Harmer, pp. 3, 75 f.) to 843 (B. 442), and on 8 November 845 exchanged a piece of land in Middlesex with Werenberht *minister regis ac praefectus* (B. 448).

Æthelhard dux. His signature is attached to Mercian charters from 831 (B. 400) to 855 (B. 488).

l. 29. *Hunberht dux.* He is found in Mercian charters from 835 (B. 414) to 872 (B. 535).

Aldbert dux. His name without a title appears for the first time in 836 (B. 416) and again in 840 (B. 430). In 845 (rightly 844) he signs as *dux* (B. 450, see above) and continues to do so until Easter 857 (B. 492).

Beornhard dux. This seems to be Beornhard's first appearance. His signature continues till 869 (B. 524).

Mucel ď. The younger earl of the name, see p. 268.

Osmund dux. Perhaps to be identified with the *Omund dux* who signs a charter of 855 (B. 487). The name does not appear elsewhere in contemporary Mercian documents.

l. 30. *Ælfstan dux.* His signature is found from 831 (B. 400) until its last appearance in this document. He received a grant of land from the Bishop of Hereford (B. 429), so that his earldom probably lay in the west of England.

Aldred ď. This name appears only twice elsewhere in Mercian charters of the period with the title *dux*, viz. B. 378 (dated 824) and B. 452 (844–845). The second of these is witnessed by two other men of the same name to whom no title is applied.

Wenberht dux. Two charters of 855 (B. 487 f.) are signed by *Werberht dux* and *Weremberht dux* respectively, while the former is witnessed also by another man named *Werberht* to whom no title is applied. For Werenberht *minister regis ac praefectus* see above.

Eadulf. He appears as a witness between 840 (B. 430) and 855 (B. 487).

l. 33. *Aldberht ƥpo^9*, i.e. *praepositus*, A.S. *prafost*, the title applied to the monastic official later called the prior. The remaining witnesses represent the members of the community at Peterborough who were parties to the transaction.

VIII

MSS. (a) University Library, Edinburgh, Laing Charters, No. 18.
(b) British Museum, Additional MS. 15350, f. 84 (or 86 by the new numbering). This is a twelfth-century cartulary from Winchester Cathedral, generally known as the *Codex Wintoniensis*.

EDITIONS. K. 1053, from (b).
B. 478, from (a).
Haddan and Stubbs, III, p. 643, from K., with a translation.

The text is taken from (a), a small and clearly written parchment which seems to have been used at one time as the binding of a book. The left-hand edge has been cut close to the writing, hence the loss of the crosses prefixed to the names in the first column of witnesses. Part of the MS. is stained and illegible, but it is not, as Birch says, defective. It was the top portion of a chirograph.

DATE. It is apparent from the reference to the 'Old Minster' (see below) and from the occurrence of forms with *e* for earlier *ea* (e.g. *gepehte, geres, ehta*) that this document is later in date than the grant which it records. Two twelfth-century copies of what purports to be the original grant (in Latin) have survived, one of which is a chirograph preserved at Winchester, while the other precedes the Anglo-Saxon version in the *Codex Wintoniensis*. The Anglo-Saxon gives the substance of the Latin version in a briefer form. It omits the boundaries of the estate included in the latter, and in the *Codex Wintoniensis* is followed immediately by another set dating from the time of Stigand who became Bishop of Winchester in 1047.

p. 14, l. 2. *Æþeluulf cyning*. King of Wessex from 839 to 858.

l. 3. *on ealdan mynstre*. This name was applied at a later date to the earlier foundation to distinguish it from the New Minster which was founded by Edward the Elder.

l. 4. *Wænbeorgon*. Wanborough, near Swindon. The boundaries given in the Latin version correspond to those of the parish of Hinton which adjoins Wanborough on the east. Those attributed to the time of Stigand are the boundaries of Wanborough proper (see Grundy, 'The Saxon Land Charters of Wiltshire', in the *Archaeological Journal*, LXXVI, pp. 172–180).

ll. 4 ff. *ða ða he teoðode* etc. This is a reference to Æthelwulf's famous donation the exact nature of which has been the subject of much controversy. The statement made here agrees very closely with that of the Saxon Chronicle (where the donation as in Asser and later writers is referred to the year 855), the only noteworthy differences being in the use of the verb *teoðode* instead of *gebocade* and the addition of the phrase *into halgun stowun*. It appears that the scheme was actually set on foot in 854. There are in existence, at any rate, several late copies of charters, said to have been drawn up at Wilton on 22 April 854, which incorporate what may be described as a general statement of the king's policy of granting one-tenth of his (private) lands, not only to holy foundations direct (Malmesbury, Glastonbury and Winchester appear as beneficiaries, B. 470, 472, 474), but also to private individuals (B. 468 f.), the estates so granted being ultimately destined, no doubt, to pass into the possession of the church. These charters are by no means free from suspicion, but it is difficult to account for the uniformity with which they reproduce the general statement, unless there was actually something of the kind drawn up.

ll. 13 f. *on þara witena gewitnesse*. The same list of witnesses is attached to B. 474, see above.

l. 15. *Osric dux*. Osric's signature appears for the first time in a highly suspicious Malmesbury charter dated 5 November 844 (B. 447) and makes its last appearance (in the form *Oric*) in a Kentish charter (B. 502) granted by Æthelbert, King of Wessex and Kent, sometime between 860 and 862. He is mentioned twice in the Saxon Chronicle, first (s.a. 845) as Earl of Dorset, and later (s.a. 860 A, D, E) as Earl of Hampshire. On both occasions he took part in defeating the Danes.

Ælfred fil regis. The king's sons, Æthelred and Alfred, make their first appearance as witnesses in 854, when the latter could scarcely have been more than six years of age. In 855 he accompanied his father to Rome.

l. 16. *Alhstan episc̄*. Bishop of Sherborne, see p. 268. He took a leading part in several campaigns, see Plummer, II, p. 71.

Wulfhere dux. Wulfhere's signature appears for the first time among the *duces* in 854 and for the last in two charters of 871–877, see pp. 285, 287. Two charters of 863 and 869 respectively (B. 508, 886) record the grant of estates in Wiltshire to Wulfhere *principi*, so that he was probably Earl of Wiltshire. A charter of 901 (B. 595) which relates to a third estate in Wiltshire, formerly in his possession, says that he deserted both his king and his country but gives no particulars. He is not mentioned in the Saxon Chronicle.

ll. 16 ff. *Esne miñ* etc. Esne and the other thegns who sign this grant generally appear as witnesses of Æthelwulf's charters of 854.

l. 17. *Suiðhun episc̄*. Swithhun first appears in the charters in 838, when he signs as deacon (B. 423). In 852 he became Bishop of Winchester and held this position until his death, which the Saxon Chronicle F. records in 861 (the only time that he is mentioned), Fl. Wig. in 862 and Simeon of Durham in 863. He witnesses charters dated 862 and 863 (B. 504 f., 508).

Lullede dux. This signature is found in charters of 854, 855 and one of 856 (B. 491, see following note).

l. 18. *Æþelbald dux*. Æthelwulf's son, see B. 459 where he signs as *Aedelbaldus Dux filius Regis*. He probably acted as King of Wessex during his father's absence at Rome (855–856) and succeeded him as sole king in 858. He died in 860 and is accredited with a reign of five years in the Saxon Chronicle. Asser records that during his father's absence he conspired, along with Ealhstan, Bishop of Sherborne, and Eanwulf, Earl of Somerset, to keep him from the throne on his return but failed to find general support. Civil war was avoided by dividing the kingdom between father and son, the former retaining the eastern portion of the realm (Kent), the latter the western (Wessex). Asser (c. 12) is the sole authority for these events. There is one charter dated 856 (B. 491) which, if genuine, must belong to the period after Æthelwulf's return from Rome. It is preserved in the *Codex Wintoniensis* and in the list of witnesses Æthelbald is erroneously described as *episcopus* and Wullaf as *dux*. It records a grant of land in Berkshire by Æthelwulf, described (as in the earlier charters) as *rex occidentalium Saxonum*, and its list of witnesses agrees with those of 854 and 855.

Uullaf abb. Wullaf and Werferth sign all the charters of 854 which refer to the donation. They appear for the last time as witnesses in B. 502.

l. 19. *Eanuulf dux*. Eanwulf (see above) was Earl of Somerset (Sax. Chr. 845 A, B, C; Asser, c. 12). He regularly appears as a witness of Æthelwulf's charters and may have been associated with him in Kent before he became King of Wessex (see B. 418, 421). His name occurs twice, probably by mistake, in the list of *duces* attached to B. 468 ff. (three of the charters dated 22 April 854). In the first of these Osric's name is missing and in the second Wulfhere's. A charter in the *Codex Wintoniensis* (B. 590) records that Eanwulf was a benefactor of Winchester and grandfather of Earl Ordlaf.

Æðered fil reg̃. See p. 275.

l. 20. *Æþelberht dux*. Probably the king's son of the name. His signature appears for the first time in 854, and it would seem from the evidence of the charters (B. 467, 486) that he was King of Kent in 855. He succeeded Æthelbald as King of Wessex in 860 and reigned for five years (Sax. Chr.).

IX

MSS. (*a*) Rochester Cathedral, *Textus Roffensis*, f. 140. The second part of this MS. is a cartulary written in the twelfth century.

(*b*) British Museum, Stowe 940, p. 43, a late transcript of parts of the *Textus Roffensis*.

EDITIONS. Hearne, *Textus Roffensis*, p. 103.
K. 276.
T. p. 478.
B. 486.
The text is from (*a*).

DATE. The estate which Dunn disposes of here was granted to him by King Æthelwulf in 855 *pro decimatione agrorum quam Deo donante cęteris ministris meis facere decreui* (see p. 274). The copy of the will preserved in the *Textus Roffensis* follows immediately after a copy of the king's charter and it is probable that it was drawn up at the same time or soon afterwards, and written on the same parchment, the *boc* to which he refers. The two are printed as one document by K. and B.

l. 21. *Dunn*. The signature *Dun* is attached to a Kentish charter of 858 (B. 496), otherwise the name seems unrecorded at the time. In his grant King Æthelwulf describes him as *minister meus*.

ll. 21 f. *ðæt land*. King Æthelwulf's grant comprised *unam uillam quod nos Saxonice an haga dicimus in meridię castelli Hrobi · et decem iugera a meridiano plaga uilluli illius adiacentia · necnon et duo iugera prati · et .x. carros cum siluo honestos in monte regis · et communionem marisci quę ad illam uillam antiquitus cum recto pertinebat*, i.e. a messuage in Rochester with land adjoining, meadowland, marshland and so many loads of wood.

l. 24. *ðam hirode*, i.e. the community attached to Rochester Cathedral which was dedicated to St Andrew.

l. 25. *hi*. Is it possible that in the copy the word *cildran* has been misread as *eldran* or that a phrase such as 7 *cildran* has dropped out after *eldran*? The similarity of the two words would account for a mistake of the kind.

p. 16, l. 3. *geearnian*. This is a good example of the use of this verb in the sense 'acquire by means of services'.

X

MS. British Museum, Cotton Augustus, II, 66, a contemporary parchment.

FACSIMILE. Bond, *Facsimiles of Ancient Charters in the British Museum*, Part II, No. 33.

EDITIONS. K. 281.
T. p. 120.
B. 496.

DATE. This brief Anglo-Saxon summary of the transaction between King Æthelbert and Wullaf is written on the back of the parchment which contains King Æthelbert's charter, dated 858. The handwriting is the same and the dialect is Kentish.

l. 5. *Wassingwellan*. This name has not survived, but it is possible that the place meant is Westwell, which appears in D.B. simply as *Welle*. It is clear, at any rate, that *Wassingwellan* was in the neighbourhood of Westwell, as the boundaries given in the Latin charter run: *ab occidente cyninges folcland quod abet Wighelm 7 Wulflaf, ab aquilone Cuðrices dun heregeðeland, ab oriente Wiʒhelmes land, a meritie biscepes land to Cert* [i.e. Chart]. It is possible that the *Wulflaf* mentioned here

278 NOTES

as the holder of *cyninges folcland* to the west of *Wassingwellan* is the same as the Wullaf who makes the exchange. Wallenberg, p. 198, suggests that by *heregeðeland* is meant Challock, which was held by Heregyth, the wife of the reeve Abba, about 835 (Harmer, No. 11).

ll. 5 f. *Eðelbearht cyning.* See p. 276.

l. 6. *Wullafe...his ðegne.* Wullaf signs Kentish charters from 838 (B. 421) to 862 (B. 506).

l. 9. *him to folclande.* There is no mention of such a change in the Latin charter. A few years later King Æthelbert granted an estate of 9 *aratra* at Mersham (lying between the Stour and Eadweald's *bocland* at Brabourne) to Æthelred (described as his *minister et princeps*) to be held as a perpetual inheritance, subject only to military service and the construction of fortifications and bridges (B. 507). *Bocland*, i.e. land held by *boc* or charter, was exempt from many of the burdens attached to *folcland*, i.e. land held by national custom.

ll. 11 f. *butan ðem wioda* etc. In the Latin charter mention is made of a salthouse at Faversham 7 .11. *wena gang mid cyninges wenum to blean ðem wiada* (i.e. the forest of Blean). For *wena gang*, 'a going of wagons', i.e. the right of carting wood, see Whitelock, p. 207.

XI

MS. The Sherborne Cartulary, f. 16 b. This MS., which is one of the Phillipps collection, is now in the possession of T. FitzRoy Fenwick, Esq., at Thirlestaine House, Cheltenham. It was written in the twelfth century.

EDITIONS. T. p. 124.
B. 510.

The text is from the MS. A charter of Edward the Confessor to Horton Abbey, also preserved in the Sherborne cartulary, is almost word for word the same as this one, see No. CXX. In some cases it seems to preserve a better reading.

ll. 14 ff. *Ricsiendum* etc. The preamble is a translation of one which occurs with slight variations in Latin charters, e.g. B. 468–470, 472, 474 (Æthelwulf's charters of 22 April 854, see p. 275), B. 495 (a grant of 858) and B. 499 (a grant of Æthelbert dated 860).

l. 19. *Æþelbreht.* See p. 276.

l. 26. *Æþelredes 7 Ælfredes.* See p. 275.

p. 18, l. 2. *Æþelwulfes.* See p. 274.

Æþelbaldes. See p. 275. King Æthelbald's coffin, which had been first discovered in 1801, was revealed during excavations in the Lady Chapel at Sherborne Abbey in 1858 (see *The Times*, 6 June 1925, p. 9).

ll. 5 f. *alra domlicra þeowdoma.* The reading *ealdordomlicra* of Edward the Confessor's charter (see p. 222, l. 10) is probably to be

NOTES

preferred, although that of the present text is also possible. For *domlic* see B.T., *Suppl.* s.v.

l. 6. *ðeoffenges*, i.e. the necessity of arresting thieves and handing them over to the jurisdiction of the public courts presided over by the king's officers. The grant amounts to one of *infangenþeof*, i.e. the right of jurisdiction over thieves with receipt of the fines involved. A charter granted by King Egbert to St Andrew's, Rochester (B. 395), carries with it freedom of the same kind: *ab omnibus difficultatibus regalis vel secularis servitutis notis et ignotis cum furis comprehensione intus et foris majoris minorisve*, while one of his to Abingdon (B. 413) makes a distinction between thieves captured on church property and those captured elsewhere: *Fures quos appellant 'weregeld ðeofas' si foris rapiantur · pretium ejus dimidium illi æcclesiæ et dimidium regi detur. Et si intus rapitur totum reddatur ad æcclesiam*.

l. 26. *Alhstan .eps*. Bishop of Sherborne, see p. 268.

Cyma .miÑ. A witness of this name and title attests Æthelwulf's group of charters dated 22 April 854 (B. 468–470, 475 f.), and the name is attached also to one of King Alfred's grants, see p. 286.

Æþelwulf .miÑ. This witness attests charters of 862, 863 and 867 (B. 506 f., 516).

l. 27. *Eanwulf .dux*. See p. 276. This seems to be his last appearance.

Beocca .miÑ. An earl of this name attests B. 550 (dated 882), B. 611 (dated 904) and B. 740 (attributed to Alfred but dated 939).

Wynsige .miÑ. This witness attests B. 519 (dated 888, probably for 868).

l. 28. *Ælfstan .dux*. This would seem to be the earliest occurrence of Ælfstan's signature with the title *dux* (apart from B. 505 which is dated 862 but attributed to Æthelred). He signs a charter of Æthelbert dated 863 as *minister* (B. 507). His signature as *dux* continues till 875.

Æþelmod .miÑ. A thegn of the name signs Æthelwulf's charters from 841 (B. 437) to 845 (B. 449) and in 843 received a grant of land in Kent (B. 442). In 855 and 858 the name appears with the title *dux* (B. 467, 486, 496), and a charter of 859 (B. 497) records the purchase of land in Kent from an earl of the name. No thegn called Æthelmod appears as a witness after 845 except here and in two lists of names associated with Æthelwulf but attached to charters dated 873 and 874 respectively (B. 536, 538).

Goda .miÑ. This signature is attached also to B. 520 (dated 868).

l. 29. *Beorhtnoþ .miÑ*. A witness of this name attests charters of 867 and 868 (B. 516, 518, 520). The name is attached also to B. 538 (see above).

Coenwald .miÑ. This signature appears also in B. 506 (dated 862).

l. 30. *Denegils .miÑ*. No witness of the name appears elsewhere.

Æþelric .miÑ. A witness of this name appears in 845 (B. 449) and also in the lists attached to B. 536, 538 (see above).

l. 31. *Osmund .miÑ*. Osmund's signature is frequently found from 838 (B. 421) onwards. In 860 he received grants of land in Dorset and Wiltshire (B. 499 f.).

280 NOTES

Wulfred .miN̄. A witness of this name attests several of Æthelwulf's charters of 22 April 854 (B. 469 f., 475 f.) and appears also in 859 (B. 497) and 863 (B. 507).
Wulfhelm .miN̄. This witness does not seem to appear elsewhere in contemporary charters.

l. 32. *Wulfhere .miN̄.* This signature is not found elsewhere in contemporary charters. For the signature *Wulfhere dux*, which is found from 854 till Alfred's reign, see p. 275.
Ecgbreht .miN̄. This witness attests charters of 862 (B. 506) and 868 (B. 518-520, 522).
Hunred .miN̄. This witness is found also in 859 (B. 497).

l. 33. *Alhhard .aƀƀ.* An abbot of this name signs B. 504 (dated 862 but attributed to Æthelred), B. 516 (dated 867) and B. 522 (dated 868), and his signature without the title 'abbot' is attached also to another of Æthelbert's charters dated 862 (B. 506).
Monnel .miN̄. This name in the form *Mannel* is attached to charters of 867 and 868 (B. 516, 520).
Ecgulf .miN̄. This name appears among the witnesses of Æthelwulf's charters dated 22 April 854 (B. 469, 475 f.).

l. 34. *Heahmund .pr̄.* This witness attests B. 507 (see above).
Eadwulf .miN̄. This witness is found also in 862 and 863 (B. 506 f.). For Eadwulf *dux* see p. 285.
Ælfhere .miN̄. This witness attests B. 506 (see above).

l. 35. *Hwita .ppo⁹s.* The signature *Hwita m̄s* is attached to B. 538 (see p. 279).
Wistan .miN̄. Wistan signs B. 507 and appears with the title *dux* in 868 (B. 518, 520, 522).

p. 20, l. 1. *þan ilcan geare.* The year was probably reckoned as beginning on September 24 (see 'The Beginning of the Year in the Alfredian Chronicle' in *E.H.R.* XXXIII, 1918, pp. 328-342).

l. 25. *Ceolred .miN̄.* A thegn of this name attests a charter of 838 (B. 421) but does not seem to appear again.

l. 27. *Luhha .miN̄.* This witness does not appear elsewhere in contemporary charters but a man of the name signs a grant of Edward the Elder to Asser, Bishop of Sherborne (B. 610).

l. 29. *Beorhtmund .miN̄.* This witness appears also in 868 (B. 520).
Æþelwulf .miN̄. See above.

l. 30. *Eanwulf .miN̄.* This witness is found also in 862 (B. 506).

l. 31. *Ealhferþ .miN̄.* Neither this witness nor a considerable number of those who follow is found elsewhere in contemporary charters. The unrecorded names are Ceofa, Herewulf, Ærcmund, Ceolred, Burgred, Wulfric, Cyrred, Ceolhelm, Ecgstan, Heorhtric, Ceolheah and Wulfheah.

l. 32. *Babba .miN̄.* The signature *Babba þ⁹* occurs in B. 538 (see p. 279).
Ceolwulf .miN̄. The sale of land in Canterbury by a certain Ceolwulf to his kinsman Eanmund is recorded in B. 519.

NOTES

l. 33. *Mucel .miÑ*. This name with the title *miles* is attached to one of Æthelwulf's charters dated 850 (B. 460). It appears also in 858, 862, 863 and 867 (B. 496, 506 f., 516). A charter of 868 (B. 520) is witnessed by one *dux* and one *minister* of the name, while another of the same year (B. 522) is also witnessed by Mucel *dux*.

Cynemund .miÑ. A witness of this name signs a charter of 901 (B. 585) but does not seem to appear earlier.

l. 34. *Cynelaf .miÑ*. Cynelaf is found also in 858, 862 and 868 (B. 496, 506, 520).

Ealhstan .miÑ. A witness of this name signs Æthelwulf's charters from 839 (B. 421) to 856 (B. 491) and also appears in 863 (B. 507).

l. 35. *Torhthelm diāc p̄po⁹s*. A charter of 867 (B. 516) is witnessed by *Torhthelm presbyter*, who was apparently one of the community at Christchurch, Canterbury. The name, which is an uncommon one, does not occur elsewhere in contemporary charters, nor have I found another instance of the double title *diaconus praepositus*.

Æþelmund .miÑ. A witness of this name signs B. 519.

ll. 36 ff. *Burhghelm .p̄r*. etc. These members of the community at Sherborne do not appear elsewhere as witnesses.

l. 37. *Duda .miÑ*. A witness of this name appears at intervals from 858 (B. 495) to 877 (B. 544).

Eardulf .miÑ. A witness of this name signs a charter of Edward the Elder dated 901 (B. 595) but does not seem to appear earlier.

l. 38. *Wulfheard .miÑ*. A witness of this name is included in the list attached to B. 536 (see p. 279).

Cuðred .miÑ. A witness of this name signs Æthelbert's charter of 862 (B. 506). For an earl of the name in the reign of Alfred see p. 285.

XII

MS. British Museum, Harley 61, f. 20. This is a late mediaeval register from Shaftesbury Abbey.

EDITIONS. K. 302; boundaries, III, p. 398.
B. 526.

DATE. In the same register (f. 18 *b*) is preserved a copy of a Latin charter (B. 525) which records the grant of *duos cassatos* at Cheselbourne to Ælfstan *principi*. It was drawn up at the same place as the present charter, the few recorded witnesses are the same and the boundaries of the estate are almost identical (see below). It would seem at first sight, therefore, as if both refer to the same grant, and the difference in the recorded size of the estate might be due, as Birch suggests, to confusion at some stage between *ii* and *u* (for *v*). The differences between the two charters, however, are also significant and show, in the first instance, that the Middle English version is not a direct translation from the Latin but may represent an Anglo-Saxon predecessor. The latter, in turn, must have been drawn up to some extent independently of the Latin charter, and may actually represent a separate grant. There is evidence, likewise (see below), for an estate of 7 hides at Cheselbourne some seventy years later.

In the Latin charter the year is given as 859. This cannot be accepted, as Æthelred did not become king until 866, but it is possible that the change of DCCCLIX to DCCCLXX would give the necessary correction. The year 870, likewise, suits the Indiction number which is III.

p. 22, l. 2. *Atheldred.* Æthelred I (see p. 276) succeeded his brother Æthelbert and reigned from 866 to 871.

ll. 3 f. *mine ðare seleste [w]iotene.* The Latin charter reads *omnibus optimatibus gentis nostre.*

l. 5. *Elfstane.* See p. 279. He may have been Earl of Dorset.

l. 6. *Alchene idal landes.* The Latin charter reads *aliquam partem,* so that it is conceivable that it represents an earlier and less comprehensive grant.

be Chiselburne. Cheselborne, Dorset. Two other charters relating to Cheselborne are preserved in the Shaftesbury Register. The first of these (B. 775) records the restitution of 7 hides and the grant of 8 hides by King Edmund in 942 to *cuidam religiose sancte conversacionis monialis femine vocitate nomine Wenflede.* The second (K. 730) records the grant of 16 hides by Cnut to Agemund *minister* in 1019. D.B. records that the estate of Cheselborne held by the Abbey of Shaftesbury in 1086 had paid geld for 16 hides in the time of King Edward and was worth 16 pounds.

l. 8 · *i·sien,* cf. *segen,* l. 11. Do these forms represent the past pcp. of the A.S. verb *seon,* 'to see'?

ll. 8 f. *alderdomelere pinghe.* The reference is apparently to dues or services exacted by an ealdorman by virtue of his office.

l. 9. *i·witradenne,* A.S. *witeræden(ne),* the payment of fines. The meaning is that no fines were to go to any outside authority but that all of them were to be paid to the owner of the estate.

l. 10. *angieldes,* A.S. *angild.* This term is of frequent occurrence in the laws in the sense of the simple unaugmented value of a thing (the reference is generally to stolen goods). The meaning here is the same, i.e. that in the case of damage or theft the plaintiff should receive the value of his goods but no additional payment. All fines, as already noted, were made over to the owner of the estate.

It is in their lists of immunities and liabilities that the two charters differ most noticeably. The Latin reads *omnium regalium debitum et principalium rerum ceterarumque causarum furisque comprehencione et ab omnium secularium servitutum molestia secura et inmunis equaliter sine expeditione et arcis municione.* The inclusion of the 'arrest of thieves' in the list of immunities is noteworthy, also the omission of *angild* from the liabilities and the inclusion of the more usual 'defence of fortresses'. These differences suggest that the two grants are independent, and it is possible that the boundaries belong to one only and have been wrongly incorporated in the other (see p. 343 for a modern instance of a similar mistake). The fact that they are not word for word the same in the two grants suggests further that the one set was not copied directly from the other.

ll. 11 ff. *gief donne* etc. The promises and threats which follow differ from those of the Latin charter which foretells only reward *cum sanctis angelis Dei* in the one case and separation *a consorcio sanctorum* in the other.

l. 20. *þus ute þinsald*. The same phrase is used to introduce the boundaries in the Latin charter (B. 525). I owe to Miss Whitelock the suggestion that *þinsald* is a mistake for *ym[b]sald*.

ll. 22 f. *ceat[w]anberge*. Does this name survive in Chebbard Farm to the south of Cheselborne? B. 525 has *Scaftesbury* which is impossible if Shaftesbury itself is meant.

l. 23. *castel*. The reference is apparently to a hill fort. The use of the description *stancastel* later shows that those mentioned earlier were probably earthworks. A good number survive in the vicinity at the present day.

l. 24. *swindone*. The name does not seem to have survived. B. 525 reads *upward of dy castele*.

burnstowe. This compound does not seem to occur elsewhere, but for others of the kind see *Chief Elements in English Place-Names*, p. 57.

ll. 26 f. *op ðe herepað*. B. 525 has *over herepaþ*.

l. 27. *crundel*, 'quarry, chalkpit', see *Chief Elements in English Place-Names*, p. 19.

l. 28. *cineþ*. B. 525 has *cnap*, O.E. *cnæpp*, see *op. cit.* p. 17.

l. 30. *ereðe*. B. 525 has *herepaðe*, which seems to be the correct reading.

hendune. Is this represented by the modern Highdon? B. 525 has *heandene*.

beorch. There are numerous tumuli in the neighbourhood.

l. 31. *deflisch*. The stream on which Dewlish stands is now called the Devil's Brook.

p. 24, l. 1. *stancastel*. Perhaps of Roman origin.

blieqȝmannes beorg. B. 525 has *bleomannes berge*.

l. 2. *frume*. Is this the river Frome a few miles distant?

l. 5. *[w]udegate*. There is a hamlet of this name near Culmstock on the borders of Devon and Somerset.

l. 7. *Ealferð eþc*. Ealhferth succeeded Swithhun as Bishop of Winchester. His signature occurs for the first time in 868 (B. 518, 520, 522) and his successor Tunbriht appears in a charter of 877 (B. 544).

l. 8. *Heahmund eþc*. Heahmund succeeded Ealhstan as Bishop of Sherborne. He fell in battle against the Danes in 871 (Sax. Chr.).

XIII

MS. British Museum, Harley 61, f. 21 b. See p. 281.
EDITIONS. Dugdale, II, p. 477.
K. 310.
B. 531.

DATE. Between 871, when Alfred became king, and 877, when Bishop Ealhferth's successor makes his appearance.
The English version of this grant is followed immediately by a Latin version (B. 532).

l. 9. *Alured king.* See above. The date of Alfred's death is uncertain. It is entered under the date 26 October 901 in the Saxon Chronicle but may have taken place as early as 899 (see *E.H.R.* XXXII, 1917, pp. 526–530).

Sceaftesburi. The foundation of the Benedictine Nunnery at Shaftesbury is generally attributed to Alfred, and his daughter Æthelgifu is said to have been the first abbess (Asser, c. 98; William of Malmesbury, *Gesta Regum*, R.S. I, p. 131).

l. 11. *on halre tungan*, cf. p. 84, l. 10 and p. 92, l. 2. The Latin version has *vivens et in prosperitate adhuc vigens*. It is possible, however, that the meaning is rather 'unequivocally', but see note on p. 338.

l. 12. *Agelyue.* Æthelgifu (see above) was Alfred's second daughter. In his will he leaves her estates at Kingsclere and Candover in Hampshire, also one hundred pounds, see Harmer, pp. 17 f.

l. 13. *onbroken.* The Latin version reads *cogente infirmitate*.

ll. 14 f. *forsteal · and hamsocne and mundebreche.* This is the earliest recorded instance of the grant of these three fines which were generally paid to the king, see II Cnut, 12; 14; 15. The term *hamsocn* makes its first appearance in the laws (along with *mundbryce*) in II Edmund, 6, *forsteall* in III Edmund, 6. Their inclusion here is therefore highly suspicious. From the time of Æthelred II onwards the three are generally classed together, the fine for each being five pounds.

l. 16. *Dunheued.* Donhead St Andrew, Wiltshire. D.B. f. 67 b records that this estate paid geld for 40 hides in the time of King Edward. One of Edwy's charters dated 956 (preserved in the Shaftesbury Register) records the grant (or probably re-grant) of 90 hides to the Abbey at Shaftesbury, consisting of 50 hides at Donhead St Andrew, Easton-Bassett and Compton Abbas and 40 hides at Handley and Iwerne Minster, subject only to the usual obligations of military service and the construction of fortifications and bridges (B. 970). The boundaries are given.

Cumtune. Probably Compton Abbas, Dorset, although this estate is entered separately in D.B. as one which paid geld for 10 hides in the time of King Edward. In Edwy's charter (see above) the amount of land at Compton is also given as 10 hides.

l. 17. *Terente.* According to D.B. Tarrant paid geld for 10 hides in the time of King Edward. A charter of Æthelstan dated 935 by which he grants *bis sex manencium* at Tarrant to the community at Shaftesbury in return for their prayers is preserved in the Register (B. 708). It is perhaps to be regarded as a renewal of ownership (possibly on different terms) as it explicitly states that it is to take the place of any earlier charters. The estate is freed from all burdens except the usual three.

l. 18. *Ywern.* Iwerne Minster. D.B. records that this estate paid geld for 18 hides in the time of King Edward.

ffuntemel. Fontmel. The Shaftesbury Register contains a copy of a charter of Æthelstan dated 24 December 932 by which he grants to the community .xi. *et dimidia adtecta carattarum* at Fontmel on condition that they daily sing psalms for his soul (B. 691). In 1086 Fontmel was held by the abbey and had paid geld for 15 hides in the time of King Edward.

l. 19. *Adward mine sune.* Edward the Elder who succeeded his father as king.

Apered arceb. Æthelred was Archbishop of Canterbury from 870 to 889.

l. 20. *Alcheferd bissop.* Ealhferth, Bishop of Winchester, see p. 283. The Latin version has *Alfredus episcopus.*

Adelheach b. Æthelheah became Bishop of Sherborne in 871. He makes his last appearance in a charter of 879–881 (B. 549). His successor Wulfsige appears for the first time in a charter dated 889 (B. 561).

Wlfhere alderman. See p. 275. This is one of the last times that his signature appears.

l. 21. *Adwlf Alderman.* His name appears in dated charters of 863 (B. 508) and 868 (B. 520, 522). The Latin version reads *Raduulfus.*

Cuðred Alderman. For a lease of land in Hampshire to Earl Cuthred see p. 26. He does not appear elsewhere, but may be identical with the thegn of the name who signs two of Æthelbert's charters, see p. 281.

Tumbert Abb. He appears as a witness to the lease mentioned in the preceding note (see p. 26, l. 14). The name is an uncommon one and it may have been he who succeeded Ealhferth as Bishop of Winchester. The Latin version has *Turebertus.*

l. 22. *Midred mine þegen.* He also witnesses the lease mentioned above. The name appears earlier in charters of Æthelwulf dated 844, 847, 854 and 855 (B. 447, 451, 467 etc.) and in one of Æthelred I dated 868 (B. 520). It is probably his name in the form *Mired* which is attached also to B. 539, dated 875.

Apelwulf. See p. 279.

Osric. One of Alfred's charters dated 882 (B. 550) is signed by a man of the name.

Berthful. The Latin version reads *Berthwlfus.* The signature *Berhtwulf minister* is attached to B. 516 (dated 867), while *Berhtwulf miles* signs a charter attributed to Æthelwulf but dated 880 (B. 548).

l. 23. *Cyma.* See p. 279. He is omitted from the Latin version, which ends the list of witnesses with *Berthwlfus et curia mei.* Does this represent a misreading of the name *Cyma*? It seems proof, at any rate, of the independence of the two versions.

XIV

MS. British Museum, Additional MS. 15350, f. 73 (or 75 by the new numbering). See p. 274.
EDITIONS. K. 1062.
B. 543.
DATE. Between 871, when Alfred became king, and 877, when Ealhferth's successor makes his appearance.

p. 26, l. 2. *Ealhferð Bisceóp.* See p. 283.
l. 3. *EASTVNE.* Easton on the River Itchen near Winchester. Grundy, *Archaeological Journal,* LXXXI, p. 88, notes that the boundaries are not those of the present parish of Easton and suggests that the grant may refer to a detached piece now included in the eastern part of the parish of Avington. Another set of boundaries which can be more easily identified is attached to a grant of 7½ hides at Easton made by King Edgar to Brihthelm, Bishop of Winchester, in 961 (B. 1076).
l. 4. *CUÐRED dux.* See p. 285.
Wulfriðe. For Wulfthryth, a not very common feminine name.
l. 7. *eahta ciricsceattan.* The unit of assessment for church dues was the hide. Cuthred, therefore, pays eight times the recognised amount due from 1 hide.
mæsseprestes gereohta. There were two chapels on the manor of Easton in 1086 (D.B. I, f. 40; V.C.H. *Hants.* I, p. 460) and it would seem from this reference to the priest's dues that there was at least one in Alfred's time. The rules for the payment of tithes to churches and chapels on private estates are given in II Edgar, 2 f.
ll. 7 f. *saulsceattas.* These were legally enforced payments (see I Æthelstan, 4 and later codes) made to the church of the parish to which the deceased person belonged, even although he was buried elsewhere (see V Æthelred, 12, 1 and later codes). Special provision is frequently made by testators in their wills for the discharge of this obligation (see Whitelock, pp. 30, 52, 54).
l. 10. *laborðe,* i.e. the Bishop of Winchester.
l. 14. *Ælfred Rex.* See p. 284.
Tunberð abb. See p. 24, l. 21 for his only other appearance as a witness.
Milred miñ. See p. 285.
ll. 15 ff. *Ælfreð pb.....Aðeuulf Diac.* These witnesses represent the community attached to the cathedral. Their names do not appear elsewhere in the charters.

NOTES 287

l. 15. *Beorhtnoð miñ.* See p. 279.
l. 16. *Æðelheah eþc.* See p. 285.
Æðelnoð miñ. Perhaps identical with the later Earl of Somerset of the name (Sax. Chr. 894 A) who attests B. 549 (a charter of 879-881), B. 550 (dated 882) and B. 568 (see below).
l. 17. *Wulfhere Dux.* See p. 275. This is one of the last times that his signature appears.
Dudig miñ. B. 568 (an undated charter) records the grant of an estate in Wiltshire by King Alfred to Dudig with reversion to Malmesbury. The same estate was afterwards purchased by Earl Ordlaf from Dudig and given to Malmesbury in exchange for land elsewhere (B. 585, dated 901). Dudig witnesses another Wiltshire charter in 901 (B. 595).
l. 18. *Æðelstan Dux.* There is no other instance of this name with the title *dux* in contemporary charters. Two *ministri* of the name sign B. 549, while B. 550 records the grant of an estate in Somerset to a *minister* of the name. One of Alfred's messengers to Rome and India in 883 (Sax. Chr. B, C, D, E) was called Æthelstan. The title *dux* may have been attached to the name by mistake in the present instance. Such errors are of common occurrence in the *Codex Wintoniensis*, see pp. 276, 289, 306.
Heremod miñ. This name occurs with the title *clericus* in another Winchester charter, see p. 40, l. 20.
l. 19. *Eadwulf Dux.* See p. 285.
Æðelferð miñ: This signature occurs in two Berkshire charters dated 862 and 868 respectively (B. 505, 522).
l. 20. *Ordulf Dux.* His name appears in two other charters, B 549 and B. 550 (see above).
Ælfhere miñ. This witness appears four times between 862 and 882 (see p. 18, l. 34, B. 506, 549 f.) and the name occurs again between 901 and 904 (B. 595, 603, 607).
l. 21. *Elfstan Dux.* See p. 279.
Wigred miñ. This name appears, without any title, in one MS. of B. 575 (dated 897) and as *Wired* in B. 587 (dated 901).
l. 23. *ycenan.* For a discussion of the origin and distribution of this river name see Ekwall, *English River Names*, pp. 217-219.
ll. 23 f. *earna bæce.* There is no name of the kind in the vicinity at the present day.
l. 25. *þone midlestan beorg.* Probably one of a group of tumuli.
ll. 25 f. *ædeswyrðe...heringesleah.* The first element in each of these compounds seems to be a proper name. A form similar to the first survives in Adsdean House (Pl.N. *Sussex*, p. 55), while the second appears again in a thirteenth-century *heringeshame* (Pl.N. *Worc.* p. 397). For *wyrþ*, 'an enclosure', and probably here 'an enclosed homestead', see *Chief Elements in English Place-Names*, p. 66. The form *worðig*, an expanded form of *worþ* (which is found along with *wyrþ*), survives in the neighbourhood in the place-names King's Worthy and Martyr

Worthy. For *leah*, probably used here in its original sense of a clearing in one-time forest land, see *op. cit.* p. 45.

l. 26. *on þa roda*. For *rod* in the sense of 'clearing' see B.T., *Suppl.* p. 689, s.v. v.

l. 27. *smalan dune*. This is mentioned also in the boundaries of Avington, B. 1068.

l. 28. *Wulfred*. I have not been able to find any other reference to a landowner of this name in the vicinity.

ll. 28 f. *on ðone mylensteall*. D.B. records two mills at Easton.

XV

MS. British Museum, Additional MS. 15350, f. 59 (or 61 by the new numbering). See p. 274.

EDITIONS. K. 1086.
B. 617.

DATE. Sometime during the episcopate of Denewulf (879–909) and possibly during the reign of Alfred. The list of witnesses corresponds very closely with one which seems to belong to 909 (see No. XX), but the grant was probably earlier in date if the events which followed are faithfully recorded in the later charters, see below.

p. 28, l. 2. *Alresforda*. Alresford, Hampshire. There are a number of charters relating to this estate. The earliest of these, B. 102 (a charter of Ine dated 701), states that it was originally granted to Winchester Cathedral by Cenwalh, King of Wessex (d. 672), and this is repeated in later charters. B. 623 (a charter of Edward the Elder dated 909), B. 938 (a charter of Edwy dated 956) and B. 1150 (an undated charter of Edgar) give the history of the estate after it was leased to Alfred, as recorded in the present document. According to the first of these it was forfeited on account of his misdeeds, but redeemed by Bishop Denewulf from the king *qui tunc temporis Angul Saxoniam regebat*—a suspicious phrase in a charter attributed to Edward the Elder, in view of the fact that the king referred to must be his father, Alfred. The charter of 956 briefly records the grant of the estate by King Edwy to a certain Ælfric. Edgar's charter repeats the story of Alfred in greater detail and describes him as a kinsman of Bishop Denewulf. It records also that it was his son who succeeded in regaining possession of Alresford (from King Edred not from King Edwy, but the reference is surely to the Ælfric of B. 938) and proceeds to annul this grant and restore the estate to the Old Minster. In every case the amount of land involved is given as 40 hides. In 1086 it was held in demesne by Walchelin, Bishop of Winchester. Its assessment in the time of King Edward is entered as 51 hides, reduced to 42 hides in 1086 with land for 40 ploughs (D.B. I, f. 40; V.C.H. *Hants.* I, p. 459).

l. 3. *Tunbryht bisceop*. Denewulf's predecessor, see pp. 283, 285.

agan. See B.T., *Suppl.* p. 28, s.v. 11 *a*. A lease granted by Bishop Oswald for three lives contains a clause which must represent a later endorsement or marginal insertion: *þis is agan twegera manna dæg 7 þa nam Ealdulf hit 7 sealde þam þe he wolde to earnignclande* (K. 679). Ealdulf was Oswald's successor as Bishop of Worcester.

ll. 4 f. *to hærfestes emnihte* etc. September 24. For a similar arrangement see B. 599 (Harmer, p. 29).

l. 5. *cyresceatweorc*. A tenant of the Bishop of Worcester had to undertake to plough two acres every year 7 *þæron his circsceat gesawe 7 þæt eft geripe 7 in gebringe* (see p. 64, ll. 17 f.). Is this the type of work referred to here?

l. 6. *tó ripe*, cf. *Rectitudines*, caps. 2, 3, 4 *a*, where details are given of the amount of work due in harvest from the various grades of peasants.

ll. 11 f. *Tata bisc̄. And Byrnstan bisc̄.* The title following these two names should undoubtedly be 'priest' not 'bishop'. They sign charters relating to the Old Minster between 900 (B. 594) and about 909 (see No. xx). For other mistakes of the kind in the *Codex Wintoniensis*, see pp. 276, 287.

l. 13. *Wighelm Diāc.* He signs No. xx and appears as a witness also in 904 (B. 604, 613).

Wulfred miñ. He also witnesses B. 590 (see below), 594, 613.

ll. 14 ff. *Æþelstan cler* etc. The only other Winchester charter with a long list of *clerici* is No. xx, p. 40. It includes all the names given here with the exception of Wulfred's. Another of Denewulf's charters (B. 590, dated 900) has a long list of *ministri*, some of whom are apparently the *presbyteri* and *clerici* of other contemporary charters.

Beornulf miñ. He also attests No. xx. For a lease of land at Ebbesbourne Wake, Wiltshire, by Bishop Denewulf to a kinsman of his named Beornulf, see Harmer, No. xvii.

l. 15. *Winstan miñ.* This witness does not seem to appear elsewhere in contemporary charters.

l. 16. *Aðulf miñ.* Two men of this name sign a group of Winchester charters dated 909 (B. 620 f., 623–625, 627–629).

XVI

MS. This document was included in the Somers Collection, see p. 266.

EDITIONS. Smith, *Beda: Historiæ Ecclesiasticæ*, Appendix, p. 771.
K. 305.
B. 560.

DATE. Between 899 and 904, see below. It is not possible to date this grant more exactly owing to the scarcity of contemporary Worcester documents.

ll. 18 f. *Uuerfriþ biscop.* Bishop of Worcester from 872 to 915.

l. 21. *Alhmundingtune.* Probably Elmstone (also known as Elmstone-Hardwicke) near Bishop's Cleeve in Gloucestershire[1]. In D.B. an estate of 5 hides at Hardwicke is entered as a berewick of Deerhurst.

higen me gebocedan. The record of this grant is extant (B. 559) and is dated 889. The transference of part of the estate to Cyneswith must have been carried out some years afterwards, to judge by the evidence of the witnesses. The signature *Cynelm abbas et diaconus* appears for the first time in a charter of 899 (B. 580), while Ecgfrith who signs there as *diaconus* had become a priest by 904 (see pp. 34, l. 19, 38, l. 7). The remaining witnesses, with the exception of Eamberht, Wigfrith and one of the two named Cynhelm, are all included in the lists attached to the grants of 904. Werfrith *presbyter*, Wigheard, Wulfred and the two named Cynhelm sign B. 559 but the remaining witnesses are entirely different in the two grants.

l. 22. *mid hina leafe.* The estate, in the first instance, had been leased to the bishop for three lives only. The surrender of his rights over 3 hides in favour of Cyneswith, therefore, had to be made with the leave of the community.

l. 24. *ða ceorlas.* The grant of Elmstone was made to Werfrith *cum hominibus ad illam pertinentibus quarum nomina paulisper inferius scripta sunt.* Actually the only names given in the cartulary are those of the witnesses, but the omission of the others may be due to the copyist. Were they the *ceorlas* mentioned here? It is certainly unusual to have the names of the men belonging to an estate recorded, and in this case there may have been something exceptional about their status. On the other hand it is possible that the reference is to a separate community of *ceorlas* attached in some way to the church of Worcester. That such communities were found in the neighbourhood is proved by the occurrence of the names Charlton Abbots, near Prestbury, and Charlton Kings.

ll. 25 f. *ðæt twega hida lond ꝼ ða ceorlas.* Does this mean the two remaining hides with their tenants, or did the *ceorlas* form a community apart? The context seems to suggest the second interpretation.

l. 26. *snæd.* An isolated wood or a clearing in a wood.

Preosdabyrig. Prestbury, Gloucestershire.

ll. 26 f. *ða hwile hit unagaen seo.* See B.T. p. 1089, s.v. *unagan*, and cf. *agan*, p. 289.

p. 30, ll. 1 f. *geearnigan.* Cf. Harmer, p. 5, l. 28: *mid eaðmodre hernisse...geeornigan*; ibid. p. 21, l. 12: *he hit geearnode...mid rihtre eadmodnysse.* The reference in both cases is to an estate.

l. 4. *Clife.* Bishop's Cleeve. The estate at Elmstone had formerly belonged to the monastery at Cleeve, see B. 559.

ll. 7 f. *to minum bure*, i.e. to the bishop's private room.

ll. 10 f. *ðreo mittan hwætes to ciricsceatte.* The payment of church dues is frequently the only obligation imposed upon its leaseholders by

---

[1] See W. St Clair Baddeley, *Place Names of Gloucestershire*, p. 60.

the church of Worcester. The amount due is rarely specified but appears as *duos modios de mundo grano* in a grant of 2 hides at Bentley (B. 1087). According to D.B. i, f. 174 (V.C.H. *Worc.* i, p. 298) the bishop was entitled to one load (*summa*) of the best grain from every hide at Martinmas. For *mitta* see p. 272.

l. 13. *Cynhel abb.* The name *Kinelm* is included in the list of the abbots of Evesham in the *Chronicon Abbatiæ de Evesham*, R.S. p. 77. He signs four Worcester grants altogether, and in 907 received a lease of Bengeworth from Bishop Werfrith who describes him as *propinquus meus* (B. 616).

XVII

MS. British Museum, Additional MS. 15350, f. 75 (or 77 by the new numbering). See p. 274.

EDITIONS. K. 1070.
T. p. 492.
B. 566.

DATE. The Anglo-Saxon version of this grant is preceded by a Latin one which seems to be a translation, see below. There is no means of dating it exactly. The reference to King Alfred suggests that it was drawn up after his death and it may therefore belong to the early years of Edward the Elder's reign.

l. 20. *CEOLWIN*. Not mentioned elsewhere.

l. 21. *AWELTVNE*. Alton Priors, Wiltshire. The *Codex Wintoniensis* contains also a charter of King Egbert (B. 390) whereby he grants this same estate of 15 hides at Alton Priors to the church of St Peter and St Paul at Winchester (see p. 305). This document has several suspicious features and can scarcely be accepted as it stands. In the first place the estate is said to have reverted to the king on the death without heirs of his *praefectus Burhghardus* to whom it had formerly been granted. Burgheard *praefectus* signs two of Egbert's charters of 824 and 825 (B. 377, 389), while Burgheard *dux* signs three of 826 (B. 391 ff.). The difference is probably only one of title (see Chadwick, *Anglo-Saxon Institutions*, p. 282), and it seems natural to identify this witness with the former owner of Alton Priors. In that case the date and the list of witnesses attached to Egbert's charter cannot be accepted. The grant is said to have been drafted on 19 August 825 *quando Egcbergtus rex exercitum Gewissorum movit contra Brettones ubi dicitur Criodantreow* and completed at Southampton on 26 December, but Burgheard, from what evidence we possess, was alive at that date (see above) and the name actually occurs twice over (once as *dux* and once as *praefectus*) in the list of witnesses attached to the grant. It is noteworthy that another charter in the *Codex Wintoniensis* (B. 389) is said to have been drafted on the same occasion and completed at the same time and it may have served as a model for the Alton one. Another

NOTES

irreconcilable fact is that the Old Minster is twice referred to by that name (*vetus monasterium*), which came into use only after the foundation of the New Minster, see p. 308. Egbert's grant, therefore, cannot be accepted in its present form, although it may be true in fact, i.e. it is possible that the estate passed at one time from Burgheard to King Egbert and from him to the foundation. There is no record of its later history until the present grant. For a lease of the estate by the community in the eleventh century see No. CVII.

ll. 21 f. *him man ón agene æht gereahte*. There is no record of this transaction. It is possible that the estate had been made over by the community itself (perhaps in return for money) during the troublous times of the Danish wars in Alfred's reign. The Latin version reads *pro qua ei pretium datum fuit*, which may be merely a mistranslation or may record an actual money transaction (apparently, however, the wrong way round).

l. 24. *yrfe*. The Latin has *pecunia*, which seems again like a bad translation of the Anglo-Saxon.

l. 25. *Osmodes*. Ceolwin's husband does not seem to be mentioned elsewhere.

l. 26. *his gemunde dege*. Either the anniversary of his birth or of his death but more probably the latter.

ll. 29 f. *gehændre...7 behefre*. The Latin version reads *vicinior vel utilior*.

p. 32, l. 1. *an hiwissce ægefæles landæs*. The Latin reads *aliquam hidam liberam*, i.e. free from the payment of *gafol* or rent. The use of *hiwisc* as the equivalent of 'hide' is noteworthy, see p. 455.

l. 3. *Aweltunæ metæ*. For a detailed analysis of the boundaries as they appear in Egbert's grant (B. 390) see Grundy, *Archaeological Journal*, LXXVI, pp. 159–164.

ll. 4 f. *þam westmæstan æwylle*. The boundaries given in Egbert's charter differ only incidentally from those given here, and in some instances they seem to have preserved a better reading. At this point they add *þe is bradewlle gehate*. Grundy identifies this spring with one between the villages of Alton Priors and Alton Barnes.

l. 5. *upp to ðam ealdan hærepaðe*. Grundy suggests that this old track is represented by the present boundary running north between the two villages.

l. 6. *wodnes beorge*. Apparently, as Grundy suggests, this is the tumulus now called Adam's Grave. The substitution of the Christian Adam for the heathen Woden is interesting.

ll. 6 f. *ceorlacumbes...woncumb*. Grundy suggests for these two the now unnamed combes to the east of Walker's Hill and the north of Knap Hill respectively.

l. 8. *ufeweard hol*. This undoubtedly refers to the stone just mentioned. Grundy interprets it differently, viz. '(and the stone is?) above the hollow'.

þæm ealdan díc. The Wansdyke.

NOTES

ll. 9 f. *þane gemænan garan.* A 'gore' was a triangular piece of land, see *Chief Elements in English Place-Names*, p. 28. By 'common' is meant 'held in common'.

l. 10. *of þæt eft* etc. A more correct reading seems to be preserved by B. 390, *oþ þæt hit æft geð in on* etc. The boundary at this point comes back to the Wansdyke.

ll. 10 f. *þet read geát.* A gap cut by the Ridgeway in the Wansdyke and now called the Red Shore.

l. 11. *þera hlinca.* The word *hlinc*, which has the general sense of 'a raised piece of ground, a bank', is used especially of a ridge of unploughed turf dividing one cultivated strip from another. The name 'lynchet' is frequently used in the same way at the present day.

l. 13. *woddes geat.* Both sets of boundaries have the same reading. Grundy takes *woddes* as equivalent to *wodnes* and suggests that Woden's Gate lay near the barrow called Woden's Barrow above. He identifies the track with the road running north-east past New Town. For a similar interchange between *Woddes* and *Wodnes* see Sax. Chr. 592 A, E.

l. 14. *of þam suðhliðe.* B. 390 reads more correctly *on* etc.

l. 15. *inne of þem díc.* B. 390 has *inne on þære dic.*

ciceling wege. Grundy suggests that this is a local name for the Ridgeway.

l. 16. *moxes dune.* Is *Mox* a proper name? Grundy identifies the hill with Knap Hill.

þane ealdan walweg. Grundy suggests that this way is now represented by the road called Workway Drove.

l. 17. *wearcingwege.* B. 390 has *weascingwege.*

l. 21. *ewelforda*, cf. *æwelforda*, B. 390. Grundy reads by mistake *æpelforda*, 'the ford of the appletree'. The first element of the compound is probably the same as that in *Aweltun* itself, i.e. A.S. *æwelle*, *æwylle*, 'spring, source'.

þæs broces. B. 390 adds *be þam ealden eadenne*, 'by the old river valley'.

l. 22. *to þæm æwelle.* Here the boundary returns to its starting-point. What follows must refer, as Grundy points out, to another parcel of land.

Fram moxes dune. See above.

l. 23. *wið eastan cealfa mære.* B. 390 reads *wið ealdan* etc. I have taken *mære* as equivalent to *mere*, cf. *hærepaðe* with similar substitution of *æ* for *e*. Grundy takes it as equivalent to *gemære.*

l. 24. *on þawæres leáge.* B. 390 reads *on howeres leage.* There is no recorded proper name of either form.

l. 26. *gewyrpes.* Literally 'something thrown up'.

l. 27. *creodan hylle*, cf. the *criodantreow*, of B. 390.

l. 28. *tesan mede.* The name survives in Tawsmead Farm to the east of Alton Priors.

XVIII

MS. British Museum, Additional Charter, 19791, the bottom portion of a chirograph.
FACSIMILE. Bond, *Facsimiles of Ancient Charters in the British Museum*, Part III, No. 2.
EDITION. B. 609.

p. 34, l. 1. *Rixiendum* etc. The construction corresponds to the Latin Ablative Absolute.
l. 4. *Uuerfrid bisco͑p'*. See p. 289.
l. 7. *Easttune*. White Ladies Aston, see Pl.N. *Worc.* p. 88. A hide of land there (perhaps the same one) was leased by Oswald to a certain Cynulf in 977 (K. 615). In 1086 it was part of the manor of Northwick (D.B. I, f. 173 b; V.C.H. *Worc.* I, p. 294).
l. 8. *ðæt Innlond*, i.e. the land retained by the tenant for his own use.
l. 13. *Cynehelm aƀƀ*. See p. 291.

XIX

MSS. (a) British Museum, Cotton Nero E. I, Part II, f. 182. See p. 263.
(b) British Museum, Cotton Tiberius A. XIII, f. 6 b (see p. 259). The text of this grant is unfortunately so badly stained as to be partly illegible.
EDITIONS. Hearne, *Hemingi Chartularium* etc., I, p. 13.
K. 339, from (b).
B. 608, from (a).
The text is from (a).

l. 23. *ĘÐEREDES...ĘÐELFLEDE*. Æthelred, Earl of Mercia, and his wife Æthelflæd, who was King Alfred's eldest daughter, see Harmer, p. 17, l. 35.
ll. 23 f. *WERFRIÐ Ƀ*. See p. 289.
l. 27. *criminum*. It is possible that this word has been substituted for the less familiar *erumnarum* which appears in the copy in MS. (b).
p. 36, ll. 1 ff. *nisi litterarum apicibus* etc. This idea is frequently expressed in similar words in the preamble of Latin charters.
l. 4. *indictione* .1. The year and the Indiction number do not fit. The evidence of the witnesses, however, supports the year 904, as all the members of the community who sign here are included in the list attached to the preceding charter, which belongs to that date (*Bernhelm* seems to be a slip for *Berhthelm*). The only difference is in the status of Oslac, who appears there as deacon and here as priest, so that, unless a mistake has been made in the preceding charter, the present grant must be later in date. Oslac signs as deacon in 892 (B. 570) but appears

as priest in a grant (B. 582) which seems to fall between 892 and 899. It is impossible, therefore, through lack of evidence, to be certain when he attained the rank of priest.

l. 6. *gewritað*. Literally 'make over in writing'.

heora hlafordum. Æthelred and Æthelflæd, who are referred to later in the charter as *Myrcna hlafordas*, seem to have had almost absolute control in Mercia.

l. 8. *bi þæm norðwalle*. The fortifications at Worcester had been constructed by Æthelred and Æthelflæd, see B. 579. It is possible that they were of stone, see V.C.H. *Worc.* IV, p. 378.

l. 10. *þ medwe land*. In 816 Bishop Deneberht had purchased from Coenwulf, King of Mercia, immunities for various estates including 30 *manentes* in the Worcester meadowland (*in Weogorna leage*) west of the Severn (B. 357). The boundaries show that this land stretched from Mosely to the Teme.

l. 14. *Beferburnan*. It is possible that the reading of the copy in MS. (*b*) is nearer the original. I cannot, however, explain the form *ludading wic*.

l. 17. *fulgodes mædlandes*. It seems unnecessary to assume here a proper name *Fulgod* not otherwise recorded (see Pl.N. *Worc.* p. 397). For instances of the combination of the adv. *ful* with adjs. see B.T. s.v. *fulclæne, fulcuð, fulgeomor* etc.

l. 22. *Ælfw̄*, i.e. Ælfwyn, their daughter. The Saxon Chronicle C records that in 919 (after the death of her mother) she was deprived of all authority in Mercia and taken to Wessex. Nothing further seems to be known of her. Her signature is attached to a charter granted by Edward the Elder in 903 (B. 603, see below), and seems to occur also, followed by the erroneous title *episcopus*, in a charter of Æthelflæd (B. 632) of which only a late copy (with the impossible date 878) survives.

ll. 30 f. *þara* .XII. *noman*. It would seem natural to take these as the first twelve names in the list of witnesses which follows, running from Bishop Werfrith to Ealhmund. They would then include Abbot Cynehelm (see p. 291), but it is possible that the last name of all, Wulfhun, should be taken as one of them.

p. 38, l. 6. *Aldred*. This name occurs in the list of witnesses attached to a charter of 901 (B. 587) recording an exchange of lands between Æthelred and Æthelflæd and Wenlock Abbey in Shropshire.

l. 7. *Æþelfrið ealdormann*. Æthelfrith's signature with the title ealdorman or *dux* is attached to dated charters from 883 (B. 551) to 904 (B. 607). It is recorded that he lost all the title-deeds in his possession by fire but was allowed to have them rewritten (B. 603, 606). His name is attached to Æthelflæd's grant (B. 632, see above) which was probably made after her husband's death.

l. 9. *Ælfred*. Two men of this name witness a charter of Earl Æthelred dated 888 (B. 557), elsewhere only one appears (B. 551, 552, 574). The name with the title *minister* is attached likewise to B. 603, but appears twice in Mercian charters (B. 537, 632) with the title *dux*. In B. 537 (a grant made by Earl Æthelred in the lifetime of King Burgred) the title is applied also to the preceding witness Eadnoth, who does not appear elsewhere among the *duces*. For B. 632 see preceding page. Neither would seem to be completely reliable.

l. 10. *Ælfstan*. Ælfstan signs here for the first time and also witnesses B. 632. He had kinsmen called Eadnoth and Alfred (B. 582).

l. 11. *Eadric*. Eadric signs B. 603 and is probably the grantee of B. 632. In the latter Æthelflæd describes him as her *minister*.

l. 12. *Edgar b.* Bishop of Hereford. He signs from 901 to 930.

Wlfhun. Perhaps a member of the community at Worcester. He signs B. 559 (dated 889), B. 570 (dated 892) and B. 582 (892–899), and Wulfhun, a priest of Worcester, is referred to in B. 574 (dated 896).

XX

MS. British Museum, Additional MS. 15350, f. 61 (or 63 by the new numbering). See p. 274.

EDITIONS. K. 1088.
T. p. 158.
B. 622.

DATE. There is a difficulty about dating this grant as the list of witnesses contains the name of Bishop Frithestan who was Denewulf's successor at Winchester, and the entries in the Saxon Chronicle and Fl. Wig. which refer to Denewulf's death (s.a. 909) and Frithestan's appointment (s.a. 910) do not suggest that they had already been associated in the episcopate. It is conceivable, however, that this document was drawn up only shortly before Denewulf's death, when through age or illness he desired to make provision for his commemoration, and that Frithestan was actually then in the position of coadjutor or acting bishop. The possibility that the copyist has made one of his frequent mistakes in giving Frithestan's title must be taken into account, but is not self-evident in view of the fact that his name occurs in the position generally occupied by the bishops who act as witnesses.

Frithestan's name appears twice (along with Wighelm's) in earlier Winchester charters (B. 604, 613) with the title *diaconus*, while in B. 612 both are erroneously described as *ministri*. These charters all belong to the year 904.

l. 16. *EADWARD cyning 7 þa hiwan*. It is curious to find the king so closely associated with the community in a grant of the kind. It suggests that Frithestan's position, if he was acting as bishop at the time, was irregular.

l. 17. *Ticceburnan*. Apparently this name was originally applied to the upper course of the Itchen. It survives in the village name

Tichborne, but Grundy (*Archaeological Journal*, LXXVIII, p. 58) points out that the grant applies to the neighbouring parishes of Cheriton and Beauworth, not to what is now Tichborne proper.

l. 20. *gemynd*. Thorpe takes this to mean King Edward's commemoration, but it seems more likely that the reference is to the bishop's.

l. 21. *swa swa hé*, i.e. the tenant.

l. 24. *ambra*. For the relationship of the amber to the *mitta* see p. 272. The capacity of the amber, unfortunately, is unknown.

ll. 25 f. 7 *feower* 7 *swin*. The second 7 is redundant or else something has been omitted after *feower*. In the second case the translation would run 'four...and a swine'.

l. 27. *þ þæ þonne* etc. The translation follows B.T., *Suppl.* p. 419, s.v. *gestrinan*, 1.

l. 28. *forgenge*. The meaning of this word is uncertain as it does not occur elsewhere, see B.T. *Suppl.* p. 242, s.v.

p. 40, l. 1. *hæres unæmetta*. The meaning is again uncertain. The form *hæres* for *heres* is parallel, however, to the form *hær* for *her*, l. 11, and a few years before the Danes of East Anglia (under the leadership of Æthelwold) had harried Wiltshire (Sax. Chr. 905).

ll. 1 ff. *þonne bid hic hiwan.....þonne bebeodað hie* etc. The construction is confused and it is possible that the text is corrupt. The simplest explanation is that the phrases enclosed in brackets have been wrongly incorporated at this point. They are correctly repeated below, and if they are omitted here, the construction is normal and the sense clear. It is possible that the mistake arose through the repetition of the phrase *for Godes lufan*.

l. 13. *Plegmund arceð*. Plegmund was Archbishop of Canterbury from 889 or 890 to 923 (Sax. Chr. A; see Armitage Robinson, *The Saxon Bishops of Wells*[1], pp. 56–58). Alfred mentions him as one of his instructors in the preface to his translation of Gregory's *Cura Pastoralis*.

Beornulf m. See p. 289.

l. 14. *Friðestan bisc̄*. He appears alone in a number of Winchester charters dated 909 (B. 620 f., 623–627), most of which are of doubtful authenticity. He continues to sign up to 931, when he resigned the see and was succeeded by Beornstan. B. 727, which records a grant made to Frithestan in 938, must be spurious or wrongly dated as he died in 932 or 933.

Æþelstan cl. etc. See p. 289. The list of *clerici* given here is much longer than appears elsewhere. It would seem from the evidence of contemporary charters that the last two names at least should have the title *minister*.

l. 15. *Osulf Dux*. Osulf witnesses Edward the Elder's charters between 901 (B. 588) and 909 (B. 624).

l. 16. *Deormod miñ*. This witness makes his first appearance in B. 549 (a charter of 879–881) and continues to sign until 909. His

---

[1] *British Academy Supplemental Papers*, IV.

name frequently heads the list of *ministri*. In two charters from the *Codex Wintoniensis* (B. 595, 611) he appears by mistake with the title *dux*. An undated charter (B. 581) records the grant of land in Berkshire to Deormod by King Alfred.

l. 17. *Tata pð*. See p. 289.

l. 18. *Beornstan pð*. See p. 289.

l. 19. *Æpelstan pð*. He appears as a witness in Winchester charters between 900 (B. 594) and 909 (B. 620, etc.).

l. 20. *Ælfstan pð*. He appears in the second list of witnesses attached to one of Bishop Denewulf's charters (see Harmer, p. 30) but not apparently elsewhere.

l. 21. *Ealhstan pð*. He is a regular witness of the Winchester group of charters dated 909.

l. 22. *Wulfric pð*. He appears also in the second list of witnesses attached to Bishop Denewulf's charter, see above. The two names, Ealhstan and Wulfric, occur in the list of *ministri* attached to B. 590, which obviously includes the members of the community at Winchester who have not been distinguished by their proper titles.

ll. 23 f. *Æpelbyrth pð*... *Yðelbeard pð*. These names are not apparently found elsewhere in contemporary charters.

l. 25. *Wigelm Diāc*. See p. 289.

l. 26. *ða gemæro*. The boundaries are traced in detail by Grundy, *Archaeological Journal*, LXXVIII, pp. 150–156.

ellen forð. Grundy points out that this name survives as a field name in Elford.

l. 27. *æpphangran*. This appears more correctly as *æpshangran* in the bounds of Kilmeston (B. 1077).

l. 28. *hormæres wudu*. In the bounds of Kilmeston this appears as *hormes wudu*.

l. 29. *mælanbeorh*. Now Milbarrow, the name being derived from the tumulus which is a feature of the parish.

l. 32. *torscagan*. Grundy notes the occurrence of the name Torshawe among the field names of Cheriton in 1611. It has now disappeared.

ll. 32 f. *gandran dune*. The name survives in the modern Gander Down.

l. 34. *cupænes*. This looks like a proper name but is otherwise unrecorded.

p. 42, l. 1. *tornagéat*. This appears as *tyrngeat*, 'turnstile', in the survey of Chilcomb (B. 620).

ll. 1 f. *beaddes scagan*. The name survives in the modern Badshear Lane.

l. 3. *hindsceata*. For *sceat*, 'nook, corner, point' (a common element in field names), see *Chief Elements in English Place-Names*, p. 51. I am uncertain how to interpret the form *hindsceata*.

l. 4. *ostercumb*. Grundy notes that this name survives in the field-name Great Eastercombe in Bramdean parish.

NOTES

XXI

MS. British Museum, Harley 4660, f. 8. See p. 263.
EDITIONS. Hickes, *Thesaurus*, I, p. 174.
K. 1097.
B. 636.

l. 7. *Disponente* etc. For the same preamble in a later Worcester charter see No. LXIV.
l. 8. *notantur*. The later charter reads *mutantur*.
l. 12. *Wilfrið biscop*. Bishop of Worcester from 922 to 929 (Fl. Wig.).
l. 14. *Clifforda*. Clifford-Chambers, Gloucestershire. An estate of 2 hides at the same place, leased by Oswald to his thegn Wihthelm in 966, was made up of *oþer healf hid gedallandes 7 healf hid on þære ege* (B. 1181), i.e. '1½ hides of partible land and half a hide on the island'.
p. 44, l. 2. *binnan ðissum gemærum*. The boundaries which follow run counter-clockwise and seem to define what is now the neighbouring parish of Milcote rather than Clifford-Chambers itself.
of Sture. The River Stour.
l. 3. *on ðone herpað*. Apparently the road called Clifford Lane.
ll. 3 f. *to Westtunniga gemære*. The boundary of Weston-on-Avon.
l. 4. *in Afene*. The River Avon.

XXII

MSS. (*a*) British Museum, Cotton Claudius C. IX, f. 194 *b*. This is an Abingdon cartulary, written in a hand of the early thirteenth century.

(*b*) British Museum, Cotton Claudius B. VI. f. 21. This is another Abingdon cartulary, written about fifty years later.

EDITIONS. *Historia Monasterii de Abingdon*, R.S., ed. Stevenson, I, p. 72.
K. 1129, from (*b*).
B. 688, from (*b*).

There is a modern English translation in Stenton's *Early History of the Abbey of Abingdon*, pp. 34 f.

The text is from (*a*).

DATE. The grant itself cannot be later than 931, see below under Archbishop Hrothward. It is possible that the record was drawn up later, when Æthelstan had attained the rank of earl. He signs consistently with this title from 932 (B. 689) onwards. The earlier charters where he appears as *dux* (B. 667, dated 930; B. 670 f., dated 931) are probably of later date.

The Anglo-Saxon version of this grant is preceded by a Latin one in both MSS. (see B. 687).

l. 6. *Æðelstan ealdorman*. Earl of East Anglia, see p. 306. He is described in the Latin version as *senator*.

NOTES

Uffentune. Uffington, Berkshire. In 1086 the Abbey of Abingdon was holding this estate. Its assessment had been reduced from 40 hides to 14 hides and there was land for 14 ploughs. On the other hand its value had risen from 15 pounds to 21 pounds and then to 26 pounds (D.B. I, f. 59; V.C.H. *Berks.* I, p. 341).

l. 8. *Winsies biscopes.* The Latin version reads *Kynsii episcopi* and it is possible that this is the correct form of the name, as a bishop called Cynesige signs contemporary charters, see p. 305. The Bishop of Berkshire at the time may have acted as assistant to Oda, Bishop of Ramsbury. The latter became Archbishop of Canterbury in 942, and this might account for the disappearance of Cynesige's signature in that year. If the reading of the Anglo-Saxon version is correct, it is impossible to distinguish Wynsige, Bishop of Berkshire, from the contemporary Wynsige, Bishop of Dorchester (see p. 307), unless we regard this as the former's only appearance (see Stenton, *op. cit.* p. 36, n. 1).

l. 9. *Wulfhem arcebiscop.* Wulfhelm was Bishop of Wells before he succeeded Athelm as Archbishop of Canterbury. There is a good deal of doubt with regard to the date of his appointment to either see, but it is probable that he was Bishop of Wells from 923 to 926 and Archbishop of Canterbury from 926 to 942 (see Armitage Robinson, *The Saxon Bishops of Wells,* pp. 28-40, 45).

Rodward biscop. Hrothward, Archbishop of York, signs in 928 (B. 663 f.), 929 (B. 665) and 930 (B. 667, 669). His successor Wulfstan begins to sign in 931. Hrothward does not appear in connection with any other see before his appointment to York, and the title 'bishop', here as elsewhere, may be equivalent to 'archbishop'.

l. 11. *be þyssan gemæran.* The boundaries are attached to the Latin version.

ll. 17 f. *cwæþ eall þ folc* etc. An interesting sidelight on the nature of the proceedings. It is noteworthy that neither the king nor any of his earls is said to have been present at this meeting. The only laymen mentioned are thegns.

XXIII

The register of Milton Abbey, Dorset, which contained this charter, has been either lost or destroyed. In Dugdale's time it was in the King's Remembrancer's Office, the contents of which were afterwards transferred to the Public Record Office. Birch failed to find it there, and a note in the V.C.H. *Dorset,* II, p. 58, records that it is no longer in existence.

EDITIONS. Dugdale, II, p. 349.
K. 1119 (from Dugdale).
B. 738 (from Dugdale).
The text is from Dugdale.

DATE. The date 843, given at the end of the charter, is impossible and should probably be corrected to 934. It is evident from the signatures that it cannot be later than that year or earlier than 933. Milton Abbey, Dorset, is said to have been founded by Æthelstan in memory of his brother Edwin, for whose death by drowning (Sax. Chr. 933 E) he was held, according to later writers, either directly or indirectly responsible (see Simeon of Durham, R.S. II, p. 93; William of Malmesbury, *Gesta Regum*, I, pp. 156 f.). William of Malmesbury's account (derived from *cantilenae*), which tells of the setting adrift of Edwin in an open boat as a punishment for his share in a conspiracy against Æthelstan at the time of his accession, was repeated in the lost register of the abbey, see Dugdale, II, p. 349. The authenticity of the story is discussed by Plummer, II, pp. 137 f.

It is recorded that in 1309 Milton Abbey lost all its charters and muniments in a disastrous fire, caused by lightning. Edward II thereupon appointed a commission to inquire into its claims to lands, rents etc. and in 1311 confirmed it in its possession of the gifts and privileges thereby established (Pat. Roll, 3 Edw. II, m. 32; *ibid.* 5 Edw. II, pt. 1, m. 17). It seems possible, therefore, that the present document may represent an attempt to reproduce in the speech of the time one which had been lost or badly damaged. A faulty memory (or a fragmentary original) might account, at any rate, for the corrupt form of some of the attesting signatures (see below); it is perhaps less satisfactory to explain in this way the use of phrases which are not characteristic of Æthelstan's other charters. Unfortunately no other copies or versions of pre-Conquest charters from this lost register (if any such ever existed) are extant, so that there is nothing of the kind with which to compare the present document. The possibility remains that the whole thing is a fabrication, although the grants which it records may actually and rightly have been associated with Æthelstan.

The lost register also contained a Latin version said to have been derived from an Inspeximus of Henry I (Dugdale, II, p. 350; B. 739). The differences between the two preclude the possibility that the Middle English version was directly translated from the Latin.

ll. 19 f. *kyng welding...Brytone*. For an instance of the title *brytænwalda* used by Æthelstan, see p. 48, l. 24. The Latin version has simply *rex Brittonum* which can scarcely be accepted as a genuine reading. The dates of Æthelstan's reign were probably 925 to 939 (see *E.H.R.* XXXII, 1917, pp. 517–521).

l. 20. *mid alle mine wytene* etc. Nowhere else in Æthelstan's charters does he mention, at this point, the co-operation of his councillors and bishops.

ll. 24 f. *sainte Sampsone · and sainte Branwaladre*. Relics of both these saints were bestowed upon the abbey by Æthelstan (see William of Malmesbury, *Gesta Pontificum*, R.S. pp. 186, 400). St Sampson was Bishop of Dol in Brittany about the middle of the sixth century.

St Branwalader's name occurs in a Breton liturgy of the tenth century (Haddan and Stubbs, II, p. 82), and his day is given as January 19 in two mediaeval calendars (Hampson, *Medii Aevi Kalendarium*, I, pp. 422, 435).

l. 25. *Muleburne*. Milbourne, Dorset. This estate is not mentioned by name either in D.B. or in Edward II's confirmation. In both of these its place seems to be taken by the manor of Milton itself which according to D.B. was rated at 24 hides for the payment of geld, and according to Edward II's confirmation charter consisted of 26 hides.

ll. 25 f. *mid ðan þ ðereto liþ*. There is no corresponding phrase in the Latin version.

p. 46, l. 1. *Wonlonde*, cf. D.B. *Winlande*. Woolland, Dorset.

l. 2. *atte yle ðan ye* etc. The Latin version has *apud insulam quæ dicitur la Ye, duas in mari et unam in terra, scilicet apud Ore*. It would seem as if the A.S. word *ieg* (island) had been taken as a proper name. Edward II's charter of confirmation, which recites the return made by the commission of inquiry, includes (by gift of King Æthelstan) 'at Fromemouthe which is called the Island of St Helen, 2 hides of land with wreck of sea; at Ore 1 hide of land with wreck of sea'. According to Hutchins, *History of Dorset*, 3rd ed., I, p. 538, St Helen's is the island called Green or Stony Island which lies in Poole Bay to the north of Ower. The manor of Ower is now represented by the farm of that name situated on an arm of Poole Bay.

l. 3. *Clyve*. Clyffe, a hamlet near Tincleton.

l. 4. *Liscombe*. Lyscombe, a detached part of Milton Abbas, now amalgamated with Cheselborne for civil purposes only.

Burdalueston. Burleston.

l. 5. *Cattesstoke*. This seems to be a late form of the name. In D.B. it appears simply as *Stoche*, cf. the *Stoke* of the Latin version of the charter.

Comptone. Probably Compton Abbas.

l. 6. *Holewertþe*. Holworth, a detached part of Milton Abbas, now amalgamated with Owermoigne for civil purposes.

l. 7. *seuene and sixty hyden*. The total actually amounts to 66½ hides.

ll. 7 f. *and anne were* etc. There is nothing in the Latin version about the weir and its accessories, the water at Weymouth or the three thegns in Sussex. The order in which the estates are enumerated also differs in some instances from that of the Middle English version so that the two would seem to be independent.

l. 8. *Twynham*. Christchurch Twyneham, Hampshire, see Chadwick, *Anglo-Saxon Institutions*, p. 211.

l. 10. *twelf acres to þan were*. In 1086 Edward, the sheriff of Wiltshire, held 12 acres of land in Hampshire of the Abbey of Milton (D.B. I, f. 43 b; V.C.H. Hants. I, p. 473).

ll. 11 f. *Sidemyntone*. Sydling. The Latin version has nothing corresponding to the phrase *to fosterland*. In 1086 there was land for 20 ploughs at Sydling.

l. 12. *Chelmyntone*. Chalmington, a hamlet near Cattistock.

NOTES

l. 13. *Ercecombe*, cf. D.B. *Ertacomestoche*. Edward II's confirmation charter has *Stokelonde*, i.e. Stockland, once a detached part of Dorset but now included in Devon.

to tymberlonde. There is no corresponding phrase in the Latin version. In 1086 there was a wood at *Ertacomestoche* worth 9 pounds.

l. 14. *almeslonde*. Literally 'land given as alms', cf. *in rigte clene almesse*, l. 18, rendered *in puram et perpetuam elemosinam* in the Latin version.

ll. 14 f. *and freo beo in alle ðinge · and freo custumes*. The construction seems confused and it is possible that something has been omitted. The Latin version reads ...*tota ista terra cum pertinentiis suis et libertatibus omnibus et liberis consuetudinibus*. The French loanword *custumes* and the Latin *consuetudines* correspond to the Anglo-Saxon *gerihta*, 'dues', which implied customary services as well as payments in money and in kind. Land held in frankalmoin (to use the regular post-Conquest term for land given 'in alms') involved spiritual but not secular service.

ll. 15 f. *þ is for mine saule* etc. It seems likely that *ich* should be read for *is*.

l. 20. *myn ogen ore*. This represents A.S. *ar*, cf. the *dominica terra* of the Latin version.

l. 23. *ungewemmed* etc. Rendered *illibata et immutabilis ac inpervertibilis* in the Latin version.

l. 31. *mid ðisse gewitnesse*. The names and the attesting clauses are the same in both versions. They may have been taken over from the Latin version.

l. 33. *Wolfhelmus* etc. See p. 300.

p. 48, ll. 1 f. *Atheldredus* etc. This is apparently a mistake for Theodred, Bishop of London, who signs from 926 (B. 658 f.) to 951 (B. 892). His will is preserved, see Whitelock, No. 1.

l. 2. *Cenwaldus episcopus*. Cenwald succeeded Wilfrith as Bishop of Worcester in 929. Fl. Wig. records his death in 957, but a grant of 958 (B. 1042), preserved in the *Codex Wintoniensis*) is signed both by him and by Dunstan, his successor.

l. 3. *Alfredus episcopus*. Bishop of Sherborne from 933 till 943.

l. 4. *Caynan episcopus*. Conan, Bishop of Cornwall, signs Æthelstan's charters from 931 to 937.

Egwynus episcopus. There is no record of a bishop of this name at the time. Two likely witnesses omitted from the list are Wulfhun, Bishop of Selsey (see p. 306), and Wynsige, Bishop of Dorchester (see p. 307), but neither of these is suggested by the *Egwynus* of the text.

l. 5. *Radulphus episcopus*. This seems to be a mistake for Eadulf, who was Bishop of Crediton from 909 to 934.

l. 6. *Brinstanus episcopus*. Bishop of Winchester from 931 to 934.

l. 7. *Alla episcopus*. Ælla or Ælfwine, Bishop of Lichfield. His signature is attached to a grant of Æthelflæd, Lady of the Mercians, which is wrongly dated 878 (B. 632), and continues until 937. His successor's appears in 941.

Offerdus princeps. Osferth *dux* signs from 909 (B. 620) to 934 (B. 702). He is mentioned in King Alfred's will (Harmer, p. 18) and was related in some way to the royal family. He signs a charter of Edward the Elder (B. 624) as *propinquus regis*, and appears in an earlier one (preserved in the *Codex Wintoniensis*) with the erroneous title *frater regis* (B. 611).

l. 8. *Alfledus minister.* This is probably for Alfred, a name which is found among the *ministri* throughout Æthelstan's reign.

l. 9. *Athelmundus minister.* This name also appears regularly among the witnesses of Æthelstan's charters.

XXIV

The MS. from which this text was derived, British Museum, Cotton Otho B. 9, was destroyed by fire in 1731. It was a copy of the gospels given by King Æthelstan to St Cuthbert's.

EDITION. Wanley, *Catalogue of Anglo-Saxon MSS.* p. 238, in Hickes, *Thesaurus*, II.

DATE. Æthelstan on his way north to invade Scotland in 934 visited the shrine of St Cuthbert, then at Chester-le-Street, and bestowed rich gifts upon it (see Simeon of Durham, I, pp. 75 f.). A list of these survives (see B. 685) and includes lands, vestments, sacred vessels, ornaments and books. One of the last of these, a MS. of Bede's *Life of St Cuthbert*, is still in existence, see p. 480.

l. 14. *þas boc.* The gospel book appears also in his list of gifts as *hunc textum euuangeliorum.* Two others are mentioned as well, *duos evangeliorum textus auro et argento ornatos.* These, apparently, have not survived.

l. 17. *ne nane þara geofena.* Simeon of Durham, *loc. cit.*, records that Æthelstan's gifts to St Cuthbert were still preserved at Durham in his time.

XXV

MS. British Museum, Additional MS. 15350, f. 93 (or 95 by the new numbering). See p. 274.

EDITIONS. K. 1110.
B. 706.

The Anglo-Saxon version of this grant is preceded by a Latin one (B. 705) to which are attached the boundaries of Enford, see Grundy, *Archaeological Journal*, LXXVI, p. 228. The two versions correspond fairly closely, but neither seems to be a direct translation from the other. The forms of the place-names are older in the Anglo-Saxon version.

ll. 23 f. *Ongolsaxna cyning 7 brytænwalda* etc. The Latin version has *rex et rector totius hujus Brittanniæ insule.* For a list of eight kings to whom the title *bryten-* (*bret-*)*walda* was applied see Sax. Chr. s.a. 827, and for a discussion of its meaning see Stenton, 'The Supremacy of the Mercian Kings', *E.H.R.* XXXIII, 1918, pp. 433 ff.

l. 25. *sc̄e TRinitatan.* For a reference to Winchester Cathedral as St Peter's see p. 28, l. 7. Its dedication to St Peter and St Paul (the most usual one in early charters) appears on p. 40, ll. 7 f., while the Holy Trinity is named along with these two saints on pp. 68, ll. 16 f.; 92, ll. 19 f. It is referred to, as here, under the name of the Holy Trinity alone on p. 52, ll. 29 f.

l. 27. *ENEDforda.* Enford, Wiltshire.

Ceolbaldinctuna. Chilbolton, Hampshire. This estate was held by the Bishop of Winchester in 1086. Its assessment had been reduced from 10 hides to 5 hides (D.B. I, f. 41; V.C.H. *Hants.* I, p. 464).

p. 50, l. 1. *Æscmeresweorðæ.* Ashmansworth, Hampshire. This estate formed part of Whitchurch, which is said to have been granted for the support of the cathedral community by Earl Hemele, then appropriated by the bishops of Winchester and finally restored to the community by Edward the Elder in 909, when a new charter was drawn up to replace the old one which had been lost (B. 624). It would seem from the final injunction which follows the boundaries in the copy of this charter preserved in the *Codex Wintoniensis* that Ashmansworth was actually on lease at the time, probably to the king (*Friðestan 7 þa hiwan...bebeodad...þæt ðæt land...sie agifen ofer Eadwardes cingæs dæg umbæsæcæn to Winteceastræ þam hiwon into heore beoddærn*), and if so, this would account for its inclusion in the present grant. It is possible, on the other hand, that Æthelstan's grant is in the nature of an addition to the original holding, but the fact that no boundaries are given suggests that this is not the case.

ll. 14 f. *And se ðæt sæ bisceop* etc. The sentence corresponding to this one in the Latin version comes immediately after the announcement of the grant and before the names of the estates and runs as follows: *et quicunque episcopus qui tunc superfuerit illiusque æcclesiæ regimen teneat eos de suis propriis episcopalibus villis pleniter pascat sicut ab antiquis temporibus illi honorabili familiæ a venerabilibus patribus constitutum fuit.*

l. 23. *Huwal Vndercyning.* Howel the Good, King of Dyved, is one of the kings named as subject to Æthelstan in the Saxon Chronicle, 926 D. He frequently attended Æthelstan's councils and attests charters from 928 (B. 663) to 949 (B. 883). He is famous as a legislator and to him was due the codification of the Welsh laws[1].

Tidhelm bisceop. Tidhelm, Bishop of Hereford, signs from 931 to 937, see below.

l. 24. *Wulfhelm Arcebisceop.* See p. 300.

Cynæsige bisceop. A bishop of this name signs from 931 (B. 674) to 942 (B. 771). Cynesige, Bishop of Berkshire, appears in B. 687, see p. 300. In B. 872 (a Crowland charter dated 948) Cynesige, Bishop of Lichfield, makes his appearance and continues to sign up to 963. He may be identical with the earlier bishop (? of Berkshire) but this is not certain.

[1] See 'Hywel Dda, 928–1928' (*Aberystwyth Studies*, vol. x).

NOTES

l. 25. *Wulfhelm bisceop.* Fl. Wig. 1, p. 238, in his list of the bishops of Hereford names Wulfhelm after Tidhelm. The two names, however, occur together, as here, in another charter of the same year (B. 702) and also in one of 937 (B. 716) where Wulfhelm II, Bishop of Wells, makes his first appearance. A bishop named Wulfhelm witnesses charters of the years 930, 931 (B. 667, 670), 933 (B. 695 f.) and possibly 934 (B. 703), where Tidhelm does not sign, while the latter is found in charters of 931, 932 (B. 677, 689) and possibly 934 (B. 700 f.) where Wulfhelm's name is lacking. Is it possible that for some reason they held office together? Only one bishop called Wulfhelm signs in 938 and 939. Ælfric, Bishop of Hereford, appears for the first time in 940 (B. 746 etc.).

l. 26. *Wulfstan Arcebisceop.* Wulfstan I, Archbishop of York from 931 to 956.

l. 27. *Alfwald ealdorman.* His signature is regularly found from 925 to 938.

l. 28. *þeodred bisceop.* Bishop of London, see p. 303.

Æþelstan miÑ. This is apparently a mistake (common to both versions) as Odda almost invariably signs at the head of the *ministri* in Æthelstan's charters, and Æthelstan seems to have attained the rank of *dux* by 932 (see p. 299). He was Earl of East Anglia and was known as Æthelstan Half-king. According to the *Historia Ramesiensis*, R.S. c. 3, he ended his life, in the reign of Edgar, as a monk at Glastonbury.

l. 29. *Wulfhun bisceop.* Bishop of Selsey. He signs from 931 (B. 675) to 940 (B. 753, 758).

ll. 29 ff. *ODDA miÑ.* etc. The list attached to the Latin version omits the first Wulfric and ends with Eadric. Ælfhere, one of the two named Wulfgar, Æthelmund, Æthelwold and one of the two named Æthelstan were later promoted to earldoms, the first two by Æthelstan, the last three by Edmund in 940, the first year of his reign.

l. 30. *Ælfheah bisceop.* There were two contemporary bishops of this name, both of whom sign the present grant, namely Ælfheah, Bishop of Wells, and Ælfheah, Bishop of Winchester. The former succeeded Wulfhelm I and probably held office from 926 to 937 or 938 (see Armitage Robinson, *The Saxon Bishops of Wells*, p. 45). The latter, frequently distinguished as Ælfheah the Bald, succeeded Beornstan in 933 or 934 and died in 951. The two appear together in B. 699, 707 and 714, the last being a grant of 937.

l. 31. *ODA bisceop.* Oda was Bishop of Ramsbury and succeeded Wulfhelm as Archbishop of Canterbury. His signature appears for the first time (with the title Bishop of Sherborne) in a doubtful charter of 927 (B. 660), where Ælfheah, Bishop of Wells, is described as Bishop of Winchester. He was consecrated by Wulfhelm, Archbishop of Canterbury, so that his appointment must be dated 926 at the earliest.

l. 32. *Ælfred bisceop.* Two bishops of the name sign the present grant, also B. 702 f. of the same date. One was Bishop of Sherborne (see p. 303), the other may have been Bishop of Elmham, which was restored sometime in the tenth century, but, if so, he apparently did not at first have Suffolk in his diocese, as Theodred, Bishop of London, speaks in his will of 'my bishopric at Hoxne' (see Whitelock, pp. 4, 102).

l. 34. *Æðelgar bisceop.* Bishop of Crediton from 934 to 953.

l. 35. *Burhric bisceop.* Burhric became Bishop of Rochester about 933 (his predecessor signs for the last time on 26 January of that year). His signature appears for the last time in 946 (B. 813).

l. 36. *Cenwald bisceop.* Bishop of Worcester, see p. 303.

l. 37. *Ælla bisceop.* Bishop of Lichfield, see p. 303.

l. 38. *Wunsige bisceop.* Wynsige, Bishop of Dorchester, signs from 925 to 937. His successor, Oscytel, appears in the charters in 951.

XXVI

MSS. (*a*) British Museum, Cotton Charters, VIII, 16. This is a contemporary parchment containing the grant of Ham, Wiltshire, to Wulfgar by Æthelstan (see below) to which is attached on a separate parchment a copy of Wulfgar's will.

(*b*) British Museum, Additional MS. 15350, f. 83. See p. 274.

FACSIMILE. Of (*a*), Bond, *Facsimiles of Ancient Charters in the British Museum*, Part III, No. 3.

EDITIONS. K. 353, from (*a*).
T. p. 495, from (*a*).
B. 678, from (*a*).
The text is from (*a*).

DATE. King Æthelstan's grant of Ham to Wulfgar is dated 12 November 931. His will may have been drawn up either at the same time or within the next few years. No title is applied to him, and there is reason to believe that by 939 at the latest he had been promoted to an earldom, see below.

p. 52, l. 1. *Wulfgar.* The signature *Wulfgar minister* occurs for the first time in 928 (B. 663) and from 931 to 938 two men of this name and title frequently appear as witnesses. The signature *Wulfgar dux* is found in two charters dated 931 (B. 670 f.) which probably belong to the time of Edmund, in one dated 933 (B. 694) which is certainly later in date, and in three suspicious Devonshire grants (B. 721, 724, 726) of which the first is dated 937 and the remaining two 670, probably for 938 at the earliest (see Chadwick, *Anglo-Saxon Institutions*, p. 183, n. 3). From 939 to 948, however, *Wulfgar dux* is a regular witness and the other Wulfgar likewise continues to sign with the title *minister* until 946. It is probable that the testator in the present instance was the former, see below.

Collingaburnan. Collingbourne, Wiltshire. A copy of a charter which records the grant of this estate to Wulfgar is preserved in the *Liber Monasterii de Hyda* (see B. 635). It is attributed to Edward the Elder and dated 921, but from the style and the witnesses it is obvious that it belongs to the time of Æthelstan and should probably be dated 931. The estate consisted of 10 hides and was granted on condition that Wulfgar should yearly supply 10 poor people with food and drink at the feast of All Saints. Collingbourne, rated at 50 hides, was one of the estates granted by Edward the Elder to the New Minster in 903 (B. 602) and was still in its possession in 1086 (D.B. 1, f. 67 *b*). There is no mention of Wulfgar's estate as a separate unit.

l. 6. *þam niwan hierede*. The New Minster at Winchester was built by Edward the Elder and consecrated in 903 (Sax. Chr. F). The earlier foundation was thereafter distinguished as the Old Minster.

l. 8. *Ingepenne*. Inkpen, Berkshire.

l. 9. *to þam tune*, cf. the use of 'farm-town' in Scotland at the present day for a farmhouse and its out-buildings.

l. 10. *Cynetanbyrig*. Kintbury, Berkshire. Nothing further is known of the community there.

ll. 13 f. *for Wulfrices 7 for Wulfheres*. Presumably, from what precedes, these are the names of Wulfgar's father and grandfather. There seems to be no means of tracing his father, but it is more than likely that his grandfather was the Wulfhere *princeps* who received grants of land in Wiltshire in 863 and 869 (see below and p. 275). This fact supports the suggestion that Wulfgar was the earl of the name, since earldoms were frequently hereditary at the time, and the latter almost certainly held office south of the Thames (see Chadwick, *Anglo-Saxon Institutions*, p. 187). If this identification is correct, there seems every reason for believing that the district under Wulfhere's control, and subsequently under Wulfgar's, included Wiltshire, since both are associated with estates there. Wulfgar's father does not seem to have held office as earl, but this may be accounted for by Wulfhere's final disaffection.

l. 15. *Cræft*. Not identified.

l. 16. *Wynsige 7 Ælfsige*. A certain Wynsige *minister* attests Æthelstan's charters in 931, 932 and 934 (B. 677, 689, 702). The name Ælfsige is too common for identification.

l. 17. *Denforda*. Denford, now a detached part of the parish of Kintbury, was held by William de Ow in 1086 in succession to a tenant of King Edward named *Alward* (D.B. 1, f. 61; V.C.H. Berks. 1, p. 352).

Æþelstane. The name is again too common for identification.

l. 18. *Cynestane*. There seems to be no other reference to anyone of the name at the time.

l. 19. *Butermere*. Buttermere, Wiltshire. This estate was granted to Wulfhere *princeps* by Æthelred I, King of Wessex, in 863 (B. 508), hence the identification of Wulfgar's grandfather (see above). It consisted of 6 hides along with *Æscmere*. In 1086 Buttermere was held in three different portions by three different tenants (see D.B. 1, ff. 70, 72, 74 *b*).

Byrhtsige. Brihtsige is not found elsewhere in contemporary charters.

ll. 19 f. *Ceolstanes sunum.* Unidentified.

l. 21. *Æscmere.* This name has disappeared but is represented by its offshoot, Ashmansworth in Hampshire (see p. 305). Grundy, *Archaeological Journal*, LXXVI, p. 184, suggests that the *Æscmere* land is now included in the parishes of Linkenholt and Vernham Dean which lie between Buttermere and Ashmansworth on the Hampshire side of the border.

l. 26. *Hamme.* Ham, Wiltshire. Wulfgar's estates are all on the borders of Wiltshire and Berkshire. This estate was held by the Bishop of Winchester in 1086 (D.B. I, f. 65 *b*) and was *de victu monachorum*. It was at Winchester Cathedral that the parchment containing Æthelstan's grant and Wulfgar's will was preserved.

ll. 29 f. *to sce Trinitate.* See p. 305.

XXVII

MS. *Liber Monasterii de Hyda*, f. 19 *b*. This MS., which was prepared in the fourteenth century, is in the possession of the Earl of Macclesfield at Shirburn Castle, Watlington, Oxfordshire. Each Anglo-Saxon document is followed by translations into Middle English and Latin.

EDITIONS. Edwards, *Liber Monasterii de Hyda*, R.S. p. 132, with a modern English translation on p. 342.
B. 649; M.E. version 650; Latin version 651.
Birch, *Liber Vitæ etc. of Hyde Abbey*, p. 221.

DATE. Not earlier than 932, when Alfred received the estate of Stoneham, and not later than 939, if King Æthelstan's death is rightly attributed to that year. The signature of Ælfwine, Bishop of Lichfield, disappears from the charters in 937, but the date of his death is not recorded and his successor does not sign until 941.

p. 54, l. 1. *Ælfreod ðein.* From 928 onwards Æthelstan's charters are generally witnessed by one man of this name and title (Latin *minister*). Two sign an earlier grant of 926 (B. 659) and Edward the Elder's charters are witnessed by as many as three (B. 623, 627) and in one case four men of the name (B. 624).

Stanham. North Stoneham, Hampshire. This estate of 12 hides was granted to Alfred by Æthelstan in 932 (B. 692), upon condition that he and his successors should daily supply 120 poor people with food and drink until the Day of Judgment. In 1086 it was still in the possession of the New Minster. Its assessment is given as 8 hides with land for 11 ploughs (D.B. I, f. 43; V.C.H. *Hants.* I, p. 471). An estate of 20 hides at Chiseldon in Wiltshire was granted to Alfred by the New Minster sometime in the reign of Æthelstan in return for 80 mancuses of gold and a yearly payment of 80 shillings on the anniversary of Edward the Elder's death (B. 648). Compensation for the non-payment of this yearly sum on the appointed day was fixed at 60 pence on the first occasion and 30 shillings on the second with confiscation of the estate on the third, unless satisfactory terms were made with the community. In 1086 this estate also was held by the New Minster (D.B. I, f. 67 b).

l. 9. *Ælfyn biscop*. Ælfwine, Bishop of Lichfield, see above.

l. 10. *Ælfryc ðeyn*. Ælfric, Eadric, Odda and Wihtgar are regular witnesses of Æthelstan's charters.

XXVIII

MS. *Liber Monasterii de Hyda*, f. 21. See p. 309.

EDITIONS. Edwards, *Liber Monasterii de Hyda*, R.S. p. 146. B. 804; M.E. version 805; Latin version 806. Birch, *Liber Vitæ etc. of Hyde Abbey*, p. 232.

DATE. Between 946, when Edred succeeded his brother Edmund as king, and about 950 (see under Bishop Ælfric below).

l. 11. *Basyngum*. Basing, near Basingstoke. Basing was bequeathed by King Edred in his will to his mother Eadgifu (see Harmer, p. 35). It is entered in D.B. as held by Hugh de Port and previously in the hands of a tenant of King Edward. Its assessment, which was 11 hides in 1066, had been reduced to 6½ hides in 1086, with land for 10 ploughs (D.B. I, f. 45; V.C.H. *Hants.* I, p. 479). The New Minster was still in possession of 2 hides at Lickpit (see below) with Hugh de Port as its tenant (D.B. I, f. 43; V.C.H. *Hants.* I, p. 471).

l. 12. *cining Edmund*. A copy of King Edmund's grant, dated 30 March 945, is preserved in the *Liber Monasterii de Hyda* (see B. 803). It describes the estate and its appurtenances as *mansionem monasticam ad Basyngum quæ nostro dicitur famine cynniges hors croht et duos cassatos cum pertinente silva in Acrycge in loco qui dicitur Licepyt suis cum certissimis territoriis pascuisve ab antiquis temporibus pertinentibus ad Beomnitfelda et Middesellum....Hujus agelli* XII. *jugera juxta locum sunt qui dicitur Totdesford et* XXIIII. *ubi dicitur Wealagærstune*. *Acrycge* and *Licepyt* are now represented by Oakridge Farm and Lickpit Farm respectively. *Beomnitfelda* appears later as 'Benetfield' in Basingstoke, while *Totdesford* may be Totford in Northington, although it seems to be rather far distant from Basing for this identification to be certain. The phrase *cynniges hors croht* is apparently a corruption of *cyniges hors croft* and the name 'King's Horse Croft' is applied at the present day to a mounded meadow close to the old ford of Pyot's Hill (see V.C.H. *Hants.* IV, p. 123, n. 117). *Wealagærstune* is represented by Woodgarston Farm in Wootton St Lawrence (see Grundy, *Archaeological Journal*, LXXVIII, p. 101).

ll. 13 f. *æc to fremdon 7 mæge ut to seallan*. The M.E. version has *for the helpynge of my sowle; they evyr for to have hem, and nevyr to do hem awey*. It is possible that the Anglo-Saxon is corrupt, as a stipula-

NOTES 311

tion that it should never be alienated would be more usual in a grant of land to a religious foundation than a clause which allowed for its bestowal upon 'strangers or kinsmen'.

l. 15. *Æthelgar biscop*. Bishop of Crediton, see p. 307.

l. 16. *Ælfric biscop*. There were two contemporary bishops of this name—Ælfric, Bishop of Hereford, whose first signature appears in 940 and his last in 951, and Ælfric, Bishop of Ramsbury, who succeeded Oda on his translation to Canterbury in 942 and signs until 949.

XXIX

MS. *Liber Monasterii de Hyda*, f. 23 b. See p. 309.

EDITIONS. Edwards, *Liber Monasterii de Hyda*, R.S. p. 165, with a modern English translation on p. 350.
B. 825; M.E. version 826; Latin version 827.

DATE. After 947, when Leckford was granted to Eadulf by King Edred (B. 824), and before 955, the year of King Edred's death.

l. 17. *of pyses stowan* etc. The text of this grant is corrupt and suspicious especially in the use of *stowan* for the *mansas* of Edred's charter. The M.E. version has *of the ten dwellyn placys at Legford*; the Latin version *de decem mansis apud Legford*.

ll. 18 ff. *fifan stowan on Leahtford* etc. The terms of Edred's grant were that five of the ten *mansas* at Leckford should be bequeathed by Eadulf to the Nunnery at Winchester and the remaining five to the monastery where he was buried.

These two estates, the latter afterwards distinguished as Leckford Abbots and the former as Leckford Abbess, were held by the New Minster and the Nunnery respectively in 1086. The assessment of each had been reduced, the one to 2½ hides, the other to 1 hide (see D.B. I, ff. 42, 43 b; V.C.H. Hants. I, pp. 469, 474). Each had land for 3 ploughs.

ll. 22 f. *7 seo wæron gewitenesse* etc. The reading here is obviously corrupt. No witnesses are named and they are not mentioned either in the M.E. translation or in the Latin one.

XXX

MS. The Society of Antiquaries of London, MS. 60, f. 51. See p. 271.

EDITIONS. K. 433 (without the boundaries).
B. 909.

DATE. King Edmund was killed on 26 May 946 and Edred succeeded him as king in the same year. The year 955, therefore, falls partly in the ninth and partly in the tenth year of Edred's reign.

312 NOTES

p. 56, l. 1. *En onomatis cyrion doxa.* The scribe does not seem to have been a very good Greek scholar and the phrase as it stands is corrupt and ungrammatical.

ll. 1 f. *ge for Gode ge for werolde.* This phrase is regularly employed to express the antithesis between the spiritual and the secular, see Whitelock, p. 238, for references to its occurrence in the wills; Robertson, p. 393, for references to its occurrence in the laws.

ll. 6 f. *þet mæg to soðe seggan* etc. It is noteworthy that Edred's grant of Haddon to Ælfsige *miles* (see following note) opens in a similar way; *Eadredus rex Anglorum quos vult honorifice larga manu locupletat. Hoc potest veraciter miles iste Ælfsige nunc cum cæteris intimare.*

l. 7. *Ælfsige Hunlafing.* It is probable, as Miss Whitelock suggests (p. 130), that this Ælfsige is identical with the Ælfsige, Wulfstan's father, who received Ailsworth in Northamptonshire in 948 (see pp. 323 f.), and that it was also he who received Haddon, Huntingdonshire, in 951 (B. 893) and Kettering in 956 (B. 943). The name Hunlaf appears twice among the witnesses of King Æthelstan's charters, namely in B. 665 (dated 929) and B. 689 (dated 932).

l. 8. *Æpelwoldingtune.* Alwalton, Huntingdonshire. In 1086 the Abbot of Peterborough held this estate, which was assessed at 5 hides with land for 9 ploughs (D.B. 1, f. 205; V.C.H. *Hunts.* 1, p. 346).

l. 9. *ferdnoðes.* This is perhaps a local word. It is not recorded elsewhere but there are not many texts from this quarter.

l. 10. *geþencend londagende.* The adj. *geþencend* would seem to correspond to the Latin *prudens* and the meaning is perhaps 'a landowner who has a sense of his obligations'. It is possible that some words have been omitted between *ferdnoðes* and *geþencend* as the text contains characteristic Mercian forms and has probably been translated from a Latin original. I am indebted to Professor Chadwick for the suggested explanation of the phrase. The three estates, Ailsworth, Haddon and Kettering, mentioned above, were granted subject only to the usual obligations of military service and the repair of fortifications and bridges.

saulsceat. See p. 286.

l. 16. *Oda ærcabiscup.* Oda, who had been Bishop of Ramsbury (see p. 306), became Archbishop of Canterbury in 942 and died in 958 (Fl. Wig.). He was the uncle of Oswald, Bishop of Worcester and Archbishop of York (see p. 319), and a good deal of information about him is given in the *Vita S. Oswaldi*[1], pp. 401–410, 412, etc. His life was written by Eadmer, see Wharton, *Anglia Sacra*, II, pp. xxxiii, 78.

Wulstan þsul. Wulfstan I, Archbishop of York, see p. 306.

Ælfsie biscup. Ælfsige I was Bishop of Winchester from 951 to 958 when he succeeded Oda as Archbishop of Canterbury. He was frozen to death in the Alps in 959 on his way to Rome to receive his pallium (Fl. Wig.). His will is extant (Whitelock, No. IV).

[1] Ed. Raine, *Historians of the Church of York*, R.S., I.

NOTES

Wulfsie pontifex. Bishop of Sherborne from 943 to 958.

l. 17. *Oscetel antistes.* Bishop of Dorchester. His first signature appears in 951 (B. 890 f.) and he succeeded Wulfstan as Archbishop of York in 956, see p. 341.

Cynsige biscup. Bishop of Lichfield, see p. 305.

Osulf p̄sul. Bishop of Ramsbury. He signs for the first time in 950 (B. 887) and for the last in 970 (B. 1268 f.), the year of his death (Fl. Wig.).

Koeuuald monachus. Cenwald's signature occurs in two other charters of Edred (B. 883 and 911, dated 949 and 955 respectively) and in one of Edwy (B. 937, dated 956).

l. 18. *Wulfelm pont⁹.* Bishop of Wells. His signature appears for the first time in a charter dated 21 December 937 (B. 716) and is not found after 955.

Berhtsige biscup. Brihtsige's signature is found in 949 (B. 880, a Kentish charter), 951 (B. 892, a charter relating to Berkshire) and in one other of 955 (B. 911, relating to Derbyshire). His see is unknown but may have been Rochester, see Searle, *Anglo-Saxon Bishops*, p. 20.

Berhthelm p̄sul. Bishop of London. He signs for the first time in 950 (B. 887) and for the last in 959 (B. 1051).

Ælfuuold ant⁹. Bishop of Crediton from 953 to 972.

l. 19. *Ędgefu euax.* Eadgifu is described in the same way in B. 911, 1346 and appears as *Eadgeofu felix* in B. 883. All of these are charters of Edred. She was the third wife of Edward the Elder and the mother of Edmund and Edred. Her signature is generally attached to her sons' charters. King Edred in his will (Harmer, No. XXI) leaves her a number of estates, including all those he held by title-deed in Kent, Surrey and Sussex. Her property was confiscated in Edwy's reign but restored in Edgar's (see Kurmer, No. XXIII).

Eadwi æpeling · 7 Eadgar. Edmund's two sons who in turn succeeded Edred, their uncle.

Morcant regl. Probably Morgan the Aged, King of Glamorgan, whose signature is attached to about a dozen charters from 931 (B. 675) to 956 (B. 937)[1]. He is mentioned in the *Book of Llandaff* (ed. Evans and Rhys, 1893, p. 240) as a contemporary of Edgar, and an account is given (p. 248) of the settlement by Edgar in his favour of a dispute with Howel the Good (see B. 1350).

Owen. Probably the son of Morgan the Aged who became one of the joint kings of Glamorgan in 983 (see *Book of Llandaff*, p. 252). The Owen who is mentioned in the Saxon Chronicle, 926 D, as one of the kings subdued by Æthelstan was probably the father of Morgan, and it is presumably his name in the form *Eugenius* which is attached to a charter of 931 (B. 675).

l. 20. *Syferð 7 Iacob.* Siferth may be identical with the king of the name who committed suicide in 962 (Sax. Chr. A) and was buried at Wimborne. Nothing further is known of him (see Plummer, II, p. 154).

[1] See J. E. Lloyd, *A History of Wales to the Edwardian Conquest*, I, p. 353, where the Welsh signatories to A.S. charters are tabulated.

NOTES

Jacob or Iago was one of the sons of Idwal Voel and ruled in North Wales. He is mentioned several times in the *Annales Cambriae*. The two names are attached also to a very doubtful charter of Edgar (B. 1185) which is signed by seven dependent kings.

Eadmund dux. Edmund, who signs as *dux* from 949 (B. 877) to 963 (B. 1125), may have been Earl of Devon (see Chadwick, *Anglo-Saxon Institutions*, p. 176).

Epelmund. Æthelmund signs as *dux* from 940 (see p. 306) to 965 (B. 1165). It would seem that his earldom was somewhere north of the Thames as he signs the charters issued by Edgar as King of Mercia in 958 (B. 1036, 1040, 1043 f.).

l. 22. *Earninga stræte.* Ermine Street, see Pl.N. *Beds. and Hunts.* pp. 2 ff.

l. 23. *Ceastertuninga.* Chesterton, *ibid.* p. 181.

l. 25. *goldege.* This name was applied to a small island in the Nen, and the name *goldiford* was formerly given to a neighbouring ford, *ibid.* p. 195.

ll. 25 f. *ofertuninga gemęre.* The Orton boundary, *ibid.* pp. 193 f.

l. 26. *be þen Æfden.* I have taken this as the plural form of *heafod*, 'a headland'.

ll. 26 f. *to fægran broce.* Probably the unnamed brook which still forms part of the eastern boundary of Alwalton.

XXXI

MS. British Museum, Cotton Claudius B. VI, f. 54. See p. 299.

EDITIONS. *Historia Monasterii de Abingdon*, R.S. I, p. 218.
    K. 1201.
    T. p. 191.
    B. 972.

DATE. This transaction cannot be earlier than 956, when Brihthelm became Bishop of Wells, or later than 957, when the division of the kingdom between Edwy and Edgar took place, see below.

p. 58, l. 8. *Byrhtelm Biscop.* Brihthelm is described as bishop elect in one of Edwy's grants dated 956 (B. 986). In 959 he was made Archbishop of Canterbury (Fl. Wig.; cf. B. 1045) but deposed in the same year. He returned to Wells which he held till his death in 973 (Fl. Wig.).

Apeluuold abb. Abbot of Abingdon and afterwards Bishop of Winchester, see p. 323.

l. 10. *Cenintune.* Kennington in Sunningwell, Berkshire.

ll. 11 f. *Crydanbrigce.* Creedy Bridge, Devon, see Pl.N. *Devon*, II, p. 405.

l. 14. *Eadwiges leaf cyninges.* Edwy succeeded Edred in 955. From 957 till his death in 959 he was king south of the Thames only, while Edgar ruled north of the Thames.

NOTES 315

l. 15. *Ælfgifu þæs cininges wif.* Her signature does not occur elsewhere. In 958 she was divorced from the king by Archbishop Oda on the ground that they were too closely related (Sax. Chr. D). For a will which may possibly be hers see Whitelock, No. VIII.

ll. 15 f. *Æþelgifu þæs cyninges wifes modur.* The testatrix Ælfgifu (see above), who may be identical with King Edwy's divorced wife, leaves an estate to Bishop Æthelwold and prays him to intercede for her mother and herself. Unfortunately her mother's name is not mentioned.

l. 16. *Ælfsige biscop.* Bishop of Winchester, see p. 312.

Osulf biscop. Bishop of Ramsbury, see p. 313.

l. 17. *Coenwald biscop.* Bishop of Worcester, see p. 303.

Byrhtnoð ealdorman. Brihtnoth, Earl of Essex, the hero of the poem on the Battle of Maldon, where he died, fighting against the Danes, in 991. He appears as *princeps* in a charter dated 29 November 956 (B. 966), and may have been Earl of Huntingdon before he became Earl of Essex. The inclusion of his name and Bishop Cenwald's shows that this document was drawn up before the division of the kingdom in 957.

ll. 17 f. *Ælfheah cyninges discðen.* It is probable that this witness was afterwards Earl of Hampshire, see pp. 338 f.

l. 18. *Eadric his brodur.* See p. 339.

XXXII

MS. British Museum, Stowe Charters, No. 27, the bottom portion of a chirograph.

FACSIMILE. *Ordnance Survey Facsimiles*, Part III, No. 28.

EDITIONS. Lye, *Dictionarium Saxonico et Gothico Latinum*, II, 1772, App. II, No. 3.
K. 477, from Lye.
T. p. 509.
B. 1010.

DATE. This bequest is dated 958 in a late Canterbury list of benefactors (Dugdale, I, p. 96). It cannot be later, if Archbishop Oda's death is rightly attributed to that year (see Stubbs, *Memorials of St Dunstan*, R.S. pp. xciv f.).

l. 19. *Æðelwyrdæs.* A brief entry in the Canterbury MS. Lambeth 1212 records the grant of an estate at *Mulatun* (identified as Milton-next-Sittingbourne) by a certain *Ageluuord minister regis* in 959 (B. 1049). It is possible, but by no means certain, that he is identical with the donor of Ickham. I have not been able to find any other reference to a man of the name in Kent at the time.

Odan ærcebisscopæs. See p. 312.

l. 21. *Geocham.* Ickham near Canterbury. In 1086 it was one of the estates of the monks held by the archbishop. Its assessment is given as 4 *solins* with land for 12 ploughs (D.B. I, f. 5; V.C.H. *Kent*, III, p. 217).

316 NOTES

l. 23. *Eadric.* Eadric was perhaps Æthelwyrd's son. The endorsement shows that he survived Æthelwyrd and so inherited the estate.

ll. 24 f. *æne dæg feorme* etc. For similar lists of provisions to be given as food-rents to religious houses see Harmer, pp. 1, 5.

p. 60, l. 1. *læuw*, see B.T. p. 635, s.v. *leow*; *Suppl.* p. 614. A later form of the will is contained in the Canterbury Registers A, f. 151 *b* (see B. 1011) and E (formerly C. v), f. 9 *b*. In both of these the reading is *ane reperes liap* (not *anne wepere shap* as given by Birch) which shows that the original was not understood.

to beðe. Toller suggests that *beðe* here may represent *bæðe*, 'bath' (see B.T., *Suppl.* p. 62, s.v. *bæþ*, 1). Confusion of *æ* and *e* is characteristic of Kentish texts and there are numerous examples in the present document of the substitution of the former for the latter. On the other hand the use of *e* for *æ* is of much less frequent occurrence (cf. *wes*, l. 16 and *hebbe*, l. 27 with *ærceb., ðæs, æt, dæg, ðæt, ælce, gelæst, mæsse, hæfð*) and I am not certain that it can be taken for granted here. There is, besides, no parallel for any such payment 'for the bath' and it would be difficult to understand its purpose. I am unable, however, to suggest any explanation of the phrase. It is retained unaltered in the M.E. version in both registers.

l. 2. *ælces wites wyrðe*, i.e. the grant carries with it the right of private jurisdiction.

l. 3. *hiowan gesæce*, i.e. for sanctuary.

l. 8. *unætnessa gebidan*. An unusual periphrasis for 'die'.

l. 10. *ða ðe him · land fram com.* This suggests that Æthelwyrd had inherited Ickham from some previous holders (perhaps his parents), but there is no record of any earlier transaction in connection with the estate, and the fullness of the details given here suggests that the arrangement made was a new one. In that case the reference must be simply to those who had leased him the estate.

ll. 11 ff. *Byrhtere · mæsse · p̃re* etc. These witnesses represent the members of the community at Christchurch.

l. 16. *Eadelm · abbod æt sc̃e Agustine.* No abbot of this name is mentioned by Thorne in his *Chronica de rebus gestis abbatum S. Aug. Cant.* (see Twysden, *Historiæ Anglicanæ Scriptores Decem*, 11) and he is not included in the list given in the V.C.H. *Kent*, 11, pp. 131 f. His signature occurs in two other instances, however, namely B. 880 (a Kentish charter dated 949) and B. 890 (dated 951), so that his existence seems vouched for.

ll. 16 ff. *Byrhtsige · diāc* etc. These witnesses represent the community at St Augustine's.

l. 20. ...*stan · cynges ðægen.* It is possible that Leofstan is meant as a *minister* of that name signs two Kentish charters of Edgar's reign, namely B. 562 (endorsement) and B. 1212 (dated 968).

l. 21. *ða .iii⁰. geferscipas.* The later version in both registers mentions by name only Archbishop Oda and the priest Brihthere then continues *and þo þri yuershipes binne burȝ an bute þet is al se hird a*

NOTES

Cristescheriche and seynt Austynes · and at seynt Gregories and manie opre yhodede and liauuede of binne burʒ and bute (Register A, cf. B. 1011). This explanation of the three *geferscipas* cannot be accepted, as the foundation of the Priory of St Gregory at Canterbury is generally attributed to Lanfranc, and it is apparent from the context that Christchurch and St Augustine's are not meant to be included in the description. A Kentish charter dated 968 (B. 1212) also includes among its witnesses *se hioræd to Cristes ciricean* 7 *se hioræd to Sancte Agustine* 7 *ða preo geferscipas innanburhwara* 7 *utanburhwara* 7 *micle gemettan*. The *innanburhwara* 7 *utanburhwara* are obviously the representatives of the lathe of Canterbury (the *Boruuar Lest* of D.B., see Chadwick, *Anglo-Saxon Institutions*, p. 250) distinguished as city members and country members respectively. I cannot understand what is meant by the *micle mættan* (or *micle gemettan* of B. 1212) and am not certain whether they formed one of the three associations or were a separate body. B.T., *Suppl*. p. 372, s.v. *gemetta* gives the meaning 'one that eats with another, a guest'.

ll. 25 f. *to gerisenum*. The same phrase occurs in the will of Ælfwold II, Bishop of Crediton, see Napier and Stevenson, *Crawford Charters*, p. 23, l. 9.

XXXIII

MS. British Museum, Additional MS. 15350, f. 54 (or 56 by the new numbering). See p. 274.

EDITIONS. K. 1231.
B. 1078.

DATE. A charter of King Edgar (B. 1077) whereby he grants an estate at Kilmeston to his thegn Athulf, with the leave of the bishop and the community, precedes the present one in the *Codex Wintoniensis* and is dated 961. It would seem that originally they were written on the same parchment, see below.

p. 62, l. 1. *Byrhtelm bisceop*. Brihthelm was Bishop of Winchester from 960 to 963.

l. 2. *Cenelmestune*. Kilmeston, Hampshire. The amount of land is given as 10 hides in Edgar's charter to which the boundaries are attached, see Grundy, *Archaeological Journal*, LXXXIII, p. 160. In 1086 the estate was divided into two parts (each assessed at 5 hides), one of which was held by the bishop and the other by a tenant of his (D.B. I, f. 40; V.C.H. *Hants*. I, pp. 459 f.).

l. 4. *hær bufan*. Presumably at the end of Edgar's charter.

ll. 4 f. *ægperes hiredes* etc. It was not until Æthelwold became Bishop of Winchester in 963 that monks were established at the Old and New Minsters. The community of nuns was the Nunnery of St Mary, generally referred to simply as the *Nunnena mynster*.

l. 6. *þæs cericlican weorces.* In King Edgar's charter it is stipulated that Athulf should render yearly .I. *cyricsceat et* .v. *scindlas* 7 .I. *bord omni anno*, i.e. '1 measure of church dues and 5 shingles and 1 board'. For *scindel* see B.T., *Suppl.* p. 697, s.v., N.E.D. s.v. *shindle*, 'a local variant of shingle, a wooden roofing tile'. No other instance of the word is recorded in B.T., and no such stipulation is found elsewhere. The supply of roofing tiles and boards demanded seems remarkably small from an estate of 10 hides.

þæs woruldweorces, cf. Edgar's charter which reads more explicitly *excepto communi labore · expeditione pontis arcisve coedificatione*.

Following the survey of Kilmeston in Edgar's charter comes the additional clause 7 .VIII. *mæd æceras undær wanexan dúne · þa gebyriad to Cenelmestune · 7 se haga on worte* (for *porte*) *bynnan suþ ealla þæ to þam lande gebyred*, i.e. 8 acres of meadow at the foot of a certain hill, and a messuage in the town within the south wall are also attached to the estate. This in turn is followed by the boundaries of a wood south of Millbarrow from which the shingles and boards due yearly to the church may have been obtained.

XXXIV

MS. British Museum, Cotton Tiberius A. XIII, f. 59. See p. 259.
EDITIONS. Hearne, *Hemingi Chartularium* etc., I, p. 125.
K. 494.
B. 1086.

l. 13. *Æpelmodestreow.* This grant is one of a group of eight in the MS. which relate to estates in Gloucestershire at Bishop's Stoke, *Uptun*, *Æpelmodestreow*, Itchington, and Compton. It seems probable, therefore, that *Uptun* and *Æpelmodestreow* represent respectively Upton and Elmestree in Tetbury. Unfortunately no boundaries are given for either and they are not mentioned again in the cartulary.

Æþelme 7 *Ælfstane* 7 *Wulfrice.* Marginal notes such as this, where the name of the original grantee is followed by one or more not mentioned in the body of the charter, are commonly found in the section of the cartulary which contains the copies of Oswald's grants. The additional names are obviously those of the successive inheritors of the estates in question, and it seems likely that they were officially recorded somewhere—perhaps on the back of the chirographs retained at Worcester. Hemming, in his section on the lands unjustly taken from the church, mentions the custom of making notes on the charters themselves with regard to the history of the estates to which they referred (Hearne, I, p. 249), and it is possible that notes of the kind were used in the present instance. Very frequently, likewise, in the case of the charters under discussion a clause is found near the end of the type *A wæs se forma man* 7 *B is se oðer*, repeating the names mentioned in the heading. Generally such a clause occurs before the signatures, but occasionally it is more awkwardly placed and is found, for example,

NOTES 319

between the sentences *scriptum est hæc carta* etc. and *sit autem terra ista libera* etc. (Hearne, I, p. 149), after the first signature *Oswald arcebisceop* (ibid. p. 151) and after the statement *Her is seo hondseten* (ibid. p. 164). In two instances charters which are found in the cartulary both with headings and incorporated clauses are also printed by Smith but without either (cf. Hearne, I, pp. 147, 153 and Smith, *Beda*, pp. 773 f., 778). In the former case the incorporated clause reads *Osulf wæs se forma man 7 Æpelstan munuc is se oðer*, while the marginal heading mentions a third name *Ufede* in addition to these two. In the latter case there seems to be a curious discrepancy between the heading which reads *Wulfringtun · Eadwige · Wulfgeofu 7 heora dohtor* and the incorporated clause which runs *Eadwig wæs se forma man 7 Wulfgyuu wæs se oðer nu hæft Æpelsige hit to þan þe þu wylle*. According to the text of the charter the estate was to pass from the survivor to their child if they had one, but the name *Æpelsige* can scarcely be that of the daughter mentioned in the heading. The explanation which suggests itself is that the two clauses represent notes or endorsements made at different dates, and that the daughter, although at one time recognised as heir, was subsequently replaced by the unknown Æthelsige. For a declaration made either at the time of a grant or later and added at the end of a charter see p. 66.

l. 14. *Oswald*. Oswald, who became Bishop of Worcester in 961 and Archbishop of York in 972, held both sees until his death in 992. He was one of the promoters of monastic reform in Edgar's reign, and along with Æthelwine, Earl of East Anglia, founded the monastery of Ramsey. His merits are extolled by his biographers (see *Historians of the Church of York*, ed. Raine, R.S. I, pp. 399–475; II, pp. 1–59) and seem to have been generally recognised.

l. 15. *Ælferes*. Ælfhere became Earl of Mercia early in 956. He signs two charters of that year as *minister*, one as *miles*, two as *comes* and all the rest, including one dated 13 February (B. 919), as *dux*. His antimonastic policy, which he carried into effect after the death of Edgar, made him very unpopular with later monastic chroniclers. He died in 983.

l. 16. *pridde hid*. Apparently *healf* has been omitted by mistake, cf. l. 23.

ll. 19 f. '*anum*' *yrfeweardum*. A mistake seems to have been made in the numeral, cf. the marginal heading and l. 24. The majority of Oswald's grants are made for three lives without restriction in the choice of heirs. Interesting exceptions occur, however. An estate leased to a certain Gardulf for life was to pass first to his wife, if she survived him, whether she married again or not (with the proviso that her second husband must be *episcopali dignitati subiectus*), and then to their son, if they had one, and if not, to any children of the second marriage (K. 637). The marginal heading names Gardulf and Leofflæd only. More complicated arrangements still are found in the grant of an estate to a certain Osulf (see p. 96).

NOTES

The practice of granting church lands for three lives led to difficulties, as might have been expected, when the time came for the church to reassert its claim. Many were lost, according to Hemming (Hearne, I, p. 259), not only through the refusal of powerful men (or men with powerful friends) to give them up, but also through the negligence of the church in claiming its rights at the proper time.

ll. 21 f. *omni regi*. This reading is frequently found in Oswald's grants.

l. 22. *ęcclesiastici censi*, i.e. A.S. *ciricsceat*.

p. 64, l. 3. *Wulfric prb*. Wulfric signs at the head of the priests from 962 until 977 when the first place is taken by Wynsige (see p. 360). His last signature occurs in 983 (K. 637).

Eadgar diac̄. Edgar signs both as cleric and deacon in 962, and in 963 both as deacon and priest. His signature continues till the last of Oswald's dated charters, issued in 991.

Cyneþen cl. Cynethegn signs in 962 and 963 but not in 966 or 967. His name appears again in 969 (it is missing, however, in seven charters of that year) and from that time onwards he generally signs at the head of the *clerici*. He appears for the last time in a grant of 996 (K. 695).

l. 4. *Ælfric prb*. Ælfric signs charters of 962 both as deacon and priest. By 966 he is no longer found.

Wulfhun · cl. Wulfhun signs from 962 till 984.

Byrhstan cl. Brihtstan signs from 962 to 977.

l. 5. *Ælfred cl*. Ælfred's signature continues till 969.

XXXV

MS. British Museum, Cotton Tiberius A. XIII, f. 63. See p. 259.

EDITIONS. Hearne, *Hemingi Chartularium* etc., I, p. 133.
K. 508.
B. 1106.

l. 6. *Coddanhrycce*. Cotheridge, Worcestershire. Hemming records that this estate was afterwards granted by a wealthy reeve named Earnwig to his brother Spiritus, who enjoyed the favour of the Danish kings, Harold and Hardacnut, but was eventually banished from England. Cotheridge was then seized by Richard Scrob and in this way was lost by the church of Worcester (Hearne, I, p. 254). In 1086 it was part of the manor of Grimley and Richard is said to have held it 'by such service as the Bishop willed' (D.B. I, f. 172 b; V.C.H. *Worc*. I, p. 289). There is a reference to the banishment of Spiritus in the survey of Shropshire (D.B. I, f. 252 b; V.C.H. I, p. 313), from which it appears that he was exiled in the time of King Edward.

l. 7. *Osuuald*. See p. 319.

l. 9. *ÆLFERE*. See p. 319.

l. 14. *immunem*. The meaning is probably 'without any liabilities incurred during their tenure'.

NOTES 321

l. 17. *his circsceat*. When paid in kind church dues generally took the form of grain, hence the association of the ending *-sceat* with 'seed' which ultimately led to the substitution by legal antiquaries of the familiar compound 'church seed' for the original term. In Cnut's Proclamation of 1027, cap. 16, the English *ciricsceat* has been rendered *primitiae seminum* by the Latin translator.

l. 19. *þa landgemæru*. For the boundaries of Cotheridge, worked out in detail, see Grundy, *The Saxon Charters of Worcestershire*, pp. 61 f. They are repeated in the cartulary (Hearne, II, p. 350), followed by another and more detailed set running apparently in the opposite direction. It is evident from a reference to 'Wulfgar's boundary' that this second set is later in date than the first, as the adjoining estate of *Cloptun* (see below) was leased to Wulfgar by Oswald in 985 (K. 649). The boundaries of *Cloptun* run by 'Ælfric's boundary.'

l. 21. *ætincweg*. The name survives in Atchen Hill.

l. 22. *bricgeburnan fordes*. This ford is mentioned also in the boundaries of *Cloptun*, a neighbouring estate no longer distinguished by that name (see Pl.N. *Worc.* p. 91). Grundy identifies the Bridge Bourne with the brook which forms part of the eastern boundary of the parish, and places the ford where the road from Worcester to Cotheridge crosses the brook.

l. 24. *rixuc*. The name may possibly survive in the modern Rushwick, see Pl.N. *Worc.* p. xliii.

hihtes gehæg. Grundy takes *Hiht* as a proper name (otherwise unrecorded). Is it possible that there is any connection between this landmark and the *hina hege* of the second set of boundaries?

l. 25. *in þa stræte*. The Worcester-Hereford road.

bregnesford. The name survives in Bransford.

l. 27. *testibus*. For the priests Wulfric and Ælfric, the deacon Edgar and the clerics Alfred, Wulfhun, Cynethegn and Brihtstan see the preceding page.

l. 28. *Cynestan clr*. Cynestan signs from 962 to 983.

Æþelstan cirward. Æthelstan signs another lease of 963 with this title (B. 1105). From 966 onwards he signs as priest. In 984 another priest of the same name makes his appearance, and from that time onwards both are regular witnesses of Oswald's grants. K. 695 (dated 996) is signed by one of them.

l. 30. *Wynstan clr*. Wynstan signs from 962 to 978.

Æþelwold clr. Æthelwold's signature is attached to one other grant dated 963 (B. 1105) and is regularly found from 977 to 985.

l. 31. *Eadwine clr*. Edwin signs from 962 to 980.

l. 32. *Wulfeah clr*. Wulfheah signs as cleric from 962 to 969, and as priest from 977 to 981.

l. 33. *Cynesige clr*. Cynesige signs in 962, 963 and 969.

Wulfgar clr. Wulfgar is a regular witness of Oswald's grants. His signature appears for the last time in 996 (K. 695).

p. 66, ll. 1 ff. *Ic Ælfric* etc. This declaration may have been made at the time of the lease or later and may represent an original endorsement.

l. 4. *þa spere hand*, as distinct from 'the spindle side', see Harmer, p. 19.

XXXVI

MS. British Museum, Cotton Tiberius A. XIII, f. 88. See p. 259.
EDITIONS. Hearne, *Hemingi Chartularium* etc., I, p. 189.
K. 511; boundaries, III, p. 463.
B. 1110.

DATE. This grant must be rather later in the year than the preceding one, as Edgar who signs there as deacon signs here as priest.

l. 5. *Ælfheres*. See p. 319.
l. 7. *O.Swald*. See p. 319.
l. 8. *þorndune*. Thorne in Inkberrow, see Pl.N. *Worc.* p. 329. An additional grant of 1 hide at Inkberrow was made to Æthelstan by Oswald in 977 (K. 613) and in 984 a grant of 4 hides at Inkberrow was made to a certain Wulfflæd (K. 644). It is impossible, through lack of boundaries, to be certain whether her holding corresponded to his, but there seems to be a likelihood that this was the case. No additional names are mentioned in connection with the grants to Æthelstan, and it is possible, therefore, that he died without appointing any heirs. The estate on Wulfflæd's death was to revert to the church of Worcester.

ll. 10 f. *þ he* etc. A verb seems to have been omitted.

l. 14. *þa landgemæra*. For the boundaries see Grundy, *The Saxon Charters of Worcestershire*, pp. 157 f.

amman. The name *amman* is found elsewhere associated with streams, see Grundy, *op. cit.* p. 157, n. 2. He identifies the brook of the present survey with the large brook which runs into the Piddle Brook near Great Nobury Farm.

l. 15. *oredeshamme*. The first element is apparently a proper name, see Pl.N. *Worc.* p. 398. For diminutives in *-ede* see Redin, *Uncompounded Personal Names in Old English*, pp. 161 f.

ll. 16 f. *incsetena gemære*. See Pl.N. *Worc.* p. 324.

l. 17. *þa stræt*. This is identified by Grundy as the former Roman road from Worcester to Alcester.

l. 24. *testibus*. For Wulfric, Ælfric, Edgar, Alfred, Brihtstan, Wulfhun and Cynethegn see p. 320; for Cynestan, Wulfgar, Edwin, Cynesige, Æthelstan, Wynstan and Wulfheah see p. 321.

XXXVII

MS. The Society of Antiquaries of London, MS. 60, f. 54 *b*. See p. 271.
EDITIONS. K. 591.
T. p. 229.
B. 1131.

NOTES 323

DATE. Between 963, when Æthelwold became Bishop of Winchester and also received an estate of 24 hides at Washington from King Edgar (B. 1125), and 975, the year of King Edgar's death.

p. 68, l. 1. *Apelwold bisceop.* Æthelwold, who had been Abbot of Abingdon, was Bishop of Winchester from 963 to 984. He was one of the leaders of the movement for monastic reform and replaced the priests of the Old and New Minsters by monks. He likewise restored Ely and Peterborough and filled them with monks. He was associated with Dunstan and Oswald in the reform movement.

l. 2. *Wulstan Uccea.* He appears as Wulfstan *Ucca* in the will of his relatives Brihtric and Ælfswith, who bequeathed him the estate of Walkhampstead (now Godstone) in Surrey and a short sword worth three pounds (Whitelock, pp. 26, 28).

l. 4. *Hwessingatune.* Washington, Sussex, see B. 1297 (the foundation charter of Thorney Abbey, dated 973), in which this exchange is also recorded. At an earlier date (946–7) Washington was included among the estates bequeathed by Earl Æthelwold to his brother Eadric (Harmer, p. 33) and 20 hides of land there were granted (or confirmed) to the latter by King Edred in 947 (B. 834). This is its next appearance in the charters.

Jaceslea. Yaxley, Huntingdonshire. A charter of Edwy dated 956 records the grant of 10 hides at Yaxley and 5 at Farcet to a certain Ælfwine described as *ministro ac militi* (B. 940). There is nothing to show when or how Wulfstan obtained his holding there.

Edgar's charter to Thorney (see above) is given in two forms in the register of the abbey known as the Red Book of Thorney (C.U.L., Additional MS. 3020). According to the first of these (f. 2; cf. B. 1297, which has been printed from a late copy) two transactions were involved in the bishop's acquisition of Yaxley, namely first the exchange with Wulfstan, which is briefly recorded here, and secondly the purchase from Ælfric *cild* (see p. 330) of the remainder of the estate. The passage in question runs: *Viginti quoque mansas que Geakeslea nominantur...... mutuauit a Wulstano primo cum .xxiiii. mansis in Wassingatune in Suðsexon · rursumque cum ille totum hoc in aliud transferre moliretur · eps alteram comparationem innouans cum .lx. purissimi libris argenti ab Ælfrico supranominato* (i.e. Ælfric *cild*) · *predictas .xxv. mansas æt twam Geakeslean 7 æt Farresheafde comparauit.* The account given in the second version of the charter (f. 3 *b*) is somewhat different. There is no mention of the second transaction and the amount of land acquired from Wulfstan, by exchange for Washington, is said to have been 17 hides at Yaxley, which were given to Thorney, and 8 hides at Farcet, which were given to Peterborough (see p. 329).

In 1086 the Abbot of Thorney had 15 hides at Yaxley, assessed to the geld. There was land for 20 ploughs (D.B. i, f. 204 *b*; V.C.H. *Hunts.* i, p. 345).

l. 5. *Ægeleswurðe.* Ailsworth, Northamptonshire. This estate was granted to Ælfsige by King Edred in 948 (B. 871), so that the forfeiture must have taken place sometime before then. In 1086 the Abbey of Peterborough held an estate of 6 hides there with land for 12 ploughs (D.B. I, f. 221; V.C.H. *Northants.* I, p. 313).

l. 6. *þornige.* Thorney Abbey, Cambridgeshire, which originally consisted of a community of anchorites (Dugdale, II, p. 571), was refounded by Bishop Æthelwold at the time of the monastic revival in Edgar's reign.

Buruh. See p. 271.

l. 8. *hi drifon serne stacan.* The Penitential of Egbert, Archbishop of York, prescribes a period of fasting for such an offence (see Thorpe, *Ancient Laws and Institutes of England,* II, p. 208) and this is repeated in the 'Canons enacted under King Edgar' (*ibid.* p. 274). The present document supplies the only recorded instance of 'pin-sticking magic' in actual practice in the Anglo-Saxon period.

Ælsie Wulfstanes feder. See p. 312.

l. 9. *hire inclifan.* The word is used also of a lion's den, see B.T. p. 590, s.v. *incleofa; Suppl.* p. 591, s.v. *incleof*[u, -e].

XXXVIII

MS. British Museum, Additional MS. 15350, f. 8 (or 10 by the new numbering). See p. 274.

EDITION. B. 1148.

DATE. Between 963, when Æthelwold became Bishop of Winchester, and 975, the year of King Edgar's death.

The Anglo-Saxon version of this charter is preceded by a Latin one (B. 1147) which ends with these words: *Hujus quoque libertatis renovationem · patria lingua hoc est Anglica scribere jussi · ne quis secularium de ignorantia se excusare possit · quia Latinam sermocinationem forte non didicit · Neque eam quamvis coram se legeretur intelligere novit.* For another instance of the kind, see p. 345. The Latin version is drawn up in regular charter style but no witnesses are named. The Anglo-Saxon version omits the preamble and uses narrative style throughout.

l. 14. *Aþelwold.* See p. 323.

l. 16. *Ciltancumbes.* Chilcomb, Hampshire.

l. 19. *Cynegils.* King of Wessex from 611 to 643.

Cynewald. For *Cynewalh* (*Cenwalh*), who succeeded his father as King of Wessex and built the Old Minster at Winchester (Sax. Chr. 643 A, 641 E, 648 F).

ll. 20 f. *ealswa hit lið* etc. A list of the estates included in the manor of Chilcomb is entered on f. 4 of the *Codex Wintoniensis* immediately after a writ of Æthelred the Unready confirming the freedom of the manor. It is given as B. 1160. They lay mainly in the valley of the Itchen, both above and below Winchester, and taken in order from Kilmeston (5 hides) to Bishopstoke (5 hides) included Tichborne

NOTES

(25 hides), Ovington and Avington (5 hides each), Easton (4 hides), Twyford (20 hides), Broombridge and Otterbourne (5 hides). To these were added the two outlying estates of Chilbolton near Andover (20 hides) and Nursling near Southampton (5 hides), making a total of 99 hides altogether.

l. 22. *Egcbirt.* King of Wessex from 802 to 839.

Apulf. A copy of the charter attributed to Æthelwulf is given in the *Codex Wintoniensis* (B. 493). It claims to be the first to put the freedom of Chilcomb into writing but cannot be accepted as genuine.

Ælfred. Alfred's charter has not been preserved although it is said to have been extant in Æthelred's time and sent to him for confirmation (see K. 642).

l. 23. *Eadweard.* Two copies of Edward's charter—one an independent parchment, the other in the *Codex Wintoniensis* (B. 620 f.)—are extant, also one of Æthelstan which is not mentioned here (B. 713).

p. 70, l. 1. *for ane hide werode.* Literally 'defended, i.e. discharged the obligations upon, at the rate of 1 hide'. In 1086 Chilcomb retained its pre-Conquest assessment of 1 hide with land for 68 ploughs (D.B. 1, f. 41; V.C.H. *Hants.* 1, p. 463).

l. 5. *portmen.* The Latin version reads less explicitly, *nec alicui secularium pro munere quolibet eam dare presumat.*

ll. 10 f. *þa modigan preostas* etc. The expulsion of the priests from the Old Minster is entered in the Saxon Chronicle, s.a. 964 A. A full account is given in Eadmer's *Vita S. Dunstani* (see *Memorials of St Dunstan*, R.S. pp. 211 ff.) and in Ælfric's *Vita S. Æthelwoldi* (see *Historia Monasterii de Abingdon*, R.S. II, p. 260). According to both of these the priests were replaced by monks brought from Abingdon. B. 1159 (a charter relating to Chilcomb and the other estates which supplied food for the monks) describes at length the vices of the ejected priests and extols the virtues of the monks.

l. 12. *æfter sc̄e Benedictes tæcinge.* The Rule of St Benedict was translated by Æthelwold for use in the reformed monasteries.

ll. 21 f. *on eallan halgan bocan.* The Latin version has *in veteri et novo testamento* and adds immediately afterwards a clause which is not represented in the Anglo-Saxon version, *sitque cœlum ferreum super capud ejus · et tellus énea sub pedibus ejus.*

XXXIX

MS. The Society of Antiquaries of London, MS. 60, f. 39 b. See p. 271.
EDITIONS. Dugdale, I, p. 382.
B. 1128.

DATE. The story of the restoration of Peterborough by Æthelwold is entered under the year 963 in the Sax. Chr. E. It tells there how the earlier foundation had been completely destroyed by the Danes (cf. 870 E) and how the bishop found on the site nothing but 'old walls and wild woods'.

326 NOTES

p. 72, l. 1. *Adeluuold bisceop.* See p. 323.

l. 2. *Medeshamstede.* See p. 271.

l. 7. *syluren pipe.* See p. 476.

l. 9. *subumbrale.* This form seems to be derived from the Latin *subhumerale*. It occurs also in the *Canons enacted under King Edgar*, cap. 33 in MS. Bodley Junius 121, where the version in MS. C.C.C., Cambridge 201 reads *subuculam* (see Thorpe, *Ancient Laws and Institutes of England*, II, p. 250). The *subucula* (see N.E.D. s.v.) was a tunic worn beneath the alb serving as a kind of cassock. For a reference to the *superhumerale*, worn above the alb, see p. 194, l. 19.

pistolclapas, cf. *pistelroccas*, p. 226, l. 26.

ll. 9 f. *corporale.* See p. 476.

l. 10. *pælles.* A.S. *pæll*, derived from Latin *pallium*, is used of a robe, cloak or covering of costly material. The merchant in Ælfric's *Colloquy* brought *pællas* from abroad. For other references see B.T. p. 771, s.v.

l. 11. *blace rẹgl cẹsternisce.* The meaning is uncertain as the word *cẹsternisce* is not found elsewhere, see B.T., *Suppl.* p. 120, s.v. *ceasternisc*.

l. 14. *weofodsceatas.* These were the cloths which covered the front and sides of the altar, see p. 477.

l. 15. *antwentig is para boca.* This is the earliest extant list of Peterborough books. Another is preserved in MS. Bodley, 163 (a copy of Bede's *Historia Ecclesiastica*) of the early twelfth century (see M. R. James, *Lists of MSS. formerly in Peterborough Abbey Library*, Suppl. to the *Bibliographical Society's Transactions*, No. 5, pp. 27 f.), while a late fourteenth-century catalogue entitled the *Matricularium Librarie Monasterii Burgi Sancti Petri* is preserved in the Chapter Library at Peterborough (see James, *op. cit.* pp. 30–81).

For other book-lists see pp. 228, 250.

l. 16. *Liber miraculorum.* Also entered (as No. 64) in the early twelfth-century list. Dr James suggests that either the Seven Wonders of the World or the Dialogues of Gregory may be meant.

l. 17. *Expositio Hebreorum nominum.* Two works of the kind are entered in the *Matricularium*, namely No. 161, *Exposicio Hebraicorum Nominum sec. Alphabetum*, and No. 289, *Interpretacio Hebraicorum Nominum*.

Prouisio futurarum rerum. Dr James suggests that probably the *Pronosticon futuri saeculi* of Julian, Bishop of Toledo, is meant, a work which appears as No. 40 in the twelfth-century catalogue.

l. 18. *Vita sci Felicis metrice.* Dr James identifies this as the work of Paulinus of Nola (d. 431). It appears as No. 38 in the twelfth-century list and was seen by Leland at Peterborough shortly before the dissolution of the monasteries (see James, *op. cit.* p. 29, where Leland's list is given). Paulinus was Bishop of Nola from about 409 and thirteen poems and the fragments of a fourteenth which he composed in honour of St Felix have been preserved.

NOTES

l. 19. *Vita Eustachii*. This appears as No. 60 in the twelfth-century list and as No. 11 in Leland's.

Descidia Parisiace polis. Dr James identifies this with Abbo of St Germain's poem on the siege of Paris by the Normans.

Medicinalis. One of the entries (No. 96) in the *Matricularium* refers to an *Ars Medicinalis*.

l. 20. *De duodecim abusiuis*. The *Matricularium* records several works of this type. The nearest in title is No. 52, *Tract. Cipriani de xii abusiuis seculi*. In every other case the form used is *abusionibus*, cf. Nos. 229 f., 300, 316.

Sermo super quosdam psalmos, cf. No. 55 in the twelfth-century catalogue, *Expositio super L^{ta} psalmos*.

ll. 20 f. *Commentum cantica canticorum*. Entry No. 116 in the *Matricularium* includes *Moralis exp. super Cant. Cant. Rithmice composita*.

l. 21. *De eucharistia*. Entry No. 289 in the *Matricularium* includes *Tract. de Eukaristia et aliis festiuitatibus anni*.

ll. 21 f. *Commentum Martiani*. Martianus Capella was the author of a widely used work entitled *De nuptiis philologiae et Mercurii*.

l. 22. *Alchimi · Auiti*. Dr James points out that this must represent not two titles but one. The total number of books is therefore twenty, not twenty-one.

Alcimus Avitus was Bishop of Vienne and died in 518. He was the author of an epic written in hexameters which dealt with the history of the world from the Creation to the Flood and Exodus. His prose writings consist of sermons and letters.

Liber differentiarum. This appears as No. 37 in the twelfth-century list. It was one of the most popular works of Isidore of Seville (d. 636), whose *Synonyma* is entered earlier in the list.

ll. 22 f. *Cilicius Ciprianus*. The correction to 'Caecilius' follows Dr James. The twelfth-century list includes (No. 56) *Epistolaris Cipriani*; the *Matricularium* (No. 52) *Septuaginta quinque Epp. Cipriani*. Cyprian, Bishop of Carthage, was a widely famed saint and martyr of the third century A.D.

l. 23. *Liber bestiarum*. The *Matricularium* records several books of the kind, e.g. No. 55, *Tract. de naturis bestiarum et volucrum*, No. 330, *Quedam summa de naturis animalium*, cf. also Nos. 70, 270.

Dr James notes that the number of Peterborough books known to exist at the present day is very small. It includes the Laud MS. (E) of the Saxon Chronicle, now in the Bodleian Library, Oxford.

l. 25. *his dryhtene*. The word *drihten* by this time was used in prose only with reference to God.

l. 26. *berewican*, i.e. outlying estates attached to the central manor. They are given in a charter attributed to Edgar (B. 1280) as Dogsthorpe, Eye and Paston, cf. Sax. Chr. 963 E, which mentions Eastfield in addition.

l. 27. *Anlafestun*. Unidentified.

l. 28. *Farresheafde*. Farcet, Huntingdonshire. For other inventories of the kind see pp. 248, 254.

weorcwurðe men. The meaning may be 'men liable for service'. For the only other recorded instance of the word see p. 248, l. 19.

l. 29. *Witlesmere`h'alfendel.* The boundaries of the half of Whittlesey Mere acquired by Bishop Æthelwold are given in Edgar's charter (see p. 327). They begin on the north *ubi primum intratur Merelade de amne Nen* and run *ad Kingesdelf* on the east (now represented by King's Delph Gate, see Pl.N. *Hunts.* pp. 185 f. It is noteworthy that the cutting of this channel is associated with King Cnut). They then continue south to *Alduuines baruue,* which is located *contra medietatem viæ ubbemerelade* (the lode connecting Ugg Mere with Whittlesey Mere, see *ibid.* p. 216), and end in the west *ubi aqua deopbece finitur ad terram.* To this was added in the time of Cnut another part purchased by Ælfsige, Abbot of Peterborough, from Thored *optimate regis* (K. 733). The description of the boundaries (which follow the same course) is more detailed and among the additional names which it supplies are Trundle Mere on the east (Pl.N. *Hunts.* p. 202) and *Scælfemære* on the south, represented by the modern Chalderbeach Farm which must have stood on its eastern shore (*ibid.* p. 188).

In 1086 the Abbot of Ramsey had one boat in Whittlesey Mere, the Abbot of Peterborough one, and the Abbot of Thorney two, one of which, along with two fisheries, two fishermen and one virgate of land, was held of him by the Abbot of Peterborough. The fisheries and meres of the Abbot of Peterborough in Huntingdonshire are valued at four pounds altogether in D.B. (see V.C.H. *Hunts.* I, p. 346).

ll. 29 f. *Vndelum...Keteiringan.* Oundle and Kettering, Northamptonshire.

p. 74, l. 1. *æt Wellan,* cf. *Wyllan,* p. 100, l. 22. According to Ekwall, *English River Names,* p. 447, the name of what is now the Old Croft River (on which stand Welney, Outwell and Upwell) must once have been *Well.* It seems likely that the reference here is to some place in the neighbourhood.

l. 4. *þam twam undredum ute o`n' þam nesse* etc. Later known as the double hundred of Nassaborough, see Pl.N. *Northants.* pp. 223 f. The ness or promontory of higher land juts out into the fens between the Welland and the Nene.

l. 5. *of six tunan.* Does this mean that the manors paid in groups of six, or is the reference to six particular manors? Details of the amount paid by six different manors are actually given in the part that follows, see below.

l. 6. *tioþunge æt ælcere sylh,* cf. VIII Æthelred, 7 (repeated I Cnut, 8, 2), where tithes are defined as the produce of every tenth acre traversed by the plough.

l. 7. *þreues.* 'Thrave' is a Scandinavian loanword in use chiefly in Scotland and the north of England, see N.E.D. It is defined as two 'stooks' of corn generally containing 12 sheaves each but varying in different localities.

l. 8. *þonne letan þa tioþunge.* The word *letan* seems unintelligible. Something has perhaps been omitted.

of þan .XXIIII. *tunan*, i.e. presumably the manors in the double hundred of Nassaborough. Maxey (two estates), Ashton (two estates), Nunton (now represented by Nunton Lodge, see Pl.N. *Northants.* p. 239) and Pilsgate, of which details follow, all lie within it. Are they the six manors mentioned in the preceding paragraph?

ll. 11 f. .v. *georde sed*, i.e., in this case, 5 quarter-acres, see Maitland, *Domesday Book and Beyond*, p. 384. The same word is used of a quarter-hide (or yardland) but it is generally clear from the context which of the two is meant.

ll. 15 f. .XIIII. *giorde sed* · 7 .III. *roda sed*. Both terms denote the same quantity of land, namely a quarter of an acre consisting of a strip 40 rods, poles or perches in length and 1 rod, pole or perch in breadth, see Maitland, *op. cit.* p. 373.

l. 17. *þ erfgewrit æt Geaceslea*. This inventory should be compared with the fragmentary entry in a Bury St Edmunds MS., see p. 248.

l. 19. *fal'd'repere*. See B.T., *Suppl.* p. 204, s.v. *faldhriper*, 'a beast kept in a fold (?)'. The word occurs also in the fragment from Bury St Edmunds, see above, but is not recorded elsewhere.

l. 20. *þa smean*. For the compounds *smeamete* (delicacy) and *smealicran* (Latin *exquisitiores*) see B.T. p. 887. The sense of *smea* in the present instance would seem to be 'titbit' or something of the kind.

l. 21. *egþwirf*. W. H. Stevenson suggested that this might mean 'part of the tackle of a harrow (A.S. *egeþe*) or a beast (*weorf*) allotted for harrowing', see *Transactions of the Philological Society*, 1895–1898, p. 530. The former seems the more likely.

l. 23. *winterstellas*. See Napier, 'Contributions to Old English Lexicography' in *Transactions of the Philological Society*, 1903–6, p. 351. *fedelsswin*, 'a fattened pig', *ibid.* p. 343.

l. 24. *Ætheluuine aldorman*. Æthelwine, Earl of East Anglia, was a friend of Bishop Oswald (with whom he founded the monastery of Ramsey) and a supporter of the monastic movement of Edgar's reign. He was the son of Æthelstan Half-king (see p. 306) and succeeded his brother Æthelwold in office. He signs for the first time as *dux* in 962 (B. 1083) and died in 992.

Ealdulf biscop. The reading 'bishop' is probably a mistake for 'abbot'. Ealdulf was appointed abbot of the restored monastery of Peterborough by Æthelwold and held office there until he succeeded Oswald as Bishop of Worcester in 992. If the reading 'bishop' is correct, the transaction must have taken place in 992 between the death of Oswald (29 February) and that of his friend Earl Æthelwine which followed soon after (see Raine, *Historians of the Church of York*, R.S. I, pp. 474 f.).

l. 25. *Iacesle*. Yaxley, Huntingdonshire, see p. 323. Yaxley and Farcet, which were acquired by Bishop Æthelwold, were bestowed upon Thorney and Peterborough respectively. Yaxley is entered in D.B. as the property of Thorney Abbey and there is nothing in its earlier or later history to associate it with Peterborough. It would

NOTES

seem, therefore, as if only Farcet were meant to be included in the description given here of the payment *for þan lande into Burch.* There is no record of any such transaction elsewhere.

l. 26. *feste`r'men,* cf. Icel. *festu-maðr,* 'a bail, surety'. The form in use in Scandinavian England points to an original compound with *festar* (the plural of *festr*) as the first element, cf. *festarpenningr,* 'a pledge, bail'.

Frana. The preponderance of Scandinavian names in the lists of sureties which begin here and continue in the following document is very striking.

l. 27. *Æthelsige·þes ealdormannes eam.* He appears also as the witness of a transaction recorded in the *Historia Ramesiensis,* R.S. p. 75. He was presumably the brother-in-law of Æthelstan Half-king.

XL

MS. The Society of Antiquaries of London, MS. 60, f. 47. See p. 271.

EDITION. B. 1130.

DATE. The transactions recorded here must fall at various dates between 963 at the earliest and 992 at the latest (see following notes)[1].

l. 29. *Osferð swade beard.* It seems possible that the MS. reading *swade* is a mistake for *spade* as the runic *w* is frequently confused with *þ*. The nickname 'spade beard' is so easily understood, however, that there seems to be no reason for such a mistake.

ll. 29 f. *Adeluuolde biscē.* The transactions in which Bishop Æthelwold is mentioned cannot be later than 984, the year of his death.

l. 30. *þane feste,* cf. Icel. *festa,* 'a bail, pledge'. The corresponding native word is *wedd* which is used in the last paragraph of the document, see p. 82, l. 27. It would seem as if something tangible—perhaps money—were meant.

l. 31. *Wyrmingtune.* For the identification of the Northamptonshire place-names see Pl.N. *Northants.* (English Place-Name Society, Vol. x), for those of Huntingdonshire see Pl.N. *Hunts.* (*ibid.* Vol. III).

p. 76, l. 1. *Finnesthorpe.* Unidentified. The same personal name is found in Fineshade (i.e. *Finnes heafod*), see Pl.N. *Northants.* pp. 164 f.

ll. 3 f. *Oswið æt Æthelingtune.* The personal name should probably be corrected to *Oswig,* cf. p. 82, ll. 2, 16.

l. 8. *Ælfrice cylde.* The transaction recorded here must be earlier than 983 when Ælfric became Earl of Mercia, see p. 369.

l. 14. *borhhand.* The English equivalent of *festerman.*

l. 18. *Elfric ealdorman.* The transaction recorded here must belong to Ælfric's period of office, 983–985.

l. 19. *Leobrantestune.* Unidentified.

on ealles heres gemote. The use of the word *here* is a reminder that the

[1] They are discussed by Vinogradoff, *The Transfer of Land in Old English Law,* Collected Papers, I, pp. 149 ff.

NOTES

Scandinavian settlement was that of a population organised on a military basis, see Stenton, *The Danes in England*, pp. 5 f.

l. 20. *clenes lande's'*, see B.T., *Suppl.* s.v. *clæne*, I (2), 'free from hurtful growth'. The meaning is more likely 'clean' in the sense of 'free from burdens or obligations incurred by the previous owner'. The sale, in other words, is a sound one. According to the *Liber Eliensis*, II, c. 26, no sureties (*vades*) were required for the purchase of land, if the transaction were carried out at Cambridge, Norwich, Thetford or Ipswich. A case in point is quoted of the purchase of an estate by Brihtnoth, Abbot of Ely, at Cambridge *coram tota civitate*.

l. 29. *eal wepentac*. The reference is still, apparently, to land at Maxey or in the same neighbourhood. It is noteworthy that Nassaborough is the only hundred in Northamptonshire to which the name 'wapentake' is sometimes applied (see Pl.N. p. xxvi). In D.B. it is applied also to Witchley Hundred (see V.C.H. *Northants*. I, p. 304), which is now part of Rutland.

p. 78, l. 5. *an hide buton anes oxangang*. For other instances of the term 'oxgang' in its English form see No. LXXXIV. In its Latinised form *bovata* it is of common occurrence in the Scandinavian districts of England, and particularly in East Anglia and the district of the Five Boroughs. The measure of land represented by the oxgang was one-eighth of a 'ploughland', Lat. *carucata*, a term which appears in its English form *plogesland* in the document referred to above. The carucate represented the amount of land that could be ploughed by a team of eight oxen, cf. the use of the term *sulung* in Kent (p. 269). The use of the Scandinavian 'oxgang' as a fraction of the English 'hide' is noteworthy, but is found elsewhere as well, see p. 166.

l. 10. *Vlf eorles suna*. It seems from the context that *eorl* is used here as a proper name. It is not recorded as such, however, by Björkman or Searle.

l. 15. *Martine*. For a contemporary abbot of the name see p. 347.

l. 17. *Esctune*. Ashton in Nassaborough Hundred (Pl.N. *Northants*. p. 229).

l. 18. *Wyðreðe crosse*. Unidentified.

l. 27. *Dicon*. The traditional meeting-place of Nassaborough Hundred was at Langdyke Bush in Ufford where the 'long dyke', i.e. King Street, a branch of Ermine Street, is intersected by the 'dyke' or road from Peterborough to Barnack (see Pl.N. *Northants*. p. 223).

p. 80, l. 3. *gedale*. Perhaps 'strips of land', cf. *gedalland*, p. 299.

l. 10. *mid anum ýre*. See B.T., *Suppl.* s.v. *ire*. This form corresponds to the Icel. sing. *eyrir*; the plural *oran* corresponds to the Icel. pl. *aurar*.

l. 11. *æt Tuce*. This seems to represent an otherwise unrecorded feminine name corresponding to the masc. *Tuc(c)a* (B. 426, 437).

l. 19. *metere*. Glossed *pictor*, see B.T. p. 681, s.v.

l. 21. *sixti sticca...xxx. æcerum*. Each *sticca*, therefore, was equal to half an acre. The word seems to be of Scandinavian origin (cf. Icel. *stika*, 'a yard measure equal to two ells').

NOTES

l. 34. *Tufes on Hylpestune.* The Christian name is of an unusual form. It occurs again in this document but is not recorded elsewhere.
p. 82, ll. 23 ff. *seo swutelung...þet is Frena* etc. The construction is unusual and it seems as if some phrases have been omitted.
l. 27. *on his wedde.* It is not clear whose security is meant. Is it the abbot's or his own?

XLI

MSS. (*a*) British Museum, Cotton Charters, VIII, 20, a single sheet of parchment in a contemporary hand.
(*b*) Rochester Cathedral, *Textus Roffensis*, f. 147, where it is followed by a Latin version (B. 1098). See p. 276.
(*c*) British Museum, Harley MS. 311, f. 22, copied from (*b*) in the seventeenth century.

FACSIMILE. Of (*a*), Bond, *Facsimiles of Ancient Charters in the British Museum*, Part III, No. 34.

EDITIONS. Hickes, *Dissertatio Epistolaris*, p. 58 in *Thesaurus*, I, from (*b*).
Herne, *Textus Roffensis*, p. 115.
K. 1288.
T. p. 271.
E. p. 211, from (*a*) with the Latin version from (*b*).
B. 1097, from (*a*).
Essays in Anglo-Saxon Law, Appendix No. 21, from K.
The text is from (*a*).

DATE. Between about 964 and 988, i.e. after the appointment of Ælfstan to the see of Rochester but before the death of Archbishop Dunstan (see below).

p. 84, l. 1. *Wuldaham.* Wouldham, Kent. In 1086 this estate was held by the Bishop of Rochester. Its assessment had been reduced from 6 *solins* in the time of King Edward to 3. There was land for 5 ploughs (D.B. I, f. 5 b; V.C.H. *Kent*, III, p. 219).
sċe Andrea. Rochester Cathedral was dedicated to St Andrew.
l. 2. *Æðelbryht.* Æthelbert II was King of Kent from 748 to 762.
l. 3. *Eardulfe.* Eardwulf became Bishop of Rochester in 747. His signature appears for the last time in 765 (B. 199) while his successor Deora signs for the first time in 772 (B. 208).
l. 5. *Eadmund cinc.* Edmund reigned from 940 to 946.
l. 6. *hundtwelftigan mancesan goldes.* The mancus of gold was equivalent to 30 silver pence.
ll. 6 f. *ðrittigan pundan,* i.e. 30 pounds of silver.
l. 8. *Eadred cinc.* Edred reigned from 946 to 955.
l. 10. *þ he beleac on halre tungon.* The Latin version has *qui statim conclusit et omnino confirmavit totum quod pater suus in vita sua fecerat,* and B.T., *Suppl.* p. 77, s.v. *belucan*, VII, 1 *a*, gives the meaning 'to complete a transaction or bargain'. The verb *lucan* occurs with this sense elsewhere (see Whitelock, p. 32) and the meaning 'conclude, establish', with or without the implication of a bargain, seems a natural

NOTES

development from the root idea 'to lock'. For the phrase *on halre tungan* see also pp. 284, 338.

Ælfrice his breðer. Ælfheah and his brother Ælfric appeared as witnesses sometime before 958 when the Ælfric associated with Bromley, Fawkham and Snodland (see pp. 352, 355) confirmed his father's bequest of Snodland to Rochester (see Whitelock, pp. 28, 132).

l. 11. *butan he hwæt æt him geearnode.* It is probable, as Miss Whitelock suggests (p. 178), that the meaning of *geearnian* is 'to hold under him', i.e. to become his tenant and be liable for the usual payments and services. It would seem, at any rate, that land so 'earned' was held at the good pleasure of the donor and was granted for life only.

l. 12. *Earhiðes.* Erith.

Crægan. The name Cray is found in a group of adjoining parishes in the neighbourhood of Sidcup at the present day, namely North Cray, Foot's Cray, St Paul's Cray, St Mary Cray and South Cray.

Ænesfordes. Eynsford.

ll. 13 f. *feng to his læne,* i.e. the estates named above which had been leased to Ælfric and which, with the exception of Eynsford, were afterwards leased to Eadric.

l. 18. *morgengife.* This gift was received by a wife from her husband on the morning after their marriage. A widow retained her morning gift unless she remarried within a year, see II Cnut, 73 a. Frequently, as here, the gift took the form of land.

æt Cræ gan. This seems to be an instance of the idiomatic use of the preposition *æt* with a place-name, see English Place-Name Society, Vol. I, Part II, p. 2.

l. 19. *Lytlanbroc.* Littlebrook.

l. 20. *ða nam he his feorme* etc. By *feorm* is meant payment of rent in kind, e.g. hens, butter, eggs, cheese, honey etc., see Harmer, pp. 5, 73. Ælfheah, apparently, was in the habit of travelling round to his various estates in order to receive the supplies to which he was entitled.

l. 22. *Dunstane.* Dunstan, who had been Abbot of Glastonbury, then Bishop of Worcester and of London, was Archbishop of Canterbury from 960 to 988.

Scylfe. Perhaps Shelve in Lenham, if Ælfheah was able to travel as far to meet the archbishop.

cwæþ his cwide, see Whitelock, pp. xiv f. regarding the oral nature of Anglo-Saxon Wills.

ll. 23 f. *sette æne cwide* etc. The Latin version at this point reads: *Ibi coram archiepiscopo fecit Ælfegus commendationem sive distributionem omnium rerum suarum et constituit unam partem æcclesiæ Christi Cantuariæ et alteram partem æcclesiæ Sancti Andreæ et terciam partem uxori suæ.* This is not necessarily the meaning of the Anglo-Saxon, as three copies of important documents were frequently made, one of which might be entrusted to a disinterested party. There is nothing to show that Christchurch was a beneficiary under his will. For examples of wills drawn up in triplicate see Whitelock, pp. 68, 70 etc.

ll. 27 f. *ðam biscope...se biscop,* i.e. the archbishop.

NOTES

l. 28. *gelædde...ahnunga.* A formal legal process, see p. 366. In this case proof of ownership, which rested on the terms of Ælfheah's will, was furnished by the archbishop (to whom the will had been declared) by means of an oath taken with supporters in the presence of witnesses.

p. 86, l. 1. *Ælfstanes biscopes on Lundene.* Ælfstan became Bishop of London in 961. His signature occurs for the last time (along with that of Ælfstan, Bishop of Rochester) in 995 (K. 691). His successor Wulfstan was appointed in 996 (Sax. Chr. F) and signs for the first time in the same year (K. 1291).

ll. 2 f. *Ælfstanes an Hrofesceastre.* The date of Ælfstan's appointment to the see of Rochester is uncertain. He signs as bishop in 964 (B. 1134) along with Ælfstan, Bishop of London. His last signature appears in 995 (K. 691).

l. 3. *Wulfsies pre'o'stes pæs scirigmannes.* This is the earliest recorded instance of a shireman or sheriff presiding at a shire-meeting. The title *scirman* (cf. also p. 140, l. 20) was later replaced by *scirgerefa* (see p. 398). It is noteworthy that the sheriff in this case was a priest.

ll. 5 f. *hit wæs gecnæwe* etc. Should this statement and the reference to the 'ten hundred men who gave the oath' be taken as exaggerations?

l. 7. *mid his selfes aðe.* Apparently there were no witnesses present when Ælfheah declared his will to the archbishop.

mid þam bocan. The Latin version reads *cum libris æcclesiastici juris,* but it is possible that the title-deeds of the estates are meant.

ll. 8 f. *ðæne aþ* etc. The meaning adopted is that of the Latin version, *ipsum vero juramentum archiepiscopi accepit Uulfsi scirman...quandoquidem ipse Leofsunu illud suscipere nolebat.*

ll. 9 f. *þær wæs god eaca* etc. The Latin version gives a much fuller account: *Insuper ad hoc perficiendum fuit hoc quoque maximum adjumentum, temporibus futuris maximum securitatis probamentum · quod decies centum viri electissimi ex omnibus illis supradictis comitatibus juraverunt post archiepiscopum in ipsa cruce Christi ratum et æternæ memoriæ stabile fore sacramentum quod archiepiscopus juraverat.*

XLII

MS. British Museum, Cotton Tiberius A. XIII, f. 80. See p. 259.

EDITIONS. Hearne, *Hemingi Chartularium* etc. I, p. 170.
K. 530.
B. 1180.

l. 11. *Hindehlyp.* Hindlip, Worcestershire.

l. 16. *for uncre sibbe,* cf. p. 96, l. 6 and note p. 343.

l. 21. *circanlade.* This term is found in another of Oswald's charters (see p. 114, l. 12) but does not occur elsewhere. B.T., *Suppl.* p. 599, s.v. *lad,* IV, suggests that it may have the same meaning as *ciricsceat,* but this seems unlikely. The meaning of the term *lad* is clear from a passage in the *Northumbrian Priests' Law*, cap. 55, *Sunnandæges cypingc we forbeodað*...7 *ælce lade ægðer ge on wæne ge on horse ge on byrdene*, while the compounds *wudulade* and *cornlade* are used for the carting of wood and of corn respectively in the *Rectitudines*, cap. 21, 4. In view of these examples, therefore, I have taken *-lade* in the compound *circanlade* in the same sense.

l. 28. *Wulfric prbt.* For Wulfric, Edgar, Alfred, Wulfhun and Brihtstan see p. 320; for Æthelstan, Wulfgar and Wulfheah see p. 321.

Ælfgar cl. Ælfgar signs as cleric from 966 to 969 and as deacon from 977 to 981.

l. 29. *Ælfstan cler.* Ælfstan signs from 962 to 983.

Vfic cl. Ufic signs from 966 to 985.

l. 31. *Leofwine cl.* Leofwine is a regular witness of Oswald's grants from 966 onwards.

XLIII

MS. British Museum, Cotton Tiberius A. XIII, f. 96 *b*. See p. 259.
EDITIONS. Hearne, *Hemingi Chartularium* etc. I, p. 206.
K. 529.
B. 1182.

p. 88, l. 1. *Eanulfestune.* Alveston, Warwickshire.

[*Ea*]*drice 7 Wulfrune.* Two later charters with the same heading record the grant of 3 hides (K. 617) and 5 hides (K. 651) at Tiddington (which adjoins Alveston) to Eadric in 977 and 985 respectively. In both cases it is stated that merely a change of tenure was involved, namely from *lænland* to *bocland*. The holder of one of Oswald's written leases was doubtless more secure in his tenure and was protected, moreover, against the exaction of payments or services other than those specified in his *boc*.

ll. 6 f. *on þære gesyndredan hide* etc. A grant of 1 hide at Bishopton in 1016 (K. 724) carried with it *synderlice* xv. *mæd aceras on ðære eafurlunga fornegean Tidingtun 7 nigoðe healf æcer on Scothomme* (the Shottery river pasture) 7 XII. *aceras yrplandes betwyx ðare ea 7 ðare dic æt ðæm stangedelfe...7 ðone ðriddan æcer beanlandes on Biscopesdune* (Bishopton).

ll. 7 ff. *Fachanleage...biccenclife.* These names do not seem to have survived.

ll. 8 f. *æt þære eorðbyrig.* There seems to be no trace of an earthwork in the vicinity at the present day.

l. 11. *meo compatri.* The Anglicised form was *cumpæder* (see Sax. Chr. 894 A) and the name was applicable to either of the two men who were godfathers to the same child or to a godfather and the child's own father. There is nothing to show which relationship is meant here.

NOTES

l. 18. *testibus.* For Wulfric and Edgar see p. 320. For Æthelstan, Wulfgar, Edwin, Wulfheah and Wynstan see p. 321. For Ælfstan, Ælfgar, Ufic and Leofwine see p. 335.

l. 21. *Eadward clr.* Edward signs as cleric in 966 and 969 and as priest from 977 to 985.

l. 22. *Tuna clr.* Tuna signs from 966 to 982.

l. 23. *Wistan prŏt.* Wistan signs as cleric in 962 and 963 and as priest from 966 to 991.

l. 25. *Ælfred prŏt.* The title 'priest' has been attached by mistake to Alfred and the two following witnesses. All three continue to sign as clerics after this date, see p. 320.

l. 26. *Wulfnoð clr.* Wulfnoth is a regular witness of Oswald's charters from 966 onwards. He signs for the last time in 996 (K. 695).

XLIV

MS. Westminster Abbey Charters, No. VIII, a contemporary parchment.

FACSIMILE. *Ordnance Survey Facsimiles,* Part II, No. 7.

EDITIONS. Kemble, *Archaeological Journal,* XIV, 1857, p. 59.
T. p. 206.
E. p. 201, from K.
B. 1063.

DATE. This document is an interesting example of the process of vouching to warranty in actual practice. The rules for such procedure are stated very fully in II Æthelred, 8–9, 4 and in the Laws of William I, 21–21, 5.

The events described here covered a period of years. They began towards the end of Edred's reign and were apparently completed in 968 when the archbishop purchased the estates concerned from Earl Ælfheah (see below).

p. 90, l. 1. *Ieceslea.* Perhaps Yaxley, Huntingdonshire, which appears on p. 68, l. 4 as *Jaceslea* and on p. 74 as *Geaceslea* (l. 17) and *Iacesle* (l. 25).

l. 2. *þurwif.* This feminine name is not recorded elsewhere in any pre-Conquest document. Its form suggests a Scandinavian origin, but there is no exact Scandinavian equivalent, and Björkman (pp. 163 f.) suggests that it may have been formed in England by analogy with the Scandinavian masculine *þorkarl.* The name *Turewif* occurs in a twelfth-century record (see Björkman, *Zur Englischen Namenkunde,* p. 88).

l. 3. *þone mann.* Used here in its original sense of 'human being', the reference clearly being to the *wifman* (a compound formed for purposes of differentiation) already mentioned.

l. 4. *Sunnanbyrg.* Sunbury, Middlesex.

l. 7. *Byrhferð ealdormann.* Brihtferth's signature as *dux* is attached to charters of 955 and 956. It is possible that B. 887 (dated 950), where it also occurs, belongs by rights to 955, but it is at any rate not earlier than 953 (see Chadwick, *Anglo-Saxon Institutions*, p. 187, n. 1). Brihtferth apparently held office in the eastern counties and may have been Earl of Essex between Ælfgar (who signs regularly till 951) and Brihtnoth (whose earliest dated signature appears on 29 November 956, see Chadwick, *op. cit.* p. 180). The signature Ælfgar *dux* appears in two charters of 956 (B. 930, 957) and in one of 958 (B. 1027). In the last of these, as an examination of contemporary charters shows, the title has been attached by mistake to a certain Ælfgar *minister* and two other witnesses of the same rank whose names follow his in the list. It is possible, therefore, that a mistake has likewise been made in the two charters of 956, but as Ælfgar's name occurs at the head of the list of earls, this explanation cannot be regarded as entirely satisfactory. Another possibility is that Ælfgar continued to sign as earl after he had retired from office (see Chadwick, *op. cit.* p. 187, n. 2). If the assumption that Brihtferth succeeded Ælfgar is right, the present document shows that Middlesex lay within the jurisdiction of the Earl of Essex at the time.

hys wer. According to the Laws of William I, 21, 2, the forfeiture of wergeld in a case of the kind was characteristic of Mercia and the Danelaw.

ll. 9 ff. *íc · hæbbe Sunnanburges bóc* etc. It is curious to find one brother holding the title-deeds and the other the estate itself. Liebermann suggests that they may have held the estate jointly at one time (*Gesetze*, II, p. 327, s.v. *bocland*, 25 *b*).

l. 15. *Wulfgare æt Norðhealum.* Probably so called to distinguish him from Wulfgar, Wulfstan's son. I have not been able to identify the place meant. The ending *-healum* probably represents the dative pl. of *healh*, see *Chief Elements in English Place-Names*, p. 34.

l. 16. *wendun gewyrda.* This seems like a half-line of poetry. The use of poetical alliterative phrases is a noteworthy characteristic of the document.

gewat Eadræd cyng. Edred died on 23 November 955 (Sax. Chr. A).

ll. 17 f. *ungebetra þinga.* This is an example of the genitive absolute, cf. (possibly) *beotra gylpa*, Sax. Chr. 1006.

l. 18. *Byrnrice.* A thegn of this name signs Edwy's charters from 956 (B. 927) to 958 (B. 1029) and received estates in Wiltshire and Hampshire in 956 (B. 934, 974).

l. 20. *Myrce gecuran Eadgar.* This took place in 957 (Sax. Chr. B, C).

l. 25. *Æðelstan' e' ealdormenn.* This must be the earl of the name who is a regular witness of Edgar's charters both before and after he became sole king. His earldom is not known, but the fact that he was granted this estate in Middlesex suggests that he was connected with the southeast Midlands (see Chadwick, *Anglo-Saxon Institutions*, pp. 177 f.).

l. 26. *for life · 7 for legere*, cf. *ge on life ge on legere*, V Æthelred, 9, 1, etc. Is the meaning the same in both cases?

p. 92, l. 2. *on halre tungan*, cf. p. 284. It seems possible from what follows that the phrase here (and perhaps elsewhere) corresponds to the Latin *viva voce* (cf. K. 819). The arrangement was apparently made sometime before Ecgferth's death, and probably when he acquired the estate.

l. 3. *Dunstane arcebisceope.* See p. 333.

ll. 6 f. *mine witan* etc. The circumstances are not explained, presumably because they were generally known at the time, but it would seem that Ecgferth had been guilty of some serious crime. Kemble regards the case as one of escheat for suicide—the only one of the kind of which any record has survived—and Liebermann also supports this view (*Gesetze*, II, p. 479, s.v. *Grab*). The entire absence of any reference elsewhere to forfeiture in the case of suicide, however, seems an important consideration, while the charters supply numerous examples of its enforcement in the case of serious crime such as theft (B. 158 and 727, 1198, K. 692), bloodshed in some specially protected place (K. 719, cf. II Edmund, 2), treason (B. 595, K. 1312) or desertion from the army (K. 1307, where this crime was one of many). The adverse attitude of the church towards suicide is expressed in homilies (see the quotations given in B.T., *Suppl.* p. 29, s.v. *agenslaga*), but as far as I know there is no legal pronouncement anywhere on the subject. The reference to the sword 'that hung on his hip' suggests that Ecgferth was a royal official. There seems to be nothing about him elsewhere, and it is impossible to say why he died by drowning.

l. 8. *Sendan.* Send, Surrey.

l. 9. *Ælfhege ealdormenn.* Edgar's charter granting 10 hides at Sunbury to his kinsman Ælfheah is extant and is dated 962 (B. 1085).

I am inclined to think that Ælfheah did not become an earl till 959. His signature generally occurs with the title *minister* up to and including 958, and one of Edwy's grants (B. 1030), made in the fourth year of his reign and the second Indiction, which describes him by that title, must belong to the early part of 959, although it is actually dated 956. He was an earl by 17 May 959 (B. 1046), but it is obvious, except in one case, that the title has been erroneously ascribed to him in charters of an earlier date such as B. 979, 982 (both dated 956), 994, 1004 (both dated 957) and 1027 (dated 958, where the title is wrongly attached also to the two preceding witnesses). Four of these charters are from the *Codex Wintoniensis*, and in every case he is the last witness described as *dux* instead of the first (in B. 1027 the third) described as *minister*. The one exception is B. 1005 which records a grant of land in Berkshire to Ælfheah *dux* by Edwy in 957. This charter has been copied into both MSS. of the *Historia Monasterii de Abingdon* (see p. 299), but three later charters dated 958, which have been preserved in one of these MSS. (Cotton Claudius B. VI), are signed by Ælfheah *minister* (B. 1022, 1028, 1032) and would seem to refute the evidence of the earlier one, the date of which may have been wrongly copied.

NOTES

There is a second Ælfheah who occasionally signs as *minister* from 955 onwards (see B. 917 where the first Ælfheah is distinguished as the brother of Earl Ælfhere). His name generally occurs considerably lower in the list than that of the first Ælfheah, and I feel certain, therefore, that the majority of the signatures where only one of them occurs belong to the latter. It is certainly he who signs at the head of the *ministri*, and I am inclined for that reason to identify him with the Ælfheah *discifer* of B. 941 and 949 and the Ælfheah *cyninges discðen* of No. XXXI (see p. 315). If this identification is correct, the last of these three charters is particularly interesting as it supplies the name of another brother, Eadric (see Whitelock, pp. 24, 125).

Ælfheah was Earl of Hampshire. His will is extant (Whitelock, No. IX) and shows that he held very wide estates.

his wér. This was the highest sum that could be paid as compensation by or for anyone.

ll. 10 f. *wið clænum legere.* The same idea is expressed by the phrase *binnon gehalgodum lictune*, II Æthelstan, 26 (cf. I Edmund, 1), while the opposite is found in the phrase *on ful(an) lecgan*, I Æthelred, 4, 1, II Cnut, 33, 1, rendered *in loco latronum sepeliri* in the *Instituta Cnuti* (see Liebermann, I, p. 337)./ The burial in consecrated ground of two brothers who had fallen in defence of one of their men (a thief) is made a cause of complaint to the king in K. 1289.

l. 12. *þæs ón syxtan gere.* The purchase of Sunbury is recorded in a spurious charter attributed to Dunstan and dated 959 (B. 1050). It cannot have taken place earlier than 968, if it was not granted to Ælfheah till 962 (see above).

ll. 15 f. *he...geagnian derr.* It would seem from this as if Dunstan's title to these estates had been called in question at some later date, hence the drawing up of this document. His declaration of ownership is in accordance with the second of the three formulae given in the document beginning *Hit becwæð* (see Liebermann, I, p. 400). It runs *swa ic hit hæbbe swa hit se sealde ðe to syllanne ahte, unbryde 7 unforboden.*

XLV

MS. (*a*) British Museum, Additional MS. 15350, f. 22 *b* (or 24 *b* by the new numbering). Another copy (*b*) is given on f. 23 *b* (or 25 *b* by the new numbering). See p. 274.

EDITIONS. K. 598.
B. 1220.
The text is from (*a*).

DATE. The Anglo-Saxon version of Edgar's charter is preceded by a Latin version (B. 1219). Both are dated 978 which should probably be corrected to 968 (see below).

l. 19. *Tantunes freols.* The original grant of Taunton was attributed to Frithegyth, the wife of Æthelheard, King of Wessex. It was afterwards augmented by Æthelwulf (B. 475).

l. 21. *Eadweard cyning.* The *Codex Wintoniensis* contains a copy of Edward's charter, dated 904 (B. 612).

l. 22 *ægþer ge twelfhynde men ge twyhynde,* i.e. both those whose wergeld was 1200 shillings and those whose wergeld was 200 shillings. The Latin version reads *tam nobiles quam ignobiles.* Edward's charter and the Latin version of Edgar's give the terms of the grant in almost the same words.

ll. 25 f. *þes tunes ciyping 7 seó ínnúng þara portgerihta.* The corresponding Latin phrase is *ville mercimonium censusque omnis civilis.* It is possible, therefore, that the A.S. *portgerihta* should be translated 'taxes' rather than 'market-dues' but I am uncertain as to its exact meaning.

Edward's charter gives additional and valuable information with regard to the previous obligations of Taunton: *Erat namque antea in illo supradicto monasterio pastus unius noctis regi · et.* VIII. *canum et unius caniculari pastus et pastus novem noctium accipitrariis regis et quicquid rex vellet inde ducere usque ad Curig vel Willettun cum plaustris et equis · et si advene de aliis regionibus advenirent debebant ducatum habere ad aliam regalem villam · quæ proxima fuisset in illorum via.*

p. 94, l. 1. *Ælfeage biscope.* See p. 306.

l. 8. *AÐELwold biscop.* See p. 323.

l. 10. *Ælfþryde.* See below. She was applied to at a later date in the case of a dispute about one of the estates attached to Taunton. Her evidence is given in K. 717 and is valuable for the additional information which it supplies regarding the events of Edgar's time.

ll. 13 f. *Crawancumbe...Cumbtune...Bananwille.* Crowcombe, Compton and Banwell are all in Somerset.

l. 14. *Scealdeburnan stoce.* Stoke near Shalbourn, Wiltshire. A copy of Bishop Denewulf's grant of this estate to Edward is preserved in the *Codex Wintoniensis* (B. 611).

l. 16. *þan hiwon æt Ceodre.* The Latin version reads *famulis famulabusque domini on Ceodre degentibus.* The only other reference to a community at Cheddar occurs in King Alfred's will (Harmer, pp. 17, 96).

Carintune. Carhampton, Somerset. An estate there was bequeathed to Edward the Elder by King Alfred (Harmer, p. 17).

l. 19. *þe teoþan geáre* etc. It would seem from this that the year 968 is meant as Edgar became sole king in 959.

l. 25. *DVNSTAN archieþs.* See p. 333.

Ælfþryþ regina. Ælfthryth, who was the daughter of Ordgar, Earl of Devon, and according to Fl. Wig. the widow of Æthelwold, Earl of East Anglia, became Edgar's second wife in 964 (Fl. Wig.) or 965 (Sax. Chr. D, F). She frequently appears in the charters as a witness and on more than one occasion was appealed to in lawsuits. Osbern and later writers attribute to her the responsibility for the death of her stepson, Edward the Martyr (see *Memorials of St Dunstan,* R.S. p. 114) and other stories and legends were current about her (see p. 374).

NOTES 341

l. 26. *OSCYTEL archieps.* Oscytel, who had been Bishop of Dorchester (see p. 313), was Archbishop of York from 956 to 971.

Æpestan dux. Æthelstan (see p. 337) seems to have been promoted to an earldom sometime in 940 as he signs some charters of that year as *minister*, others as *dux*. He continues to sign till the last years of Edgar's reign.

l. 27. *Ælfhere dux.* Earl of Mercia, see p. 319.

l. 28. *ÆLFSTAN eps.* Bishop of London, see p. 334.

Elfheah dux. Earl of Hampshire, see pp. 338 f.

l. 29. *BYRHTELM eps.* Bishop of Wells, see p. 314.

Ordgar dux. Earl of Devon (Fl. Wig.; B. 1178) and the father of Ælfthryth. He signs as *dux* from 964 (B. 1135) onwards. He died in 971 (Fl. Wig.).

l. 30. *OSWOLD eps.* Bishop of Worcester, see p. 319.

Æpelwine dux. Earl of East Anglia, see p. 329.

l. 31. *ALFWOLD eps.* Bishop of Crediton, 953–972.

Byrthnoð dux. Earl of Essex, see p. 315.

l. 32. *OSVLF eps.* Bishop of Ramsbury. He signs for the first time in 950 (B. 887) and died in 970 (Fl. Wig.).

Oslac dux. Oslac signs as *dux* in 963 (B. 1113), although his appointment to an earldom is first entered under the year 966 in the Sax. Chr. E. According to Simeon of Durham and the tract entitled *De primo Saxonum Adventu* (Simeon of Durham, R.S. II, pp. 197, 382) he was Earl of York and the districts dependent upon it. He was banished after Edgar's death (Sax. Chr. 975), 'unjustly' according to Fl. Wig. (s.a. 976).

l. 33. *WYNSIGE eps.* Bishop of Lichfield. His first signature appears in 964 (B. 1134) and his last in 973 (B. 1292).

Eadulf dux. His signature is found in two other charters only (B. 1230, 1266), dated 969 and 970 respectively. The tract mentioned above describes him as *Eadulf cognomento Yvelcild* and says that he governed Northumbria *a Teisa usque Myreford*.

l. 34. *Ælfric abb.* Abbot of St Augustine's, Canterbury, from 956 to 971.

Eanulf min. His signature appears for the first time in 958 (B. 1042) and continues till the end of Edgar's reign. Estates in Oxfordshire and Cornwall were granted to him by Edgar (B. 1036, 1056).

l. 35. *Osgar abb.* Abbot of Abingdon from 963 to 984.

Ælfwine min. Two men of this name occasionally appear as witnesses of Edgar's charters from 958 to 970, while three sign B. 1047 (dated 958) and 1055 (dated 960). B. 1051, 1227 record grants of estates to a man of the name.

l. 36. *Elfstan abb.* Abbot of Glastonbury (see Fl. Wig. s.a. 970; B. 1179). He signs as abbot from 964 (B. 1135, 1143) to 970, and it was probably he who became Bishop of Ramsbury in that year.

Æpelweard min. Two men of this name (as here) are frequent witnesses of Edgar's charters throughout his reign. It was probably one of them who later became Earl of the Western Provinces (see p. 373).

l. 37. *Æscwig abb̃.* Abbot of Bath (see B. 1164, 1257). His signature first appears in 963 (B. 1120) and continues until the reign of Edward the Martyr (K. 1276 f.). It was probably he who became Bishop of Dorchester about 977.

Wulfstan miñ. Edgar's charters are generally witnessed by one man, and sometimes by two men, of the name. One of them was probably Wulfstan of Dalham (see p. 367).

l. 38. *Æþelgar abb̃.* Abbot of the New Minster, Winchester. His first signature appears in 964 (B. 1135). In 980 he became Bishop of Selsey and in 988 Archbishop of Canterbury.

Byrtferð miñ. Brihtferth is a regular witness of Edgar's charters.

l. 39. *Cynewerd abb̃.* Abbot of the reformed monastery of Milton Abbas, Dorset, from 964 (Sax. Chr. A; Fl. Wig.) to 973, when he became Bishop of Wells (Fl. Wig.).

Oswerd miñ. The two names, Osweard and Osulf, generally occur together in Edgar's charters. It is noteworthy that Bishop Oswald had a brother called Osulf (B. 1139, cf. B. 1204) and that B. 1314 records the grant of an estate by Edgar to his kinsman Osweard in 975.

l. 40. *Þyrcytel abb̃.* Thurcytel was a kinsman of Oscytel, Archbishop of York, and was Abbot of Bedford at the time of the latter's death (Sax. Chr. 971 B, C). According to the *Liber Eliensis*, II, c. 31, he was expelled from Bedford. His signature occurs also in B. 1230 (dated 969) and 1266 (dated 970).

l. 41. *Ælfheah abb̃.* His signature occurs also in dated charters of 970, 972 and 974.

Elfwerd miñ. Ælfweard is a regular witness of Edgar's charters and his name is frequently found beside Æthelweard's.

l. 42. *Ealdred abb̃.* His signature occurs three times in charters of 969 and 970 (B. 1228, 1264, 1266).

XLVI

MSS. (*a*) British Museum, Additional Charter 19792, the top portion of a chirograph.

(*b*) British Museum, Cotton Tiberius A. XIII, f. 83 *b*. See p. 259.

FACSIMILE. Of (*a*), Bond, *Facsimiles of Ancient Charters in the British Museum*, Part III, No. 28.

EDITIONS. Hearne, *Hemingi Chartularium* etc. I, p. 177.
K. 557, from (*b*).
B. 1233, from (*a*).

The text is from (*a*).

p. 96, l. 1. *Oswold bisceop.* See p. 319.
l. 2. *Ælfheres Mercna heretogan.* See p. 319.

NOTES 343

ll. 3 f. *þæt sint...hida*. A blank has been left and the number of hides has not been recorded.

ll. 4 f. *Teottingctun* 7 *Ælfsigestun*. Teddington and Alstone, Worcestershire. The boundaries of Teddington are given independently in the cartulary (Hearne, II, p. 362) and have been wrongly incorporated by Kemble in the grant of an estate of 3 hides at Tiddington, Warwickshire (K. 617). The amount of land there as here is unspecified. A charter of Offa, dated 780, records the grant of 5 hides at Teddington to the monastery of Bredon, while a charter of Bishop Ealdred records the grant of 3 hides at Teddington and Alstone to Worcester, free of service to the episcopal manor of Bredon to which it is said to have belonged in former times. In D.B. 3 hides at Teddington are entered as belonging to the manor of Bredon (D.B. I, f. 173; V.C.H. *Worc.* I, p. 291).

l. 5. *cnihte*. See p. 394.

Osulf. There are two grants by Oswald to his brother Osulf, namely B. 1139 (which from the list of witnesses should be dated about 966) and B. 1204, dated 967. The estate to which the second of these refers was re-granted to his nephew Ælfwine in 988 (B. 1205; the date is correctly given in the full copy of the charter, Hearne, I, p. 173). The Osulf of the present grant is probably this brother. A charter of 979 (K. 623) records the grant of an estate by Oswald to a certain Æthelstan *meo carnaliter fratri*, and relatives called Gardulf and Edwy also appear as lessees of estates (K. 637, 670; 645).

l. 9. *Eadleofu*. The arrangement seems a curious one and it would seem from the marginal heading in the cartulary that Eadlifu never actually inherited the estate. Was she perhaps Osulf's second wife?

l. 20. *þæs hierdes*. For Wulfric, Edgar, Alfred, Wulfhun and Brihtstan see p. 320; for Æthelstan, Wulfgar, Cynesige, Edwin and Wulfheah see p. 321; for Wistan, Edward, Tuna and Wulfnoth see p. 336; for Ælfstan, Ælfgar, Ufic and Leofwine see p. 335.

XLVII

MS. Bodleian Library, Oxford, Bodley 579, f. 11 *b*, generally known as the Leofric Missal.

EDITIONS. J. B. Davidson, Appendix to 'Some Anglo-Saxon Boundaries' etc. in *Transactions of the Devonshire Association*, VIII, 1876, p. 419 (with a translation).

F. E. Warren, *The Leofric Missal*, p. 8 (text), p. lx (translation and comments).

E. p. 256.

B. 1244.

DATE. Between about 969 (the earliest recorded instance of Abbot Leofric's signature, see B. 1228, 1264) and 993, when that of his successor Brihthelm makes its appearance.

p. 98, l. 1. *anburge*. There is no other recorded instance of this word, the closest parallel to which seems to be the verb *onbyrgan*, 'to be surety for', cf. the noun *byrgea*, 'one who acts as surety'. The compound *inborh* occurs in II Edward, 3, 1 and also in the O.E. Homilies (see B.T. p. 590, s.v.), but the form in general use in the sense of 'surety' is *borg*. Toller suggests, therefore, that the reading of the present text may represent original *on borge* (see B.T., *Suppl.* p. 102, s.v. *borh*, 1). The form *anburge*, however, must be accepted as it stands, especially in view of the fact that the text shows no other signs of corrupt forms.

Eadgyfe abbedysse. She was presumably abbess of a Devonshire and probably of an Exeter foundation. For an abbess of the same name at the Nunnery in Winchester in the time of Edgar see p. 102, l. 24. According to one tradition the community attached to the church of St Peter at Exeter to which Leofric, Bishop of Crediton, removed his episcopal see in 1050 (see p. 474) was one of nuns (William of Malmesbury, *Gesta Pontificum*, R.S. p. 201), according to another one of monks (Leland, *Itinerary*, ed. Hearne, 2nd ed. III, p. 54). The present transaction seems to point to the existence of two communities—one of nuns and one of monks—towards the close of the tenth century, the second of which, if not the first as well, was attached to the church of St Peter, and hence bequeathed its claim to Stoke Canon (see below) to Bishop Leofric (see p. 226, l. 9). Of the community of nuns nothing can be learned from the present transaction except its interest in an estate which according to a spurious charter had been bequeathed to St Peter's at Exeter by Æthelstan (B. 723).

l. 2. *Sto῾c'tune*. The reference is apparently to Stoke Canon, see Pl.N. *Devon*, II, p. 447.

ll. 2 f. *Wulfsige EDwig*. The absence of a stop or conjunction between these two names is noteworthy. A double name of this type would be very unusual, however, and it is probable that a stop has been omitted by mistake. A certain Wulfsige of Lamerton (*æt Lamburnan*) appears as a witness in the first of a series of manumissions entered on f. 8 *b* of the same MS., see B. 1247.

l. 3. *Denisc*, i.e. 'the Danish man'.

Hunwine. It is noteworthy that the estate of Stoke Canon was granted to a thegn of this name by Cnut in 1031 (see *Journal of the British Archaeological Association*, 1883, p. 289) and in this way, probably, was alienated from the church of St Peter at Exeter. For a later Devonshire witness of the name see p. 200, l. 25.

l. 4. *Edwig boga*. The name *boga* is used of anything curved or bent, see B.T., *Suppl.* p. 100, s.v.

Brun þ. This witness appears in four of the above-mentioned series of manumissions, see B. 1245, 1248 f., 1253.

l. 5. *into mynstre*. Presumably the community attached to St Peter's at Exeter is meant.

XLVIII

MSS. (*a*) British Museum, Stowe Charters, No. 31, a single parchment, the handwriting of which may be of later date.
(*b*) British Museum, Additional MS. 5819, f. 4*b* (by the new numbering). This is an eighteenth-century copy made by William Cole.
FACSIMILE. Of (*a*), *Ordnance Survey Facsimiles*, Part III, No. 32.
EDITIONS. K. 563, from (*b*).
T. p. 239.
B. 1267.
The text is from (*a*).

DATE. The Anglo-Saxon version of this charter is represented as subsidiary to the more complete Latin version (B. 1266) which precedes it on the same parchment and supplies the date and the list of witnesses. It is said to have been drawn up by command of the king and entered on the parchment (*sceda*) in order that the arrangements made might reach the ears of the common people (*in auribus vulgi sonare*). It cannot be regarded, however, as a direct translation of the Latin version, from which it differs considerably (see following notes).

In the Latin version the date given is 970, described as the thirteenth year of Edgar's reign. As he became king north of the Thames in 957 (see p. 337) this description is correct for the part of the country in which Ely is situated.

l. 8. *cining...ofer Engla þeode*. The Latin version reads *basileus dilectæ insulæ Albionis*.

ll. 9 f. *Scottas 7 Cumbras 7...Bryttas*, i.e. Scots, Cumbrians (the inhabitants of Strathclyde) and Britons (the Celtic inhabitants of Wales and Cornwall). Edgar frequently appears in the charters with the title *rex Anglorum ceterarumque gentium in circuitu persistentium gubernator et rector*.

l. 12. *his lof arære*. The poem in praise of Edgar entered in the Saxon Chronicle, 959 E, says of him, *He arerde Godes lof wide*.

l. 17. *oð þissere geendunge*. The Latin version reads *usque in finem sæculi*.

ll. 19 f. *7 he us gewissige...forgife*. There is nothing corresponding to this in the Latin version.

ll. 23 f. *mid agenum freodome* etc. The Latin version reads *hoc privilegio rebusque copiosis*.

p. 100, l. 2. *Atheldrythe*. The account given in the Latin version is not quite so full. Bede is not mentioned by name, but the source of information is said to be the *Historia Anglorum*. Bede's account of Etheldreda is given in his *Historia Ecclesiastica*, IV, c. 19, and is closely reproduced here.

ll. 9 f. *gehwyrfed* etc. The Latin version omits this personal reference and reads instead *regali fisco subditus*.

l. 10. *Atheluuold.* See p. 323. The Latin version describes him as *diocesi Uuintoniensis civitatis fungens.*

l. 12. *Heartingas.* Harting, Sussex. In 1066 it was held of the king by the Countess Gytha, the widow of Earl Godwine (D.B. I, f. 23; V.C.H. *Sussex,* I, p. 422).

on sixtigum hidum. In 1066 this estate was assessed at 80 hides (D.B. *loc. cit.*).

l. 14. *Meldeburna.* Melbourn, Cambridgeshire.

Earningaford. The name survives in Armingford Hundred in the south-west of Cambridgeshire. There is no mention in D.B. of any estate or village called Armingford, but the land held by Ely at Whaddon, Meldreth, Melbourn and Shepreth all lay within the hundred of the name (cf. the *Inquisitio Eliensis,* ed. Hamilton, p. 107).

l. 15. *Norðwold.* Northwold, Norfolk (see D.B. II, f. 213 b; V.C.H. *Norfolk,* II, p. 135).

l. 17. *Brihtnoð.* See p. 374. He is described in the Latin version as *quendam sapientem ac bene morieratum virum.*

l. 20. *to þære ærran sylene.* The restoration of Ely by Æthelwold and the appointment of Brihtnoth as abbot are entered under the year 963 in the Saxon Chronicle E, so that the earlier part of this charter would seem to be in the nature of a recapitulation of what had already taken place some years before. For a separate charter of Edgar, which covers part of the same ground as this one, see below.

l. 21. *for fyrdinge.* The Latin version (which is reproduced also in the *Liber Eliensis,* II, c. 5) reads *pro expenditione,* which, in view of the Anglo-Saxon, would seem to be a mistake for *expeditione.* Ducange quotes this one instance only of the term *expenditio,* explained as 'expensæ', but if the Latin term is correct, it is difficult to understand what is meant.

l. 22. *binnan þam iggoðe,* i.e. the isle of Ely.

æt Wyllan. See p. 328. The reference is probably again to the neighbourhood of the Old Croft River.

ll. 22 f. *þa socna* etc. The Latin version reads *intra paludes causas seculares duorum centuriatuum.* The reference is to the proceeds of justice within the two hundreds of Ely. A full account of the privileges enjoyed by Ely is given in the *Liber Eliensis,* II, c. 54: *Et hæ sunt dignitates et consuetudines ecclesiæ de Ely...infra insulam et infra duos centuriatus insulæ; scilicet omnia placita et jura quæ pertinent ad coronam regis; et omnes homines duorum centuriatuum insulæ de quindecim in quindecim diebus debent convenire ad Ely vel ad Wicheforda quæ caput centuriatuum insulæ dicitur vel ad Modich quæ quarta pars est centuriatuum, ad discernenda jura S. Æthedredæ; et nemo infra insulam habeat terram vel jus aliquod nisi S. Æthelreda; et nullus baronum regis infra duos centuriatus insulæ habeat curiam suam, sed calumpniator et calumpniatus ad prædicta loca venient et ibi judicabuntur.*

ll. 23 f. *him to scrudfultume.* There is no such stipulation in the Latin version.

l. 24. *on East Englan æt Wichlawan.* The Latin version reads *in Uuichlauuan in provincia Orientalium Saxonum,* i.e. Essex. This cannot be accepted, as 'Wicklow' was certainly in Suffolk, but the mistake is a curious one. The exact site of 'Wicklow' is unknown.

l. 25. *fif hundredum.* These five hundreds were Plumesgate, Loes, Wilford, Carlford and Colneis, all in the south-east of Suffolk (see V.C.H. *Suffolk,* I, p. 387, n. 195).

ll. 28 f. *pone feorðan pening.* The Latin version reads *omnem quartum nummum reipublicæ.* This fourth penny was usurped by Picot the sheriff and was claimed in the Ely suit which was heard before Geoffrey of Coutances sometime between 1072 and 1075, see the *Inquisitio Eliensis,* ed. Hamilton, p. 195.

l. 29. *on folclicre steore.* The reference is to fines levied in the public courts to which no private person had any claim. A more commonly found division is into three parts, two of which went to the king and the third to the earl.

ll. 30 f. *gif ænig mann* etc. There is nothing corresponding to this in the Latin version and the exact meaning of the *socn* 'pertaining to one day's food-rent' is difficult to understand. It is noteworthy that a copy of a separate charter of Edgar (in Latin) is also found (B. 1265) which records the exchange of Melbourn and Armingford for Harting, carried out at Easter 970 at *Wulfamere.* It is difficult to determine the relationship of this charter to the present one. Both were drawn up in the same year at the same place, the names of the witnesses (which end with the bishops in B. 1265) and the attesting clauses are the same in both, except for the omission of the second bishop named Ælfwold in B. 1265. The wording of the charter in general is entirely different from that of the present one, but there is one clause which connects it with the Anglo-Saxon version. It follows the account of the exchange and runs: *cui enimvero libens mutuacioni per totam prefatam insulam omnis emendacionem reatus specialiter, communionemque in eadem re extra insulam, quantum ad noctis pastum regalem jure pertinere censetur unius, adjungere decrevi,* i.e. the receipt of all the fines within the isle is made over to Bishop Æthelwold, on behalf of Ely, and a share in those outside the isle to consist of the profits of all the pleas arising out of the assessment, collection etc. of the king's food-rent (I am indebted to Professor Stenton for this explanation). It would seem as if the writer of the Anglo-Saxon version of the present charter had borrowed the reference to the profits arising from the king's food-rent and inserted it here without properly understanding its meaning or application.

The Latin version names as witnesses the king, the two archbishops, 12 bishops, the queen, 11 abbots (including a certain Martin who does not seem to appear elsewhere), 9 *duces* (including a certain Malcolm, not found elsewhere, unless he is to be identified with the Malcolm *rex Cumbrorum* of B. 1185) and 41 *ministri.* As many of these as can be identified suit the date to which the charter is assigned.

NOTES

XLIX

MS. British Museum, Additional MS. 15350, f. 6 *b*. See p. 274.
EDITIONS. K. 594.
T. p. 231.
B. 1163 and *An Ancient Manuscript of Nunnaminster*, Appendix D, p. 129 with a modern English translation.

DATE. With this document should be compared B. 1302 (from the *Codex Wintoniensis*), which records Edgar's grant of the land adjoining the two Minsters and the Nunnery to these respective foundations, clear of all secular dwellings *ut cenobite inibi degentes a civium tumultu remoti tranquillius Deo servirent*. This grant is dated 984 but cannot be later than 970, if the death of Osulf, Bishop of Ramsbury, who appears as a witness, is rightly attributed to that year by Fl. Wig. The present document seems to represent a slightly later arrangement.

p. 102, l. 16. *Apelwold bisceop*. Bishop of Winchester, see p. 323.

l. 17. *þæs hiredes his bisceopstoles*, i.e. the community at the Old Minster.

l. 20. *se abbod Æþelgar*. Abbot of the New Minster, see p. 342.

l. 22. *þa ylcan mylne*. There seems to be some omission or mistake in the record of the transaction given here, as the only mill mentioned passed into the possession of the Old Minster in exchange for two plots of ground.

ll. 24 f. *Eadgyfe abbedesse* etc. There is no reference elsewhere to a daughter of King Edgar of this name and it seems impossible that he could have had one old enough to attain the rank of abbess in his own lifetime. His daughter Eadgyth (the only one recorded elsewhere) became Abbess of Wilton and died there in 984 at the age of twenty-three (see William of Malmesbury, *Gesta Pontificum*, R.S. pp. 188–191). The name of the abbess of the Nunnery at Winchester in the time of Edgar is given in later records as St Edith (see Birch, *An Ancient Manuscript of Nunnaminster*, p. 7) but this seems due to confusion with Edgar's daughter Eadgyth. An abbess Eadgifu, who may very well be identical with the one named here, appears as a witness of a transaction in the time of Æthelred (see p. 136, l. 20), so that the name seems vouched for. I cannot explain the phrase *þæs cinges dohter* except (unsatisfactorily) as an interpolation.

p. 104, l. 1. *se tige*. See B.T. p. 1028, s.v. *tyge, tige*, III.

l. 3. *Ælfdryðe ðære hlæfdian*. See p. 340. The title regularly applied to the king's wife is 'the Lady'.

l. 14. *þe on...ðe on*. One of these relative clauses is incomplete.

cyrografum. These were made by writing two or more (generally three) copies of a document on the same parchment, with some word (generally *cyrograph*) in large capital letters filling most of the space between the copies. The parchment was then cut through the capitals so that the upper halves of the letters ran along the bottom of one portion and the lower halves of the same letters along the top of the corresponding portion. They could then be fitted together, if required, to show that they came from the same parchment.

In the present instance one of the chirographs is given to each of the parties concerned, but it is frequently found that one is deposited in a church or monastery which has no immediate interest in the transaction recorded.

L

MS. The Sherborne Cartulary, f. 8 *b*. See p. 278.

EDITION. B. 1308.

DATE. Probably between 970 and 975 (see notes below).

l. 20. *Cristes boc*. The Sherborne MS., from which this grant is taken, consists of two parts, the first a cartulary, the second a collection of divine offices. Both are in the same handwriting. This reference shows that Edgar's charter was originally entered in a gospel book.

Womburnan. Oborne, near Sherborne. Edgar is entered in a list of kings who were benefactors of the abbey as the donor of 5 hides there (see Dugdale, I, p. 337). This estate is included in Æthelred's Sherborne charter dated 998 (K. 701) and in D.B. is one of the nine described as *de victu monachorum*.

ll. 21 f. *mine yldran* etc. Æthelbald and Æthelbert were the brothers of Alfred, Edgar's great-grandfather. For the discovery of Æthelbald's coffin at Sherborne see p. 278. On 5 June 1925 a coffin, supposed to be Æthelbert's, was also discovered in the Lady Chapel there (see *The Times*, 6 June 1925, p. 9).

p. 106, l. 3. *Dunstan archieps*. See p. 333.

l. 5. *Wulsin eps*. Probably Wulfsige, Bishop of Cornwall, whose first signature appears in 963 (B. 1118) and his last in 980 (K. 624).

l. 6. *Alfstan eps*. There were three contemporary bishops of the name—at London, Rochester (see p. 334) and Ramsbury respectively. It is noteworthy that the two names Wulfsige and Ælfstan come at the end of the list of bishops attached to a charter of 973 (B. 1292). The two other Ælfstans (to be identified from other charters as the Bishop of London and the Bishop of Rochester respectively) come earlier in the list, and the last signature, therefore, must be that of Ælfstan, Bishop of Ramsbury, the most recently appointed of the three. It is possible, therefore, that the Ælfstan of the present grant is also the last-named. The charter in that case cannot be earlier than 970 (the year of his appointment) or later than 975 (the year of King Edgar's death).

ll. 7 ff. *Eanwulf.dux*. etc. The names which follow are all, without exception, attached to Æthelbert's Sherborne charter (see pp. 18, 279 ff.) and cannot agree with the date 970-975. It seems, therefore, that a mistake must have been made in copying this charter into the cartulary. A possible explanation may be found in the similarity between the names *Alfstan eps* of Edgar's charter and *Alhstan .eps*. of Æthelbert's, which may have led the copyist to confuse the two lists.

LI

MS. British Museum, Cotton Claudius C. IX, f. 200 (see p. 299). This record follows two sets of boundaries relating to Kingston and is introduced by the heading in red: *Item de hac eadem terra in uetustissimis et pene consumptis litteris · ita scriptum repperimus.*

EDITIONS. *Historia Monasterii de Abingdon*, R.S. I, p. 355.
B. 1262.
Stenton, *The Early History of the Abbey of Abingdon*, p. 36, gives a modern English translation.

DATE. Between the death of Earl Ælfheah in 971 and the promotion of Æthelgar, Abbot of the New Minster, to the see of Selsey in 980.

l. 13. *Ælfheah ealdorman.* Earl of Hampshire, see pp. 338 f.

Ælfhere ealdormenn. Earl of Mercia and the brother of Earl Ælfheah, see p. 319.

l. 14. *Kingestune.* Kingston Bagpuize, Berkshire. There is no mention of this estate in Ælfheah's will (Whitelock, No. IX), but Professor Stenton suggests that it was probably included in Faringdon (see *op. cit.* p. 37). Seven hides at Kingston had been granted by Edgar to the deacon Brihtheah in 970 (B. 1260)—a charter which is signed both by Ælfhere and Ælfheah.

Osgar abbud. Abbot of Abingdon, see p. 341.

l. 17. *Apelwarabirig.* This place is mentioned also in the boundaries of an unnamed estate on the Avon granted to the Abbey of Wilton (B. 1286). The description, which starts at the Avon, runs: *east...oð hit cymð to ðæm wege þe scæt fram hambres buruh* (Amesbury) *to Æpelwarebyrig oð hit cymð to þam wege þe scæt eastan fram winterburnan* (Winterbourne) *west to billancumbe to þæm ealdan wuduforda* (Woodford) etc. It is probable, therefore, that *Æpelwaraburg* is the modern Alderbury near Salisbury. It appears in D.B. as *Alwarberie* and was important enough to give its name to the hundred in which it was situated. From the entries in D.B. I, ff. 68 b, 72, 74 b, it would appear that the land there belonged to the king.

l. 19. *Adelwold bisceof.* Bishop of Winchester, see p. 323.

Ælfstan bisceop. Probably the Bishop of Ramsbury of the name (970–981).

Æthelgar abb. Abbot of the New Minster, see p. 342.

ll. 19 f. *Eadwine.* Probably the thegn of the name who was afterwards Earl of Sussex (see p. 366).

l. 20. *Ælfric cild.* Ælfhere's successor as Earl of Mercia, see p. 369.

ll. 20 f. *Ælfric Sirafes sunu · 7 Brihtric* etc. Both names, Ælfric and Brihtric, are frequently found among the witnesses of Edgar's charters. B. 1171 is signed by three men called Ælfric, B. 1172 and 1260 by two, while two men of the name Brihtric sign B. 1230 and 1282. Siraf does not seem to appear elsewhere.

ll. 22. *þysses gewrites geclofan*, i.e. the document was drawn up in the form of a chirograph, see p. 348.

NOTES

LII

MS. Rochester Cathedral, *Textus Roffensis*, f. 166 *b*. See p. 276.
EDITIONS[1]. Lambarde, *Perambulation of Kent*, 3rd ed. pp. 419-424, with an interlinear translation.
Hearne, *Textus Roffensis*, Appendix, pp. 379-382, from Lambarde's *Perambulation* etc. 1596, pp. 386-389.
B. 1322.

DATE. There is a good deal of doubt with regard to the date of this document and it is not certain that it is actually pre-Conquest. The use of the word *per* (mediaeval Latin *pera*) is in favour of a post-Conquest date for the existing English version (no other instance is recorded until the end of the fourteenth century, see N.E.D. s.v.), unless it can be regarded as a substitution by the twelfth-century scribe for an earlier and less familiar term. The English version is preceded in the MS. by a Latin version (B. 1321) which may have supplied the word *pera* but seems itself to have been derived from an English original in view of its use of the word *suliuas* throughout, representing A.S. *syll* and accompanied on its first appearance by the explanation *id est tres magnas trabes*, and also of its mistake in translating the place-name *Ufanhylle* (see below). Neither version seems to have been derived directly from the other.

If the document is actually pre-Conquest in origin, it seems possible, from what is known of the history of the estates assigned for the support of the bridge, that it was drawn up sometime between 942 at the earliest (see note on Malling) and 988 at the latest (see note on Wouldham) and probably not before 973 (see note on Fawkham). It is difficult, however, to determine the date with any certainty.

The wooden bridge at Rochester, after undergoing many vicissitudes and frequently falling into disrepair (it was burned in 1264 and severely damaged by a great flood in 1281), was replaced by a stone one in 1387. The contributory lands, as set forth in these regulations, were still held liable to a certain extent for the maintenance of the new bridge, but other estates were granted to the newly appointed bridge corporation to be held in trust for that purpose alone. For the history of the bridge in full see Hasted, *History of Kent*, II, pp. 15-22.

l. 26. *ærest* etc. The Latin version has a somewhat different reading and it is possible that it represents the original more exactly. It runs *primum ejusdem civitatis episcopus incipit operari in orientali brachio primam peram de terra*.

l. 26. *þære burge biscop*, i.e. the Bishop of Rochester.

l. 27. *þreo gyrda*. As the rod, pole or perch measures 16½ feet, the total length of the bridge, which can be calculated from the particulars given, was 437½ feet.

p. 108, l. 1. *Borcstealle*. In 1086 the Bishop of Rochester had

---

[1] For a translation and commentary see also Gordon Ward, 'The Lathe of Aylesford in 975' in *Archaeologia Cantiana*, XLVI.

80 burgage properties (*mansuras terrae*) in Rochester which belonged to Borstall and Frindsbury, 'his own manors' (D.B. I, f. 5 *b*; V.C.H. *Kent*, III, p. 220). It is possible that the tenants of these properties supplied the work for the bridge. Frindsbury had been granted to the Bishop of Rochester by Offa in 764 (B. 195), Borstall by Coenwulf, King of Mercia, in 811 (B. 339).

Cucclestane. For the grant of Cuxton to Rochester by Æthelwulf in 880 see B. 548.

l. 2. *Stoce.* It is recorded in D.B. that this estate belonged to the bishopric of Rochester, but that Earl Godwine bought it from two men who held it of the bishop without the latter's knowledge. Archbishop Lanfranc, however, in King William's time proved his claim to it against the Bishop of Bayeux, so that by 1086 it was again in the possession of the church of Rochester (D.B. I, f. 5 *b*; V.C.H. *Kent*, III, p. 220).

Gyllingeham. In 1086 Gillingham was held by the Archbishop of Canterbury except for half a *solin* which belonged to the Bishop of Bayeux (D.B. I, ff. 3 *b*, 8; V.C.H. *Kent*, III, pp. 211, 229).

l. 3. *Cætham.* In 1086 Chatham was held by the Bishop of Bayeux (D.B. I, f. 8 *b*; V.C.H. *Kent*, III, p. 229).

l. 5. *Heallingan.* For the grant of Halling to Rochester by King Egbert see B. 260.

ll. 5 f. *Trotescliue.* For the grant of Trottiscliffe to Rochester by Offa in 788 see B. 253.

l. 6. *Meallingan.* Three ploughlands at Malling were granted to the Bishop of Rochester by Edmund (see B. 779). This grant cannot be earlier than 942 in view of the fact that it is signed by Archbishop Oda, see p. 312.

Fliote. A later hand has added the word *suth* in the Latin version. South Fleet was held by the Bishop of Rochester, North Fleet by the Archbishop of Canterbury, see below.

Stane. Stone near Dartford.

l. 7. *Falchenham.* The reversion of Fawkham was bequeathed to Rochester by the parents of a certain Ælfric (see Whitelock, p. 28). It was forfeited, along with Bromley, by the latter's widow, but both estates were purchased from King Edgar by the Bishop of Rochester in 973 (see p. 365). The bishop then retained the title-deeds but allowed the widow, Brihtwaru, the usufruct of the estates. After the death of Edgar, however, he was forced to give up the title-deeds to Brihtwaru and her kinsman Brihtric, and it is not recorded when or how he obtained his rights again. The will of Brihtric and his wife is extant (Whitelock, No. XI) and there it is stated that both estates were to pass to Rochester after Brihtwaru's death. This must have occurred before 987, as by that date Bromley was held by the cathedral (K. 657).

The inclusion of Fawkham among the bishop's estates in the present document would suggest that it was drawn up sometime between 973 and the death of Edgar in 975, or else after Brihtwaru's death, the

NOTES

date of which is not recorded. See, however, under Snodland below.

l. 7. *se feorðe þe per* etc. The Latin version reads simply *quarta pera pertinet ad regem*. It is possible that in the Anglo-Saxon the *þe* is merely a repetition of the ending *-ðe* of the preceding ordinal number.

ll. 8 f. *of Ægelesforda · 7 of ellan þam læþe*. For the lathe of Aylesford see V.C.H. *Kent*, III, pp. 179 f. In 1086 Aylesford was held by the king (assessed at 1 *solin* with land for 15 ploughs), while a tenant of his was holding close to Rochester as much of the land of the manor as was valued at 7 pounds (D.B. I, f. 2 b; V.C.H. *Kent*, III, pp. 208 f.).

l. 9. *of Ufanhylle*. The Latin version reads *de super montaneis* with *et de vfenhylle* written above the line in a later hand. For the manor of 'Ovenhill', later Overhill, see Hasted, *History of Kent*, II, p. 16. It has ceased to exist as a separate property, see Cave-Browne, *The History of Boxley Parish*, p. 13.

l. 10. *of þam smalanlande*. The Latin version has *de smalalande* but the name seems to be merely descriptive. For a reference to *smale londe* elsewhere see Whitelock, p. 2, l. 29, and for the suggestion that the reference is to 'strips of land' see *ibid*. p. 102.

ll. 10 f. *Dudeslande...Gisleardeslande*. These cannot now be identified. Both forms seem to be derived from proper names. A certain Gislheard appears among the witnesses in two Kentish charters (B. 536, 538 dated 873 and 874 respectively).

l. 11. *Wuldeham*. For the history of Wouldham see No. XLI. It is noteworthy that here it is included among the king's lands, so that this document would seem to have been drawn up before its recovery by Rochester which was accomplished by 988 at the latest.

Burhham. In 1086 Burham was held by a tenant of the Bishop of Bayeux. It is recorded, however, that the Bishop of Rochester had the houses of this manor (in Rochester) and that they were worth 7 shillings (D.B. I, f. 7 b; V.C.H. *Kent*, III, p. 226). The tenants of these houses may possibly have supplied the work for the bridge.

l. 12. *Æcclesse*. According to D.B. there were three houses in Rochester which had belonged to this manor (D.B. f. 7; V.C.H. *Kent*, III, p. 225).

Horstede. Horsted near Aylesford.

Fearnlege. A grant of land at Farleigh was made by King Alfred to Earl Sigelm in 898 (B. 576). In 960 or 961 this estate was given to Christchurch by his daughter Eadgifu, the third wife of Edward the Elder (see Dugdale, I, p. 96; B. 1065).

Cærstane. A mistake has been made by the copyist of the Anglo-Saxon version in writing initial *c* for *t*. The estate meant is Teston, cf. the Latin version which has *Terstane*.

l. 13. *Cealce*. In 1086 there were three messuages (*hagas*) in Rochester attached to this manor (D.B. I, f. 9; V.C.H. *Kent*, III, p. 231).

Ædune. The Latin version has *Hathdune*, cf. D.B. *Hadone*, which is identified with Haven Street near Frindsbury (see V.C.H. *Kent*, III, pp. 231, 268).

NOTES

sy fifte per. An inquisition of 1340 shows that practically the same estates were responsible for the repair of the fifth pier, each by that time being liable for a certain fixed sum instead of the actual labour (see Flower, *Public Works in Mediaeval Law*, Selden Society, I, pp. 203-209). Hadlow and Swanton are not mentioned in the later list and instead of the two Peckhams it names *Oppeham* and West Peckham, but the lists otherwise are the same.

l. 15. *Wopringabyran.* Wateringbury and *Hæselholt* (see below) are both mentioned in the will of Brihtric and Ælfswith (Whitelock, pp. 26, 28), which was apparently drawn up sometime between 973 and 987. Both estates there are bequeathed to private individuals (Wateringbury to Wulfsige and *Hæselholt* to Sired) with the stipulation that two days' food-rent should be paid for each yearly to the church of St Andrew at Rochester. In 1086 there were 4 messuages (*hagae*) in Rochester which belonged to the manor of Wateringbury (D.B. I, f. 8 *b*; V.C.H. *Kent*, III, p. 230).

Netlestede. An estate of 6 hides at Nettlestead was bequeathed by Earl Alfred between 871 and 889 to his wife and daughter, to pass after the former's death to his kinsman Sigewulf (Harmer, pp. 13 f.). It is stipulated that Sigewulf and his heirs should pay 100 pence to Christchurch from the estate. In 1086 it was held by the Bishop of Bayeux (D.B. I, f. 8 *b*; V.C.H. *Kent*, III, p. 230).

þam twam Peccham, i.e. East and West Peckham. By 1086 one of them had passed to the Bishop of Bayeux. Peckham was one of the estates granted by Eadgifu to Christchurch in 960 or 961 (see above).

l. 16. *Hæselholte.* Probably Hadlow, which appears in D.B. as *Haslow*. For a case arising out of the refusal of two men to contribute to the repair of Rochester Bridge, which, it was stated, they were bound to do by reason of their tenements in Hadlow, held of the manor of West Peckham, see Flower, *op. cit.* p. 208, n. 1.

l. 17. *Swanatune.* Now Swanton Street, a hamlet about 4 miles south of Sittingbourne.

Offaham. For the grant of Offham to Christchurch by Æthelwulf see B. 407 f. In 1086 there was one house in Rochester attached to this estate (D.B. I, f. 7 *b*; V.C.H. *Kent*, III, p. 226).

Westerham. This estate was one of those left by Earl Alfred to his wife and daughter, see above.

l. 19. *Holinganburnan.* Hollingbourn was bequeathed to Christchurch by the Ætheling Æthelstan about 1015 (see Whitelock, p. 58). There is no mention elsewhere of a lathe attached to it. In 1086 there were three burgage properties (*mansiones terrae*) in Rochester which belonged to the manor of Allington in Hollingbourn, held by Hugh de Port of the Bishop of Bayeux (D.B. I, f. 8; V.C.H. *Kent*, III, p. 227).

l. 21. *Howaran.* The Latin version reads *homines de hou*. In 1086 Hoo itself, which had been held by Earl Godwine, was in the hands of the Bishop of Bayeux. Nine houses in Rochester which belonged

NOTES 355

to the manor and which paid 6 shillings had been taken away from it (D.B. I, f. 8 *b*; V.C.H. *Kent*, III, p. 229).

l. 23. *syo landper æt þam west ænde.* It is described in the Latin version as *nona pera quæ ultima est in occidentali brachio.*

l. 24. *Flyote.* Distinguished in the Latin version as *Northfleta*, see above.

Hehham. For the grant of Higham by Offa to the Archbishop of Canterbury in 774 see B. 213. Two ploughlands there were bequeathed to Rochester Cathedral by Brihtric and Ælfswith, see above.

Denetune. Denton near Gravesend.

l. 25. *Melantune.* Milton next Gravesend.

Hludesdune. In 1086 there were four houses in Rochester which belonged to this manor (D.B. I, f. 7 *b*; V.C.H. *Kent*, III, p. 225).

Meapeham. In 940 Earl Eadwulf granted an estate of 12 hides at Meopham to Christchurch (see B. 741, 747). It is included also in the list of estates given by Eadgifu (see p. 353) and an estate there passed to Christchurch likewise by the will of Brihtric and Ælfswith. In 1086 Meopham was held by Christchurch. Its assessment had been reduced from 10 *solins* in the time of King Edward to 7 and there was land for 30 ploughs (D.B. I, f. 4 *b*; V.C.H. *Kent*, III, p. 216).

ll. 25 f. *Snodilande.* This estate was also connected with Ælfric and his family (see above under Fawkham). It was bequeathed to Rochester in reversion by Ælfric's father (Whitelock, p. 28) and the title-deeds relating to it were given to the cathedral by his mother, but afterwards sold to Ælfric without the bishop's knowledge (see p. 122, ll. 3 f.). The case brought against Ælfric's widow for the recovery of the title-deeds was successful and led to the forfeiture of Bromley and Fawkham (see above), but after King Edgar's death the previous decision was reversed and the bishop was forced once more to give up the title-deeds. When or how a settlement of the dispute was come to is uncertain, but according to Brihtric's will this estate also was to pass to Rochester Cathedral after Brihtwaru's death. It is curious, therefore, to find it included here among the archbishop's lands. It was alienated from Rochester Cathedral again at a later date and recovered probably in 995 or soon afterwards (see No. LXIX), but there is nothing in what is known of its history to connect it with Canterbury.

l. 26. *Berlingan.* This estate is mentioned along with Wateringbury and *Hæselholt* in the will of Brihtric and Ælfswith. Like them it was bequeathed to a private individual—Wulfheah—who had to pay 1000 pence to St Andrew's at Rochester and also render two days' food-rent yearly on behalf of the souls of Brihtric and Ælfswith and their ancestors.

Peadleswyrþe. Paddlesworth near Snodland.

ealla þa dænewaru. The Latin version reads *de omnibus illis hominibus qui manent in illa valle.* It has an additional paragraph at the end which enjoins that the beams should be of sufficient size to support the weight of the planks and of the traffic crossing the bridge.

LIII

MS. British Museum, Additional MS. 15350, f. 6 (or 8 by the new numbering). See p. 274.

EDITION. K. 1347.

DATE. Between 975 and 978 or 979, i.e. sometime during the reign of Edward the Martyr. It cannot be dated more exactly.

The Anglo-Saxon version of this exchange is preceded by a Latin one, which seems to be a translation.

p. 110, l. 1. *Aðelwold biscop.* Bishop of Winchester, see p. 323.

l. 2. *Eadwardes cyninges.* Edward, the elder son of Edgar, succeeded his father as king in 975. He was murdered in 978 or 979 (Sax. Chr.) and came to be regarded as a saint and martyr. In 980 his body was removed by Earl Ælfhere from Wareham, where it was first buried, to Shaftesbury, and many miracles were performed at his tomb there. His festival was celebrated on 18 March (see V Æthelred, 16).

l. 3. *Æðelhilde.* I have taken this as the genitive of the feminine name Æthelhild. The Latin version reads *contra Ælfwinum...et Æðelhildam matrem ipsius* but there is nothing to show that Æthelhild was directly concerned in the exchange, as the singular pronoun 'he, his, him' is used throughout. She appears as a witness, so that her approval was accorded to the transaction.

l. 4. .XII. *hida landes æt Mordune.* There are three charters in the *Codex Wintoniensis* which relate to an estate of 20 hides at *Mordun* and it is clear from the boundaries (which are the same in every case) that the place meant is Moredon in the parish of Rodbourne Cheney near Swindon, Wiltshire[1]. The earliest of these (B. 788, dated 943) is a grant by King Edmund to his thegn Ælfsige, the second (B. 983) is a grant by King Edwy in 956 to his thegn Wynsige, while the third (B. 1217) is a grant by King Edgar in 968 to his thegn Edwin. Two charters in the Abingdon MS., Cotton Claudius B. VI, relate (as the boundaries show) to the same estate. The first (B. 1093, dated 962) is a grant by Edgar to the thegn Edwin (cf. B. 1217 above), while the second (K. 1305, dated 1008) records the restitution of the estate to the Abbey of Abingdon by King Æthelred, into whose hands it had come by forfeiture. The boundaries in these two grants are the same and are rather fuller than those given in the Winchester charters. In both the amount of land is given as 20 hides.

If the *Mordun* of the present exchange is identical with the Wiltshire Moredon, then Ælfwine's father Ælfsige must have succeeded Edwin in the ownership of the estate and was probably not long dead when the exchange was effected by his son. There is no mention in any of the Moredon grants of any obligation to pay a food-rent to the Old Minster, but this seems to have been a private arrangement between the owner of *Mordun* and the community and may supply a reason for the interest taken at Winchester in the descent of the Wiltshire estate of the name.

[1] See Grundy, *Archaeological Journal*, LXXVI, pp. 283 f.

NOTES

There is nothing to show how or when Moredon came into the possession of the Abbey of Abingdon, and the charters supply no further account of its history. The fact that the exchange concerns an estate of only 12 hides may be regarded as casting doubt on the identification of the present *Mordun* with the Wiltshire Moredon. It is noteworthy, however, that although the size of the Wiltshire estate is invariably given as 20 hides in the charters, the survey attached to the earliest surviving grant (B. 788) refers to 16 hides only. This may point to a possible subdivision of the estate on a 4-hide basis.

ll. 5 f. *his yldran* etc. There is nothing in the royal grants of Moredon to show that there was any relationship between the successive grantees, but this does not necessarily mean that none existed. If the *Mordun* of the present charter is actually the same estate it would seem to have passed regularly from father to son.

ll. 6 ff. *Ælfsige* etc. There is no separate record of Ælfsige's grant.

ll. 8 f. *he him on þæt ylcan gera*. The reference, I take it, is to Ælfwine. The Latin version, however, reads: *Ælfsige...genitor illius hanc eandem tellurem familiae in uetusto monasterio...pro pastu designauit et eis eodem tenore e contra concessit intra ciuitatem Wintoniae duo iugera ruris* etc.

l. 13. *Ælfred cining*. There is no record of any grant of the kind by Alfred whose surviving charters are very few in number.

l. 15. *Æþælmær ealdorman*. Æthelmær, Earl of Hampshire, died in 982 and was buried at the New Minster (Sax. Chr. C, Fl. Wig.). He signs as *dux* from 977 onwards and may have succeeded Ælfheah, who died in 971. His will is extant (Whitelock, No. x). A later earl of the name held office in the Western Provinces, see pp. 386 f.

Æþelgar abbod. See p. 342.

ll. 17 f. *Þonne synt ðyses gehwerfes* etc. There is no corresponding clause in the Latin version.

LIV

MSS. (*a*) British Museum, Harley 55, f. 4 *b*. This is a codex executed by various hands. Oswald's statement is preceded by a number of medical prescriptions in Anglo-Saxon (written about 1040) and a copy of the Laws of Edgar (written about 1050).

(*b*) British Museum, Harley 6841, p. 129. This is a late paper copy of (*a*).

EDITION. B. 1278 f.

The text is from (*a*).

DATE. It is probable that this statement was drawn up soon after Oswald became Archbishop of York in 972 (see p. 319).

l. 22. *Ottanlege*. Otley in Wharfedale. There is no record of the grant of Otley to York.

ll. 23 ff. *Haddincham* etc. Of the list which follows Ilkley, Menston,

Burley, Guiseley, Middleton, Denton and Little Timble are entered as berewicks of Otley in D.B. I, f. 303 b (V.C.H. *Yorks.* II, p. 213).

l. 24. *Scefinc.* This seems to be represented by the modern name Chevin, which is applied to a line of hills south of the Wharfe and appears also in a number of farm names in the vicinity.

p. 112, l. 1. *Becwudu.* For the identification with Beckwith see *Introduction to the Survey of English Place-Names* (English Place-Name Society, Vol. I, Part I), p. 66.

Byllinctun. I have not been able to find any modern name corresponding to this in Wharfedale.

l. 2. *Rypum.* Æthelstan was by tradition the chief benefactor of Ripon (see his rhyming charter, B. 647). The monastery there was destroyed by Edred when he harried Northumbria (Sax. Chr. 948 D) but was restored by Oswald (see *Historians of the Church of York*, R.S. I, p. 462).

Heawic. The two villages of this name are now distinguished as Copt Hewick and Bridge Hewick.

Ansætleh. I have not been able to identify this name as it stands. Can it be a misrepresentation of Sawley which is included among the berewicks belonging to Ripon (D.B. I, f. 303 b; V.C.H. *Yorks.* II, p. 214)?

l. 3. *Myðtune.* Myton-on-Swale (see below).

l. 4. *Scirebunnan.* Sherburn in Elmet. It is recorded in the Chronicle of the Archbishops of York (see *Historians of the Church of York*, R.S. II, p. 340, n. 5) that King Edgar gave Sherburn to Archbishop Oscytel in 963. A charter of that year, however, of which a copy is preserved in the *Liber Albus* of York (B. 1112), records the grant of 20 *casati* at Sherburn to a man of the name of Æslac, and there is no further record of the grant of the estate to York. In D.B. Sherburn is entered as a manor which had been and still was in the demesne of the Archbishop of York. With its berewicks, which are left unspecified, it was assessed at 96 carucates for geld (D.B. I, f. 302 b; V.C.H. *Yorks.* II, p. 210).

ll. 4 f. *Ceoredesholm...Gisferþ[es] dæll.* Unidentified.

l. 7. *Oscytel yrcebiscop.* Oscytel (see p. 341) was Oswald's predecessor at York. He died on 1 November 971.

l. 8. *for unrihtan hæmede.* Warnings against illicit unions are frequent in the later Anglo-Saxon Laws (cf. V Æthelred, 10 = VI Æthelred, 11 = I Cnut, 6, 3; I Cnut, 24) but no penalties are specified. According to the early Kentish laws offences of the kind involved excommunication and the payment of 100 shillings in the case of a nobleman, 50 shillings in the case of a commoner. Forfeiture of the offender's goods, if a native of the country, is expressly forbidden (Wihtred, 3–5, 1).

Æffeltune. There are several places named Appleton in Yorkshire but none of them was in the possession of the archbishop in 1086. The transaction recorded here is not mentioned elsewhere.

NOTES

ll. 9 f. *Yferingaham.* Everingham in the East Riding. There is no other record of this purchase. In 1086 Everingham with its berewicks was rated at 17 carucates for geld (D.B. I, f. 302 *b*; V.C.H. *Yorks.* II, p. 211).

ll. 10 f. *fæge Osulfes fæder.* Miss Whitelock has pointed out a parallel use of the corresponding O.N. word on the Rök stone, see Gordon, *Introduction to Old Norse*, p. 168, No. 12, l. 2.

l. 11. *Neoweboldan.* Now represented by North and South Newbald in the East Riding. A charter of Edgar dated 963 (B. 1113) by which he grants 30 *casati* at Newbald to Earl Gunner is preserved in the *Liber Albus* of York. There is no other record of the transaction mentioned here. In 1086 the estate was rated at 28 carucates and 2 bovates for geld with land for 16 ploughs (D.B. I, f. 302 *b*; V.C.H. *Yorks.* II, p. 211).

l. 12. *[ge]mancsun.* The mancus was equivalent to 30 pence so that the sum paid was 15 pounds.

l. 13. *Heolperbi.* Helperby was rated at 5 carucates and had land for 3 ploughs. In 1086 it was waste (D.B. I, f. 303; V.C.H. *Yorks.* II, p. 213).

ll. 13 f. *wæron twegen gebroþra* etc. Reference is made by Wulfstan II, Archbishop of York, in his homilies to occurrences of the kind, see Napier, *Wulfstan*, p. 161, note.

l. 14. *Mytun.* Myton-on-Swale.

l. 15. *Wibustan.* Probably identical with the *Wipestune* of D.B. now represented by Wide Open Farm in Skelton (see Pl.N. *North Riding of Yorks.* pp. 17 f.). Both Myton and Wide Open are included in D.B. in the list of lands the soke of which belonged to Helperby (1, f. 303; V.C.H. *Yorks.* II, p. 213).

Þurulfestun, cf. the *Turulfestorp* of D.B. (also included in the list of lands the soke of which belonged to Helperby) which has now become Tholthorpe—an instance, apparently, of the substitution of the Scandinavian *þorp* for the English *tun* (see Pl.N. *North Riding of Yorks.* pp. 21 f.).

Ioletun. Youlton, see Pl.N. *Devon*, Part I, p. liii.

Þorp. For the distribution of the name 'Thorpe' in the North Riding, see Pl.N. *North Riding of Yorks.* Introd. p. xxiv. The absence of any distinguishing prefix makes identification impossible.

l. 16. *Scyteby.* Skidby in the East Riding near Beverley. In 1086 the archbishop had 14 carucates and the third part of a carucate there (D.B. I, f. 381 *b*; V.C.H. *Yorks.* II, p. 318).

l. 17. *Bracenan.* Bracken, a hamlet about eight miles north of Beverley. There are no charters extant relating to the purchase of either Skidby or Bracken.

l. 18. *into sc̄e Iohanne.* It would seem that the collegiate church of St John at Beverley is meant. According to tradition it was founded by Æthelstan (see the two versions of his rhyming charter, B. 644 f.).

ll. 19 f. *min hlaford*, i.e. the king. W. H. Stevenson suggests that

360 NOTES

the reference is to Edward the Martyr or Æthelred rather than Edgar, who is mentioned by name immediately before (see *E.H.R.* XXVII, 1912, p. 14, n. 65).

l. 20. '*into sc̄e Pe*[*tre*]'. York Minster which was dedicated to St Peter.

ll. 21 ff. *pas opre land* etc. I have found it impossible to establish the remainder of the text satisfactorily.

LV

MS. British Museum, Cotton Tiberius A. XIII, f. 77 *b*. See p. 259.

EDITIONS. Hearne, *Hemingi Chartularium* etc. I, p. 163.
K. 612.

p. 114, l. 1. [*Wulf*]*ringctun*. Wolverton, Worcestershire. In 1086 an estate of 2 hides at Wolverton was held by Roger de Laci of the manor of Kempsey and tenanted by *Aiulf*. The name of the previous holder, who continued in possession after the Conquest, is given as *Alric* (D.B. I, f. 172 *b*; V.C.H. *Worc*. I, p. 288).

l. 3. *EADWARDES*. Edward the Martyr, see p. 356.

l. 6. *Cymesige*. Kempsey, Worcestershire. In 1086 this manor was assessed at 24 hides, 13 of which were in demesne.

l. 12. *cyrcanlade*. See pp. 334 f.

l. 18. *Æpelwold*. As no additional names are given it is possible that Æthelwold died without appointing any heirs.

Kemble has incorporated in this charter a survey of Wolverton which actually occurs quite independently in the cartulary, see Hearne, II, p. 359.

l. 21. *Godingc diac̄*. Goding and Leofstan are regular witnesses of Oswald's charters from 977 onwards. They also sign in 996 (K. 695).

l. 22. *Winsige prb̄t*. Wynsige's name first appears in 969. A grant of Oswald of that year (B. 1243) is said to have been made with his cognisance and that of all the monks at Worcester (no other names are given), while his appointment as *decanus* at Worcester is recorded by Fl. Wig. in the same year. The latter states further that in 969 Oswald expelled from the community all those who refused to become monks, but if this is true they must have been allowed to return later (probably after the death of Edgar in 975) as his grants from 977 onwards are invariably witnessed by a number of *clerici*, the majority of whom are found before 969. Only one of Oswald's grants, unfortunately, falls between 969 and 977, namely B. 1298 dated 974, and it too is said to have been made with the cognisance of Wynsige (here described as *decanus*) and all the monks at Worcester. There are altogether seven grants dated 977, one of which (K. 615) is signed by 10 witnesses with the title *monachus*, 1 (Edgar) with the title *presbyter*, 1 (Leofstan) with the title *diaconus* and 15 with the title *clericus*. The witnesses described as monks include 5 who are found in Oswald's earlier grants, namely Æthelstan (who signs there as priest), Ælfsige (who signs as

NOTES 361

deacon), Wulfheah, Leofwine and Ælfgar (who sign as *clerici*), while all but two of the *clerici* are found in 969 or earlier. Edgar who signs as priest is likewise a regular witness of Oswald's earlier grants (see p. 320). The list of witnesses attached to the remaining six charters of 977 is well represented by the present grant. The number of priests, when compared with the grants of 969, has been increased, but the only actually new name is that of Wynsige, for Wulfric, Edgar and Æthelstan sign the earlier grants as priests, Ælfsige as deacon, Wulfheah and Edward as *clerici*. Four of the deacons' names are new, but Ælfgar signs as *clericus* up to 969. The only new witnesses among the *clerici* are Ælfnoth and Æthelric.

When this list is compared with K. 615 (the exceptional charter of 977) it is found that all those signing as priests and deacons appear there as monks with the exception of Wulfric (the only man of the name is described as *clericus*), Edgar (who signs both as priest), Edward (who signs as *clericus*), Goding (who does not appear) and Leofstan (who signs both as deacon). It seems possible, therefore, that K. 615 is the first of the 977 series, and that the present grant and the remaining five represent the community as it was finally constituted. The course of the reform movement at Worcester, however, is by no means easy to follow or to piece together from such fragmentary evidence. Fl. Wig.'s statement with regard to the introduction of monks and the transference of Wynsige from Ramsey to Worcester in 969 is supported by the one exceptional charter of that year (B. 1243), while the fact that only one grant of later date is found until the year 977 (B. 1298) may point to an unusual or unsettled state of affairs during the eight intervening years (although Oswald's appointment to York in 972 must also be taken into account). The fact that these two charters are exceptional in their account of the witnesses is not to my mind a proof that they are not genuine, while the statement that Wynsige was transferred from Ramsey to Worcester in 969 is not necessarily invalidated by the fact that the former was a very recent foundation to which the earliest date assigned is 968. It seems likely from the evidence of the charters that Wynsige came to Worcester late in 969 (there are ten grants of that year with the usual and earlier list of witnesses) and, since nothing is known of his career before that date, it is possible (if such an assumption is necessary) that part of his training was received elsewhere than at Ramsey. That he had a Worcestershire connection seems evident from K. 616, a grant made to him by Oswald in 977 of land at Washbourne, *swa swa Wulfstan his fæder hit hæfde*.

For a different view of the evidence and the course of events see Armitage Robinson, *St Oswald and the Church of Worcester* (British Academy Supplemental Papers, No. v), App. B, pp. 33-37.

ll. 23 ff. *Wulfric* etc. For Wulfric, Edgar, Cynethegn, Wulfhun and Brihtstan see p. 320; for Wulfheah, Æthelstan, Wulfgar, Cynestan, Wynstan, Edwin and Æthelwold, see p. 321; for Edward and Wulfnoth see p. 336; for Ælfgar, Leofwine and Ælfstan see p. 335.

NOTES

l. 23. *Æþelsige diāc.* Æthelsige signs as deacon up to 981, then as priest until 996.
l. 24. *Wulfweard diāc.* Wulfweard continues to sign up to 990.
Ælfnoð cl. Ælfnoth's signature continues till 989.
l. 27. *Æþric cl.* A cleric of this name signs from 977 to 980.
l. 28. *Ælfsige prb̄t.* Ælfsige signs three charters of 969 as *diaconus*. His signature as priest continues up to 996 (K. 695).

LVI

MS. British Museum, Cotton Tiberius A. XIII, f. 72. See p. 259.
EDITIONS. Hearne, *Hemingi Chartularium* etc. I, p. 151.
K. 680.
DATE. This grant and the two following ones should probably be attributed to the year 977, as Brihtstan's signature is not found after that date.

p. 116, l. 1. *Hymeltune*. According to Hemming Himbleton, Spetchley, Wolverton and 1 hide at Whittington were given by Bishop Brihtheah along with the manor of Hallow to his brother Æthelric. They were afterwards seized by William, Earl of Hereford, and so were alienated from the church of Worcester (Hearne, I, p. 266). This is corroborated to a certain extent by the evidence of D.B., where Æthelric is named as the former holder of lands at Himbleton and Spetchley to which Roger de Laci had succeeded. Himbleton is described as waste (D.B. I, f. 173 *b*; V.C.H. *Worc.* I, p. 296).

l. 3. *Eadwardes*. Edward the Martyr, see p. 356.

ll. 13 f. *þære are hide*. The inflected form *are* for *anre* occurs several times in the cartulary.

l. 14. *landgemæru*. For the boundaries worked out in detail see Grundy, *The Saxon Charters of Worcestershire*, p. 152. They are repeated in the cartulary followed by another set taken from a charter which has not been preserved (see Grundy, *op. cit.* pp. 291–295). A third set is attached to a grant of 5 hides at Himbleton by Earl Æthelred to Æthelwulf (B. 552, dated 884, see Grundy, *op. cit.* pp. 147–151). Grundy points out that the surveys seem actually to apply to the neighbouring parish of Huddington. His investigations have shown that the survey attached to B. 552 seems to include the whole parish, while the unattached set apparently defines the part of Huddington outside the 1 hide leased to Wulfgeat.

ll. 14 f. *egcbrihtingcþirne*. One of the landmarks of the 5 hides at Himbleton is *egcbyrhttigccroft*. It lay between the Bow Brook and the pit which has given its name to Blackpit Lane (see Pl.N. *Worc.* p. 136).

l. 16. *on efene lea þæt to mægdenne brigce*. These are mentioned also in the unattached set of boundaries. There is a reference to *mægidna brycg* in the boundaries of Crowle and, as Grundy points out, it must have been situated at or close to the junction of the Crowle, Grafton Flyford and Huddington boundaries.

NOTES

l. 20. *se fifta æcer*. The estate as a whole consisted apparently of 5 hides (B. 552), so that the amount of meadow is exactly proportioned to Wulfgeat's 1 hide.

ll. 20 f. *þære dalmædue*, cf. *gedallandes*, p. 299.

l. 21. *þæs wuda gemære*. As Grundy points out two pieces of timberland which meet at the *ceastergeat* are included in the survey which follows.

ll. 22 f. *æt ceastergeate* etc. This *ceaster* reference is extremely difficult to understand as there are no traces of earthworks or Roman remains in the vicinity (see Grundy, *op. cit.* p. 154). I can only suggest that Worcester is meant, see p. 267.

l. 25. *to deorleage*. This appears also in the boundaries of Oddingley (B. 1108).

l. 27. *wicwege*. Droitwich appears simply as *Wich* in D.B. and forms without the prefix are found as late as the fifteenth and sixteenth centuries (see Pl.N. *Worc.* pp. 285, 286, n. 1). I have taken *wic* in the same sense here.

ll. 28 f. *Wulfgeat* etc. This probably represents an endorsement or marginal note which has been incorporated by the copyist.

ll. 33 ff. *Wynsige* etc. For Wynsige, Goding and Leofstan see p. 360; for Wulfric, Edgar, Cynethegn, Wulfhun and Brihtstan see p. 320; for Wulfheah, Æthelstan, Wulfgar, Cynestan, Edwin and Wynstan see p. 321; for Ælfsige, Æthelsige, Ælfnoth and Ætheric see p. 362; for Edward and Wulfnoth see p. 336; for Ælfgar and Leofwine see p. 335.

l. 38. *Wulfweard cl.* A mistake seems to have been made here as Wulfweard invariably signs Oswald's other grants as *diaconus*, see p. 362.

LVII

MS. British Museum, Cotton Tiberius A. XIII, f. 67. See p. 259.

EDITIONS. Hearne, *Hemingi Chartularium* etc. I, p. 141.
K. 681.

DATE. Probably 977, see p. 362.

p. 118, l. 1. *Genanofre*, cf. p. 124, l. 15. The name has now disappeared.

l. 3. *Eadwardes*. Edward the Martyr, see p. 356.

l. 5. *Wulfheah*. See p. 321.

l. 12. *lipperdes gemære*. The name survives in Leopard Grange (see Pl.N. *Worc.* p. 161) in the parish of St Martin's without Worcester.

l. 14. *Wulfgares gemære*, i.e. the boundary of an estate *æt þære Pirian* (cf. Perry Wood) leased to him by Bishop Oswald in 969 (B. 1240).

ll. 20 f. *seo hondseten*. The list of priests is the same as in the two preceding charters except for the omission of Wulfheah (who as grantee does not sign) and the inclusion of Wistan (see p. 336). The list of deacons is the same and rightly includes Wulfweard (see p. 362). The list of clerics is the same as in the grant of Wolverton (see p. 114) except for the omission of Wulfnoth and the inclusion of Ufic (see p. 335).

LVIII

MS. British Museum, Cotton Tiberius A. XIII, f. 65 b. See p. 259.
EDITIONS. Hearne, *Hemingi Chartularium* etc. I, p. 138.
K. 682.
DATE. Probably 977, see p. 362.

p. 120, l. 1. *Witlea.* Little Witley, Worcestershire. In 1086 a hide of land at Little Witley was held by Urse d'Abitot of the bishop's manor of Wick Episcopi (D.B. I, f. 172 b; V.C.H. *Worc.* I, p. 288). It had formerly been held by the priest *Arnwin* who, according to Hemming, received it from Bishop Ealdred at the request of Eadric the Wild (Hearne, I, p. 256).

l. 3. *EADWARDES.* Edward the Martyr, see p. 356.

l. 5. *sumum preoste.* The word *preost* is used with the general sense of a member of the priesthood in Anglo-Saxon and here the reference is obviously to the Wulfgar who regularly signs as *clericus* (see p. 321). The word *mæssepreost* is used to distinguish those who were qualified to perform the office of mass.

Wulfgar, who signs among the *clerici* from 962 to 996, received altogether four grants from Oswald. The earliest of these, B. 1240 dated 969, comprised a hide of land at Battenhall (on the outskirts of Worcester), a messuage by the south wall of Worcester, a church and various accessories described in a paragraph which follows the signatures and may be a later addition to the original grant. It runs as follows: *Eac we writað him þa circan ⁊ þone circstall ⁊ þone worþig to þære burnan ⁊ þone croft be suþan þære burnan · 7 .vi. æcras mæde on þa gerefmæde ⁊ ic on him be Godes bletsunga ⁊ be ure ægþer ge wuda ge on felda · swa his bóc him wisaþ.* In 980 he received 5 hides at Waresley (K. 627) and in 985 1 hide at *Cloptun* in the parish of St John's in Bedwardine (K. 649). All these grants were for three lives, but his is the only name recorded in connection with any of them.

ll. 13 f. *þæs landes gemæra.* For the boundaries worked out in detail see Grundy, *The Saxon Charters of Worcestershire*, pp. 268–270. They are repeated in the cartulary (Hearne, II, p. 352) and are followed by another set taken from a grant of 4 hides at Witley made by Oswald to Eadmær in 969 (Hearne, I, p. 159).

ll. 15 f. *of ðrym gemæran* etc. The same line from the 'three boundaries' to the *Doferic* is followed in the Latin version of the boundaries of Wick Episcopi and the lands attached thereto (B. 219). The Anglo-Saxon version runs differently. The 'three boundaries' appear again in connection with Bentley (K. 765, 1313). Grundy identifies them as those of Wichenford, Holt and Little Witley.

l. 16. *kyllan hrigc*. Probably 'Cylla's ridge', see Pl.N. *Worc*. p. 396.
l. 17. *sylweg*. Grundy suggests the meaning 'Pillar (?) Way'.
l. 18. *buttingc graf*. This may represent a genitival compound, 'Butt(a)'s copse', see Pl.N. *Worc*. p. 395.
eccles bróc. For other instances of the prefix *eccles-* in stream names see Ekwall, *English River Names*, p. 141.
l. 19. *doferic*. The old name of the Shrawley Brook, see Ekwall, *op. cit*. p. 136.
ll. 20 ff. The witnesses are the same as in the preceding charter except for the inclusion of Wulfheah and the omission of Wulfgar (the grantee).

LIX

MSS. (*a*) Rochester Cathedral, *Textus Roffensis*, f. 162 *b*. See p. 276.
(*b*) British Museum, Harley MS. 311, f. 24, copied from (*a*) in the seventeenth century.
EDITIONS. K. 1258.
T. p. 264.
B. 1296.
Essays in Anglo-Saxon Law, App. No. 19, from K.
The text is from (*a*).

DATE. The Bishop of Rochester who figures in the events described here must be Ælfstan (see p. 334). The only stages in the proceedings which can be dated more or less exactly are the purchase of Bromley by the bishop from the king, of which an independent record survives, dated 955 for 973 (B. 1295), and the enforced relinquishment of the title-deeds by the bishop which must fall between the date of Edwin's appointment to an earldom (probably by Edward the Martyr) and that of his death in 982 (see below). By 987 Bromley was again in the possession of the cathedral, from which it was taken by Æthelred but restored in 998 (K. 657, 700).

p. 122, l. 1. *Bromleage...Fealcnaham*. Bromley and Fawkham, Kent. Both of these estates were held by the Bishop of Rochester in 1086, Bromley assessed at 3 *solins* (as compared with 6 *solins* in the time of King Edward) and with land for 13 ploughs, Fawkham assessed at 2 *solins* (D.B. I, f. 5 *b*; V.C.H. *Kent*, III, p. 219).
l. 2. *Snodinglandes*. Snodland, Kent. For a later lawsuit about this estate see No. LXIX. It was held by the Bishop of Rochester in 1086, assessed at 3 *solins* (as compared with 6 *solins* in the time of King Edward) and with land for 6 ploughs (D.B. *loc. cit*.).
l. 4. *Ælfrice Æscwynne sunu*. His father's name was Ælfhere, see Whitelock, p. 28 (the will of Brihtric and Ælfswith). According to this will Ælfric's ancestors (or parents) bequeathed Fawkham to Rochester, his father bequeathed Snodland and he himself bequeathed Bromley.

ll. 10 f. *se arcebiscop Dunstan.* See p. 333.
l. 11. *Aðelwold biscop.* Bishop of Winchester, see p. 323.
ll. 11 f. *Ælfstan biscop·7 oðer Ælfstan.* Probably Ælfstan, Bishop of London (see p. 334), and Ælfstan, Bishop of Ramsbury (see p. 350), unless one of the two is the Bishop of Rochester himself.
l. 12. *Ælfere ealdorman.* Earl of Mercia, see p. 319.
ll. 13 f. *ða stod ðara wydewan áre* etc. This shows that Ælfric must have been regarded as an accessory to the theft. His widow's name was Brihtwaru (see Whitelock, *loc. cit.*).
l. 14. *Wulfstan se gerefa.* Probably Wulfstan of Dalham (see below), who seems to have acted as sheriff in Cambridgeshire as well as in West Kent (see Chadwick, *Anglo-Saxon Institutions*, p. 231, n. 1).
ll. 17 f. *se byscop gebohte ða bécc.* The reversion of these estates had been granted to Rochester, hence the bishop's anxiety to secure them.
l. 18. *on Godeshylle.* Is it possible that Gadshill near Rochester is meant?
l. 20. *þurh forespræce·7 costnunge*, i.e. the bishop used not only argument in favour of his claim but the added inducement of payment in order that the king might waive his right to the estates. According to the Bromley charter (B. 1295) a certain sum was contributed by the reeve Wulfstan in order that the grant might be made incontrovertible.
l. 22. *gewatt se cing.* Edgar died in 975.
ll. 22 f. *Byrhtric ðare wydewan mæg.* It is his will and his wife's that is referred to on the preceding page (Whitelock, No. XI).
l. 24. *on reaflace.* For the use of *reaflac* elsewhere with reference to the illegal seizure of an estate see p. 128, l. 16.
ðane ealdorman Eadwine. Edwin, Earl of Sussex, died in 982 (Sax. Chr. C) and was buried at Abingdon. His signature as *dux* appears for the first time in a charter of Edward the Martyr (K. 1276) but he is probably to be identified with the Edwin whose signature as *minister* is found in earlier charters and continues till the reign of Edward the Martyr (K. 1277). It would appear from the present document that his earldom included Kent as well as Sussex.
ll. 25 f. *geneddan ðane biscop* etc. It would seem, from what we know of Anglo-Saxon legal procedure, that this could only have been done by clearing Ælfric of the charge of complicity in the theft of the Snodland title-deeds. According to the evidence supplied by Brihtric's will an amicable settlement was finally made whereby the reversion of the estates to Rochester was once more agreed upon, see Whitelock, p. 28.
ll. 27 f. *Tale·ne teames·ne ahnunga.* These represent the three types of legal procedure which could be adopted in a case of disputed possession. The term *talu* does not occur in the laws but its meaning—the formal statement of a claim—is clear from its use elsewhere in the charters (cf. pp. 384, 401). The process of vouching to warranty—*team*—was the subject of frequent legislation (see Robertson, p. 423

NOTES 367

for references). The process called *ahnung*—declaration of ownership—is also frequently referred to in the laws and the mode of procedure, in the case of livestock, is given in II Æthelstan, 9.

The formula employed in a declaration of the kind, where land was in question, is given in the treatise which opens with the words *Hit becwæð* (see p. 339), cap. 3 ff. It begins: 7 *ic agnian wylle to agenre æhte ðæt ðæt ic hæbbe 7 næfre ðe myntan ne plot ne ploh, ne turf ne toft, ne furh ne fotmæl, ne land ne læse, ne fersc ne mersc, ne ruh ne rum, wudes ne feldes, landes ne strandes, wealtes ne wæteres.*

l. 29. *ðæs ceapes*. It would seem that the purchase of the estates by the bishop is meant. Two of the bishops named as witnesses cannot be accepted, however, as they were not appointed to their respective sees until after Edgar's death. They are Æthelgar, Bishop of Selsey, 980–988, and Æscwig, Bishop of Dorchester, whose first signature appears in 979 and whose predecessor signs a charter of Edward the Martyr (K. 1276). Their names are not included in the list attached to B. 1295, where Æthelgar's place is taken by his predecessor Eadhelm, and where Ælfwold, Bishop of Sherborne, and Brihthelm, Bishop of Wells, also appear. It is obvious from the reference to Ælfthryth as 'the king's mother' that this paragraph (and probably, therefore, the document as a whole) was drawn up in the time of Æthelred, hence the mistakes.

l. 30. *Oswald arceð*. See p. 319.

p. 124, l. 1. *Sideman .b.* Bishop of Crediton from 973 to 977.

l. 2. *Ælfðryð*. See p. 340.

Osgar .ab. Abbot of Abingdon, see p. 341.

ll. 2 f. *Wulfstan on Dælham*. Wulfstan of Dalham (near Newmarket) is frequently mentioned in the *Liber Eliensis*, e.g. II, c. 2, where he is described as *quidam qui erat regi a secretis, vir prudens, consilio pollens, opibusque potens, cœlitus inspiratus*. Ælfric in his *Life of Æthelwold* says that he was sent by Edgar to assist the bishop in expelling the priests from the Old Minster at Winchester, see *Historia Monasterii de Abingdon*, R.S. II, p. 260.

l. 3. *Ælfric · on Ebbesham*. Ælfric of Epsom does not seem to appear elsewhere with this title.

l. 4. *læð*. The name 'lathe', applied to an administrative district, is peculiar to Kent.[1] In 1086 there were six of these divisions (the D.B. form is *lest*), the names of which, derived from royal estates and meeting-places of the Kentish council, can be traced back to early Saxon times (see Chadwick, *Anglo-Saxon Institutions*, pp. 249 f.).

The alliterative phrase *ne læðes ne landes* occurs in the treatise *Hit becwæð* (see above), cap. 3, 2: *ne gyrne ic ðines, ne læðes ne landes, ne sace ne socne*. The phrase itself corresponds to the Scandinavian *land ok láð*, but the spelling suggests that the writer had the Kentish lathe in mind.

[1] See J. E. A. Jolliffe, *Pre-Feudal England: The Jutes*, pp. 40 ff.

LX

MS. British Museum, Cotton Domitian A. VII, f. 43 b. This is the *Liber Vitae* of St Cuthbert's.

FACSIMILE. *Liber Vitae Ecclesiae Dunelmensis*, Surtees Society, Vol. CXXXVI, 1923.

EDITIONS. *Liber Vitae Ecclesiae Dunelmensis*, Surtees Society, XIII, 1841, p. 56.
B. 1255.

DATE. See under Earl Thured below.

l. 5. *Þureð eorl*. An earl of this name signs Æthelred's charters between 979 (K. 621) and 989–990 (see p. 374) and is heard of for the last time on his appointment as one of the joint leaders of the fleet in 992 (Sax. Chr. E). It is possible, though by no means certain, that he was identical with the Thored, son of Gunner, who ravaged Westmorland in 966 (Sax. Chr. E; see Plummer, II, pp. 159 f.). This grant suggests that he was associated with Yorkshire, but neither the extent nor the duration of his earldom is known.

l. 6. *sće Cuðberhtes stowe*. St Cuthbert's body was originally buried at Lindisfarne, but the monks who fled from the Danish invasion of 875 carried it with them. After many wanderings it reached Chester-le-Street and remained there from 882 till 995 when it was finally moved to Durham. It seems likely that the monks in their flight carried their *Liber Vitae* with them. The early lists of names which it contains seem to have been left without continuation until they settled at Durham.

Smiþatune. Smeaton, Yorkshire.

l. 7. *Creic*. Crayke, about twelve miles north of York. This estate is said to have been given by King Ecgfrith to St Cuthbert to provide a convenient stopping place for him on his way to and from York (Simeon of Durham, R.S. I, pp. 32, 199; cf. B. 66). It was forcibly occupied for a time by Ælla, King of Northumbria, but according to tradition the monastery which St Cuthbert founded there was still in existence in 883 and provided a resting-place for his body for four months (*ibid.* pp. 68, 208). Nothing more is heard of Crayke until it appears in the present grant. In 1086 it was held by the Bishop of Durham, and had a church and a priest. It was assessed at 6 carucates with land for 4 ploughs (V.C.H. *Yorks.* II, p. 217).

Suþtune. Sutton-on-the-Forest, Yorkshire (see *Liber Vitae Dunelmensis*, Surtees Society, CXXXVI, 1923, p. xxv). D.B. has no record of any estates held by St Cuthbert's either there or at Smeaton.

LXI

MSS. (*a*) British Museum, Cotton Tiberius A. XIII, f. 66. See p. 259.

(*b*) British Museum, Cotton Vespasian A. v, f. 188 *b*, contains a summary of the grant, also the boundaries, from (*a*).

NOTES

EDITIONS. Hearne, *Hemingi Chartularium* etc. I, p. 139.
K. 683.

DATE. This grant cannot be later than 985, if the banishment of Ælfric, Earl of Mercia, is rightly attributed to that year (see below). The list of witnesses agrees with those of 987 to 989, but there are no grants of 986 and only three dated 985. It is noteworthy that the signatures of Wynsige and Edward are no longer found. Both make their last appearance in the three charters of 985. Oswig's signature first appears in a dated charter in 987 and is not found after 989.

l. 11. *Bradingccotan*. Bredicot, Worcestershire.
Godingce. Goding is apparently the deacon of the name (see p. 360). It is related elsewhere in the cartulary (Hearne, I, p. 265) that this grant was made on condition that he should act as scribe for the monastery, a stipulation which he gladly accepted and faithfully carried out, *multosque postmodum huic monasterio libros scribebat*. It is related further that he retained Bredicot till his death and that his heirs after him held it until it was seized by the Normans. It is entered among the lands of the church of Worcester in D.B. when it was held by Walter Ponther (D.B. I, f. 173 b; V.C.H. *Worc*. I, p. 295).
Genenof[*re*]. See p. 363.

l. 13. *Æþelredes Angulcyningces*. Æthelred II, the son of Edgar and Ælfthryth, succeeded his brother Edward the Martyr in 978 or 979 (see p. 356). He died in 1016.
Ælfrices aldermannes. Ælfric succeeded Ælfhere as Earl of Mercia in 983 and was banished in 985 (Sax. Chr. C, D, E) or 986 (Fl. Wig.). He is referred to in a grant of Oswald dated 985 (K. 651), but thereafter the charters are witnessed by one earl of the name only (the Earl of Hampshire). Two of Æthelred's charters included in the *Historia Monasterii de Abingdon*, R.S. I, pp. 367-370, 373-377, which record the banishment of a certain Ælfric on a charge of treason *in ducatu suo* (p. 368), seem to refer to the same event. From them we learn that the sentence of banishment was pronounced at Cirencester and that it had not been reversed at any rate by the year 999 to which one of the charters belongs (p. 373; K. 703). The other (p. 367; K. 1312) is undated. In the dated charter (a copy of which is found also in MS. C.C.C., Cambridge 111, f. 169) Ælfric is described as *quidam comes*, in the other as *cognomento puer* (A.S. *cild*, cf. p. 106, l. 20 where he appears as a witness to a sale of land by Earl Ælfhere to Osgar, Abbot of Abingdon). Ælfric *cild* figures elsewhere in transactions relating to Ely (*Liber Eliensis*, II, cc. 7, 11, 46) and Peterborough (see p. 76, l. 8). It is evident from these references that he was a man of importance and a likely successor, therefore, to Ælfhere in Mercia. The charge against him as recorded in Æthelred's charters is comprehensive but vague, *cum in ducatu suo contra me et contra omnem gentem meam reus existeret* (K. 1312); ...*contra deum meumque regale imperium multa et inaudita miserabiliter committens piacula* (K. 703), and Henry of Huntingdon (R.S. p. 168) speaks of *Alfricus quem rex crudeliter exulavit*.

Fl. Wig. seems to be the only authority for the statement that he was Ælfhere's son, and although this is possible, as earldoms were frequently hereditary at the time, confirmatory evidence is lacking. One of Edwy's charters dated 956 (B. 946) records the grant of an estate at Wormleighton, Warwickshire, to Earl Ælfhere, while one of the Abingdon charters referred to above (K. 1312) is concerned with the restitution of certain estates, including Wormleighton, which had been seized by Ælfric from a certain widow named Eadflæd. The other Abingdon charter (K. 703) relates to one of these estates in particular, and repeats the story of its seizure by Ælfric from the widow Eadflæd. Ælfhere died in 983 and it seems possible, therefore, that it was his widow who was holding Wormleighton. Nothing is said of any relationship between Ælfric and her or of any reasonable claim that he might have had to any of her estates. He is not mentioned either in Earl Ælfheah's will (see p. 339).

l. 21. *Tidbrihtingctune.* Tibberton is a little to the north of Bredicot.

on anum stede. As a place-name element *stede* is found in combination with descriptive adjectives such as 'green' and 'fair' and with names of trees, crops, animals, etc. The name Medstead in Hampshire represents the compound *mædstede,* see *Chief Elements in English Place-Names,* p. 55, s.v. *stede.*

l. 22. *alswa hit to gedale gebyrað,* cf. the use of the phrase *to gedale* with regard to the division of estates between two or more holders, Whitelock, p. 32, ll. 9, 12, 19.

p. 126, l. 3. *landgemæru.* The boundaries are repeated in the cartulary see Hearne, II, p. 357. They are discussed in detail by Grundy, *Saxon Charters of Worcestershire,* pp. 34–37.

l. 4. *of calawan hylle.* Grundy identifies this with Sneachill, but the latter appears as *fnætes* (for *sn*-) *wyllan* in a charter of 977 (K. 612), see Pl.N. *Worc.* p. 166.

l. 5. *to þære mære stowe.* The word *stow,* which in the first instance means simply 'place' or 'site', is commonly used of a religious foundation, and the evidence of place-names shows that it was generally employed with some sacred or religious association (see *Chief Elements in English Place-Names,* p. 57). The name Merstow Green, which probably represents A.S. *mære stow,* 'famous place', survives in the vicinity of Evesham Abbey and may have been applied originally to the whole site of the abbey and its grounds (see Pl.N. *Worc.* p. 263). I cannot explain the reference in the present instance. Grundy takes *mære* in the sense of *gemære,* 'boundary'.

l. 6. *to þære saltstræte.* Grundy identifies this with the road from Evesham to Droitwich via Martin Hussingtree.

l. 7. *to Spæchæme gemære.* The Spetchley boundary.

ll. 10 f. *to wynne mæduan.* For *wynna* see p. 261. Has it the same meaning here?

l. 11. *be þære stræt.* Grundy suggests that this must be part of the old Roman road from Worcester to Alcester.

l. 15. *Huniburnan.* This brook appears also in the boundaries of

NOTES

Crowle (B. 428) and of Pershore (B. 1282). It forms the whole south boundary of Crowle (Grundy, p. 67).

l. 29. *Leofstan diaĉ.* See p. 360.

l. 30. *Æþelstan prbt.* For the two Æthelstans and Wulfgar see p. 321.

Æperic diaĉ. It is difficult to know whether there were two men of this name at Worcester or only one. A cleric of the name signs five charters of 977 and the only three of 978, while in the exceptional charter of 977 (see p. 360) the name appears with the title 'monk', and in one other of the same year with the title 'deacon'. The only charter of 979 is signed by a deacon of the name, while one of 980 is signed both by a deacon and a cleric of the name. From that time onwards the name appears regularly among the deacons and is found for the last time in a grant made by Archbishop Wulfstan (K. 1313). It would seem, therefore, as if the Ætheric who signs once as monk and once as deacon in 977 were distinct from the Ætheric who signs as cleric up to 980.

l. 30 f. *Osuui clr...Leofwine clr.* These two appear together in one charter of 987 (K. 660), three of 988 (K. 666 ff.) and two of 989 (K. 669 f.) with the title *monachus*, and are the only two witnesses so described. In one of 987 (K. 661) and two undated ones (K. 679, 683) they sign together with the title *clericus*. Leofwine, who signs as *clericus* from 966 onwards, is described as *monachus* in the exceptional charter of 977 (K. 615), but does not appear again with that title until 984. From that time onwards, when he appears without Oswig, he is described sometimes as *monachus* and sometimes as *clericus*. It is noteworthy that in a grant of 990 (see p. 132, l. 27) he is described as *clr* in the cartulary copy but as *moñ* in the version given by Hickes (cf. MS. Harley 4660). It seems more than likely, therefore, that at least from 984 onwards the title *clericus* is ascribed to him by mistake and that both Oswig and he should invariably appear as monks. Oswig's signature is only found from 987 to 989.

l. 32. *Ælfsige prbt.* For Ælfsige, Æthelsige and Wulfweard see p. 362.

Wulfric clr. Wulfric is a regular witness from 984 to 996.

l. 33. *Eadgar prbt.* For Edgar and Cynethegn see p. 320.

l. 34. *Wistan prbt.* For Wistan and Wulfnoth see p. 336.

Wulfwine clr. A cleric of this name signs a grant dated 967 (B. 1206) and one dated 977 (K. 616) and is a regular witness from 981 to 996.

LXII

MS. Corpus Christi College, Cambridge, MS. 286, f. 77 *b*. This is a gospel book from St Augustine's, Canterbury, traditionally believed to be one of the two copies sent by St Gregory to St Augustine.

EDITIONS. Hickes, *Dissertatio Epistolaris*, p. 10, in *Thesaurus*, I.
    Wanley, *Catalogue of Anglo-Saxon MSS.*, p. 15, in *Thesaurus*, II.
    K. 429.

DATE. Kemble, following Wanley, dates this charter wrongly about 949. It must be at least forty years later, as Wulfric was Abbot of

St Augustine's from 989 to 1006. The witnesses likewise fit the later but not the earlier date.

p. 128, l. 2. *Lifinges*. Perhaps Lyfing of Malling, see p. 385.
l. 3. *sammæle*. A Scandinavian loan-word.
Clife. Probably Cliffe or Cliffe at Hoo near Rochester.
ll. 3 f. *he gebéh...mid lande*. See B.T., *Suppl*. p. 300, s.v. *gebugan*, I, 3 *a*. This verb is regularly used with reference to commendation.
l. 7. *swá gewerud* etc. For *gewerian* in the sense of 'to stock land' see B.T., *Suppl*. p. 449, s.v.
l. 9. *Siweard · 7 Sired his broðor*, cf. p. 142, ll. 13 f. The two names frequently appear together among the *ministri* from 995 (K. 688) to 1005 (K. 714, 1301) and are attached also to K. 715, a charter of Æthelred to Christchurch, Canterbury (see p. 428, n.). For the signature *Sigeward on Cent* see p. 130, l. 19. A charter of 990 (K. 1285) records the grant of land at Sibertswold, Kent, to *Sigered minister*. It is possible that the Sired of the present charter is also identical with the *Sired ealda* who witnesses a Kentish marriage agreement of 1016–1020 (see p. 150, l. 10), with the *Sigeryd minister* of another Kentish charter of 1018 (*Ordnance Survey Facsimiles*, Part III, No. 39) and with the *Siræd minister* of Cnut's charter of 1023 to Christchurch, Canterbury (see p. 160, l. 39).
ll. 9 f. *Wulfstan æt Sealtwuda · 7 oðer Wulfstan*, cf. p. 142, l. 15. K. 715 (see above) is witnessed by Wulfstan *senex* (*ealda*) and Wulfstan *iuuenis* (*geonga*).
l. 10. *Siferð*. A man of this name, described as *miles*, signs a Rochester grant of 1012 (K. 719).

LXIII

MS. *Liber Monasterii de Hyda*, f. 34 *b*. See p. 309.
EDITION. Edwards, *Liber Monasterii de Hyda*, R.S. p. 244, with a modern English translation on p. 359.
DATE. The events described in this narrative must have been spread over several years, but reached their culmination in 989–990, i.e. after the appointment of Ordbriht as Bishop of Selsey but before the death of Archbishop Æthelgar (see below). The narrative occurs in a Latin charter of Æthelred (dated 993) by which he grants the delinquent's forfeited estates to his mother Ælfthryth in return for Cholsey. The M.E. version which follows is a free translation of the Anglo-Saxon and frequently misses the point of the original. The Latin is in the nature of a brief summary.
l. 16. *þ reaflac*, cf. p. 122, l. 24.
his wer. See p. 339. The reference to wergeld has not been understood and is omitted throughout in the M.E. translation.
l. 19. *Byrhtmæres æt Burnan*. Perhaps the grandfather of Godric of Bourne, see p. 439.
l. 24. *Æþelwine ealdorman*. Earl of East Anglia, see p. 329.

p. 130, ll. 6 f. *Æþelgare arcebisceop.* Æthelgar, who was Abbot of the New Minster, then Bishop of Selsey (see p. 342), was appointed Archbishop of Canterbury in succession to Dunstan, who died on 19 May 988. According to the Saxon Chronicle, C, E, he held the see for a year and three months, corrected in F (a Canterbury MS.) to a year and eight months. His *obitus* is given as 13 February (see *Liber Vitae etc. of Hyde Abbey*, ed. Birch, p. 270), so that his period of office should be dated 988–990.

l. 8. *hine 7 ealle his are.* The reference seems to be to Wulfbold (even although he was already dead) and all his property (or is it perhaps to his son?). By her action after his death his widow had confiscated her share of his possessions (see VI Æthelstan, 1, 1). The M.E. version is wide of the mark, *Wlfbold was take to the kyng with alle hys goode.*

l. 9. *Oswold arcebiscop.* See p. 319.

l. 10. *Ælfstan biscop of Londone.* See p. 334.

Sigeric biscop. Sigeric, who had been Abbot of St Augustine's, was Bishop of Ramsbury from 985 to 990. He succeeded Æthelgar as Archbishop of Canterbury.

ll. 10 f. *Ælfstan bisceop on Hrofeceastre.* See p. 334.

l. 11. *Ordbyrht bisceop.* Ordbriht, who had been Abbot of Chertsey (Sax. Chr. 964 A), was Bishop of Selsey from 989 to 1009.

Ælfeah bisceop. Ælfheah became Bishop of Winchester in 984 and Archbishop of Canterbury in 1006. In 1012 he was killed by the Danes and under the name of St Alphege (or Elphege) was afterwards celebrated as a saint and martyr. Osbern's *Vita Elphegi* is printed by Wharton in *Anglia Sacra*, II, pp. 122–147.

The M.E. version has seven additional names at this point, ending with that of Ælfheah, Bishop [of Lichfield]. These would seem to have been omitted by mistake from the Anglo-Saxon transcript. The missing names are those of Æthelsige, Bishop [of Sherborne], Ælfwold, Bishop of Devonshire, Ealdred, Bishop [of Cornwall], Sigegar, Bishop [of Wells], Æscwig, Bishop [of Dorchester] and Theodred II, Bishop [of Elmham]. The reason for the mistake can be found in the occurrence twice over of the name Ælfheah.

ll. 11 f. *Aþulf bisceop.* Athulf or Æthelwulf became Bishop of Hereford between 951 and 955. His last signature appears in 1012 (K. 719).

l. 12. *Byrhnoþ ealdorman.* Earl of Essex, see p. 315.

ll. 12 f. *Aþelweard ealdorman.* Earl of the Western Provinces; he signs as *dux* from 975 to 998. His interest in vernacular literature is vouched for by Ælfric, some of whose works were addressed to him, while he was himself the author of a Latin chronicle—the first historical work in that language since the time of Bede.

l. 13. *Alfric ealdorman.* Earl of Hampshire or probably of a wider area, since he is described as *Wentaniensium Prouinciarum dux* (K. 698). He witnesses charters from 983 to 1016 and can almost certainly be identified with the earl of the name who was slain at *Assandun*. Twice in the Saxon Chronicle he appears as a traitor (s.a. 992, 1003). He is described, however, as *an of þam þa se cyng hæfde mæst truwe to* (Sax. Chr. 992 F) and it is evident from the charters that he never forfeited to any extent the confidence which the king so unwisely placed in him. From 999 onwards his signature invariably heads the list of *duces* until the last years of the reign (1012–1016) when it is ousted by that of Eadric Streona (see p. 393).

Þeodred eorl. The name Theodred has undoubtedly been substituted for the English *Þored* or *Þured* representing the Scandinavian *Þórðr*. For Earl Thored see p. 368. The title *eorl* here corresponds to the Scandinavian *jarl*.

ll. 13 f. *Eadulf abbod.* Abbot of Peterborough, see p. 329.

l. 14. *Byrnoþe abbod.* Abbot of Ely, see p. 100, ll. 16 f. His death (through the magic arts of Ælfthryth) is attributed to the year 981 (*Liber Eliensis*, II, c. 56), but his signature continues till 996 (K. 696, 1292) and that of his successor Ælfsige does not occur for certain until 999 (K. 703).

Germanus abbod. According to the *Historia Ramesiensis* Germanus, who had been a monk at Fleury, became Prior of Westbury on Trym, Gloucestershire (founded by Oswald), then Dean of Ramsey, then Abbot of Winchcombe. In 975 when the monks were expelled from Winchcombe after the death of Edgar, he returned to Fleury, but was recalled to Ramsey in the same year. In 992 (according to the same authority) he was made Abbot of Cholsey, but his signature with the title Abbot of Ramsey is attached to a charter of 993 (K. 684). In 997 (K. 698) he is described as Abbot of Cholsey, and although the abbey is said to have been destroyed by the Danes in 1006, his signature continues until 1019 (K. 729).

Wlfsige abbod. Wulfsige was Abbot of Westminster from *c.* 959 to *c.* 997. In 992 he was made Bishop of Sherborne, see Harmer[2], p. 579.

l. 15. *Leofric abbod of Miclanige.* Between the names of Wulfsige, Abbot of Westminster, and Leofric, Abbot of Michelney, the M.E. version has two others, namely *Leofryc abbot and Sygeward abbot*. The only possible Leofric, apart from the Abbots of Michelney and Exeter who are included in both versions, is the Abbot of St Albans of the name, who succeeded his brother Ælfric when the latter became Bishop of Ramsbury in succession to Sigeric. The present document, however, belongs to the period before Archbishop Æthelgar's death and Sigeric's promotion, so that Leofric's signature as abbot cannot be genuine. There is no mention elsewhere of any Abbot Siweard at the time, so that it seems most likely that in the M.E. text the names *Leofryc* and *Sigeward*, which occur together among the lay witnesses, have been erroneously incorporated among the abbots as well.

Leofric, Abbot of Michelney, witnesses two charters of 993 and 997 respectively (K. 684, 698) and is named in an original charter of the abbey dated 995 (see *Somerset Record Society Publications*, XIV, p. 44). He was abbot at any rate as early as 983, when he signs along with Leofric, Abbot of Exeter (K. 636).

NOTES 375

Leofric abbod of Eaxcestre. See p. 343.

l. 16. *Ælfhun abbod.* An abbot of this name signs a few Winchester and Abingdon charters between the years 982 (K. 633) and 995 (K. 1289). In one instance (K. 684, dated 993) he is described as Abbot of Milton Abbas, Dorset.

Ælfelm. See *Ælfhelm polga* below. The signature Ælfhelm *minister* is of frequent occurrence from 982 (K. 632) to 990 (K. 673), when that of Ælfhelm *comes* makes its appearance (K. 672). A Kentish charter of 995 (K. 688) is signed both by Ælfhelm *dux* and Ælfhelm *minister*, while the latter appears as a witness also in 1007 and 1008 (K. 1303, 1305).

Wlfeah. The signature Wulfheah *minister* is found from 986 (K. 654) to 1005 (K. 714, 1301), when it disappears altogether from the charters of Æthelred's reign. It is possible, therefore, that this witness should be identified with the Wulfheah who was blinded in the year 1006 (Sax. Chr. E).

Wulfric Wulfrune suni. In 995 Wulfric, Wulfrun's son, was granted the forfeited estate of Dumbleton, Gloucestershire (K. 692). He appears as a witness also at the confirmation of Ætheric of Bocking's will about 997 (K. 704; Whitelock, p. 44). His own will is extant (Whitelock, No. XVII). The signature Wulfric *minister* is found during Æthelred's reign from 980 (K. 624) to 1003. In 982 (K. 633) and 988 (K. 663 f.) two men of the name sign.

l. 17. *Stir Wulfes suni.* Stir, the son of Ulf (the Anglicised form of the name has been substituted here), appears as a benefactor of the new church at Durham in 998. He is seen in rather a different light when his daughter Sige became the second wife of Earl Uhtred *quam pater suus ideo ei dedit ut Turbrandum sibi inimicissimum interficeret* (Simeon of Durham, R.S. 1, pp. 83, 216). The signature *Styr* is attached to K. 710, a charter dated 1004.

Nafena 7 Norwina[n] his broðor. In 1016 Thurketel, Nafena's son, was murdered along with Uhtred, Earl of Northumbria (Sax. Chr. D, E; Fl. Wig.). I have not found any other reference to Northwine, and neither he nor his brother appears elsewhere as a witness to any of the charters.

l. 18. *Leofwine Leoftætan suni.* The name Leofwine is a common one among the witnesses of Æthelred's charters. The name *Leoftæta* (or *-tæte*) is not recorded elsewhere but it is connected with names such as *Tata* (see p. 28, l. 11 and cf. *Taeta*, B. 598) and *Tatæ* (the alternative name of Æthelburg, the daughter of Æthelbert of Kent and the wife of Edwin of Northumbria, see Bede, *Historia Ecclesiastica*, II, c. 9). For a *matrona* named Leoftæt who forfeited her Warwickshire estates *suis ineptiis*, see T. p. 299 and *The Eynsham Cartulary*, ed. Salter, I, p. 21.

Leofsige æt Mordune. Perhaps Morden in Surrey. A thegn named Leofsige signs four of Æthelred's charters, namely K. 633, 654, 657, 687 (dated 982, 986, 987 and 994 respectively). The last of these charters is witnessed also by Leofsige *dux*.

Bonda. This name does not occur elsewhere among the witnesses of Æthelred's charters. In 1023 Cnut granted a charter to Leofwine *Bondan sunu* in respect of land in Hampshire which he had bought from King Æthelred (K. 739).

l. 19. *Ælfhelm polga*. Ælfhelm Polga's will is extant (Whitelock, No. XIII). He is mentioned several times in the *Liber Eliensis* in connection with transactions of Edgar's reign and appears as a benefactor of Westminster in the spurious charter B. 1050. He had a brother of the same name as himself (*Liber Eliensis*, II, c. 10) who might be the witness of the present charter (see above). A certain Leofwine Polga appears as a legatee of Ælfwold II, Bishop of Crediton, about 1010 (see Napier and Stevenson, *Crawford Charters*, p. 23).

Apelwold, cf. *Apelwold pes greta* (l. 20). A witness of this name appears in Æthelred's charters between 986 and 1012. In 1005 (K. 714) and 1007 (K. 1304) two *ministri* of the name sign, but neither of them is distinguished as *pes greta*.

Leofric. The signature Leofric *minister* is found from 980 to 1008. In 982, 984, 995 and 997 (K. 1278, 641, 692, 698) two men of the name sign and in 987 (K. 657) three.

Sigeward on Cent. See p. 372.

l. 20. *Leofsunn*, for *-sunu*, cf. the *Leofsune* of the M.E. version. The name does not appear elsewhere among the witnesses of Æthelred's charters. A certain Leofsunu was connected with a Rochester lawsuit (see p. 84, l. 25) and one of the warriors who fell at Maldon in 991 bore the same name.

Ælfgar se Hunitunisca. The name Ælfgar is found throughout Æthelred's reign among the *ministri* who witness his charters. In 1007 (K. 1303) and 1008 (K. 1305) three men of the name sign. Nowhere else is any one of them distinguished by the descriptive title of the present charter.

l. 21. *Wulsegat*, for *Wulfgeat*, cf. the *Wlfgeat* of the M.E. version. Wulfgeat signs from 986 to 1005. In 1006 his estates were forfeited (Sax. Chr. C, D, E) *propter injusta judicia et superba quae gesserat opera* (Fl. Wig.), cf. also K. 1305 where his wife is associated with him in his crimes (*de qua modo non est dicendum per singula*) and K. 1310 where the reason given is *quia inimicis regis se in insidiis socium applicavit*.

Æpelmer. Probably the founder of Cerne and Eynsham, see pp. 386 f.

Æpelric. The signature Æthelric *minister* is found in Æthelred's charters from 987 (K. 657) to 1008 (K. 1305). Two men of the name sign K. 658.

Æpelnoðe Wiftanes suni. The M.E. version has *Athenoth Wystanus sone*. In 991 Æthelnoth, Wistan's son, was one of the ambassadors who negotiated peace between Æthelred and Richard, Duke of Normandy (see William of Malmesbury, *Gesta Regum*, R.S. I, p. 192; *Memorials of St Dunstan*, R.S. p. 398). The name Æthelnoth is found among the *ministri* from 982 to 996.

l. 22. *Leofwine Æpulfes suni*. Edgar's foundation charter of Thorney Abbey (B. 1297) records the sale of land to the abbey by Leofwine,

NOTES

Athulf's son. He appears also as a benefactor of Ely (*Liber Eliensis*, II, c. 60). The name Leofwine is found among the *ministri* of Æthelred's charters from 980 to 1015. In several instances two men of the name sign and in one case three (K. 714).

Sigebrht. This name does not occur elsewhere among the witnesses of Æthelred's reign.

Leofstan on Supseaxan. A certain Leofstan, son of Ælfwold, took part in the embassy to Richard, Duke of Normandy, in 991 (see above). The name Leofstan appears about half a dozen times among the *ministri* between 983 and 990.

The boundaries of the forfeited estates follow immediately. They are described in Æthelred's charter as consisting of VII. *sulunga in loco qui Bradanburna vocitatur, et quartam semis ipso in loco qui æt Weofacotan dicitur*, II. *quoque nec minus æt Burhwarefelda*, III. *itidem eo in loco quem solicolæ æt Natincgdune appellare solent. Item quoque* III. *æt Cealconæt* .I. *æt Wirigenn*. The places named include Brabourne, near Ashford, Evegate in Smeeth (formerly *Thevegate*; the scribe has apparently misread initial þ as the runic w) and Nackington. For *Burhwarefelda* (the open country attached to Canterbury) see p. 270. The last two names have not been identified. Wallenberg, p. 350, suggests that *Cealconæt* is a bogus form due to misreading on the part of the scribe and that *Wirigenn*, if initial w has been written by mistake for original þ, may be connected with Perry Wood which adjoins Saltwood.

LXIV

MSS. (*a*) British Museum, Cotton Tiberius A. XIII, f. 84 *b*. See p. 259.
(*b*) British Museum, Harley 4660, f. 9. See p. 263.

EDITIONS. Hickes, *Thesaurus*, I, p. 140.
Hearne, *Hemingi Chartularium* etc. I, p. 180.
K. 674, from (*a*).

The text is from (*a*).

l. 23. [*M*]*ortun*. The name is preserved in the present Moreton Farm in Lower Westmancote (see Pl.N. *Worc.* p. 102). A charter in the British Museum MS. Cotton Vitellius C. 9 (see Hearne, II, p. 567) records the grant of 2 hides at Moreton by King Æthelstan to the thegn Æthelnoth, but there is nothing to show when or how this estate came into the possession of the church of Worcester. This charter is the last of a group of five which includes the grant of Teddington and Alstone (see p. 96) and it is followed in the cartulary by the sentence Ðas .v. bec locyaþ into Breodune.

ll. 24 f. *Disponente regi* etc. For the same preamble in an earlier Worcester charter see No. XXI.

l. 25. *mutantur*. The earlier grant reads *notantur*.

p. 132, ll. 7 f. *se eldra...se iungra* etc. Other instances are found of intermixed acre-strips assigned to different holders, see pp. 88, 335.

378   NOTES

l. 8. *ge innor ge utter*. The same phrase occurs in the grant of an estate at Clifford Chambers (K. 667), *mid were 7 mid mylene ge inner ge utter swa to þæm preom hidan gebyrige*. It seems, therefore, to have the same meaning as *ge neor tune ge fir*, which occurs in the grant of 5 hides at Tiddington to Eadric in 985 (K. 651).

l. 9. *Uppþrop*. This name does not seem to have survived.

l. 14. .iiii. *pund*. For the purchase of a Worcestershire estate of 5 hides for 10 pounds see p. 162. It is noteworthy that the hide is valued at 2 pounds of silver in both cases. An early ninth-century grant of Bishop Deneberht to a certain Eanswith was made on condition that she should continue to renovate, clean and augment the furnishings of the church, see B. 307.

l. 23. *þara broþra naman*. The witnesses are the same as in Oswald's lease of Bredicot (see p. 126) except for the inclusion of Goding (see p. 360) and the omission of Oswig (see p. 371).

LXV

MSS. (*a*) Fragments of three Worcester charters, of which this is one are found among the Middleton MSS. (see p. 263) on two strips of parchment which had been attached as guards to a sixteenth-century book to prevent the threads cutting through the paper (see W. H. Stevenson's *Report on Lord Middleton's* MSS. p. 197).

(*b*) British Museum, Cotton Tiberius A. XIII, f. 60 *b*. See p. 259.

(*c*) British Museum, Cotton Vespasian A. v, f. 179 *b*, from (*b*), with omissions.

EDITIONS. Stevenson, *op. cit.* p. 211.
            Hearne, *Hemingi Chartularium* etc. I, p. 129.
            K. 675, from (*b*).
The text is from (*b*).

p. 134, l. 1. *Cumtune*. Grundy (*Saxon Charters of Worcestershire*, pp. 158 f.) identifies the *Mersc* of the present grant with Mearse Farm in Inkberrow and associates 'Æthelstan's boundary' with the estate at Thorne in Inkberrow granted to a man of the name in 963 (see p. 66). This charter, however, as it appears in the cartulary, is the last of a group of eight introduced by the words *Geanbec into Gleweceaster* and followed by the statement *þas genbec hyrað into Wincescumbe*. The three charters immediately preceding refer to grants of land in Itchington in Thornbury, and it seems more likely, therefore, that the *Cumtun* of the present charter is represented by the villages of Compton Greenfield and Easter Compton both in the parish of Henbury. This identification has been confirmed by Sir Allen Mawer, who identifies *Merse* with the tithing of Mars(h) in Thornbury.

It is noteworthy that four of these Gloucestershire charters record grants of land to a certain Æthelweard, and that in three cases out of the four (with reference, namely, to two estates at Bishop's Stoke

NOTES 379

and one at Upton) the marginal heading reads 'Æthelweard and Æthelmær'. The earliest of these grants is dated 969 and the latest 988, and it is possible that by 990 Æthelmær (as Æthelweard's heir) had already succeeded to these estates. The fourth estate granted to Æthelweard consisted of 1 hide at Itchington. No additional names are mentioned and no boundaries are given, but in 991 a hide at the same place (which may represent the same estate if no heir was appointed) was granted to a certain Ælfstan and two heirs (K. 677).

ll. 9 f. xxx. *euwna* etc. This probably represents the stock made over to Æthelmær rather than part payment in kind on his side. Grammatically either interpretation is possible.

l. 15. *Biles hamme.* Probably Bilsham in Olveston.

ll. 15 f. *to þam middel ge[m]are.* It is obvious from the reading *gema-* of the Middleton fragment that a mistake has been made by the transcriber, perhaps due to the *geare* of the following sentence.

l. 18. *naman.* The witnesses are the same as in the preceding charter, the only difference being that Leofwine, who signs there as cleric, signs here as monk (see p. 371).

ll. 28 ff. *Ic gean him* etc. This probably represents an additional grant made at a rather later date and perhaps endorsed on the original charter.

l. 28. *Brynes hamme.* For the personal name *Bryne* see Redin, *Uncompounded Personal Names in Old English,* p. 121.

ll. 28 f. *þe Æþelm ahte.* Æthelm was the grantee of an estate at Elmestree in Tetbury (see No. xxxiv). It may be a former holding of his in the same region that is referred to here.

LXVI

MS. British Museum, Cotton Augustus, II, 15, a contemporary parchment.

FACSIMILE. Bond, *Facsimiles of Ancient Charters in the British Museum,* Part III, No. 37.

EDITIONS. K. 693.
T. p. 288.
Essays in Anglo-Saxon Law, App. No. 22, from K.

DATE. Sigeric became Archbishop of Canterbury in 990, while Æthelsige I, Bishop of Sherborne, signs for the last time in the same year (K. 672 f.). His successor Wulfsige was appointed in 992 and his signature occurs for the first time in 993 (K. 684). The events described here must fall, therefore, sometime between 990 and 992.

p. 136, l. 1. *Wynflæd.* For a testatrix of the name see Whitelock, p. 109. Miss Whitelock is of opinion that this Wynflæd was probably entirely different from the Wynflæd of the lawsuit and possibly identical with the *religiose sancte conversacionis monialis femine Wenflede* to whom King Edmund granted two estates in Dorset in 942 (B. 775). She points out that there is no reference in the will to the estates concerned in the dispute, but this does not seem to me conclusive, especially in view of the fact that there is no mention either of Cheselborne and Winterborne, the two estates of King Edmund's grant. It is noteworthy that the Wynflæd of the will is associated with estates in Wiltshire, Dorset, Somerset, Berkshire, Hampshire and Oxfordshire, and that representatives of all these counties took part in the case arising out of the claim made by the Wynflæd of the lawsuit to the two estates of Hagbourne and Bradfield in Berkshire. The impossibility of dating the will exactly, however, leaves the identity of the testatrix a matter of surmise.

l. 2. *Wulfamere.* It seems possible that the name survives in Woolmer Forest in Hampshire. *Wulfamere* occurs also as the scene of royal grants in B. 576 (dated 898), B. 1266 (the Latin version of Edgar's Ely charter, see p. 345) and B. 1265 (another Ely charter of the same date as the preceding one). In the last two it is described as a royal manor. In the thirteenth century the name of Woolmer Forest appears as *Ulmere, Wolvemare* (see V.C.H. *Hants.* III, p. 16).

l. 3. *Sigeric arcebiscop.* Sigeric (see p. 373) was Archbishop of Canterbury from 990 to 994.

Ordbyrht biscop. Bishop of Selsey, see p. 373.

Ælfric ealderman. Earl of Hampshire, see pp. 373 f.

l. 4. *Ælfþryþ þæs cyninges modor.* See p. 340.

l. 5. *Ælfric.* Presumably Ælfric was Leofwine's father.

ll. 5 f. *Hacceburnan...Bradanfelda.* Hagbourne and Bradfield, Berkshire.

l. 6. *Deccet.* Datchet, Buckinghamshire.

l. 10. *be Æluere abbude.* Ælfhere signs as abbot from 985 (K. 648) to 1007 (K. 1303 f.). In K. 684 (dated 993) and K. 698 (dated 997) he is described as Abbot of Bath.

his insegel. It seems from what follows that, unless Abbot Ælfhere delivered the king's message verbally, *insegel* is used here in the sense of *gewrit 7 insegel*, see p. 140, l. 16 and cf. *mid þæs cynges gewrite 7 insegle*, Sax. Chr. 1048 E.

Cwicelmeshlæwe, cf. Sax. Chr. 1006 C, D, E. It is not certain whether it should be identified with Cuckhamsley Barrow or with Scutchamfly Knob, Berkshire.

l. 12. *Æþelsige biscop · 7 Æs`c´wig biscop · 7 Ælfric abbud.* Æthelsige (see above) became Bishop of Sherborne in 978; Æscwig, Bishop of Dorchester, signs from 979 (K. 621) to 1002 (K. 1297); two abbots of the name Ælfric sign in 990–991 (K. 672, 712 f.), in 997 (K. 698, where they are distinguished as Abbot of Malmesbury and Abbot of Evesham respectively) and again in 1002 (K. 707). Ælfric, Abbot of Malmesbury, signs also in 993 (K. 684) and it is probably he who is meant here. It is very curious that Ælfric, Bishop of Ramsbury, is not mentioned in connection with this shire-meeting, since Berkshire

NOTES

in all probability formed part of his diocese, and according to III Edgar, 5, 2 (repeated II Cnut, 18, 1) the presence of the bishop of the diocese was necessary at a meeting of the kind. There is no mention either of the earl whose presence was likewise required. It is possible, however, that Earl Ælfric, who had been a witness in support of Wynflæd's claim, was thereby excluded from taking any further part in the proceedings. The only explanation I can offer for the absence of the Bishop of Ramsbury is that the case actually arose in the interval between Sigeric's promotion to Canterbury and Ælfric's appointment as his successor at Ramsbury. If this is correct, the lawsuit should be definitely attributed to the year 990.

l. 15. *his swutelunga.* It is noteworthy that while Archbishop Sigeric and Bishop Ordbriht are expressly said to have sent their declarations to the meeting, there is no mention of Earl Ælfric and his.

l. 16. *hit hyre geahnian.* The various modes of procedure in lawsuits about land according to the nature of the case are discussed by J. L. Laughlin, 'The Anglo-Saxon Legal Procedure' in *Essays in Anglo-Saxon Law*, pp. 240–262. Wynflæd, by proving the earlier transaction which had taken place between Ælfric and herself, had invalidated Leofwine's right of possession, and to her, therefore, was awarded the right of substantiating her claim. Such an award practically amounted to a decision in her favour, as it only remained for her to produce the necessary number of supporters to take the oath on her behalf.

l. 18. *Wulfgar abbud.* Wulfgar was Abbot of Abingdon from 990 (Sax. Chr. C, 989 E) to 1016 (Sax. Chr. C, E; 1017, Fl. Wig.).

ll. 18 f. *Æfic þara æþelinga discsten.* Perhaps identical with Æfic, the king's high-reeve, who was killed by Earl Leofsige in 1002 (Sax. Chr. E and K. 719).

ll. 20 f. *Eadgyfu abbudisse.* Perhaps abbess of the Nunnery at Winchester, see p. 348.

l. 21. *Liofrun abbudisse.* Leofrun, Abbess of Reading, is mentioned in the *Liber Vitae etc. of Hyde Abbey*, ed. Birch, p. 58.

ll. 21 f. *Leofecanoran.* Lewknor, Oxfordshire. I am indebted to Professor Stenton for this identification.

ll. 24 f. *menig god þegen* etc. It is noteworthy that 24 people are mentioned altogether, namely 11 men and 13 women, without counting Wynflæd herself and Ælfthryth who seems to have played a special part in the case as a whole. It seems possible, since the whole list of names is not given, that an oath of at least 36 was called for.

l. 25. *se fulla.* It is possible that a noun has been omitted by mistake.

ll. 26 f. *þ man þene aþ aweg lete.* The amicable settlement of disputes as in this case, is not uncommon.

l. 29. *forgyldan,* i.e. pay compensation for Wynflæd's loss of rents and other payments.

þam cyninge his wer. See p. 339.

p. 138, l. 1. *Æþelsige biscope.* It is more than likely that the disputed estates were handed over to Æthelsige in his capacity as president of the shire-meeting. It is possible, on the other hand, that Wynflæd had already agreed to make them over to him. There is nothing, however, to connect them with Sherborne, as in 1086 they were in private hands and had been so at the Conquest (see V.C.H. *Berks.* I, pp. 350, 354, 366).

l. 3. *his fæder gold 7 siolfor.* The exact nature of the original transaction between Wynflæd and Leofwine's father (? Ælfric) is not explained and is not clear. Apparently there was something to be said on Leofwine's side as well as on Wynflæd's.

l. 4. *þa dyde hio* etc. The meaning seems to be that Wynflæd did as little as she dared without thereby invalidating her oath.

l. 7. *Ælfgar þæs cyninges gerefa.* This is probably the *Ælfgarus præpositus* of K. 1305, an Abingdon charter dated 1008.

l. 8. *Leofric æt Hwitecyrcan.* This is probably Whitchurch in Oxfordshire, near the Berkshire border. The later history of this witness, who by his various crimes forfeited both his life and his possessions, is told in K. 1307, which records the grant of his estate at Whitchurch to another Leofric in 1012. The Leofric of Whitchurch who was slain in battle against the Danes in 1001 (Sax. Chr. A) was presumably the tenant of Whitchurch in Hampshire.

There is no mention at the end of the document of the number of copies made but a series of capital letters, cut in half, runs along the bottom margin which suggests that there was more than one.

LXVII

MS. British Museum, Cotton Tiberius A. XIII, f. 91. See p. 259.

EDITIONS. Hearne, *Hemingi Chartularium* etc. I, p. 195.
K. 676.

l. 10. *Tætlinctune.* This estate is now represented by Talton Farm in the parish of Tredington (Pl.N. *Worc.* p. 173). Newbold-on-Stour is in the same parish. Both were probably included in the 23 hides at Tredington held by the Bishop of Worcester in 1086 (D.B. I, f. 173; V.C.H. *Worc.* I, p. 293). The two preceding charters in the cartulary refer to Tidmington and Blackwell respectively and the present grant is followed by the statement *þas .*III*. bec lociað into Tredintune.*

l. 16. *Leofinc.* I have not found any reference elsewhere to this earlier tenant.

l. 22. *þara broðra gewitnesse.* The witnesses are the same as in the two grants of 990 (see pp. 132, 134) except for the omission of Wulfweard and the inclusion of Godwine. The latter's name is attached to a charter of 982 (K. 634) but is not found again in dated charters until 991. It appears in one which is undated (B. 1184) but which must be earlier than 987 as it is signed by Wynsige (see p. 360).

LXVIII

MS. British Museum, Cotton Domitian A. VII, f. 43 b. See p. 368.
FACSIMILE. *Liber Vitae Ecclesiae Dunelmensis*, Surtees Society, Vol. CXXXVI, 1923.
EDITIONS. *Liber Vitae Ecclesiae Dunelmensis*, Surtees Society, XIII, 1841, p. 57.
K. 925.
B. 1256.
DATE. See under Earl Northman below.

p. 140, l. 1. *Norðman eorl*. According to Simeon of Durham (R.S. I, p. 83) Bishop Aldhun leased certain estates belonging to St Cuthbert's to the Northumbrian earls whose names are given elsewhere (p. 213) as *Ethred eorl, Northman eorl* and *Uhtred eorl*. The list of estates includes Escomb, so that the present record may have been made when it was restored to the foundation.

Of Earl Northman little or nothing is known. It is probably his signature which accompanies Earl Waltheof's at the end of the list of *duces* attached to one of Æthelred's charters dated 994 (K. 687). Earl Leofwine had a son named Northman whom Fl. Wig. (s.a. 1017) describes as *dux*, but the two cannot be identical. The latter, described as *minister*, received a grant of land from Æthelred (K. 662, dated 988 although the list of witnesses belongs to 996 at the earliest) which later passed to his brother Earl Leofric (K. 938) and was restored by him to the abbey of Evesham (see also *Chronicon Abbatiae de Evesham*, R.S. p. 84), and it is probably he who signs as *minister* in 1016 (K. 723, another Evesham document) and 1017 (K. 1313, a Worcester document). The available evidence, therefore, associates him exclusively with Worcestershire and Earl Northman must be regarded as a northern contemporary. A certain Northman, described both as *miles* and *princeps*, received an estate at Twywell in Northamptonshire from King Æthelred in 1013 (K. 1308) and a sheriff of Northamptonshire in the time of Edward the Confessor bore the same name (K. 863, 904).

Ediscum. Escomb, near Bishop Auckland, County Durham. There is an almost complete Saxon church there dating from about the seventh century (see Baldwin Brown, *The Arts in Early England*, II, 2nd ed. 1925, pp. 136–142).

l. 2. *Feregenne*. Identified as Ferryhill, 6 miles south of Durham (*Liber Vitae Ecclesiae Dunelmensis*, Surtees Society, CXXXVI, p. xxv).

l. 3. *Ulfcytel Osulfes sunu*. Two of Edgar's grants (B. 1044, 1052) which apply to lands in Nottinghamshire and Yorkshire and are dated 958 and 959 respectively (before he became king of the whole of England) are witnessed by Ulfketel *minister*. He may be identical with the donor of the present grant, but the impossibility of dating it exactly

384 NOTES

makes this uncertain. For a reference to an Osulf associated with Yorkshire, who was apparently alive in the time of Archbishop Oswald, see p. 112, l. 11.

Norðtun. Norton, County Durham. This gift is the earliest record of this estate which seems thereafter to have remained in the possession of the bishopric (see V.C.H. *Durham*, III, pp. 305 f.).

ll. 4 f. *mið sace 7 mið socne.* This phrase, which is regularly employed at a later date, seems to have come into use at any rate as early as the middle of the tenth century (see Stenton, *Types of Manorial Structure in the Northern Danelaw*, pp. 78–81). The term *socn* is also used alone in the same sense, see III Æthelred, 11. *mið* is a Northumbrian form.

LXIX

MSS. (*a*) Rochester Cathedral, *Textus Roffensis*, f. 155. See p. 276.
(*b*) British Museum, Harley 311, f. 29 *b*, copied from (*a*) in the seventeenth century.

EDITIONS. Hickes, *Dissertatio Epistolaris*, p. 43, in *Thesaurus*, I.
K. 929.
T. p. 301.
Essays in Anglo-Saxon Law, App. No. 25, from K.
The text is from (*a*).

DATE. Probably soon after the appointment of Godwine as Bishop of Rochester in 995. There may have been two successive bishops of this name as it is found there from 995 till 1045.

l. 9. *Snoddinglande.* For an earlier dispute in which Snodland was involved see No. LIX.

l. 12. *swutelunga*, i.e. documents affording written evidence of the cathedral's right to the estate in question, cf. the common opening *Her swutelað on þisum gewrite.*

l. 15. *seo talu.* The statement of the plaintiff's case, cf. *ontalu* below and see p. 366.

l. 16. *gewrit 7 his insegl.* See p. 380.

þam arcebisceope Ælfrice. Ælfric, who had been a monk at Abingdon, then Abbot of St Albans, became Bishop of Ramsbury in 990 and Archbishop of Canterbury in 995. He died in 1005 (Sax. Chr. A) or 1006 (*ibid.* C, D, E, F; Fl. Wig.). In his will (Whitelock, No. XVIII) he makes bequests to all the places with which he had been connected.

l. 18. *be ontale · 7 be oftale.* By *ontalu* is meant the statement of the claimant or plaintiff in the case; by *oftalu* the counter-statement of the defendant refuting the claim or charge.

l. 20. *se scyresman Leofric.* I have not found any mention of this sheriff elsewhere.

Ælfun abb. For a contemporary Abbot of Milton Abbas of the name see p. 375. There would seem to be no reason for the abbot of a south-western monastery taking a leading part in Kentish affairs, and it is possible, therefore, that the Abbot Ælfhun of the present document should be sought for elsewhere. The name is not a common one, however, and there is a possibility that the Abbot Ælfhun of the charters (if one and the same) was the Ælfhun who appears as Bishop of London in 1004 (K. 709 f.). In 1013 the latter accompanied Ælfgifu Emma and her sons to Normandy *þ he hi bewitan sceolde* (Sax. Chr. E, cf. Fl. Wig. who calls him the princes' *magister*). He seems, therefore, to have stood in a particular relationship to the royal family and may have enjoyed the special confidence of the king even before his appointment to London. The identification of Abbot Ælfhun with the later bishop of the same name is, however, entirely conjectural.

ll. 23 f. *oþ hy ealle bædon þone biscop* etc. The case, like numerous others, ends in a compromise.

p. 142, l. 7. *Wulfric abbod.* Abbot of St Augustine's, see pp. 371 f.
Siweard, cf. l. 13. See p. 372.
l. 8. *Wulfstan æt Sealtwuda*, cf. l. 15. See p. 372.
Ælfelm Ordelmes sunu. Two later Kentish documents are witnessed by Æthelwine, Ælfhelm's son, see pp. 170, l. 1; 204, ll. 9 f.
l. 11. *Orpedingtune.* Orpington, Kent.
l. 13. *Lifing æt Meallingan.* Perhaps the Lyfing of No. LXII. A witness of the name signs K. 715 (see p. 372).
l. 14. *Leostan æt Mærseham.* Perhaps the Leofstan who also witnesses K. 715.
ll. 14 f. *Godwine Wulfeages sunu*, cf. p. 150, l. 10.
l. 17. *Sidewine æt Pealleswyrðe.* There is a Paddlesworth near Folkestone but in this case the hamlet of the same name 1 mile west of Snodland is probably meant. The D.B. form is *Pellesorde*.
l. 18. *Wærelm.* This witness signs another Kentish charter dated 1003 (*Ordnance Survey Facsimiles*, III, No. 36). For the appearance of Leofwine, Wærelm's son, in another Kentish document see p. 150, ll. 15 f.
on byrig, i.e. Canterbury.
Guðwold. Guthwold signs the same Kentish charter as Wærelm, see above.

LXX

MS. *Liber Monasterii de Hyda*, f. 36 b. See p. 309.

EDITION. Edwards, *Liber Monasterii de Hyda*, R.S. p. 258, with a modern English translation on p. 365.

DATE. Sometime between 995 and 1005 or 1006, i.e. while Ælfric was Archbishop of Canterbury, see p. 384.

ll. 23 f. *Ælfsige abbod.* Ælfsige succeeded Æthelgar as Abbot of the New Minster in 980. His first signature appears in 988 (K. 663). He died in 1007 (see Birch, *Liber Vitae etc. of Hyde Abbey*, p. 276, an entry of his *obitus* under that year with which the evidence of the charters agrees).

l. 24. *Wlfmære*. A writ issued by Æthelred about 984 is addressed to Earl Ælfric and to Wulfmær and Æthelweard and all the thegns in Hampshire (K. 642). The signature Wulfmær *minister* occurs about half a dozen times between 986 and 1005.

l. 25. *Bertune*. Barton Stacey near Andover, Hampshire.

l. 26. *Dregtune*. Drayton, now a tithing in the parish of Barton Stacey. Four hides at Drayton were granted to the New Minster by Edward the Elder in 903 (B. 602). The estate was held of the abbey by a freeman in 1066 (D.B. I, f. 42 *b*; V.C.H. *Hants.* I, p. 470) but was one of those seized by Hugh de Port (*ibid.* p. 418, n. 1).

ll. 26 f. *swa gewered* etc. See p. 372.

p. 144, l. 4. *Ælfheges bisceopes*. Bishop of Winchester and Ælfric's successor at Canterbury, see p. 373.

Ælfrices ealdermannes. Earl of Hampshire, see pp. 373 f.

Eðelmæres. The signature *Æpelmær minister* occurs for the first time in 983 (K. 1279). The two names Ordulf and Æthelmær are found together in that order in four charters of the years 986 to 988 (K. 655, 657 f., 664). In 990 (K. 672) Æthelmær signs for the first time at the head of the *ministri* and from 994 (K. 686) to 1005 (K. 1301) his name is generally found in that position and is almost invariably followed by Ordulf's. Another *minister* of the name Æthelmær makes his appearance in 994 (K. 686) and continues to sign at intervals along with the first Æthelmær until 1005 (K. 1301). In a charter of 999 (K. 703) the second Æthelmær is described in MS. C.C.C., Cambridge, 111 as the son of Æthelwold, which is likewise the name of the witness signing immediately after him both in that charter and in two others of the year 1002 (K. 1295 f.). Six charters of the years 1007 to 1012 (K. 1303-1307, 719) are signed by one Æthelmær only. In four of these his name heads the list of *ministri*, while in the remaining two (K. 1304 f.) it comes second. In three cases out of the six (K. 1303 ff.) it is followed immediately by the name Æthelwold, and this evidence, slight as it is, seems to suggest that the Æthelmær of these later charters is the second one of the two.

The first Æthelmær, who is the witness of the present charter, can almost certainly be identified with Æthelmær, the founder of Cerne and Eynsham and the patron of Ælfric the homilist, by the fact that, as grantee, he does not sign the charter obtained from Æthelred in 1005 for his newly founded monastery at Eynsham (K. 714). Æthelmær, the founder of Eynsham, can be identified further with the earl of the name (see below) by the fact that the estate of Lawling, Essex, bequeathed to the latter by Ælfflæd about 1002 (Whitelock, p. 40) was one of those given by the former in exchange for Eynsham in 1005 or somewhat earlier (see Æthelred's charter in *The Eynsham Cartulary*, ed. Salter, I, p. 20 for the correct reading *decem in Litlan Cumtune decemque in Lellincge* which should be substituted for Kemble's incorrect and misleading version, following Dugdale, *decem in Litlan Cumtune in Lellincge*, K. 714). Æthelmær apparently held office as

NOTES 387

Earl of the Western Provinces. His connection with Dorset is proved by the occurrence of his signature as *dux* or *ealdorman* in two Sherborne documents of the years 1012 and 1014 respectively (see p. 146, l. 24 and K. 1309) and by the fact that an undated writ is addressed to him by name, though without any title, by Æthelric, Bishop of Sherborne (K. 708). In 1013 he submitted to Swegn along with the western thegns (Sax. Chr. E), and Fl. Wig. in recording the same event calls him *Domnaniae comes*.

It is uncertain at what date he succeeded to the office of earl. Æthelweard, Earl of the Western Provinces, signs until 998 but, as Miss Whitelock points out (p. 145), he was alive in the episcopate of Burhwold, Bishop of Cornwall (see K. 981), whose predecessor signs till 1002. The title *dux* attached to Æthelmær and the two following witnesses in K. 1291 (a charter of 996 from the *Codex Wintoniensis*) is undoubtedly a mistake. Ælfflæd's will (see above) cannot be later than 1002 (see Whitelock, *loc. cit.*) and there is one other document of the same year (K. 1296, an Abingdon charter) where the title *dux* is also applied to Æthelmær. In 1004 (K. 710) and 1005 (K. 1301, a Sherborne charter), on the other hand, he appears again simply as *minister*, and in view of his professed intention in 1005 of living with his newly established community at Eynsham (K. 714) it seems possible that after acting as earl for a brief period in 1002 he resigned office but took it up again some years later.

Neither Æthelmær nor his father Æthelweard is called *dux* in Æthelred's Eynsham charter, but it is practically certain that the latter was the Æthelweard who preceded him as Earl of the Western Provinces (see Ælfric's *Lives of the Saints*, ed. Skeat, p. 4). It is clear from Æthelred's charter that Æthelweard was dead in 1005 and it is possible that he died sometime in 1002 and was succeeded immediately by his son.

The Saxon Chronicle records that in 1017 Æthelweard Æðelmæres sunu þæs grætan was killed, and this entry is generally taken to refer to the son of Earl Æthelmær. It seems to me possible, however, that the other Æthelmær is meant and that his nickname has been introduced for the express purpose of distinguishing him from the earl[1]. It is noteworthy that one of the witnesses in a case dating from about 990 is *Apelwold þes greta* (see p. 130, l. 20) and it is certainly possible that this is the father of the second Æthelmær and that he bequeathed his nickname to his son. A parallel can be found in the case of Æthelric Bigga and his son Esbearn Bigga, see p. 436.

l. 5. *Ordulfes.* Ordulf signs from 980 (K. 624) to 1005 (K. 1301). He is probably to be identified with the founder of Tavistock (Sax. Chr. 997 C, D, E) and, if so, was the son of Earl Ordgar and the brother of King Edgar's wife Ælfthryth.

[1] Miss Whitelock has drawn my attention to the fact that Fl. Wig. describes him as *Æthelwardus filius Agelmari Ducis* so that I am probably mistaken in my attempt to connect him with the other Æthelmær.

388 NOTES

Sulgeates. For *Wulgeates,* see p. 376.
Æðelrices. See p. 376.
Æðelweardes. Two *ministri* of this name sign in 981 and 982 (K. 629, 1278), then one only until 1005, 1007 and 1008 when again there are two. One only signs from 1012 to 1015.

LXXI

MS. British Museum, Cotton Tiberius B. v, Part I, f. 75 *b* (or 74 *b* by the new numbering). Three folios, beginning at f. 75 (or 74), are different from the rest of the MS. and did not originally form part of it. They seem to have belonged to a gospel book.
EDITION. K. 1352.
DATE. Not later than 999, see below.

l. 10. *on þysse Crystes bec.* See above.

l. 11. *Pottune.* Potton, Bedfordshire. The Ælfhelm of the present grant is undoubtedly the Ælfhelm Polga who appears elsewhere (see p. 130, l. 19; B. 1050; *Liber Eliensis,* II, cc. 10, 11, 29) and whose will is extant (Whitelock, No. XIII, dated 975–1016). The history of his estate at Potton is obscure. In his will (see Whitelock, p. 32) he bequeathes the estates of Hatley and Potton to two brothers, Ælfstan and Ælfmær, apart from an unspecified amount of land granted to a certain Osgar. According to the *Historia Ramesiensis,* R.S. p. 62, however, he and his wife Æffa gave these two estates to Ramsey Abbey. In 1086 the estate of Potton, assessed at 10 hides, was held by the Countess Judith, the widow of Earl Waltheof, and Ramsey Abbey had no holding there or at Hatley.

Ælfhelm's grant of half a hide to his goldsmith Leofsige probably preceded the drawing up of his will. It is possible, therefore, that the Osgar mentioned in connection with land at Hatley and Potton in the latter was Leofsige's heir.

Leofsige...hys goldsmiþe. Ælfhelm had a relative of this name (see *Historia Ramesiensis,* R.S. *loc. cit.*) who may be the Leofsige mentioned as a legatee in his will (Whitelock, p. 32, ll. 14–17). For a grant of land by King Edred to his goldsmith Ælfsige *ob studium quam mihi auri argentique fabrica sollicite deservit atque decorat,* see B. 879.

l. 13 f. *Byrhtnoþ abbod.* Abbot of Ely, see p. 374. His inclusion as a witness shows that the grant was made before the year 999 at the latest.

l. 14. *Ælfhelm se gunge.* Probably Ælfhelm Polga's younger brother, see p. 376.

l. 15. *Æþelhric 7 Alfwold.* These two names appear together twice in Ælfhelm's will (Whitelock, p. 32, ll. 10, 20).

Wulfmær þæs bisceopes broþar. One of Ælfhelm's legatees bears this name (Whitelock, p. 32, l. 22), but it would appear from the context that one of his own three brothers is meant. The description *þæs bisceopes broþar* in the present instance may be intended, therefore, to

NOTES 389

distinguish another holder of the name. The bishop referred to is probably either the Bishop of Elmham or the Bishop of London.

ll. 15 f. *Ælmær cild*. Perhaps the Ælfmær of Ælfhelm's will, see above.

l. 16. *Leofric æt Holewelle* etc. Holwell is now in Hertfordshire. A certain Godric is mentioned in Ælfhelm's will as a joint legatee along with the latter's daughter. It is probable, therefore, as Miss Whitelock suggests, that he was Ælfhelm's son-in-law, and he may or may not be identical with the Godric, the son of Leofric of Holwell, mentioned here.

l. 17. *Hernicwelle*. Unidentified.

Ælfsige preost...Osferþ preost. In his will Ælfhelm makes a bequest to his priest (Whitelock, p. 32, l. 8). The reference to Ælfsige's son is noteworthy.

LXXII

MS. Corpus Christi College, Cambridge, MS. 383, f. 107. This MS. originally belonged to St Paul's and is dated 1125–1130 by Liebermann.

EDITION. Liebermann, *Archiv für das Studium der Neueren Sprachen*, CIV, 1900, pp. 23 f. It is discussed in the preceding pages.

DATE. This document is entered in the MS. in a twelfth-century hand, but is attributed by Liebermann to a date about 1000. No other record of the kind seems to survive, but it recalls the obscure annal 1008 in the Saxon Chronicle. It contains a list of the number of 'shipmen', i.e., presumably, men required for service on a warship, supplied by estates in Essex, Middlesex and Surrey (three or four seem to belong to adjacent counties), most of which, then or later, were in the possession either of the Bishop of London or of the community at St Paul's. We are reminded of the *manege sciran þe mid weorce to Lundene belumpon* mentioned in the Saxon Chronicle, s.a. 1097.

The basis of assessment is difficult to understand. Two estates, Fulham and Southminster, contribute five men each. At Fulham, according to D.B., the bishop himself held 40 hides and the canons 5 hides, while at Southminster he held 30 hides in demesne. Four men, on the other hand, are contributed by St Osyth, an estate assessed at only 7 hides in D.B., while Clacton, assessed at 20 hides, contributes only two men, and Stepney, where the bishop held 32 hides, is combined with Islington, where the canons held two estates of 2 hides each, to contribute the same number. A few of the places named are on or near the coast, but the majority are inland, and proximity to or distance from the sea supplies no clue to the assessment.

The total number of men provided is 45. Alfred's longships had 60 oars or more (Sax. Chr. s.a. 897) and Ælfwold II, Bishop of Crediton, bequeathed a warship of 64 oars to the king (Napier and Stevenson, *Crawford Charters*, p. 23). The 60 helmets and 60 coats of mail left by Archbishop Ælfric along with his best ship to King Æthelred (Whitelock, p. 52) were probably intended as equipment for the crew. It would seem, therefore, from these few indications, that ships of about 60 oars were commonly in use during the Danish wars.

l. 18. [*S*]*cipmen*. See B.T., *Suppl.* p. 698, s.v., 'a fighting man who goes in a ship'.

Ticc. For *Cicc*, i.e. Chich, now St Osyth (see D.B. I, f. 11; V.C.H. *Essex*, I, p. 439). For similar confusion of *t* and *c* in the same name see Whitelock, p. 2, l. 16, where it appears as *Tit*.

The first three estates named in the list—St Osyth, Tillingham and Dunmow—were bequeathed to St Paul's by Theodred, Bishop of London, sometime between 942 and 951 (see Whitelock, pp. 2, 99). Tillingham, assessed at 20 hides 6 acres, was held by the canons of St Paul's in 1086 (D.B. I, f. 13; V.C.H. *Essex*, I, p. 442), but Dunmow is not entered either among their lands or those of the Bishop of London. It appears by that date as a number of small estates under different holders, and the same is true of Tolleshunt, the estate which comes next in the list.

l. 19. *Næsingstoce*. According to D.B. I, f. 13 (V.C.H. *Essex*, I, p. 443) Navestock had been held by two freemen before the Conquest but had since passed into the possession of St Paul's 'by the king's gift', as the canons claimed. 'The other Navestock' is said to have been seized by the canons. It is possible that their claim to these estates had some foundation. A charter, attributed to Edgar but dated 867, records the grant of 15 hides there to St Paul's (B. 1210).

Neosdune. Neasden, Middlesex, is not mentioned in D.B.

l. 20. *Hinawicun*, i.e. Wickham St Paul's, the estate held by the community, as distinct from Wickham Bishops, the estate held by the bishop. It appears in D.B. simply as *Wicam* but, as Liebermann points out, the forms of the place-names in the present document are considerably earlier than those of D.B. Both Neasden and Wickham are included among the estates confirmed to St Paul's in a charter granted by Æthelstan, B. 737.

Tollandune. No Essex manor of the name is entered in D.B., and if Tollington, North London (D.B. *Tollentone*), is meant, it is curious that two such widely separated estates should be combined for the purpose of supplying two men.

Gnutungadune. I have failed to identify this estate.

l. 21. *Bræmbelege*. A convent was founded at Bromley by William, Bishop of London (1051–1075).

þottanheale. In 1086 the canons held Tottenham, Middlesex, assessed at 5 hides (D.B. I, f. 128).

Clopham. In 1086 Clapham was held by Geoffrey de Maundeville in succession to *Turbern*, the pre-Conquest holder (D.B. I, f. 36; V.C.H. *Surrey*, I, p. 323). There is no mention of any connection between this estate and St Paul's.

Bærnun. In 1086 Barnes was held by the canons as part of the Archbishop's manor of Mortlake (D.B. I, f. 34; V.C.H. *Surrey*, I, pp. 311 f.). It was assessed at 8 hides. It is one of the estates mentioned in Æthelstan's charter, see above.

l. 22. *Drægtune.* Drayton, Middlesex, is also mentioned in Æthelstan's charter. In 1086 it was held by the canons and was assessed at 10 hides (D.B. I, f. 128).

Caddandune. Caddington was at one time partly in Hertfordshire and partly in Bedfordshire but has now been transferred entirely to Bedfordshire. Both the Caddington estates were held by the canons of St Paul's in 1086, and both had been in the possession of a certain Leofwine *cild* before the Conquest (D.B. I, ff. 136, 211; V.C.H. *Herts.* I, p. 316; V.C.H. *Beds.* I, p. 230). The canons, moreover, had the king's writ to show that they held the Bedfordshire manor by Leofwine's gift. A copy of the will of Edwin, Leofwine's father, is extant by which he bequeathes Caddington and other estates to his son (K. 920).

l. 23. *Sandune.* Sandon is mentioned as the property of St Paul's in Æthelstan's charter (see above). In 1086 it was held by the canons and was assessed at 10 hides (D.B. I, f. 136; V.C.H. *Herts.* I, p. 317).

Ceaddingtune. Unidentified.

Fullanhamme. Fulham, see p. 389 and D.B. I, f. 127 *b*.

l. 24. *Forþtune.* Unidentified.

Stybbanhype. Stepney is entered in D.B. I, f. 127 among the lands of the Bishop of London.

Gislandune. Islington (see p. 389) is entered among the lands of the canons (D.B. I, f. 128).

l. 25. *Orseapun*, cf. *of þam westrum Orseapum.* There is now only one village of the name. In 1086 it was held by the Bishop of London (D.B. I, f. 9 *b*; V.C.H. *Essex*, I, pp. 437 f.).

Ligeandune. In 1086 Leyton was divided amongst various holders and had no connection with St Paul's.

Seopinglande. There is nothing in D.B. to connect Shopland with St Paul's.

l. 26. *Bylcham.* Belchamp St Paul is mentioned in Æthelstan's charter. In 1086 it was held by the canons. Its pre-Conquest assessment had been 5 hides (D.B. I, f. 12 *b*; V.C.H. *Essex*, I, p. 442).

Coppanforda. For the bequest of Copford to Ælfstan, Bishop of London, by Æthelric see Whitelock, p. 42. This will was confirmed by Æthelred probably in 997 (*ibid.* p. 147). In 1086 Copford was held by the bishop (D.B. I, f. 10 *b*; V.C.H. *Essex*, I, p. 439).

l. 27. *Holande.* Neither the Bishop of London nor the canons of St Paul's had any holding there in 1086.

Suðmynster. It is recorded in D.B. that this estate was taken away by Cnut but recovered by Bishop William in King William's time (D.B. I, f. 10; V.C.H. *Essex*, I, pp. 438 f.). It is probable, therefore, as Liebermann suggests, that this document was drawn up before the time of Cnut.

Claccingtune. Clacton was held by the bishop in 1086 (D.B. I, f. 11; V.C.H. *Essex*, I, p. 439).

l. 28. *Hæplege...Codanham.* It would seem from the combination of these two estates that the reference is to Hadleigh and Coddenham in Suffolk; otherwise, as Liebermann points out, it would seem more likely that either Hadleigh, Essex, or Hadley, Middlesex, is meant by the former. There was apparently no connection between any of these estates and St Paul's.

LXXIII

MSS. (*a*) Cambridge University Library, Ff. 2. 33, f. 49 *b*. This is the Sacrist's Register of the Abbey of Bury St Edmunds, written about the beginning of the fourteenth century.

(*b*) British Museum, Additional MS. 14847, f. 19 *b* (by the new numbering), another fourteenth-century Bury cartulary generally inferior to (*a*).

The text is from (*a*). The grant is referred to and the opening words quoted in the list of Bury benefactors in C.U.L., Ee. 3. 60, f. 321. It is recorded also without quotation in the similar lists in C.U.L., Additional MS. 6006, ff. 73 *b*, 74 *b* and C.U.L., Mm. 4. 19, f. 167.

EDITIONS. K. 1349, from (*b*).
B. 1013, from (*b*).

DATE. This grant is attributed to the time of Æthelred in the records mentioned above and is dated 1005 in the margin of Ee. 3. 60, f. 321. There is no means of verifying or establishing the exact date.

p. 146, l. 1. *Vlfketel.* The title *comes* is applied to the donor of these estates in the entries referred to above. In Additional MS. 6006, f. 74 *b* he is more fully described as *Alderman, dux et inclitus comes*. There is little doubt, therefore, that he is identical with the stalwart defender of East Anglia against the Danes (Sax. Chr. s.a. 1004, 1010) who fell at *Assandun* in 1016. It is curious that neither in the Saxon Chronicle nor in the charters does Ulfketel appear with the title *ealdorman* or *dux*. He signs about a dozen of Æthelred's charters as *minister*.

ll. 2 ff. *Rikínghale...Rucham...Wlpet...Hilderíclea*. Rickinghall, Rougham, Woolpit and Hinderclay are all in Suffolk. They were held by the abbey in 1086 (see V.C.H. *Suffolk*, I, pp. 498, 501).

l. 4. *Redfares þorpe*. I have been unable to identify or to find any further record of this estate.

l. 5. *mid Sake and Sokne.* See p. 384.

LXXIV

MS. The Sherborne Cartulary, f. 14 *b*. See p. 278.
EDITIONS. K. 1302.
T. p. 300.

DATE. The only possible year for Æthelric, Bishop of Sherborne, and Ælfsige, Bishop of Winchester, to appear as witnesses together is 1012 (see below).

NOTES 393

l. 8. *Eadmund æþeling.* Edmund Ironside, the son of Æthelred. The stubborn resistance which he offered to Cnut led to the division of the kingdom between them, but he died in 1016, a few months after his father.

ll. 8 f. *þone hyred æt Scireburnan.* Sherborne was reconstructed and filled with monks in the reign of Æthelred (see V.C.H. *Dorset*, II, p. 63).

l. 9. *Holancumbe.* This estate is included among the possessions of the abbey in Æthelred's charter (K. 701, dated 998). It is the subject of a later agreement, see No. cv.

l. 12. *gewærþ hym.* See B.T., *Suppl.* p. 448, s.v. *geweorðan*, v. *se prafost.* See p. 273.

l. 14. *Wulfstan archebisceop.* Wulfstan became Archbishop of York and Bishop of Worcester in 1002 (K. 1296). In 1016 he resigned Worcester but retained York until his death on 28 May 1023.

l. 23. *Lyfing b.* Bishop of Wells from 999 to 1013 and Archbishop of Canterbury from 1013 to 1020. His other name is said to have been Ælfstan (Sax. Chr. s.a. 1019 D, cf. *Ordnance Survey Facsimiles*, III, No. 39) or Æthelstan (Fl. Wig. s.a. 1005).

Æþelric b. Bishop of Sherborne. He was appointed in 1001 or 1002 and his signature appears for the last time in a charter dated 1009 (K. 1306). There are no dated charters of 1010 or 1011 but his successor Æthelsige II signs in 1012 (K. 719). If the present document is genuine (and there seems no reason for thinking otherwise) Æthelric must have been alive in 1012 (see following note).

Æþelsie b. This is apparently a mistake for Ælfsige, Bishop of Winchester. His first signature in a dated charter appears in 1013 (K. 1308) but he may have succeeded Æthelwold II in the previous year.

l. 24. *Eadric ealdorman.* Eadric Streona was Earl of Mercia from 1007 to 25 December 1017 (Fl. Wig.). He is described by Fl. Wig. s.a. 1007 as *hominem humili quidem genere sed cui lingua divitias ac nobilitatem comparaverat, callentem ingenio, suavem eloquio, et qui omnes id temporis mortales tum invidia atque perfidia, tum superbia et crudelitate, superavit.* All accounts agree as to his unscrupulous self-seeking (by which he won his nickname) and his treachery (cf. Sax. Chr. s.a. 1009, 1015, 1016). When Cnut divided the kingdom into four in 1017 he was granted the earldom of Mercia (which he had previously held), but was put to death the same year and his body cast without burial outside the wall of London (Fl. Wig. s.a. 1017). Hemming, who had reason to remember him as a despoiler of the church of Worcester, finds in his ignominious end an instance of justly earned retribution, *Deo sibi dignam ultionem reddente, ut qui multorum monasteriorum destructor, et cunctorum fere extiterat oppressor, a cunctis etiam ad sepulturam sperneretur* (Hearne, I, p. 281).

Æðelmer ealdorman. Earl of the Western Provinces, see pp. 386 f.

ll. 24 f. *Æþelfand Æþelmeres suna.* This name is not recorded elsewhere and may be a misreading of *Æðelward*, see p. 387.

NOTES

l. 25. *Leofsuna abbud æt Cernel.* The name of this Abbot of Cerne is not recorded elsewhere.

ll. 25 f. *Ælfget Hengþes suna.* This witness does not appear elsewhere.

p. 148, l. 1. *Siwærd.* Is this Siweard of Kent (see p. 372)? The two signatures *Sigwerd* and *Sigered* are found together in one of Æthelred's grants in the Sherborne Cartulary (K. 1301, dated 1005).

Brihtric reada. Two men of the name witness the grant referred to in the preceding note. One of them may be the witness of the present agreement.

l. 2. *Ealdwine þ · 7 Wulfric þ.* Perhaps chaplains to Edmund the Ætheling.

ll. 2 f. *Lofwine...discpen.* For the office of *discpegn* or seneschal see Larson, *The King's Household in England before the Norman Conquest,* p. 125.

l. 3. *Ælfget 7 Ælwerd his cnihtas.* The fact that these two (along with the seneschal) are the only members of the Ætheling's household mentioned by name shows that they were of considerable standing. For an account of the O.E. *cniht* see Stanton, *The First Century of English Feudalism,* pp. 132 ff. Bequests to *cnihtas* are frequent in wills, see Whitelock, p. 235, s.v. *cniht* for references.

LXXV

MS. A single sheet of parchment in the possession of Lady (Herbert) Dering of Hamptons, Tonbridge, Kent. The top halves of the letters CYROGRAPFHVM run along the bottom edge showing that it is the top portion of a chirograph.

The Dering family (formerly of Surrenden Dering, Kent) traces its descent from Saxon times. A certain Dering FitzSired (identified as the son of one of the witnesses of the present grant) was slain at the Battle of Hastings in 1066. He is entered in D.B. as a former tenant at Deal, while a man of the same name, not however described as the son of Sired, had formerly held Farningham (V.C.H. *Kent,* III, pp. 205 f., 222). On the history of the family see Hasted, *History of Kent,* III, p. 228, note (*a*).

EDITION. K. 1315.

DATE. This grant is traditionally ascribed to Earl Godwine, and as he is entered as the former holder of lands both at Boughton Aluph and Boughton Malherbe (see below), it is possible that this is correct. If so, it was presumably made before his promotion to an earldom (see p. 409), as no title is applied to him. It is at any rate earlier than the death of Archbishop Lyfing in 1020.

All the names mentioned in connection with the present grant (except the last) appear also in the marriage agreement of a certain Godwine who has been identified more doubtfully with the earl of the name (see p. 397). The signature of a certain Godwine *minister*

NOTES

is attached to a grant made by Cnut to Christchurch, Canterbury (see p. 160, l. 40), which is also witnessed by Earl Godwine, while three men of the name appear as witnesses or sureties of the marriage agreement (see p. 150). It was, therefore, a common name in Kent at the time.

l. 5 f. *Leofwine readan.* He acted as a surety for the Godwine of the marriage agreement.

l. 6. *Swiðrædingdænne.* This is generally identified with Surrenden Dering, near Pluckley, but as Wallenberg points out (pp. 331 f.) there is a Southernden near Boughton Malherbe which seems to be derived from a similar Anglo-Saxon form and might satisfy the conditions of the grant more closely.

l. 8. *æt þon sceatte.* For a grant of swine-pasture in Kent in return for 1450 pence see B. 1212.

Leofsunu. A man of the name, who may be identical with the present one, acted as a surety for the Godwine of the marriage agreement along with his brother Godwine, Eadgifu's son.

l. 10. *Boctun.* There are several places named Boughton in the neighbourhood of Ashford and Maidstone, e.g. Boughton Aluph (with the hamlets of Boughton Corner and Boughton Lees in the same parish), Boughton Malherbe and Boughton Monchelsea (with the two adjacent hamlets of Boughton Green and Boughton Quarry).

Boughton Aluph, which had been held by Earl Godwine, is distinguished as *Earlesboctun* in the *Domesday Monachorum* (see V.C.H. *Kent*, III, p. 257). Its D.B. assessment is 7 *solins* with land for 33 ploughs and woodland to render 200 swine (*ibid.* p. 251). Boughton Malherbe is said to have been held by *Alwin* of Earl Godwine. It was assessed at 1 *solin* with land for 2 ploughs and woodland to render 20 swine (*ibid.* p. 228). It seems possible, therefore, that the latter is the Boughton mentioned in the present grant.

l. 11. *Lyfingc bisceop.* Archbishop of Canterbury, see p. 393. He signs two charters of the same period (K. 728, 1310) as *Dorobernensis ecclesiae episcopus.*

Ælfmær abbud. Abbot of St Augustine's, see p. 410.

l. 12. *Stred.* See p. 372.

l. 13. *Ælfsige cild.* He acted as a witness at the drawing up of the marriage agreement (see above). The title *cild* is of comparatively rare occurrence and its exact significance is uncertain.

Æþelric. Perhaps Æthelric Bigga, see p. 409.

LXXVI

MS. This document was included in the Somers Collection, see p. 266.

EDITIONS. Hickes, *Dissertatio Epistolaris*, p. 76, in *Thesaurus*, I.
Wanley, *Thesaurus*, II, pp. 302 f.
Smith, *Beda: Historiæ Ecclesiasticæ* etc. Appendix, p. 778.

Hearne, *Hemingi Chartularium* etc. II, p. 598, from Wanley.
K. 738, from Hickes.
T. p. 320, from Hickes and Hearne.
The text is from Smith. The differences in the other copies are slight and generally only orthographical.

DATE. This agreement seems to fall between 1014, when Ælfweard became Abbot of Evesham, and 1016, when Archbishop Wulfstan resigned Worcester. Had it been later, his successor Leofsige would almost certainly have acted as a witness.

l. 16. *se arcebisceop*. Wulfstan, Bishop of Worcester and Archbishop of York, see p. 393.

l. 17. *Ealretune*. Orleton, Worcestershire.

ll. 17 f. *Ribbedforda*. Ribbesford, Worcestershire. According to Hemming (Hearne, I, p. 256) this manor was taken from the church of Worcester first by the Danes and then by Turstan the Fleming, who suffered the usual consequences of his act, *ipseque non multo post et ipsam et omnem terram suam perdidit exilioque multatus est. Sic qui parum Deo injuste abstulit, omnia sua juste perdidit*. In 1086 it was held by the king as a berewick of Kidderminster (D.B. I, f. 172; V.C.H. *Worc.* I, p. 286).

l. 18. *Cnihtewican*. Knightwick was part of the manor of Grimley. This manor belonged to the church of Worcester and in 1086 1 hide at Knightwick was held of it by Robert the Despencer. It had formerly been leased to a nun Eadgyth who had restored it to the monastery in the time of King William, when the increase in the number of the monks forced them to reclaim it for their own use (D.B. I, f. 173 b; V.C.H. *Worc.* I, p. 295). There seems to be no mention elsewhere of its connection with Winchcombe.

l. 20. *Eanulfintune*. This estate is now represented by Alton Lodge in the parish of Rock (see Pl.N. *Worc.* p. 70). In 1066 it was held by Godric, a thegn of Earl Ælfgar (D.B. I, f. 176; V.C.H. *Worc.* I, p. 309).

l. 24. *Leofwine ealdorman*. Leofwine is described in K. 698, a document of 997, as Earl of the Hwicce, and he probably succeeded Eadric Streona as Earl of Mercia in 1017 (see Freeman, *Norman Conquest*, 3rd ed. I, p. 418). He seems to have died sometime in the course of 1023, as his signature is lacking in two charters of that year (K. 737, 739) and does not appear again in any of the later ones which can be dated with certainty.

Aeþelstan bisc. Bishop of Hereford from 1012 till his death on 10 February 1056. Fl. Wig. (s.a. 1055) records that he was blind for the last thirteen years of his life.

ll. 24 f. *Aelfword abb*. Ælfweard, who had been a monk at Ramsey, became Abbot of Evesham in 1014 and Bishop of London in 1035. In 1044 he resigned both charges because of ill-health and wished to

NOTES

retire to Evesham, but the monks refused to admit him. He betook himself to Ramsey, therefore, with many of the books and treasures which he had formerly bestowed upon Evesham, and died there in the same year. The disease from which he suffered is said to have been leprosy (*Historia Ramesiensis*, R.S. p. 157). He is described in the *Chronicon Abbatiae de Evesham*, R.S. p. 83 as a kinsman of Cnut.

l. 25. *Brihteh munuc.* This is probably Archbishop Wulfstan's nephew Brihtheah who later became Abbot of Pershore, then Bishop of Worcester, see p. 421.

LXXVII

MS. Somner, *A Treatise of Gavelkind*, pp. 75 f., describes the MS. of this agreement as 'an old Saxon tripartite deed or charter' and gives the text from 'that part of it left and laid up at Christchurch'. K. and E. quote as their authority a MS. in the *Arc. C.C. Cantuar.*, while T. describes it as *Ch. Antiq. Cantuar.* I have not been able to find any trace of this MS. at Canterbury and it is not apparently in the British Museum.

EDITIONS. Somner, *op. cit.* p. 196.
K. 732.
T. p. 312.
E. p. 228.
The text is from Somner.

DATE. This agreement must have been drawn up between 1016 (the year of Cnut's accession) and 1020 (the year of Archbishop Lyfing's death). It should be compared with the treatise *Be Wifmannes Beweddunge* (Liebermann, I, pp. 442-444), which Liebermann dates roughly between 970 and about 1060 but regards as probably the work of a contemporary of Cnut (see III, pp. 241 f.).

p. 150, l. 1. *Godwine.* It has been suggested that the Godwine of this marriage agreement was the earl of the name (see p. 409), but there seems to be no means of establishing such an identification. Earl Godwine is known to have been married to Gytha, the sister of Earl Ulf (see p. 418), but there is no record of an earlier marriage. William of Malmesbury (*Gesta Regum*, R.S., I, p. 245) states, however, that he was twice married, and although he was certainly misinformed with regard to these marriages (the first, he says, was to a sister of Cnut), he may have had some authority for his statement. There is a possibility that the Godwine of this agreement was identical with the Godwine who granted a piece of swine-pasture in Kent to Leofwine the Red about the same time (see No. LXXV), and a further possibility that the latter was identical with the earl of the name, but the whole matter of identification is uncertain (see p. 394).

l. 2. *Byrhtric.* A thegn of this name witnesses a charter granted by Cnut to Christchurch, Canterbury, see p. 160, l. 37.

ll. 3 f. *anes pundes gewihta goldes* etc. A gift of this kind was apparently a regular part of the proceedings, cf. *Be Wifmannes Beweddunge*, cap. 3: *Ðonne syððan cype se bridguma hwæs he hire geunne wið ðam ðe heo his willan geceose*. The treatise contains in addition traces of archaic practice no longer found in the present record, e.g. the payment of *fosterlean*, 'remuneration for maintenance' by the prospective husband (cap. 2).

ll. 4 f. *Stræte...Burwaramersce*. There seems to be no village or hamlet called 'Street' in the vicinity of Burmarsh at the present day. The name was probably derived from the Roman road which ran from Canterbury to Studfall Castle, cf. the modern Court-at-Street, a hamlet three miles west of Hythe.

l. 7. *Cincgestune*. Kingston, Surrey.

beforan Cnute cincge etc. It would seem from the public nature of the ceremony and the rank of the witnesses that the prospective bride and bridegroom belonged to important families. In the treatise referred to above the bridegroom's kinsmen act as sureties for him throughout.

ll. 7 f. *Lyfinges arcebiscopes*. See p. 393.

l. 9. *Ælfmeres abbodes*. Abbot of St Augustine's, see p. 410.

ll. 9 f. *Æþelwines sciregerefan*. Æthelwine is called *scirman* in a writ of 1013–1020 (K. 731).

l. 10. *Siredes ealdan*. See p. 372.

Godwine Wulfeages sunu, cf. p. 142, ll. 14 f., where he also appears. The signature *Wulfheh minister* occurs in the endorsement to a Kentish charter (B. 562). This endorsement cannot be dated more exactly than 963–975.

l. 11. *Ælfsige cild*. See p. 395.

Eadmer æt Burham. For his appearance as a witness elsewhere see pp. 170, l. 2, 188, l. 29.

ll. 11 f. *Godwine Wulfstanes sunu*. The signature *Wulfstan minister* also occurs in B. 562 (see above).

l. 12. *Kar þæs cincges cniht*. The signature Carl *minister* is found in the charters from 1019 (K. 730) to 1045 (K. 781). In one case (K. 751, dated 1033) the title attached is *miles*. Two Kentish landholders called Godric *Carlesone* (*filius Carle*) and Goduin *filius Carli* respectively are found in D.B. I, ff. 1, 6 *b*, 9; V.C.H. *Kent*, III, pp. 204, 223, 231.

þa man þ mædan fette, cf. *Be Wifmannes Beweddunge*, cap. 6: *Gif hy þonne ælces ðinges sammæle beon ðonne fon magas to 7 weddian heora magan to wife 7 to rihtlife ðam ðe hire girnde*. This constitutes the second part of the ceremony and some time might elapse between the betrothal and the bringing home of the bride.

l. 13. *Byrhtlingan*. Brightling, Sussex.

þa eode þyses ealles on borh etc. The sureties who now make their appearance for the first time were probably drawn from the bridegroom's kin. It is noteworthy that eleven names are given, and that an oath of twelve (of whom one is the person concerned in the case) is of very frequent occurrence in the settlement of legal business.

NOTES

Ælfgar Syredes sunu. For Sired see above.

l. 14. *Frerþ preost* etc., cf. *Be Wifmannes Beweddunge,* cap. 8: *Æt ðam giftan sceal mæssepreost beon mid rihte se sceal mid Godes bletsunge heora gesomnunge gederian on ealre gesundfulnesse.*

ll. 14 f. *Leofwine preost,* 7 *Wulfsige preost.* Probably members of the community of St Martin's at Dover. This community had been established in the first instance by Eadbald, King of Kent, in the chapel of St Mary in the castle of Dover, but in 696 it was removed by Wihtred to the church of St Martin (V.C.H. *Kent,* II, p. 133). The lands of the canons of St Martin's are entered in D.B. I, ff. 1 *b,* 2 (V.C.H. *Kent,* III, pp. 204–208).

l. 15. *Eadræd Eadelmes sunu.* The signature *Eadelm minister* is found in B. 562 (see above).

ll. 15 f. *Leofwine Wærelmes sunu.* For Wærelm see p. 385.

l. 16. *Cenwold rust.* Not apparently found elsewhere.

Leofwine Godwines sunu æt Hortune. The tenant of Monks Horton in the time of King Edward is entered as *Leuuinus* (D.B. I, f. 13 *b*; V.C.H. *Kent,* III, p. 248).

ll. 17 f. *Godwine Eadgeofe sunu* etc. See p. 395.

l. 19. *þe ic heom gæf.* The sudden change to the first person is surprising and it is difficult to know who is the speaker. It would seem most likely that the bride's father is meant.

l. 21. *þyssa gewrita synd ðreo.* An earlier stage of development is represented in the legal treatise *Be Wifmannes Beweddunge* where apparently a tangible pledge of some kind is used as a guarantee of good faith, cf. cap. 6: 7 *fo to þam borge se ðe ðæs weddes waldend sy.*

l. 22. *þ þridde hæfð Byrhtric self.* It is noteworthy that a copy of the document is retained by the bride's father who acts throughout as her representative. The *weddes waldend* (see preceding note) has by this time disappeared from the proceedings.

LXXVIII

MS. Hereford Cathedral, P. I. 2, f. 134. The existence of this MS was intimated to me by Mr N. R. Ker.

FACSIMILE. From the words *þær ðær heo wæs* (p. 152, l. 9) to the end—*New Palaeographical Society,* Part x, pl. 234. For a transcript of the first part I am indebted to Mr G. T. Shepherd of the University of Birmingham.

EDITIONS. Hickes, *Dissertatio Epistolaris,* p. 2, in *Thesaurus,* I.

K. 755.

T. p. 336.

Essays in Anglo-Saxon Law, Appendix, No. 28, from K.

NOTES

C. B. Judge, *Harvard Studies and Notes in Philology and Literature*, XVI (1934), pp. 93-95.

DATE. Sometime in the reign of Cnut, 1016 to 1035.

ll. 23 f. *Ægelnoðesstane*. Aylton near Ledbury, Herefordshire.
l. 24. *Æþelstan ƀ.* Bishop of Hereford, see p. 396.
l. 25. *Ranig Ealdorman*. The signature *Ranig dux* occurs in 1018 (K. 728) and *Hrani dux* in 1023 (K. 739), 1026 (K. 743) and 1031 (K. 744). The name does not occur again in either form in any of the remaining charters of Cnut's reign, but the signature *Reoni comes* occurs once in a doubtful charter of Hardacnut (K. 761), and according to Fl. Wig. *Roni [comes] Magesetensium* took part in the punitive expedition sent by Hardacnut against Worcester in 1041.

Edwine. From the context it seems as if Earl Ranig's son is meant, but it is noteworthy that Leofwine, Earl of Mercia, had a son of the name, and he may have been present as his father's representative.

l. 26. *Þurcill hwita*. Thurkil the White and Leofflæd his wife both held considerable estates in Herefordshire according to D.B. In 1086 most of them had passed to Hugh Lasne (D.B. I, f. 187; V.C.H. *Hereford*, I, pp. 342 f.). Thurkil appears as a witness in a transaction (see No. XCIX) in which a certain Leofwine, Leofflæd's brother, is concerned.

Tofig pruda. To Tofi the Proud is ascribed the foundation of the first church of Waltham in the reign of Cnut, after the discovery of the holy cross at his estate of Montacute in Somerset (see *De Inventione Sanctae Crucis* etc., ed. Stubbs, pp. 1-13). According to the same authority Waltham was lost after his death by his son Æthelstan, *degenerans a patris astutia et sapientia*, and granted by Edward the Confessor to Harold who refounded it. In 1042 Tofi married Gytha, the daughter of Osgod Clapa, and during the marriage feast King Hardacnut was taken ill and died. Tofi must have been advanced in years at the time of the marriage, if the authority quoted above is right (p. 13) in calling him the grandfather of Esgar the Staller (see p. 464). He himself is described with considerable exaggeration as *Tovi le Prude qui totius Angliæ post regem primus, stallere, vexillifer regis monarchiam gubernabat* (p. 6). The statement which follows to the effect that he was *regiis implicitus negotiis* is borne out, however, by his appearance as the king's messenger in the present instance. His signature occurs in K. 749 (a charter of 1033) and he is named as one of the executors of a will of 1042 or 1043 (Whitelock, p. 74). It is probable that the signature Tofi *minister* which is commonly found from 1018 (K. 728) onwards is his in most cases, although two men of the name sign K. 746 and three sign K. 751 (both Abingdon charters dated 1032 and 1033 respectively). One of Cnut's charters (K. 741) is signed by *Toui hwita* and *Toui reada*.

p. 152, l. 1. *Bryning scirgerefa.* The title *scirgerefa* is not found till the reign of Cnut, but the title *scirman* with which it is then interchangeable (see p. 398) appears considerably earlier (see p. 334) and a *gerefa* is already associated with a *scir* in VI Æthelstan, 10. It is probable that the office of sheriff arose early in the tenth century when the great earldoms were formed after the midland counties were taken over, and that the sheriff normally was in charge of a county (see Chadwick, *Anglo-Saxon Institutions,* pp. 229-231).

ll. 2 f. *Godric æt Stoce.* Grifin son of Mariadoc is entered in D.B. as the successor of Godric at Stoke Prior (D.B. 1, f. 187 b; V.C.H. *Hereford,* 1, p. 343).

l. 4. *Enneawnes sunu.* The name is obviously corrupt. K. and T. take it to represent the feminine name *Eanwen,* but the genitive ending *-es* is against this assumption and it seems better to regard it as a masculine form in *-wine,* e.g. *Eanwine.* The name given is not necessarily that of Edwin's mother.

ll. 5 f. *Weolintun · 7 Crydes læh.* Wellington and Cradley, Herefordshire. In D.B. Wellington is entered among the estates of Hugh Lasne which had formerly belonged to Thurkil the White (D.B. 1, f. 187; V.C.H. *Hereford,* 1, p. 342). Cradley is included among the lands of the canons of Hereford (D.B. 1, f. 182; V.C.H. *Hereford,* 1, p. 322).

l. 8. *ða talu.* See p. 366 and cf. the corresponding terms Lat. *narratio,* Fr. *conte* used in the thirteenth century (Pollock and Maitland, *History of English Law,* II, p. 602). In the present instance Thurkil is referring to the defendant's side of the case which he is prepared to present once it is known. It is interesting to notice that he is not one of the three thegns sent to discover it.

l. 9. *of þam gemote þær* etc. It seems as if a verb of motion (cf. *ridon,* l. 23) has been omitted.

l. 10. *Fæliglæ.* Fawley is about 9 miles south-west of Aylton.

l. 11. *Wynsige scægðman.* In Ælfric's Vocabulary *pirata vel piraticus vel cilix* is glossed *wicing vel scegðman* (Wright-Wülcker, I, p. 111, l. 26; cf. also Ælfric's *Grammar,* ed. Zupitza, p. 24, l. 9) and in II Æthelred, 7 *an sceiðman,* i.e. a member of the invading Danish fleet, is contrasted with *an landesman,* i.e. a native of the country. In the present instance the name must denote a member of the crew of an English longship (*scægð*), see Whitelock, p. 137.

l. 12. *hwylce talu heo hæfde.* Her defence takes the form of a simple denial of her son's claim to any part of her property, followed by the formal disposal of all her possessions to her kinswoman Leofflæd, wife of Thurkil the White, to take effect after her death. The existing document, unfortunately, gives no account of Thurkil's formal refutation of Edwin's claim. It concerns itself only with the establishment of Leofflæd's right to the inheritance verbally bestowed upon her by her enraged kinswoman.

402 NOTES

l. 26. *þa land clæne*, i.e. free from any claim such as Edwin had brought against them, see p. 331.

ll. 27 f. *sče Æðelberhtes mynstre*. The cathedral church of Hereford was dedicated to St Æthelbert.

l. 29. *let settan* etc. The order of proceedings is interesting, namely (1) the oral will declared before witnesses, (2) the authorisation obtained from the shire-meeting, (3) the written record entered in a gospel book.

LXXIX

MS. British Museum, Harley Charter 83, A. 3, a contemporary parchment.

FACSIMILE. Bond, *Facsimiles of Ancient Charters in the British Museum*, Part IV, No. 43.

EDITIONS. K. 924.
B. 1318.
T. p. 434.

DATE. See below.

p. 154, l. 1. *Her swutelað* etc. The reading of the MS. can scarcely be accepted as it stands, hence the emendation.

l. 2. *Fuldre*. The name Fulder is probably, but not certainly, of Scandinavian origin, see Björkman, p. 44.

l. 3. *Ludintune*. Luddington, Warwickshire. According to Hemming (Hearne, I, p. 278) estates at Luddington and elsewhere in Warwickshire were lost by the monks of Worcester in the time of Cnut through their tardiness in the payment of geld, since a rule had been established whereby he who first paid the overdue geld for an estate became its owner. In this way, he says, those who coveted any of their estates were able to acquire them by cunningly forestalling the monks in their payment. These fraudulent transactions, however, did not escape divine retribution, *nam unusquisque eorum qui huic fraudi operam dederunt digna ultione perpercussi aut luminibus privati, aut paralisi dissoluti aut in insaniam versi sunt, plurimi etiam semet ipsos interfecerunt*.

The present transaction seems to belong to a date early in the eleventh century, when the monastery was still in possession of this particular estate, but was already in difficulties for money.

LXXX

MSS. (*a*) Lambeth Palace Library, *Gospels of MacDurnan*, f. 115. This MS., which had belonged to Maelbright MacDurnan, Abbot of Armagh and Raphoe (d. 927), was given by King Æthelstan to Christchurch, Canterbury, and there had certain charters written in it.

(b) British Museum, Additional MS. 14907, f. 18 b, an eighteenth-century copy of (a) made by the Welsh antiquary, Lewis Morris.
EDITIONS. K. 1321, from (b).
T. p. 331, from (b).
The text is from (a).
DATE. Between 1020 and 1038, i.e. while Æthelnoth was Archbishop of Canterbury.

l. 12. *Tokiges.* The name is of Scandinavian origin and is of frequent occurrence in England, see Björkman, pp. 142 f.
Healtune. Halton, Buckinghamshire. At the Conquest this estate was held by Leofwine, son of Earl Godwine, but was restored to the archbishop instead of passing to the Bishop of Bayeux along with Leofwine's other estates (D.B. I, f. 143 b; V.C.H. *Bucks.* I, pp. 210, 233).

l. 13. *Hrisbeorgan.* Monks Risborough, Buckinghamshire.

l. 14. *Wulfnoðes cwyde.* It seems at first sight as if Toki were applying for an extension of the terms of Wulfnoth's will, but the archbishop's commendation of his course of action suggests that this is not the case, and that he was prompted in his application merely by the desire for security in his tenure of the estate. If this is the correct interpretation, it seems likely that Wulfnoth was Toki's father-in-law. If, however, the archbishop's concession carries with it an actual extension of tenure on Toki's behalf, it seems possible that Wulfnoth was Æthelflæd's first husband from whom she had inherited Halton.

l. 15. *æfter his dæge 7 his wifes,* i.e. either after Toki's death or after Wulfnoth's, according to the interpretation adopted.

l. 19. *his mannum,* i.e. the monks of Christchurch.

l. 20. *for ðam cwyde.* The use of this phrase suggests that Toki was merely reminding the archbishop of the terms of the original bequest in accordance with which he desired to continue as sole tenant of the estate for the rest of his life. For a later application by Toki to Æthelnoth's successor on behalf of the same estate see No. XC.

l. 22. *Bleddehlæwe.* Bledlow, Buckinghamshire.

l. 23. *Eaningadene.* Unidentified.

LXXXI

MS. British Museum, Additional Charter 19796, the bottom portion of a chirograph.

FACSIMILE. Bond, *Facsimiles of Ancient Charters in the British Museum,* Part IV, No. 15.

EDITION. E. p. 235.

DATE. This transaction cannot be later than 28 May 1023, the date of Archbishop Wulfstan's death. It was probably not much earlier, see note on Abbot Leofsige, p. 405.

NOTES

p. 156, l. 1. *Ælfwerd abb.* Abbot of Evesham, see p. 396.

l. 3. *Norðtune.* Seven hides at Norton and one at Lenchwick are said to have been granted in 709 to Bishop Ecgwine for his monastery at Evesham by Coenred of Mercia and Offa of East Anglia (B. 125). In 976 the Abbey of Evesham and its lands were seized by Ælfhere, *dux quidam sceleratissimus* (see p. 319) and later, in fear of death, bestowed by him on a monk named Freodegar who became abbot but afterwards gave the abbey to a certain powerful man named Godwine in exchange for Towcester. Godwine continued to hold certain of the abbey lands (including Lenchwick and probably Norton) until they were redeemed from him by Abbot Brihtmær about 1010. In 1013 he seized them again but was finally expelled from them by Abbot Ælfweard in 1014 (*Chronicon Abbatiae de Evesham*, R.S. pp. 78–82). Norton and Lenchwick, which are immediately north of Evesham, were held by the abbey in 1086 (D.B. I, f. 175 b; V.C.H. *Worc.* I, p. 306).

l. 4. *to inware...to utware.* The possession of 5 hides of land *to cynges utware* is found as a necessary qualification for the attainment of the legal status of a thegn in the late Anglo-Saxon period (see *Be Leode geþincþum*, cap. 3 and *Norðleoda laga*, cap. 9; Liebermann, I, pp. 456, 460). Liebermann assigns both of these treatises to the period 1030–1060. The land *to inware* was presumably subject only to the claims of the owner, in this case the Abbey of Evesham.

l. 5. *þa ða hit weste læg.* This condition was probably the result of the wars between the English and the Danes which marked the end of Æthelred's reign and continued until the establishment of Cnut as sole king. Hemming describes the county at that time as *depredata et atrocissime devastata* and attributes the loss of a number of church lands to the action of *comes Hacun et sui milites* (Hearne, I, p. 251).

æt Hacune 7 æt Leofrice, cf. p. 162, l. 13 where Hakon and Leofric are also named in connection with a Worcester shire-meeting. From one of Cnut's writs (K. 757), which survives only in a post-Conquest form but may represent an Anglo-Saxon original, it would appear that Hakon was earl and Leofric sheriff of Worcestershire.

l. 7. *Egwines.* Ecgwine, Bishop of Worcester, was the founder of the original monastery at Evesham. An account of the miraculous events leading up to his choice of that particular site for his foundation is given in the *Chronicon Abbatiae de Evesham*, R.S. pp. 4–11 and a slightly different version by William of Malmesbury, *Gesta Pontificum*, R.S. pp. 296 f.

l. 8. *cyricsceat ge teoðunge.* Injunctions regarding the payment of church dues and tithes are frequent in the laws. Church dues were payable at Martinmas (Ine, 4, II Edgar, 3 etc.), the tithe of young livestock at Pentecost (II Edgar, 3 etc.) and that of the fruits of the earth at the Equinox (*ibid.*) or at the feast of All Saints (V Æthelred, 11 etc.).

NOTES

l. 9. *toll 7 team.* This seems to be the earliest occurrence of these two terms in conjunction. Later they are generally found in lists of privileges following *sacu 7 socn* and preceding *infangenþeof* (cf. K. 829, 843, 853). For the process of vouching to warranty see No. XLIV. Alternative forms of the oath employed by the plaintiff and defendant respectively in a case of the kind are given in the compilation which Liebermann entitles *Swerian*, caps. 2–4 (see *Gesetze*, I, p. 396).

l. 20. *Ælfgeofu seo hlæfdie* etc. It is curious to find any controlling influence in the Abbey of Evesham ascribed to Ælfgifu, and there seems to be no other reference to anything of the kind. Perhaps nothing more is meant than that she was the patroness of the monastery, or does it mean that she was actually lay abbess? It is possible, again, that the idea involved is that of commendation and lordship.

l. 21. *Wulfstan arcebiscop.* See p. 393.

Leofsige abb. An abbot of this name witnesses an undated charter (K. 736), which, like the present one, cannot be later than 1023 as it is signed by Archbishop Wulfstan. If in both cases the witness is Leofsige, Abbot of Ely, neither charter can be earlier than 1022 as his predecessor Leofric was holding office in that year (K. 734). The date of Leofsige's appointment to Ely is uncertain, but if it is put as early as 1023, his predecessor must have held office for a very short time, and there is no special note to that effect in the *Liber Eliensis*. For the death of Leofsige, Abbot of Ely, see p. 467.

Leofric · 7 Eadwine. Probably Earl Leofwine's sons, see pp. 400, 412.

l. 22. *Bryhtteg munuc.* See p. 397.

l. 23. *Leofsige biscop.* Bishop of Worcester from 1016 to 1033.

Hacun eorl. See pp. 404, 412.

Byrhtwine. Brihtwine signs two Worcester charters, K. 1313 and E. p. 234.

Ælfsige m̃. This name is perhaps a later addition.

l. 24. *Byrhtwold biscop.* Bishop of Ramsbury. Brihtwold's predecessor Ælfric was promoted to Canterbury in 995 (see p. 384) and Fl. Wig. attributes Brihtwold's appointment to the same year. Ælfric's death and Brihtwold's appointment are entered together in the Saxon Chronicle, s.a. 1006 E; the former only is recorded s.a. 1005 A. Brihtwold's first signature occurs in 1005 (K. 714) and it seems possible, therefore, that Ælfric retained Ramsbury after his promotion to Canterbury, and that Fl. Wig. has antedated Brihtwold's appointment. He died in 1045.

Eglaf eorl. See p. 410.

l. 25. *Ælfsige abb.* Probably Ælfsige, Abbot of Peterborough from 1005 to 1055.

Leofwine ealdorman. See p. 396.

LXXXII

MS. A parchment contained in the Red Book of Canterbury, No. 16, at Canterbury Cathedral.
FACSIMILE. *Ordnance Survey Facsimiles*, Part I, No. 19.
EDITIONS. K. 737.
T. p. 316.

In addition to the Anglo-Saxon version there is a Latin version of this charter of which four exemplars are extant, viz. two in the Red Book of Canterbury (Nos. 15, 17), one in the Stowe Collection of Charters and one in the Crawford Collection. Facsimiles of the first three are given in the *Ordnance Survey Facsimiles*, Part I, Nos. 20, 21; Part III, No. 40. The last has been edited by Napier and Stevenson, *Crawford Charters*, No. XII. Kemble and Thorpe print the Latin version along with the Anglo-Saxon one. Napier and Stevenson note that both the Anglo-Saxon version and the Latin one, No. 15, in the Red Book of Canterbury are in an Old English hand of the eleventh century and may be older than the Norman Conquest. The others are later in date. A Middle English translation of the Anglo-Saxon version is given in the two Cathedral registers A. f. 154 and E. f. 11 *b*, followed in each case by a copy of the Latin version. A summary of the charter in Latin is entered in the Gospels of MacDurnan (see Westwood, *Palaeographia Sacra Pictoria*, p. 12) and is given in K. 1328 from an eighteenth-century copy of this entry (B.M. Additional MS. 14907, f. 20 *b*) made by the Welsh antiquary Lewis Morris.

Kemble regarded the charter as spurious and the editors of the Crawford Charters likewise view it with suspicion, chiefly on the grounds 'that there is no exact parallel in Old English charters for the grant of such privileges and immunities'. They concede, however, that it is 'a very skilful imitation of a genuine Old English one', and conclude that it is founded upon a genuine charter of Cnut which may or may not have been a grant of the port of Sandwich. They point out further that the formulae and the list of witnesses agree with the date to which it is assigned, and it seems to me, therefore, that the weight of evidence is on the side of regarding it as genuine. The fact that there are no earlier examples of the grant of privileges of the kind does not necessarily prove that none were granted by Cnut; the possibility even that such rights were a matter of local usage in the Anglo-Saxon period 'and needed no other sanction' does not seem to me to preclude their ratification by the representative of a new dynasty in England. It seems to me, therefore, that the charters of this type attributed to Cnut have been regarded with undue suspicion.

p. 158, ll. 1 ff. *On ðas hegestes Godes* etc. Napier and Stevenson (p. 137) note that the preamble of the Latin version occurs word for word the same in the charters of Cnut's predecessors, e.g. K. 388, 611. There is no exact parallel to the Anglo-Saxon.

NOTES

l. 15. *mines heouodes kinehelm*. The late Canterbury list of benefactors (Dugdale, I, p. 97) records Cnut's grant of Sandwich in 1023 *cum corona sua aurea que adhuc servatur in capite crucis majoris in navi ejusdem ecclesie.*

l. 17. *ða hæuene on Sandwic*. The tidal estuary of the Stour from Sandwich to the sea is still known as Sandwich Haven.

ll. 17 ff. *ealle ða lændinge* etc. The Latin version reads simply *portum de Sanduuic et omnes exitus eiusdem aquae ab utraque parte fluminis*, cf. Ducange, s.v. *exitus* (5), '*vectigal pro evehendis mercibus ex aliquo loco*'. This is the only instance of the word *lænding* quoted in B.T. p. 629, s.v. *lending*. Its use here is probably due to Scandinavian influence, cf. *taperæx* below.

l. 19. *fram Pipernæsse to Mærcesfleote*. The former of these names survives in the modern Pepperness, the point of land on the east coast of Kent to the north of the estuary of the Stour (see *Crawford Charters*, p. 137), while the latter has left no trace as a place-name in the vicinity. The reason for this is obvious. The word *mearcfleot* appears frequently in Kentish boundaries and in every case refers to one of the tidal inlets, characteristic of the coast, which form natural and well-marked dividing lines between one area and another (cf. B. 348, *ab occidente unum fretum qui nominatur nostra propria lingua mearcfleot*). The difficulty here is to decide which of the tidal inlets is meant. The editors of the *Crawford Charters* have pointed out that in the summary of this grant included in the Saxon Chronicle s.a. 1029 F the name *Nortmuthe* has been substituted for *Mærcesfleote*, cf. *norðmutha* in the entry in MacDurnan's Gospels (the reading *Northuuicha* in K. 1328 is a mistake which is not found in the eighteenth-century transcript which it reproduces), and they suggest that the point intended is that where the North Stream flows into the Stour just outside the northeast corner of Sandwich. In their view, therefore, the grant 'embraces the whole stretch of the river from Sandwich to the sea'. I am inclined to think that *a Pipernæsse usque Nortmuthe* includes even more and that it is meant to define the whole of the wide tidal channel which at that time separated Thanet from the mainland. The name *norðmuþa* occurs twice in the Saxon Chronicle (s.a. 1049 C, 1052 E) and it seems clear from the second reference that the mouth of this channel on the north coast of Kent is meant. Whether or not the later summaries by substituting *Nortmuthe* for *Mærcesfleote* have justifiably defined the limits of the original grant it is impossible to say. The form *Mærcesfleote* with the genitive ending attached to the first element of the compound is a curious and unusual one. In a grant of Reculver made to Christchurch by Edred in 949 (B. 880) the boundaries of the surrounding area include among the points enumerated along the north coast *norþmuþa*, *eanflæde muþa* and *mearcfleotes muþa*, all of which probably represent different branches of the same tidal channel. A form such as the last would have been more comprehensible in the present instance, but the reading *mærcesfleote* is common to both versions (English and Latin).

l. 20. 7 þ scip bið aflote. The summary of the charter given in the Saxon Chronicle, 1031 A, adds a further detail at this point, namely *beo an scip flotigende swa neh þan lande swa hit nyxt mæge.*

l. 21. *taperæx*. This word occurs only in the present charter and its summarised versions in the Saxon Chronicle. The first element of the compound has been traced to Russian, so that it probably reached England by way of Scandinavia (see Björkman, *Scandinavian Loanwords in England*, p. 256).

l. 22. *gereflanges*. No other instance of this word is known and its exact meaning is uncertain. The Middle English translation reads *yreulinges*, while the Latin version has *ministri*.

ll. 24 f. *þ scip 7 si ouerfæreld*. The Latin version reads *nauicula et transfretatio*. The reference seems to be to a small ship or ferry boat for the conveyance of passengers and goods across the haven.

l. 25. *si tolne*. This payment on incoming goods is distinct from the dues (*gerihta*) paid on outgoing merchandise. Both alike fell to the monks of Christchurch.

l. 29. *ænne spreot*. The Latin version reads *lignum quod Angli nominant spreot*. The word is one which is generally associated with ships, see N.E.D. s.v. *sprit*.

These methods of measuring distance (cf. the use of *taperæx*) are curious but at the same time practical from the point of view of sailors and of an element as variable as the sea. An axe was probably chosen in the first instance, because it was commonly carried on board ship and could be thrown in such a way as to mark the point reached in the ground with its blade. A pole (again a sailor's implement), which could be held in the outstretched hand, was obviously more suited for measuring distance which could not be fixed by a mark on the surface of the sea.

p. 160, l. 1. *of ðas healue þare middelsæ*. The Latin version reads *ex hac parte medietatis maris*. The *middelsæ* is literally the 'middle sea', i.e. the sea which lies between two others. The reference, as far as I can understand it, is once more to the wide tidal channel running between the sea on the north coast of Kent and that on the east coast. 'On this side of the middle sea' would then mean on the Sandwich side. The 'middle sea', as the result of silting, no longer provides a navigable channel between the two coasts, but there is evidence that it was used not only by small boats but by merchant ships up to the latter half of the fifteenth century (see Hasted, *History of Kent*, IV, p. 289).

l. 27. *Ægelnoð*. Æthelnoth, Archbishop of Canterbury, see p. 403.

l. 29. *Ælfric*. Archbishop of York from 1023 to 1051. He is called *Ælfricus Puttuc* by Fl. Wig. (s.a. 1023) and is said to have been dean (*præpositus*) of Winchester Cathedral before his appointment to York. Cnut's proclamation of 1027 is addressed to the two archbishops, Æthelnoth and Ælfric, by name.

ll. 31 f. *Ælfwine se b of Lundene...Ælfwine b of Wincæstre*. These names are both correctly given in the Latin version as it appears in the

Red Book of Canterbury, No. 17, and the *Crawford Charters*, No. XII, and should be emended accordingly to *Ælfwig* and *Ælfsige* respectively. The copy in the Red Book of Canterbury, No. 15, gives the second one correctly but has *Ælfwinus* for the first, while the copy in the Stowe Charters has the first one correct but reads *Ælfwinus* for the second.

Ælfwig became Bishop of London in 1014 (Sax. Chr. D) and his signature occurs for the last time in 1035 (K. 753). Ælfsige II was Bishop of Winchester from 1014 to 1032 (Sax. Chr. E) or 1033 (K. 750). He was succeeded by Ælfwine.

l. 33. *Brihwald b̃.* Brihtwold seems to have succeeded Burhwold as Bishop of Cornwall in 1019 (cf. K. 730 which is signed by *Buruhwold* and K. 729 of the same year which is signed by two bishops called *Brihtwolf* for *-wold*, i.e. the Bishop of Ramsbury and the Bishop of Cornwall respectively). In 1027 he was succeeded by his nephew Lyfing, Bishop of Crediton (Fl. Wig. I, p. 238). His signature occurs also in K. 1324, a charter of about 1023–1027.

l. 34. *Ægelric b̃ of Dorsætscire.* The Latin version reads correctly *dorccensis eccle eps*, i.e. Bishop of Dorchester, not of Dorset, the see of which was Sherborne. Æthelric was Bishop of Dorchester from 1016 to 1034. His predecessor Eadnoth was killed at *Assandun*.

l. 35. *Ælmer b̃.* Bishop of Selsey from 1009 to about 1032.

Wulnoð abb̃. Wulfnoth, Abbot of Westminster, witnesses K. 748 (a charter dated 1032) and No. LXXXV. He died in 1049 (Sax. Chr. C; Fl. Wig.) or 1050 (Sax. Chr. D).

Ægelric .m̃. This witness, as the editors of the *Crawford Charters* suggest, is probably to be identified with Æthelric Bigga who was a Kentish landowner and a benefactor both of Christchurch and St Augustine's (see p. 436 and K. 1338). For his appearance elsewhere as a witness see pp. 170, ll. 1 f., 172, l. 5, 192, l. 8.

l. 36. *Godwine b̃.* Bishop of Rochester, see p. 384.

Godwine eorl. Godwine's first signature as *dux* occurs in 1018 (K. 728). His earldom is said by Fl. Wig. (s.a. 1051) to have included Kent, Sussex and Wessex. In 1051 he and his sons were exiled but were restored to favour and office the following year. He died at Winchester in 1053 and was buried in the Old Minster (Sax. Chr.; Fl. Wig.).

Ælfwine .m̃. This signature is found in Cnut's charters from 1019 (K. 729) to 1035 (K. 753). In two charters of 1033 (K. 749, 1318) and one of 1035 (K. 1322) the name appears with the title *dux*, probably by mistake, that is to say Ælfwine is the last described as *dux* instead of the first described as *minister* (cf. K. 751 f., dated 1033 where he signs at the head of the *ministri*). For a witness called *Ælfwine se reada* in two later Kentish charters see pp. 188, l. 30, 204, l. 11.

l. 37. *Brihtwine b̃.* Either Brihtwine I who preceded Ælfmær as Bishop of Sherborne (see over) or Brihtwine, Bishop of Wells between 1013 and 1024 (see William of Malmesbury, *Gesta Pontificum*, R.S. p. 194).

Ægelaf eorl. Eglaf, Scand. *Eilífr.* For a full account of his career see *Crawford Charters*, pp. 139–142. Fl. Wig. names him as joint commander along with Heming of one of the Danish fleets which came to England in 1009. He signs as *dux* from 1018 (K. 728) to 1024 (K. 741), and seems to have been connected with Gloucestershire (K. 1317). His death is not recorded. He was the brother of Ulf (see p. 418) and the brother-in-law of Earl Godwine through the marriage of the latter with his sister Gytha.

Brihtric .m̃. See p. 397.

l. 38. *Æðelstan ƀ.* Bishop of Hereford, see p. 396.

Þrim eorl. The title *dux* is applied to Thrym in the copies of the Latin version preserved in the Red Book of Canterbury, No. 17, and the Stowe Charters, whereas in the remaining two copies he is more correctly described as *minister*. The signature *Þrumm minister* is attached to K. 734 (an Ely charter of 1022) and that of *Þrim miles* to K. 735 (a Bury St Edmunds charter). The editors of the *Crawford Charters* suggest that he may have been identical with the Thrum who ended the sufferings of Archbishop Ælfheah (see p. 373) with the blow of an axe (Fl. Wig. s.a. 1012).

Leofric .m̃. Perhaps Earl Leofwine's son, the later Earl of Mercia, see pp. 412 f.

l. 39. *Ælmær aƀƀ.* Abbot of St Augustine's. The date of his appointment as Bishop of Sherborne is given once as 1017 and once as 1022 (see Thorne, *Chronica de rebus gestis abbatum S. Augustini Cantuariæ*, cols. 1782 f. in Twysden, *Decem Scriptores*, II). The earlier date is not supported by the evidence of the charters and it is possible that a mistake has been made in writing M.xvij for M.xxij. His signature as abbot occurs in K. 734, a document of 1022, and if the present charter is genuine and correctly dated, it would appear that his appointment did not actually take place until 1023 at the earliest. His successor Ælfstan does not sign until 1032, but was already in office in 1027 (see p. 420).

Yric eorl. Eric, Scand. *Eiríkr*, was the son of Hakon the Bad, Earl of Hlathir, and is a prominent figure in the Scandinavian historical sagas. A full account of his career is given by Napier and Stevenson, pp. 142–148. He was the brother-in-law of Cnut and came to England in his service. In 1016 he was made Earl of Northumbria in place of Uhtred and signs as *dux* from 1018 (K. 728) to 1023 (K. 739). William of Malmesbury, followed by Henry of Huntingdon, states that he was exiled by Cnut, but there is no evidence in support of this in any early authority. The sagas, on the other hand, relate that he died in England either before or after a pilgrimage to Rome.

Siræd .m̃. See p. 372.

l. 40. *Brihtmær aƀƀ.* Perhaps Abbot of Crowland, see p. 468.

Þord minister. The Scandinavian name *Þórðr* appears in various Anglicised forms among the names of the *ministri* who witness royal charters from 1018 (K. 728) to 1045 (K. 776, 780). In 1023 (K. 739) and 1024 (K. 741) two men of the name sign. Sometime before 1022 a certain Ðored, described as *optimas regis*, sold land to Peterborough (K. 733), while the signature *Þored steallara* is attached to a Kentish charter (No. LXXXV, p. 168, l. 29) and a certain *Þorð Þurkilles nefa* witnesses another Kentish charter of 1032 (No. LXXXVI, p. 172, ll. 5 ff.). It is possible that one or other of these is identical with the present witness and perhaps with the *Þórðr* who is said to have warned the thingmen of London of the plot against them after Swegn's death (see *Crawford Charters*, p. 148) or with *Þórðr* 'the Viking' who, according to the *Flateyjarbók* version of the Saga of St Olaf, assisted Cnut in his attack on London Bridge (see Ashdown, *English and Norse Documents*, p. 178).

Godwine .m̃. A witness of this name appears in Cnut's charters in 1018 (*Ordnance Survey Facsimiles*, III, No. 39), 1022 (K. 734, with the title *satrapa*), 1026 (K. 743), 1033 (K. 749) and 1035 (K. 1322, where the signature is actually *Godwine Brytæl minister*).

l. 41. *Brihtwine abb̃.* For Brihtwig, Abbot of Glastonbury and afterwards Bishop of Wells. The Latin version gives his name correctly in all four exemplars. His signature as abbot occurs in dated charters from 1018 (K. 728) to 1023 (K. 739) and his first signature as bishop appears in 1024 (K. 741).

Agemund .m̃. This name represents the Scand. *Qgmundr*. The same witness signs another Kentish charter (No. LXXXV, p. 168, l. 29), and it may have been he who received a grant of land in Dorset from Cnut in 1019 (K. 730) and who signs a Dorset charter of 1024 (K. 741).

Eadmær .m̃. Perhaps the *Eadmær æt Burham* of Godwine's marriage agreement (see p. 150, l. 11), of Cnut's grant of Folkestone to Christchurch (see p. 170, l. 2) and of Æthelric's agreement of 1044 (see p. 188, l. 29). The signature *Eadmær minister* is attached to two other Kentish documents of 1035 (*Ordnance Survey Facsimiles*, III, No. 42) and 1038–1044 (K. 769) respectively.

LXXXIII

MS. British Museum, Cotton Charters, VIII, 37, the top portion of a chirograph.

FACSIMILE. Bond, *Facsimiles of Ancient Charters in the British Museum*, Part IV, No. 14.

EDITIONS. Hickes, *Thesaurus*, I, Praefatio, p. xxi.
K. 898, from Hickes.
T. p. 375.
Essays in Anglo-Saxon Law, Appendix, No. 27, from K.

DATE. Æthelstan did not become Bishop of Hereford until 1012. Ælfheah, Archbishop of Canterbury, was a prisoner of the Danes from before Michaelmas 1011 until his death the following April

(Sax. Chr.). A mistake must have been made, therefore, in naming him as one of the witnesses of the earlier transaction recorded here, if it is rightly associated with Bishop Æthelstan. The dispute which followed seems to belong to 1023. It cannot be later, if the death of Earl Leofwine is rightly attributed to that year, while the fact that Wulfstan, Archbishop of York, is not called upon for evidence in support of Bishop Æthelstan suggests that it arose either during his last illness or after his death which took place on 28 May 1023.

p. 162, l. 1. *Æþelstan bisceop.* Bishop of Hereford, see p. 396.
l. 2. *Leofrice æt Blacewellan.* The estate of Blackwell was afterwards in the possession of Leofric, Earl of Mercia (see p. 461). The reference here must be to a previous owner of the same name.

fif hide landes. In 1086 the Bishop of Hereford held 15½ hides at Inkberrow *in capite* and 5 hides of the Bishop of Worcester (D.B. I, ff. 173, 174; V.C.H. *Worc.* I, pp. 289, 299). It is the latter estate which is under dispute here.

l. 3. *Ælfeges arcebisceopes.* Archbishop of Canterbury, see p. 373.
l. 4. *Wulfstanes Arcebisceopes.* Archbishop of York, see p. 393.
ll. 5 f. *mid ten pundan* etc. This means that the money was paid partly in gold and partly in silver to the value in all of ten pounds of silver. For the valuation of the hide see p. 378.

l. 7. *sibban oððe fremdan,* cf. the Scotch phrase 'freend or fremd'.
l. 9. *þærto boc settan.* Æthelred's later codes of law show a remarkable resemblance in phraseology to the sermons of Wulfstan. The business of drawing up a charter entrusted to him here confirms the view that he was directly responsible for much of the text of these later laws.

l. 11. *on sum þæt land.* For this construction see B.T. p. 934, s.v. *sum,* II (2).

l. 13. *Leofwine ealdor[m]an.* See p. 396.
Hacu[n]. Hakon was Cnut's nephew and the husband of his niece Gunnhild. Fl. Wig. states that he was banished in 1029 and the Saxon Chronicle C records his death at sea in the following year. For a summary of the Norse evidence with regard to his career see Ashdown, *English and Norse Documents,* p. 282, s.v. *Hákon.* He is accused by Hemming of despoiling the church of Worcester of several of its manors (Hearne, I, p. 251). He signs Cnut's charters as *dux* in 1019 and again from 1023 to 1026. His signature appears also in a charter dated, perhaps wrongly, 1031 (K. 744).

Leofric. This is probably Leofwine's son, the later Earl of Mercia. His first signature as *dux* in a dated charter occurs in 1032 (K. 746). It is attached, however, to an undated charter of the Abbey of Athelney (K. 1324) which survives only in an eighteenth-century transcript and has *Æðeluold,* Archbishop of Canterbury, for Æthelnoth, and *Bryðwig,* Bishop of Wells, for Brihtwine. This charter (if genuine) should probably be dated 1023 as it is signed by Brihtwig, Abbot of Glastonbury (the successor of Brihtwine at Wells), whose last signature as abbot is found in a dated charter of that year (K. 739) and his first as bishop in one of 1024 (K. 741). The signature Leofric *minister* occurs, however, in the list attached to a grant of 1026 (K. 743) and has generally been taken as that of the Leofric under discussion. I am not certain that this is necessarily the case, as a man of the same name and title attests a grant of 1033 (K. 1318). Unfortunately only three other dated charters of Cnut fall between 1023 and 1032, namely one of 1024 (K. 741) and two of 1031 (K. 744 and *Ordnance Survey Facsimiles*, Part II, Exeter Charters, No. XI). None of these is witnessed by Leofric either as *minister* or *dux*, so that the date of his appointment must remain uncertain.

l. 14. *his land clæne.* See p. 402.

l. 16. *hit e....an.* The reading was perhaps *hit edniwan* or something of the kind.

l. 23. *þa se þær geanwyrde wæs.* See B.T., *Suppl.* p. 287, s.v. *geanwyrde.*

l. 25. *heora seht* etc. There seems to be no other instance of any construction of the kind with *seht* (see B.T. p. 857, s.v.) and the original reading is uncertain.

l. 26. [*sa*]*ce.* Perhaps used in its legal sense, i.e. 'suit'.

p. 164, l. 2. *gehealden.* See B.T., *Suppl.* p. 339, s.v. -*healdan*, XI a.

l. 11. *Cyneword æt Pebbewurðy.* The only place of the name in the vicinity seems to be Pebworth, Gloucestershire.

Ælewig etc. Is it possible that the original reading was *Feccanham*? The A.S. letters *s* and *f* are easily confused.

l. 12. *Wulfri*[*c*] *æt Cloddesheale.* Cladswell in Inkberrow, see Pl.N. *Worc.* p. 325.

ll. 12 f. *Sæword æt Uptuny.* It is not possible to tell which 'Upton' is meant.

l. 13. *Bynningtune.* Unidentified.

l. 15. *æt SCA Marian.* The cathedral church which was built by Oswald and dedicated to St Mary. It was completed in 983 (see Hearne, I, p. 188).

l. 16. *æt Sce Æþelbrihte.* See p. 402.

LXXXIV

MS. The York Gospels in the Dean and Chapter Library, York, ff. 156 *b*, 157. The text begins on the verso of the last page of St John's gospel. This MS. is in a handwriting of the late tenth or very early eleventh century. The Anglo-Saxon entries were probably made about 1020–1030.

EDITIONS. W. H. Stevenson in *E.H.R.* XXVII, 1912, pp. 15-19, with a modern English translation and notes, reprinted by W. Farrer, *Early Yorkshire Charters*, 1914, I, p. 21.

DATE. W. H. Stevenson dates this document about 1030.

l. 23. *seo socn*. The term is used here in a territorial sense, i.e. with reference to the land over which the lord of the manor of Sherburn exercised jurisdiction without being the actual proprietor. This type of land (also called *socnland* later in the document) is carefully distinguished from the *inland* which comprised the central manor and any outlying portions appurtenant to it which were in the actual possession of the lord of the manor (i.e. *agenland*). The terms *weorcland* and *læn* refer to other varieties of tenure, see notes.

Scyreburna. Sherburn in Elmet, see p. 358. The identifications which follow are taken from W. H. Stevenson's article.

folcrihte. For references to the occurrence of this term in the laws see Attenborough, s.v. *folcriht*, also Robertson.

l. 24. *twa oxnagang*. See p. 331.

Fleaxlege. Now represented by Flaxley Lodge in the parish of Selby.

l. 25. *plogesland*, cf. the Scandinavian *plógsland*, and see p. 331.

l. 26. *Burhtun*. Now represented by Burton Hall in the parish of Brayton.

l. 27. *twegen þorpas*. Now represented by Thorpe Willoughby and Thorpe Hall near Selby.

twa Hyrst. Now distinguished as Temple Hirst and Hirst Courtney.

ll. 27 f. *twa Haðelsæ...priddan Haðelsæ*. East, West and Chapel Haddlesey.

l. 29. *eall Byrum ⁊ Breiðetun eal*. Farrer suggests for these Byrom in Brotherton and Burton Salmon.

p. 166, l. 3. *Fristun*. Now Monk Fryston.

Styfetun. Now represented by Steeton Hall in South Milford.

l. 4. *Myleford*. South Milford.

Fenntún. Now Church Fenton.

l. 5. *Luteringtun*. Now represented by Lotherton Hall.

Edgar's grant of 20 hides at Sherburn to Æslac in 963 (B. 1112) contains the boundaries of what is described as the *inland*, i.e. apparently the central manor of Sherburn, followed immediately by a list of scattered pieces of land also made over to Æslac's ownership, and dependent, it would seem, upon the central manor (see Stenton, *Types of Manorial Structure in the Northern Danelaw*, p. 82). The list, which is useful for comparison with the present one, runs as follows (see B. 1112, 1352): half a hide at *Hibaldestofte*, 1 hide at Fryston, 2 oxgangs at Hillam, 2 oxgangs at Lumby (uncertain, the reading is actually 7 *on on Lundby twegra oxenagang*), 2½ hides at Milford and at Steeton, 2 hides at Micklefield, the whole of Lotherton except 1 hide, 1½ hides at Fenton and 1½ hides at Cawood. The mixture of hides and oxgangs is interesting. It is noteworthy that jurisdiction over the whole of these lands, according to the present document, belonged to Sherburn, with the exception of Fenton (where half a ploughland is excluded), Cawood (where two parts only are included) and *Hibaldestofte*, which seems to be unrepresented in the present list.

l. 6. *Hehferðehegðe*. Unidentified.

Hudelestun. Now represented by Huddleston Hall.

l. 7. *þam inlande*. See above and p. 294.

ll. 7 f. *weorclandes*. This compound is not found elsewhere. It would seem that land subject to labour services is meant, which was not, however, in the absolute possession of the lord of the manor of Sherburn.

l. 11. *agenland*. This compound is also unrecorded elsewhere. It would seem to mean land that was held in absolute possession.

læn. Land held on lease. Edgar's grant of 963 conveyed 1½ hides at Fenton to Æslac, see above.

l. 13. *Ottanleage*. Otley, see p. 357.

l. 14. *On oðeran Hafecesweorðe*. There is only one Hawksworth at the present day.

l. 15. *Ectune*. Unidentified. The name occurs in D.B. I, f. 303 b (V.C.H. *Yorks*. II, p. 213), in the list of berewicks belonging to Otley. The editor suggests that Lindley may be meant, but this is unlikely as the latter occurs in the form *Lindeleage* in the present document along with *Ectune*, see ll. 22 f.

l. 16. *unbesacen agenland*. All the places mentioned are included in the D.B. list of berewicks belonging to Otley, see above.

l. 17. *socnland*. There is no separate list in D.B. of the lands over which Otley had rights of jurisdiction. All the places mentioned here, with the exception of *Scefinge* and Lindley, are included in the list of berewicks, see above.

l. 19. *Scefinge*. See p. 358.

l. 20. *Meðeltune*. A Scandinavian-English compound. The D.B. form is *Middeltune* which already shows the substitution of the English form of the adjective for the Scandinavian.

l. 21. *Biceratune*. This name has not survived. It appears in D.B. as *Bichertun* (see V.C.H. *Yorks*. II, p. 213). It is suggested there that Newhall near Otley may be meant.

l. 24. *Rypum*. Ripon, see p. 358.

milegemet etc. This represents the limit of the special privilege of sanctuary bestowed upon Ripon by Æthelstan, see *Memorials of Ripon*, I, Surtees Society, LXXIV, p. 33, also his rhyming charter, B. 647.

l. 25. *on þam .ii. hida*. It is noteworthy that the term 'ploughland' is not found in this section, its place being taken by 'hide'. The term 'oxgang' continues to be used. It is not clear what two hides are meant here. According to D.B. there was land for 10 ploughs at Ripon, extending 1 league round the church (see V.C.H. *Yorks*. II, p. 214).

Carlewic. Unidentified.

Munecatun. Now Bishop Monkton.

l. 27. *Hereleshó.* This is the pre-Conquest name of How Hill near Fountains Abbey. In the fourteenth century it was frequently called 'Michael How' from the chapel of St Michael de Monte which had been built there, see *Memorials of Fountains Abbey*, Surtees Society, XLII, pp. 54, 156 ff., 201, 220.

Stodlege. Studley is not included in the list of berewicks in D.B. but is found among the lands over which Ripon had jurisdiction (see below).

l. 28. *Suðtune.* Now represented by Sutton Grange. It is included in D.B. in the list of lands over which Ripon had jurisdiction, but not among the berewicks.

Nunnewic. Nunwick is not included in D.B. in the list of berewicks belonging to Ripon. It is entered separately as consisting, for geld, of 4½ carucates of *inland* and half a carucate in the soke of Ripon. In 1086 it was held by a tenant of the archbishop (D.B. I, ff. 303 b, 380; V.C.H. *Yorks.* II, pp. 214, 306).

Þorntune. Now Bishop Thornton. Of the places enumerated here Bishop Monkton, Markington, How Hill and Bishop Thornton are included in D.B. in the list of berewicks belonging to Ripon, see above.

l. 30. *weste land.* The places enumerated are all included in D.B. in the list of berewicks belonging to Ripon. In 1086 the land included in the berewicks was waste except for a certain amount at Markington, Bishop Monkton and How Hill. This was the result of William the Conqueror's devastation of Yorkshire in 1069. The places that were waste at the time of this survey all lie to the south-west of Ripon at a distance of about 4 to 6 miles.

l. 32. *Cnearresweorð.* This appears in D.B. as *Kenaresforde,* identified as Skelden (V.C.H. *Yorks.* II, p. 214, n. 21). The substitution of *-ford* for the less familiar *-weorð* is frequently found in place-names.

l. 33. *preostaland,* i.e. as distinct from the archbishop's.

l. 35. *Hotune.* Hutton Conyers.

p. 168, l. 1. *socnland.* The list of lands in D.B., over which Ripon had jurisdiction, includes two Stainleys, Sutton, Sleningford and Bridge Hewick (V.C.H. *Yorks.* II, p. 214).

Gypingadeal. Now Givendale.

l. 2. *Eastwic.* Westwick is found at the present day but not 'Eastwick'.

LXXXV

MSS. (*a*) British Museum, Stowe Charter, No. 40 (late eleventh century). The Anglo-Saxon version follows a Latin one on the same parchment.

(*b*) British Museum, Cotton Vitellius D. VII, No. 30, f. 39. This MS. is very ragged at the edges and the first letters of the line are frequently missing.

FACSIMILE. Of (*a*), *Ordnance Survey Facsimiles*, Part III, No. 41.

NOTES

EDITIONS. Dugdale, I, p. 109, from (b).
K. 1327, from (b).
T. p. 324.
The text is from (a).

DATE. It is impossible to accept this charter in its present form as genuine. The date 1032 (entered as an endorsement in a hand of the thirteenth century) is the only possible one to include Ælfsige, Bishop of Winchester, Æthelric, Bishop of Selsey, and Ælfwine, Abbot of the New Minster, but it cannot fit Ælfmær, Abbot of St Augustine's, or Earl Leofwine (the Latin version, however, has *Lifricus* and MS. (*b*) *Leofric*). Even if *Ælmær* is regarded as a mistake for *Ælfstan* and *Lyfwine* for *Leofric*, it seems impossible to accept the evidence of this one isolated document for the presence in England at such a late date of the Danish earls Ulf, Eglaf and Eric whose signatures are not found elsewhere after 1024. The use of the double name *Ælfgyua Imma* is also suspicious. It appears as well in K. 779, dated 1045, which is certainly spurious, and in K. 962 of about the same date, which comes from a St Albans MS. containing a number of charters of very doubtful form.

l. 8. *Folkenstane*. Folkestone is included among the lands of the Bishop of Bayeux in D.B. and had previously been held by Earl Godwine (D.B. I, f. 9 *b*; V.C.H. *Kent*, III, p. 233). There is no mention of any former connection with Christchurch, but there were five churches there in 1086 from which the archbishop received 55 shillings.

ll. 8 f. *Eadsi his preost*, cf. p. 170, l. 8. Eadsige's signature as priest is attached to K. 741, a charter dated 1024, but does not appear again. In a grant dated 1035 he is referred to by Cnut as bishop, see p. 420. He succeeded Æthelnoth as Archbishop of Canterbury in 1038.

ll. 11 f. *ne gyfen ne syllan* etc. The rhyme and alliteration are noteworthy.

l. 12. *ne forspekan · ne forspillan*, cf. *Leges Henrici*, 61, 13 *b*: *Nemo potest de feodo domini sui placitare sine eo, nec cogi debet rectum eius forspeken nec forspillan* (Liebermann, I, p. 582). The use of the phrase without translation into Latin shows that it was regularly established in the legal terminology of the time. The Latin version of the present charter renders it *nec verbis forisfacere nec extirpare*.

l. 16. *on Æðelstanes dæge*. Two copies of Æthelstan's supposed grant of Folkestone to Christchurch are preserved in MS. B.M. Cotton Tiberius A. II and MS. Lambeth 1212 respectively (see B. 660).

l. 17. *Odan arceb*. Archbishop of Canterbury, see p. 312.

hit wearð syððan ut gedon. There seems to be no record of its history from the time of Æthelstan's grant (which is dated 927 but witnessed by Ælfheah who did not become Bishop of Winchester until 934) until the present charter. As both are of doubtful authenticity it is uncertain whether Christchurch's claim to Folkestone was justly founded or not.

ll. 23 f. *Ælfgyua Imma*. Ælfgifu was the wife first of Æthelred and afterwards of Cnut.

418 NOTES

l. 24. *Ægelnoð arcebiscop*. See p. 403.
ll. 24 f. *Ælfwi*'*né ƀ on Lundene*. This witness is omitted in MS. (*b*). His name had been correctly given in the first instance (see p. 409) with *-ne* afterwards inserted above.
l. 25. *Ælfsi ƀ on Winceastre*. See p. 409.
Ægelric ƀ on Suðsexan. Æthelric, Bishop of Selsey, signs for the first time in 1032 (K. 746) along with Æthelric, Bishop of Dorchester. He died in 1038 soon after Archbishop Æthelnoth.
l. 26. *Ælmær abbud æt sc̄e Augustine*. See p. 410.
Wulnoð aƀƀ æt Westminstre. See p. 409.
l. 27. *Ælfwine aƀƀ æt Niwan Mynstre*. See p. 437. His first signature occurs in 1032 (K. 746).
Wulfsi aƀƀ æt Certesige. The signature Wulfsige *abbas* occurs in K. 762 (dated 1042), K. 767 (dated 1043), K. 777 and 778 (both dated 1045). The list of the abbots of Chertsey given in V.C.H. *Surrey*, II, p. 63, has no names between Daniel (about 1025) and Siweard, who became Bishop of Rochester in 1058.
l. 28. *Ulf eorl*. Ulf was the brother of Eglaf and the brother-in-law of Cnut, whose sister he married, as well as of Earl Godwine. His signature occurs elsewhere only twice, namely in K. 735 (a Bury St Edmunds charter of 1020–1023) and K. 740 (a charter of 1020–1024 relating to St Benedict's of Hulme). He may have become Viceroy of Denmark (see Napier and Stevenson, *Crawford Charters*, p. 141, n. 5).
Eglaf eorl. See p. 410.
Lyfwine eorl. This is probably a mistake for Leofric, see above and pp. 412 f.
Harold eorl. K. 764, a Worcester charter of 1042, is attested by *Harald dux*. The witness both there and here is probably the Danish earl Harold, the son of Thurkil and the second husband of Cnut's niece Gunnhild, who was killed on his return journey from Rome by Duke Ordulf of Saxony in 1042 (see Adam Bremensis in *Scriptores Rerum Germanicarum*, 3rd ed. 1917, Lib. II, c. LXXVIIII). His widow was banished from England with her two sons, Hemming and Thurkil, in 1044 (Fl. Wig.).
ll. 28 f. *Yric eorl*. See p. 410.
l. 29. *Þored steallara*. See pp. 410 f. This is the earliest reference in English sources to the office of staller, for which see Larson, *The King's Household in England*, pp. 146–152.
Agamund. See p. 411.
Osgod Clapa. This witness appears only twice elsewhere in the charters with his double name (K. 749, 1319), also in Thurstan's will (Whitelock, No. XXXI), but there can be little doubt that he is identical with the Osgod *minister* who signs from 1026 (K. 743) to 1046 (K. 783, 1335). He appears in the Saxon Chronicle both with and without his second name and in one instance (s.a. 1047 D) is described as Osgod *stallere*. He was outlawed in 1046 (which accounts for the disap-

NOTES

pearance of his signature in that year) and in 1049 had a fleet of ships, part of which made a raid on Essex. He died in 1054 (Sax. Chr. C, D).

Tofig. Probably Tofi the Proud, the son-in-law of Osgod Clapa, see p. 400.

p. 170, l. 1. *Ægelwine Ælfhelmes sunu,* cf. p. 204, ll. 9 f.

Siword æt Cilleham. In 1066 estates at Chilham and elsewhere (D.B. I, ff. 10, 10 *b*; V.C.H. *Kent*, III, pp. 235, 236 f.) were held by a certain Sired, probably the son of the present witness, and possibly the descendant of Siweard or Sired his brother who appear as witnesses of earlier Kentish charters, see p. 372. *Siret de Cilleham* is included also in two lists of Kentish landowners who enjoyed special exemptions and privileges (D.B. I, ff. 1, 2; V.C.H. *Kent*, III, pp. 204, 206).

ll. 1 f. *Ægelric bigga.* See p. 409.

l. 2. *Ælfword 'se' Kæntisca.* This witness does not seem to appear elsewhere.

Eadmer æt Burhham. See p. 398.

ll. 5 f. *mid þæs kynges haligdome.* Literally 'with the king's relics'. The phrase is found for the first time in one of Æthelred's charters of about 997 (see Whitelock, pp. 46, 151).

LXXXVI

K. does not mention the source of his text; T., who apparently took his from K., suggests British Museum, Cotton Augustus, II, 70 (?), but this is not correct. I have taken mine from Somner (see below) as I have been unable to discover any early MS. copy. There is a M.E. version in the Cathedral Registers A. f. 153, E. f. 10 *b* at Canterbury.

EDITIONS. Somner, *A Treatise of Gavelkind,* p. 214.
K. 745.
T. p. 328.

DATE. In the late Canterbury list of benefactors Eadsige's grant of Appledore, Orpington, Palster and Wittersham is attributed to the year 1032 (Dugdale, I, p. 97).

l. 8. *Eadsige.* See p. 417.

l. 9. *Apoldre.* Appledore, Kent. Of the estates mentioned in this charter Appledore, Warehorne and Orpington are entered among the lands of the monks held by the archbishop in 1086, Berwick was held of him by knight service, while Palster was in the possession of the Bishop of Bayeux and held by one of his tenants (D.B. I, ff. 4 *b,* 5, 10 *b*; V.C.H. *Kent,* III, pp. 215, 218, 238). The name of the pre-Conquest tenant of Palster is given as *Eduui 'presbyter'.* Is this by any chance a slip for *Eadwine* (see below)?

ll. 11 f. *Ædwines.* Edwin was Eadsige's brother, see p. 204, ll. 10 f.

l. 13. .III. *wæga cyses.* Cheese is generally measured by the wey (Latin *pondus*). According to the *Historia Monasterii de Abingdon*, R.S. 1, p. 345, the *pondus Abbendunense* contained 22 stone in the tenth century but the monks complained that it had been reduced to 18 stone in the twelfth. It is possible that local variations always existed.

ll. 13 f. *þreo gebind æles.* See B.T., *Suppl.* p. 296, s.v. *gebind*, 11; N.E.D. s.v. *bind*, sb. (5), where all the instances quoted of the use of the word as a measure of quantity refer either to salmon or eels. The latest instance (dated 1728) defines a bind of eels as '10 sticks and every stick of 25 eels'. In D.B. 6 fisheries are entered at Appledore.

l. 20. *Berwican.* A charter which records the grant by Cnut of land at Berwick in perpetuity to Eadsige (described as bishop) is dated 1035 (*Ordnance Survey Facsimiles*, III, No. 42). If he was already holding an estate there in 1032 it is possible that only a change of tenure was involved.

ll. 23 f. *hundeahtigan marcan hwites seolfres.* The mark of silver was equivalent to 8 ores (i.e. 160 pence in accordance with the common reckoning of 20 pence to the ore). Both are Scandinavian standards of weight and the mark makes its first appearance in England in Alfred and Guthrum, 2.

l. 24. *be hustinges gewihte.* Uniformity of weights and measures was demanded in III Edgar, 8, 1, *swylce mon on Lundenbyrig* 7 *on Wintanceastre healde*. The *husting* (the word is of Scandinavian origin) was the court of London (see Liebermann, II, p. 522, s.v.).

l. 25. *Palstre...Wihtriceshamme.* The name *Palstre* survives in Palster Court Manor in the parish of Wittersham.

p. 172, l. 4. *Æðelnoð Arceb.* See p. 403.

Ælfstan Abb. If the date 1032 is correct, this is the earliest occurrence of Ælfstan's signature as Abbot of St Augustine's. He succeeded Ælfmær (see p. 410) and is named as abbot in Cnut's grant of St Mildred's body and lands to St Augustine's in 1027 (Thorne, *Chronica* etc., col. 1783 in Twysden, *Decem Scriptores*, II). He took part likewise in the translation of the body of St Mildred to Canterbury in 1030. His signature appears for the last time in 1045 (see p. 437).

l. 5. *Brihtric geounga.* For an older Brihtric see p. 397.

Æþelric bigenga. The M.E. version in both registers gives the second name more correctly as *bigge*. For Æthelric Bigga see p. 409.

ll. 5 f. *Þorð Þurkilles nefa.* See pp. 410 f.

l. 6. *Tofi.* Perhaps Tofi the Proud, see p. 400.

Ælfwine preost, 7 *Eadwold preost*. Probably members of the community at Christchurch.

NOTES

LXXXVII

MS. British Museum, Additional Charter 19797, the bottom portion of a chirograph.

FACSIMILE. Bond, *Facsimiles of Ancient Charters in the British Museum*, Part IV, No. 19.

EDITION. E. p. 238.

DATE. Probably soon after the appointment of Brihtheah as Bishop of Worcester, see below.

l. 10. *Byrhteh .b.* Brihtheah, who was the nephew of Wulfstan, Archbishop of York, was Abbot of Pershore before he became Bishop of Worcester in 1033 (Fl. Wig.). He died on 20 December 1038. He is accused by Hemming of alienating many of the church lands in order to enrich his relatives (Hearne, I, p. 266).

l. 13. *Easttune.* This is probably Cold Aston or Aston Blank, a village 20 miles east of Gloucester in the neighbourhood of Notgrove where land was held by the church of Worcester.

ll. 14 f. *Leofsige .b.* Leofsige was Brihtheah's predecessor at Worcester, see p. 405.

LXXXVIII

MS. British Museum, Cotton Claudius A. III, f. 5 (or 6 by the new numbering). The first part of this MS. consists of a fragmentary gospel book which at one time belonged to Christchurch, Canterbury.

EDITIONS. Dugdale, I, p. 100.
K. 958.
T. p. 579.
Birch, *Liber Vitæ etc. of Hyde Abbey*, p. xxii, n. 1.

DATE. In the Canterbury list of benefactors (Dugdale, I, p. 97) this grant is attributed to the year 1036 but is said to have been made with the knowledge and consent of King Cnut. If this date is even approximately correct, the donor can scarcely be identified (as Birch, *op. cit.* pp. xxi f. suggests) with the Earl Thored whose signature appears for the last time in 989–990 and who is not heard of again after 992 (see p. 368). One section of the composite MS. volume which contains the text of the present grant apparently belonged at one time to a man of the name, as it opens with a poetical dedication in his honour: *Ic eom halgung boc healde hine dryhten þe me fægere þus frætewum belegde. Þureð to þance þus het me wyrcean· to loue 7 to wurðe þampe leoht gesceop* etc. (see Birch, *op. cit.* p. xxii).

For the occurrence of the signature Thored in the charters both during and after Cnut's reign see p. 410.

l. 20. *Horslege.* East Horsley, Surrey. In 1086 this estate was held by the Archbishop of Canterbury for the sustenance of the monks. Its assessment had been reduced from 14 hides in the time of King Edward to 3 hides and 1½ virgates. There was land for 5 ploughs (D.B. I, f. 31; V.C.H. *Surrey*, I, p. 300).

LXXXIX

MS. British Museum, Cotton Claudius A. III, f. 5 (or 6 by the new numbering). See p. 421.

EDITIONS. Dugdale, I, p. 100.
K. 974.

DATE. This grant is dated 1036 in the late Canterbury list of benefactors (Dugdale, I, p. 97).

p. 174, l. 1. *Æpelnoð...arceb.* See p. 403.
ll. 1 f. *Godmæresham.* Godmersham, Kent. In 1086 Godmersham was held by the Archbishop of Canterbury and was assessed at 8 *solins* with land for 12 ploughs. Its value in the time of King Edward is given as 12 pounds (D.B. I, f. 5; V.C.H. *Kent*, III, p. 217).
l. 2. *Sirede eorle.* The signature *Syhrod dux* occurs in 1019 (K. 729) and *Siræd dux* in 1023 (K. 739).

XC

MSS. (*a*) Lambeth Palace Library, *Gospels of MacDurnan*, f. 114. See p. 402.
(*b*) British Museum, Additional MS. 14907, f. 22, an eighteenth-century copy of (*a*).

EDITION. K. 1336, from (*b*).
The text is from (*a*).

DATE. This document should be compared with No. LXXX. Toki's application in this instance was probably made soon after Eadsige became archbishop in 1038. The fact that he did not appear in person suggests that by this time he was an old man.

l. 7. *Eadsige arceb.* Eadsige (see p. 417) was Archbishop of Canterbury from 1038 to 1044 when he resigned because of ill-health but took up office again in 1048. He died in 1050.
Tokig. See p. 403.
l. 8. *Hrisbeorgan.* See p. 403.
his twegen cnihtas. Two of his superior servants are probably meant (see p. 394). The fact that he makes no application on behalf of his descendants suggests that he had no family.

XCI

MS. British Museum, Cotton Augustus, II, 90, a contemporary parchment.

FACSIMILE. Bond, *Facsimiles of Ancient Charters in the British Museum*, Part IV, No. 20.

NOTES

EDITIONS. Dugdale, I, p. 108.
K. 758.
T. p. 338.
E. p. 297.

DATE. The events related here may have taken place shortly before Harold Harefoot's death, as according to the Saxon Chronicle E (1039 for 1040) he died at Oxford. The reference to Lyfing as Bishop of Devonshire only may point, however, to an earlier date (see below) and a thirteenth-century endorsement attributes the document to the year 1038.

l. 14. *Harold king.* Harold Harefoot's claim to be the son of Cnut and Ælfgifu of Northampton was doubted even in his own day (Sax. Chr. 1035 C, D; 1036 E). He ruled England from the time of Cnut's death in 1035 but was apparently not generally recognised as king until 1037 (see *Sax. Chr.* ed. Earle and Plummer, II, p. 209). He died in 1040.

Sandwic. For the grant of Sandwich to Christchurch by Cnut see No. LXXXII.

l. 16. *twegen hæri'n'gc timan.* The herring season at Ipswich lasts from St Michael's Day to St Clement's, i.e. from 29 September to 23 November (see *Black Book of the Admiralty*, II, p. 158). At Dover, according to D.B. I, f. I (V.C.H. *Kent*, III, p. 203), the king's peace was established in the town from St Michael's Day to St Andrew's (30 November), which Maitland interprets as during the herring season (*Domesday Book and Beyond*, p. 193). Two complete herring seasons, therefore, would mean rather more than a year.

l. 19. *Ælfstan abb. æt sc̄e A.* Abbot of St Augustine's, see p. 420.

l. 21. *Steorran.* This Steorra is perhaps identical with the *Stir̃* who is described as Hardacnut's *major domus* (Fl. Wig. s.a. 1040).

p. 176, l. 1. *Eadsige arceb.* See pp. 417, 422.

l. 3. *binnan Oxanaforde.* See above.

l. 5. *Lyfingc b̃ of Defenanscire.* Lyfing had been Abbot of Tavistock and accompanied Cnut on his journey to Rome (Fl. Wig. s.a. 1031 for 1027). On his return he was made Bishop of Crediton and Cornwall and in 1038 became Bishop of Worcester as well. In 1040 he was deprived of the see of Worcester by Hardacnut but was restored the following year. He died on 23 March 1046.

ll. 7 f. *Oswerd æt Hergerdesham.* Osweard of Harrietsham appears elsewhere in Kentish charters, see p. 192, l. 9. An Osweard of Norton was also a landholder in Kent in the time of King Edward and it is impossible to say which is meant when only the name *Osward* is given in D.B. Their lands with one exception had passed to the Bishop of Bayeux and were held in 1086 by various Norman tenants, chief among them being Hugh de Port. A man named Osweard had been sheriff of Kent in the time of King Edward (D.B. I, f. 2 *b*; V.C.H. *Kent*, III, p. 208).

l. 32. *Mildrype æker.* Mildred was the daughter of Domneva, who founded the Abbey of Minster in Thanet, and was herself the second abbess. In 1027 Cnut granted her body and all her land to the Abbey of St Augustine, and her body was translated to Canterbury on 18 May 1030 (see p. 420). This grant was confirmed by Edward the Confessor in 1043. I have been unable to identify 'Mildred's field'.

wið þone wodan. There is no instance in B.T. of *woda* used elsewhere as a substantive except when applied to persons, and it seems possible, therefore, that a noun has dropped out, e.g. *flod* where the recurrent *-od* might to some extent account for the omission. Examples of the adj. *wod* applied to the sea or to floods are quoted in B.T. p. 1261, s.v., and the context suggests that something of the kind is meant, i.e. that protection was required against flooding, due perhaps to the rapidly flowing tide. At a later date an embankment known as the Abbot's wall was made to protect the low-lying ground round Ebbsfleet from flooding at high tide (see Hasted, *History of Kent,* IV, pp. 289, 325). If *se woda* is taken as a substantive, it seems most likely that the racing fast-flowing tide is meant. Leo, *Angelsächsisches Glossar,* col. 13, takes it as 'storm' and renders the passage 'ein Damm (Kai) gegen den Sturm'.

p. 178, ll. 1 f. *geweard...æt.* See B.T., *Suppl.* s.v. *geweorðan,* IV.

ll. 2 f. *Hyppeles fleote.* Traditionally Ebbsfleet was the landing place of Hengest and Horsa, of St Augustine and of Mildred herself who received her early training in France. Its loss of importance was undoubtedly due to the gradual silting up of the channel on that side, and the abbot's failure to divert ship-traffic from Sandwich, as described here, should probably be attributed to the same cause.

XCII

MS. Cambridge University Library, Ff. 2. 33, f. 50. See p. 392.

EDITION. K. 978.

The grant is referred to and the opening words quoted in the list of benefactors in C.U.L., Ee. 3. 60, f. 322 *b*, while it is recorded also without quotation in the similar lists in the C.U.L. MSS., Additional 6006, f. 74 and Mm. 4. 19, f. 167.

DATE. In C.U.L., Ee. 3. 60, *loc. cit.,* this grant is attributed to the time of Hardacnut and dated 1040. There seems to be nothing against the acceptance of this date as at any rate approximately correct.

l. 12. *Stigand.* In the records of the grant mentioned above Stigand is described as *lauerd,* perhaps to distinguish him from the bishop of the same name (see p. 431). He is perhaps the Stigand who appears as a beneficiary under the will of Leofgifu, see Whitelock, p. 76.

ll. 13 f. *Playford.* Near Ipswich. Either the grant of this estate to Bury never took effect or else it was alienated at a later date. In 1086 it was held by Humphrey, son of Robert, of Robert Malet and had been held in the time of King Edward by *Godwin,* son of *Alfer,* under the queen (D.B. II, f. 314 *b*; V.C.H. *Suffolk,* I, p. 454).

NOTES

l. 18. *gentale*, i.e. *geantalu*, see B.T., *Suppl.* p. 286. A better translation might be 'counter-claim'.

ne forsegen ne forwerken, cf. *ne forspekan ne forspillan*, p. 168, l. 12. It was a well-established principle that an estate in which the holder had only a life interest could not be forfeited by any action on his part, cf. Whitelock, p. 46, l. 30; p. 70, l. 8.

ll. 18 f. *þis aren* .II. *witnesse*. It seems curious to use the numeral two when actually eight names are given, but this seems to be the reading of the text. The reference must be to the two most important witnesses whose names head the list.

l. 19. *Alfric bisscop*. A passage included in both the C.U.L. MSS., Additional 6006, f. 73 and Ee. 3. 60, f. 322 b, states that there were altogether three bishops of East Anglia called Ælfric, *unus bonus, alter niger et tertius parvus ob differentia vocati*. The first Ælfric held the see in the reign of Edgar, the second died about Christmas 1038 and was succeeded by the third, who in turn was succeeded by Stigand in 1043 or 1044. Both Fl. Wig. I, p. 233, and William of Malmesbury, *Gesta Pontificum*, R.S. p. 150, include both the second and the third Ælfric in their lists of the bishops of East Anglia, although the former, apparently by mistake, refers elsewhere (s.a. 1038) to Stigand as the immediate successor of the earlier of the two. In the present instance the reference must be to the third bishop of the name.

Vut Abbot. Ufi, who had been Prior of St Benedict's at Hulme, was appointed first abbot of the Benedictine house at Bury, founded in the reign of Cnut. He died in 1044.

l. 20. *seynt Eadmundes biri*. The relics of St Edmund were originally at Hoxne but were removed to *Bedericesworth*, later known as Bury St Edmunds, early in the tenth century. They were in the keeping of a community of secular canons until the foundation of the Benedictine abbey.

Stigand. Probably the donor of the estate.

ll. 20 f. *Aelfwine Wluardes sune*. Perhaps the Ælfwine who witnesses an agreement between Æthelmær and Abbot Ufi, see p. 184, l. 13; perhaps also the Ælfwine *Wulfredes sunu* who appears elsewhere as a witness along with Ælfric Wihtgar's son, see K. 962 and Whitelock, p. 78.

l. 21. *Alfric Withgares sune*. This witness is described as *comes famosus* in an entry in the C.U.L. MSS., Ee. 3. 60, f. 324 and Additional 6006, f. 74, which records his grant of Melford to Bury and his foundation of a house of secular canons at Clare. He acted as Queen Ælfgifu Emma's deputy in the exercise of her rights of jurisdiction in the eight and a half hundreds later granted to Bury (K. 874, 883, 905) and on the evidence of D.B. was himself an important landowner in the eastern counties. He appears as a legatee in the will of his kinswoman Leofgifu (Whitelock, p. 76) and as a witness to a grant by his kinsman Æthelwine the Black to St Albans (K. 962). He likewise disputed a will of the latter in favour of Ramsey Abbey (*Historia Ramesiensis*, R.S. p. 169).

426 NOTES

Eadric. Perhaps Eadric of Laxfield who was a prominent landowner both in Norfolk and Suffolk. According to D.B. he was outlawed by Edward the Confessor at one stage of his career, then pardoned and restored to his lands (see V.C.H. *Suffolk*, I, p. 450).

Ordger. A writ of William the Conqueror confirming Edward the Confessor's grant of jurisdiction over eight and a half hundreds to Bury names a certain Ordgar along with Ælfric, Wihtgar's son, as the former representative of Queen Ælfgifu Emma in its administration (see Davis, *Regesta Regum Anglo-Normannorum*, I, p. 119, No. vii). This may be the witness of the present charter. A man of the same name was sheriff of Cambridgeshire in the time of King Edward (D.B. I, ff. 197, 199).

l. 22. *Lemmer.* This name appears elsewhere in a list of Suffolk witnesses (see Whitelock, p. 82).

XCIII

MSS. (*a*) British Museum, Cotton Augustus, II, 84, an eleventh-century parchment.

(*b*) Cambridge University Library, Ff. 2. 33, f. 50. See p. 392.

(*c*) British Museum, Additional MS. 14847, f. 19 *b* (by the new numbering). See p. 392.

FACSIMILE. Of (*a*), Bond, *Facsimiles of Ancient Charters in the British Museum*, Part IV, No. 44.

EDITIONS. Dugdale, III, p. 132, n. 5.
K. 961, from (*a*).
B. 1018.

The text is from (*a*). The grant is referred to and the opening words quoted in the list of benefactors in C.U.L., Ee. 3. 60, f. 322 *b*. It is recorded also without quotation in the similar lists in the C.U.L. MSS., Additional 6006, f. 73 *b* and Mm. 4. 19, f. 167.

DATE. There is no means of dating this grant exactly. It is included among those of the time of Hardacnut in C.U.L., Ee. 3. 60, *loc. cit.*

l. 24. *Þurkytel.* Thurketel is described as *dreing inclitus* in the entries referred to above. For bequests by two other men of the same name (a common one in East Anglia at the time) see Whitelock, Nos. XXIV and XXV. For *dreng* see Björkman, *Scandinavian Loanwords in England*, p. 208.

ll. 25 ff. *Culeforde...Wridewellan...Gyxeweorðe.* Culford, Wordwell and Ixworth in Suffolk, near Bury St Edmunds. In 1086 these three were all included in the lands held by the abbey. At Wordwell and Ixworth the holders could dispose of their land but the abbey had the right of jurisdiction and commendation (D.B. I, ff. 364, 366 *b*, 367 *b*; V.C.H. *Suffolk*, I, pp. 500, 503 f.).

XCIV

MS. British Museum, Additional Charter 19799, the top portion of a chirograph.

FACSIMILE. Bond, *Facsimiles of Ancient Charters in the British Museum*, Part IV, No. 23.

EDITION. E. p. 242.

p. 180, ll. 1 f. *LEOFINC bisceop*. Bishop of Worcester, see p. 423.
l. 2. *HEARÐACNUTES cynges*. Hardacnut, who was the son of Cnut and Ælfgifu Emma, succeeded his half brother Harold Harefoot in 1040 and died in 1042.
l. 5. *EADMUNDDescótan*. Armscott in Tredington, see Pl.N. *Worc.* p. 172.
ll. 12 ff. *gif ænig* etc. It would appear from the list of witnesses that this charter was formally drawn up at a shire-meeting at which both the king and his mother were present. The anathema is of the type found in the royal charters of the period.
l. 19. *Ælfgeofu his modor*. Ælfgifu is a regular witness of Hardacnut's charters.
l. 20. *Ælfward .b.* Abbot of Evesham and Bishop of London, see pp. 396 f.
l. 21. *Godwine abbod*. Godwine, Abbot of Winchcombe, died in October 1053 (Sax. Chr. C, D; Fl. Wig.). The signature *Godwine abbas* occurs for the first time in 1042 (cf. K. 764).
l. 22. *Leofric .eorl*. Earl of Mercia, see pp. 412 f.

XCV

MS. British Museum, Cotton Claudius A. III, f. 5 *b* (or 6 *b* by the new numbering). See p. 421.

EDITIONS. Dugdale, I, p. 100.
K. 896.

DATE. This charter gives the impression of having been drawn up soon after Edward the Confessor's accession.

l. 24. *Eadwerd cyng*. Edward the Confessor, the son of Æthelred and Ælfgifu Emma, reigned from 1042 to 1066.
l. 25. *Certham*. Chartham, Kent. In 1086 this estate was held by the archbishop. It was assessed at 4 *solins* with land for 14 ploughs (D.B. I, f. 5; V.C.H. *Kent*, III, p. 217).
l. 27. *mund 7 upheald*, cf. T. p. 391, where the parallel phrase *geheald 7 mund* is used in a similar connection. There is no other instance in B.T. of the use of the word *upheald*; the corresponding Icelandic *upp-hald* is quoted.

p. 182, ll. 7 f. *on þissere Xpes béc.* The record of this grant is preserved in a gospel book, see p. 421.

l. 10. *Ðis synd þara landa nama.* The list of estates which follows is written in paler ink and seems to be a later addition.

l. 10. *Sandwic.* See Nos. LXXXII, XCI.

Eastryge. Eastry had passed to the community at Christchurch by exchange with Archbishop Wulfred in 811 (B. 332). There seems to be no record of its later history until the time of Æthelred (K. 715). In 1086 it was one of the estates belonging to the monks and held by the archbishop (D.B. I, f. 5; V.C.H. *Kent*, III, p. 218). It was assessed at 7 *solins*.

Tænet. The manor of Monkton, comprising nearly all the western half of the island of Thanet, was granted to Christchurch by Eadgifu, the third wife of Edward the Elder and the mother of Edmund and Edred, along with Farleigh, Meopham, Cooling etc. (B. 1065). In 1086 it was assessed at 18 *solins* with land for 31 ploughs (D.B. I, f. 4 b; V.C.H. *Kent*, III, p. 216).

l. 11. *Ieoccham.* According to the late Canterbury list of benefactors (Dugdale, I, p. 96) Ickham was given to Christchurch by *Athelward* in 958. In 1086 it was assessed at 4 *solins* with land for 12 ploughs (D.B. I, f. 5; V.C.H. *Kent*, III, p. 217).

Godmæresham. For the grant of Godmersham see No. LXXXIX.

l. 12. *Wyll.* Westwell was bequeathed to Christchurch by Archbishop Ælfric (Whitelock, p. 52). Probably, however, as in the case of Monks Risborough (see below), it was not his private property. In D.B. it is entered among the estates of the monks held by the archbishop.

East Cert · 7 oþer Cert. Both of these estates were held by the archbishop in 1086, Great Chart assessed at 3 *solins* with land for 12 ploughs, Little Chart assessed at 2½ *solins* as compared with 3 *solins* in the time of King Edward (D.B. I, p. 5; V.C.H. *Kent*, III, p. 217).

Berwica. Berwick in Lympne, see p. 420.

ll. 12 f. *Werhornas · Apuldra.* For the grant of Warehorne and Appledore see No. LXXXVI.

l. 13. *Merseham.* According to the late Canterbury list of benefactors Mersham was given to the monks of Christchurch by Siweard and his wife Matilda in 1051. For a writ confirming the gift see K. 847[1] (a Latin version is given by Thorne, col. 2224 in Twysden, *Decem Scriptores*, II). It is addressed to Archbishop Stigand and cannot be earlier, therefore, than 1052. In 1086 Mersham was held by the archbishop in demesne. Its assessment had been reduced from 6 *solins* in the time of King Edward to 3 with land for 12 ploughs (D.B. I, f. 3 b; V.C.H. *Kent*, III, p. 212).

Orpedingtun. For the grant of Orpington see No. LXXXVI.

Preostatun. Preston is one of a number of estates said to have been restored to Christchurch by Edmund, Edred and Edwy in 941 (B. 766, 811).

---

[1] The names of the five witnesses attached to it by K. belong by rights to the A.S. version of K. 715 (see p. 372).

NOTES

l. 14. *Meapaham Culingas.* See above under Thanet. An earlier grant of Meopham to Christchurch by Eadwulf *dux* is recorded in B. 747, while land at Meopham was also bequeathed to Christchurch by Brihtric and Ælfswith (Whitelock, No. xi). The history of Cooling from the time that Eadgifu inherited it from her father until she bestowed it upon Christchurch is told in B. 1064 f. (Harmer, No. xxiii). In 1086 Meopham was assessed at 7 *solins* as compared with 10 *solins* in the time of King Edward. There was land for 30 ploughs (D.B. 1, f. 4 *b*; V.C.H. *Kent*, iii, p. 216).

Frinningaham. In the list of benefactors this estate is said to have been given to Christchurch by Archbishop Ælfheah in 1010. In 1086 Farningham, assessed at 1 *solin*, was held by knight-service of the archbishop. It was worth 11 pounds of which the monks received 4 *ad uestitum suum* (D.B. 1, f. 4; V.C.H. *Kent*, iii, pp. 213 f.).

Holingaburnan. Hollingbourn was bequeathed to Christchurch by the Ætheling Æthelstan (see Whitelock, pp. 58, 169). In 1086 it was held by the archbishop. It was assessed at 6 *solins* with land for 24 ploughs (D.B. 1, f. 4 *b*; V.C.H. *Kent*, iii, p. 216).

l. 15. *Fernlege · Peccham.* Farleigh and Peckham were given to Christchurch by Eadgifu along with Monkton, Meopham and Cooling sometime about 960 (see above). In 1086 Farleigh was assessed at 6 *solins* with land for 26 ploughs.

l. 16. *Pæccingas.* Patching was held by the archbishop in 1086 but was *de vestitu monachorum*. Its assessment had been reduced from 12 hides in the time of King Edward to 3 hides and 3½ virgates. There was land for 9 ploughs (D.B. 1, f. 16 *b*; V.C.H. *Sussex*, 1, p. 389).

Wudutun. In 1086 Wootton was held by the archbishop but was also *de vestitu monachorum*. It had been assessed at 6 hides in the time of King Edward but 1½ hides had been annexed by the Count of Mortain. There was land for 5 ploughs (V.C.H. *Sussex*, 1, p. 388).

l. 17. *Wealawurð.* Walworth, according to the late Canterbury list of benefactors, was granted to Christchurch along with Chartham by Edward the Confessor. The story told is that King Edmund granted it *cuidam joculatori suo nomine Hitardo*, and that later, in the time of King Edward, the same *Hitardus*, before setting out on a pilgrimage to Rome, granted the estate and its title-deeds to Christchurch. The inclusion of Walworth in Æthelred's charter (K. 715) shows, however, that if Christchurch was actually in possession of the estate at that date, the kings referred to in the story must be Edmund I (d. 946) and Edward the Martyr (d. 978 or 979) rather than Edmund Ironside (d. 1016) and Edward the Confessor. In 1086 Walworth was assessed at 3½ hides as compared with 5 hides in the time of King Edward. There was land for 3 ploughs (see V.C.H. *Surrey*, 1, pp. 299 f.).

Mersetham · Ceigham. These two estates, according to the Canterbury list of benefactors, were given to Christchurch in 1018 by *Ethelstanus qui et Livingus*. For Lyfing, Archbishop of Canterbury, see p. 393. In 1086 both estates were held by the archbishop, the one to provide clothing, the other food for the monks. The assessment of

NOTES

Merstham (which had land for 8 ploughs) had been reduced from 20 hides to 5, that of Cheam (with land for 14 ploughs) from 20 hides to 4 (see V.C.H. *Surrey*, I, pp. 299 f.).

Horslege. For the grant of Horsley see No. LXXXVIII.

l. 18. *Suðcyrcean·Middeltun.* In 1086 Southchurch was held by Christchurch as a manor and 4 hides, Milton (in Prittlewell) as a manor and 2 hides (D.B. I, f. 8 *b*; V.C.H. *Essex*, I, p. 437).

Læellingc...Hæðleh·Illaleh. These three estates—Lawling, Hadleigh and Monks Eleigh—are said to have been given to Christchurch by Earl Brihtnoth in 991 (see Palgrave, *The Rise and Progress of the English Commonwealth*, 1921, Part II, p. 314; Whitelock, p. 107). The gift is recorded also in the late Canterbury list of benefactors with the date 941 for 991. The reversion of Monks Eleigh to Christchurch had been left by Earl Ælfgar, Brihtnoth's father-in-law (see Whitelock, pp. 6, 38). In the list of benefactors mentioned above Hadleigh is entered again separately under the impossible date 835 as the gift of *Elfleda* with the cognisance and consent of King Æthelred. Ælfflæd was the wife of Brihtnoth and the daughter of Ælfgar. There is no mention of the bequest of Hadleigh in her will (see Whitelock, pp. 38–42).

Boccing. This estate was bequeathed to Christchurch by Æthelric about 995 (see Whitelock, pp. 42, 44, 146 f.).

l. 20. *Hrysebyrgan.* Monks Risborough was pledged by Archbishop Sigeric to Æscwig, Bishop of Dorchester, in return for money to buy off an attack of the Danes (K. 689). Soon afterwards, however, Æscwig restored it to Archbishop Ælfric (Sigeric's successor) and the community at Christchurch (K. 690). It was apparently held by the archbishop himself as he bequeathes it to Christchurch in his will (Whitelock, p. 52). It is entered in D.B. as an estate of 30 hides and had been held of Christchurch in the time of King Edward by Esgar the Staller (D.B. I, f. 143 *b*; V.C.H. *Bucks.* I, p. 233).

l. 21. *Niwantun·Brutuwylle.* See below. The latter is now called Brightwell Baldwin.

XCVI

MS. British Museum, Cotton Claudius A. III, f. 5 (or 6 by the new numbering). See p. 421.

EDITIONS. Dugdale, I, p. 100.
K. 965.
T. p. 368.

DATE. Between the accession of Edward the Confessor and the death of Ælfgifu, i.e. between 1042 and 1052. This document is in the nature of a declaration of what had already taken place in the lifetime of King Cnut. It was probably drawn up shortly after Edward's accession.

l. 23. *Niwantune.* Probably Newington, Oxfordshire, although Ælfgifu's grant of Newington and Brightwell to Christchurch is

NOTES

attributed to the year 997 (K. 697; Dugdale, I, p. 97). The form of this grant is suspicious (Ælfgifu's double name is used, see p. 417) and it is noteworthy that Newington and Brightwell are not included by Æthelred in the list of estates belonging to Christchurch in 1001 or 1002 (K. 715). They are both mentioned, however, in the list attached to Edward the Confessor's charter (see p. 430) and in D.B. Newington (assessed at 15 hides with land for 18 ploughs) is entered as the only estate belonging to the Archbishop of Canterbury in Oxfordshire. No estate of the name in Kent is included among the lands of the archbishop or his monks, but it is noteworthy that the former was entitled to a payment of 6 pounds from Newington near Milton, although the estate was held by Albert the Chaplain and had been occupied by a tenant of Queen Edith in 1066 (D.B. I, f. 14 b; V.C.H. *Kent*, III, p. 252). Four messuages in Canterbury belonged to the manor.

l. 24. *Ælfric se þegen.* There seems to be no record of this forfeiture elsewhere.

XCVII

MS. Cambridge University Library, Ff. 2. 33, f. 49. See p. 392.

The agreement is referred to also and the opening words quoted in the list of benefactors in C.U.L., Ee. 3. 60, f. 324.

DATE. Either 1043 or 1044, i.e. after the appointment of Stigand to the see of East Anglia (see below) but before the death of Abbot Ufi (see p. 425).

p. 184, ll. 1 f. *Ailmer þe biscopes brother.* Æthelmær succeeded Stigand his brother as Bishop of Elmham in 1047 and shared in his downfall in 1070.

l. 2. *Vui Abbot.* See above.

l. 4. *Swanetone...Hildoluestone.* Swanton Novers and Hindolveston, Norfolk.

l. 6. *his day.* Æthelmær, after he became bishop, drew up a document whereby he bequeathed these two estates among others to Bury (Whitelock, No. xxxv), but his successor, Bishop William, succeeded in retaining them (D.B. II, ff. 192 ff.; V.C.H. *Norfolk*, II, p. 115).

ll. 9 f. *Stigande bisscop.* C.U.L., Additional MS. 4220, f. 61, drawing, as it says, from Marianus Scotus, attributes to the year 1044 the death of Ælfric III, Bishop of Elmham, the appointment and ejection of Stigand, followed by the appointment and ejection of Grimketel (for simony, see Fl. Wig. s.a. 1038; William of Malmesbury, *Gesta Pontificum*, R.S. pp. 150, 205) and the reappointment of Stigand. It is wrong in saying that Grimketel (who was Bishop of Selsey at the time of his appointment to Elmham) was ejected from both sees at the same time, as he continues to witness charters as Bishop of Selsey until 1046 (K. 784) and held the see until his death in 1047. There is no reason, however, for distrusting its evidence with regard to the history of the

NOTES

East Anglian see. Stigand's appointment and subsequent ejection are recorded in the Saxon Chronicle 1043 C, where the latter event is connected very plausibly with the disgrace of Queen Ælfgifu Emma. His re-instatement is given only in E (1043 for 1044), and neither MS. mentions the temporary appointment of Grimketel, but a writ of Edward the Confessor is addressed to Bishop Grimketel, Ælfwine, Ælfric and all his thegns in Suffolk (K. 832). Stigand, after his reinstatement, held the see until 1047 when he became Bishop of Winchester.

l. 10. *Lefstan þe dean*. Leofstan was a beneficiary under the will of Bishop Ælfric (see Whitelock, pp. 72, 183) and appears also as a witness to a will of about 1045 (*ibid.* pp. 82, 196). It was probably he who succeeded Ufi as abbot.

l. 11. *Lefsi Abbot*. Abbot of Ely, see p. 405.

l. 12. *Alfsy Abbot*. The Abbey of St Benedict at Hulme, Norfolk, was founded by Cnut in 1019 and Ælfsige was appointed first abbot. The date of his death is not recorded, but he was still abbot when Edward the Confessor granted his charter to the abbey in 1046 (see *Chronica Johannis de Oxenedes*, R.S. p. 292).

l. 13. *Alfwine*. Perhaps Ælfwine, the son of Wulfweard (or Wulfred), see p. 425.

Alfric. Perhaps Ælfric, Wihtgar's son, see p. 425.

Edric. Perhaps Eadric of Laxfield, see p. 426.

Godwine. The name is too common for identification. A thegn of the name held land at Eriswell and Wixoe in the time of King Edward (D.B. II, ff. 402 *b*, 414; V.C.H. *Suffolk*, I, pp. 539, 550).

ll. 13 f. *Fredegist*. Land at Scarning near East Dereham was held by *Fredregis*, a freeman, in the time of King Edward (D.B. II, f. 165 *b*; V.C.H. *Norfolk*, II, p. 88). The name is not a common one.

l. 14. *Vlf aet Welle*. The place meant might be Wells, Norfolk, but no one of the name is connected with Wells in D.B. A thegn called Ulf held lands in the neighbourhood of Norwich in the time of King Edward (D.B. II, ff. 150, 180 f.; V.C.H. *Norfolk*, II, pp. 75, 103 f.). Ulf the thegn also held lands in Suffolk (D.B. II, ff. 429 f.; V.C.H. *Suffolk*, I, p. 564). For *Wellan, Wyllan* see pp. 328, 346.

Scule Leofwoldes sune. Scula, a thegn of King Edward, held land at Barnham near Thetford in the time of King Edward (D.B. II, f. 299; V.C.H. *Suffolk*, I, p. 440). The name is of Scandinavian origin, see Björkman, p. 124.

ll. 14 f. *Godwine æt Cringelforð*. Cringleford is in the neighbourhood of Norwich.

l. 15. *Eadwine Vlfketeles sune*. Unidentified. Was he the son of Ulfketel, Earl of East Anglia (see p. 392)?

XCVIII

MS. British Museum, Additional MS. 15350, f. 41 *b* (or 43 *b* by the new numbering). See p. 274.

EDITION. K. 768.

DATE. The date of the transaction recorded here is determined by the presence of Earl Swegn, the Lady Ælfgifu and Bishop Ælfweard among the witnesses. Swegn's first signature as earl occurs in 1043 (see below), while Ælfgifu is not found as a witness after 1044 (see below) and Ælfweard, Bishop of London, died in the same year.

l. 18. *Ælfwine bysceop.* Bishop of Winchester from 1032 to 1047.
l. 19. *Osgoð.* A certain Osgot is entered in D.B. as the holder in the time of King Edward of land at *Scaldeford* which was apparently in the vicinity of Wroxall (D.B. 1, f. 53; V.C.H. *Hants.* 1, p. 522; V, pp. 166 f.). Wroxall itself in 1086 was in the king's hands and had been held before the Conquest by the Countess *Gueda* (i.e. Gytha) of Earl Godwine (her husband). There is nothing to show how or when it had come into his possession.

The identity of the Osgod of the present transaction is difficult to determine. If he were identical with the Osgot of *Scaldeford* there would seem little reason for effecting such an exchange as that of Wroxall for Adderbury, unless at the time Wroxall were his only holding in the vicinity. If, on the other hand, he were identical with the Osgod *minister* whose signature disappears from the charters in 1046, and if the latter, as already suggested, were identical with Osgod Clapa who was outlawed in the same year (see pp. 418 f.), then an explanation might be found for the state of affairs in 1086, namely that Osgod's forfeited estate of Wroxall had been bestowed by the king on Earl Godwine, while the Old Minster had regained possession of Adderbury. The chief objection to this is that Osgod Clapa is generally associated with the eastern counties only.

l. 20. *EADBVRGEbyrig.* Adderbury, Oxfordshire. This estate, which was held by the Bishop of Winchester in 1086, had been bequeathed to the Old Minster by the Ætheling Æthelstan (see Whitelock, p. 56).

l. 25. *Ælfgyfu.* In 1043 Ælfgifu Emma was deprived of her lands and possessions by order of her son the king (Sax. Chr. C, D; 1042 E). Her signature is attached to four charters of 1044 (K. 771, 773 ff.) but does not occur again, her place as a witness being taken by Queen Edith from 1045 onwards. The only exception is a spurious Westminster charter dated 1045 (K. 779) which includes both Ælfgifu and Edith in its list of witnesses.

l. 26. *EADSIGE arceb.* See p. 422.
Ælfric archebisceop. See p. 408.

l. 27. *Brihtwold b.* Bishop of Ramsbury, see p. 405.
Lyfincg b. Bishop of Worcester, see p. 423.
Duduc b. Bishop of Wells from 1033 to 1060 (Sáx. Chr. D; Fl. Wig.; 1061, Sax. Chr. E). According to Fl. Wig. he was a native of Lotharingia. He signs K. 1318, a charter of 1033, as *presbyter* and was probably one of the king's chaplains before his promotion.
Æpestan b. Bishop of Hereford, see p. 396.
l. 27 f. *Eadnod .b.* Bishop of Dorchester from 1034 to 1049.
l. 28. *Ælfwerð .b.* Bishop of London from 1035 to 1044 and at the same time Abbot of Evesham, see pp. 396 f.
Grimcytel b. Bishop of Selsey from 1039 to 1047 and for a short time Bishop of Elmham as well, see p. 431.
Godwine eorl. See p. 409.
ll. 28 f. *Leofric eorl.* See pp. 412 f.
p. 186, l. 1. *Siwerd eorl.* Siweard was Earl of Northumbria. His first signature as *dux* appears in 1033 (K. 749) and he continues to sign up to 1053 or 1054 (K. 797, 800). He died in 1055.
Swegen eorl. Swegn was the eldest son of Earl Godwine and was himself Earl of Oxfordshire, Gloucestershire, Herefordshire, Somerset and Berkshire (Fl. Wig. s.a. 1051). He is first mentioned in the Saxon Chronicle in connection with his expedition into South Wales (1046 C), but his signature as *dux* occurs as early as 1043 (K. 767). It appears for the last time in a document of 1046 (K. 784). From 1047 to 1050 he was in exile, and in 1051 was outlawed again along with his father and brothers. According to the Saxon Chronicle C he died at Constantinople in 1052 on his way back from Jerusalem. Fl. Wig. says that he died in Lycia *invalitudine ex nimio frigore contracta*, while William of Malmesbury states that he was slain by the Saracens (*Gesta Regum*, R.S. 1, p. 245).
Ordgar. Ordgar's signature occurs for the first time in 1031 (K. 744) and for the last (with the title *nobilis*) in a charter dated 1049 (K. 787). He is perhaps to be identified with the *Ordgarus Deuonensis* who witnesses Earl Leofric's undated charter relating to Coventry (K. 939). He generally signs along with Odda, Ælfgar and (less frequently) Osgod.
Odda. See pp. 456 ff.
l. 2. *Ælfgar.* Two men of this name sign Cnut's earliest charter (K. 728) and continue to appear together as witnesses until 1033 (K. 1318). Thereafter only one signs, except in the case of No. cv where the witnesses include Ælfgar, the brother of Ordgar, and Ælfgar of Minehead. The signature Ælfgar *nobilis* is attached to a charter of 1049 (K. 787) where the same title is applied also to Ordgar and Odda, while Ælfgar *þe Erles sune* (i.e. Earl Leofric's) witnesses a will of about 1045 (Whitelock, p. 82). The last-mentioned Ælfgar was Earl of East Anglia during Harold's exile (1051–1052) and succeeded him there again in 1053 when he became Earl of Wessex.
l. 4. *Þyssa gewrita syndon þreo.* The copy in the *Codex Wintoniensis* was made from the bottom portion of a chirograph.

XCIX

MS. Hereford Cathedral, P. i. 2.
FACSIMILE. *New Palaeographical Society*, Part x, pl. 234.
EDITIONS. Hickes, *Dissertatio Epistolaris*, p. 9, in *Thesaurus*, I.
K. 802.
C. B. Judge, *Harvard Studies and Notes in Philology and Literature*, XVI (1934), pp. 95 f.
DATE. Between 1043 and 1046, i.e. during Swegn's tenure of office. see p. 434.

l. 6. *Leofwine Leofflæde broðor*. Probably the brother-in-law of Thurkil the White, see p. 400.

l. 7. *Mælueshylle*. The name survives in the adjacent villages of Mansell Gamage and Mansell Lacy, Herefordshire.

l. 8. *Ufices suna*. The name *Ufic* is a diminutive of Ufa, see Redin, *Uncompounded Personal Names in Old English*, p. 152.

ll. 8 f. *mid healfe marce goldes...7 twegen oran*. The employment of the Scandinavian system of money reckoning is interesting in a transaction which is apparently carried out between two Englishmen. The mark of gold seems to have been equivalent to 300 West Saxon shillings (see Chadwick, *Anglo-Saxon Institutions*, p. 50).

l. 9. *to fane*. For *to faren(n)e*?

l. 10. *Swegnes eorles*. See above.

l. 11. *Æpelstanes bisceopes*. Bishop of Hereford, see p. 396. *Purceles hwitan*. See above.

l. 13. *sće Æpelberhtes mynstre*. Hereford Cathedral, see p. 402. *sće Guðlaces*. For an earlier reference to this foundation see Whitelock, p. 54, l. 12. It appears in D.B. as the holder or former holder of lands both in Herefordshire and Worcestershire (see V.C.H. *Hereford*, I, pp. 282, 325 f., 335, 338; V.C.H. *Worc*. I, p. 308).

C

MSS. (*a*) Cambridge University Library, Ff. 2.33, f. 49 *v*. See p. 392.
(*b*) British Museum, Additional MS. 14847, f. 19. See p. 392.
EDITIONS. K. 1340, from (*b*).
T. p. 593, from (*b*).
The text is from (*a*). The grant is referred to and the opening words quoted in the list of benefactors in C.U.L., Ee. 3. 60, f. 324, while it is recorded also without quotation in the similar lists in the C.U.L. MSS., Additional 6006, f. 74 and Mm. 4. 19, f. 167.

DATE. Between 1043 and 1047, i.e. while Stigand was Bishop of Elmham, see pp. 431 f.

l. 14. *Wlfgeat*. Wulfgeat is described as *barun notus* in the entries referred to above.

l. 16. *Gyselingham*. Gislingham, Suffolk. In 1086 the greater part of this estate had been lost by the abbey. It had been leased by Abbot

Leofstan to a certain Ælfsige for life but had passed into the possession of Gilbert 'Balastarius' at the Conquest (D.B. II, f. 444 b; V.C.H. *Suffolk*, I, p. 578).

l. 17. *Aelfwines*, cf. the reading *Æthelwine* of MS. (b). The relationship between Wulfgeat and Ælfwine (or Æthelwine) is not clear, but probably they were father and son.

l. 18. *ffakenham*. Fakenham, Norfolk. In 1086 the abbey enjoyed rights of jurisdiction and commendation with regard to this estate, although the men occupying it could give and sell their land (D.B. II, f. 367 b; V.C.H. *Suffolk*, I, p. 503).

CI

MS. British Museum, Cotton Augustus, II, 70, the middle portion of a chirograph.
There is a M.E. version in the cathedral registers A. f. 153, E. f. 11, at Canterbury.

FACSIMILE. Bond, *Facsimiles of Ancient Charters in the British Museum*, Part IV, No. 27.

EDITIONS. K. 773, with the M.E. version.
T. p. 354, with the M.E. version.
E. p. 243, with the M.E. version.

DATE. The British Museum parchment is endorsed with the name Æthelric Bigga and the date 1044, and both the name and the date are repeated in the heading of the M.E. version in the registers at Canterbury and in the late Canterbury list of benefactors (Dugdale, I, p. 97). That this identification of Æthelric is correct is proved by the mention of his son Esbearn in the charter. The latter, who inherited his father's nickname, appears in D.B. as *Esber, Sbern(e) Biga*. The only difficulty with regard to the date 1044 is the presence among the witnesses of Wulfric, Abbot of St Augustine's, see below.

p. 188, l. 2. *Eadsige arcebisceop*. See p. 422.
Cert. Chart, Kent, see p. 428.
l. 3. *Ceolnoð*. Archbishop of Canterbury, see p. 270. The transaction mentioned here is dated 839 in the late Canterbury list of benefactors. A copy has been preserved in the Lambeth MS. 1212, from which it has been printed as B. 427.

l. 4. *Apelulf cing*. King of Wessex, see p. 274.

l. 14. *to ecere ælmessan*. For the use of the same phrase with reference to land, see Harmer, pp. 21, 24.

l. 15. *Esbearn his sunu*. According to D.B. Esbearn Bigga was one of a group of *alodiarii* for whose land no relief was paid to the king on the death of the holder (D.B. I, f. 1; V.C.H. *Kent*, III, p. 204).

l. 17. *Stuting·7 Melentun*. Stowting and Milton, Kent. In 1086

NOTES

Stowting was held of the archbishop by the Count of Eu. Its assessment had been reduced from 1½ *solins* to 1, with land for 8 ploughs (D.B. I, f. 4; V.C.H. *Kent,* III, p. 213). There is no mention of Milton among the lands of the archbishop or his monks.

ll. 17 f. *se haga binnan port.* In 1066 Esbearn held 11 messuages in Canterbury (D.B. I, f. 2; V.C.H. *Kent,* III, p. 206). These passed with the majority of his estates to the Bishop of Bayeux (see V.C.H. *Kent,* III, pp. 224, 226, 229, 237).

l. 21. *sum heora freonda.* It is possible that *freond* is used here with the sense of the Scandinavian *frændi,* i.e. 'relation' rather than 'friend'. It is noteworthy that although *Æthelric* is an English name, *Esbearn* is of Scandinavian origin, see Björkman, p. 10, s.v. *Asbeorn.*

l. 22. *to rihtan gafole.* The force of *riht* is perhaps not exactly rendered by the translation 'fair'. The meaning is rather 'duly appointed, legally established'.

l. 25. *Ælfwine b.* Bishop of Winchester, see p. 433.

Stigand b. Bishop of Elmham, see pp. 431 f. He succeeded Ælfwine as Bishop of Winchester.

Godwine b. Bishop of Rochester, see p. 384.

ll. 25 f. *Godric decanus.* Dean of Christchurch.

l. 26. *Wulfric abbud.* Wulfric's appointment as Abbot of St Augustine's during the lifetime of Ælfstan, because of the latter's ill-health, is entered in the Saxon Chronicle E, 1043[2] for 1045. Ælfstan, whose signature is found in two charters dated 1045 (K. 776, 779), died on 5 July 1046 (Sax. Chr. 1044 E for 1046). Wulfric died in 1061.

l. 27. *Ælfwine abbud.* Ælfwine, Abbot of the New Minster, signs for the first time in 1032 (K. 746). He died in 1057. The M.E. version gives no names after Abbot Wulfric's but reads simply *and manie abotes · and erles and manie opre men · yhodede · and lewede binne burʒ and bute* (Reg. A).

ll. 27 f. *Siweard abbud.* Abbot of Abingdon. He became coadjutor bishop to Archbishop Eadsige in 1044 but resigned in 1048 because of ill-health and retired to Abingdon (Sax. Chr. C). He died in the same year. There was a contemporary Abbot of Chertsey of the same name (K. 776, 778) who became Bishop of Rochester in 1058.

l. 28. *Wulfnoð abb.* Abbot of Westminster, see p. 409.

Godwine eorl. See p. 409.

Leofric eorl. Earl of Mercia, see pp. 412 f.

l. 29. *Atsur roda.* This witness appears as *Azor Rot* in D.B. I, f. 13 (V.C.H. *Kent,* III, p. 248) where he is entered as the tenant in the time of King Edward of an estate in the hundred of Newchurch, assessed at 1 *solin* but with land for 5 ploughs. There was an *Azor* who held *Loisnes* (Lessness) at the time of the Conquest (D.B. I, f. 6 *b*; V.C.H. *Kent,* III, p. 222) and who is described as *Atsere optimas* in a grant of land there to the Abbey of Westminster (K. 824, dated 1066). The name *Azor* is of frequent occurrence in the charters and in D.B. One other man of the name is distinguished as *Atsere swerte* (K. 824,

438   NOTES

870). The adj. *roda* represents the Scandinavian *rauðr* and the name itself is of Scandinavian origin.

Ælfstan steallære. The signature Ælfstan *minister* is common in the charters of Edward's reign, but nowhere else does the name appear with the title 'staller'.

Eadmær æt Burhham. See p. 398.
l. 30. *Godric æt Burnan.* See p. 439.
Ælfwine se reada, cf. p. 204, l. 11.

CII

MS. A parchment in the Red Book of Canterbury, No. XXI. It is the top portion of a chirograph.

FACSIMILE. *Ordnance Survey Facsimiles*, Part I, No. 23.

EDITION. K. 790.

DATE. This agreement would seem to belong to the year 1044 or 1045 since it was drawn up before the retirement of Abbot Ælfstan, but after the appointment of Siweard as coadjutor bishop to Archbishop Eadsige (see p. 437).

p. 190, l. 8. [*þa forew*]*eard*. There seems no doubt that this was the reading of the text.

ll. 8 f. *Godwine eorl.* See p. 409.

l. 10. *Leofwine preoste.* Perhaps the priest of the name who appears elsewhere and seems to have been associated with St Martin's at Dover, see pp. 150, l. 14, 192, l. 9 f., 204, l. 8.

embe sča Myl[*dryþe a*]*re.* I would suggest that this was probably the reading of the text. The grant of St Mildred's body and lands to St Augustine's was traditionally ascribed to Cnut, see p. 420. It was disputed later by St Gregory's, Canterbury (Thos. of Elmham, R.S., p. 224).

l. 12. *þa halig* etc. I have found it impossible to reconstruct the text at this point, but the translation suggests what should probably be understood.

ll. 12 f. *eama wergeld.* The reference is to the story associated with the foundation of the Nunnery at Minster in Thanet by Domneva, the mother of St Mildred. The land there is said to have been granted to her by King Egbert in compensation (i.e. as wergeld) for the murder of her brothers (the king's nephews) by a councillor of his named Thunor. The story is related at length in K. 900 (a charter from St Augustine's), see also Hardy, *Descriptive Catalogue of MSS.*, R.S. I, pp. 263 f., 376 ff., 381 ff.; Cockayne, *Leechdoms* etc., R.S. III, p. 426; Simeon of Durham, R.S. II, pp. 3–13; William of Malmesbury, *Gesta Pontificum*, R.S. pp. 318 f.

l. 17. *Lang*[*a*]*dune.* Now represented by East and West Langdon near Dover.

Gildinge. Ileden, see Wallenberg, p. 325.

NOTES 439

l. 18. ...*es mæssan*. Perhaps *sēe Martines mæssan*.
l. 20. *mid*...*ā*. Perhaps *mid mannā*, if *magum* is rightly interpreted as 'women'.

CIII

MS. British Museum, Cotton Augustus, II, 35, the top portion of a chirograph.
FACSIMILE. Bond, *Facsimiles of Ancient Charters in the British Museum*, Part IV, No. 28.
EDITIONS. Madox, *Formulare Anglicanum*, p. 176, No. CCLXXXIV.
K. 789.
T. p. 350.
E. p. 247.
DATE. Between 1044 and 1048 as it is witnessed both by Archbishop Eadsige and his coadjutor Bishop Siweard, see p. 437.

p. 192, l. 1. *Godric æt Burnan*, cf. p. 188, l. 30. In 1066 Godric of Bourne was one of the *alodarii* whose land was exempt from the payment of relief to the king on the death of the holder (D.B. I, f. 1; V.C.H. *Kent*, III, p. 204). He is entered as the tenant of Brabourne in the time of King Edward (D.B. I, f. 13 *b*; V.C.H. *Kent*, III, p. 249). In other cases where the name Godric occurs it is impossible to distinguish him from Godric *Carlesone*.

l. 2. *Offaham*. In 1086 this estate was held by Hugh de Port of the Bishop of Bayeux. In 1066 it had been held by Godric. Its assessment was 1 *solin* with land for 3 ploughs. It was worth 30 shillings as compared with 20 shillings when it was received and 40 shillings in the time of King Edward (D.B. I, f. 7; V.C.H. *Kent*, III, p. 225).

l. 3. *an marc goldes*. See p. 435.
on geceapodne ceap. See B.T., *Suppl.* p. 119, s.v. *ceap*, I.
l. 5. *Wii*. Wye, a village 4½ miles north-east of Ashford. Meetings of the Kentish council are recorded there in 839 and 845 (B. 426, 449) and it appears elsewhere as an administrative centre (see p. 270 and Chadwick, *Anglo-Saxon Institutions*, p. 249). By 1066 it would appear that the usual meeting-place of the shire was at Penenden Heath near Maidstone, cf. D.B. I, f. 1 (V.C.H. *Kent*, III, p. 204), where Godric of Bourne is named as one of those exempted from attending shire-meetings held at any greater distance.

l. 6. *Eadsige arceƀ*. See p. 422.
Siward ƀ. See above.
Godric decanus. See p. 437.
l. 7. *Wulfric aƀƀ*. See p. 437.
l. 8. *Ægelric bygga*. See p. 409.
þurgar Ælfgares sunu. See p. 150, l. 13 for a witness called Ælfgar, the son of Sired.
l. 9. *Osweard æt Hergeardesham*. See p. 423.

ll. 9 f. *Leofwine preost.* See p. 438.

l. 10. *Godric portgerefa.* Presumably reeve of Canterbury.

Wulfsige þæs cynges gerefa. Perhaps also a Canterbury official. A *præpositus regis* at Canterbury, whose duty it was to collect on behalf of the king the fines payable directly to him for obstruction of the highways, is mentioned in D.B. 1, f. 2 (V.C.H. *Kent,* III, pp. 206 f.).

CIV

MS. Corpus Christi College, Oxford, MS. CXCVII, f. 106 *b*. This MS., which originally belonged to Bury St Edmunds, contains a bilingual copy of the Rule of St Benedict which ends near the top of f. 105; ff. 105 *b* and 106 are blank. The earlier part of the survey is entered in a handwriting which is of the same type, though not exactly the same, as that of the Rule.

EDITION. D. C. Douglas, *E.H.R.* XLIII, 1928, pp. 376–383.

DATE. This record seems to have been compiled from various notes and memoranda relating to Bury. It is not possible to date any of it with certainty except the paragraphs which contain references to Abbot Leofstan (1044–1065) and Abbot Baldwin (1065–1097 or 1098), but as a whole it probably belongs to the eleventh century (see Douglas, p. 376, n. 2).

l. 14. *wið ðan abbode.* It would seem from what follows that Leofstan's predecessor is meant, i.e. Ufi, see p. 425.

l. 15. *Niwentune.* Probably Newton, D.B. *Niwetuna,* an estate of 2 carucates where in 1066 there were 3 *villani* and 4 *bordarii* (D.B. II, f. 360; V.C.H. *Suffolk,* I, p. 496).

sceppe. This word is derived from O.Norse *skeppa,* 'a measure, a bushel', see Napier, 'Contributions to Old English Lexicography' in *Transactions of the Philological Society,* 1903–6, p. 319. In modern dialects the word *skep* is used in the sense of 'a basket, beehive'.

l. 16. *slægryðer.* See Napier, *op. cit.* p. 321, and cf. *slegneat,* p. 12, l. 11.

ll. 17 ff. *doð to...into þan ealdan fyrme.* Dr Douglas (p. 377) remarks that 'the abbot seems to be having some difficulty in maintaining the old farm in its entirety'. It seems to me, however, that what is specified here is an addition to the old food-rent, i.e. an innovation made by Abbot Leofstan. For *don to* in the sense of 'add', followed by the accusative as here (*þis fermfultum*), see B.T., *Suppl.* s.v. *don,* IV (2a). I take *to fyllincge* with what precedes, i.e. *oþer* .VI., and the phrase *into þan ealdan fyrme* as explanatory of *doð to.*

l. 18. *fermfultum.* This word is not of frequent occurrence. It appears in Earl Alfred's will (Harmer, p. 14) and in II Cnut, 69, 1, and in both cases seems, as here, to refer to an additional contribution to an already established *feorm.* This meaning is clear in Cnut's regulation which makes a contribution of the kind voluntary instead of obligatory. Earl Alfred's provision for the annual payment of 200 pence to Chertsey by the holder of Clapham *for Ælfredes sawle to feormfultume* seems to require the same interpretation. It can hardly represent the full rent of the estate and is indeed parallel to the payment of 100 pence to Christchurch from another of Alfred's estates, which is described as 'a pious gift' (*elmesse*).

l. 20. *Brihtric p̄r.* This might stand for *preost* but a man of the name was prior (*praepositus*) at Bury in the time of Edward the Confessor, see p. 444.

ll. 21 f. *twegan oran....*XVI. *peñ.* It would seem from this that the ore of 20 pence is meant, unless the second sum is to be regarded as equivalent to half the first. The ore of 16 pence appears later in the document.

l. 23. *On Elsingtun-hundred* etc. The section which follows down to *landemacan* seems to have no connection with what precedes. Dr Douglas notes that the units specified are apparently the small Danish hundreds of 12 carucates, and discusses the importance of this document in establishing their identity with the later East Anglian leets (pp. 378–380).

manslot. See Napier, *op. cit.* p. 307, for a philological note on this word with Scandinavian parallels of which the closest in form is O.Norse *mannshlutr.* The English term seems to mean 'a man's share or holding'. A later instance of its use in the same corner of Norfolk is quoted by Vinogradoff, *English Society in the Eleventh Century,* p. 281, with reference to the manor of Walpole where divisions known as *tenmanlots* or *tenmanlands* appear. An earlier instance is found in one of Edwy's charters (B. 1029) which records the grant of the manor of Southwell, Nottinghamshire, to Oscytel, Archbishop of York, in or about the year 956. This charter is preserved in the *Liber Albus* of York, and the Anglo-Saxon portions are given in a very corrupt form. The relevant passage reads *on Fearnesfelda gebyrað twega mannahlot landes into Sudwellan on Healum a se seoxta acer 7 dreon mannahlot on Normantune a se dridda acer on Fiscestune da twegen dales 7 feower mannahlot ealles dans landes,*[1] i.e. at Farnsfield two 'manslots' of land belong to Southwell, at Halam every sixth acre and three 'manslots', at Normanton every third acre, at Fisherton two-thirds of the whole estate and four 'manslots' (see Stenton, *Types of Manorial Structure in the Northern Danelaw,* p. 79). The *tenmanlots* at Walpole contained 120 acres, so that a single holding of the kind contained 12 acres. There is nothing to indicate the size of the 'manslot' either in Edwy's charter or here.

l. 24. *Spelhoge.* Dr Douglas points out (p. 378) that the name Spellow is applied at the present day to six fields lying between Islington and Clenchwarton.

[1] The passage has been corrected from the MS.

ll. 24 f. *In...Fuwelege...Ærnehogo.* I have not been able to identify these three. Islington, Clenchwarton and Lynn are all in Marshland, Norfolk, and the other places named were presumably in the same region.

ll. 27 f. *Apolfes suðtun.* I have not been able to trace the name Athulf in connection with any Sutton in the vicinity. Dr Douglas suggests that Long Sutton, Lincolnshire, is meant.

p. 194, l. 1. *dlde Walbec.* Was this anywhere in the region of Walsoken? *Watlingetune.* Watlington, a few miles south of King's Lynn.

ll. 3 ff. *Ures drihtnes* etc. Here begins a new section which would seem to have been drawn up originally soon after Leofstan became Abbot of Bury.

l. 13. *Bædericeswyrðe.* The old name of Bury St Edmunds. This seems to be the latest instance of its use so far recorded, see Whitelock, p. 183.

l. 14. *.x. bec.* At the time of the dissolution of the monasteries the library of Bury St Edmunds seems to have contained over 2000 volumes, see M. R. James, *The Abbey of St Edmund at Bury*, pp. 3, 99–103.

ll. 16 f. *Sĉe Eadmundes uita.* Leland, who visited Bury at the time of the dissolution and examined the remains of the library, notes among the books found there *Abbo Floriacensis de vita S. Edmundi martyris ad Dunstanum Archiep. Cantuar.* (see *Collectanea*, ed. 1770, IV, p. 162; M. R. James, *op. cit.* p. 10). This copy of Abbo's Life of St Edmund has not survived.

l. 18. *pella.* The A.S. *pæll*, derived from the Latin *pallium*, is used of coverings, robes or cloaks of costly material. It is difficult to be certain of its exact meaning here. The number given is a large one.

l. 19. *superumerale.* Described as 'an imitation of Aaron's ephod worn by bishops in the tenth and eleventh centuries and consisting of two golden pieces like epaulettes on the shoulders, joined round the neck by an embroidered band', Atchley and Wyatt, *Glossary of Ecclesiastical Terms*, p. 182.

l. 20. *scufrægl*, i.e. curtains which could be drawn at will.

l. 21. *corporale.* See p. 476.

l. 22. *marmarstan gesmiðede.* The reference is probably to portable altars, see p. 476.

l. 23. *Brihtric.* It is curious that four of the names in this list, namely Brihtric, Leofstan, Ætheric and Thurstan, occur also in the first note or memorandum. There is a reference in the list of benefactors in the C.U.L. MSS., Ee. 3. 60, f. 324 *b* and Mm. 4. 19, f. 167 *b*, to Leofstan, the seneschal (*dapifer*) of Abbot Leofstan.

ll. 27 f. *Ad te leuaui.* These are the initial words of the office or introit for Advent Sunday, see Atchley and Wyatt, *op. cit.* s.v.

l. 28. *Sĉe Eadmundes byrig.* This name, which begins to appear in the eleventh century, ultimately ousted the old one.

l. 29. *into þæra byrig.* This seems to mean the demesne land.

manna earningaland. It is recorded in D.B. II, f. 372 (V.C.H. *Suffolk,* I, p. 508) that in 1066 Abbot Baldwin held 118 men in Bury *ad victum monachorum.* These, however, could give and sell their land, so that it is doubtful if they correspond to the holders of *earningaland* mentioned here. There is much uncertainty with regard to the meaning of the term, but it would seem from its occurrence elsewhere that the land to which it was applied was not at the disposal of the holder (see Whitelock, p. 80, l. 17; p. 88, l. 31; p. 178). By 1086 the town of Bury St Edmunds had extended greatly over the land which had formerly been arable so that there were altogether 342 houses on demesne land which was under the plough in the time of King Edward (V.C.H. *Suffolk,* I, p. 509).

ll. 29 f. *On Wirlingaweorðe* etc. The list which follows gives the names of the estates which singly or in groups were responsible for supplying food-rents to Bury every month. The final note of the document gives the amount of this monthly purveyance.

There seems to be a reference to this section of the document in C.U.L., Additional MS. 6006, f. 75 *b*, at the end of an account of the food-rents of a later date, differently arranged, where it says that all the estates with the exception of one were in the possession of Bury St Edmunds in the time of Abbot Leofstan when the food-rents of the monks and the abbot were rendered *per menses integros...ut de Bertone firma unius mensis et de Lakforde cum Heringiswelle similiter....*

Worlingworth was granted to Bury by Bishop Ælfric in the reign of Harold Harefoot (see Whitelock, p. 70).

l. 30. *Saham.* Soham near Worlingworth. This estate is said to have been given to Bury by Ælfric, Bishop of Elmham, *cognomento bonus* (C.U.L., Ee. 3. 60, f. 322 *b*), see p. 425.

l. 31. *Pallegrafe.* A certain Wulfstan granted 4 *cassati* at Palgrave to Bury in 962 (B. 1084) and in 1066 the abbey was holding 4 carucates there. Palgrave is included likewise among the bequests of a certain Thurketel to Bury in the early eleventh century (see Whitelock, p. 68). This may represent a re-grant of the estate (which may have been alienated sometime after 962) or else it may represent the grant of a separate one which was afterwards alienated (see Whitelock, p. 179).

Porpa. The nearest place of the name is Westhorpe, D.B. *West Torp*, where in 1066 eight freemen under the abbot's soke and commendation held 60 acres, and a man who could not sell his land held 7 acres (D.B. II, f. 370 *b*; V.C.H. *Suffolk,* I, p. 507). A separate entry (D.B. f. 371) refers to a freeman who held 1 acre.

Redgrafe. This estate is said to have been given by Ulfketel, the donor of Rickinghall etc., see p. 392.

l. 33. *Stoca.* Perhaps Stoke Ash where in 1066, according to one entry in D.B., 7 freemen under the abbot's soke and commendation held 10 acres and half a plough, and according to another 14 freemen with 33½ acres and 2 ploughs were under the abbot's soke and

NOTES

commendation with one exception (D.B. II, f. 370; V.C.H. *Suffolk*, I, p. 506).

Brocaforde. Part of Brockford is said to have been given by Bishop Ælfric *cognomento bonus* (see above).

Byrtune. Great Barton was bequeathed to his kinsman Osgot, Eadulf's son, by Bishop Theodred of London, sometime between 942 and about 951 (see Whitelock, p. 4). There is no record of its transference to Bury, but it is recorded in the list of benefactors that one part of the estate was given by Bishop Theodred, another by a certain Edwin, while the third part was acquired by Brihtric *praepositus* (i.e. prior) in the time of Edward the Confessor (C.U.L. MSS., Ee. 3. 60, f. 320 b, Additional 6006, ff. 73, 74 b, Mm. 4. 19, f. 167).

l. 34. *Ruhham*. Rougham was also left by Bishop Theodred to Osgot. It was granted to Bury by Ulfketel along with Rickinghall and Woolpit, see p. 392.

Elmeswella. Elmswell is included in a list of estates of which no record was preserved (C.U.L., Ee. 3. 60, f. 326).

p. 196, l. 1. *Grotene*. Groton is also included among the estates of which no record was preserved (see above and C.U.L., Additional MS. 6006, f. 75).

ll. 1 ff. *Koccefelda...Ceorlesweorðe*. Cockfield was left by Ælfgar to his daughter Æthelflæd with reversion to Bury. The latter in turn left it along with Chelsworth to her sister Ælfflæd (the wife of Earl Brihtnoth) who bequeathed both estates directly to Bury St Edmunds (see Whitelock, pp. 6, 36, 38).

l. 2. *Hwipstede*. Whepstead was bequeathed to Bury St Edmunds by Bishop Theodred (Whitelock, p. 4).

l. 3. *Bradefeldæ*. According to C.U.L., Additional MS. 6006, f. 75, the donor of this estate was uncertain. In C.U.L., Ee. 3. 60, ff. 321, 322 b, it is included among the gifts of Ulfketel (see above) and of Bishop Ælfric the Good.

Horningasearðe. Horringer, also known as Horningsheath, is included by Bishop Theodred among the estates bequeathed to Bury. According to the lists of benefactors only part of it was his. Another part was given by Robert le Manaunt (*sine carta*, according to C.U.L., Ee. 3. 60, f. 320 b) while the third part was *de socagio*, cf. also the C.U.L. MSS., Additional 6006, f. 73, Mm. 4. 19, f. 166 b.

l. 4. *Rysebi*. Risby is said to have been given by Edward the Confessor (C.U.L., Ee. 3. 60, f. 324). According to C.U.L., Additional MS. 6006, f. 75, however, the donor was uncertain.

Lecforde. Lackford is said to have been given by a certain *matrona*, *sed sine carta* (C.U.L., Ee. 3. 60, f. 325). The grant would seem to be attributed to the time of King William and Abbot Baldwin.

Hyrningcwylle. It is stated in the list of benefactors that Herringswell was given by a certain Wulfric *vir dives* (C.U.L., Ee. 3. 60, f. 324 b), but according to C.U.L., Additional MS. 6006, f. 75, the donor was uncertain.

l. 5. *Runcgetune.* Is this South Runcton, Norfolk (which was held by Bury) or was there a place of the name in the neighbourhood of Culford and Fornham? *Culeforde.* For the grant of Culford see No. XCIII.

l. 6. *Fornham.* In C.U.L., Ee. 3. 60, ff. 320, 324 *b*, it is said that King Edmund gave *minorem Fornham* while a certain Alnothus *praepositus* gave *maiorem Fornham*, the latter *sine carta*. According to C.U.L., Additional MS. 6006, f. 75, the donor of Fornham was uncertain.

ll. 7 f. *Her syndon* .xxx. *boca* etc. It is uncertain to what this applies as the note is probably misplaced. It would seem to belong to the inventory which precedes the list of food-rents.

l. 9. *Paccenham.* Pakenham was among the estates left by Bishop Theodred to his kinsman Osgot, Eadulf's son (see above). In the lists of benefactors it is said to have been held by Osgot *Claf*, i.e. Clapa, and to have been given to the abbey by Edward the Confessor (see also *Memorials of St Edmund's Abbey*, R.S. I, p. 364). A writ addressed to Bishop Stigand and Earl Harold gives notification of this grant (K. 851) and there the former owner of the estate is referred to simply as Osgod. It seems to me, however, that the identification with Osgod Clapa is probably correct. The writ must have been issued between 1045 and 1047, and as Osgod Clapa was exiled in 1046, the estate might easily have passed into the king's hands then. It is noteworthy that another of the estates (Rougham) left to Osgot, Eadulf's son, passed to Bury from another owner at a much earlier date (see above), so that the former does not seem to have enjoyed a preternaturally long life, and it would be curious to find him referred to without explanation in a document of Edward the Confessor as the previous owner of the estate. It is possible that Osgod Clapa was a descendant or relative of the earlier Osgot.

Stantune. Stanton is said to have been given to Bury by Edward the Confessor (C.U.L., Ee. 3. 60, f. 324).

ll. 11 ff. *Her onstent gewriten* etc. This seems to be an entirely detached note or memorandum. It is noteworthy that the accompanying interlinear Latin translation retains the Anglo-Saxon numerals in most cases and renders 1 *flicce* by *an bacun*.

l. 11. *Eggemere.* Egmere, Norfolk. It is difficult to understand the reference to this estate. It appears in the will of Ælfric, Bishop of Elmham, where he bequeathes 30 acres to Ælfwine, his priest at Walsingham, and the rest to Ufi the prior (Whitelock, p. 72). The latter, as Miss Whitelock points out, can scarcely be identical with Ufi, Prior of St Benedict's at Hulme, who became Abbot of Bury in 1020, for the will was not drawn up till the reign of Harold Harefoot. In 1066 three carucates at Egmere were held by Æthelmær, Bishop of Elmham, and half a carucate is entered also under the king's lands as an outlying estate belonging to the manor of Wighton (D.B. II, ff. 113, 192 *b*; V.C.H. *Norfolk*, II, pp. 43, 115). Its connection with Bury is therefore obscure.

l. 13. *Cole.* This represents the Scandinavian name *Koli.* For its occurrence elsewhere in the Anglicised form *Cola* see p. 210, l. 8.

l. 15. *stottas,* cf. Napier, *op. cit.* p. 323.

scora. A Scandinavian loan-word, cf. O.N. *skor,* see Napier, *op. cit.* p. 320.

l. 20. *Her stant gewriten.* This represents the beginning of a new section, the separate paragraphs of which may belong to different dates but are all probably to be attributed to the time of Abbot Baldwin.

l. 21. *to caritatem,* i.e. Anglo-Saxon *to ælmesse.*

ll. 21 f. *hælf pund...*XII. `or`. It would seem that here the ore of 16 pence is meant, as 12 ores of 20 pence would be equivalent to a pound, and the distinction between *þæt healf pund* and *ða* VI. *or* of ll. 22 f. would be lost. The Latin translation, which substitutes Norman shillings for the ores of the original, supports this view as the sums given there correspond to those arrived at by taking the ore as one of 16 pence.

l. 23. *natiuitatem scæ Mariæ.* 8 September.

ll. 23 f. `Sce' Dionisius messe.` 9 October. Baldwin had been a monk of St Denys (i.e. Dionysius) at Paris before coming to England.

l. 24. `Sce' Nicholaus.` 6 December.

l. 33. *Ixewyrðe.* For the grant of Ixworth see No. XCIII.

p. 198, ll. 1 ff. *Ad anniuersarium* etc. This section is obviously later in date and the use of Latin instead of English is noteworthy.

l. 1. *diem depositionis regis Willi.* William the Conqueror died on 9 September 1087.

l. 3. *.x. solidi,* i.e. 10 Norman shillings.

die obitus reginę. Matilda, the wife of William the Conqueror, died on 3 November 1083.

l. 8. `Werkentune'.` Warkton, Northamptonshire. According to the lists of benefactors Warkton was given to Bury by Matilda with William the Conqueror's consent (C.U.L. MSS., Ee. 3. 60, f. 325, Additional 6006, ff. 73 *b*, 75, Mm. 4. 19, f. 167).

l. 14. *Ad anniuersarium...regis Æduuardi.* This is a translation of the English note on the commemoration of King Edward. It may be of later date than the original memorandum. The x *solidos* of this version correspond to the *healf pund* of the earlier one, showing that the Norman shilling of 12 pence is meant.

l. 15. *ad pitantiam.* The English version is more definite with its *to fisce.*

l. 27. *.IIII. sol ad festum sci Nicholai.* This seems to be a mistake for VIII *solidos,* cf. the 6 ores of the English version and the VIII *solidos* paid at the feast of St Dionysius, which represents half the total amount paid by one of the two mills.

l. 30. *Ðis is Sce Eadmundes ferme.* It would seem at first sight as if this note were misplaced and ought to follow on after the earlier section dealing with the food-rents of the abbey. The division into months is the same and the grouping of the estates likewise, with one noteworthy difference, namely the substitution of Coney Weston for Lackford. This suggests that the two accounts are actually of different date, and that the second was probably drawn up after Abbot Baldwin had arranged that the contributions in money and in kind for the celebration of Abbot Ufi's anniversary should come from Lackford. Stoke is not included along with Rickinghall and Brockford, but the omission may be accidental.

met. The word *(ge)met* is used as a rule with the general sense of 'measure', cf. V Æthelred, 24; VI Æthelred, 32, 2, etc. I have not found any other instance of its employment with what seems to be a precise meaning.

l. 31. *masc 7 grut.* 'Mash' is the mixture of malt and hot water which after fermentation becomes beer; 'grout' is the name applied to the infusion during the process of fermentation and also to the sediment left after the beer has been poured off, see N.E.D. s.v.

p. 200, l. 2. *Cunegestune.* Coney Weston was granted to Bury by Edward the Confessor (K. 880).

l. 8. *Tifteshale.* Tivetshall is an addition to the earlier list. It was left to Bury by a monk named Siweard who was made dean by Abbot Leofstan (C.U.L. MSS., Ee. 3. 60, f. 324, Additional 6006, f. 74 *b*, Mm. 4. 19, f. 167 *b*).

l. 9. *lepene.* Is this derived from the O.E. *leap,* 'a basket'? The word 'leap' is still used locally in this sense, and as late as the eighteenth century was employed as a measure denoting half a bushel (see E.D.D. s.v.). The diminutive form 'lippy' is still in use in Scotland to denote a quarter peck.

CV

MS. The Sherborne Cartulary, f. 21. See p. 278.
EDITIONS. K. 1334.
T. p. 346.

DATE. Either 1045 or 1046, i.e. after the accession of Ælfwold to the see of Sherborne but before the death of Lyfing, Bishop of Worcester, on 23 March 1046.

l. 12. *Godwine eorle.* See p. 409.

l. 13. *Alfwolde bisceope.* Ælfwold's predecessor, Brihtwine, signs for the last time in 1045 (K. 776 etc.) while Ælfwold himself signs for the first time in 1046 (K. 784). He held the see until 1058.

ll. 13 f. *Care Tokies suna.* Both names are Scandinavian. For Care (Sc. *Kári*) see Björkman, p. 76. The signature Toki *minister* appears twice in connection with grants of land in Devon, see *Ordnance Survey Facsimiles,* II, Exeter Charters, No. XI (a charter of Cnut dated 1031) and K. 1332 (a charter of Edward the Confessor dated 1042). This witness may be identical with the *Toki praepotens et diues minister regis* whose bequest of the estates of Teddington and Alstone to Ealdred, Bishop of Worcester, was disputed by his son Aki (K. 805).

l. 14. *Holacumbe.* It seems possible that Holcombe Rogus, Devonshire is meant. It is noteworthy, at any rate, that the monks of Sherborne held 9 *cassatos* at *Holancumb* in 998 (K. 701) and that in 1086 the estate of Holcombe Rogus paid geld for 9 hides. None of the other Holcombe estates approaches this size. In 1086 (D.B. I, f. 299 *b*; V.C.H. *Devon*, I, p. 455) it was in the possession of Baldwin the sheriff and had been held in the time of King Edward by *Ulf* (corrected to *Seward* in the Exeter D.B.; the reading of the Exchequer D.B. is *Seward*). Is it possible that the original reading of the Exeter D.B. was right? It is noteworthy, at any rate, that the present agreement leaves the estate in the hands of a man named Ulf.

l. 18. *unbesacun* 7 *unbefliten*, cf. II Cnut, 72.

l. 20. *Lyfing ƀ be norðan.* Bishop of Worcester. He held also the united sees of Crediton and Cornwall, see p. 423. The same description is applied to Stigand, Bishop of Elmham, and Eadnoth, Bishop of Dorchester, in the Saxon Chronicle E (a Canterbury MS.), s.a. 1045 and 1046[2].

ll. 20 f. *Ælfwine aƀƀ on Bucfæsten.* The date both of the foundation and of the dissolution of the Benedictine Abbey of Buckfast is unknown. In 1137 its site was granted to a colony of Cistercian monks and a new house was established there. The possessions of the earlier abbey are recorded in D.B. I, ff. 182 f. (V.C.H. *Devon*, I, pp. 432 f.), from which it appears that Ælfwine was alive at the Conquest. An entry in the *Rotuli Hundredorum*, p. 75, No. 25, attributes to Cnut the grant of Zeal Monachorum *in perpetuam elemosinam*.

l. 21. *Sihtric aƀƀ on Tæfingstoce.* The occurrence of Sihtric, Abbot of Tavistock, as a witness along with Lyfing, Bishop of Worcester, is difficult to explain, as it would seem that the former only became abbot when Ealdred, who preceded him, was promoted to Worcester on the death of Lyfing (Fl. Wig. s.a. 1046). Is it possible that Ealdred held some other office before becoming Bishop of Worcester? Sihtric died in 1082. He is given a bad character by William of Malmesbury who says of him in his *Gesta Pontificum*, R.S. p. 204: *sub rege Willelmo piraticam aggressus, religionem polluit, ecclesiam infamavit.*

ll. 21 f. *Odda · 7 Ælfric his broðor.* See pp. 456 ff.

l. 22. *Ordgar 7 his twegen gebroðra.* For Ordgar see p. 434.

l. 23. *Dodda cild.* The signature Dodda *minister* is of frequent occurrence between 1042 (K. 764) and 1050 (K. 791).

Alon. This witness does not seem to appear elsewhere. The name is Norman.

Æþelmær Cola sunu. A witness named Æthelmær signs four of Edward the Confessor's charters between 1043 (K. 767) and 1052 (K. 796).

Osmær. Osmær's signature is attached to four Devonshire charters, namely K. 1332 (dated 1042), K. 770 (dated 1044) and *Ordnance*

NOTES

Survey Facsimiles, II, Exeter Charters, Nos. XII (dated 1044) and XIII (dated 1050). The first two are witnessed also by Odda, Ordgar, Ælfgar, Dodda and Ælfweard, while Toki's name is attached to the first as well.

l. 24. *Leofwine æt Exon.* This witness does not seem to appear elsewhere.

Ælfweard Alfwoldes sunu. The signature Ælfweard *minister* is found from 1042 (K. 1332) to 1054 (K. 800).

Wiking. The name represents the Scandinavian *Víkingr* see Björkman, p. 176.

l. 25. *Ælfgær æt Mynheafdon.* In 1086 Minehead, assessed at 5 hides with land for 12 ploughs, was held by William de Moion but had been held by *Algar* in 1066 (D.B. I, f. 95 *b*; V.C.H. *Somerset*, I, p. 502).

Wulfweard æt Winesham. There is a Winsham in Somerset and a hamlet of the same name in north-west Devon.

ll. 25 f. *Hunewine Héca sunu.* In 1031 Cnut granted an estate in Devonshire to a thegn called Hunewine (see p. 344). The name is an uncommon one.

l. 26. *Ælfwig æt Hægdune.* The name Haydon is found both in Dorset (near Sherborne) and Somerset.

Godman preost. The priest Godman signs two other charters, namely K. 767 (dated 1043) and K. 791 (dated 1050). Godric, who became Abbot of Winchcombe in 1054, is described as the son of Godman, the king's chaplain, by Simeon of Durham, R.S. II, p. 171.

l. 27. *Lutsige on Wiht.* The name *Lutsige* does not occur elsewhere. Is it by any chance a corruption or misreading of *Wulfsige*? In 1086 *Ulsi* held half a hide at Chale in the Isle of Wight which he had held in the time of King Edward (D.B. I, f. 54; V.C.H. *Hants.* I, p. 525).

CVI

MS. British Museum, Additional MS. 15350, f. 94. See p. 274.

EDITION. K. 820.

DATE. The transaction took place while Stigand was Bishop of Winchester (see below) and cannot be more exactly dated.

p. 202, l. 6. *Stigand Bisceop.* Stigand, who had been Bishop of Elmham (see pp. 431 f.), became Bishop of Winchester in 1047 and Archbishop of Canterbury in 1052 or 1053 (see p. 463). He was deposed in 1070.

l. 8. *Spæresholte.* Sparsholt seems to be included in the manor of Chilcomb in D.B. (see V.C.H. *Hants.* III, p. 444). One of the former tenants there, holding land for 1 plough, is said to have been *Æilmer* (D.B. I, f. 41; V.C.H. *Hants.* I, p. 464).

NOTES

l. 9. *sceattæ*. The reference is perhaps to money paid as rent (see B.T., *Suppl.* p. 696, s.v. *sceatt*, 1 a). It is curious that the amount is so vaguely stated, cf. the following document.

l. 11. *Ælfwinæ abbod.* See p. 437.

CVII

MS. British Museum, Additional MS. 15350, f. 74 *b*. See p. 274.

EDITIONS, K. 949.
B. 390 (end).

DATE. This transaction belongs to the period when Stigand was Bishop of Winchester (see p. 449).

l. 16. *AWeltune.* Alton Priors, Wiltshire, see p. 291.

l. 18. *gereflande*, i.e. land held by the reeve in return for his services, cf. *gerefmæd*, B.T., *Suppl.* p. 393, and the thirteenth-century *Rentalia Glastonbury (Somerset Record Society Publications*, v), p. 118: [*Prepositus*] *habebit j pratum quod appellatur Refmede*, and p. 140: [*Prepositus*] *debet habere ij hammes prati...que vocantur Refhammes*.

ll. 18 f. *forð mið þas hlafordes*, cf. the *Rentalia Glastonbury*, p. 64: *Prepositus de Winterburne...debet habere unum afferum cum afferis domini in pastura.*

l. 20. *swylce hæ best geunne.* See B.T. p. 1122, s.v. *unnan*, III.

ll. 20 f. *wið swylcan sceatte* etc. See above.

l. 22. *Godwine eorl.* See p. 409.

l. 23. *Ælfwine abb.* See p. 437.

CVIII

MS. British Museum, Stowe Charter, No. 42, the bottom portion of a chirograph.

FACSIMILE. *Ordnance Survey Facsimiles*, Part III, No. 43.

DATE. Probably between 1048 and 1050, i.e. after Bishop Siweard had resigned office (see p. 437).

p. 204, l. 1. *Eadsi arcebisceop.* Archbishop of Canterbury, see p. 422.

ll. 2 f. *butan reada gatan.* Later called Redingate, then Ridingate. This gate gave access to the city on the south-east side from the Roman road between Dover and Canterbury. The original Roman gateway was later replaced by what Hasted describes as 'a very ordinary structure' (*History of Kent*, IV, p. 414). This also has disappeared without leaving any trace.

l. 3. *wiðutan Wiwergatan*, see p. 270. It guarded the south entrance to the city but has now disappeared.

ll. 6 f. *Godwine b on Rofeceastra.* See p. 384.

NOTES

l. 7. *Godwine b æt sc̄e Martine.* Godwine, Bishop of St Martin's, witnesses K. 1338 (a charter of 1048–50) and his death on 9 March 1061 is recorded in the Saxon Chronicle E. According to Gervase of Canterbury, *Opera*, R.S. II, p. 361 : *Habebat...quondam Cantuariensis archiepiscopus corepiscopum quendam qui in ecclesia Sancti Martini extra Cantuariam manebat; qui adveniente Lanfranco deletus est.* Godwine probably became Bishop of St Martin's when Siweard resigned office. *Godric decanus.* See p. 437.

l. 8. *Leofwine preost.* See p. 438.

l. 9. *Ægelric bicga.* See p. 409.

Esbearn. Probably the son of Æthelric Bigga, see p. 436.

l. 9 f. *Ægelwine Ælfelmes sunu,* cf. p. 170, l. 1.

l. 10. *þurgar,* cf. p. 192, l. 8.

Eadric æt Æþelham. Eadric of Elham is entered in D.B. as the tenant in the time of King Edward of estates at Ewell and Tickenhurst as well as at Elham, all of which had passed to the Bishop of Bayeux (D.B. I, ff. 9 *b*, 11 f.; V.C.H. *Kent,* III, pp. 234, 239, 241). He is possibly the Eadric of other entries as well.

ll. 10 f. *Eadwine þæs arceb broðor,* cf. No. LXXXVI.

l. 11. *Ælfwine se reada,* cf. p. 188, l. 30.

Godric æt Burnan. See p. 439.

l. 12. *Ælfred · 7 his broðor Gyldewine.* These witnesses do not seem to appear elsewhere in Kentish charters.

CIX

MS. Corpus Christi College, Cambridge, MS. 111, f. 73. This is a twelfth-century cartulary of the Abbey of Bath.

EDITIONS. K. III, p. 450.
E. p. 376.
B. 928.
Hunt, *Two Chartularies of the Priory of St Peter at Bath,* p. 18.

DATE. This survey follows King Edwy's grant of Tidenham to the Abbot of Bath in 956 (B. 927) and precedes the lease of the same estate to Archbishop Stigand (see No. CXVII). Seebohm (*English Village Community,* p. 149) connects it with the former transaction, Maitland (*Domesday Book and Beyond,* p. 330, n. 2) with the latter. Liebermann (I, p. 445, note (*a*); III, p. 245) dates it about 1050 in view of its apparent relationship to the *Rectitudines.*

l. 16. *Dyddanhamme.* Tidenham, Gloucestershire. The lands of the manor lie in the triangle formed by the Wye and the Severn. The boundaries, which run up the Wye (beginning at the mouth), then across by a series of landmarks to the Severn and down that river to the mouth of the Wye again, are given in Edwy's charter.

inlandes, i.e. land held in demesne.

NOTES

l. 17. *gesettes landes.* Apparently synonymous with *gafol-landes*, i.e. land occupied by rent-paying tenants, cf. Ine, 64 f.

Stræt. Stroat on the Roman road from Gloucester to Cærleon (Seebohm).

ll. 18 ff. *cytweras...hæcweras.* See Seebohm, *op. cit.* pp. 150–153, for a full description of the basket weirs and hackle weirs in use on the Wye and the Severn.

l. 18. *Middeltune.* Now Milton.

l. 20. *Cingestune.* Now Sedbury.

l. 21. *bufan dic,* i.e. Offa's Dyke.

ll. 21 f. *utan hamme,* i.e. outside the area enclosed by the dyke which, after running south along the cliffs on the left bank of the Wye, cuts across the promontory from Tallards Marsh to Sedbury Cliffs on the Severn, leaving the point of the triangle outside. For a detailed study of Offa's Dyke in the Wye valley (from which this description is drawn) see Fox, *Archaeologia Cambrensis,* June 1931, pp. 1–74. I am indebted to Sir Cyril Fox for much information and help with regard to the topography of the district and the boundaries of the Tidenham estate.

l. 22. *þan scipwealan,* i.e. the Welsh sailors who plied up and down the Wye (see Fox, pp. 65–67). The form *scipwealh* may be compared with *horswealh* (Ine, 33) used of a Welsh horseman.

l. 24. *Bispestune.* Now represented by Bishton Farm (Seebohm).

l. 25. *Landcawet.* Landcaut lies in a loop of the Wye outside Offa's Dyke. The name shows that it had long remained a Welsh village.

l. 26. *at gyrde* .XII. *pæneġ.* The rate of payment is slightly higher than at Hurstbourne Priors, see p. 455.

l. 27. .IIII. *ælmespeneġ.* Perhaps synonymous with the payment called *ælmesfeoh* which was due from the *geneat* (*Rectitudines,* cap. 2) and in some cases from the thegn (*ibid.* cap. 1, 1). In VII Æthelred, 7 it appears under the name *pecunia elemosinæ* which is the translation of *ælmesfeoh* in the Quadripartitus version of I Edmund, 2. It is possible that the *Romfeoh* 7 *sulhælmessan* of I Edmund, 2 (MS. D), represent the separate payments which together made up *ælmesfeoh* (see Robertson, pp. 6, 295).

p. 206, l. 5. *Se geneat.* His duties are set out more fully in the *Rectitudines,* cap. 2.

ll. 5 f. *swa on lande·swa of lande.* According to the *Rectitudines* the duties of the *geneat* included *nigefaran to tune feccan...ærendian fyr swa nyr swa hwyder swa him mon to tæcð.*

ll. 6 f. *ridan·7 auerian·7 lade lædan.* The same list of duties occurs in the same order in the *Rectitudines,* cap. 2 and suggests some relationship between the two documents. The indebtedness seems most likely to be on the side of the present one, as there is no reference in the *Rectitudines* to any of the special local conditions characteristic of Tidenham, particularly the duties connected with fishing. It is possible, as Liebermann suggests, that the writer was the same in both cases.

NOTES

l. 7. *Se gebur.* The duties of the *gebur* are set out in detail in the *Rectitudines,* caps. 4-4, 2.

l. 8. *erian healfne æcer.* The *gebur* of the *Rectitudines* had to plough 1 acre every week.

ll. 8 f. *7 ræcan sylf* etc. The same expression is used in the *Rectitudines,* cap. 4, 1 *b.* Liebermann (I, p. 447; III, p. 249) takes *ræcan* as the opposite of *gebringan* and translates the passage 'das Saatkorn selbst in des Herrn Scheune erholen'.

l. 9. *gehalne.* Liebermann, I, p. 446, note (*b*), following Birch, reads *ge halne* and emends the second word to *halue* which he takes as the M.E. form of A.S. *healfne.* The MS., however, has *gehalne* which is perfectly comprehensible as it stands, see B.T., *Suppl.* p. 337, s.v. *gehal.*

to cyrcscette. There is no mention of church dues in connection with the *gebur* of the *Rectitudines.* A tenant of the Bishop of Worcester had to undertake to plough 2 acres every year *7 þæron his circsceat gesawe 7 þæt eft geripe 7 in gebringe* (see p. 64, ll. 17 f.).

sahweþere. For *swa hwæðere,* see B.T., *Suppl.* p. 577, s.v. *hwæþer,* v *a.*

l. 10. *mæra.* This word does not occur elsewhere, see B.T., *Suppl.* p. 628, s.v. Seebohm takes it to mean 'large rods', as both long and short rods are required to construct the basket weirs used for catching salmon in the Wye and the Severn.

l. 11. .VIII. *geocu byld* etc. Both the construction and the meaning are difficult to understand. Seebohm (p. 154) translates it 'build eight yokes and wattle three ebbs', and explains the latter by the necessity of providing three fences to correspond to the heights of the spring, middle and neap tides. In spite of the punctuation (which is frequently astray) I am inclined to take *tyne* with what follows and have translated it accordingly. I have taken *byld* as a mistake for *bylde* (pres. subj.) parallel to *tyne* etc.

æcertyninge, cf. the *gauoltininga* demanded from the peasants at Hurstbourne Priors (l. 27 below). For the importance of fencing see Ine, 40; 42.

l. 12. *tyne · 7 dicie .1. gyrde burhheges.* Among the duties of the *geneat* in the *Rectitudines* are included *bytlian 7 burh hegegian.* There is no mention of any such obligation in the case of the *gebur.* I have taken *tyne* as a verb (Seebohm's *fiftyne* is not the reading of the MS.) and have connected it with what follows. The very small amount of *burhhege* for which the *gebur* was responsible is more comprehensible if the care both of the fence and the ditch is attributed to him. There is, besides, no other instance in the document of a number such as 'fifteen' written in the form v *tyne.* The hardness of the work involved might account for the small quantity of digging required as compared with the amount of fencing.

l. 13. *ripe oðer healfne æcer · mawe healfne.* It is stated in the *Rectitudines* that the *gebur* was obliged on some estates to give three days as 'week-work' during harvest. There is no special mention of mowing,

454 NOTES

but he might have to give two days' work every week throughout the year. The peasants at Hurstbourne Priors had also to mow half an acre, see 1. 24 below.

l. 14. .VI. *penneg ofer Estre*. The only Easter payment specified in the *Rectitudines* in the case of the *gebur* is a young sheep or twopence.

l. 15. *healfne sester hunies*, cf. the *Rectitudines*, cap. 4, 5: *on sumen landa gebur sceal syllan huniggafol.*
to hlafmæssan. 1 August.

ll. 15 f. .VI. *systres mealtes* etc. The food-rent due at Martinmas from the *gebur* is given in the *Rectitudines*, cap. 4, 1, as 23 sesters of beer and 2 hens.

l. 17. .VII. *swyn* etc. According to D.B. the common rate of payment by the villein in Sussex for the pasturage of swine was one in seven (see V.C.H. *Sussex*, 1, p. 365). A similar arrangement is found on certain estates in Surrey along with the surrender of every tenth pig elsewhere (see V.C.H. *Surrey*, 1, p. 291).

l. 18. *mæstenrædene*. Payments in swine for mast are generally distinguished in D.B. from payments for pasture (see V.C.H. *Surrey, loc. cit.*). The *gebur* of the *Rectitudines* had to give 6 loaves to the *inswan* (the herdsman in charge of the swine belonging to the demesne) when he drove his herd to feed on mast.

CX

MS. British Museum, Additional MS. 15350, f. 70 (or f. 72 by the new numbering). See p. 274.

EDITIONS. K. 977.
B. 594.

DATE. This account of the dues rendered at Hurstbourne Priors is incorporated in a charter of Edward the Elder dated 900, but is generally attributed to the eleventh century from its resemblance to the *Rectitudines* and the description of the manor of Tidenham (see No. CIX).

l. 19. *þa gerihta*. This term includes both payments in money or in kind and services.

ða ceorlas. The term *ceorl* here as elsewhere, e.g. Ine, 40, 42, Alfred and Guthrum, 2, denotes (without taking account of distinctions) the free but dependent tenant on an estate who owes both rent and services to the lord of the manor. The term 'peasant', though unsatisfactory, seems to be the nearest modern equivalent.

l. 20. *Hysseburnan*. Hurstbourne Priors, Hampshire. In 1086 this estate (which was held by the Bishop of Winchester) had land for 51 ploughs. In the demesne there were 4 ploughs, and there were 55 *villani* and 38 *bordarii* with 45 ploughs (D.B. I, f. 41; V.C.H. *Hants*. I, p. 465). These may be regarded as the successors of the *ceorlas* of the present document.

NOTES 455

æt hilcan hiwisce feorwerti penega. The word *hiwisc*, 'family, household', is related to the word *hid*, 'hide', and is frequently used interchangeably with it, cf. *Norðleoda laga*, 7 where the expression *hiwisc landes* corresponds to the *hide landes* of Ine, 32; B. 879, where grants of *unam mansam* are followed by the boundaries *þæs hiwisces*; B. 470, 691, where the *þrid half heyweshe* of the one and the *oþer half hewisse* of the other, at specified places, clearly refer to estates of 2½ hides and 1½ hides respectively.

In the present case it would seem from the rate of the money payment that the term *hiwisc* has the same meaning. Forty pence is a comparatively large sum but it is exactly four times the amount demanded from the *gebur* of the *Rectitudines* (cap. 4, 1) whose holding was apparently a yardland (cap. 4, 3). The unit of assessment, therefore, here as elsewhere, is the hide.

ll. 20 f. *tó herfestes emnihte.* 24 September, cf. p. 28, l. 4 and B. 599 (two Winchester grants). In the *Rectitudines* the date fixed for the payment of his *gafolþ*[9] by the *gebur* is Michaelmas, i.e. 29 September. The autumn equinox was probably identified with Michaelmas for practical purposes.

l. 21. VI. *ciricmittan eálað.* This compound does not seem to appear elsewhere but may be compared with *chircheambre* which is given as an alternative name for *chirchesed* (A.S. *ciricsceatt*) in the Peterborough Register (Society of Antiquaries of London, MS. 60, f. 228 *b*) and quoted by Kemble, *Saxons in England*, II, p. 493, n. 2. For the capacity of the *mitta* see p. 272.

ll. 21 f. III. *sesðlar hlafhwetes.* Probably three sesters are meant, see p. 272.

ll. 22 f. III. *æceras géerian* etc., cf. the *Rectitudines*, cap. 4, 2, where the same regulation applies to the *gebur*. The land so ploughed is described as *gauolyrðe*.

l. 24. *ðreo púnd gauolbærer.* This seems a very small quantity, especially when compared with the amount of *beregafol* prescribed by Ine, 59, 1, namely 6 weys (*wæga/pundwæga*) for every labourer. Liebermann suggests, therefore, that *pund* in this case and in the *Rectitudines*, cap. 8 f., where the (? yearly) allowance of grain for an *esne* and a female slave is given as XII *pund godes cornes* in the one case and VIII *pund cornes* in the other, is equivalent to *pundwæg* (see *Gesetze*, II, p. 473, s.v. *Gewicht*, 2–2 *c*; III, p. 79). It is possible, since considerable variety was certainly found in the Anglo-Saxon period with regard to measures of weight, that the *pundwæg* may represent one kind of *wæg* (i.e. wey), but it is difficult to understand the use of *pund* alone with this sense in view of the ambiguity involved. I have therefore retained the translation 'pound'.

heafne æcer gauolmæde. The tenants on the manor of Tidenham had also to mow half an acre, see l. 13 above.

l. 27. XVI. *gyrda gauoltininga.* This corresponds to the *æcertyninge* .XV. *gyrda* at Tidenham, see ll. 11 f. above.

to easran, cf. the *Rectitudines*, cap. 4, 1: *on Eastran an geong sceap oððe* II *p*.

l. 30. *ælce wucan wircen*. The amount of work demanded from the *gebur* is specified in the *Rectitudines*, cap. 4: *on sumen lande is þæt he sceal wyrcan to wicweorce II dagas swilc weorc swilc him man tæcð ofer geares fyrst ælcre wucan* 7 *on hærfest* III *dagas to wicweorce* 7 *of Candelmæsse oð Eastran* III. The demands made on the tenants at Hurstbourne Priors were less onerous than these. The compiler of the *Rectitudines* frequently insists that customs vary in different parts of the country and on different estates.

butan ðrim, cf. Alfred, 43, where a more generous allowance of holidays for 'all free men' is made, namely 37 days altogether in the year.

ll. 30 f. *to middan wintra*, i.e. at Christmas.

l. 31. *to ganddagan*, for *gang-*. Rogation Days are the three days before Ascension Day.

CXI

MS. This document was included in the Somers Collection, see p. 266.

EDITIONS. Smith, *Beda: Historiæ Ecclesiasticæ* etc., Appendix, p. 782. K. 804, from Smith.

DATE. Not earlier than 1046 or later than 1053, and probably about 1051–1052, see notes on Bishop Ealdred and Earl Odda.

p. 208, l. 1. *Ealdred b.* Ealdred, who was first a monk at Winchester then Abbot of Tavistock (Fl. Wig.), succeeded Lyfing as Bishop of Worcester in 1046 and in 1056 became Bishop of Hereford as well. In 1060, on his appointment as Archbishop of York, he resigned Hereford, and two years later was replaced at Worcester. He died in 1069.

l. 3. *Dicford*. Ditchford in the manor of Blockley, Worcestershire, which was held by the Bishop of Worcester.

l. 7. *ænigne frambyge don*. For *frambyge* see B.T., *Suppl*. p. 262, s.v., where only one other instance of its use is recorded. One example of the corresponding verb *frambugan* is given in B.T. p. 330, s.v.

ll. 9 f. *Leofric eorl*. Earl of Mercia, see pp. 412 f.

l. 10. *Odda eorl*. Odda signs as *minister* from 1014 (K. 1309) to 1045 (K. 781). His name occurs four times between 1038 and 1043 with the title *miles* (E. p. 239, K. 760, 764, 767) and twice in charters of 1049 and 1050 respectively with that of *nobilis* (K. 787, 791). In 1051 after the exile of Earl Godwine he was made Earl of Devon, Somerset, Dorset and Cornwall (Sax. Chr. 1048 E for 1051) and it is possible that he held office as Earl of Worcestershire (and perhaps Gloucestershire) for some time after Earl Godwine's reinstatement in 1052 (see Freeman, *Norman Conquest*, 3rd ed. II, pp. 581 f.). His name occurs with the title *eorl* or *dux* in three charters only, including the present one, and all of them are grants made by Ealdred, Bishop of Worcester.

One of these (K. 805), as well as the present one, probably belongs to the period of Earl Godwine's exile, as neither he nor any of his sons appears as a witness; the other[1] is apparently later in date, as Odda signs along with Harold *dux* and Raulf *dux*, and must be attributed at the earliest to the year 1053. It is noteworthy that the signature Ælfric *minister* is also attached to it; if it is that of Odda's brother, the charter must fall between the date of Earl Godwine's death (15 April 1053) and Ælfric's (22 December). In another of Ealdred's charters Odda is named as a witness along with his brother but without any title (see p. 210, l. 5).

Before his death which took place on 31 August 1056 (Sax. Chr. C, D; Fl. Wig.) Odda became a monk, and the signatures Odda *monachus* and Ælfric *monachus* actually occur in an undated charter (K. 797) preserved in a twelfth-century register of the Abbey of Evesham (Cotton Vespasian B. xxiv). Unfortunately this charter cannot be accepted as it stands. One of the witnesses is Ælfric, Archbishop of York, who died on 22 January 1051; and it is certain that Odda had not become a monk at such an early date. It is more than likely that *miñ* (i.e. *minister*) has been misread by the copyist as *moñ* (i.e. *monachus*) in the case of Odda and Ælfric (and possibly also of Ælfstan who precedes them in the list). These three names are the last on the list and come immediately after those of Æthelwine *decanus* and three of the monks of Worcester, so that such a mistake might easily have occurred. It is not recorded that Ælfric ever became a monk, but it is noteworthy that, like Odda, he died at Deerhurst, and he may possibly have been a member of the community there.

Odda is specially associated with Deerhurst and Pershore. At Deerhurst he built a chapel in memory of his brother, and both the building itself and an inscribed stone recording its dedication by Bishop Ealdred on 12 April 1056 are still extant (see Baldwin Brown, *The Arts in Early England*, 2nd ed. II, pp. 307 f.). He himself died at Deerhurst (Fl. Wig.) but like his brother was buried at Pershore. In 1259 his coffin was discovered and its inscription recorded in the annals of the monastery (see Leland, *Collectanea*, I, p. 244). He is there described as Odda *dux quondam priscis temporibus Ædwinus vocatus in baptismo* and Fl. Wig. also attributes to him another name, viz. *Agelwinus*, i.e. Æthelwine. The reasons either for his change or for his choice of name are unknown, but a parallel is found in the case of his contemporary, Manni, Abbot of Evesham, who is described as *Wlmarus* (i.e. Wulfmær) *qui et Manni* (Fl. Wig. s.a. 1044).

Another problem suggested by the *Annals of Pershore* is Odda's connection with the wicked Earl *Delfer*, i.e. Ælfhere of Mercia. He is stated there to have been Ælfhere's heir and to have restored to the abbey all that the latter had wrongfully taken away from it. The statement that he was Ælfhere's son (Leland, *Itinerary*, V, p. 2) can scarcely

---

[1] Bond, *Facsimiles of Ancient Charters* etc., Part IV, No. 32.

be accepted as Ælfhere died in 983. It is possible, however, that he may have been his grandson. Nothing is known of Ælfhere's descendants, unless the Godwine of Ælfheah's will is to be regarded as his son rather than the latter's (see Whitelock, p. 22). It is noteworthy that Fl. Wig. calls Ælfhere *regis Anglorum Eadgari propinquus* (s.a. 983), while William of Malmesbury describes Odda and Ralph of Hereford as *comites et regis cognati* (*Gesta Regum*, R.S. 1, p. 243). I have not been able, however, to find any definite proofs of the relationship between Ælfhere and Odda.

All the authorities quoted (Sax. Chr., Fl. Wig., etc.) speak of Odda in terms of the highest praise. The *Annals of Pershore* record of him that he took a vow of celibacy in order that no heir of his should ever again deprive the abbey of its possessions. Edith, 'the sister of Earl Odo' (i.e. Odda), is entered in D.B. as the former tenant of an estate at Leadon in Bishop's Frome, Herefordshire (D.B. 1, f. 186; V.C.H. *Hereford*, 1, p. 337), while Odda himself appears as the former holder of the manor of Longdon (D.B. 1, f. 180 b; V.C.H. 1, p. 317).

ll. 10 f. *Berhtric Ælfgares sunu.* D.B. shows that in 1066 Brihtric Ælfgar's son was a landowner in Dorset, Devon, Gloucestershire and Worcestershire. In 1086 most of his lands were in the possession of Queen Matilda. According to legend he had refused the offer of her hand in earlier days, hence her revenge (see Freeman, *Norman Conquest*, 2nd ed. IV, pp. 165, 761–764).

l. 11. *Owine.* For the appearance of this witness elsewhere see p. 210, l. 6, K. 805, 912, 956.

Wagan. The name is of Scandinavian origin, cf. O.Danish *Vagn*. The present witness signs two other charters of Ealdred (see p. 210, l. 6; K. 805) and is probably identical with the Wagan who heads the list of *barones Leofrici comitis* in the post-Conquest version of a deed relating to St Albans (K. 950). A *Wagene de Wotton* (see D.B. 1, f. 170) appears as a witness in a charter of Earl Leofric relating to Coventry (K. 939) and is possibly the same man. The connection of the Scandinavian names Wagen and Atsur (see below) with Worcestershire is discussed by Napier and Stevenson, *Crawford Charters*, p. 144.

Aeglric etc. Æthelric was the brother of Brihtheah, Bishop of Worcester (see p. 421) from whom, according to Hemming, he received certain church lands at Wolverton and Whittington, Himbleton and Spetchley (Hearne, 1, p. 266). Later he was deprived of all of them by William, Earl of Hereford.

ll. 11 f. *Ceolmær.* Ceolmar witnesses two other charters of Ealdred, see p. 210, l. 7; E. p. 248. He is perhaps identical with the *Celmar* who had held the manor of Doddenham in the time of King Edward 'and could betake himself where he would' (D.B. 1, f. 176 b; V.C.H. *Worc.* 1, p. 314).

l. 12. *Atsur*, cf. O.Norse *Qzurr*. His signature is attached to half a dozen Worcester charters between 1042 (K. 764) and about 1062 (K. 823). It is possible, though not certain, that the *Asserus filius*

NOTES

Tolrii (? Toki) of K. 950 is the same person. Hemming (Hearne, I, p. 269) states that Bishop Brihtheah gave 5 hides at Bengeworth to *Atsere*, his kinsman and chamberlain, from whom they were seized by Urse the sheriff. In D.B. *Azor* is entered as a former tenant of the church of Worcester at Bengeworth, Redmarley d'Abitot and Churchill near Bredicot (V.C.H. *Worc.* I, pp. 297, 291, 295), while he appears also as a tenant of the Abbey of Pershore at Pershore and Comberton (*ibid.*, p. 304). Particulars are given of the terms on which he held the estate at Pershore, and it is stated further that after his wife's death, which took place after the Conquest, he became an outlaw.

Esebearn. Esbearn is another name of Scandinavian origin, cf. O.Danish *Esbern*. The signature *Esbern miles* first appears in 1043 (K. 767) while a charter of 1045–1046 is signed by Ordgar and his two brothers Ælfgar and *Escbern* (see p. 200, l. 22). In King Edward's charter granted to Waltham Abbey in 1062 (K. 813) occurs the signature *Esbernus princeps*. For Esbearn Bigga see p. 436.

Ordwig. Ordwig witnesses three other Worcester charters, see p. 210, l. 7 and K. 807, 823. He is probably to be identified with the Ordwig *minister...vir...magna largitate et laudabili probitate* who had held Acton Beauchamp of the church of Worcester but restored it before his death to Wulfstan II who was then prior (Hearne, I, p. 250). The estate, Hemming records, was afterwards seized by Æthelwig, Abbot of Evesham, only to fall into the clutches of Urse the sheriff. The monks of Evesham gave a different account of its history (*Chronicon Abbatiæ de Evesham*, R.S. p. 95).

Aeþestan fætta. See p. 460.

l. 13. *Aelfward æt Langadune*. According to D.B. 18 of the 30 hides which formed the manor of Longdon were held in the time of King Edward by nine freemen of whom one was *Elward* (D.B. 1, f. 174 *b*; V.C.H. *Worc.* I, pp. 300 f.). Longdon is entered elsewhere as Earl Odda's (see p. 458). In 1086 it was in the possession of Westminster Abbey to which it had been given by the king along with his manor of Pershore.

l. 14. *denisce* 7 *englisce*. The order is noteworthy.

ll. 14 f. *hredde he* etc. The verb *hreddan*, 'to redeem', seems to be used here in the same way as *werian*, 'to defend', is used elsewhere, see p. 460. The word *landhredding* occurs in a mortgage of about 1018 where from the context it appears that the redemption of the land in question took the form of a money payment (see Napier and Stevenson, *Crawford Charters*, pp. 9, 76). There is nothing in the present grant to show whether money or service is meant.

l. 15. *for are*. See p. 362.

to cinges banne. A list of the services due by a thegn on behalf of his lord at such a summons is given in the *Rectitudines*, cap. 1, 1: ...*swilce is deorhege to cyniges hame* 7 *scorp to friðscipe* 7 *sæweard* 7 *heafodweard* 7 *fyrdweard, ælmesfeoh* 7 *cyricsceat* 7 *mænige oðere mistlice ðingc*.

CXII

MS. British Museum, Harley 4660, f. 10. See p. 263.
EDITIONS. Hickes, *Thesaurus*, I, p. 142.
K. 923.
The text is from Hickes.
DATE. It is possible that this grant also belongs to the years 1051–1052, see under Odda below.

l. 17. *Ealdred .b.* See p. 456.
Æpestane fættan. He witnesses the preceding charter but does not seem to appear elsewhere.

ll. 18 f. *mid þam hrofleasan lande.* No other instance is recorded of the use of the adj. *hrofleas* in the sense which seems to be required here, i.e. 'land with no houses upon it' (see B.T., *Suppl.* p. 568, s.v.). Perhaps a part of the moor or swampy ground adjoining Hill is meant.

l. 19. *he hig eac wérige for twa hida,* i.e. the amount of his holding was assessed at 2 hides for the purpose of answering the claims upon it, cf. the *Rectitudines*, cap. 3, 4: *werige se cotsetla his hlafordes inland, gif him man beode æt sæwearde 7 æt cyniges deorhege 7 æt swilcan ðingan swilc his mæð sy,* also II Cnut, 79: *se ðe land gewerod hæbbe on scypfyrde 7 on landfyrde...habbe he hit unbesaken* etc. Other examples of the use of *werian for* in this connection are quoted in B.T. p. 1207, s.v. III c, and to these may be added *Osferð bohte .v. hida landes...on ða gerad ðæt he werað hi for .*II. (K. 797).

l. 22. *Hylle.* Hill near Fladbury, Worcestershire (see Pl.N. *Worc.* p. 135).

p. 210, l. 3. *Manni abb.* Manni was Abbot of Evesham from 1044 to 1058 or 1059 when he resigned because of paralysis. He died in 1066 (*Chronicon Abbatiæ de Evesham,* R.S. pp. 87 f.).

l. 4. *Ælfric abb.* Ælfric may have succeeded Brihtheah as Abbot of Pershore (see p. 421), as the signature Ælfric *abbas* occurs in a charter of 1033 (K. 1318) and again in 1035 (K. 1322). His signature continues, generally along with that of Manni, Abbot of Evesham, until about 1055 (e.g. K. 807, 912, 939).

l. 5. *Leofric eorl.* Earl of Mercia, see pp. 412 f.
Odda. See pp. 456 ff. The title *eorl* may have been omitted by accident. The fact that Earl Godwine does not sign suggests that the charter belongs to the period of his exile, 1051–1052.
Ælfric his broþor. See p. 457.

l. 6. *Æglric þæs .b. broþer.* See p. 458.
ll. 6 f. *Owine...Ordwig.* See pp. 458 f.
ll. 7 f. *Ælfric æt Cumbrintune.* In 1086 Comberton was held by

NOTES

Gilbert Fitz Turold. The previous tenant is said to have been *Edric* (D.B. I, f. 175; V.C.H. *Worc.* I, p. 303).

l. 8. *Godric finc*. Godric Finch, according to Hemming, had been the holder of 7 hides at Charlton. On his death the estate was due to revert to the church of Worcester, as the lease had now run for three lives. Bishop Wulfstan by means of a *calicem aureum magni pretii* obtained the king's support for his claim, but was ultimately despoiled of the estate by Robert the Despencer, the brother of Urse the sheriff (Hearne, I, pp. 268 f.; V.C.H. *Worc.* I, p. 296, n. 8).

Berhtwine. This is perhaps the *Brihtwinus predives* who figures in the cartulary (Hearne, I, p. 263) as the donor of Hadzor to the church of Worcester when his grandson Edwin became a monk there. The gift was confirmed by Edwin's father, Brihtmær, but according to Hemming the manor was seized after the Conquest by William, Earl of Hereford, and given to Gilbert Fitz Turold, an officer of his (cf. D.B. I, f. 177; V.C.H. *Worc.* I, p. 315). Brihtwine signs two other charters of Ealdred (E. p. 247, K. 823).

Cola. See p. 446.

CXIII

MS. British Museum, Cotton Tiberius A. XIII, f. 180 (or 183 by the later numbering). See p. 259.

EDITIONS. Hearne, *Hemingi Chartularium* etc. II, p. 408. K. 766.

DATE. According to Hemming the two estates of Wolverley and Blackwell were restored to Worcester by Earl Leofric while Wulfstan II was prior (Hearne, II, p. 404). Wulfstan's predecessor Æthelwine signs a charter of 1052-1053 (K. 807), so that the gift cannot be earlier in date. On the other hand it cannot be later than 1057, the year of Earl Leofric's death.

l. 21. *Wulfweardiglea...Blaca'wyllan'*. The two estates of Wolverley and Blackwell, Worcestershire, are said to have been taken from the monastery by *Denicemen 7 wiðerwearde deman*, rendered *Dani ceterique Dei adversarii* in the Latin version of the same document (Hearne, II, pp. 404, 406). Earl Leofric is alleged, moreover, to have held them unjustly for a long time (Hearne, I, p. 261). He retained certain other estates which the church of Worcester claimed, under promise to restore them at his death, but the grant was extended to his widow Godgifu. Thereafter they were seized along with her other possessions by Edwin and Morcar (her grandsons) *ad sui (ut postmodum patuit) non solum confusionem verum etiam ad honoris, in quo diu fuerant, celerem amissionem, nam alter eorum Edwinus videlicet a suis peremptus, alter vero in captivitate mortuus est* (Hearne, I, p. 262). This is one of the many cases of divine retribution which Hemming takes particular delight in recording.

ll. 26 f. *hæbbe he...Godes curs*. This recalls the rhymed curse said to have been pronounced against Urse the sheriff by Bishop Ealdred of Worcester: *Hattest þu Urs, haue þu Godes kurs* (William of Malmesbury, *Gesta Pontificum*, R.S. p. 253).

CXIV

MS. British Museum, Additional MS. 15350, f. 98 b. See p. 274.
EDITIONS. K. 1337.
T. p. 586.
B. 980.
DATE. Probably about 1053.

p. 212, l. 2. *Heilincigæ*. Hayling Island. This estate, along with eight others, was said to have been given to the Old Minster by Queen Ælfgifu Emma after she had safely passed through the trial by ordeal in answer to the charge that they were lovers brought against her and Bishop Ælfwine of Winchester (see *Historia Major Wintoniensis* in *Anglia Sacra*, I, pp. 233-235). The whole story is of late date and very doubtful authenticity. In 1086 the manor was held by the Abbey of Jumièges near Caen in succession to Wulfweard the White who is said to have held it of Queen Edith. The monks of St Swithin (i.e. the Old Minster), however, claimed it as their right, asserting, on the lines of this charter, that it had been given to them by Queen Ælfgifu Emma with seisin of one half and reversion of the other on the death of Wulfweard to whom it had been granted for life (see D.B. I, f. 43 b; V.C.H. *Hants.* I, p. 473). Wulfweard died in the time of King William who thereupon granted the manor to the Abbey of Jumièges (see Round, *Calendar of Documents preserved in France*, I, p. 526). Sometime after the Domesday evidence had been adduced, however, the king acknowledged the claim of the monks and confirmed Queen Emma's gift on their behalf (see B.M., Additional MS. 29436, f. 11 b; *E.H.R.* 1920, pp. 388 f.). Henry I regranted Hayling Island to the Abbey of Jumièges and the matter was not finally settled until later in the twelfth century (1139-1142) when the bishop and monks of Winchester, at the request of Pope Innocent, resigned all claims upon 'a portion of Hayling Island which the church of Jumièges had long possessed' (see Round, *op. cit.* p. 55).

There is nothing in D.B. to show that the monks of Winchester produced any documentary evidence in support of their claim to Hayling Island. It is said, however, to have been attested by *Elsi* (i.e. Æthelsige), Abbot of Ramsey, and by the whole hundred.

l. 3. *Wulfweardæ hwitan*. Wulfweard the White, according to D.B., held lands in Kent, Middlesex, Buckinghamshire, Oxfordshire, Gloucestershire, Wiltshire, Hampshire, Somerset, Dorset and probably

NOTES

Berkshire and Lincolnshire (see V.C.H. *Somerset*, I, p. 399). He seems to have had some special connection with Queen Edith and continued to hold his lands after the Conquest.

l. 7. *sæ bisceop Stigandæ*. Wulfweard's request was obviously made after Ælfgifu Emma's death (6 March 1052). Stigand succeeded Robert Champart as Archbishop of Canterbury when the latter was deprived of his see in 1052, but did not receive his pallium until 1058, and his position seems to have been generally regarded as irregular (see Sax. Chr. 1053 C; Freeman, *Norman Conquest*, 3rd ed. II, pp. 652–655). He appears as a witness to a grant of 1053 (K. 798) with the title *episcopus*, and it is probable that the present document belongs to the same year. His signature with the title archbishop seems to appear for the first time in a dated charter in 1059 (E. p. 300; the date 1055 attached to K. 801 cannot be accepted as Ealdred, who also signs as archbishop, did not succeed to the see of York until 1060). He is addressed as archbishop, however, in several royal writs which cannot be exactly dated but might be earlier than 1058, and is similarly described in a document which seems to belong to the period 1053–1055 (see p. 214, l. 22).

l. 15. *Harold eorl.* Harold, the second son of Earl Godwine, seems to have become Earl of East Anglia in 1045. He signs an Exeter charter of 1044 with the title *nobilis* (*Journal of the British Archaeological Association*, XXXIX, 1883, p. 294) and two of 1045 as *minister* (K. 776, 780, which were apparently issued at the same time as both record grants of land to Bishop Ælfwine of Winchester and have identical lists of witnesses), while his name with the title *dux* also appears for the first time in a dated and authentic charter of the same year (K. 781, a Winchester charter, the original of which is preserved). Two earlier charters of the years 1043 (K. 916) and 1044 (K. 771) respectively, where his name appears with the title *dux*, are both highly suspicious, and so too is K. 748 (a Crowland charter dated 1032) where he makes his first appearance as a witness (*Haroldus filius Godwini comitis*). He was banished along with his father and brothers in 1051 and restored along with them in the following year. In 1053 he succeeded his father as Earl of Wessex.

ll. 15 f. *Ælfwine aƀƀ*. See p. 437.

ll. 16 f. *Leofing stæallære* etc. The same three witness a charter of about the same date (see p. 214, ll. 29 f.). Lyfing's signature does not occur again.

l. 17. *Raulf stæallære.* Ralph the Staller had a son of the same name. The elder Ralph, according to the Saxon Chronicle 1075 E, 1076 D, was born in Norfolk, and his son 'for that reason' (D) was given the earldom of Norfolk and Suffolk by William I. It seems that his father had held this position before him, as four writs in favour of Bury St Edmunds, issued by William I soon after the Conquest, are addressed to Earl Ralph along with the Bishop of Elmham (Davis, *Regesta Regum Anglo-Normannorum*, I, Nos. 40–43). He is referred to also as *Comes R. vetus* in two Norfolk entries in D.B. II, ff. 128 *b*, 129, but appears frequently elsewhere with his English title of *stalra*. It is proved by a charter granted by the Conqueror to the Abbey of St Riquier in Ponthieu (see H. M. Cam, *E.H.R.* xxxi, 1916, p. 443) that he was alive in February 1068, while an entry in D.B. II, f. 194 (see V.C.H. *Norfolk*, II, p. 116) seems to show that he had died before Bishop Æthelmær of Elmham was deposed in 1070. His signature with the title *minister, steallere, regis dapifer, regis aulicus* is found from 1050 (K. 791) onwards. His son Ralph, Earl of East Anglia, forfeited his estates as the result of his share in the rising of 1075.

Æscar steallære. The estates formerly held by Esgar *steallere* in Berkshire, Middlesex, Hertfordshire, Oxfordshire, Northamptonshire, Warwickshire, Essex and Suffolk were given by the Conqueror to Geoffrey de Mandeville (see V.C.H. *Essex*, I, p. 343). He attests charters throughout the reign of Edward the Confessor, sometimes as *minister*, once as *regiae procurator aulae* (K. 813) and once as *regis dapifer* (K. 808). He is said to have been the grandson of Tofi the Proud (see p. 400).

l. 18. *Wulfric æt Wernæforda.* Wulfric (*Ulvric*) is mentioned in D.B. as the holder along with *Olward* of the manor of Warnford in parage of King Edward (D.B. I, f. 45; V.C.H. *Hants.* I, p. 481). It was assessed at 4 hides and there were 2 halls. Another manor of Warnford belonged to the Abbey of Hyde (D.B. I, f. 43; V.C.H. I, p. 471). In 1086 they were both held by Hugh de Port.

Ælfwine. The name *Alwin* occurs frequently in the D.B. survey of Hampshire, and it is possible, though not certain as the name is a common one, that the same man is meant in each case. He is entered twice as a tenant of the Bishop of Winchester (D.B. I, ff. 40, 41 *b*; V.C.H. *Hants.* I, pp. 460, 465) and elsewhere appears as a tenant of King Edward. In the section relating to the land held by the king's thegns occurs an entry to the effect that *Alwin* held a certain estate of the king in 1086 which his father *Ulviet* had held (D.B. I, f. 50 *b*; V.C.H. *Hants.* I, p. 509).

l. 19. *Ælfweard.* The name *Alward* also occurs fairly often in the Domesday survey of Hampshire, and again there is nothing to show whether the entries refer to the same man or not. The name is found among the tenants of the New Minster, King Edward and Earl Godwine.

Cupping. There is a manor called Kippings (fourteenth century *Cuppyngs*) in the parish of Church Oakley which was held at the beginning of the reign of Henry III by Nicholas Kipping, see V.C.H. *Hants.* IV, p. 226. Can there be any connection between the A.S. name Cupping and this later surname?

CXV

MSS. (a) The Eynsham Cartulary in the possession of the Dean and Chapter of Christ Church, Oxford, f. 9 b. It was begun in the last years of the twelfth century.
(b) British Museum, Cotton Vespasian B. xv, f. 6 (or f. 8 by the new numbering). This MS. contains late copies of documents from various sources.
(c) British Museum, Harley 258, f. 3. This MS. contains copies of documents from various sources made in the seventeenth century.

EDITIONS. Dugdale, III, p. 13, from (a).
K. 956, from (b) and (c).
T. p. 370, from (b) and (c).
H. E. Salter, *The Cartulary of the Abbey of Eynsham*, I, p. 28, with a translation p. 29.
The text is from (a).

DATE. Between 1053 and 1055, i.e. after the appointment of Leofwine to the see of Lichfield (see below) but before the death of Earl Siweard (see p. 434).

l. 24. *Wlwig .b.* Wulfwig was Bishop of Dorchester from 1053 to 1067.
Leofric eorl. Earl of Mercia, see pp. 412 f.
Godgife þæs eorles wif. Godgifu is generally associated with Leofric in his endowments and benefactions, cf. p. 210, ll. 15 f. (Worcester), K. 938 (Evesham), Fl. Wig. s.a. 1057 (Coventry etc.). She survived her husband but the date of her death is not recorded. By the time of Henry of Huntingdon (R.S. s.a. 1057) her fame had entirely eclipsed his.
l. 25. *Sĉe MARIAN stowe.* Stow St Mary was a foundation of secular canons established early in the eleventh century. It seems to have come to an end in 1066 but was revived by Remigius, who transferred the see of Dorchester to Lincoln and likewise removed his refounded monastery of Eynsham to Stow. It was finally constituted in 1091 but the succeeding bishop, Robert Bloet, moved the monks back to Eynsham and attached Stow and its endowments to the see of Lincoln.
p. 214, ll. 2 f. *þæt him þærto fylstan wolde.* See B.T., *Suppl.* s.v. *fylstan* (3).
l. 4. *þeowdom.* Here used in the sense of divine service, cf. I Cnut, 3, 2.
l. 5. *þa land.* These are given as Newark and Fledborough in Nottinghamshire, Brampton and Marton in Lincolnshire (see K. 818).
l. 7. *into his feorme*, i.e. as food-rent or payment in kind.
ll. 7 f. *Æðeric .b. 7 Æðnoð .b.* Æthelric was Bishop of Dorchester from 1016 to 1034, Eadnoth (the second of the name) from 1034 to 1049. If Roger of Hoveden (R.S. I, p. 103) is correct, therefore, in

assigning the foundation of Stow St Mary to a bishop called Eadnoth, the reference must be to the first of the name who preceded Æthelric and died in 1016.

ll. 9 f. *þa twegen deles* etc. Remigius received the manor of Sleaford *pro commutatione altaris de Stou*, i.e. in place of his share of the offerings made to the abbey (see Salter, *op. cit.* I, p. 32, No. 3).

ll. 12 f. *ðære ærre · Sc̄e Maria mæssan* etc. The festivals of the Virgin celebrated by the Anglo-Saxon church were the Purification (2 February), the Annunciation (25 March), the Assumption (15 August) and the Nativity (8 September). The Feast of the Immaculate Conception (8 December) is said to have been introduced by Anselm in 1068. The earlier and later festivals mentioned here are probably those of 15 August and 8 September, when offerings would be more plentiful than at the two winter festivals. The phrase *betwyx þam twam sc̄a Marian mæssan* is used in the Saxon Chronicle, 1069 E, with reference to the period between the Assumption and the Nativity.

l. 22. *Eadgyðe his gebeddan*. Edith was the daughter of Earl Godwine and was married to Edward the Confessor in 1045.

Stigandes arceƀes. See p. 463.

ll. 22 f. *Kynsiges arceƀes*. Cynesige, described as *regis capellanus* (Fl. Wig.), was appointed Archbishop of York in 1051 (Fl. Wig.) but did not receive his pallium until 1055 (Sax. Chr. D). He died in 1060.

l. 23. *Heremannes ƀes*. Hereman, a chaplain of the king (described as *de Lotharingia oriundus* by Fl. Wig. and as *natione Flandrensi* by William of Malmesbury, *Gesta Pontificum*, R.S. p. 182), became Bishop of Ramsbury in 1045. In 1055 he resigned and left England, but three years later he returned and was made Bishop of Sherborne in addition to Ramsbury. In 1075 he transferred the see of Sherborne to Old Sarum. He died in 1078.

Dodika · ƀes. Bishop of Wells, see p. 434.

ll. 23 f. *Leofrices · ƀes*. Leofric was made Bishop of Crediton in 1046. In 1050 he moved the see to Exeter (see p. 474).

l. 24. *Ealdredes · ƀes*. Bishop of Worcester, see p. 456.

Heka · ƀes. Heca, described as *regis capellanus* by Fl. Wig., succeeded Grimketel as Bishop of Selsey in 1047 and died in 1057.

ll. 24 f. *Ægelmæres · ƀes*. Bishop of Elmham and the brother of Archbishop Stigand, see p. 431.

l. 25. *Alfwoldes · ƀes*. Bishop of Sherborne, see p. 447.

Willelmes · ƀes. William, described as *regis capellanus* by Fl. Wig., was Bishop of London from 1051 to 1075.

l. 26. *Leofwines · ƀes*. Leofwine, who had been Abbot of Coventry, became Bishop of Lichfield on the death of Wulfsige in October 1053 (Sax. Chr. D; Fl. Wig.). See Harmer[2], p. 567.

Sigweardes eorles. See p. 465.

Haroldes eorles. See p. 463.

l. 27. *Raulfes eorles*. Ralph, the nephew of Edward the Confessor (Fl. Wig. s.a. 1051, 1055), is said to have accompanied him to England

NOTES

in 1041 (*Historia Ramesiensis*, R.S. p. 171). He signs three charters of 1050 as *dux* (K. 791 ff.) and in 1051 raised forces in his earldom (probably Worcestershire) to oppose Earl Godwine and his sons. On Swegn's final banishment in that year he probably succeeded him as Earl of Herefordshire. In 1052 (Sax. Chr. E) he was made joint commander with Earl Odda of a fleet stationed at Sandwich to watch Earl Godwine, but the latter succeeded in evading them and they were replaced. In 1055 he was unsuccessful in defending Herefordshire against the forces of Earl Ælfgar and Gruffydd of Wales (see below). He died in 1057 and was buried at Peterborough. He is frequently referred to as Earl Ralph the Timid, cf. Fl. Wig. s.a. 1055.

Ælfgares eorles. Ælfgar was the son of Leofric and Godgifu. He held the earldom of East Anglia during Harold's exile (1051–1052) and succeeded him there again in 1053. In 1055 he was banished and attacked Hereford with the help of Gruffydd of Wales and a body of Norsemen from Ireland. Peace was made and he was restored to his earldom in the same year. In 1057 he succeeded his father as Earl of Mercia. In the following year he was again banished but won back his position once more with Welsh and Norse assistance. The date of his death is not recorded but his last signature appears in 1065 (K. 815) and the first of his son Edwin, who succeeded him, in 1066 (K. 824 f.). The reasons for his banishment are nowhere stated. His daughter Ealdgyth became the wife of Gruffydd of Wales (killed 1063) and then of Harold. His son Morcar was Earl of Northumbria at the time of the Conquest.

Manniges abb. Abbot of Evesham, see p. 460.

l. 28. *Ælfwines abb*. Abbot of the New Minster, see p. 437.

Leofsiges abb. The death of Leofsige, Abbot of Ely, is dated 1045 in the *Liber Eliensis*, II, c. 94, although at the same time it is said that his successor Wulfric was consecrated by Archbishop Stigand. The two statements are incompatible as Stigand did not become archbishop until 1052, and there seems good reason for believing that the date of Leofsige's death has been put ten years too early. An Abbot Leofsige signs two charters of 1054 and 1055 respectively (K. 800 f., see below) and Leofsige, Abbot of Ely, is named along with Leofric, Abbot of Peterborough, and Wulfgeat, Abbot of Crowland (see below), in an undated charter of Edward the Confessor (K. 904) which cannot be earlier than 1052.

Leofrices abb. Leofric, the nephew of Earl Leofric, was Abbot of Peterborough from 1052 to 1066 and held in addition the abbeys of Burton, Coventry, Crowland and Thorney before his death (Sax. Chr. 1066 E). He was taken ill during the early part of the Hastings campaign (in which he assisted) and returned to Peterborough where he died.

l. 29. *oðres Leofsiges abb*. There seems to be no trace of this abbot elsewhere (unless he is the witness of the charters of 1054 and 1055 which relate to Abingdon and Evesham respectively, see above) and I have been unable to identify him.

NOTES

Brihtmæres abb. Brihtmær, Abbot of Crowland, was succeeded by Wulfgeat, Abbot of Peakirk, who in turn was succeeded by Ulfketel, a monk of Peterborough. There is a good deal of doubt as to the dates of these successive abbots. Ulfketel, who was appointed *jubente Leofrico abbate suo*, ruled for twenty-four years, according to Ordericus Vitalis, and was followed by Ingulf (died 17 December 1108) who also ruled for twenty-four years. In the *Acts of Lanfranc* (Plummer, I, p. 290) the deposition of Ulfketel is assigned to Lanfranc's sixteenth year as archbishop (i.e. August 1085–August 1086) so that his appointment would fall in 1061 or 1062. His predecessor Wulfgeat is said by Ordericus to have ruled Crowland for a long time but no dates are given. He appears in two spurious charters of the abbey (K. 794 f.) of which the second is dated 1051 and the first cannot be later than 1050 as it is witnessed by Eadsige, Archbishop of Canterbury (d. 1050), but no reliance can be placed on these. According to the evidence of K. 904 he was abbot before the death of Leofsige, Abbot of Ely, which should perhaps be attributed to the year 1055 (see above). If the evidence of the present charter is trustworthy, Brihtmær was still alive at any rate as late as 1053.

ll. 29 f. *Esgeres stealres.* See p. 464.
l. 30. *Raulfes steallres.* See pp. 463 f.
Lifinges steallres. See p. 463.
l. 31. *huscarlan.* A Scandinavian loan-word, see Björkman, *Scandinavian Loanwords in England*, p. 214, s.v. 'a member of the bodyguard or household troops of a king or noble'.

ll. 31 ff. *ón þurgodes lagen* etc. In the Lincolnshire D.B. *Turgot lag* appears in several entries as a tenant in the time of King Edward (see Foster and Longley, pp. 95 ff.) and it is recorded also that one of the lawmen of Lincoln before the Conquest was called Godric (*ibid.* p. 3). It is probable, therefore, that Thurgod and his companions were the lawmen of Lincoln at the time that this charter was drawn up. Thurgod was a landholder in Yorkshire, Nottinghamshire and Oxfordshire, as well as in Lincolnshire, see V.C.H. *Yorks.* II, pp. 145 f.

p. 216, ll. 7 f. *mid þæs kyngces haligdome.* See p. 419.

CXVI

MSS. (*a*) Register A in the Chapter Library, Canterbury, f. 153 *b*.
(*b*) Register E in the Chapter Library, Canterbury, f. 11 *b*.
Both of these are fourteenth-century copies.

EDITIONS. K. 799, from (*b*).
T. p. 372.
The text is from (*a*).

DATE. In the late Canterbury list of benefactors this grant is dated 1054 (Dugdale, I, p. 97).

l. 11. *Gerschereche.* The name survives in Gracechurch Street, London.
Stigant archebiscop. See p. 463.
l. 12. *Godric pane den.* See p. 437.
l. 14. *alre haleʒene cheriche.* There is a church of All Hallows on the west side of Gracechurch Street at the present day.
l. 18. *adeswen.* I cannot understand this form. It might represent A.S. *adwæscan* but the latter is active in meaning, see B.T. *Suppl.*, p. 9, s.v.
l. 20. *Lyefstan portireue and biscop.* Two writs addressed by Edward the Confessor to William, Bishop of London, and Leofstan and Ælfsige *porterefen* are extant (K. 857, 861). The name of the bishop has apparently been omitted here by mistake.
ll. 20 f. *Eylwíne stikehare.* In D.B. in the list of those having *sac and soc* in the lathe of Sutton and the lathe of Aylesford occurs the name *Aluuinus 'hor'* (D.B. 1, f. 1 *b*; V.C.H. *Kent*, III, p. 204).

CXVII

MS. Corpus Christi College, Cambridge, MS. 111, f. 74. See p. 451.
EDITIONS. K. 822.
T. p. 379.
E. p. 377.
B. 929.
Hunt, *Two Chartularies of the Priory of St Peter at Bath*, p. 19.

DATE. Between 1061 and the expulsion of Earl Tostig in 1065 (see below).

l. 22. *Ælfwig abbud.* Ælfwig's signature appears only twice in the charters (K. 813, 817, dated 1062 and 1065 respectively).
l. 23. *Stigande archeb.* See p. 463.
l. 24. *Dyddanhamme.* Tidenham, Gloucestershire, see p. 451. This estate was included among those forfeited by Stigand in 1070. In 1086 it was held by William, Earl of Hereford.
p. 218, l. 4. .VI. *merswun.*7 .XXX. *pusenda hæringys.* The estate held valuable fisheries both in the Wye and the Severn.
l. 5. *Eadgyð seo hlæfdige.* See p. 466.
l. 6. *Ealdryd archeb.* Ealdred was elected Archbishop of York in December 1060 and went to Rome for his pallium in the following year (Sax. Chr. D; Fl. Wig.).
Hereman .b. Bishop of Ramsbury, see p. 466.
Gisa .b. Gisa, who had been one of the king's chaplains, succeeded Duduc as Bishop of Wells in 1060 and went to Rome for consecration in the following year (Fl. Wig.). He is said by Fl. Wig. to have been a native of Lotharingia. He died in 1088.
Harold eorl. See p. 463.
l. 7. *Tosstig eorl.* Tostig, who was one of Earl Godwine's sons, was

made Earl of Northumbria in succession to Siweard in 1055. In 1061 he accompanied Archbishop Ealdred to Rome. In 1065 he was driven out by the Northumbrians and took refuge in Flanders. In 1066 he returned and plundered in the Isle of Wight, Sandwich and Lindsey, and after an interval in Scotland joined Harold Hardrada in his invasion of Northumbria. He was killed at the Battle of Stamford Bridge.

Æþelnoð abb. Æthelnoth became Abbot of Glastonbury in 1053. In 1067 he was taken to Normandy by the Conqueror and remained in exile there until he was formally deposed in 1078.

Ægylwig abb. Æthelwig succeeded Manni as Abbot of Evesham in 1058 or 1059 (see p. 460). He died in 1077.

ll. 7 f. *Ægylsige abb.* Æthelsige succeeded Wulfric as Abbot of St Augustine's. Sometime after the Conquest he fled to Denmark and was followed at St Augustine's by Scotland who was appointed abbot in 1070.

l. 8. *Ordric abb.* Ordric was Abbot of Abingdon from 1052 to 1066.
Esegar steallere. See p. 464.
Roulf steallere. See pp. 463 f.
l. 9. *Bondig steallere.* Bondig's signature is attached to two charters (K. 813, 945) with the title *regis palatinus* and *stabulator* respectively. He appears in D.B. as *Bondi stalrus* in connection with a Bedfordshire estate (D.B. 1, f. 218 *b*; V.C.H. Beds. 1, p. 264), and as *Boding constabularius* in connection with two Buckinghamshire estates which in 1086 had passed to Henry de Ferrers (D.B. 1, f. 151; V.C.H. Bucks. 1, p. 265). He is probably the *Bondi* or *Bundi* likewise to whose lands the latter had succeeded in Essex, Berkshire, Oxfordshire and Northamptonshire (see V.C.H. Essex, 1, pp. 350, 504).

CXVIII

MS. British Museum, Cotton Charters, X, 17 (see below).

FACSIMILE. Bond, *Facsimiles of Ancient Charters in the British Museum*, Part IV, No. 37.

DATE. This charter has part of the tag remaining to which presumably the king's seal was attached. In spite of this it is almost certainly spurious. Bond, judging it by palaeographical tests, regarded it as doubtful, and it is impossible to reconcile the signature of Ealdred as archbishop (see p. 456) with that of Earl Godwine (see p. 409). Wargrave, according to tradition, was one of the nine manors granted by Queen Ælfgifu Emma to the Old Minster after she had vindicated her innocence with the aid of St Swithin (see p. 462). According to D.B., however, it had been held by Queen Edith before the Conquest and in 1086 was in the king's hands. It is noteworthy that according to D.B. Hayling Island had also been in the possession of Queen Edith, so that if there is any truth at all in the statement that these two manors had been given to the Old Minster at one time by Queen

NOTES

Ælfgifu Emma, the gift must have been revoked or annulled at a later date. The most likely time for this to have happened was in 1043 when Ælfgifu Emma was deprived of her possessions. The *Historia Major Wintoniensis* states (p. 235) that after the triumphant issue of her trial *redditum est reginae et episcopo quicquid illis sublatum fuerat*, but there is nothing to this effect elsewhere and the whole story seems to be a fabrication.

l. 17. *Weregrauæ*. Wargrave.
l. 26. *Stigandus arc̄*. Archbishop of Canterbury, see p. 463.
l. 27. *Ealdred arc̄*. Archbishop of York, see p. 456.
Hæreman eps̄. Bishop of Ramsbury, see p. 466.
ll. 27 f. *Ræimballd cancell*. Regenbald, who signs between 1050 and 1054 as *presbyter* (K. 791 ff., 796, 800), generally appears with the title *cancellarius* from 1060 till the end of the reign (K. 809, 813, 824 f.). He apparently continued to act as one of the king's chaplains after the Conquest (cf. Davis, *Regesta Regum Anglo-Normannorum*, p. 3, No. 9; p. 5, No. 19) and may have held office as chancellor for some time also, although this is more doubtful (cf. Davis, *op. cit.* p. 57, No. 213). He is referred to once in D.B. with the title *canceler* but is generally called *presbyter*. He became dean of a college of secular canons at Cirencester before his death, and in 1133 Henry I granted to the monastery which he had refounded there the rich possessions of Regenbald, comprising lands and churches in Gloucestershire, Wiltshire, Somerset, Dorset, Berkshire, Oxfordshire, Buckinghamshire and Northamptonshire. Leland records that he was buried in the abbey church at Cirencester and quotes the epitaph from his tomb (*Itinerary*, v, p. 62).

CXIX

MSS. (*a*) Cambridge University Library, Additional MS. 6006, f. 51. This is a thirteenth-century *Liber de Consuetudinibus* of Bury St Edmunds.

(*b*) Cambridge University Library, Ee. 3. 60, f. 161. This is the *Registrum Vestiarii* of Bury St Edmunds also known as the Pinchbeck Register. It was begun in 1333.

(*c*) Cambridge University Library, Gg. 4. 4, f. 317, where it has been copied from (*b*). This is the *Registrum Cellerarii* I, also called the *Registrum Alphabeticum*.

EDITIONS. K. 944, from (*b*).
T. p. 438, from (*b*).
Lord Francis Hervey, *The Pinchbeck Register*, I, p. 360.
The text is from (*b*).

DATE. The heading describes this agreement as *Carta sc̄i Edwardi regis*. There is no means of dating it exactly.

p. 220, l. 2. *husfast*, cf. *heorðfæst*, II Cnut, 20.
l. 3. *Bideripe*. Literally 'reaping by request', cf. *Rectitudines*, cap. 5, 2.

on pent. A Latin account of the dues paid to the cellarer which precedes the transcript of this agreement describes this payment as *Repsiluer.*

Petermasse. The reference is apparently to the feast of St Peter's Chains (*ad Vincula*) celebrated at Lammas (1 August).

l. 7. *7 sea cnytes....* I cannot make sense of the words following *cnytes.* The Latin account of the dues paid to the cellarer reads with reference to this payment: *Et antequam villa fuit libera solebant homines metere vt serui. Sola hospicia militum et*[1] *capellanorum et seruiencium curie quieta erant a tali censu* (MS. (*a*), f. 49; MS. (*b*), f. 159 *b*). This establishes the reading *cnihtas* corresponding to the *milites* of the Latin account but sheds no light on what follows.

CXX

MS. The Sherborne Cartulary, f. 29 (see p. 278). The charter breaks off unfinished at the end of f. 29 *b* as f. 30 is unfortunately missing.

EDITIONS. K. 1341.
T. p. 388.

In the cartulary this charter is introduced with the words (in red): *Ðis is se freols ðe Eadweard cyngc 7 Eadgyð seo hlæfdige geuðon into þam haligum mynstre æt Hortune Criste to lofe 7 Sča MARIAN 7 eallon Cristes halgon.*

It is practically word for word the same as that of Æthelbert of Wessex to Sherborne, dated 864 (see No. XI). As the witnesses are wanting, it is impossible to verify the date assigned to it.

l. 18. *Hortune.* Horton, according to William of Malmesbury, *Gesta Pontificum,* R.S. p. 203, was founded by Ordulf, the son of Ordgar, the founder also of Tavistock. In the twelfth century it was reduced from an abbey to a priory and annexed as a cell to Sherborne (see V.C.H. *Dorset,* II, p. 72).

p. 222, ll. 11 f. *burhgeweorce.* This is an addition to the list of exceptions in Æthelbert's charter. The system of establishing fortified centres against the Danes was begun by Alfred and continued by his son Edward the Elder.

l. 24. *tacncircule.* This refers to the lunar cycle of 19 years, see B.T. p. 967, s.v. II. The place occupied by any given year in the cycle is indicated by the golden number of the year, which is found as the remainder when the given year + 1 is divided by 19. The golden number of the year 1061 is therefore correctly given here as 17.

[1] MS. (*a*); om. MS. (*b*).

APPENDIX I

POST-CONQUEST DOCUMENTS

I

MSS. (*a*) Bodleian Library, Oxford, MS. Auct. D. 2. 16, f. 1. This is a copy of the gospels in Latin, see below.
(*b*) *The Exeter Book* in the Chapter Library, Exeter Cathedral, f. 1. The lists in both these MSS. were written in the second half of the eleventh century and most likely during the last quarter of the century.
(*c*) Corpus Christi College, Cambridge, MS. 101, f. 62. This is a sixteenth-century transcript of (*b*).
(*d*) British Museum, Harley MS. 258, f. 125 *b*. This is a seventeenth-century copy of (*a*).

FACSIMILES. (1) British Museum, Additional MS. 9067, a facsimile transcript of the *Exeter Book*.
(2) *The Exeter Book*, 1933.

EDITIONS. Dugdale, II, p. 527, from (*a*).
K. 940, from (*d*).
E. H. Pedler, *The Anglo-Saxon Episcopate of Cornwall*, p. 136, from K.
T. p. 428, from (*d*).
E. p. 249, from (*a*).
Kershaw, *Anglo-Saxon and Norse Poems*, p. 206, based on (*b*).
The Exeter Book Facsimile, 1933, pp. 18–30, gives the text of (*b*) with full critical apparatus and notes by Dr Max Förster.

The text is from (*a*).

A M.E. version of this document is preserved as Charter No. 2570 in the Cathedral Library, Exeter. Its relationship to the A.S. copies is discussed by Dr Förster (p. 14) and the text is printed (p. 30). A Latin abstract made in the twelfth century and entered on f. 3 of the *Exeter Book* is also reproduced (p. 32).

DATE. Between 1069, when William I granted permission to Leofric to give 7 hides at Bampton, Aston, Chimney and Holcombe to St Peter's, Exeter (see below), and 10 February 1072, the date of Leofric's death.

p. 226, l. 1. *on þissere Xþes bec*, i.e. the copy of the Latin Gospels from which the present text is taken. The reading of the Exeter Book, which is an anthology of poetry, is simply *on ðissere bec*.

Leofric .б̄. Leofric, according to William of Malmesbury (*Gesta Pontificum*, R.S. p. 201), had been brought up and trained in Lotharingia. He probably accompanied Edward the Confessor to England in 1042, as in a grant of 1044 he appears as the king's chaplain (*Ordnance Survey Facsimiles*, II, Exeter Charters, No. XII). In 1046 he was appointed Bishop of Devon and Cornwall (see Sax. Chr. 1044 E, where he is described as *þæs cynges preost*; Fl. Wig. s.a. 1046, where he is called *regis cancellarius*) and in 1050 he removed his episcopal see from Crediton to Exeter.

l. 4. *þurh his gærsuma*. This Scandinavian loan-word appears several times in the Saxon Chronicle, e.g. 1035 D, 1047 E, 1070 E (*gersumas on sceat 7 on scrud 7 on bokes*), 1128 E (*gersumes on gold 7 on silure*). Dr Förster suggests that its use in the present instance may imply 'that the money was paid out of the extraordinary imposition which the bishop as lord of the manor could exact from his tenants as a kind of subsidy', but I am not certain (in view of the general sense of 'treasure' with which the word is employed in the Saxon Chronicle) that such an interpretation is necessary. It is possible that Leofric sacrificed some of his own private 'treasure' in order to indemnify the holders of the estates which he regained for St Peter's, Exeter.

l. 5. *Culmstoke*. The grant of an estate of 5 hides at Culmstock was attributed to Æthelstan, see B. 724 (a spurious charter). In 1086 this manor was held by the Bishop of Exeter. It had paid geld for 5 hides and had land for 15 ploughs (see V.C.H. *Devon*, I, p. 416).

Brancescumbe. An estate at Branscombe was bequeathed by King Alfred to his younger son Æthelweard (Harmer, p. 17). In 1086 it was held by the Bishop of Exeter and was for the support of the canons. It had paid geld for 5 hides and had land for 16 ploughs (V.C.H. *Devon*, I, p. 417).

Sealtcumbe. Salcombe Regis near Sidmouth. In 1086 this manor was held by the Bishop of Exeter. It had paid geld for 3 hides and had land for 6 ploughs (V.C.H. *Devon*, I, p. 416).

l. 6. *Scē Maria circean*. The manor of St Mary Church was likewise for the support of the canons and was held by the Bishop of Exeter in 1086. It had paid geld for 2 virgates and had land for 3 ploughs.

Stofordtune. In 1086 the manor of Staverton was held by the Bishop of Exeter and was also for the support of the canons. It had paid geld for $2\frac{1}{2}$ hides and had land for 20 ploughs (V.C.H. *Devon*, I, p. 417).

l. 7. *Spearcanwille*. Sparkwell is near Staverton and has no separate entry in D.B. among the lands of St Peter's, Exeter. Baldwin the sheriff held a manor there which Brihtric had held in the time of King Edward (V.C.H. *Devon*, I, p. 465).

Morceshille. Now represented by Marshall Farm near Ide (Pl.N. *Devon*, Part II, p. 498).

Sidefullan hiwisc. For references to St Sidwell, of whom little is known, see Dr Förster's note (p. 18, n. 28). Her name (*S. Satiuola*) appears in the list of saints whose relics were given by Æthelstan to

NOTES 475

St Peter's, Exeter, and she is said there to have been 'innocently slain by her father's mowers' (see Dugdale, II, p. 529). According to an eleventh-century account of the resting-places of the English saints she was buried outside Exeter (Liebermann, *Die Heiligen Englands*, p. 17). The *hiwisc*, 'hide' or 'holding' referred to here appears in the fifteenth century as *Seynt Sidewill fee* (see Pl.N. *Devon*, Part II, p. 437).

l. 8. *Brihtricesstane.* This appears in D.B. in the forms *Bretricestan* (Exeter MS.), *Bedricestan* (Exchequer MS.) and is identified with the farm of Treasbeare in the parish of Honiton Clyst (V.C.H. *Devon*, I, p. 416, n. 7). In 1086 it was held by the Bishop of Exeter. It had paid geld for 1 hide and had land for 5 ploughs.

ll. 8 f. *þ land æt Toppeshamme* etc. In both MSS. (*a*) and (*b*) this has been inserted above the line by the original scribe. It is not found in the M.E. version. The estate of Topsham (1 hide) had been given to St Peter's, Exeter, by Æthelstan in 937 (B. 721). According to D.B. it was held by the king in 1086 and had been Earl Harold's in the time of King Edward (V.C.H. *Devon*, I, p. 410). It had paid geld for 1 hide and had land for 12 ploughs. It would appear, therefore, as if Leofric's acquisition of the estate were only temporary.

l. 9. *Stoce.* A spurious Exeter charter (B. 723) records the grant of Stoke Canon by Æthelstan. In 1031 the same estate was granted by Cnut to his thegn Hunewine (see p. 344). In 1086 it was held by the Bishop of Exeter. It had paid geld for 1 hide and had land for 6 ploughs (V.C.H. *Devon*, I, p. 416).

l. 10. *Sydebirig.* According to D.B. this manor had been held by *Alwin* and *Godwin* in parage in the time of King Edward (V.C.H. *loc. cit.*).

Niwantune. Newton St Cyres, near Crediton. In 1086 this manor was held by *Domne* but was claimed by the Bishop of Exeter who produced his charters in witness that the church of St Peter had been seised of it before the reign of King Edward. He asserted besides that in King William's time he had a suit concerning it and proved his right with the support of Frenchmen as witnesses (V.C.H. *Devon*, I, p. 415).

Norðtune. Norton is not included among the lands of St Peter's, Exeter in D.B.

ll. 10 f. *þ land æt Clist* etc. This entry has been made above the line by the original scribe in both MSS. (*a*) and (*b*) and is included in the M.E. version. Numerous manors of the name (derived from the river Clyst) are mentioned in D.B. but none of them appears among the lands of St Peter's, Exeter. The name *Wid* is found also in the *Liber Vitae Ecclesiae Dunelmensis*, Surtees Society, XIII, p. 107 (*Wid le Franceis*), and probably represents the Norman *Wido*.

ll. 14 f. *þ land æt Bemtune* etc. For William I's grant of Bampton, Aston and Chimney (Oxfordshire) to Leofric see Davidson, *Journal of the British Archaeological Association*, XXXIX, 1883, pp. 298-301. In 1086 the Bishop of Exeter was holding 6 hides at Bampton with land for 6 ploughs. Aston and Chimney are hamlets in the parish of Bampton.

l. 15. *Doflisc.* A grant of 7 hides of land at Dawlish had been made by Edward the Confessor to Leofric, his worthy chaplain, in 1044 (see Davidson, *op. cit.* pp. 292–295). In 1086 this manor was held by the Bishop of Exeter and was for the support of the canons. It had paid geld for 7 hides and had land for 30 ploughs (V.C.H. *Devon*, I, p. 415).

l. 16. *Holacumbe...Supwuda.* The boundaries of 1 hide and 1½ yardlands at Holcombe are given in William I's charter (see above) and correspond roughly to those of East Teignmouth parish (see Davidson, *Transactions of the Devonshire Association*, XIII, p. 125). Southwood is in Dawlish and does not appear elsewhere as a separate estate.

l. 18. *Ide.* This estate had been given by Æthelstan in 937 (see Davidson, *op. cit.* p. 119).

l. 23. .II. *mycele Xpes bec gebonede.* One of these, as Dr Förster suggests, was probably the Latin copy of the gospels in the Bodleian Library from which the present list is taken. From its inscription it is known to have belonged to Leofric. It may once have had an ornamented cover.

An interesting account of an ornamented cover of the kind is preserved in Additional MS. 40000 in the British Museum (a Latin Gospel book which at one time belonged to Thorney Abbey). It reads as follows: ☩*Ælfric 7 Wulfwine Eadgife goldsmiðes geafen to broþerrædenne twegen orn weghenes goldes* (i.e. 2 ores of weighed gold) *þ is on þis ilce boc her for uten gewired* (i.e. made into filigree ornament). This ornamentation, unfortunately, has entirely disappeared.

l. 24. *scrin.* Dr Förster suggests that these were reliquaries or small ornamented boxes for the preservation of saints' relics.

.I. *geboned altare.* Dr Förster suggests that this was probably a portable altar.

l. 25. .IIII. *corporales.* The *corporale* in the present context is explained by Dr Förster as the linen cloth upon which the consecrated elements were placed during the Eucharistic celebration and with which they were sometimes covered. The word is also used of a Eucharistic vestment.

.I. *silfren pipe.* Dr Förster explains that by this 'pipe' is meant a tube for drinking the sacramental wine out of the chalice.

l. 26. .II. *dalmatica.* The dalmatic was the outer vestment worn by the assisting deacon.

.III. *pistelroccas,* cf. *pistolclapas,* p. 72, l. 9. In both cases the reference is probably to the vestment worn by the epistoler or sub-deacon who read the epistles. In the *Visio Leofrici* (a dream attributed to Earl Leofric, see pp. 412 f.) a great company is described *ealle mid snawhwítum réafe gescrydde 7 þ on þa wisan þe se diacon bið þonne he godspell ret* (see Napier, *Transactions of the Philological Society*, 1907–10, p. 182).

NOTES 477

l. 27. .III. *cantercæppa*. The cantor, as Dr Förster explains, was the leader of the choir.

ll. 27 f. v. *pællene weofodsceatas* etc. The difference between the *weofodsceatas*, i.e. the cloths of rich material covering the front and sides of the altar and hence termed 'frontals', and the *oferbrædelsas*, i.e. the white linen cloths spread over the top of the altar, is explained by Dr Förster. The adj. *pællene* means 'purple', then 'rich or costly'.

l. 29. .II. *wahreft*. A description of a wall-hanging of the kind is given in the *Visio Leofrici*, ed. Napier (see above), pp. 184 f.: *Ða wæs þær án prilig wahrægl 7 swyðe picce gewefen þæt hangode bæftan þam weofode · 7 stod þær án medmycel ród on ðære eorðan on ðam norðeasthyrnan 7 wæs swa mycel þæs treowes gesyne swa wolde beon god hande brad beneoþan þam wahrifte 7 se oðer dæl wæs betwyx þam wahrifte 7 þam wahe.*

ll. 29 f. .VI. *mæsene sceala*. Dr Förster explains these bowls as the basins for receiving the water poured out of a cruet over the hands of the celebrating priest. The meaning of the adj. *mæsene*, which is not recorded elsewhere, is uncertain, but obviously some material of which the bowls were made is meant. The reading *mæseren*, 'of maple', cf. Icel. *mösur*, is suggested by B.T. Others, e.g. Thorpe and Earle, suggest 'brazen', cf. O.E. *mæstling*, 'brass'. The M.E. version has *massyn*, an unknown word apparently carried over from the A.S.

l. 30. *hnæppas*. These are described by Dr Förster as cruets or bowls for carrying the water and wine used during mass.

l. 32. *storsticcan*. The meaning 'incense spoon' is that suggested by Dr Förster, cf. B.T. s.v. *sticca*, II.

p. 228, l. 1. .II. *guðfana*, i.e. military standards. Among the gifts made by Æthelstan to St Cuthbert's were included *duo vexilla et unam lanceam* (see B. 685).

'.I.' *merc*, i.e. an ecclesiastical banner.

ll. 3 f. .II. *fulle mæssebec*. One of these is the Leofric Missal, MS. Bodley 579 in the Bodleian Library, Oxford. It is one of the nine MSS. containing an inscription to the effect that it was given by Leofric to St Peter's, Exeter.

l. 4. .I. *collectaneum*. The British Museum MS. Harley 2961 is a collectarium which may have been Leofric's.

l. 5. .I. *adteleuaui*. See p. 442. Dr Förster suggests that Leofric's book of the kind may have been an *Antiphonarium Missae*, i.e. a collection of the musical texts for the mass which opened with these words.

.I. *tropere*, i.e. a book containing the phrases introduced as an embellishment into some part of the text of the mass or of the breviary office that is sung by the choir (see N.E.D. s.v. *trope*, 5).

l. 6. *swa man singð on Rome*. The *Psalterium Romanum* was the form of the psalter generally used in England. The preceding two, as Dr Förster points out, must have been of the Gallican type. The British

NOTES

Museum MS. Harley 863 may represent one of them, as it contains the psalter according to the Gallican version and probably came from Exeter.

l. 7. .i. *deorwyrðe bletsingboc.* The British Museum Additional MS. 28188 is a benedictional which probably came from Exeter.

.i. *englisc Xp̄es boc.* The reading of MS. (*b*) *p̄eos* instead of .i. is inappropriate as the book to which it is prefixed is not a gospel book. Dr Förster suggests, however, that the list now attached to the Exeter Book was written for an English gospel book, probably the C.U.L. MS. Ii. 2. 11, which is proved by the inscription on the first page to have been given by Leofric to Exeter. He suggests further that the first seven folios of the Exeter Book, i.e. those containing the list and the manumissions which follow, probably belonged originally to the Cambridge MS., and points out that f. 8, where the Exeter Book proper begins, is rubbed and stained and was probably for some time the outside leaf of the MS.

ll. 8 f. *regula canonicorum,* i.e. the Rule of Bishop Chrodegang of Metz which Leofric imposed upon the regular canons whom he introduced into the monastery of St Peter at Exeter. This copy is probably to be identified with MS. 191 in the library of Corpus Christi College, Cambridge, which contains a copy of Chrodegang's rule both in Anglo-Saxon and in Latin.

l. 9. *martyrlogium.* It is possible that this is identical with MS. 196 in the library of Corpus Christi College, Cambridge.

ll. 9 f. .i. *scriftboc on englisc.* This has been identified with MS. C.C.C., Cambridge, No. 190, which contains a Latin and two Anglo-Saxon penitentials.

ll. 10 f. *Boeties boc on englisc,* i.e. King Alfred's translation of the *De Consolatione Philosophiae* of Boethius. The Exeter copy has not survived.

ll. 11 f. .i. *mycel englisc boc* etc., i.e. the Exeter Book itself.

l. 15. *þus fela leden boca* etc. This does not mean, as Dr Förster points out, that the books already mentioned were all in English. The service books, at any rate, must have been in Latin and only four books altogether are actually said to have been in English, namely a gospel book, a penitential, King Alfred's translation of Boethius and the Exeter Book itself.

l. 16. *liber pastoralis · 7 liber dialogorum,* i.e. Gregory's *Cura Pastoralis* and *Dialogues.* The former survives as MS. Bodley 708 in the Bodleian Library, Oxford. It contains the Leofric inscription.

l. 17. *liber Boetii de consolatione.* This copy still survives and is now in the Bodleian Library as the first part of MS. Auct. F. 1. 15. It contains the Leofric inscription.

isagoge Porphirii, i.e. the commentaries of Boethius on the *Isagoge* of Porphyry. The latter was an upholder of Neo-Platonism and a follower of Plotinus.

l. 18. *liber Prosperi.* Prosper of Aquitaine was a disciple of St

NOTES

Augustine. The work referred to here may be his *Liber Sententiarum*, compiled from the writings of St Augustine.

liber Prudentii psicomachie. The *Psychomachia* of Prudentius was an allegorical poem dealing with the conflict between Christian virtues and heathen vices. It was very popular throughout the Middle Ages. His *Liber Hymnorum*, a collection of 12 hymns, is generally referred to as the *Cathemerinon*. His book on the martyrs was a poem entitled *Peristephanon.* Leofric's copy of the works of Prudentius survives as MS. Bodley, Auct. F. 3. 6. It contains the Leofric inscription.

l. 21. *onsundron,* i.e. apart from the copy in the volume of the four prophets mentioned above.

liber Isidori ethimolagiarum. Isidore of Seville (d. 636) was a voluminous and influential writer. His *Etymologiae* remained an important work of reference for centuries. MS. Bodley 394 is a copy of the *Liber S. Isidori de Miraculis Christi* and as it came from Exeter, it may have been Leofric's.

ll. 21 f. *passiones apostolorum.* This was a collection of apocryphal legends of the apostles compiled in Gaul in the sixth century.

l. 23. *expositio Bede super apocalipsin.* Now included in MS. 149 in the Lambeth Palace Library.

ll. 23 f. *expositio Bede super* VII. *epistolas canonicas.* A copy of this work, which came from Exeter, is now in MS. Bodley 849.

l. 25. *liber Oserii.* No author of the name is known and it is usually taken as a mistake for *Orosii.* Dr Förster suggests *Aserii* as a possible alternative, i.e. Asser's *Life of King Alfred.*

ll. 25 f. *liber Machabeorum,* i.e. the Book of the Maccabees, an apocryphal work dealing with the oppression and deliverance of the believing Israelites. It survives in three versions.

l. 26. *liber Persii,* i.e. the satires of Persius Flaccus, one of the two volumes of classical Latin included in the list. This copy survives as the second part of MS. Bodley, F. 1. 15.

Sedulies boc. Probably, as Dr Förster suggests, the *Carmen paschale* of Coelius Sedulius (a Christian poet of the early fifth century) which deals with the miracles of Christ.

liber Aratoris. Arator was a Christian poet of the sixth century whose epic and didactic poem *De Actibus Apostolorum* was widely read in the Middle Ages.

l. 27. *diadema monachorum.* The author of this ninth-century work was Smaragdus, Abbot of St Mihiel, in the diocese of Verdun. It was a collection of ascetic rules. The reading of MS. (*b*) at this point, i.e. *liber de sanctis patribus* (written on an erasure), probably refers to the fifth-century *Vitae Patrum* of Rufinus of Aquileia.

glose Statii, i.e. probably the glosses of Lactantius Placidus to the *Thebais* of Statius, the second of the classical Latin works included in the list.

liber officialis Amalarii. Amalarius of Metz was a liturgical writer of the ninth century. His chief work, which is the one meant here, was entitled *De Ecclesiasticis Officiis*. This copy, with the Leofric inscription, is preserved in the library of Trinity College, Cambridge.

l. 28. *his capellam*. It would seem from the context that the word *capella* is used here in a particular sense, cf. Ducange, s.v. (3), *Ministeria ac vasa sacra quae sacerdoti ad sacra peragenda necessaria sunt*, and the examples quoted there from Matthew Paris. The M.E. version has *chapel* which could be used in the same sense, see N.E.D. s.v. (8). The construction of the last part of the sentence (particularly the force of the prepositions in the phrases *on eallum...pingum þe he...dide* and *mid Godes ðeninge*) is difficult to understand, and the M.E. version (which has misinterpreted the word *ann*) gives little help ...*he and hys chapel was broust yn with hym and al þat he hymsylue dyde with Godys seruys.*

p. 230, ll. 3 f. *ætbredan* etc. The Leofric inscription (which is invariably given both in Latin and in English) generally ends with a similar curse directed against anyone who should remove the book in which it occurs. In the Cambridge Gospels this sentence has been erased in both versions.

II

MS. Corpus Christi College, Cambridge, MS. 183, f. 96 *b*. The record is entered on the last leaf of the MS. which probably belonged to Durham. It contains Bede's *Life of St Cuthbert* and has been identified, therefore, with the copy given by King Æthelstan to the see of St Cuthbert (then at Chester-le-Street), described as *unam sancti Cuthberti vitam metrice et prosaice scriptam* (B. 685). A picture at the beginning of the MS. may represent the king offering the volume to St Cuthbert.

EDITION. M. R. James, *Descriptive Catalogue of the Manuscripts in Corpus Christi College, Cambridge*, p. 441.

DATE. Between 1071 and 1080, see under Bishop Walcher below.

l. 6. *Walchear b*. Walcher, who was a native of Lotharingia (Sax. Chr. 1080 E; Fl. Wig. s.a. 1072, 1080; Simeon of Durham, R.S. II, p. 208) became Bishop of Durham in 1071 and succeeded Waltheof as Earl of Northumbria in 1075. He was murdered in 1080 (see below).

Ealdgyðe. It is possible that the Ealdgyth of the present grant was the daughter of Ealdred, Earl of Northumbria, and the wife of the Northumbrian thegn Ligulf (see Simeon of Durham, R.S. I, p. 219; II, p. 209).[1] The latter and his family were slain by Gilbert, the bishop's kinsman and his deputy in the government of Northumbria, who was instigated to the crime by the bishop's chaplain. The story of his death and the bishop's which followed at a meeting with Ligulf's kinsmen

[1] Miss Whitelock suggests as another possible candidate Aldgitha, daughter of Earl Uhtred and King Æthelred's daughter Elfgiva. She married Maldred, son of Crinan, and was the mother of Earl Cospatric (*De Obsessione Dunelmi*, § 2).

is told at length by Fl. Wig. s.a. 1080; Simeon of Durham, R.S. II, pp. 208-211; William of Malmesbury, *Gesta Pontificum*, R.S. pp. 271 f. The Saxon Chronicle, 1080 E, records simply that Walcher was slain *æt anum gemote* and a hundred men with him, both French and Flemish.

l. 7. *Ðornhlawa*. Probably Thornley, 7 miles east of Durham.

to þyse male. The word *mal*, derived from O.Scand. *mál* (see Björkman, *Scandinavian Loanwords in England*, p. 103), is found (chiefly in the Saxon Chronicle) in the various senses of 'action at law, terms, agreement, pay'.

l. 8. *æt deadum oððe æt cwicvm*. This phrase seems to be used idiomatically, cf. III Æthelred, 1, 2; 2. It is difficult to understand to whom it can apply unless to Ealdgyth herself.

l. 10. *Windegatum*. Probably Wingate, 9 miles east of Durham.

III

MS. The Society of Antiquaries of London, MS. 60, f. 52. See p. 271.

EDITION. Ellis, *Introduction to Domesday Book*, I, pp. 184-187.

A translation of this document is given by Cockayne, *The Shrine*, pp. 205-208. It is discussed by Round, *Feudal England*, pp. 147-156, and his analysis of its contents (p. 153) is reproduced in his introduction to the Domesday Survey in the V.C.H. *Northants*. I, p. 259. He calls it the Northamptonshire Geld Roll and dates it not later than 1075 in view of its references to 'the Lady, the king's wife' whom he takes to be Edith, the widow of Edward the Confessor. It seems possible, however, that Matilda, the wife of the reigning king is meant, otherwise either her own or the king's name would almost certainly have been introduced. Matilda is referred to as 'the Lady' in the Saxon Chronicle, 1067 D, but as 'King William's queen' when her death is recorded. She does not appear in D.B. as she died in 1083. She is not referred to, for example, in connection with Warkton which had been held in 1066 by Ælfgifu, the wife of Earl Ælfgar and the mother of Morcar, but had subsequently passed to Bury St Edmunds by Matilda's gift (V.C.H. *Northants*. I, pp. 285, 318). If the identification of Osmund *þes kynges writere* with Osmund the chancellor is correct, the document may be earlier than 1078 when he became Bishop of Salisbury (see below), unless he continued to hold office as chancellor after his appointment.

l. 11. *Suttunes hundred*. The hundred takes its name from Sutton, now King's Sutton, see Pl.N. *Northants*. p. 58.

an hundred hida. According to this document Northamptonshire consisted of 22 hundreds, 4 'hundreds and a half' and 2 double hundreds, which agrees exactly with its assessment of 3200 hides in the County Hidage (see Chadwick, *Anglo-Saxon Institutions*, p. 208). The actual hidage, however, is shown to be only 2663½ hides, as neither of the double hundreds and only 9 of the hundreds contained their full complement of hides. The assessment in every case is said to be the same as it was in King Edward's day.

l. 13. *inland*, i.e. land exempt from the payment of geld. Round notes the frequent occurrence of figures such as 40 hides (seven times), 30 hides (twice), 20 hides (twice), 15, 25, 35, 45, 60 hides under this heading and concludes that such arbitrary sums represent a reduction in the number of hides assessed to the geld which had been granted on the hundreds since the Confessor's death. The reason for this reduction he finds in the amount of land lying waste, probably as the result of the devastation which the county suffered in 1065 (V.C.H. I, pp. 260 f.).

l. 15. *Werdunes hundret*. This takes its name from Warden, now Chipping Warden (Pl.N. pp. 36 f.).

an hundret hida. There are occasional discrepancies between the number of hides assigned to a hundred and the total arrived at by adding together the different amounts in the analysis which follows. In this case the total of the separate amounts is only 99 hides, but the discrepancy can be easily accounted for by the accidental omission of the figure I, e.g. in the reading .XVIII. for .XVIIII.

l. 22. *Grauesende hundred*. Now part of Fawsley Hundred (Pl.N. p. 9). The old name has not survived.

ll. 25 f. *Eadboldesstowe hundred*. This now forms the N.E. part of King's Sutton Hundred (Pl.N. p. 47).

p. 232, l. 1. *Egelweardesle hundred*. Now part of Fawsley Hundred (Pl.N. p. 9).

l. 4. *Osmund þes kynges writere*. The Latin *notarius* is rendered *writere* in the Anglo-Saxon translation of Gregory's Dialogues (see B.T., *Suppl.* s.v.). Osmund was Bishop of Salisbury from 1078 to 1099.

l. 6. *Uoxle hundred*. Now Green's Norton Hundred (Pl.N. p. 38).

l. 10. *Uyceste hundred*. Apparently for Towcester with loss of the first two letters of the name, cf. *Tofeceaster* (Sax. Chr. 921 A), *Tovecestre* (D.B.).

l. 14. *Hocheshlawa hundred*. The name *Huxloe*, *-low* is found as a field name within the hundred (Pl.N. p. 177).

l. 17. *Wilebroce hundred*. The hundred derives its name from the Willow Brook beside which the hundred court was held (Pl.N. p. 198).

l. 21. *Uptunegrene*. Now Nassaborough Hundred (see p. 328), which coincides with the soke of Peterborough.

l. 22. *nigeða healf hida*. This has been wrongly interpreted by Round as 9½ hides.

l. 24. *þridde healf hide*. This has been wrongly interpreted as 3½ hides by Round. The total of the separate amounts is 109 hides which shows a discrepancy of half a hide.

l. 25. *Ricard engaigne*. The lands of Richard Engayne are entered in D.B. I, f. 229 (V.C.H. I, p. 356). They lay at Stibbington (now in Hunts.), Benefield (in Huxloe Hundred), Abington (in Spelhoe Hun-

NOTES 483

dred) and Kirby (in Corby Hundred). He also held four houses in Northampton (D.B. 1, f. 219; V.C.H. 1, p. 301).

l. 26. *Nauereslund.* Now part of Huxloe Hundred (Pl.N. pp. 176 f.).

.VIII. *'syðe' twenti hide.* The total of the separate amounts of land comes only to 108½ hides, so that something must have been omitted.

l. 29. *twelfta healf hide.* This has been wrongly interpreted by Round as 12½ hides.

l. 30. *si læfdi* etc. Edith, the widow of Edward the Confessor, is entered in D.B. as the former holder of the widespread manor of Finedon which, with its appendages, was assessed at 27 hides with land for 54 ploughs. Part of this manor (9½ hides) lay in *Neueslund* Hundred (D.B. 1, f. 220; V.C.H. 1, p. 308). In 1086 it was in the hands of William the Conqueror, but may have been held by Matilda between 1075 and 1083.

l. 31. *Nęresforda hundred.* Now Navisford Hundred (Pl.N. p. 216).

p. 234, l. 1. *Pocabroc hundred.* This name (originally *puca broc*, i.e. goblin brook, Pl.N. p. 215) has now become Polebrook.

l. 4. *Neowbotlegraue.* Now Nobottlegrove (Pl.N. p. 78).

l. 16. *byrigland*, i.e. land belonging to the borough of Northampton which lies within this hundred.

Ricardes land. See p. 232, l. 25 above. The D.B. assessment of Abington is given as 4 hides with land for 8 ploughs.

l. 17. *into Multune...Willmes land.* Moulton was held by William Engayne of Robert de Buci (D.B. 1, f. 225 b; V.C.H. 1, p. 335). He was the holder also of Pytchley and Laxton in Orlingbury Hundred (D.B. 1, f. 229; V.C.H. 1, p. 356) and of a house in Northampton attached, apparently, to his estate at Moulton (D.B. 1, f. 219; V.C.H. 1, p. 301).

l. 19. *Hwicclesłea.* Now in Rutland where the name of the hundred survives in Witchley Warren near Ketton (V.C.H. *Rutland,* 1, p. 121).

l. 25. *Stotfalde hundred.* Now the west part of Rothwell Hundred (Pl.N. p. 109).

ll. 27 f. *ferðe healf gerde*, i.e. 3½ yardlands or seven-eighths of a hide. Round has one-eighth which makes the total wrong.

l. 29. *Stoce hundred.* The name formerly given to part of Corby Hundred with its centre at Stoke Albany (Pl.N. p. 155).

l. 30. *eahtetende healf hide.* Round takes this as 18 hides (*Feudal England,* p. 153), 18½ hides (V.C.H.). Both are wrong.

l. 31. *ælleofte healf hide.* Round interprets this wrongly as 11½ hides (V.C.H.).

l. 32. *Hehhám.* Higham Ferrers Hundred (Pl.N. p. 189).

l. 35. *Anforðesho.* Hamfordshoe Hundred (Pl.N. p. 136). The total of the different amounts of land is 149½ hides without the 10 hides belonging to Hamfordshoe. There is a discrepancy, therefore, of half a hide which might be the result of an accidental omission.

l. 36. *Maleslę hundred.* Now included in Orlingbury Hundred but the name survives in Mawsley (Pl.N. pp. 122, 128).

p. 236, ll. 2 f. .VIII. *healf hide* 7 .XII. *healf hide*. Wrongly interpreted by Round as 8½ hides and 12½ hides respectively.

l. 5. *ðe Scotte kyng*. It is surprising to find the Scottish king entered as a landowner in Northamptonshire at such an early date. David I by his marriage with Matilda, daughter of Waltheof, Earl of Northumbria, and widow of Simon de St Liz, Earl of Northampton, came into possession of the earldom of Northampton and the honour of Huntingdon, but there is no reference in D.B. to any previous holding in the neighbourhood by any of the Scottish kings. The lands held by David of Scotland in Corby Hundred, according to a Northamptonshire survey of the twelfth century, had been held in 1086 by the Countess Judith, the widow of Earl Waltheof, and Gunfrid de Cioches, i.e. Chocques near Bethune (see V.C.H. *Northants.* I, pp. 386 f.). Professor Stenton has drawn my attention to a passage in the *Chronica Majora* of Matthew Paris (R.S. I, pp. 467 f.) which records the grant of Lothian by Edgar to Kenneth III, King of Scotland, *hac conditione ut annis singulis in festivitatibus præcipuis quando rex et ejus successores diadema portarent, venirent ad curiam et cum cæteris regni principibus festum cum lætitia celebrarent; dedit insuper ei rex mansiones in itinere plurimas ut ipse et ejus successores ad festum venientes ac denuo revertentes hospitari valuissent*. The statement adds that these *mansiones* remained in the possession of the Scottish kings until the time of Henry II. Unfortunately no names are given, and, as stated above, there is nothing to show that the Kings of Scotland held any land in Northamptonshire until the time of David I. The only explanation (suggested to me by Professor Chadwick) seems to be that the reference to the Scottish king is due to the twelfth-century copyist who in this instance at least has brought the document up to date.

Vrs. There is no reference in D.B. to any landowner of the name in Northamptonshire. A certain Ralph, son of Urs, witnesses a writ of 1087–1097 with regard to Bury St Edmunds (Davis, *Regesta*, No. 393; Appendix, No. lxiv).

l. 7. *Roðewelle hundred....* .LX. *hida*. The total of the separate amounts comes only to 45 hides. There is no mention of waste land which may have been omitted by mistake.

l. 10. *ðes kynges wif*. It seems from the context as if the allusion must be to the Conqueror's wife. According to D.B. three-quarters of a hide of land in Rothwell Hundred belonged to the manor of Finedon which had been Queen Edith's.

ll. 10 f. *Rodbertes wif heorles*. Identified by Round as Maud, the wife of Robert, Count of Mortain. In 1086 the Abbey of Grestain was holding land at Harrington in Northamptonshire (V.C.H. I, p. 320) of which she had been the donor (see Dugdale, VI, p. 1090).

ll. 13 f. *is gewered* etc. It is obvious that either the amount of land which had paid geld or the amount in demesne has been omitted by mistake. The missing number would seem to be VI. 7 XX.

l. 18. *Witeget preost*. I have not found any other reference to a priest of the name.

IV

MS. British Museum, Additional MS. 15350, f. 25 (or f. 27 by the new numbering). See p. 274.
EDITIONS. K. 897.
T. p. 432.
DATE. The presence of Wulfweard the White as a witness shows that this document was drawn up earlier than D.B. (see below).

l. 25. TANTVNE. The manor of Taunton, which was assessed at 54 hides, 2½ virgates (D.B. I, f. 87 b; V.C.H. *Somerset*, I, p. 442), was one of several wide tracts of country, such as Chilcomb in Hampshire and Downton in Wiltshire, held by the Bishop of Winchester.

ll. 25 f. *cucu 7 dead*. The corresponding Latin phrase, *vivus et mortuus*, is used throughout D.B. in the same connection.

l. 26. *Nigonhidon*. Now Nynehead Flory, so called from the family of Flury which held the estate by knight service of the Bishops of Winchester in the twelfth century (see V.C.H. *Somerset*, I, p. 403, n. 6).

ll. 27 ff. *cirhsceattas* etc. The list of dues which follows should be compared with those in the Exchequer D.B. and the Exeter D.B. respectively (see V.C.H. *Somerset*, I, pp. 442-444) and with the concessions made by Edward the Elder to Taunton in 904 (B. 612). The correspondence between the dues as set forth here and in the two versions of D.B. is sufficiently close. The most notable difference is the omission in the present document of any reference to the necessity for burial in Taunton which affected the holders of all the estates mentioned in D.B. with the exception of Bagborough. The list of estates from which these dues were rendered is longer in both versions of D.B. by the addition of Maidenbrooke, Norton Fitzwarren, Bradford, Halse, Heathfield, *Scobindare* (*-alre*), Stoke St Mary and Andersleigh. The first five of these estates are included in the list with Tolland, Oake, etc. in the Exchequer D.B. as responsible for the payment of all the dues, while in the Exeter D.B. Norton, Bradford, Halse and Heathfield seem to be answerable only for Peter's Pence, Hundred Pence and attendance three times a year at the bishop's court. In both versions Bagborough is said to be exempt from military service as well as *sepulturam*, while the unknown *Scobindare* (*-alre*) and Stoke St Mary are free from the former. The present document is more detailed in the account which it gives of the separate estates. It generally specifies the exact amount of the church dues rendered by each, and distinguishes between them in certain cases in the matter of attendance at the bishop's court.

l. 27. *burhgerihtu*. (The Exchequer D.B. has *burgheristh*, the Exeter D.B. *burgerist*.) The term does not occur elsewhere but it recalls Edgar's injunction *to ælcere byrig...hæbbe ic mines cynescypes gerihta* (IV Edgar, 2 *a*). It is noteworthy that there is no mention of the receipt of toll or of market dues of any kind either in the present document or in D.B., and it seems possible, therefore, that the term *burhgerihtu* includes these and corresponds to the *portgerihta* of Edgar's Taunton charter (see p. 340). It is obvious, at any rate, that payments to, not by the borough, are meant. (For a different interpretation of the term as possibly equivalent to *burhbot* see Ballard, *Domesday Boroughs*, p. 100). The term *burgherist* occurs in only one other entry in D.B. (see V.C.H. *Somerset*, I, p. 438), where its application is equally obscure but where it is evident that a payment of some kind is meant.

heorðpenegas. This payment (the *denarii sci Petri* of D.B.) was levied on behalf of the church at the rate of one penny for every household. It is also called *Romfeoh* (cf. II Edgar, 4; I Cnut, 9).

l. 28. *hundred penegas.* There is no mention of such a payment in the laws or in any pre-Conquest document, apart from the 30 pence paid to the hundred for ignoring its authority (I Edgar, 3). The name suggests that it was a tax levied by the hundred court upon the landholders within its jurisdiction (see Liebermann, II, p. 520, s.v. *hundred*, 22 a), but in this case the place of the hundred court has been taken by the bishop as lord of the manor of Taunton. It is noteworthy that at the end of the entry referring to Halse the Exeter D.B. adds, 'This estate is in (*de*) Taunton hundred', so that the area of the bishop's jurisdiction may have corresponded to that of the hundred of Taunton.

l. 28. *teoþung* etc. There is no mention of any such payment in D.B. and it is peculiar to Nynehead Flory and Hele in the present document. It seems to be the earliest recorded instance of the substitution of a money payment for the usual payment in kind, cf. II Edgar, 3; V Æthelred, 11, 1; I Cnut, 8, 1.

l. 29. *hamsocn · 7 forsteall · gripbrice.* These three major offences are generally classed together (see p. 284).

handfangenþeof. The term does not occur in the laws but seems to mean the right of exercising justice upon a thief caught in the act and of receiving the forfeitures (cf. *æt hæbbendre handa*, Wihtred, 26; II Æthelstan, 1; *handhabbenda*, IV Æthelstan, 6). D.B. has simply *latrones.*

aþ · 7 ordel. It is more explicitly stated in D.B. that all who have to take an oath (*facturi sacramentum*) or undergo the ordeal (*judicium portaturi*) must do so in Taunton.

l. 30. *fyrdwíte*, cf. II Cnut, 12; 15. According to Ine, 51, the amount of the fine was determined by the status of the defaulter. It is noteworthy that in the present document the obligation of military service falls only upon Nynehead Flory and Hele, whereas in D.B. it is incumbent upon all the estates with the exception of those already mentioned.

ll. 30 f. *eall swa oft* etc. No distinction between the estates is made either in the Exchequer D.B. or in the Exeter D.B. with regard to this obligation. The statement *ter in anno teneri placita episcopi sine ammonitione* in both is of general application.

ll. 31 f. *Dunna wes þæs biscopes mann* etc. According to the evidence of D.B. none of the estates mentioned here (with the possible exception of Nynehead Flory) lay within the bounds of the manor of Taunton, but all of them had to pay the specified dues to the Bishop of Winchester as lord of the manor with rights of jurisdiction extending beyond its limits, probably over the hundred of Taunton. It is specially noted with regard to Hillfarrance and Hele, however, that they could not be separated from Taunton in the time of King Edward, and the application of the phrase *þæs biscopes mann* in the present document to Ealdred, the tenant of Hele, seems in this way to be accounted for satisfactorily. Its use in connection with Dunna is more difficult to understand, unless it is interpreted as 'the man responsible to the bishop for the payment of the dues' or unless it is taken to indicate a closer connection between the estates concerned and the manor of Taunton in the time of King Edward than existed in 1086. The evidence of D.B., moreover, only partially agrees with that of the present document with regard to the tenancy of these particular estates, for while *Domno* is entered as the former tenant of Oake and Upper Cheddon Fitzpaine, the name of the tenant of Tolland and Lower Cheddon Fitzpaine in the time of King Edward is given as *Ulwin*. In 1086 these estates had passed into the hands of Roger de Corcelle. Dunna's name (in the forms *Domno, Domne, Dunno, Dunne, Donno*) appears elsewhere in connection with various estates which had passed into the possession of Roger de Corcelle, William de Moion and others (see V.C.H. *Somerset*, I, pp. 494 f., 503 f., 513, 518).

p. 238, ll. 2 f. .v. *circsceattas*. Nothing is said in D.B. as to the amount of church dues rendered by the various estates. It is uncertain whether payment in money or in kind is meant.

l. 5. *þriwa secan gemot*. This agrees with D.B.

Eaforde, i.e. Ford in Norton Fitzwarren.

l. 6. *Ealdreð*. Ealdred is entered in D.B. as the former holder of Hele which paid geld for 1 hide and could not be separated from Taunton in the time of King Edward. In 1086 it was held by Alfred Pincerna of the Count of Mortain (V.C.H. *Somerset*, I, p. 478).

l. 11. *ungeboden*. In contrast to the conditions affecting Nynehead Flory and Hillfarrance respectively.

Lidigerde. Lydeard St Lawrence. In D.B. it is stated that 2½ hides at *Lidiarda* and *Lega* (i.e. Lydeard and Andersleigh) had been added to the manor of Taunton by King William 'to be held by St Peter and Bishop Walchelin'. It is likewise stated that they had always paid the customary dues to Taunton, and they are included in the list of estates from which these dues were exacted in the Exeter D.B. but not in the Exchequer copy. The truth of the statement as to their liability is supported by the inclusion of Lydeard in the present document.

l. 16. *twam Holaforda*. Holford, later Rich's Holford, in Lydeard St Lawrence, and Holford, later Treble's Holford, in Combe Florey.

l. 17. *eall þæ geylcan gerihta* etc. If the differences in the amount of church dues required are disregarded, the estates enumerated fall into the following groups according to the dues for which they were liable, namely (1) Nynehead Flory and Hele, (2) Oake, Tolland, Upper and Lower Cheddon, Ford and the two Holfords, (3) Bagborough and Lydeard, (4) Hillfarrance

l. 18. *Gisa bisceop.* Bishop of Wells, see p. 469.

Ælfsie abb. Abbot of Bath. He appears in a bond of union for prayer etc. established in 1077 (T. p. 615) and is named also in two series of manumissions (K. 933–937, 1351). He died in 1087.

Wulgeat abb. Abbot Wulfgeat witnesses a charter of 1068 in favour of Gisa, Bishop of Wells (E. p. 433), along with Wulfwold, Abbot of Bath (?), Æthelnoth, Abbot of Glastonbury, and Leofweard, Abbot of Michelney. Is it possible that he was Abbot of Athelney?

ll. 18 f. *Ælfnod · mynsterprauost.* Unidentified but probably Prior of Bath.

l. 19. *Wulfwerd wita.* See pp. 462 f. The estates of Wulfweard the White in Somerset are entered under a special heading in D.B. I, f. 87 (V.C.H. *Somerset*, I, pp. 441 f.). All of them, with the exception of one which had been mortgaged by Wulfweard, were at the time in the king's hands. In addition Wulfweard had held certain estates under the lordship of Queen Edith's manor of Keynsham, one of which had remained in his wife's possession. An entry in the *Inquisitio Geldi* (V.C.H. *Somerset*, I, p. 533) implies that he was still alive in 1084.

Godwine Eadwies sunu. There is no one so distinguished in D.B. although several men of the name are entered there. Perhaps the most likely identification of the present one is with the Godwine described as *anglicus*, whose estate of Draycott near Cheddar (which he and his mother held in the time of King Edward) is entered among the lands of the king's thegns (D.B. I, f. 99; V.C.H. *Somerset*, I, p. 524). According to the *Inquisitio Geldi* (V.C.H. I, p. 528) this estate (which was assessed at one virgate) was held free of geld. A further entry in the *Inquisitio* refers to another holding of Godwine *anglicus* in the hundred of Hartcliffe. One of the tenants in the bishop's manor of Taunton was also called Godwine (D.B. I, f. 87 *b*; V.C.H. I, p. 443).

l. 20. *Ælmer þæs abbodes broþor.* Again there is no one so described in D.B. The name *Ælmær* is of frequent occurrence in connection with estates held in the time of King Edward but in other hands in 1086. One man of the name (which appears in the forms *Almer, Almar, Elmer, Ailmar*) held in the time of King Edward a number of lands belonging to Glastonbury. Was he by any chance 'the abbot's brother'?

Ælgelric æt Healswege. Æthelric is entered in D.B. as the holder of Halsway and several other estates (including Treble's Holford) of Roger de Corcelle (D.B. I, ff. 93 *b*, 94; V.C.H. *Somerset*, I, pp. 488–492). He had held Halsway and one other in the time of King Edward, but had come into possession of the rest since the Conquest.

l. 21. *Heardinc · Eadnoðes sunu.* This witness figures elsewhere in a transaction which took place in Devon (T. p. 649) and is identified by Freeman (*Norman Conquest*, IV, pp. 755-759) with the *Harding*, son of *Elnod* or *Alnod*, who appears as an extensive landowner in D.B., and with the *Herdingus* whose father *Ednod* (Eadnoth the Staller) had been killed in repelling an attack on Somerset by Harold's sons (Sax. Chr. 1067 D; Fl. Wig. 1068; William of Malmesbury, *Gesta Regum*, R.S. II, p. 313). The signature *Herdingus reginae pincerna* is attached to Edward the Confessor's grant of Waltham to Harold in 1062 (K. 813) and *Herding* appears as a witness to a charter of the Conqueror in favour of Gisa, Bishop of Wells, in 1068 (Davis, *Regesta*, p. 7, No. 23). It is a curious fact that Eadnoth's estates did not pass to his son, but in Somerset, as well as elsewhere, are found in the possession of Hugh, Earl of Chester (see D.B. I, f. 91 *b*; V.C.H. *Somerset*, I, p. 473). In the survey of Somerset Hearding's estates are entered among those of the king's thegns, and all of them, except one, had formerly belonged to Tofi the sheriff (see V.C.H. I, pp. 522 f.). He appears also in possession of land held of the Abbot of Glastonbury since before the Conquest (D.B. I, f. 90 *b*; V.C.H. I, p. 466).

Garmund. A certain Garmund or Warmund (the forms are interchangeable in D.B.) was holding estates of various Norman lords in 1086 and is probably identical with the present witness.

Ælfric tigel. There is no one distinguished by this title in D.B. where the name *Alvric* is of common occurrence. One man of the name appears among the king's thegns as the owner of an estate which Brihtric 'his father' (Exeter D.B.) held in the time of King Edward (D.B. I, f. 99; V.C.H. *Somerset*, I, p. 524). There was an *Alvric* also holding land of the manor of Taunton (D.B. I, f. 87 *b*; V.C.H. I, p. 443).

l. 22. *Ordgar se wite.* The only Ordgar mentioned in D.B. in connection with Somerset was no longer holding land in 1086 (see V.C.H. *Somerset*, I, pp. 485, 491, 520).

Ælfwerd Leofsunes sunu. Again there is no one so called in D.B. A certain *Alward* appears among the king's thegns as the holder, along with his brothers, of an estate which their father had held in the time of King Edward (V.C.H. *Somerset*, I, p. 524), while *Alward* or *Ailward*, a thegn, appears as one of the joint holders of lands elsewhere in Somerset since before the Conquest (cf. V.C.H. I, pp. 439, 513). One of the tenants of the manor of Taunton was called *Alward* (D.B. I, f. 87 *b*; V.C.H. I, p. 443), while a man of the same name was holding *Lega* (Andersleigh) of the Bishop of Winchester by grant of King William.

ll. 22 f. *Brichtric se calewa.* A man named Brihtric is included among the king's thegns who were holding land in 1086 (D.B. I, f. 98 *b*; V.C.H. *Somerset*, I, pp. 522 f.) and the name appears frequently elsewhere as that of a former landowner in Somerset. It is impossible to know whether the same man is meant throughout and whether he can be identified with the Brihtric of the present document.

NOTES

l. 23. *Dodda æt Curi.* In the *Inquisitio Geldi* Dodo of Cori is entered as the holder of half a hide in the hundred of Williton (V.C.H. *Somerset*, I, p. 532). *Curi* is now Curry Rivel (see *Publications of the Somerset Record Society*, XIV, p. 39). The holder of Nether Stowey was also called *Dodo* (D.B. I, f. 99; V.C.H. *Somerset*, I, p. 523).

Ælmer werl. The addition to Ælfmær's name seems to be corrupt and I cannot understand what is meant.

Sæwold æt Iliacum. The place-name seems to be corrupt and I have not been able to identify it. A certain *Sirewold* is entered in D.B. as the holder of 2½ hides of the manor of Road which belonged to the Bishop of Coutances (D.B. I, f. 88 *b*; V.C.H. *Somerset*, I, p. 453). The same name appears elsewhere as that of a former holder of land in the time of King Edward (e.g. V.C.H. I, pp. 454, 473). A certain *Siwold* is entered as the former holder of Nether Stowey.

l. 24. *Wulfric æt Pauleshele.* In D.B. *Ulvric* is entered as the former holder in the time of King Edward of *Pouselle* (Poleshill in Milverton). In 1086 it was held by Dodeman of William de Moion (D.B. I, f. 96; V.C.H. *Somerset*, I, p. 506).

Ealdred æt Sulfhere. Ealdred was holding Monksilver of Roger de Corcelle in 1086 (D.B. I, f. 93 *b*; V.C.H. *Somerset*, I, p. 488). He had held it in the time of King Edward.

ll. 24 f. *Wulger æt Hiwerc.* The place-name is apparently corrupt. Is it possible that it represents original *Hiwisc* (see K. 708, 816), D.B. *Hewis* (Ludhewish in Nettlecombe) which had been held by *Ulgar* in the time of King Edward (D.B. I, f. 93 *b*; V.C.H. *Somerset*, I, p. 488)?

l. 25. *Æilwine wunge.* The name *Alwin* is of frequent occurrence in D.B. but never with any addition corresponding to the unknown *wunge* here. Only in one instance is a man of the name entered as holding land in 1086 which he held in the time of King Edward (D.B. I, f. 97 *b*; V.C.H. *Somerset*, I, p. 515). Again it is impossible to know whether the reference is to the same man throughout.

V

MS. St Paul's Chapter House Books, W.D. 16, p. 36 *b*, in the Cathedral Library. This entry is one of several dating from about the end of the thirteenth century. It is said in a note appended by the copyist to have been taken from an old Lambourn missal.

EDITION. J. Footman, *The History of Lambourn Church*, p. 183, with a translation by Birch on p. 17.

DATE. The note added by the copyist attributes this charter to Cnut and states that he granted the church of St Michael at Lambourn to St Paul's. In its present form, however, the record must be assigned to a very much later date, as the tenants of Bockhampton whom it names (Ralph and Edward) were holding their estates there in 1086 and had replaced earlier pre-Conquest tenants. None of the witnesses named can be traced to the time of Cnut except possibly the last one, *Ælfwine b*, if the abbreviation is to be interpreted as 'bishop' (see below). If the charter was originally granted by Cnut, it must therefore have been revised and brought up to date after the Conquest.

p. 240, ll. 1 f. *into þam minstre* etc. An entry in a MS. of the gospels at Bern has been printed in the *Journal of English and Germanic Philology*, XXXIII, 1934, p. 344. It is in the form of a brief announcement by a certain Æthelweard to a certain Ceolbreht that he wished two-thirds of the tithes from Bedwin (Wilts.) and Lambourn to be assigned to the maintenance of the servants of God at Bedwin. The MS. dates from the ninth century and the entry (which is the first of four in Anglo-Saxon) is in a hand of the late tenth century. It is possible that at that time Lambourn did not possess a church of its own.

Lambourn is first mentioned in King Alfred's will where he bequeathes *þone ham æt Lamburnan* to his wife Ealhswith (Harmer, p. 18). It appears again in the will of Æthelflæd, the second wife of King Edmund, whom she survived, and is there bequeathed to her lord, i.e. the king (see Whitelock, pp. 34, 138 f.). In 1086, as in 1066, it was a royal manor, assessed at 20 hides with land for 42 ploughs (D.B. I, f. 57 *b*; V.C.H. *Berks.* I, p. 331).

l. 2. *an hyde landes.* The glebe land attached to the church of Lambourn (which is entered as 1 hide in D.B.) became the manor of Lambourn Deanery. It belonged to the deans of St Paul's till 1800 (V.C.H. *Berks.* IV, p. 255).

sker 7 sacleas. The word *sker* is a Scandinavian loan-word, which corresponds in meaning to the A.S. *clæne*, cf. K. 839, where land is given *sacleas 7 clæne.* The phrase *sker 7 sacleas* is used several times in the charters of Edward the Confessor.

l. 4. *scriftækeres.* For the payment known as *shrift-silver*, i.e. the fee paid upon receiving priestly absolution, see N.E.D. s.v. *shrift*, 10. Is it possible that something of the kind is meant here, i.e. that the priest was allowed the produce of 2 acres at harvest in return for his services as confessor?

fearh. Glossed *porcellus*, see B.T., *Suppl.* p. 207, s.v.

l. 7. *to elefen.* I cannot understand what is meant.

l. 8. *his gielde hrypere.* Perhaps, as Birch takes it, *gielde* means 'gelded', see B.T., *Suppl.* p. 354, s.v. *gelde.*

mid þære hæman. I am uncertain what is meant, unless the reference is to the inhabitants of Up Lambourn and Lambourn itself which are distinguished as *uphæme toune* and *byrihæme tune* later in the document. There is, however, no recorded instance of the word *hæme* used independently in this sense (see *Chief Elements in English Place-Names*, p. 30, s.v.) and the reference may be to some kind of stock.

l. 13. *geneatlandes,* i.e. the land occupied by tenants of the *geneat* class who owed both services and rent to the lord of the manor, see

Rectitudines, cap. 2. Edgar was the first to decree that tithes should be rendered *ge of ðegnes inlande ge of (ge)neatlande* (II Edgar, 1, 1).

ll. 13 f. *vp . hæme toune*. Up Lambourn is a tithing 1 mile northwest of Lambourn.

l. 14. *byrihæme tune*. Apparently Lambourn proper is meant, now known as Chipping Lambourn. The name *burg* is frequently used of a royal residence.

l. 16. *Cobbaudoune*. Coppington Down and Coppington Hill lie to the south-west of Lambourn.

l. 17. *gebur*. For the payments and services of the *gebur* in the late Anglo-Saxon period see *Rectitudines*, cap. 4. His holding is given there as a yardland for which he received both stock and implements from his lord. These hàd to be returned at his death.

l. 19. *þegenlande*. According to D.B. the manor of Lambourn (exclusive of the king's demesne land and of Bockhampton) was divided between Hascoit Musard, Geoffrey de Mandeville and Matthew of Mortain, all of whom had succeeded pre-Conquest tenants. Their estates may have composed the 'thegnland' mentioned here.

l. 20. *on Bokhamtoune · R ·* Ralph 'son of the Earl' is entered in D.B. as the tenant of Bockhampton in succession to three freemen who held it as three manors of King Edward. Its assessment had been reduced from 8 hides to 3 hides less a virgate with land for 4 ploughs (D.B. I, f. 62 *b*; V.C.H. *Berks.* I, p. 362). This estate is identified as West Bockhampton (V.C.H. IV, p. 258).

ll. 21 f. *of Eadwardes*. Edward is entered as the tenant of [East] Bockhampton in succession to a certain Anschil. The assessment had been reduced from 3 hides to half a hide with land for 2 ploughs (D.B. I, f. 63 *b*; V.C.H. *Berks.* I, p. 368).

l. 22. *Eastbury*. Matthew of Mortain's holding in the manor of Lambourn is identified with Eastbury (V.C.H. *Berks.* IV, p. 260).

l. 27. *þare scire*. I have taken *scir* in the sense of 'parish' in view of the reference to the hundred of Lambourn which follows. In 1086 the hundred included the whole of the two parishes of East Garston and Lambourn (V.C.H. *Berks.* IV, p. 246). East Garston takes its name from its pre-Conquest tenant, Esgar the Staller, and it was to this estate of 30 hides (entered as part of the manor of Lambourn) that Geoffrey de Mandeville had succeeded (V.C.H. *Berks.* I, p. 358).

l. 28. *Croc p*[9]. I have not been able to trace any of the priests who appear as witnesses.

l. 30. *Oda*. A man of the name is entered in D.B. as the holder of 1 hide of Ralph's estate at Bockhampton (see above).

Wikyng ou Traue. I have not been able to trace this witness or to identify the place meant.

l. 31. *Ægelwine on Minbiry*. Membury, Wiltshire, on the borders of Berkshire.

Cafi. The name may be *Casi*. I have not been able to trace it in either form.

NOTES

Ealfric lif⁹ etc. It is impossible to tell whether *on* has been omitted by mistake in the case of this name and the next or whether the additional names are descriptive. It is conceivable that *Ealri [on] kin⁹* (if this is the correct reading) might be Ælfric of Kintbury, but I have not been able to find any reference to a man of the name in D.B. In 1086 Kintbury was divided into two manors, one of which was held by the king and the other by the Abbess of Amesbury.

l. 32. *Ælfwine b.* For Ælfwine, Bishop of Winchester in the reign of Cnut, see p. 433. It is noteworthy that this name retains its correct Anglo-Saxon form and it may therefore have been taken over from an earlier document.

VI

MS. British Museum, Cotton Tiberius A. XIII, f. 174 (or 177 by the new numbering). See p. 259.

EDITIONS. Hearne, *Hemingi Chartularium* etc. II, p. 393.
T. p. 439.
This page of the MS. is badly stained and in part illegible. The text is from Hearne, collated with the MS.

DATE. Perhaps about 1084, see below.

p. 242, l. 2. *hídgelde*. In the year 1083 or 1084 the heavy tax of 72 pence was levied on every hide (see Sax. Chr. 1083 E; Fl. Wig. 1084). The *Inquisitio Geldi* is the record of this levy for the south-west shires (see V.C.H. *Somerset*, I, p. 384).

Hemming records that the church of Worcester suffered severely at an earlier period, for during the wars between Æthelred and Swegn it had to sacrifice the majority of its treasures in order to pay its share of the heavy Danegeld imposed upon the country as a whole. The passage runs: *Ob hujus itaque tam gravis tributi exactionem omnia fere ornamenta hujus ecclesie distracta sunt, tabule altaris, argento et auro parate, spoliate sunt, textus exornati, calices confracti, cruces conflate, ad ultimum etiam terre et villule pecuniis distracte sunt* (Hearne, I, p. 248).

l. 3. *of þam æscene*. It would seem from this document that every article of value had a heavy tax placed upon it and had to be redeemed at its full value. The prep. *of* is literally 'from' or 'by', and the idea seems to be that the payment comes from the objects specified. The sums recorded are amazingly high. The *æscen*, see B.T., *Suppl.* p. 19, s.v., is said to be a wooden vessel, but if this was so, it is difficult to account for the cost, unless it was bound with gold or set with jewels.

l. 4. *hrygilebúc*. Taken as equivalent to *recelsbuc*, see B.T. p. 789. The combination of *hr-, hl-* initially for A.S. *r-, l-* is characteristic of the document, cf. *hrodan, hlæfle, hlangan.*

APPENDIX II

MISCELLANEOUS DOCUMENTS
(UNDATED)

I

MS. British Museum, Additional MS. 43703, a transcript of MS. Cotton Otho B. XI (c. 1025) made by Laurence Nowell, Dean of Lichfield, in 1562. The Cotton MS. was almost totally destroyed by fire in 1731 and the folio containing the Burghal Hidage is not among the surviving fragments. In the transcript it follows the Laws of Alfred and is itself followed immediately by the specifications with regard to the maintenance and defence of fortifications which are here printed along with it for the first time. The Burghal Hidage is found also in the following MSS:

(a) Liber Rubeus Scaccarii, f. 29 (c. 1230), in the Public Record Office, London.
(b) British Museum, Cotton Claudius D. II, f. 1 b (c. 1310).
(c) Corpus Christi College, Cambridge, MS. 70, f. 3 (c. 1320).
(d) Oriel College, Oxford, MS. 46, f. 2 b (c. 1330).

EDITIONS. (1) Of the Burghal Hidage:
Riley, *Munimenta Gildhallae*, R.S. II, p. 627, from MS. (b).
B. 1335, from MS. (b).

Gale, *Historiae Britannicae etc. Scriptores XV*, I, p. 748, gives a list of the boroughs and the number of hides attached to each, compiled from MSS. (a) and (b) and a third text which closely resembled, if it was not identical with, that of MS. Cotton Otho B. XI. Liebermann, *Leges Anglorum Londoniis collectae*, p. 10, n. 1, taking Riley's text as a basis, gives the different readings of MSS. (a), (c) and (d). The figures are also reproduced and the document discussed by Maitland, *Domesday Book and Beyond*, pp. 502 ff. and Chadwick, *Anglo-Saxon Institutions*, pp. 204 ff.

(2) Of the specifications which follow:
Hickes, *Dissertatio Epistolaris*, p. 109, from MS. Cotton Otho B. XI.

DATE. The Burghal Hidage would seem to have been drawn up between 911 and 919, i.e. after the death of Æthelred, Earl of Mercia, when Edward the Elder took over London and Oxford with the districts dependent upon them, but before he assumed full control in Mercia after the death of Æthelflæd (see Chadwick, *op. cit.* p. 207). It is noteworthy that the copy contained in MS. Cotton Otho B. XI (as reproduced in the sixteenth-century transcript) did not give the statistics referring to Essex, Worcester and Warwick which are added as a kind of appendix

NOTES

in the copies found in the later MSS. In some cases likewise the figures which it supplies differ from those of the later MSS.

The specifications regarding the maintenance and defence of fortifications are not found along with any of the later copies of the Burghal Hidage, nor do they appear elsewhere. They seem intended to supply the clue to the basis of assessment, i.e. that the area assigned to each borough was roughly proportioned to the amount of wall to be manned and defended there. Calculations based on these specifications (4 hides to 1 rod, pole or perch of wall) give results which can be verified in certain cases (see below) and which suggest that some such rough-and-ready reckoning was actually employed. It is difficult, however, to account for the figure attached to Watchet (513 hides), if the basis of assessment was the same in every case, and the area enclosed both at Lyng and at Lidford, by the same reckoning, must have been extremely small.

p. 246, l. 1. *Eorpeburnan.* Unidentified. The survey begins in the east of Sussex then goes westward as far as Devonshire and returns through Somerset, the north of Wiltshire, Oxfordshire, Berkshire, Buckinghamshire to Surrey.

l. 3. *Burham.* Gale gives 726 hides to Burpham.

ll. 4 f. *Portceastre.* The wall which enclosed the Roman fort at Portchester is still in existence and measures about 800 yards (V.C.H. *Hants.* I, p. 329). It is probable, therefore, that the reading of MS. Cotton Claudius D. II is to be preferred, as 650 hides on the basis of 4 hides to 1 rod, pole or perch of wall gives about 894 yards of wall. It seems impossible, likewise, to accept 150 hides as correct for Southampton which in the time of Æthelstan was important enough to be allowed 2 moneyers (II Æthelstan, 14, 2). The reading of the Liber Rubeus Scaccarii is ambiguous but should probably be taken in the same way as that of MS. Cotton Claudius D. II. It runs as follows: *Donne hyreð to Portecheastre D. ħ · 7 C.L. ħ · to Hamtona 7 to Wincheastra · hyrað* .XXIIII. *hund · ħ.*

l. 6. *Wintaceastre.* The mediaeval wall at Winchester, which probably followed the line of the Roman wall, was about 3280 yards in length (V.C.H. *Hants.* I, p. 285). The 2400 hides of the Burghal Hidage would give, according to the specifications which follow, a wall of 3300 yards in length. The two figures are strikingly close. Winchester was allowed 6 moneyers by Æthelstan (*loc. cit.*).

l. 9. *Werham.* The rampart and ditch which enclose three sides of Wareham (the fourth side being protected by the river) probably represent the Saxon fortifications of the town. They are about 2180 yards in length, a figure which corresponds closely enough to the 2200 yards derived from the 1600 hides of the present document.

Brydian. It is uncertain whether Bridport or Bredy (about 8 miles west of Dorchester) is meant.

l. 16. *Baðan.* The mediaeval wall, which is generally taken to correspond to the Roman one, measured about 1250 yards in length (V.C.H. *Somerset*, I, p. 227). The 1000 hides of the Burghal Hidage would give 1375 yards of wall.

l. 17. *Mealdmesbyring*. The 1200 hides of the present text would give 1650 yards of wall at Malmesbury. This figure seems preferable to the 2200 hides of the later copies.

l. 19. *Wælingforda*. The fortifications at Wallingford which enclose three sides of a large rectangle are about 2115 yards in length. The bank of the river, which forms the fourth side, is about 915 yards in length. The figure of the Burghal Hidage—2400 hides as in the case of Winchester—gives 3300 yards of wall. Wallingford is the only Berkshire borough included in the assessment.

l. 20. *Sceaftesige*. Unidentified.

l. 23. *anes æceres bræde*. The breadth of an acre is 4 rods, poles or perches, i.e. 1 chain.

wealstillinge. This word is not recorded elsewhere and I am uncertain of its meaning.

l. 24. *be anum men*. The hide was originally the amount of land necessary for the support of a household. A clause in a section of Æthelstan's laws which seems intended for the use of boroughs (II Æthelstan, 16) provides that 'every man shall have 2 well-mounted men for every plough in his possession'. This points to the provision of 2 men from every hide for an unspecified purpose which may have been connected with the maintenance and defence of fortifications. The obligation, therefore, is twice as heavy as in the present document and may have been an innovation of Æthelstan which superseded the earlier and customary rule of 1 man for every hide.

l. 25. *gesettan*. If *wære* is rightly taken as 'defence', *gesettan* should perhaps be interpreted as 'garrison', see B.T., *Suppl*. s.v. IV (2 *b*).

l. 27. *furlange*. The furlong is equivalent to 40 rods, poles or perches. The proportions are correctly worked out.

II

MS. The York Gospels in the Dean and Chapter Library, York, f. 157. See p. 413.

EDITIONS. J. Raine, *Fabric Rolls of York Minster* (Surtees Society, Vol. XXXV), p. 142.
B. 1324, from Raine.
W. H. Stevenson, *E.H.R.* XXVII, 1912, p. 9.

DATE. Probably entered in the MS. about 1020–1030, see p. 413.

p. 248, l. 13. *Scirburnan*. Sherburn in Elmet, see p. 358.

l. 14. *aspiciens*. This is the first word of the response to the first lesson in the first nocturn of the first Sunday in Advent.

adteleuaui. See p. 442.

ll. 16 f. *weouedsceatas...ouerbrædels*. See p. 477.

NOTES

III

MS. Pembroke College, Cambridge, MS. 88, *Excerpta de Moralibus Gregorii*, on the reverse of the last leaf. This MS. belonged to Bury St Edmunds.

EDITIONS. M. R. James, *Descriptive Catalogue of MSS. in Pembroke College Library*, p. 81.

M. Förster, *Festschrift für Lorenz Morsbach* in *Studien zur Englischen Philologie*, 1913, pp. 158 f.

l. 19. [x]l *weorcwyrðra manna*. Dr Förster referred this fragment to Liebermann, who suggested that it originally opened with the word *gafol* of which the last letter only remains. It seems to me, however, that it is undoubtedly an inventory, not an account of the yearly tribute payable by the men who owed service, as Liebermann suggested, and that the first letter probably represents a numeral. The tail of the preceding letter is visible and shows that it cannot have been *o* but might possibly have been *c* or more probably *x*, from a comparison with these numerals where they occur elsewhere in the document. I have therefore adopted the reading *xl*, although it is possible, since the leaf has been cut, that 40 does not represent the full number.

This inventory should be compared with those of Farcet and Yaxley (see pp. 72, l. 28, 74, l. 17) which also begin by specifying the number of able-bodied men on each estate.

l. 20. *faldhripera*, cf. p. 74, l. 19, for the only other recorded instance of this word.

l. 22. ...*nhund*. The reading might be *sifon* or *nigon*, i.e. 700 or 900.

ll. 22 f. *opar* [*he*]*alfhund*. Dr Förster reads *twelf*, but the preceding *opar* shows that the reading should be *healf*, and half of the letter *a* preceding the *lf* is actually visible.

IV

MS. Corpus Christi College, Cambridge, MS. 183, f. 96 b (see p. 480). This inventory of church goods precedes the lease of church lands by Bishop Walcher to Ealdgyth.

EDITION. M. R. James, *Descriptive Catalogue of MSS. in Corpus Christi College*, Cambridge, I, p. 441.

p. 250, l. 1. *Tea · calices*. This inventory is particularly interesting as an example of the Northumbrian dialect probably of the tenth century. Characteristic forms are *tea*, *ðrea* (with unrounding of the diphthong *eo* to *ea*, while the first in addition shows loss of final -*n*), also *leoda* (where the diphthong derived from P.Gmc. *au* has retained a trace of its original rounding, see Luick, *Historische Grammatik der Englischen Sprache*, Vol. I, Part 1, § 119). Forms which are characteristic

NOTES

of the Anglian dialect as a whole include *sex, twœgentig, bælt, cetel* and *gerinade*.

bleod, cf. *bleda*, l. 3. It is possible that *bleod* represents original *bleoda* with *a*-Umlaut of *e* to *eo*. It looks, however, as if more than one letter has been erased, and as these additional letters must have projected into the margin, it is not certain whether they originally formed part of *bleod* or of some other word.

l. 2. *án bælt*. King Æthelstan's gifts to St Cuthbert's included *unum cingulum* (B. 685).

án · hana. I have been unable to find any meaning for the word *hana* except 'cock' which seems out of place in the present context. Is it by any chance a misreading of *fana* 'standard'? Æthelstan's gifts to St Cuthbert's included *duo vexilla* (B. 685).

l. 4. *fíf calices · 7 feawer · discas*. It is not clear why these should be enumerated separately from the chalices and patens already mentioned. Æthelstan's gifts included *unum calicem argenteum et duas patenas, alteram auro paratam, alteram Greco opere fabrefactam*.

ll. 4 f. *sex. tene · hornas · gerinade*. Among Æthelstan's gifts are mentioned *tria cornua auro et argento fabrefacta*.

V

MS. Corpus Christi College, Cambridge, MS. 367. This is a composite volume of various works written between the eleventh and the fifteenth centuries. The list of books is entered in a small hand on the verso of the *Life of St Kenelm* and is followed by the *Visio Leofrici* (see p. 476) written in a similar but larger hand.

EDITIONS. M. R. James, *The Sources of Archbishop Parker's MSS.* p. 62.

Floyer and Hamilton, *Catalogue of MSS. in Worcester Cathedral Library*, p. 166, n. 3.

A. S. Napier in *Philological Society's Transactions*, 1907–1910, p. 188.

M. R. James, *Descriptive Catalogue of MSS. in Corpus Christi College*, Cambridge, p. 202.

l. 6. *Deo englissce passionale*. A 'passional' or 'passionale' is a book containing accounts of the sufferings of the saints and martyrs for reading on their festival days (see N.E.D. s.v.). A Latin passional which formerly belonged to Worcester is now MS. 9 in the library of Corpus Christi College, Cambridge (see M. R. James, *op. cit.* p. 21).

.II. *englissce dialogas*, i.e. two copies of Gregory's *Dialogues*. These had been translated at King Alfred's request by Werfrith, Bishop of Worcester, see Asser, *Life of King Alfred*, c. 77; William of Malmesbury, *Gesta Regum*, R.S. I, p. 131.

ll. 6 f. *Oddan boc.* Was this a book (perhaps an anthology) which had belonged to or been presented by Earl Odda? For the latter see pp. 456 ff.

l. 8. .II. *pastorales · englisce,* i.e. two copies of Gregory's *Cura Pastoralis* in King Alfred's translation. The copy sent by King Alfred himself to Worcester is preserved in the Bodleian Library, MS. Hatton 20. Another copy which came from Worcester is now MS. 12 in the library of Corpus Christi College, Cambridge, see M. R. James, *op. cit.* p. 32.

þe englisca regol, i.e. the Rule of St Benedict which was translated by Æthelwold, Bishop of Winchester, see p. 323. MS. 178 in the library of Corpus Christi College, Cambridge, which came from Worcester, contains a collection of Anglo-Saxon Homilies followed by the Rule of St Benedict both in Latin and Anglo-Saxon (see M. R. James, *op. cit.* p. 414).

Barontus, i.e. a copy of the Vision of St Barontus of Pistoia (c. 700), see *Acta Sanctorum,* III, p. 567.

VI

MS. British Museum, Cotton Domitian, I, f. 55 *b*. This consists of two books from St Augustine's bound together. The list occurs on a leaf of the first, an early Isidore, see M. R. James, *The Ancient Libraries of Canterbury and Dover,* p. lxix (where the MS. is described as Cotton Domitian, VIII, instead of I).

EDITION. M. R. James, *loc. cit.* n. 1.

l. 9. *Æpestanes.* Dr James suggests that the reference here is to King Æthelstan and that the entry gives a list of the books which were presented by him to the abbey. I do not think that this is necessarily the case, as the title *cyninges* would almost certainly have been used of a royal donor. The entry, moreover, is in the nature of an inventory rather than a list of gifts, and Æthelstan possibly, the priest Ælfwold almost certainly, had been a member of the community at St Augustine's. The absence of service books is noteworthy, but may be accounted for by the fact that only such books as were unusual or noteworthy were entered in the list. They had perhaps been bequeathed to the abbey by their former owners.

de natura rerum. One of the works of Bede which are represented also by the *De Arte Metrica* and the *Apocalipsin.*

l. 10. *Persius.* The satires of Persius Flaccus, see p. 479.

Donatem '*minorem*'. Donatus was a grammarian of the fourth century. His *Ars Grammatica* consisted of two parts, distinguished respectively as the *Ars minor,* an elementary grammar, and the *Ars maior* for more advanced pupils. Both are included here. From his name is derived the word 'donat' or 'donet' applied to an elementary treatise on grammar, see N.E.D. s.v.

l. 11. *Alchuinum.* Alcuin was one of the most distinguished scholars of the eighth century in England. He was trained at York and gained a European reputation for his scholarship and learning. The later years of his life were spent at the court of Charles the Great. He was the author of prose works on grammar, philology, theology and history, and also wrote a considerable number of Latin poems. One of his longer poems (on the Saints of York) contains a very valuable catalogue of the library at York.

l. 12. *Glossam super Catonem.* The reference is to Dionysius Cato, the author of a collection of apophthegms in verse. His work enjoyed great popularity throughout the Middle Ages. A MS. in the library of Gonville and Caius College, Cambridge, which contains (1) *Glossae super Sedulium*, (2) *Glossae super Catonis Disticha* came from St Augustine's (see M. R. James, *The MSS. in the Library of Gonville and Caius College, Cambridge,* I, No. 144).

libellum etc. I have not been able to identify or trace this work.

l. 13. *Sedulium.* See above and p. 479.

gerim. See B.T., *Suppl.* p. 396, s.v. II a, 'a calendar, numeral', i.e. a directory giving the variations in the canonical hours and in the mass caused by saints' days and festivals, see N.E.D. s.v. *numeral* (3). Ælfric in his Pastoral Letter addressed to Archbishop Wulfstan enjoins (cap. XLIV): *Mæssepreost sceal huru habban mæsseboc·sangbec·7 rædingc-bec·saltere·7 handboc·penitentialem·7 gerim·7 ða beon wel gerihte*; cf. also the *Canons of Ælfric* (addressed to Bishop Wulfsige), cap. XXI.

l. 14. *Dialogorum.* The Dialogues of Gregory.

VII

MS. Bodleian Library, Oxford, Auct. D, II, 14. This is a copy of the gospels in Latin (see *Summary Catalogue of Western MSS. in the Bodleian Library,* Part I, pp. 500 f.). The entry occurs on the last flyleaf, f. 173, the back of which contains the versicle, respond and prayer said at the church door on returning after a lustration of the monastery with holy water. The handwriting of these flyleaf entries is entirely different from that of the MS. proper and the parchment also seems to be of a different type. It is possible, therefore, that this leaf did not originally belong to the MS. The mention of Abbot Baldwin in the list of names which follows the inventory of books suggests that the leaf, if not the MS. as a whole, was connected with Bury St Edmunds.

EDITION. Macray, *Annals of the Bodleian Library,* 2nd ed. p. 30.

DATE. It is evident, particularly from the forms of the proper names, that this entry is post-Conquest. The inclusion of Abbot Baldwin in the list of names which follows the inventory points to a date between 1065 and 1097 or 1098 (see p. 440). Freoden may be the abbot's brother *Frodo* whose lands are entered under a special heading in the Domesday survey of Suffolk (see V.C.H. *Suffolk,* I, p. 490).

NOTES

l. 16. *tropere.* See p. 477.
l. 17. *atteleuaui.* See p. 442.
ll. 18 f. *Blakehad boc.* Is this a reference to a copy of the Rule of St Benedict? The Benedictines were called 'black monks' from the colour of their dress.
l. 19. *forbeande.* I cannot understand this form.
l. 20. '*do'natum.* See p. 499.
.xv. *bocas.* It is noteworthy that in spite of the erasures the total number of books named is fifteen.
ll. 21 f. *Ealfric* etc. These names are separated from the inventory by a space of about two lines so that they have possibly no connection with it.

VIII

MS. Pembroke College, Cambridge, MS. 83, *Beda super Lucam*, on the first flyleaf. This MS. belonged to Bury St Edmunds.

EDITIONS. M. R. James, *Descriptive Catalogue of the MSS. in Pembroke College Library*, p. 73.

M. Förster, *Festschrift für Lorenz Morsbach* in *Studien zur Englischen Philologie*, 1913, pp. 153–157.

This fragment, which was entered in the MS. about the middle of the twelfth century, is apparently part of a will which may have been drawn up by or for the Wægen whose signature appears at the end of the document, followed by what seems to be a double cross. No place-names are mentioned so that it is impossible to assign it to any particular locality, but the use throughout of the Scandinavian money terms 'mark' and 'ore' and the occurrence of other Scandinavian loan-words (see below) suggest that it belongs to the Danelaw. The name *Wægen* itself represents the Scandinavian *Vagn* (see p. 458). Since the fragment occurs in a MS. which belonged to Bury, it is to be assumed that the will had some connection with the abbey or at any rate with the neighbourhood. There is no means of dating it exactly, but in its present form it is clearly post-Conquest.

p. 252, l. 1. *twælf oræn.* There seems to be no means of deciding the value of the ore in the present document, i.e. whether 16 or 20 pence.

l. 2. *at his þruth.* The form *þruth* for *þruh* shows the substitution of *th* for final *h* which is frequently found in Middle English and generally attributed to the influence of French scribes.

It is difficult to determine the exact force of *at* here and throughout the passage, but it would seem that the sums specified were meant to be expended on the articles mentioned. I have not been able, however, to find any recorded instance of A.S. *æt* or M.E. *at* used in this sense. Liebermann suggested to Dr Förster that the phrase *at his þruth*, 'an seinem Sarge' was equivalent to 'bei offenem Grabe' but the force of *at* appears to be the same throughout, and it seems to me that *at hale, at wax, at milch* can hardly mean anything but 'for ale, wax, milk'.

hoferbredles, i.e. A.S. *oferbrædels*. The use of an unhistorical *h* before initial vowels is characteristic of the document, cf. *hale, hopær hæræ*, etc. The translation follows Dr Förster.

l. 3. *7 twa ore 7 an ære*. It seems better to take 7 *twa ore* with what precedes rather than with what follows, i.e. 7 pence and 2 ores for ale and 1 ore for bread, as the sums expended on ale and bread respectively seem then less out of proportion. Dr Förster's suggestion that something may have been omitted after 7 *twa ore* is also possible. The form *ære* represents the Scandinavian singular *eyrir*, cf. p. 331.

l. 5. *te fyrræ · ærflæ*. Dr Förster gives the explanation of this phrase. The form *fyrræ* represents O.Norse *fyrre*, 'first', while *ærflæ*, derived from O.Norse *erfiǫl*, 'funeral feast', is recorded in the fifteenth century in the form *arvell*, and continued in use in the dialects of N. England until the nineteenth, see N.E.D. s.v. *arval*.

at hældyggæ. Dr Förster explains this form as representing *ælding*, derived from O.Norse *elding*, 'fuel'. Two examples of its use in Middle English are recorded, and it survives in modern dialects, cf. N.E.D., E.D.D., s.v. *elding*.

l. 6. *seuentene peniges*. According to VI Æthelstan, 6, 2 the value of a pig was 10 pence.

l. 7. *an repær*. Apparently *at* has been omitted here and also before *þræ buces* and *an cese*.

l. 9. *7 half twælf ere*. This seems to represent the A.S. *healf twelfta ere*, i.e. 11½ ores. I have omitted the phrase 7 *fyf ora* which precedes, because to my mind it is not meant to be included. Although in the same handwriting and still legible, it is very much paler than the rest, and it would seem that an attempt has been made to obliterate it. I would suggest, therefore, that it was repeated by mistake from the preceding paragraph and then erased, though not completely so, by the copyist.

at te hopær · hærflæ. It was a Scandinavian custom to hold a double funeral feast, the second either a month or a year later than the first. References to this custom in the Swedish and Norwegian laws are quoted by Dr Förster (pp. 156 f.). There seems to be no other record of its occurrence in England.

IX

MS. The MS. consists of a leaf of parchment with the entries on both sides. This leaf has been cut in two (from top to bottom) and one half is in the possession of Captain Cragg of Threekingham, Lincolnshire, while the other half (again cut in two from top to bottom) is in the library of Queens' College, Cambridge, where it was found in the binding of a book. The Queens' College fragments were printed by

Skeat in the *Proceedings of the Cambridge Philological Society*, 1902, pp. 12 f., but the portion in Captain Cragg's possession has not been printed before. It was recognised as part of the Queens' College document by Professor Stenton.

It has been found impossible to reconstruct the text completely as words are wholly or partly missing at the two points in every line where the document has been cut. It is obvious that only one or two letters are lacking between the second Cambridge fragment and Captain Cragg's portion, but rather more seem to have been lost when the Cambridge portion was cut in two. Unfortunately also the writing has faded badly in patches and it is frequently impossible to make out the reading with any certainty. I am greatly indebted to Professor Stenton and Sir Allen Mawer for help in the elucidation of the document.

Four different handwritings can be distinguished in the entries, while scraps of Latin in the blanks and at the end were probably scribbled at a much later date when the document had ceased to be of value.

DATE. Thorney (see p. 324) was refounded by Bishop Æthelwold in 972 (Dugdale, II, p. 593) and it is probable that the earlier notes of the property assigned to the new foundation were made soon afterwards. The record as a whole recalls the Peterborough documents (Nos. XXXIX and XL) and may have been begun at the instigation of Bishop Æthelwold himself. The handwriting of the last entry seems to be of later date.

l. 15. *beansæde*. This compound is not recorded elsewhere.

Niwantune. Water Newton, Hunts., see Pl.N. *Hunts*. p. 193. An estate of 5 hides was held there by Thorney Abbey in 1086 (D.B. I, f. 204*b*; V.C.H. *Hunts.* I, p. 345). According to the account given in Edgar's foundation charter (B. 1297) it was acquired in the first instance from Ælfric *cild*.

l. 17. *Fearresheafde*. An estate at Farcet is included in the endowment of Thorney in Edgar's foundation charter (see above).

gegrindum. I have taken this as equivalent to *gegrynd* (see p. 102, l. 18) and have adopted the translation suggested for the latter in B.T. p. 397, s.v.

l. 19. *Stangrunde*. In 1086 Thorney Abbey held an estate at Stanground, Hunts., assessed at 8 hides with land for 10 ploughs (D.B. *loc. cit.*).

l. 20. *Geaceslea*. Yaxley, Hunts., see p. 323.

l. 22. *Witlesmere*. The purchase of Whittlesey Mere for Thorney is recorded in Edgar's foundation charter (see above).

l. 23. *mæderwerde*. I cannot understand what is meant. The final letter of the first word seems unmistakably *r* but might be a badly formed *s*. Unfortunately *mædes werde* (perhaps to be taken as one word) seems also to be inexplicable. Sir Allen Mawer has drawn my attention in connection with this form to the difficult *medes* of *Medeshamstede* and the *mædes* which lies behind Meads (Pl.N. *Sussex*, p. 431). The payment for whatever is meant is a comparatively high one.

Huntandune. Two hides of land at Huntingdon and the little monastery of St Mary outside the town are included in the endowment of Thorney in Edgar's foundation charter.

p. 254, l. 1. *Middeltune.* Milton, Cambridgeshire. For the acquisition of this estate by Ely, see *Liber Eliensis*, II, c. 31.

l. 2. `ge'eah`ta'de. See B.T., *Suppl.* p. 318, s.v. *geeahtian.*

l. 7. *mylenoxan.* This compound is not recorded elsewhere. According to VI Æthelstan 6, 2 an ox was valued at a mancus.

l. 9. `x. pund´. This probably represents the total so far.

ll. 11 f. *to isene.* Perhaps for tools.

l. 17. *Hæpfelda.* According to the *Liber Eliensis*, II, c. 7 an estate of 40 hides at Hatfield was granted to Ely by King Edgar but at his death it was successfully claimed by Earl Æthelwine and his brothers and had to be bought back by the monks.

l. 29. *byryg.* The remainder of the document is concerned with Ely and its estates. *Byryg* seems to be used as a proper name and I have taken it as a shortened form of 'St Etheldreda's *burh*'. The reference seems unmistakably to Ely itself and the use of *burh* in the same way has given us the modern Peterborough and Bury St Edmunds.

l. 30. *Strætham.* An estate of 8 hides at Stretham was bought for Ely by Bishop Æthelwold and later it was added to by the purchase of two separate holdings of 1 hide and 24 acres respectively (*Liber Eliensis*, II, c. 10).

l. 31. *Horningesige.* An interesting story is told of the unscrupulous behaviour of two priests, Æthelstan and Herulf, who were attached to a community at Horningsea. The former, who acted as deputy for the latter, was discovered to be a receiver of stolen goods but was ransomed by Herulf with the treasures belonging to the church. The estate was purchased for Ely by Bishop Æthelwold in the time of King Edgar (*Liber Eliensis*, II, cc. 32 f., 45, 49).

p. 256, l. 1. *Hafucestune.* An estate of 4½ hides at Hauxton was purchased by Bishop Æthelwold in 975 (*Liber Eliensis*, II, c. 27).

l. 2. [M]*eldeburnan.* See p. 346.

l. 3. *sige.* This form does not seem to occur elsewhere but the reference is apparently to sows. Does it perhaps represent a mutated plural *syge* derived from *sugu*?

l. 5. *Æþelflæd.* A benefactress of the name is referred to in the *Liber Eliensis*, II, c. 64. Her will is extant (Whitelock, No. XIV). She was the second wife of King Edmund and, if the *Liber Eliensis* is right in describing her as the wife of Earl Æthelstan, she must have married again after his death. Her sister was the wife of Earl Brihtnoth and was also a benefactress of Ely.

l. 10. *werum.* At Professor Stenton's suggestion I have taken this in the sense in which the word *wer* is used in the last paragraph, i.e. 'weir' or 'dam' or perhaps more correctly 'eel-trap'.

l. 14. *hyre.* See B.T., *Suppl.* p. 586, s.v. *hyr*, 1: 'payment contracted to be made for the temporary use of anything'.

l. 15. *.iiii. ðusend.* There can be no doubt that the reference is to eels.

l. 16. *snasa.* The original sense of the word is 'spit or skewer' (see B.T. p. 891) but it is used to indicate a quantity of fish, presumably because they were frequently run on to a stick. The word *sticca* is used with the same sense at the end of the paragraph, but it is possible that the two words represent different quantities and that, as Sir Allen Mawer has suggested to me, a certain number of (short) *snasa* went to make up one (long) *sticca.* The earliest example given in the N.E.D. of the use of the word 'stick' as a measure of quantity for small eels (apparently 25 or 26) is from D.B.

ll. 16 f. *tynadwere.* Presumably a fenced weir or dam of some kind, from *tynan.*

l. 17. *forwerde.* This form is difficult and the reference may be to another weir with *werde* written by mistake for *were.* Sir Allen Mawer has suggested as a possible emendation *fordwere,* 'weir by a ford'.

l. 18. *ladwere.* See B.T. p. 604, s.v. *lad*, 11. The reference is apparently to one of the fen lodes.

burhwere. Possibly the Ely weir, if, as seems probable, the *burh* referred to is once again the *burh* of St Etheldreda.

l. 19. *mudecan[wer]e.* The first element seems like a proper name.

l. 21. *wratwere.* Sir Allen Mawer has suggested that the name might mean the weir by which crosswort (*wræt*) grew, see B.T. p. 1270, s.v.

bulingge.... Sir Allen Mawer has drawn my attention to the *bulunga fenn* of a Westminster charter (B. 1048).

l. 22. *brade.* There might be some connection between this name and Bradney near March, see Ekwall, *English River-Names*, p. 138.

INDEX NOMINUM

Clarendon figures refer to pages, plain figures to lines of text

Æffa, Ælfhelm Polga's wife, **388**
Æffe, Wulfgar's wife, **52**, 2 ff.
Æfic, seneschal, **136**, 18; **381**
Ælfflæd, Earl Brihtnoth's wife, **386** f., **430**, **444**
Ælfgar, Earl of (1) East Anglia, (2) Mercia, **214**, 27; **396**, **434**, **467**, **481**
— Earl of Essex, **337**, **430**, **444**
— king's reeve, **138**, 7; **382**
— cleric (Worc.), **86**, 28; **88**, 25; **96**, 22; deacon, **114**, 20; **116**, 33; **118**, 22; **120**, 25; **335**, **361**
— monk, **144**, 14; **176**, 2 ff.
— of Minehead, **200**, 25; **434**, **449**
— Ordgar's brother, **200**, 22; **459**
— Sired's son, **150**, 13
— Stigand's priest, **178**, 13 f.
— *se Hunitunisca*, **130**, 20; **376**
— **136**, 20; **186**, 2; **192**, 8; **208**, 10; **210**, 5; **434**, **439**
Ælfgeat, Hength's son, **146**, 25; **394**
— *cniht*, **148**, 3; **394**
Ælfgifu Emma, wife of (1) Æthelred II, (2) Cnut, **156**, 20; **168**, 23 f.; **170**, 7 f.; **172**, 3 f.; **180**, 19; **182**, 22; **184**, 25 f.; **188**, 24 f.; **212**, 1; **218**, 15; **385**, **405**, **417**, **425**–**427**, **430**–**433**, **462** f., **470** f.
— wife of King Edwy, **58**, 15; **315**
— wife of Earl Ælfgar, **481**
— of Northampton, **423**
— **136**, 22 f. (2)
Ælfheah, Bishop of Lichfield, **373**
— Bishop of Wells, **50**, 30; **306**
— I, Bishop of Winchester, **50**, 33; **94**, 1; **306**, **417**
— II, Bishop of Winchester and Archbishop of Canterbury, **130**, 11; **144**, 4; **162**, 3; **373**, **386**, **410** ff., **429**
— Abbot, **94**, 41; **342**
— Earl of Hampshire, **92**, 9, 11 f.; **94**, 28; **106**, 13; **336**, **338** f., **350**, **370**, **458**

Ælfheah, Ælfstan's son, **84**, 7 ff.; **333** f.
— King Edwy's seneschal, **58**, 17 f.; **315**, **339**
— thegn, **50**, 25, 33 (2)
— **140**, 8
Elfhelm the Young, **144**, 14; **388**
— Ordhelm's son, **142**, 8, 17; **385**
— Polga, **130**, 19; **144**, 11, 13; **376**, **388**
— **130**, 16; **136**, 19; **170**, 1; **204**, 10; **375**
Ælfhere, Abbot (? of Bath), **136**, 10; **380**
— Earl of Mercia, **62**, 15; **64**, 9; **66**, 5 f.; **86**, 13; **88**, 3; **94**, 27; **96**, 2; **106**, 13 f., 22 f.; **114**, 3; **116**, 3; **118**, 3; **122**, 12; **124**, 2; **319**, **350**, **356**, **369** f., **404**, **457** f.
— thegn, **18**, 34; **26**, 20; **50**, 32, 36; **106**, 11; **280**, **287**, **306**, **349**
— **365**
Ælfhild, relative of Bishop Oswald, **86**, 11, 16
Ælfhun, Bishop of London, **385**
— Abbot, **130**, 16; **140**, 20; **142**, 7, 10; **375**, **384** f.
Ælfmær, Bishop of Selsey, **160**, 35; **409**
— Abbot of St Augustine's, Canterbury and Bishop of Sherborne, **148**, 11; **150**, 9; **160**, 39; **168**, 26; **395**, **409** f., **417**, **420**
— priest, **164**, 10
— *cild*, **144**, 15 f.; **389**
— *werl*, **238**, 23; **490**
— 'the abbot's brother', **238**, 20; **488**
— **388**
Ælfnoth, Prior (? of Bath), **238**, 18 f.; **488**
— priest, **252**, 11
— cleric (Worc.), **114**, 24; **116**, 36; **118**, 28; **120**, 26; **361** f.
— of *Creast*, **82**, 13
— of Orpington, **142**, 11
— Bada's son, **74**, 28; **78**, 23 f.; **80**, 28 f.

Ælfnoth, 254, 6; 256, 4, 11
Ælfred. *See* Alfred
Ælfric, Archbishop of York, 160, 29; 184, 26; 408, 457
— I, Bishop of East Anglia (Elmham), 425, 443 f.
— II, Bishop of East Anglia, 425, 432, 443, 445
— III, Bishop of East Anglia, 178, 19; 425, 431
— Bishop (of Hereford or Ramsbury), 54, 16; 306, 311
—— II, Bishop of Ramsbury and Archbishop of Canterbury, 140, 16; 142, 9f.; 144, 3; 374, 380f., 384f., 389, 405, 428
— Abbot of Evesham, 380
— Abbot of Pershore, 210, 4; 460
— Abbot of St Augustine's, Canterbury, 94, 34; 341
— Abbot, the homilist, 373, 386, 401, 500
— Abbot (? of Malmesbury), 136, 12; 380
— Earl of Hampshire, 130, 13; 136, 3; 144, 4; 373f., 381, 386
— Earl of Mercia, 76, 18; 124, 13; 330, 369f.
— *cild*, 76, 8; 106, 20; 323, 330, 350, 503
— priest (Worc.), 64, 4, 29; 66, 27; 320
— of Comberton, 210, 7f.; 460f.
— of Epsom, 124, 3; 367
— brother of Ælfheah, Ælfstan's son, 84, 10, 14; 333
— Æscwyn's son, 122, 4f., 7; 333, 352, 355, 365f.
— Earl Odda's brother, 200, 21f.; 208, 10; 210, 5; 457
— Siraf's son, 106, 20; 350
— Wihtgar's son, 178, 21; 425 f.
— thegn, 50, 26; 54, 10; 182, 24; 310, 431
— *km*⁹, 240, 31; 493
— *lif*⁹, 240, 31; 493
— *tigel*, 238, 21; 489
— goldsmith, 476
— 64, 6, 12; 66, 1; 118, 1; 136, 5; 184, 13; 250, 21; 288, 321, 380f., 432
Ælfsige I, Bishop of Winchester and Archbishop of Canterbury, 56, 16; 58, 16; 312

Ælfsige II, Bishop of Winchester, 146, 23 (*Æpel-*); 160, 32 (*Ælfwine*); 168, 25; 392f., 408f., 417
— Abbot of Bath, 238, 18; 488
— Abbot of the New Minster, 142, 23f.; 385
— Abbot of Peterborough, 156, 25; 328, 405
— Abbot of St Benedict's, Hulme, 184, 12; 432
— monk, 254, 10, 26
— priest, 144, 17; 389; (Worc.), 114, 28; 116, 37; 118, 28; 120, 25; 126, 32; 132, 28; 138, 28; 360ff.
— cleric (Winch.), 28, 9; 40, 23
— *cild*, 148, 13; 150, 11; 395
— Hunlafing, 56, 7; 312
— Brihtsige's son, 90, 1f., 5
— Ælfwine's father, 110, 6; 356f.
— father of Wulfstan Uccea, 68, 8, 12; 324
— King Edred's goldsmith, 388
— *portgerefa*, 469
— thegn, 50, 34f. (2); 156, 23f.; 356
— 52, 16; 72, 31; 80, 28, 32; 110, 3; 308, 436
Ælfstan, Bishop of London, 86, 1; 94, 28; 122, 11 (?); 124, 1 (?; 130, 10; 334, 366, 391
— Bishop (? of Ramsbury), 106, 6, 19; 122, 11f. (?); 124, 1 (?); 349f., 366
— Bishop of Rochester, 86, 2f.; 130, 10f.; 140, 11; 332, 334, 365
— Abbot of Glastonbury, 94, 36; 341
— Abbot of St Augustine's, Canterbury, 172, 4; 174, 19; 176, 16, 24, 27; 178, 1f., 9; 190, 9; 410, 420, 437f.
— Earl, 12, 30; 18, 28; 26, 21; 106, 8; 273, 279, 281f., 349
— Staller, 188, 29; 438
— priest (Winch.), 40, 20; 298
— deacon (Winch.), 26, 20
— cleric (Winch.), 40, 16; (Worc.), 86, 29; 88, 23; 96, 27; 114, 23; 118, 26; 120, 24; 335
— Heahstan's son, 84, 5, 8f.
— 38, 10; 60, 18 (3); 62, 13; 296, 388
Ælfswith, Brihtric's wife, 323, 354f., 365, 429

INDEX NOMINUM

Ælfthryth, King Edgar's wife, **94**, 10, 25; **104**, 3; **124**, 1 f.; **136**, 4, 17; **340** f., **348**, **367**, **369**, **372**, **381**, **387**
Ælfwaru, **136**, 23
Ælfweard, Abbot of Evesham and Bishop of London, **148**, 24 f.; **156**, 1, 26; **180**, 20; **184**, 28; **396** f., **404**, **433** f.
— of Denton, **74**, 32; **82**, 1 f., 23 f.
— of Longdon, **208**, 13; **459**
— Ælfwold's son, **200**, 24; **449**
— Leofsunu's son, **238**, 22; **489**
— the Kentishman, **170**, 2; **419**
— *cniht*, **148**, 3; **394**
— thegn, **94**, 41; **342**
— **80**, 30; **136**, 20; **212**, 19; **464**
Ælfwig, Bishop of London, **160**, 31; **168**, 24 f.; **408** f., **418**
— Abbot of Bath, **216**, 22; **469**
— of Haydon, **200**, 26
Ælfwine, Bishop of Winchester, **184**, 18; **188**, 25; **240**, 32 (?); **409**, **433**, **462** f., **493**
— Abbot of Buckfast, **200**, 20 f.; **448**
— Abbot of the New Minster, **168**, 27; **188**, 27; **202**, 11, 23; **212**, 15 f.; **214**, 28; **417** f., **437**
— priest at Walsingham, **445**
— priest, **164**, 9 f.; **172**, 6; **420**
— the Red, **188**, 30; **204**, 11
— Ælfsige's son, **110**, 3, 18; **356** f.
— Wulfweard's son, **178**, 20 f.; **425**
— Bishop Oswald's nephew, **343**
— thegn, **94**, 35; **160**, 36; **341**, **409**
— **136**, 19; **184**, 13; **186**, 17; **212**, 18; **432**, **436**, **464**
Ælfwold I, Bishop of Crediton, **56**, 18; **94**, 31; **313**
— II, Bishop of Crediton, **317**, **373**, **376**, **389**
— II, Bishop of Sherborne, **200**, 13, 19 f.; **214**, 25; **447**
— Earl, **50**, 27; **306**
— priest, **250**, 14; **499**
— son of Ælfhelm the Young, **144**, 15; **388**
— **74**, 25; **78**, 17, 21, 28; **200**, 24; **256**, 3
Ælfwyn, daughter of Earl Æthelred and Æthelflæd, **36**, 22; **295**
Ælla, King of Northumbria, **368**
— (Ælfwine), Bishop of Lichfield, **48**, 7; **50**, 37; **54**, 9; **303**, **309**
Ærcmund, thegn, **20**, 24; **280**
Æscwig, Bishop of Dorchester, **122**, 30; **136**, 12; **367**, **373**, **380**, **430**
— Abbot of Bath, **94**, 37; **342**
Æscwyn, Ælfric's mother, **122**, 4 f.
Æslac, **358**, **414** f.
Æthelbald, King of Mercia, **2**, 1 f., 18; **8**, 12, 16; **259** f.
— Earl, afterwards King of Wessex, **14**, 18; **18**, 2, 4; **20**, 10; **104**, 22; **275** f., **278**, **349**
Æthelbert II, King of Kent, **84**, 2; **332**
— Earl, afterwards King of Wessex, **14**, 20; **16**, 5 f., 19 f.; **18**, 24; **20**, 2, 23; **104**, 22; **275**, **278**, **349**; charters of, **280** f., **285**, **472**
— (-*byrth*), priest, **40**, 23; **298**
Æthelburg, wife of King Edwin of Northumbria, **375**
Æthelfand, Æthelmær's son, **146**, 24 f.; **393**
Æthelferth of Newton, **252**, 15
— the Stout, **80**, 24
— thegn, **26**, 19; **287**
Æthelflæd, Lady of the Mercians, **34**, 23; **36**, 6; **38**, 3, 13; **294** ff., **303**, **494**
— Toki's wife, **154**, 13; **403**
— Earl Ælfgar's daughter and second wife of King Edmund, **444**, **491**, **504**
— **136**, 24; **256**, 5; **504**
Æthelfrith, Earl, **38**, 7; **295**
Æthelgar, Bishop of Crediton, **50**, 34; **54**, 15; **307**
— Abbot of the New Minster, Bishop of Selsey and Archbishop of Canterbury, **94**, 38; **102**, 20; **104**, 8; **106**, 19; **110**, 15; **122**, 30; **130**, 9; **342**, **350**, **367**, **372**–**374**, **385**
Æthelgeard, **86**, 11
Æthelgeard of Frome, **152**, 1 f.
Æthelgerth, thegn, **50**, 37
Æthelgifu, King Alfred's daughter, **24**, 12; **284**
— King Edwy's mother-in-law, **58**, 15 f.; **315**
— **60**, 5, 8; **136**, 23
Æthelheah, Bishop of Sherborne, **24**, 20; **26**, 16; **285**
— priest, **20**, 23

INDEX NOMINUM

Æthelheard, King of Wessex, **339**
— Earl, **12**, 28; **273**
Æthelhelm, cleric (Winch.), **40**, 18
Æthelhild, **110**, 3, 15; **136**, 21; **356**
Æthelhun, priest, **4**, 16f., 27; **262**
Æthelm, cleric (Winch.), **28**, 9
— **60**, 14; **62**, 13ff.; **134**, 28; **379**
Æthelmær, Archbishop Stigand's brother, Bishop of Elmham, **184**, 1f., 16; **214**, 24f.; **425, 431, 445, 464, 466**
— Earl of Hampshire, **110**, 15; **357**
— **130**, 21; **144**, 4; **376, 386**f.; Earl of the Western Provinces, **146**, 24
— Cola's son, **200**, 23; **448**
— **134**, 1, 5; **146**, 25; **156**, 2, 15; **202**, 7, 13; **250**, 19; **378**f.
Æthelmod, thegn, **18**, 28; **106**, 6; **279, 349**
Æthelmund, thegn, **20**, 35; **48**, 9; **50**, 36; **281, 304, 306**
— **56**, 20; **264, 314**
Æthelnoth, Archbisnop of Canterbury, **154**, 11; **160**, 27; **168**, 24; **172**, 4; **174**, 1, 9; **188**, 16; **403, 408, 412, 417**f.
— Abbot of Glastonbury, **218**, 7; **470, 488**
— priest, **54**, 11
— reeve at Eastry, **4**, 15, 26; **262**
— thegn, **26**, 16; **287, 377**
— son of Æthelferth the Stout, **80**, 24
— Wistan's son, **130**, 21; **376**
Æthelred I, King, **14**, 20; **16**, 26; **18**, 29; **20**, 6, 25; **22**, 2f.; **24**, 7; **275, 282**; charters of, **279**f., **285, 308**
— II, the Unready, King, **124**, 13; **136**, 2; **140**, 11; **144**, 2f.; **162**, 3; **218**, 19; **360, 365, 376, 389, 391, 393, 417, 427, 431, 493**; charters and writs of, **324, 349, 356, 368**f., **372, 375**ff., **383, 386**f., **392**f., **419**; laws of, **260, 286, 328, 336, 339, 356, 358, 401, 404, 412, 447, 452, 481, 486**; time of, **284, 325, 348, 376, 392**f., **404, 428**
— Archbishop of Canterbury, **24**, 19; **285**
— Earl of Mercia, **34**, 23; **36**, 6; **38**, 3, 13; **294**ff., **362, 494**

Æthelred, reeve of Canterbury, **142**, 18
— **10**, 29; **78**, 11; **271, 278**
Æthelric, Bishop of Dorchester, **160**, 34; **214**, 7; **409, 418, 465**f.
— I, Bishop of Selsey, **168**, 25; **417**f.
— Bishop of Sherborne, **146**, 23; **387, 392**f.
— Bigga, **170**, 1f.; **172**, 5; **188**, 1ff.; **190**, 7; **192**, 8; **204**, 9; **387, 409, 411, 420, 436**f., **451**
— of Halsway, **238**, 20; **488**
— of *Hernicwelle*, **144**, 16f.
— son of Ælfhelm the Young, **144**, 15; **388**
— Æthelmund's son, **264**
— Bishop Brihtheah's brother, **208**, 11; **210**, 6; **362, 458**
— cleric (Worc.), **361**
— thegn, **18**, 30; **106**, 10; **160**, 35; **180**, 5; **279, 349, 409**
— **130**, 21; **144**, 5; **148**, 13; **376, 391, 395, 430**
Æthelsige I, Bishop of Sherborne, **136**, 12; **138**, 1; **373, 379–382**
— II, Bishop of Sherborne, **393**
— Abbot of St Augustine's, Canterbury, **218**, 7f.; **470**
— deacon (Worc.), **114**, 23; **116**, 34; **118**, 25; **120**, 28; priest, **126**, 28; **132**, 25; **134**, 26; **138**, 30; **362**
— the Red, **152**, 10
— Ælfric's son, **66**, 1f.
— uncle of Earl Æthelwine, **74**, 27; **78**, 22f.; **330**
Æthelstan, King of England, **44**, 7, 19; **46**, 29; **48**, 14, 23; **50**, 20; **54**, 3f., 9; **168**, 16; **301**f., **304–307, 309, 313, 344, 359, 377, 402, 415, 474–477, 480, 495**f., **498**f.; charters of, **285, 301, 304, 306, 312, 325, 390**f., **417**; laws of, **286, 339, 367, 373, 401, 486, 495**f., **502, 504**; reign of, **304, 308**f., **495**
— King of Kent, **270**
— the Ætheling, **354, 429, 433**
— Bishop of Hereford, **148**, 24, 28f.; **150**, 24; **160**, 38; **162**, 1, 9; **184**, 27; **186**, 11; **396, 411**f.
— Half-king, Earl of East Anglia, **44**, 6; **50**, 28 (*min*.); **299, 306, 329**f.

INDEX NOMINUM

Æthelstan, Earl, 26, 18; 90, 25, 28; 94, 26; 287, 337, 341, 504
— thegn, 50, 29 f. (2); 306
— sacristan (Worc.), 64, 28 f.; 321
— priest (Winch.), 40, 19; (Worc.), 86, 30; 88, 24; 96, 26; 114, 26; 116, 38; 118, 26; 120, 24; 126, 30; 33 (2); 132, 26 f. (2); 134, 22, 27 (2); 138, 26 f. (2); 298, 321, 360 f., 504
— cleric (Winch.), 28, 14; 40, 14; (Worc.), 66, 26; 297
— the Fat, 208, 12, 17; 460
— of Bledlow, 154, 22
— of Sunbury, 90, 4 ff.
— of Upton, 78, 2; 80, 34
— Catla's son, 80, 33; 82, 7
— son of Tofi the Proud, 400
— Bishop Oswald's brother, 343
— Bishop Oswald's thegn, 66, 8, 21; 322
— 52, 17; 78, 21; 134, 15; 250, 9; 308, 378, 499
Æthelswith, wife of King Burgred of Mercia, 272
Æthelweard, Earl of the Western Provinces, 130, 12 f.; 373, 387
— cleric (Winch.), 40, 17
— King Alfred's son, 474
— thegn, 94, 36, 42 (2); 341 f.
— 144, 5; 378 f., 386, 388, 491
Æthelwig, Abbot of Evesham, 218, 7; 459, 470
— of [? Fecka]nham, 164, 11; 413
— monk, 164, 9
Æthelwine, Earl of East Anglia, 74, 24; 78, 20; 94, 30; 128, 24; 130, 12; 319, 329, 504
— sheriff (Kent), 150, 9 f.; 398
— of Membury, 240, 31
— prior (Worc.), 457, 461
— the Black, 425
— *stikehare*, 216, 20 f.; 469
— *wunge*, 238, 25; 490
— Ælfhelm's son, 170, 1; 204, 9 f.; 385
— son of Brihtmær of Gracechurch, 216, 16
— 250, 21
Æthelwold, Bishop of Lichfield, 8, 29; 268
— I, Bishop of Winchester, 68, 1, 13 f.; 72, 1 ff.; 74, 29 f.; 76,
7 f.; 78, 5, 11; 80, 5, 27; 94, 8, 27; 98, 21; 102, 16, 21; 104, 4; 106, 19; 110, 1, 14; 122, 11, 30; 315, 317, 323 ff., 328 ff., 346 f., 499, 503
— II, Bishop of Winchester, 393
— Earl of East Anglia, 329, 340
— Earl, 323
— cleric (Worc.), 64, 30 f.; 114, 25; 118, 27; 120, 25; 321
— *cniht*, 114, 1, 7 f., 18; 360
— thegn, 50, 31; 306
— the Stout, 130, 20; 376, 387
— Frithegist's son, 82, 14 ff.
— 60, 18; 130, 19; 297, 376, 386
Æthelwulf, King of Wessex, 10, 2; 14, 2, 15; 18, 2; 20, 9 f.; 68, 22; 188, 4; 269–272, 274–277, 339; charters of, 275 f., 278–281, 285, 325, 352, 354
— deacon (Winch.), 26, 21
— thegn, 18, 26; 20, 29; 106, 10; 279, 349
— 10, 30; 24, 22; 271, 285, 362
Æthelwyrd, 58, 19 f.; 60, 5, 7; 315 f.
Ætheric, cleric (Winch.), 28, 11; 40, 22; (Worc.), 114, 27; 116, 39; 118, 29; 120, 28; deacon, 126, 30; 134, 25; 138, 29; 362, 371
— the Long, 76, 11
— of Bocking, 375
— 192, 14; 194, 26; 442
Ætlebrant of Pilsgate, 76, 15
— 78, 28; 80, 18

Ada, 80, 31
Afa, Abbot, 156, 22
Agemund, thegn, 160, 41; 282, 411
— 168, 29
Ail-, Ayl-. *See* Æthel-
Aki, Toki's son, 448
Al-. *See also* Æl-, Eal-
Albert the Chaplain, 431
Alcuin, 500
Ald-. *See also* Eald-
Alda, *cinges gefera*, 2, 21; 260
Aldhun, Bishop of Durham, 383
Alfred, King, 14, 15; 16, 26; 18, 30; 20, 7, 26; 24, 9; 26, 14; 30, 22; 68, 22; 110, 13; 259, 272, 275, 284, 286 ff., 291, 294, 297, 340, 353, 357, 389, 472, 474, 478, 498 f.; charters of, 279 f., 285;

INDEX NOMINUM

laws of, **420, 454, 456**; reign of, **280** f., **288, 292**; will of, **304, 340, 491**
Alfred, Bishop (? of Elmham), **50,** 26; **306** f.
— Bishop of Sherborne, **48,** 3; **50,** 32; **303**
— Earl of Surrey, **354, 440** f.
— Pincerna, **487**
— of Lincoln, **271** f.
— priest (Winch.), **26,** 15
— cleric (Winch.), **40,** 23; (Worc.), **64,** 5, 31; **66,** 29; **86,** 32; **88,** 25 ('priest'); **96,** 22; **320, 336**
— (*Alfledus*), king's thegn, **48,** 8; **304**
— thegn, **54,** 1; **309**
— Goldwine's brother, **204,** 12; **451**
— **28,** 2; **38,** 9; **288, 295** f.
Alhhun, Bishop of Worcester, **12,** 27 f.; **265, 273**
Alon, **200,** 23; **448**
Anfrith, **240,** 30
Anschil, **492**
Asser, Bishop of Sherborne, **259, 276, 280**
Aswig, mother of Ufi, **80,** 16
Athulf, Bishop of Hereford, **130,** 11 f.; **373**
— thegn, **28,** 16; **289**
— **62,** 2; **130,** 22; **192,** 27; **317** f., **442**
Atsur the Red, **188,** 29; **437** f.
— **208,** 12; **210,** 7; **458** f.

Babba, thegn, **20,** 32; **280**
Bada, **74,** 28; **78,** 24; **80,** 28
Badanoth Beotting, **10,** 1; **269**
— priest, **10,** 28; **269** f.
— **10,** 30; **271**
Bægmund, priest and abbot, **10,** 25; **270**
Baldwin, Abbot of Bury St Edmunds, **196,** 20, 26; **198,** 2 ff.; **250,** 21; **440, 443** f., **446** f., **500**
— sheriff (Devonshire), **448, 474**
Beocca, thegn, **18,** 27; **106,** 5; **279, 349**
Beonna, Abbot of Peterborough, **271**
Beorht-. *See* Briht-
Beornheah, brother of Brihtstan, **130,** 23; **132,** 6
— **82,** 20
Beornheard, Earl, **12,** 29; **273**
Be(o)rnhelm, **38,** 6

Beornmund, priest (Canterbury), **60,** 18
Beornric, **90,** 18; **337**
Beornstan, Bishop of Winchester, **48,** 6; **297, 303, 306**
— priest (Winch.), **28,** 12 (*bisc.*); **40,** 18; **289**
Beornwulf, King of Mercia, **8,** 3 ff.; **266**
— thegn, **28,** 14; **40,** 13; **289**
Berht-. *See also* Briht-
Berhthun, **4,** 4; **261**
Bertram, priest (Canterbury), **60,** 17
Bionna, Bishop of Hereford, **8,** 33; **268**
Biornlaf, priest (Winch.), **26,** 18
Biornoth, Earl, **8,** 32; **268**
Blacere, **194,** 23
Boia of Milton, **76,** 15 f., 23
— **78,** 2
Bolam, **8,** 39; **269**
Bonda, **130,** 18; **376**
Bondig, Staller, **218,** 9; **470**
Brada, priest, **8,** 31
Brenting, **76,** 24
Brihtferth, Earl, **90,** 7, 14; **336** f.
— thegn, **94,** 38; **342**
Brihtheah, Abbot of Pershore and Bishop of Worcester, **172,** 10; **362, 397, 421, 458** ff.
— monk, **148,** 25; **156,** 22; **397**
— deacon, **350**
Brihthelm, Bishop of London, **56,** 18; **313**
— Bishop of Wells, **58,** 8; **94,** 29; **314, 367**
— Bishop of Winchester, **62,** 1; **286, 317**
— Abbot of Exeter, **343**
— **30,** 12, 17 (2); **34,** 13, 18 (2)
Brihthere, priest (Canterbury), **60,** 11; **316**
Brihtmær, Abbot of Crowland, **160,** 40 (?); **214,** 29; **410, 468**
— Abbot of Evesham, **404**
— of Bourne, **128,** 19; **372**
— of Gracechurch, **216,** 10 f.
— **256,** 8 f.; **461**
Brihtmund, priest (Worc.), **34,** 16
— thegn, **20,** 29; **280**
— **60,** 13
Brihtnoth, Earl of Essex, **58,** 17; **94,** 31; **130,** 12; **315, 337, 430, 444, 504**

INDEX NOMINUM

Brihtnoth, Abbot of Ely, 100, 17; 130, 14; **144**, 13f.; **346, 374**
— thegn, **18**, 29; **26**, 15; **106**, 7; **279, 349**
— **32**, 18
Brihtred, Bishop of Lindsey, **12**, 28; **268, 273**
Brihtric, prior (?), Bury St Edmunds, **192**, 20; **441, 444**
— the Bald, **238**, 22f.; **489**
— the Red, **148**, 1; **394**
— the Young, **172**, 5
— Ælfgar's son, **208**, 10f.; **210**, 5f.; **458**
— brother of Ælfric, Siraf's son, **106**, 20f.
— thegn, **160**, 37; **410**
— **60**, 20; **122**, 22; **138**, 8; **150**, 2, 22; **192**, 22; **194**, 23; **323, 352, 354**f., **365**f., **397, 429, 442, 474, 489**
Brihtsige, Bishop (? of Rochester), **56**, 18; **313**
— deacon (Canterbury), **60**, 16f.
— cleric (Winch.), **28**, 16; **40**, 22
— Warmund's son, **78**, 19
— **52**, 19; **60**, 14 (2); **90**, 2; **308**
Brihtstan, cleric (Worc.), **64**, 4, 32; **66**, 27; **86**, 30; **88**, 21 ('priest'); **96**, 24; **114**, 18; **116**, 31; **118**, 23; **120**, 21; **320, 336, 362**
— brother of Beornheah, **130**, 23; **132**, 6
Brihtwaru, **352, 355, 366**
Brihtwig, Abbot of Glastonbury, **160**, 41; **411, 413**
— **60**, 14
Brihtwine, Bishop (? of Sherborne or Wells), **160**, 37; **409**
— II, Bishop of Sherborne, **447**
— Bishop of Wells, **412**f.
— **156**, 23; **164**, 8; **210**, 8; **405, 461**
Brihtwold, Bishop of Cornwall, **160**, 33; **409**
— Bishop of Ramsbury, **156**, 24; **184**, 27; **405, 409**
— of Mereworth, **86**, 3f.
Brihtwulf, deacon, **20**, 28
— **24**, 22 (*Berthful*); **285**
Brin-. *See* Beorn-
Brun, priest (Exeter), **98**, 4; **344**
Bryne, **134**, 28; **379**
Bryning, sheriff (Herefordshire), **152**, 1

Brynwald, **12**, 35
Burgheard, Earl, **291**f.
Burghelm, priest, **20**, 36
Burgred, King of Mercia, **12**, 27; **272, 296**
— thegn, **20**, 26; **280**
Burhric, Bishop of Rochester, **50**, 35; **307**
Burhwold, Bishop of Cornwall, **387**, **409**
Bynna, **8**, 39; **269**
Byrht-. *See* Briht-
Byrn-. *See* Beorn-

Cæn-. *See* Cen-
Cafi, **240**, 31; **492**
Care, Toki's son, **200**, 13f.; **447**f.
Car[l], *cniht*, **150**, 12; **398**
Catla, **80**, 33
Cenferth (-frith), priest, **12**, 33
— **30**, 17; **34**, 14
Cenric, **60**, 15
Cenwald, Bishop of Worcester, **48**, 2; **50**, 36; **58**, 17; **303, 315**
Cenwig, priest (Canterbury), **60**, 11
Cenwold *rust*, **150**, 16; **399**
Ceofa, thegn, **20**, 36; **280**
Ceolberht, Bishop of London, **8**, 39; **268**
Ceolbreht, **491**
Ceolburh, Abbess of Berkeley, **264**
Ceolheah, thegn, **20**, 35; **280**
Ceolhelm, thegn, **20**, 30; **280**
— **30**, 18; **34**, 17; **38**, 9
Ceolmær, **208**, 11f.; **210**, 7; **458**
Ceolmund, deacon, **20**, 26
Ceolnoth, Archbishop of Canterbury, **10**, 23; **12**, 27; **188**, 3f.; **270**
Ceolred, Bishop of Leicester, **12**, 27; **273**
— Abbot of Peterborough, **12**, 1; **31**; **271**
— thegn, **20**, 25, 29 (2); **280**
Ceolstan, **52**, 19f.; **309**
Ceolwin, **30**, 20; **291**
Ceolwulf I, King of Mercia, **6**, 4; **264**f.
— thegn, **20**, 32; **280**
Cichus, **10**, 28; **270**
Clac of Barnwell, **78**, 11
— of Castor, **78**, 9, 13
— of Warmington, **76**, 5
— son of Tuce, **80**, 12
— **76**, 14; **78**, 3, 7

Cnut, King, 150, 7, 24; 158, 12f.; 160, 25; 168, 7; 170, 7, 21; 172, 3; 182, 23; 190, 11f.; 282, 328, 344, 391, 393, 397, 404, 406f., 410ff., 417f., 420f., 423f., 427, 432, 438, 448f., 475, 490; charters and writs of, 372, 376, 400, 404, 406, 409, 411f., 434, 447; laws of, 284, 328, 333, 339, 358, 381, 440, 448, 460, 465, 486; proclamation of, 321, 408; time of, 328, 391, 400ff., 425, 430, 491, 493
— 76, 15
Coenred, King of Mercia, 404
Coenwald, monk, 56, 17; 313
— thegn, 18, 29; 106, 3; 279, 349
Coenwulf, King of Mercia, 295, 352
Cola, 200, 23; 210, 8
Cole, 196, 12f.; 446
Conan (*Caynan*), Bishop of Cornwall, 48, 4; 303
Creoda, 32, 27
Croc, priest, 240, 28; 492
Cupping, 212, 19; 464
Cussa, 264
Cuthbald, priest, 8, 32
Cuthbert, priest, 4, 25; 8, 34; 263
Cuthred, King of Kent, 262
— Earl, 8, 34; 24, 21; 26, 4, 22; 268, 285
— thegn, 20, 38; 281
Cuthwulf, Abbot, 8, 29; 268
Cyma, thegn, 18, 26; 20, 30; 106, 4; 279, 349
— 24, 23; 286
Cynath, deacon (Worc.), 34, 12; 38, 11
— 30, 13
Cyneberht, 10, 28; 270
Cyneferth, 76, 26
Cynegils, King of Wessex, 68, 19; 324
Cyneheah, thegn, 14, 18
Cyn(e)helm, Abbot of Evesham, 30, 13; 34, 13; 38, 6; 291
— 30, 16, 18 (2); 34, 12; 290
Cynelaf, thegn, 20, 34; 281
— 30, 15; 34, 16, 20 (2)
Cynelm, 86, 11
Cynemund, thegn, 20, 33; 280
Cynesige, Archbishop of York, 214, 22f.; 466
— Bishop of Berkshire, 305

Cynesige, Bishop of Lichfield, 56, 17; 305, 313
— bishop, 50, 24; 305
— cleric (Worc.), 64, 33; 66, 30; 96, 26; 321
— 164, 9; 254, 19
Cynestan, priest (Winch.), 26, 17
— cleric (Winch.), 28, 10; 40, 19; (Worc.), 64, 28; 66, 30; 114, 20; 116, 33; 118, 22; 120, 24; 321
— 52, 18; 308
Cyneswith, 28, 20, 27; 290
Cynethegn, cleric (Worc.), 64, 3, 29; 66, 27; 114, 26; 116, 38; 118, 28; 120, 21; 126, 28; 132, 25; 134, 26; 138, 30; 320
Cynewalh, King of Wessex, 68, 19; 288, 324
Cyneweald, priest, 12, 34
Cyneweard, Abbot of Milton Abbas, 94, 39; 342
— of Pebworth (?), 164, 11; 413
Cynewulf, thegn, 14, 17
Cynred, Bishop of Selsey, 8, 25; 267
Cynsige, 60, 19
Cynulf, 294
Cyrred, thegn, 20, 28; 280
Cytel, son of Clac of Warmington, 76, 4f.
— brother of Thurferth, Rolf's son, 82, 3ff.
— brother of Thurferth of Warmington, 76, 3
— 98, 3
Cytelbearn, 78, 10

Daniel, Abbot of Chertsey, 418
David I, King of Scotland, 484
Deneberht, Bishop of Worcester, 264, 295, 378
Denegils, thegn, 18, 30; 279
Denewulf, Bishop of Winchester, 28, 1, 9; 38, 17; 288f., 296, 298, 340
Denisc, 98, 3; 344
Deormod, thegn, 40, 16; 297f.
Deorwulf, 112, 9
Dering FitzSired, 394
Dodd, 76, 22, 27; 78, 8, 12; 80, 2
Dodda, *cild*, 200, 23; 448
— of Curry, 238, 23; 490
Dodeman, 490
Domneva, 423, 438

INDEX NOMINUM

Drabba, brother of Boia of Milton, 76, 16
— 78, 2
Drew de Beuere, 272
Duda, thegn, 20, 37; 281
— 264
Dudig, thegn, 26, 17; 287
Duduc, Bishop of Wells, 184, 27; 214, 23; 434, 469
Dunn, 14, 21; 276 f.
Dunna, 236, 31; 487
Dunstan, Archbishop of Canterbury, 84, 21 f.; 92, 3; 106, 3 f.; 122, 10 f., 29 f.; 303, 323, 332 f., 339, 373
Dyddel, 10, 27; 270
Dynne, 6, 13, 15; 265

Ead-. See also Ed-
Eadbald, King of Kent, 399
Eadberht, Bishop of London, 4, 3; 261
— Earl, 8, 31; 268
— 6, 13, 15; 265
Eadflæd, 370
Eadgifu, wife of Edward the Elder, 56, 19; 310, 313, 353 ff., 428 f.
— Abbess of the Nunnery, Winchester, 102, 24; 348
— Abbess, 98, 1; 136, 20; 344, 348, 381
— of Lewknor, 136, 21 f.
— wife of Brihtmær of Gracechurch, 216, 15
— sister of Godric of Bourne, 192, 2
— 150, 17; 476
Eadgyth, King Edgar's daughter, Abbess of Wilton, 348
— nun, 396
Eadhelm, Bishop of Selsey, 367
— Abbot of St Augustine's, Canterbury, 60, 16; 316
— 60, 14; 136, 19; 150, 15; 399
Eadlifu, 96, 9; 343
Eadmær of Burham, 150, 11; 170, 2; 188, 29; 398, 411
— thegn, 160, 41; 411
— son of Brihtmær of Gracechurch, 216, 16
— 130, 4; 364
Eadnoth I, Bishop of Dorchester, 409
— II, Bishop of Dorchester, 184, 27 f.; 214, 8; 434, 448, 465 f.
— Staller, 489

Eadnoth, 238, 21; 296
Eadric Streona, Earl of Mercia, 146, 24; 393, 396
— the Small, 76, 29 f.
— the Wild, 364
— of Elham, 204, 10; 451
— of Thorpe, 76, 24, 27; 82, 7
— Ælfric's son, 84, 14 ff.; 192, 9; 333
— Ufic's son, 186, 7
— Ælfheah's brother, 58, 18; 315, 339
— Earl Æthelwold's brother, 323
— thegn, 50, 30; 54, 10; 306, 310
— (of Laxfield?), 178, 21; 184, 13; 426, 432
— fellow-sponsor, thegn, of Bishop Oswald, 88, 1 ff.; 138, 10, 14; 335, 378
— 38, 11; 58, 23; 60, 5 ff.; 80, 17; 82, 22; 136, 20; 296, 316
Eadsige, priest, afterwards Archbishop of Canterbury, 168, 8 f.; 170, 8, 16; 172, 8; 174, 7; 176, 1 ff.; 184, 26; 188, 2 ff.; 190, 21; 192, 6; 204, 1; 417, 419 f., 422, 437 ff., 468
— sheriff (Hants.), 212, 17 f.
— 60, 14, 19
Eadstan, 60, 20
Eadulf, Bishop of Crediton, 48, 5 (*Radulphus*); 303
— Earl of Northumbria, 94, 33; 341
— priest, 54, 17; 311
Eadwald (-wold), priest, 12, 34; 172, 6; 420
— 136, 20
Eadwulf, Bishop of Hereford, 268
— Bishop of Lindsey, 8, 34; 268
— Earl, 8, 17 ff.; 24, 21; 26, 19; 267, 285, 429
— priest (Worc.), 34, 20
— cleric (Winch.), 40, 15, 24 (2)
— thegn, 18, 34; 20, 31; 106, 8; 280, 349
— 12, 30; 273
Ealdber(h)t, prior, 12, 33; 273 f.
— Earl, 12, 29; 273
Ealdgyth, Earl Ælfgar's daughter, 467
— 230, 6; 480 f., 497
Ealdhelm, 12, 34
Ealdred, Bishop of Cornwall, 373

INDEX NOMINUM

Ealdred, Bishop of Worcester and Archbishop of York, **208**, 1, 17; **214, 24**; **218**, 6, 27; **343, 364, 448, 456**f., **462**f., **469**ff.
— Abbot, **94**, 42; **342**
— Under-king of Worcester, **4**, 2 f.; **261**
— Earl of Northumbria, **480**
— Earl, **12**, 30; **273**
— of Monksilver, **238**, 24; **490**
— Lyfing's son, **128**, 2
— thegn, **14**, 20
— **8**, 25; **38**, 6; **142**, 16; **238**, 6; **267, 295, 487**
Ealdulf, Abbot of Peterborough and Bishop of Worcester, **74**, 24, 30; **76**, 8ff.; **78**, 14ff.; **80**, 32; **82**, 6ff.; **130**, 13 f.; **289, 329**
Ealdwine, priest, **148**, 2; **394**
Ealhferth, Bishop of Winchester, **24**, 7, 20; **26**, 2, 15; **283** f., **286**
— thegn, **20**, 31; **280**
Ealhheard, Earl, **8**, 38; **268**
— Abbot, **18**, 33; **106**, 9; **280, 349**
— priest, **12**, 33
Ealhhere, Earl, **10**, 24; **270**
Ealhmund, Bishop of Winchester, **268**
— **34**, 19; **38**, 11; **295**
Ealhstan, Bishop of Sherborne, **8**, 37; **14**, 16; **18**, 26; **20**, 24; **268, 276, 283**
— of Islip, **76**, 10
— priest (Winch.), **40**, 21; **298**
— thegn, **14**, 19; **20**, 34; **281**
Ealhswith, wife of King Alfred, **491**
Eanberht (*Eam-*), **30**, 14; **290**
Eanmund, Abbot, **8**, 27, 30 (2); **267** — **280**
Eanred, priest, **12**, 33
Eanswith, **378**
Ean(w)ulf, Earl of Somerset, **14**, 19; **18**, 27; **276**
— Earl, **106**, 7; **349**
— thegn, **20**, 30; **94**, 34; **280, 341**
Eardwulf, Bishop of Rochester, **84**, 3; **332**
— thegn, **20**, 37; **281**
— **30**, 14, 18 (2); **34**, 16, 20 (2); **38**, 7
Earnwig, **320**
Ecgberht (-briht), deacon, **12**, 34
— thegn, **18**, 32; **20**, 31; **106**, 6; **280, 349**

Ecgferth (-frith), King of Northumbria, **368**
— priest (Worc.), **30**, 15; **34**, 19; **38**, 7; **290**
— **90**, 27; **92**, 2, 6; **338**
Ecgmund, priest, **8**, 35 f. (2)
Ecgstan, thegn, **20**, 33; **280**
Ecgulf, thegn, **18**, 33; **106**, 9; **280, 349**
Ecgwine, Bishop of Worcester, **156**, 7; **404**
— bishop, **48**, 4; **303**
Edgar, King, **56**, 19; **62**, 3, 15; **64**, 9; **66**, 5; **68**, 2, 15; **86**, 13; **88**, 2; **90**, 20 f.; **92**, 18; **96**, 2; **98**, 8; **104**, 19; **106**, 1; **112**, 12, 17; **122**, 2 ff.; **286, 313** f., **323** f., **337, 340** f., **345, 348** f., **352, 355** f., **358, 360, 366** f., **369, 374, 387, 458, 484, 504**; charters of, **288, 314, 317** f., **323, 327** f., **337, 339** ff., **346-350, 356, 359, 380, 383, 390, 414** f., **503** f.; laws of, **357, 381, 404, 485** f., **492**; reign of, **316, 324, 340** f., **348, 376, 425**
— Bishop of Hereford, **38**, 12; **296**
— priest, **8**, 28
— deacon (Worc.), **64**, 3, 30; priest, **86**, 29; **96**, 24; **114**, 25; **116**, 39; **118**, 29; **120**, 26; **126**, 33; **132**, 29; **134**, 24; **138**, 29; **320, 360** f.
— **256**, 15
Edith, wife of Edward the Confessor, **214**, 22; **218**, 5; **431, 433, 462** f., **466, 470, 481, 483** f., **488**
— Earl Odda's sister, **458**
— St, **348**
Edmund, King, **54**, 12, 14; **84**, 5, 8; **282, 306, 310** f., **313, 332, 352, 356, 380, 428** f., **445, 491**; laws of, **284, 338** f., **452**; time of, **307**
— (Ironside), the Ætheling, **146**, 8; **393** f., **429**
— Earl, **56**, 20; **314**
— priest (Worc.), **34**, 15
— **60**, 18, 20 (2)
Edred, King, **54**, 15, 21 f.; **56**, 4, 13; **58**, 2; **84**, 8; **90**, 16; **288, 310-314, 323, 332, 336** f., **358, 388, 407, 428**

INDEX NOMINUM

Edred, Eadhelm's son, 150, 15
Edward the Confessor, King, 180, 24; 182, 22; 184, 25; 188, 24; 194, 8, 12; 196, 27; 198, 14; 210, 1f.; 214, 21; 218, 5, 14f.; 220, 16; 222, 24; 230, 12ff.; 232, 2ff.; 234, 2ff.; 236, 2ff.; 238, 1; 400, 427, 430, 444–447, 476, 481ff.; charters and writs of, 278, 431f., 438, 447f., 459, 464, 467, 469; tenants of, 308, 310, 464, 492; time of, 265, 271, 282 and *passim*
— the Elder, King, 24, 19; 38, 16; 40, 12; 68, 23; 92, 21; 94, 12, 15; 274, 280, 285, 297, 305, 308f., 313, 340, 353, 386, 428, 472, 485, 494; charters of, 281, 288, 295, 297, 304, 307, 309, 325, 340, 454; laws of, 344; reign of, 291
— the Martyr, King, 110, 2, 14; 114, 3; 116, 3; 118, 3; 340, 360, 365, 369, 429; charters of, 366f.; reign of, 342, 356
— II, King, 301ff.
— sheriff of Wiltshire, 302
— of Bockhampton, 240, 22; 492
— brother of Æthelstan of Sunbury, 90, 9ff.
— cleric (Worc.), 88, 21; 96, 23; priest, 114, 18; 116, 31; 118, 31; 120, 28; 336, 361, 369
— 60, 15
Edwin, Earl of Mercia, 265, 461, 467
— Earl of Sussex, 122, 24; 365f.
— cleric (Worc.), 64, 31; 66, 29; 88, 24; 96, 28; 114, 22; 116, 34; 118, 24; 120, 22; 321
— thegn, 356
— Earl Ranig's son (?), 150, 25; 400
— Brihtmær's son, 461
— Eadric's son, 82, 22
— *Enneawnes* son, 152, 4; 401f.
— Ulfketel's son, 184, 15; 432
— Archbishop Eadsige's brother, 170, 11ff.; 204, 10f.; 420
— King Æthelstan's brother, 301
— 106, 19f.; 136, 19; 156, 21; 350, 391, 405, 444
Edwy, King, 56, 19 (*æþeling*); 58, 14; 90, 16, 18; 288, 314f., 356, 428, 451; charters of, 284, 288, 323, 338, 370, 441, 451; reign of, 313
Edwy *boga*, 98, 4
— Æthelwig's kinsman, 164, 12
— Bishop Oswald's kinsman, 343
— 98, 3; 238, 19
Egbert, King of Wessex and Kent, 68, 22; 292, 325, 352, 438; charters of, 279, 291
— Archbishop of York, Penitential of, 324
Eglaf, Earl, 156, 24; 160, 37; 168, 28; 410, 417f.
Eincund, 76, 17ff.; 82, 5
Eorl, 78, 10, 30; 331
Eorlbriht, priest (Canterbury), 60, 17
Eric, Earl, 160, 39; 168, 28f.; 410, 417
Erneberht, deacon, 8, 39
Esbearn, son of Æthelric Bigga, 188, 15; 204, 9; 387, 436f., 451
— Ordgar's brother, 200, 22
— 208, 12; 459
Esgar, Staller, 212, 17; 214, 29f.; 218, 8; 400, 430, 464, 492
Esne, king's thegn, 4, 17; 262
— thegn, 14, 16; 275
— 4, 26
Etheldreda, St, 100, 2; 345, 504f.
Fastulf of *Finnesthorpe*, 76, 1
— priest, 76, 30
— 82, 19
Feologeld, priest and abbot, 4, 26; 263
Frana, 74, 26
Frena, 76, 14ff.; 78, 15ff.; 80, 8, 28; 82, 25
Freodegar, monk, 404
Freoden, 250, 21
Frerth, priest (Folkestone), 150, 14
Frethegod, deacon (Canterbury), 60, 12f.
Frithegist, 74, 27; 78, 10ff.; 80, 29; 82, 14ff.; 184, 13f.; 432
Fritheyth, wife of Æthelheard, King of Wessex, 339
Frithestan, Bishop of Winchester, 40, 14; 296f., 305
Frithulf, 76, 12
Fulder, 154, 2; 402

Gænburg, Æthelnoth's wife, 4, 15, 25
Gardulf, Bishop Oswald's kinsman, 319, 343

INDEX NOMINUM

Garmund, 238, 21; **489**
Geoffrey of Coutances, **347**
— de Maundeville, **390**, **464**, **492**
Germanus, abbot, **130**, 14; **374**
Gilbert Balastarius, **436**
— FitzTurold, **461**
— kinsman of Walcher, Bishop of Durham, **480**
Gisa, Bishop of Wells, **218**, 6; **238**, 18; **469**, **488** f.
Gislheard, **353**
Goda, Wulfsige's son, **142**, 16 f.
— thegn, **18**, 28; **106**, 12; **279**, **349**
Godgifu, Earl Leofric's wife, **212**, 24; **214**, 15; **461**, **465**, **467**
Goding of Walton, **76**, 17
— deacon (Worc.), **114**, 21; **116**, 35; **118**, 23; **120**, 26; **124**, 16; **132**, 27; **134**, 22; **138**, 31; **360** f., **369**, **378**
Godman, priest (Sherborne), **200**, 26; **449**
Godric, Abbot of Winchcombe, **449**
— Dean of Christchurch, Canterbury, **188**, 25 f.; **192**, 6; **204**, 7; **216**, 12
— *portgerefa* (Canterbury), **192**, 10; **440**
— Finch, **210**, 8; **461**
— of Bourne, **188**, 30; **192**, 1, 12; **204**, 11; **372**, **439**
— of Stoke, **152**, 2; **401**
— Carl's son, **398**, **439**
— son of Leofric of Holwell, **144**, 16; **389**
— thegn of Earl Ælfgar, **396**
— **214**, 32; **250**, 21; **468**
Godwine, Bishop of Rochester, **140**, 7 ff.; **142**, 10; **160**, 36; **188**, 25; **204**, 6 f.; **384**
— Bishop of St Martin's, **204**, 7; **451**
— Abbot of Winchcombe, **180**, 21; **427**
— Earl of Wessex, etc., **160**, 36; **184**, 28; **188**, 28; **190**, 8 ff.; **200**, 12, 19; **202**, 22; **218**, 28; **346**, **352**, **354**, **394** f., **397**, **403**, **409** f., **417** f. **433** f., **456** f., **460**, **463** f., **466** f., **469** f.
— cleric (Worc.), **138**, 30; **382**
— thegn, **160**, 40; **394** f., **411**
— of Cringleford, **184**, 14 f.
— of Horton, **150**, 16

Godwine, Ælfsige's son, **80**, 32; **82**, 12 f.
— Carl's son, **398**
— Eadgifu's son, **150**, 17; **395**
— Edwy's son, **238**, 19; **488**
— Wulfheah's son, **142**, 14 f.; **150**, 10; **398**
— Wulfstan's son, **150**, 11 f.; **398**
— **98**, 3; **118**, 1; **148**, 5; **150**, 1; **184**, 13; **394** f., **397**, **404**, **432**, **458**
Goldwine (*Gylde-*), Alfred's brother, **204**, 12; **451**
Grifin, Mariadoc's son, **401**
Grim of Castor, **76**, 18
— brother of Eadric of Thorpe, **76**, 24
— **78**, 2
Grimketel, Bishop of Selsey, **184**, 28; **431** f., **434**, **466**
— **82**, 9
Gruffydd, King of North Wales, **467**
Gunfrid de Chocques, **484**
Gunna, **80**, 13
Gunner, Earl, **359**
— **368**
Gunnhild, King Cnut's niece, **412**, **418**
Guthwold, **142**, 18
Gyreweard, **78**, 6; **80**, 6 ff.
Gyrping, **78**, 6, 33
Gytha, Earl Godwine's wife, **346**, **397**, **410**, **433**
— Osgod Clapa's daughter, **400**

Hæletha, thegn, **188**, 3
Hafslæin, **252**, 9
Hakon the Bad, Earl of Hlathir, **410**
— Earl, **156**, 5, 23; **162**, 13; **404**, **412**
Hama, *swangerefa*, **8**, 20; **267**
Hardacnut, King, **180**, 2, 19; **218**, 20; **320**, **400**, **423**, **427**; charters of, **400**; time of, **424**, **426**
Harold Hardrada, **470**
— Harefoot, King, **174**, 14; **176**, 3 ff.; **320**, **423**, **427**; reign of, **443**, **445**
— Earl of (1) East Anglia, (2) Wessex, **212**, 15; **214**, 26; **218**, 6; **226**, 9; **400**, **445**, **457**, **463**, **467**, **475**, **489**
— Earl, **168**, 28; **418**
Hascoit Musard, **492**

INDEX NOMINUM

Heahberht, Bishop of Worcester, 6, 4f.; 8, 27, 32; 264f., 267, 273
Heahferth, deacon, 8, 37
Heahmund, Bishop of Sherborne, 24, 8; 283
— priest, 18, 34; 20, 27; 106, 10; 280, 349
Heahred, 30, 12; 34, 19
Heahstæf, priest, 8, 30
Hearding, priest, 240, 28
— Eadnoth's son, 238, 21; 489
Heathored, Bishop of Worcester, 264
Heca, Bishop of Selsey, 214, 24; 466
— 200, 26
Hedda, Abbot of Peterborough, 271
Hemele, Earl, 305
— 264
Hem(m)ing, 410, 418
Hengest, 424
Hength, 148, 1
Henry I, King, 462, 471; Inspeximus of, 301
— II, King, time of, 484
— III, King, time of, 464
— de Ferrers, 470
Henulf, deacon (Winch.), 26, 19
Heorhtric, thegn, 20, 34; 280
Heoteman, priest, 20, 37
Heregyth, Abba's wife, 278
Hereman, Bishop of Ramsbury, 214, 23; 218, 6, 27; 466
Heremod, cleric (Winch.), 40, 20
— thegn, 26, 18; 287
Herewulf, thegn, 20, 23; 280
Herred, 34, 7
Herulf, Ada's son, 80, 31
— priest, 504
— 78, 27
Hiht (?), 64, 24
Hildefrith, priest (Worc.), 34, 18
Horsa, 424
Howel the Good, King of Dyved, 50, 23 (under-king); 305, 313
Hræthhun, Bishop of Leicester, 8, 30; 268
Hrothward, Archbishop of York, 44, 9; 299f.
Hu..., 250, 22
Hudeman of Achurch, 74, 31; 78, 20
— 78, 30f.; 80, 29; 82, 4ff.
Hugh, Earl of Chester, 489
— de Port, 310, 386, 423, 439, 464
— Lasne, 401

Humberht, Bishop of Elmham, 8, 38; 268
— deacon, 12, 34
Humphrey, Robert's son, 424
Hunberht, Earl, 12, 29; 273
Hundulf, 76, 23; 78, 28; 80, 1, 13
Hunewine, Heca's son, 200, 25f.; 449
— 475
Hungifu, 76, 29
Hunlaf, 312
Hunred, thegn, 18, 32; 106, 8; 280, 349
Hunsige, priest (Winch.), 26, 16
Hunwine, 98, 3; 344
Hwita, prior, 18, 35; 106, 11; 280, 349
Hwituc, 34, 15
Hysenoth, priest, 10, 26; 270

Idwal Voel, 313
Ine, King of Wessex, charter of, 288; laws of, 272, 453ff., 486
Ingulf, Abbot of Crowland, 468
Ingwald, Bishop of London, 2, 20; 259f.

Jacob, 56, 20; 313f.
Judith, Countess, 388, 484

Kenneth III, King of Scotland, 484
Ketel. *See* Cytel
Kipping, Nicholas, 464

Lanfranc, Archbishop of Canterbury, 317, 352, 451, 468
Lemmer. *See* Leofmær
Leofflæd, wife of Thurkil the White, 152, 15f.; 400f.
— 319
Leofgifu, 425
Leofmær, 178, 22; 426
Leofric, Bishop of Crediton (then Exeter), 214, 23f.; 226, 1; 344, 466, 473–480
— Abbot of Ely, 405
— Abbot of Exeter, 98, 2; 130, 15; 343, 374
— Abbot of Michelney, 130, 15; 374
— Abbot of Peterborough, 214, 28; 467
— Abbot of St Albans, 374
— Earl of Mercia, 180, 22; 184, 28;

INDEX NOMINUM

188, 28; 208, 9f.; 210, 5, 15f.; 212, 24; 216, 8; 383, 412f., 417f., 434, 458, 461, 467, 476
Leofric, sheriff (Kent), 140, 20; 142, 7, 13; 384
— of Blackwell, 162, 2ff.; 164, 2ff.; 412
— of *Eaningadene*, 154, 22f.
— of Holwell, 144, 16; 389
— of Stretham, 256, 6f.
— of Whitchurch, 138, 8; 382
— Ealdred's son, 142, 16
— thegn, 160, 38; 410
— 60, 14, 19 (2); 130, 19; 156, 5, 21; 162, 13; 210, 6; 376, 412f.
Leofrun, Abbess of Reading, 136, 21; 381
Leofsige, Bishop of Worcester, 156, 23; 172, 14f.; 396, 405, 421
— Abbot of Ely, 156, 21; 184, 11; 214, 28; 403, 405, 467f.
— Abbot, 214, 29; 467
— Earl, 381
— of *Mordune*, 130, 18; 375
— son of Ealhstan of Islip, 82, 15
— Thurlac's son, 80, 33f.; 82, 8f.
— goldsmith, 144, 11; 388
Leofstan, Dean, then Abbot, of Bury St Edmunds, 184, 10; 192, 17; 194, 13; 196, 7; 432, 435f., 440, 442f., 447
— deacon (Worc.), 114, 22; 116, 36; 118, 24; 120, 27; 126, 29; 132, 28; 134, 23; 138, 28; 360f.
— *portgerefa* (London), 216, 20; 469
— of Mersham, 142, 14; 385
— of Sussex, 130, 22; 377
— king's thegn, 60, 20; 316
— 60, 20; 192, 20; 194, 25; 442
Leofsunu, Abbot of Cerne Abbas, 146, 25; 394
— brother of Godwine, Eadgifu's son, 150, 17f.
— 84, 25; 86, 8; 130, 20; 148, 8; 238, 22; 376, 395
Leoftæt, 375
Leoftæta (-e), 130, 18; 375
Leofweard, Abbot of Michelney, 488
Leofwine, Bishop of Lichfield, 214, 26; 465f.
— Earl of (1) the Hwicce, (2) Mercia, 148, 24; 156, 25; 162, 13; 168, 28; 383, 396, 400, 410, 412, 417

Leofwine, cleric (Worc.), 86, 31; 88, 24; 96, 27; 114, 19; 116, 37; 118, 29; 120, 22; 126, 31; 132, 27; 134, 23 (monk); 138, 26; 335, 361, 371, 379
— priest (Dover), 150, 14; 190, 10ff.; 192, 9f.; 204, 8; 399, 438
— the Red, 148, 5ff.; 150, 17; 395, 397
— of Ditton, 142, 15f.
— of Exe, 200, 24; 449
— of Frome, 152, 2, 10
— Earl Godwine's son, 403
— son of Æthelstan of Bledlow, 154, 22
— son of Godwine of Horton, 150, 16; 399
— Ælfheah's son, 140, 8
— Athulf's son, 130, 22; 376f.
— Leoftæta's son, 130, 18; 375
— Wærelm's son, 150, 15f.; 385
— Wulfsige's son, 150, 25f.
— Leofflæd's brother, 186, 6; 400, 435
— *cild*, 391
— seneschal, 148, 2f.
— 136, 8, 13; 380ff.
Leofwold, 184, 14
Ligulf, thegn, 480
Luhha, thegn, 20, 27; 280
Lullede, Earl, 14, 17; 275
Lutsige of Wight, 200, 27; 449
Lyfing, Bishop of Cornwall, Crediton, and Worcester, 176, 5; 180, 1ff.; 184, 27; 200, 20; 409, 423, 447f.
— Bishop of Wells and Archbishop of Canterbury, 146, 23; 148, 11; 150, 7f.; 393–395, 397
— Staller, 212, 16; 214, 30; 463
— of Malling, 142, 13; 385
— Ealdred's father, 128, 2, 9
— 60, 19; 138, 16

Maneboia, 80, 30
Mannel, 78, 4; 80, 9
Manni, Abbot of Evesham, 210, 3; 214, 27; 457, 460, 470
Martin, 78, 15; 331
Matilda, wife of David I of Scotland, 484
— wife of William the Conqueror, 198, 4; 446, 458, 481, 483
— Siweard's wife, 428

INDEX NOMINUM

Matthew of Mortain, 492
Maud, wife of Robert, Count of Mortain, 484
Mildred, St, 423 f., 438
Milred, Bishop of Worcester, 2, 2, 19; 259 f.
— thegn, 24, 22; 26, 14; 285
Monn, 34, 15
Monnel, thegn, 18, 33; 106, 7; 280, 349
Morcar, Earl of Northumbria, 461, 467, 481
— 271 f.
Morgan, King of Glamorgan, 56, 19; 313
Mucel, Earl, 8, 36; 268
— the Younger, Earl, 12, 29; 268
— thegn, 20, 33; 280

Nafena, 130, 17; 375
Northman, Earl, 140, 1; 383
Northwine, Nafena's brother, 130, 17; 375

Oda, Bishop of Ramsbury and Archbishop of Canterbury, 50, 31; 56, 16; 60, 11; 168, 17; 306, 311 f., 315 f., 352
— 240, 30; 492
Odda (Earl), 186, 1; 200, 21; 208, 10; 210, 5; 449, 456–460, 467, 499
— thegn, 50, 29; 54, 9; 306, 310
— 250, 6; 499
Offa, King of East Anglia, 404
— King of Mercia, 2, 23; 4, 1; 260, 343, 352, 355
Ogga of Southwick, 76, 2
Oggod of Castor, 78, 8
— 78, 1; 80, 9, 11, 29; 82, 1
Ordbriht, Bishop of Selsey, 130, 11; 136, 3, 15; 372 f., 381
Ordgar, Earl of Devon, 94, 29; 340 f., 387, 472
— the White, 238, 22; 489
— 178, 21; 186, 1; 200, 22; 426, 434, 449, 459
Ordhelm, 142, 8
Ordlaf, Earl, 276, 287
Ordric, Abbot of Abingdon, 218, 8; 470
— cellarer, Bury St Edmunds, 220, 1
Ordulf, Earl, 26, 20; 287
— 144, 5; 386 f., 472

Ordwig, 208, 12; 210, 7; 459
Orm, 76, 27 ff.
Osbern, 76, 23
Oscytel, Bishop of Dorchester and Archbishop of York, 56, 17; 94, 26; 112, 7, 19; 307, 313, 341 f., 358, 441
— 194, 27
Osferth, priest, 144, 17; 389
— *princeps*, 48, 7 (*Offerdus*); 304
— *swade* beard, 74, 29; 330
— Frithegist's son, 74, 27; 78, 10 ff.; 80, 29; 82, 26
— Oggod's son, 82, 1
— 76, 7, 10; 78, 15; 80, 17
Osgar, Abbot of Abingdon, 94, 35; 106, 14; 124, 2; 341, 369
— 76, 21; 388
Osgod Clapa, 168, 29; 400, 419, 445
— of Bainton, 78, 26
— 184, 19, 21; 186, 5; 433 f.
Osgot, Eadulf's son, 444 f.
— 76, 31
Oslac, Earl of York, 94, 32; 341
— deacon (Worc.), 34, 22; priest, 38, 10; 294 f.
Osmær, 200, 23; 448 f.
Osmod, 30, 25; 292
Osmund of Catworth, 76, 4
— secretary of William the Conqueror, 232, 4; 481 f.
— Earl, 12, 29; 273
— priest, 10, 29; 270
— thegn, 18, 31; 20, 28; 106, 12; 279, 349
Osric, Earl, 14, 15; 275 f.
— 24, 22; 285
Osulf, Bishop of Ramsbury, 56, 17; 58, 16; 94, 32; 313, 341, 348
— Earl, 40, 15; 297
— Hudeman's son, 82, 4 ff.
— *cniht*, 96, 5; 319, 343
— thegn, 94, 40; 342
— 80, 16; 82, 19; 112, 11; 140, 3; 359, 384
Oswald, Bishop of Worcester and Archbishop of York, 62, 14, 23; 64, 7; 66, 7, 21; 86, 12 ff.; 88, 3 ff.; 94, 30; 96, 1 ff.; 110, 21; 112, 18; 114, 2, 20; 116, 2, 31; 118, 2, 22; 120, 2, 20; 122, 30; 124, 12; 126, 28; 130, 9; 132, 3, 25; 134, 2 f., 20; 138, 11, 24; 289, 294,

INDEX NOMINUM

299, 312, 318f., 322f., 329, 342f., 357f., 360f., 364, 369, 374, 384, 413
Oswald, deacon (Canterbury), 60, 12
Osweard, Sheriff of Kent, 423
— of Harrietsham, 176, 7f.; 192, 9; 423
— of Norton, 423
— thegn, 94, 39; 342
Oswig of Elton, 76, 3f.; 82; 2, 16, 22
— priest, 78, 2
— cleric (Worc.), 126, 30; 369, 371, 378
Oswulf, priest, 20, 24
Othulf of Barnwell, 74, 32
Owen, 56, 19; 313
Owine, 208, 11; 210, 6; 214, 32; 458

Picot, sheriff, 347
Plegmund, Archbishop of Canterbury, 40, 13; 297

Rædnoth, priest, 20, 38
Ralph (Raulf), Earl of East Anglia, 464
— Earl of Hereford, 458
— Earl, 214, 27; 457, 466f.
— Staller, 212, 17; 214, 30; 218, 8; 463f.
— of Bockhampton, 240, 20, 30; 492
— son of Urs, 484
Ranig, Earl, 150, 25; 400
Regenbald, chancellor, 218, 27f.; 471
Regngar, priest, 8, 33
Remigius, Bishop of Dorchester (then Lincoln), 465f.
Richard, Duke of Normandy, 376f.
— Engayne, 232, 25; 234, 16; 482f.
— Scrob, 320
Robert Bloet, Bishop of Lincoln, 465
— Champart, Archbishop of Canterbury, 463
— Earl, 236, 10f.; 484
— the Despencer, 396, 461
— de Buci, 483
— le Manaunt, 444
— Malet, 424
Roger de Corcelle, 487f., 490
— de Laci, 362
Rolf, 82, 3, 15, 21; 272
Rothin, priest (Canterbury), 60, 17

Sæman, Æthelmær's son, 202, 8

Sæwold of *Iliacum*, 238, 23; 490
Saxa, 80, 13
Scule, Leofwold's son, 184, 14; 432
Sideman, Bishop of Crediton, 124, 1; 367
Sidewine of Paddlesworth, 142, 17; 385
Sielm, 60, 15
Siferth, 56, 20; 128, 10; 194, 25; 214, 32; 313
Sigar, priest, 250, 18
— 80, 2
Sige, Stir's daughter, 375
Sigebriht, 130, 22; 377
Sigeferth, 78, 15; 80, 8, 27
Sigefrith, deacon (Canterbury), 60, 12
— 60, 19
Sigegar, Bishop of Wells, 373
Sigelm, Earl, 353
Sigemund, 10, 29; 271
Sigered, deacon (Canterbury), 60, 13
Sigeric, Bishop of Ramsbury and Archbishop of Canterbury, 130, 10; 136, 3, 14; 373f., 379ff., 430
Sigewulf, 354
Sigred, Earl, 8, 33; 268
Sihtric, Abbot of Tavistock, 200, 21; 448
Simon de St Liz, Earl of Northampton, 484
Siraf, 106, 20; 350
Sired, Earl, 174, 2; 422
— the Old, 150, 10
— Siweard's brother, 128, 9; 142, 13f.; 372, 419
— thegn, 160, 39; 410
— 150, 13; 354, 419
Siric, 214, 33
Siweard, Earl of Northumbria, 186, 1; 214, 26; 434, 465, 470
— Abbot of Abingdon, 188, 27f.; Bishop, 190, 21; 192, 6; 437ff., 450
— Abbot of Chertsey, 418, 437
— Abbot, 374
— of Chilham, 170, 1; 419
— of Kent, 130, 19; 372
— of Upton, 164, 12f.
— monk, 447
— 128, 9; 142, 7, 13; 148, 1; 394, 428
Solomon, priest, 250, 15

INDEX NOMINUM

Spiritus, 320
Steigncytel of Luddington, 76, 1 f.
— 78, 7
Steorra, Harold Harefoot's steward, 174, 21; 423
Stigand, Bishop of Elmham, Bishop of Winchester and Archbishop of Canterbury, 184, 9f.; 186, 21f.; 188, 25; 202, 6, 10, 14f., 22; 212, 7, 14; 214, 22; 216, 11, 23; 218, 26; 274, 425, 428, 431 f., 435, 437, 445, 448–451, 463, 467, 469
— 178, 12ff.; 424
Stir, Wulf's son, 130, 17; 375
Stric, 76, 10
Styrcyr of Upton, 76, 15
— 78, 1, 3; 80, 18
Sumerlida, priest, 74, 28, 30; 76, 5; 78, 19f., 24; 82, 2ff.
— of Stoke, 74, 32; 76, 11; 82, 3 (*Sumer*), 13 f., 21
— 78, 31
Sunte, 76, 23
Swædæ, 252, 10
Swægildæ, 252, 10
Swegn, King of Denmark and England, 387, 411, 493
— Earl, 186, 1, 10; 433ff., 467
Sweta, 98, 3
Swift, 78, 29
Swithberht, deacon, 10, 30; 271
Swithhun, Bishop of Winchester, 14, 17; 275, 283
Swuste, 82, 10

Tata, priest (Winch.), 28, 11 (*bisc.*); 40, 17; 289
Thancred, monk, 176, 5 f., 8
Theodred II, Bishop of Elmham, 373
— Bishop of London, 48, 1 (*Atheldredus*); 50, 28; 303, 307, 390, · 444 f.
— Earl. *See* Thored
Theodric, priest, 240, 29
Thored, Earl, 124, 5; 130, 13 (*Þeodred*); 368, 374, 421
— Staller, 168, 29; 418
— thegn, 160, 40; 410 f.
— Thurkil's nephew, 172, 5 f.; 420
— 172, 20; 328, 411, 421
Thruthgar, cleric (Winch.), 28, 12; 40, 21

Thrym, Earl, 160, 38; 410
Thunor, 438
Thur, 76, 7
Thurcytel, Abbot of Bedford, 94, 40; 342
Thurferth of Warmington, 76, 2 f.
— Rolf's son, 82, 3 ff.
— 80, 13
Thurgar, Ælfgar's son, 192, 8
— 204, 10
Thurgisl, 250, 22
Thurgod *lagen*, 214, 32; 468
Thurketel, Nafena's son, 375
— 178, 24; 426, 443
Thurkil the White, 150, 26; 152, 7ff.; 186, 11; 400 f., 435
— 418
Thurlac Farthing, 78, 13
— 78, 27; 80, 2, 11, 33; 82, 8
Thurstan, 192, 21; 194, 26; 418, 442
Thurwif, 90, 2; 336
Thurwold of Helpston, 78, 9, 12
— of Maxey, 78, 6; 80, 2
Tidbald, priest (Worc.), 34, 17
Tidhelm, Bishop of Hereford, 50, 23; 305 f.
Tile, 10, 27; 270
Tofi the Proud, 150, 26; 400, 419 f., 464
— 168, 29; 172, 6; 419 f.
— the sheriff, 489
Toki, 154, 12; 174, 7; 200, 13; 403, 422, 447 ff.
Torhthelm, prior, 8, 26; deacon and prior, 20, 35; 267, 281
Tostig, Earl of Northumbria, 218, 7; 469 f.
Tuce, 80, 11; 331
Tufes of Barnack, 82, 7 f.
— of Helpston, 80, 34; 82, 8; 332
Tuna, cleric (Worc.), 88, 22; 96, 24; 336
Tunberht, Bishop of Lichfield, 12, 27; 273
— Abbot, 24, 21; 26, 14; 285
Tunbriht, Bishop of Winchester, 28, 3; 283, 288
Tunna, father of Ufi, 80, 15
Tunwulf, 12, 35
Turstan the Fleming, 396

Uffa, cleric (Winch.), 40, 24

INDEX NOMINUM

Ufi, Abbot of Bury St Edmunds, 178, 19; 184, 2, 10; 196, 33; 198, 22; 425, 431 f., 440, 447
— prior, 445
— 72, 31; 78, 9; 80, 14
Ufic, cleric (Worc.), 86, 29; 88, 26; 96, 25; 118, 30; 120, 27; 335, 364
— 186, 8; 435
Uhtred, Earl of Northumbria, 375, 410
— Earl, 8, 37; 268
Ulf, Earl, 168, 28; 397, 410, 417 f.
— of *Welle*, 184, 14; 432
— Dodd's son, 76, 22, 26 f.; 78, 8, 12; 80, 1 f.
— *Eorl's* son, 78, 10, 30
— Eincund's brother, 82, 9
— 76, 17, 28; 80, 15; 200, 16; 271 f.; 448
Ulfketel, Abbot of Crowland, 468
— sheriff (Herefordshire), 186, 11 f.
— Osulf's son, 140, 3; 383 f.
— 146, 1; 184, 15; 392, 432, 443 f.
Urs, 236, 5; 484
Urse d'Abitot, 364
— sheriff, 459, 461 f.

Wægen, 252, 11 f.; 501
Wærelm, 142, 18; 150, 15; 385
Wagen, 208, 11; 210, 6; 458
Walchelin, Bishop of Winchester, 288, 487
Walcher, Bishop of Durham, 230, 6; 480, 497
Walter Ponther, 369
— priest, 240, 29
— deacon, 240, 29
Waltheof I, Earl of Northumbria, 383
— II, Earl of Northumbria, 388, 480, 484
Warmund, 78, 19
Wealdred, priest (Canterbury), 60, 12
Wenberht, Earl, 12, 30; 273
Wenelm, 60, 19
Werenberht, king's thegn, 273
Werferth, Abbot, 14, 19; 276
Werfrith, Bishop of Worcester, 28, 18 f.; 30, 2, 5, 12; 34, 4, 12, 23; 36, 5; 38, 5, 13; 259 f., 289 ff., 295, 498
— priest (Worc.), 30, 14; 34, 14; 290

Werfrith, 264
Werheard, Abbot, 12, 28; 273
[W]erman, priest, 240, 28 f.
Wid, 226, 11; 475
Wigar, thegn, 50, 32
Wigberht, priest, 8, 29
Wigfrith, 30, 16; 290
Wigheard, 30, 16; 34, 14; 290
Wighelm, deacon (Winch.), 28, 13; 40, 25; (Worc.), 8, 38; 289, 296
— 8, 25; 267
Wiglaf, priest (Worc.), 34, 21
— cleric (Winch.), 28, 12
Wigmund, priest, 10, 27; 270
Wigred, thegn, 26, 21; 287
Wigthegn, Bishop of Winchester, 8, 36; 268
Wigulf, Sunte's son, 76, 23 f.
Wihtgar, thegn, 54, 10; 310
— 60, 21; 178, 21
Wihthelm, 299
Wihtred, King of Kent, 399; laws of, 358, 486
— Abbot, 8, 28; 12, 28; 267
Wiking of *Traue*, 240, 30; 492
— 200, 24; 449
Wilfred I, Bishop of York, 260
— II, Bishop of York, 259
— Bishop of Dunwich, 8, 35; 266, 268
Wilfrith I, Bishop of Worcester, 2, 20; 259 f.
— II, Bishop of Worcester, 42, 12; 299, 303
Wilheard, priest, 12, 33
William I, the Conqueror, 198, 1, 8; 242, 1; charters and writs of, 426, 463, 475 f.; laws of, 336 f.; time of, 352, 391, 396, 444, 462, 475
— Bishop of Elmham, 431
— Bishop of London, 214, 25; 390 f., 466, 469
— Earl of Hereford, 362, 458, 461, 469
— Engayne, 234, 17; 236, 11, 18; 483
— de Moion, 449, 487, 490
— de Ow, 308
Wine, 42, 5
Wineman of Raunds, 82, 17 f.
Winsige, seaman, 152, 11; 401
Winstan, thegn, 28, 15; 289

INDEX NOMINUM

Wistan, priest, 20, 25; (Worc.), 88, 23; 96, 28; 118, 30; 120, 27; 126, 34; 132, 30; 134, 25; 138, 26; 336, 363
— thegn, 18, 35; 106, 9; 280, 349
Witeget, priest, 236, 18; 484
Wulf, 130, 17; 375
Wulfbold, 128, 12; 130, 1, 4 f.; 373
Wulfflæd, 322
Wulfgar, Abbot of Abingdon, 136, 18; 381
— cleric (Worc.), 64, 33; 66, 26; 88, 22; 96, 25; 114, 28; 116, 32; 118, 14, 30; 120, 1, 5; 126, 29; 132, 26; 134, 22; 138, 31; 321, 363 ff.
— of *Hiwerc*, 238, 24 f.; 490
— of *Norðhealum*, 90, 15; 337
— Wulfstan's son, 90, 3; 337
— thegn, 50, 35, 37 (2); 306
— 30, 13; 34, 21; 52, 1, 13, 31; 80, 17; 307 ff.
Wulfgeat, Abbot of (1) Peakirk, (2) Crowland, 467 f.
— Abbot, 238, 18; 488
— *cniht*, 116, 1, 5, 28; 362 f.
— 78, 33; 130, 21; 144, 5 (*Sul-*); 186, 14, 19 f.; 208, 2; 376, 435 f.
Wulfheah, cleric (Worc.), 64, 32; 66, 29; 86, 30; 88, 23; 96, 26; priest, 114, 24; 116, 35; 118, 1, 5; 120, 23; 321, 361, 363, 365
— thegn, 20, 36; 280
— 130, 16; 142, 14; 150, 10; 375
Wulfheard, thegn, 20, 38; 281
— 6, 5 f.; 264 f.
Wulfhelm I, Bishop of Wells and Archbishop of Canterbury, 44, 9, 12; 46, 33; 50, 24; 300, 306
— Bishop (? of Hereford), 50, 25; 306
— II, Bishop of Wells, 56, 18; 306, 313
— cleric (Winch.), 28, 10; 40, 18
— thegn, 18, 31; 50, 31; 106, 4; 279, 349
— 60, 19
Wulfhere, Earl, 14, 16; 24, 20; 26, 17; 275 f., 285
— thegn, 18, 32; 106, 3; 280, 349
— 52, 14; 308

Wulfhun, Bishop of Selsey, 50, 29; 303, 306
— cleric (Worc.), 64, 4, 32; 66, 28; 86, 28; 88, 26 ('priest'); 96, 23; 114, 27; 116, 39; 118, 31; 120, 23; 320, 336
— 38, 12; 295 f.
Wulfmær, *cild*, 250, 17
— *cniht*, 172, 12 f.
— thegn, 50, 24
— 'the bishop's brother', 144, 15; 388 f.
— 116, 1, 29; 142, 24; 386
Wulfnoth, Abbot of Westminster, 160, 35; 168, 26; 188, 28; 409
— cleric (Worc.), 88, 26; 96, 28; 114, 26; 116, 37; 126, 33; 132, 29; 134, 25; 138, 28; 336, 364
— Clac's son, 76, 14
— Stric's son, 76, 10 f.
— thegn, 50, 28
— painter, 80, 19, 25
— 80, 1; 154, 14; 403
Wulfred, Archbishop of Canterbury, 4, 16 ff.; 8, 14, 27; 262, 265, 428
— cleric (Winch.), 28, 15
— thegn, 18, 31; 28, 13; 106, 5; 279, 289, 349
— 12, 2, 9; 26, 28; 30, 19; 34, 21; 38, 8; 60, 15; 271, 288, 290
Wulfric, Abbot of Ely, 467
— I, Abbot of St Augustine's, Canterbury, 128, 2; 142, 7, 10; 371 f.
— II, Abbot of St Augustine's, Canterbury, 188, 26; 192, 7; 436 f., 470
— priest (Winch.), 40, 22; (Worc.), 64, 3, 28; 66, 26; 86, 28; 88, 21; 96, 22; 114, 23; 116, 34; 118, 25; 120, 22; 298, 320, 361; 148, 2; 164, 10; 394
— cleric (Winch.), 28, 13; 40, 20; (Worc.), 126, 32; 132, 28; 134, 24; 138, 27; 361, 371
— of *Bynningtune*, 164, 13
— of Cladswell, 164, 12
— of Poleshill, 238, 24; 490
— of Warnford, 212, 18; 464
— Wulfrun's son, 130, 16; 375
— Wulfstan's son, 162, 11; 164, 5
— thegn, 20, 27; 50, 27, 33 (2); 280, 306

INDEX NOMINUM

Wulfric, 30, 17; 34, 13; 52, 13; 62, 13; 148, 15; 202, 15, 25; 210, 7; 256, 9; 308, 444
Wulfrun, 130, 16
Wulfsige, Bishop of Cornwall, 106, 5; 349
— Bishop of Lichfield, 466
— I, Bishop of Sherborne, 285
— II, Bishop of Sherborne, 56, 16; 313
— III, Bishop of Sherborne, 379
— Abbot of Chertsey, 168, 27; 418
— Abbot of Westminster, 130, 14; 374
— priest and sheriff (Kent), 86, 3, 9; 334; priest (Dover), 150, 15; 399
— cleric (Winch.), 28, 11; 40, 13, 15 (2)
— 'the king's reeve', 192, 10; 440
— reeve of the Bishop of Worcester, 34, 5f.
— thegn, 50, 34
— of Lamerton, 344
— Madding, 164, 13
— 98, 2; 142, 16; 150, 26; 256, 15; 344, 354
Wulfstan I, Archbishop of York, 50, 26; 56, 16; 306, 313
— I, Bishop of Worcester and II, Archbishop of York, 146, 14, 23; 148, 23f.; 156, 21; 162, 4, 8; 359, 371, 393, 396f., 403, 405, 412, 421, 500
— Bishop of London, 334
— II, Prior then Bishop of Worcester, 459, 461
— priest, 136, 18
— cleric (Winch.), 28, 17; 40, 17, 19 (2)
— of Dalham, 124, 2f.; 342, 366
— of Saltwood, 128, 9f.; 142, 8, 15; 372
— Uccea, 68, 2ff.; 323
— the Young, 142, 15; 372
— Ceolwin's nephew, 32, 1

Wulfstan, Wynsige's father, 361
— reeve (Kent), 122, 14
— thegn, 94, 37; 342
— 60, 21; 90, 3; 128, 10; 150, 11; 162, 11ff.; 164, 5, 8; 443
Wulfthryth, Cuthred's wife, 26, 4; 286
Wulfweard, deacon (Worc.), 114, 24; 116, 38 ('cleric'); 118, 26; 120, 29; 126, 31; 132, 29; 134, 24; 362ff., 382
— the White, 212, 3ff.; 238, 19; 462f., 485, 488
— of Winsham, 200, 25
Wulfwig, Bishop of Dorchester, 212, 24; 465
Wulfwine, cleric (Worc.), 126, 34; 132, 30; 134, 26; 138, 29; 371
— goldsmith, 476
Wulfwold, Abbot of Bath (?), 488
Wulfwyn, 136, 23
Wullaf, Abbot, 14, 18; 276
— (*Wilaf*) cleric (Winch.), 40, 16
— thegn, 16, 6; 50, 23; 277f.
— 30, 15; 34, 17f. (2); 38, 10
Wynflæd, nun, 282, 379f.
— 136, 1ff.; 379ff.
Wynsige, Bishop of Berkshire, 44, 8; 300
— Bishop of Dorchester, 50, 38; 303, 307
— Bishop of Lichfield, 94, 33; 341
— priest (Worc.), 114, 22; 116, 33; 118, 24; 120, 21; 320, 360f., 369, 382
— cleric (Winch.), 28, 14; 40, 14, 21 (2)
— thegn, 18, 27; 106, 11; 279, 308, 349, 356
— 52, 16; 308
Wynstan, cleric (Worc.), 64, 30; 66, 28; 88, 25; 114, 21; 116, 35; 118, 25; 120, 23; 321
— 164, 9

Ythelbeard, priest (Winch.), 40, 24; 298

INDEX LOCORUM

Abingdon (*Abbendone, -dune*), Berks., 266; abbey of, 44, 6f., 11f.; 58, 10; 279, 325; abbots of, *see* Ordric, Osgar, Siweard, Wulfgar; cartularies of, 299, 356; *Historia* of, 325, 338, 369, 420
Abington (*Habintune*), Northants., 234, 16; 483
Achurch (*Ase(n)circan*), Northants., 74, 31; 78, 20
Acton Beauchamp, Worcs., 459
Adam's Grave (tumulus), Wilts., 292
Adderbury (*Eadburgebyrig*), Oxon., 184, 20, 22; 433
Addingham (*Haddincham*), Yorks., 110, 23
Adisham (*Edesham*), Kent, 182, 11
Adsdean House, Sussex, 287
Ærnehogo Hundred, Norfolk (?), 192, 25f.; 442
Æscmere, 52, 21; 309. See Ashmansworth
Ailsworth (*Ægeleswurðe*), Northants., 68, 5ff.; 312, 323f.
Alderbury (*Æþelwarabirig*), Wilts., 106, 17; 350
Allington in Hollingbourne, Kent, 354
Alresford (*Alresforda*), Hants., 28, 2; 288
Alstone (*Ælfsigestun*), Worcs., 96, 5; 343, 377, 448
Alton Barnes, Wilts., 292
Alton Lodge (*Eanulfintune*), Worcs., 148, 20; 396
Alton Priors (*Aweltune*), Wilts., 30, 21; 32, 3f.; 202, 16; 291f.
Alveston (*Eanulfestune*), Warwicks., 88, 1, 5
Alwalton (*Æþelwoldingtune*), Hunts., 56, 8, 21; 312
Anlafestun, Northants., 72, 27; 82, 6; 327
Ansætleh, Yorks., 112, 2; 358
Appledore (*Apoldre, Apuldra*), Kent, 170, 9; 182, 13; 419f.
Appleton (*Æffeltune*), Yorks., 112, 8; 358

Armingford (*Earningaford*), Cambs., 100, 14; 346f.
Armscott (*Eadmunddescotan*), Worcs., 180, 5; 427
Ashmansworth (*Æscmeresweorðæ*), Hants., 50, 1; 305
Ashton (*Æsctune, Esc-*), Northants., 74, 11, 15; 78, 14, 17; 329, 331
Assandun, Battle of, 373, 392, 409
Aston (*Easttune*), Glos., 172, 13; 421
Aston (*Esttune*), Oxon., 226, 15; 475f.
Aston, White Ladies (*Easttune*), Worcs., 34, 7; 294
Atchen Hill, Worcs., 321
Avington, Hants., 286, 325
Avon, River (*Afene*), 44, 4 (Glos.); 46, 8 (Hants.); 88, 9, 11 (Warwicks.)
Axbridge (*Axanbrycge*), Somerset, 246, 15
Aylesford (*Ægelesforda*), Kent, 108, 8f.; 351, note; 353
Aylton (*Ægelnoðesstane*), Herefordshire, 150, 23f.; 400

Bædericeswyrðe. *See* Bury St Edmunds
Bagborough (*Baggabeorgan, -beorge*), Somerset, 238, 8, 12; 485
Baildon (*Bægeltune, Bældune*), Yorks., 166, 13, 18
Bainton (*Badingtune*), Northants., 78, 26; 80, 33
Bampton (*Bemtune*), Oxon., 226, 14f.; 475f.
Banwell (*Bananwille*), Somerset, 94, 14, 16
Barbourne (*Beferburnan*), Worcs., 36, 14f.
Barkston (*Barcestune*), Yorks., 166, 5, 8
Barlow (*Bernlege*), Yorks., 164, 25
Barnack (*Beornican*), Northants., 82, 8
Barnes (*Bærnun*), Surrey, 144, 21; 390f.
Barnham, Suffolk, 432

INDEX LOCORUM

Barnwell (*Byrnewilla*), Northants., 76, 1; 78, 11
Barton, Great (*Byrtune*), Suffolk, 194, 33; 198, 30; 444
Barton Stacey (*Bertune*), Hants., 142, 25; 386
Basing (*Basyngum*), Hants., 54, 11; 310
Bath (*Baðan*), Somerset, 246, 16; 495 f.; abbey of, 216, 23; abbots of, *see* Ælfhere, Ælfsige, Ælfwig, Æscwig, Wulfwold; prior of, *see* Ælfnoth; cartulary of, 451
Battenhall, Worcs., 364
Beckwith (*Becwudu*), Yorks., 112, 1; 358
Bedford, abbot of. *See* Thurcytel
Belchamp St Paul (*Bylcham*), Essex, 144, 26; 391
Benefield (*Beringafelde*), Northants., 76, 9
Bengeworth, Worcs., 291, 459
Bentley, Worcs., 290, 364
Berkeley, abbess of. *See* Ceolburh
Berkshire (*Bearrucscire*), 44, 8; bishop of, *see* Cynesige, Wynsige; grants of land in, 276, 298
Berwick (*Berwica*), Kent, 170, 20; 182, 12; 419 f.
Beverley, Yorks., church of St John at, 112, 18; 359
Biccenclif, Warwicks., 88, 10; 335
Biceratune, Yorks., 166, 21; 415
Bilsham (*Bileshamme*), Glos., 134, 15; 379
Birkin (*Byrcene*), Yorks., 164, 28
Birling (*Berlingan*), Kent, 108, 26
Bishop Monkton (*Munecatun*), Yorks., 166, 25, 35; 168, 2; 415
Bishop's Cleeve (*Clife*), Glos., 30, 4, 11; 290
Bishop's Cliffe (*Cliue*), Kent, 108, 24
Bishop's Stoke, Glos., 318, 378
Bishopstoke, Hants., 324
Bishop Thornton (*Þorntune*), Yorks., 166, 28; 416
Bishopton (*Biscoptun*), Yorks., 166, 24
Bishopton, Warwicks., 335
Bishton (*Bispestune*), Glos., 204, 24; 452
Blackwell (*Blacewellan, -awyllan*), Worcs., 162, 2; 210, 21; 461
Blean, Forest of, Kent, 278

Bledlow (*Bleddehlæwe*), Bucks., 154, 22
Bluntisham (?), Hunts. (....*tesham*), 254, 20
Bockhampton (*Bokhamtoune*), Berks., 240, 20; 492
Bocking (*Boccing*), Essex, 182, 18; 430
Borstall (*Borcstealle*), Kent, 108, 1; 351 f.
Boughton (*Boctun*), Kent, 148, 10; 394 f.
Bourne (*Burnan*), Kent, 188, 30; 192, 1; 204, 11
Bourne (*Burnan*), 128, 19; 130, 5
Brabourne, Kent, 278, 377
Bracken (*Bracenan*), Yorks., 112, 17; 359
Bradfield (*Bradanfelda*), Berks., 136, 6
Bradfield (*Bradefeldæ, -felde*), Suffolk, 196, 3; 200, 5; 444
Bradley, Worcs., 264
Brampton, Lincs., 465
Brandon (*Bromdune*), Suffolk, 256, 6
Bransford (*Bregnesford*), Worcs., 64, 25; 321
Brayton (*Breiðetun*), Yorks., 164, 25, 29
Bredicot (*Bradingccotan*), Worcs., 124, 11, 15; 126, 3; 369
Bredon, monastery of, Worcs., 267, 343, 377; manor of, 343; abbot of, *see* Eanmund
Bredy (or Bridport), Dorset (*Brydian*), 246, 9; 495
Brightling (*Byrhtlingan*), Sussex, 150, 13
Brightwell (*Brutuwylle*), Oxon., 182, 21; 430
Brihtricesstane, Devon, 226, 8; 475
Broadwas (*Bradewassan*), Worcs., 2, 25; 4, 5; 261
Brockford (*Brocaforde, Broke-*), Suffolk, 194, 33; 200, 8; 444
Bromley (*Bromleah*), Kent, 122, 1 ff.; 333, 352, 355, 365
Bromley (*Bræmbelege*), 144, 21; 390
Bromsgrove (*Bremesgrefan*), Worcs., 6, 4; 264 f.
Broombridge, Hants., 325
Brotherton (*Broðertun*), Yorks., 164, 29; 414
Buckfast Abbey (*Bucfæsten*), Devon, 200, 21; 448

INDEX LOCORUM

Buckingham (*Buccingahamme*), 246, 20; Buckinghamshire (*Buccinghamscire*), 182, 19
Burham (*Burh(h)am*), Kent, 108, 11; 150, 11; 170, 2; 188, 29; 353
Burleston (*Burdalueston*), Dorset, 46, 4
Burley (*Burhleg, -leage*), Yorks., 110, 24; 166, 19f.; 358
Burmarsh (*Burwaramersce*), Kent, 150, 5
Burn (*Byrne*), Yorks., 164, 26
Burpham (*Burham*), Sussex, 246, 3; 495
Burton Abbey, Staffs., 467
Burton (*Burhtun*), Yorks., 164, 26; 414
Bury St Edmunds (*Bædericeswyrðe, seynt Eadmundes biri*, etc.), Suffolk, 178, 20, 23; 184, 3ff.; 186, 15, 21; 194, 13, 28; 220, 2; 442; foundation of Benedictine Abbey at, 425; abbots of, *see* Baldwin, Leofstan, Ufi; cartularies of, 392, 471; MSS. from, 440, 497, 500f.; lists of benefactors to, 392, 424, 426, 431, 435, 442, 444ff.; library at, 442
Buttermere (*Butermere*), Wilts., 52, 19; 308
Byllinctun, Yorks., 112, 1; 358
Bynningtune, 164, 13
Byrom (*Byrum*), Yorks., 164, 29; 414

Caddington (*Caddandune*), Beds., 144, 22; 391
Cambridge (*Grantanbricge*), 100, 29; 331; Cambridgeshire, sheriff of, 366
Candover, Hants., 284
Canterbury (*Cantwarabyrig, -berig*, etc.), Kent, 140, 9, 19; 142, 12; 158, 14; 160, 27; 168, 8; 204, 12f.; 216, 13; lathe of, 317; open country attached to, 377; associations at, 316f.; grant of land in, 269f.; sale of land in, 280; Ridingate (*reada gatan*), 204, 2f.; 450; Worth Gate (*wiwergatan*), 204, 3; 450; archbishops of, *see* Ælfric, Ælfsige, Æthelgar, Æthelnoth, Æthelred, Ceolnoth, Dunstan, Eadsige, Lanfranc, Lyfing, Oda, Plegmund, Robert Champart, Sigeric, Stigand, Wulfhelm, Wulfred Christchurch Cathedral (*Cristes cirican*, etc.), 10, 5f.; 58, 20; 60, 25; 84, 23; 128, 8; 142, 11; 148, 12; 150, 8, 21; 154, 15, 17; 158, 22, 24; 168, 8, 18; 170, 4f., 10ff.; 172, 8, 20f.; 174, 1, 4, 11, 15, 18; 176, 1ff.; 178, 8; 180, 25f.; 182, 1, 5, 24, 26; 188, 10, 26; 190, 6, 22, 24; 192, 7, 12; 204, 8, 14; 216, 12f.; members of the community at, 281, 316; late list of benefactors to, 315, 407, 419, 421, 428ff., 436, 468; Red Book of Canterbury at, 406; copy of the gospels given by Æthelstan to, 402; fragmentary gospel-book from, 421
St Augustine's (*see* Augustine), 128, 5ff.; 142, 12; 148, 12; 150, 9, 22; 168, 26; 170, 5; 172, 4f., 8; 174, 19; 178, 8; 188, 27; 190, 6f., 9ff.; 192, 7f., 12; 204, 15; 317; abbots of, *see* Ælfmær, Ælfric, Ælfstan, Æthelsige, Eadhelm, Wulfric; members of the community at, 316; MSS. from, 371, 499f.
Priory of St Gregory, 317
St Martin's, bishop of, 204, 7; 451
Carhampton (*Carintune*), Somerset, 94, 16; 340
Carlewic, Yorks., 166, 25
Carlford Hundred, Suffolk, 347
Castor (*Castre*), Northants., 76, 18, 31; 78, 8ff.; 82, 1
Cattistock (*Cattesstoke*), Dorset, 46, 5; 302
Catworth (*Catteswyrðe*), Hunts., 76, 4
Cawood (*Cawudu, -wuda, Cauda*), Yorks., 112, 5; 164, 23; 166, 10; 414f.
Ceaddingtune, 144, 23
Ceoredesholm, Yorks., 112, 4
Cerne Abbas (*Cernel*), Dorset, 146, 25; 376, 386; abbot of, *see* Leofsunu
Chalk (*Cealce*), Kent, 108, 13; 353
Challock, Kent, 278

INDEX LOCORUM

Chalmington (*Chelmyntone*), Dorset, 46, 12; 302
Charlton, Worcs., 461
Charlton Abbots and Charlton Kings, Glos., 290
Chart (*Cert*), Great and Little (*East Cert and oper Cert*), Kent, 182, 12; 188, 2, 6; 277, 428
Chartham (*Certham, Certa-*), Kent, 180, 25; 182, 11; 427
Chatham (*Cætham*), Kent, 108, 3; 352
Cheal in Gosberton (*Cegle*), Lincs., 12, 21; 272
Cheam (*Ceigham*), Surrey, 182, 17; 429 f.
Chebbard Farm, Cheselborne, Dorset, 283
Cheddar (*Ceodre*), Somerset, 94, 16 f.; 340
Cheddon Fitzpaine (*Cedon*), Upper and Lower (*twam Cedenon*), Somerset, 238, 2, 17; 487
Chelsworth (*Ceorlesweorðe, -wurðe*), Suffolk, 196, 2; 200, 5; 444
Chertsey (*Certesige*), Surrey, 168, 27; abbots of, *see* Daniel, Siweard, Wulfsige; payment to, 441
Cheselborne (*Chiselburne, Chesel-*), Dorset, 22, 6, 21; 282, 380
Chesterton, boundary of (*Ceastertuningagemærie*), Hunts., 56, 23; 314
Chevin (*Scefinc*), Yorks., 110, 24; 166, 19; 358
Chichester (*Cisseceastre*), Sussex, 246, 4
Chilbolton (*Ceolbaldinctuna*), Hants., 48, 27; 305, 325
Chilcomb (*Ciltancumbes*), Hants., 68, 16; 324 f., 485
Chilham (*Cilleham*), Kent, 170, 1; 419
Chilterns, the (*Cilternes*), 182, 20
Chimney (*Ceommenige*), Oxon., 226, 15; 475 f.
Chiseldon, Wilts., 309
Chiswick (*Ceswican*), Mdx., 144, 22
Cholsey, Berks., 372; abbot of, 374
Christchurch Twyneham (*Twynham, Tweoneam*), Hants., 46, 8; 246, 8; 302
Church Fenton (*Fen(n)tun*), Yorks., 166, 4, 11; 414 f.
Churchill, Worcs., 459

Cingestune, 204, 20, 23; 452
Cirencester, Glos., 369; abbey at, 471
Clacton (*Claccingtune*), Essex, 144, 27; 389, 391
Cladswell (*Cloddesheale*), Worcs., 164, 12; 413
Clapham (*Clopham*), Surrey, 144, 21; 390
Clare, Suffolk, house of secular canons at, 425
Clenchwarton Hundred (*Clencware*), Norfolk, 192, 26; 442
Cleyley Hundred (*Klegele*), Northants., 230, 19
Clife. *See* Bishop's Cleeve
Cliffe at Hoo (?), Kent (*Clife*), 128, 3; 372
Clifford Chambers (*Clifforda*), Glos., 42, 14; 299, 378
Clifton (*Cliftune*), Yorks., 166, 21
Clofesho(*us*), 8, 5; 266; documents issued at, 267 ff.; meetings at, 266
Cloptun, Worcs., 321, 364
Clyffe (*Clyve*), Dorset, 46, 3; 302
Clyst (*Clist*), Devon, 226, 11; 475
Cnearresweorð, Yorks., 166, 32; 416
Cockfield (*Koccefelda, Kokefelde*), Suffolk, 196, 1; 200, 4; 444
Coddenham (*Codanham*), Suffolk, 144, 28; 392
Collingbourne (*Collingaburnan*), Wilts., 52, 1; 307 f.
Colneis Hundred, Suffolk, 347
Comberton (*Cumbrintune*), Worcs., 210, 7 f.; 459 ff.
Compton Abbas, Dorset, 24, 16 (*Cumtune*); 46, 5 (*Comptone*); 284, 302
Compton (*Cumtune*), Glos., 134, 1, 7; 318, 378
Compton (*Cumbtune*), Somerset, 94, 14 f.
Coney Weston (*Cunegestune*), Suffolk, 200, 2; 447
Cooling (*Culingas*), Kent, 182, 14; 428 f.
Copford (*Coppanforda*), Essex, 144, 26; 391
Coppington (*Cobbaudoune*), Berks., 240, 16; 492
Corby Hundred (*Corebi*), Northants., 236, 1

INDEX LOCORUM

Cornwall, bishops of, *see* Brihtwold, Burhwold, Conan, Ealdred, Lyfing, Wulfsige; grant of estates in, **341**
Cossington (*Cusintune*), Kent, **108**, 10
Cotes, Great, Lincs., **272**
Cotheridge (*Coddanhrycce, -hrycge*), Worcs., **64**, 6 ff.; **261**, **320** f.
Coventry, Warwicks., abbey of, **467**; abbot of, **466**; charter relating to, **458**
Cradley (*Cyrdesleah*), Herefordshire, **152**, 5; **401**
Cræft, **52**, 15; **308**
Cray (*Crægan*), Kent, **84**, 12 ff.; **333**
Crayke (*Creic*), Yorks., **124**, 7; **368**
Creast, **82**, 13
Crediton (*Cridiantune*), Devon, **202**, 5; bishops of, *see* Ælfwold, Æthelgar, Eadulf, Leofric, Lyfing, Sideman
Creedy Bridge (*Crydanbrigce*), Devon, **58**, 11 f.; **314**
Cricklade (*Crecgelade*), Wilts., **246**, 17 f.
Cringleford (*Cringelford*), Norfolk, **184**, 15; **432**
Crowcombe (*Crawancumbe*), Somerset, **94**, 13
Crowland, Lincs., abbey of, **467**; abbots of, *see* Brihtmær, Ingulf, Ulfketel, Wulfgeat; charters of, **271**, **463**, **468**
Crowle, Worcs., **362**, **371**
Culford (*Culeforde*), Suffolk, **178**, 25; **196**, 5; **200**, 7; **426**
Culmstock (*Culmstoke*), Devon, **226**, 5; **474**
Curry Rivel (*Curi*), Somerset, **238**, 23; **490**
Cuxton (*Cucclestane*), Kent, **108**, 1; **352**
Cwicelmeshlæwe, Berks., **136**, 10; **380**

Dalham (*Dælham*), Cambs., **124**, 3; **367**
Datchet (*Deccet*), Bucks., **136**, 6
Dawlish (*Doflisc*), Devon, **226**, 15; **476**
Daylesford, Worcs., **264**
Deal, Kent, **394**
Deerhurst, Glos., **290**, **457**

Denford (*Denforda*), Berks., **52**, 17; **308**
Denton (*Denetune*), Kent, **108**, 24; **355**
Denton (*Dentune*), Northants., **74**, 32; **82**, 2 ff.
Denton (*Dentun*), Yorks., **110**, 25; **166**, 14, 21; **358**
Devil's Brook, Dorset, **283**
Devonshire (*Defenanscire*), **176**, 5; possible earl of, **314**
Dewlish (*Deflisch*), Dorset, **22**, 31; **283**
Ditchford (*Dicford*), Worcs., **208**, 3; **456**
Ditton (*Dictune*), Kent, **108**, 17; **142**, 16
Doddenham, Worcs., **261**, **458**
Dogsthorpe, Northants., **327**
Donhead St Andrew (*Dunheued*), Wilts., **24**, 16; **284**
Dorchester (*Dornwaraceaster*), Dorset, **18**, 21 f.; bishops of, *see* Æscwig, Æthelric, Eadnoth, Oscytel, Wulfwig, Wynsige
Dorset (*Dorsæton, -sætscire*), **148**, 2; **160**, 34; **200**, 20; earl of, **282**
Dover (*Doferan*), Kent, **150**, 14; **204**, 9; **399**, **423**
Downton, Wilts., **485**
Drayton (*Dræg-, Dregtune*), Hants., **142**, 26; **144**, 2; **386**
Drayton (*Drægtune*), Mdx., **144**, 22; **391**
Droitwich, Worcs., **363**, **370**
Dudeslande, Kent, **108**, 10; **353**
Dumbleton, Glos., **375**
Dunhampstead (*Dunhæmstedes*), Worcs., **116**, 25 f.
Dunmow (*Dunmæwan*), Essex, **144**, 18; **390**
Durham, bishops of. *See* Aldhun, Walcher
Dykes, the (*Dicon*), Northants., **78**, 27; **331**

Eadboldesstowe Hundred, Northants., **230**, 25 f.; **482**
Eaningadene, **154**, 23
Eashing (*Escingum*), Surrey, **246**, 21
East Anglia (*Eastenglum*), **182**, 19; king of, *see* Offa; bishop of, *see* Ælfric; earls of, *see* Ælfgar, Æthelstan, Æthelwine, Æthelwold, Harold, Ralph

INDEX LOCORUM

Eastbury (*Eastbury*), Beds., **240**, 18, 22
Eastfield, Northants., **327**
Easton (*Eastune*), Hants., **26**, 3, 23; **286, 288, 325**
Easton-Bassett, Dorset, **284**
Eastry (*Eastorege, Eastryge*), Kent, **4**, 15; **182**, 10; **262, 428**
Eastwick (*Eastwic*), Yorks., **168**, 2; **416**
Eaveston (*Efestun*), Yorks., **166**, 31
Ebbesborne Wake, Wilts., **289**
Ebbsfleet (*Hyppelesfleote*), Kent, **178**, 2f.; **424**
Eccles (*Æcclesse*), Kent, **108**, 12; **353**
Ectune, Yorks., **166**, 15, 22; **415**
Egelweardesle Hundred, Northants., **232**, 1; **482**
Egmere (*Eggemere*), Norfolk, **196**, 11; **445**
Eleigh, Monks (*Illaleh*), Suffolk, **182**, 19; **430**
Elham (*Æpelham*), Kent, **204**, 10; **451**
Elmestree in Tetbury (*Æpelmodestreow*), Glos., **62**, 13, 17; **318, 379**
Elmham, bishops of. See Ælfric, Æthelmær, Alfred, Humberht, Stigand, Theodred, William
Elmstone (*Alhmundingtune*), Glos., **28**, 21; **290**
Elmswell (*Elmeswella, -welle*), Suffolk, **194**, 34; **200**, 1; **444**
Elton (*Æpelingtune, Æilin-*), Hunts., **76**, 4; **82**, 2ff.
Ely (*Elig, Helig*), Cambs., **98**, 23; **100**, 13; **184**, 12; **252**, 24; **254**, 13; **504**; isle of, **346** f.; *Liber Eliensis*, **331, 342, 346, 367, 369, 374, 376** f., **388, 405, 467, 504**; *Inquisitio Eliensis*, **346** f.; abbots of, *see* Brihtnoth, Leofric, Leofsige, Wulfric
Enford (*Enedforda*), Wilts., **48**, 27; **304**
Eorpeburnan, **246**, 1; **495**
Epsom (*Ebbesham*), Surrey, **124**, 3
Ercecombe, Dorset, **46**, 13; **303**
Eriswell, Suffolk, **432**
Erith (*Earhiðes*), Kent, **84**, 12ff.
Ermine Street (*Earningastræte*), **56**, 22; **58**, 1f.; **314**

Escomb (*Ediscum*), County Durham, **140**, 1; **383**
Essex (*E(a)st Se(a)xan*), **86**, 6; **182**, 17; earls of, *see* Ælfgar, Brihtnoth; possible earl of, **337**
Evegate in Smeeth, Kent, **377**
Everingham (*Yferingaham*), Yorks., **112**, 9f.; **359**
Evesham (*Eofeshamme*, etc.), Worcs., abbey of, **156**, 1f., 15; **172**, 18; **180**, 20f.; **208**, 9; **210**, 4; **370, 404**f.; abbots of, *see* Ælfric, Ælfweard, Æthelwig, Brihtmær, Cynehelm, Manni; list of abbots of, **291**; *Chronicon* of, **291, 383, 397, 404, 459**f.; register of, **457**
Ewell, Kent, **451**
Exe (*Exon*), **200**, 24
Exeter (*E(a)x(an)ce(a)stre*), Devon, **200**, 12; **246**, 10f.; cathedral (St Peter's) of, **226**, 2, 20; community attached to, **344**; abbots of, *see* Brihthelm, Leofric; Exeter Book, **473**; MSS. from, **343, 476, 478**ff.
Eye, Northants., **327**
Eynsford (*Ænesford*), Kent, **84**, 12, 16
Eynsham, Oxon., **376, 386**f., **465**; cartulary of, **386, 465**
Eythorne (*Hægyðeðorne*), Kent, **6**, 1; **262**

Fachanleage, Warwicks., **88**, 7
Fairburn (*Farenburne*), Yorks., **164**, 29
Fakenham (*ffakenham*), Norfolk, **186**, 18; **436**
Farcet (*F(e)arresheafde*, etc.), Hunts., **72**, 28; **74**, 25; **252**, 17; **254**, 25; **323, 327, 329**f., **503**
Farleigh (*Fe(a)rnlege*), Kent, **108**, 12; **182**, 15; **353, 429**
Farningham (*Frinningaham*), Kent, **182**, 14; **394, 429**
Farnley (*Fearnleage*), Yorks., **166**, 22
Faversham (*Fefresham*), Kent, **16**, 11; **278**
Fawkham (*Falchenham, Fealcna-*), Kent, **108**, 7; **122**, 1ff.; **333, 352**f., **355, 365**
Fawley (*Fæliglæh*), Herefordshire, **152**, 9f.; **401**
[? Fecka]nham, Worcs., **164**, 11; **413**

INDEX LOCORUM

Ferryhill (*Feregenne*), County Durham, **140**, 2; **383**
Finnesthorpe, **76**, 1
Flaxley (*Fleaxlege*), Yorks., **164**, 24; **414**
Fledborough, Notts., **465**
Fleet (*Fliote*), Kent, **108**, 6, 24; **352**, **355**
Folkestone (*Folcestane*, *Folken-*), Kent, **150**, 14; **168**, 8; **417**
Fontmel (*ffuntemel*), Dorset, **24**, 18; **285**
Ford (*Eaforde*), Somerset, **238**, 5; **487**
Forde, Lincs. (?), **12**, 21
Fordham (*Fordham*), Cambs., **256**, 14
Fornham (*Fornham*), Suffolk, **196**, 6; **200**, 7; **445**
Forþtune, **144**, 24
Foxley Hundred (*Uoxle*), Northants., **232**, 6; **482**
Frindsbury (*Frinondesbyrig*), Kent, **108**, 1; **352**
Frome, River (*Frome*, *Frume*), Dorset, **24**, 2; **46**, 1; **283**
Frome, Herefordshire, **152**, 2, 10
Frome (*Fromæ*), Somerset (?), **50**, 17
Fulham (*Fullanhamme*), London, **144**, 23; **389**, **391**
Fuwelege Hundred, Norfolk (?), **192**, 25; **442**

Gadshill (*Godeshylle*), Kent, **122**, 18; **366**
Gander Down (*gandran dune*), Hants., **40**, 32 f.; **298**
Gateforth (*Gæiteford*), Yorks., **164**, 26
Genanofre, Genen-, Worcs., **118**, 1, 5; **124**, 11, 15; **363**
Gillingham (*Gyllingeham*), Kent, **108**, 2; **352**
Gisferpesdæll, Yorks., **112**, 5
Gisleardeslande, Kent, **108**, 11; **353**
Gislingham (*Gyselingham*), Suffolk, **186**, 16; **435** f.
Givendale (*Gyðingdale*, *Gyþingadeal*), Yorks., **166**, 34; **168**, 1
Glastonbury, Somerset, **275**; Rentalia of, **450**; abbots of, see Ælfstan, Æthelnoth, Brihtwig
Gloucester (*Glæaweceastre*), **172**, 18; Gloucestershire (*Glæaweceastrescire*), **172**, 12; **260**

Gnutungadune, **144**, 20
Godmersham (*Godmæresham*), Kent, **174**, 1 f.; **182**, 11; **422**
Gracechurch (*Gerschereche*), London, **216**, 11; **469**
Grafton Flyford, Worcs., **362**
Grantley (*Grantelege*), Yorks., **166**, 30
Grauesende Hundred, Northants., **230**, 22; **482**
Grimley, Worcs., **266**
Groton (*Grotene*), Suffolk, **196**, 1; **200**, 2; **444**
Guilsborough (*Gildesburh*), Northants., **234**, 9
Guiseley (*Gislicleh*), Yorks., **110**, 24; **358**
Gussage (*Gissic*), Dorset, **24**, 17

Haddlesey, East, West and Chapel (*twa Haðelsæ... þriddan Haðelsæ*), Yorks., **164**, 27 f.; **414**
Haddon, Hunts., **312**
Hadleigh (*Hæpleh*, *-lege*), Suffolk, **144**, 28; **182**, 19; **392**, **430**
Hadlow (*Hæselholte*), Kent, **108**, 16; **354** f.
Hadzor, Worcs., **461**
Hagbourne (*Hacceburnan*), Berks., **136**, 5
Halling (*Heallingan*), Kent, **108**, 5; **352**
Hallow, Worcs., **261**, **362**
Halsway (*Healswege*), Somerset, **238**, 20; **488**
Halton (*Healtune*), Bucks., **154**, 12; **174**, 10; **403**
Halwell (*Halganwille*), Devon, **246**, 11 f.
Ham (*Hamme*), Wilts., **52**, 26, 31; **307**, **309**
Hamfordshoe (*Anforðesho*, *Anuerðeshoh*), Northants., **234**, 35; **236**, 12; **483**
Hampshire (*Hamtunsciræ*), **202**, 12, 24; **212**, 19 f.; earls of, see Ælfheah, Ælfric, Æthelmær; possible earl of, **315**; thegns of, **386**
Handley (*Hanlee*), Dorset, **24**, 17; **284**
Harrietsham (*Hergeardesham*), Kent, **176**, 8; **192**, 9
Harting (*Heartingas*), Sussex, **100**, 12; **346** f.

534　INDEX LOCORUM

Hastings (*Hæstingaceastre*), Sussex, 246, 2
Hatfield (*Hæpfelda*), Herts., 254, 17; 256, 3, 11; 504
Hatley, Beds., 388
Hauxton (*Hafucestune*), Cambs., 256, 1; 504
Haven Street (*Ædune*), Kent, 108, 13; 353
Hawksworth (*Hafecesweorðe*), Yorks., 166, 14 ff.; 415
Haydon (*Hægdune*), Dorset or Somerset, 200, 26; 449
Hayling Island (*Heilincigæ*), Hants., 212, 2; 462
Hehferðehegðe, Yorks., 166, 6
Hele (*Hele*), Somerset, 238, 7; 487
Helperby (*Helperby*, *Heolp-*, *-bi*), Yorks., 112, 3 ff.; 359
Helpston (*Hylpestune*), Northants., 78, 9, 12; 80, 34; 82, 8
Henhurst (*Hennhyste*), Kent, 108, 13
Hereford (*Her(e)forda*), 148, 29; 164, 16; cathedral (St Æthelbert's) of, 152, 28; 164, 16; 186, 13; 402; bishops of, *see* Ælfric, Æthelstan, Athulf, Bionna, Eadwulf, Edgar, Tidhelm, Wulfhelm; list of bishops of, 306; St Guthlac's, 186, 13; 435
Herefordshire (*Herefordscire*), 186, 12; earls of, *see* Ralph, William; possible earl of, 467
Hernicwelle, 144, 17
Herringswell (*Hyrningcwylle*, *Herningwelle*), Suffolk, 196, 4; 200, 2; 444
Hewick (*Heawic*), Yorks., 112, 2; 168, 6; 358, 416
Higham (*Hehham*), Kent, 108, 24; 355
Higham Ferrers (*Hehham*), Northants., 234, 32; 483
Hilgay (*Hyllingyge*), Norfolk, 256, 14
Hill (*Hylle*), Worcs., 208, 22; 460
Hillam (*Hyllum*), Yorks., 166, 3; 414
Hillfarrance (*Hylle*), Somerset, 238, 12; 487
Hillfield (*Hylfelde*), Dorset, 46, 12
Himbleton (*Hymeltune*), Worcs., 116, 1 ff.; 362, 458
Hinderclay (*Hildericlea*), Suffolk, 146, 4; 392
Hindlip (*Hindehlyp*, *-hlep*), Worcs., 86, 11, 15

Hindolveston (*Hildoluestone*), Norfolk, 184, 4
Hinton, Wilts., 274
Hirst Courtney and Temple Hirst (*twa Hyrst*), Yorks., 164, 27; 414
Hiwerc, Somerset, 238, 25; 490
Holcombe (*Holacumbe*), Devon, 226, 16; 476
Holcombe Rogus (*Hola(n)cumbe*), Devon, 146, 9; 200, 14; 393, 448
Holford, Rich's and Treble's (*twam Holaforda*), Somerset, 238, 16; 487
Holland (*Holande*), Essex, 144, 27; 391
Hollingbourn (*Holinga(n)burnan*), Kent, 108, 19; 182, 14; 354, 429
Holt, Worcs., 364
Holwell (*Holewelle*), Herts., 144, 16; 389
Holworth (*Holewertpe*), Dorset, 46, 6; 302
Honey Bourne (*Huniburnan*), Worcs., 126, 14 f.; 371
Hoo, people of (*Howaran*), Kent, 108, 21; 354 f.
Horne (*Hornan*), Rutland, 12, 5; 272
Horningsea (*Horningesige*), Cambs., 254, 31; 504
Horringer (*Horningasearðe*, *-ingeseorðe*), Suffolk, 196, 3; 200, 4; 444
Horsley, East (*Horslege*), Surrey, 172, 20; 182, 17; 421
Horsted (*Horstede*), Kent, 108, 12
Horton (*Hortune*), Dorset, abbey of, 220, 18; 222, 8; 278, 472
Horton (*Hortune*), Kent, 150, 16
How Hill (*Herelesho*), Yorks., 166, 27; 168, 3; 416
Hoxne, Suffolk, bishopric at, 307; relics of St Edmund at, 425
Huddington, Worcs., 362
Huddleston (*Hudelestun*), Yorks., 166, 6; 415
Hulme, Norfolk, abbey of St Benedict at, 184, 12 f.; 432; abbot of, *see* Ælfsige; prior of, 425, 445
Huntingdon (*Hunta(n)dune*), 252, 23; 254, 7, 12; 504; possible earl of, 315
Hurstbourne Priors (*Hysseburnan*) Hants., 206, 20; 454
Hutton (*Hotune*), Yorks., 166, 35

INDEX LOCORUM

Huxloe Hundred (*Hocheshlawa*), Northants., **232**, 14; **482**
Hwicce, province of, **2**, 6; **260**f.; rulers of, **261**; earl of, **396**

Ickham (*Geocham, Ieocc-*), Kent, **58**, 21; **182**, 11; **315, 428**
Ide (*Ide*), Devon, **226**, 18; **476**
Ileden (*Gildinge*), Kent, **190**, 17; **438**
Ilkley (*Hyllicleg, Yllicleage*), Yorks., **110**, 23; **166**, 20; **357**
In Hundred, Norfolk, **192**, 24; **442**
Inkberrow (*Intanbeorgum, -an, Intebyrgan*),Worcs.,**6**,6,14;**162**, 2 f.; **264**f., **322**; boundary, land of the people of (*Incsetena gemære, lande*), **66**, 16f., 19
Inkpen (*Ingepenne*), Berks., **52**, 8, 23
Ipswich, Suffolk, **331, 423**
Islington (*Gislandune*), London, **144**, 24; **389, 391**
Islington Hundred (*Elsingtun*), Norfolk, **192**, 23; **442**
Islip (*Isslepe, Hyslepe*), Northants., **76**, 10; **82**, 15
Itchen, River (*Ycenan*), Hants., **26**, 23, 29; **286**f., **296, 324**
Itchington, Glos., **318, 378**f.
Iwerne Minster (*Ywern*), Dorset, **24**, 18; **284**f.
Ixworth (*Gyxeweorðe* etc.), Suffolk, **178**, 27; **196**, 33; **198**, 20; **426**

Keelby Cotes or Nun Coton, Lincs., **272**
Kempsey (*Cymesige*), Worcs., **114**, 6
Kennington (*Cenintune*), in Sunningwell, Berks., **58**, 10; **314**
Kent (*Cent, Kænt*), **130**, 19; **150**, 20; men of East Kent and West Kent (*East Cantwarena and West Cantwarena*), **86**, 4 f.; thegns of East Kent and West Kent, **140**, 17, 21; kings of, *see* Æthelbert, Æthelstan, Cuthred, Eadbald, Wihtred; sheriff of, **423**; sheriff of West Kent, **366**
Kettering (*Keteiringan*), Northants., **72**, 30; **312**
Kilmeston (*Cenelmestune*), Hants., **62**, 2; **298, 317**f., **324**
Kingsclere, Hants., **284**

Kingston (*Cincgestune, Kyng-*), Surrey, **150**, 7; **168**, 22
Kingston Bagpuize (*Kingestune*), Berks., **106**, 14; **350**
King's Worthy, Hants., **287**
Kintbury (*Cynetanbyrig*), Berks., **52**, 10ff.; **308**
Kippings, Hants., manor of, **464**
Knightwick (*Cnihtewican*), Worcs., **148**, 18; **396**

Lackford (*Lecforde, Lac-*), Suffolk, **196**, 4ff.; **198**, 24, 29; **444, 447**
Lambourn (*Lambourne*), Berks., **240**, 1ff.; **491**
Landcaut (*Landcawet*), Glos., **204**, 25; **452**
Langdon (*Langadune*), Kent, **190**, 17; **262, 438**
Langport (*Langport*), Somerset, **246**, 16
Lawling (*Lællingc*), Essex, **182**, 18; **386, 430**
Leadon, Herefordshire, **458**
Leckford (*Leahtford*), Hants., **54**, 17ff.; **311**
Ledsham (*Ledesham*), Yorks., **166**, 2
Lehcotum, Lincs., **12**, 22; **272**
Leicester, bishops of. *See* Ceolred, Hræthhun
Lenchwick, Worcs., **404**
Leobrantestune, Northants. (?), **76**, 19
Leopard Grange, boundary of (*Lipperdes gemære*), Worcs., **118**, 12; **363**
Lewes (*Læwe*), Sussex, **246**, 2
Lewknor (*Leofecanoran*), Oxon., **136**, 22; **381**
Leybourne (*Lillanburnan*), Kent, **108**, 16
Leyton (*Ligeandune*), Essex, **144**, 25; **391**
Lichfield, bishops of. *See* Ælfheah, Ælla, Æthelwold, Cynesige, Leofwine, Tunberht, Wulfsige, Wynsige
Lickpit Farm, Hants., **310**
Lidford (*Hlidan*), Devon, **246**, 12
Lincoln (*Lincolne*), **214**, 33; bishops of, *see* Remigius, Robert Bloet; lawmen of, **468**
Lindley (*Lindeleh, -leage*), Yorks., **110**, 25; **166**, 23; **415**

INDEX LOCORUM

Lindsey, bishops of. *See* Brihtred, Eadwulf
Linton (*Lindune*), Cambs., **254**, 21
Littlebrook (*Lytlanbroc*), Kent, **84**, 19
Loes Hundred, Suffolk, **347**
London (*Lundene, Londone, Lundenbyrig*), **86**, 1; **122**, 2, 10; **130**, 10; **160**, 31; **168**, 25; **214**, 5; **266**; bishops of, *see* Ælfhun, Ælfstan, Ælfweard, Ælfwig, Brihthelm, Ceolberht, Eadberht, Ingwald, Theodred, William, Wulfstan; court of, **420**; bridge of, **68**, 10; **411**; harbour of (*Lundentunes hyðe*), **2**, 12; St Paul's, **214**, 4; Chapter House Book of, **490**; MS. from, **389**
Longdon (*Langadune*), Worcs., **208**, 13; **458**f.
Long Sutton, Lincs., **442**
Lotherton (*Lutering(a)tun*), Yorks., **166**, 5, 8; **414**
Luddesdown (*Hludesdune*), Kent, **108**, 25
Luddington (*Lullingtune*), Northants., **76**, 2
Luddington (*Ludintune*), Warwicks., **154**, 3; **402**
Lumby (*Lundby*), Yorks., **166**, 3; **414**
Lutton (*Lundingtune*), Northants., **82**, 11
Lydeard St Lawrence (*Lidigerde*), Somerset, **238**, 11; **487**
Lyng (*Lengen*), Somerset, **246**, 15; **495**
Lynn Hundred (*Lynware*), Norfolk, **192**, 27; **442**
Lyscombe (*Liscombe*), Dorset, **46**, 4; **302**

Mærcesfleote, Kent, **158**, 19; **407**
Maidstone (*Mægpanstane*), Kent, **108**, 14
Maldon, Essex, Battle of, **315**, **376**
Malling (*Meallingan*), Kent, **108**, 6; **142**, 13; **352**
Malmesbury (*Mealdmesbyring*), Wilts., **246**, 17; **275**, **496**; charter of, **275**; grant in reversion to, **287**
Mansell (*Malveshylle*), Herefordshire, **186**, 7; **435**
Markington (*Mercing(a)tun*), Yorks., **166**, 26, 34; **168**, 3; **416**
Marsh (*Mersce*) in Thornbury, Glos., **134**, 8, 14; **378**
Marshall (*Morceshille*), Devon, **226**, 7; **474**
Martin Hussingtree, Worcs., **370**
Marton, Lincs., **465**
Martyr Worthy, Hants., **287**f.
Mawsley Hundred (*Malesle*), Northants., **234**, 36; **483**
Maxey (*Macuseige*, etc.), Northants., **74**, 10, 14; **76**, 22; **78**, 6, 34; **80**, 2; **329**
Medeshamstede, **72**, 26; **74**, 5. *See also* Peterborough
Melbourn (*Meldeburna*), Cambs., **100**, 14; **256**, 2; **346**f.
Meldreth, Cambs., **346**
Melford, Suffolk, **425**
Membury (*Minbury*), Wilts., **240**, 31; **492**
Menston (*Mensinctun*), Yorks., **110**, 23; **166**, 19; **357**
Meopham (*Meapeham, Meapa-*), Kent, **108**, 25; **182**, 14; **355**, **428**f.
Mercia, kings of. *See* Æthelbald, Beornwulf, Burgred, Ceolwulf, Coenwulf, Offa; earls of, *see* Ælfgar, Ælfhere, Ælfric, Æthelred, Eadric Streona, Edwin, Leofric, Leofwine
Mereworth (*Mæreweorðe, -anwyrðe*), Kent, **86**, 4; **108**, 16
Mersham (*Mersaham, Merse-, Mærse-*), Kent, **16**, 7ff.; **142**, 14; **182**, 13; **428**
Merstham (*Mersetham*), Surrey, **182**, 17; **429**f.
Merstow Green, Worcs., **370**
Michelney (*Miclanige*), Somerset, **130**, 15; abbots of, *see* Leofric, Leofweard
Micklefield (*Miclafeld*), Yorks., **166**, 2; **414**
Middlesex (*Middelseaxan*), **86**, 6; **337**
Middleton (*Middeltun, Meðel-*), Yorks., **110**, 24; **166**, 20; **358**
Milbarrow (*Mælanbeorh*), Hants., **40**, 29; **298**, **318**
Milborne (*Muleburne*), Dorset, **44**, 25; **302**
Mildenhall, Suffolk, **266**
Milford, South (*Myleford*), Yorks., **166**, 4; **414**

INDEX LOCORUM

Milton (*Middeltune*), Cambs., **254**, 1; **504**
Milton (*Middeltun*), Essex, **182**, 18; **430**
Milton (*Middeltune*), Glos., **204**, 18
Milton (*Melantun*), Kent, **108**, 25; **188**, 17; **355, 436** f.
Milton (*Mylatune, Myle-*), Northants., **76**, 16, 23
Milton Abbas (*Middeltone*), Dorset, abbey of, **46**, 7, 17; **301**; abbots of, see Cyneweard, **375, 384**; register of, **300**
Minehead (*Mynheafdon*), Somerset, **200**, 25; **449**
Minster, Kent, abbey of, **260, 423, 438**
Monk Fryston (*Fristun*), Yorks., **166**, 3; **414**
Monksilver (*Sulfhere*), Somerset, **238**, 24; **490**
Mordune (? Morden, Surrey), **130**, 18; **375**
Moredon (*Mordune*), Wilts., **110**, 4
Moreton (*Mortun* or *Uppþrop*), Worcs., **130**, 23; **132**, 5; **377**
Moulton (*Multune*), Northants., **234**, 17; **483**
Myton (*Myðtune, Mytun*), Yorks., **112**, 3, 14; **358** f.

Nackington, Kent, **377**
Nassaborough, Northants., double hundred of, **328** f., **331**
Nauereslund, Northants., double hundred of, **232**, 26; **483**
Navestock (*Næsingstoce*), Essex, **144**, 19; **390**
Navisford Hundred (*Nęresforda*), Northants., **232**, 31; **483**
Neasden (*Neosdune*), Mdx., **144**, 19; **390**
Nettlestead (*Netlestede*), Kent, **108**, 15; **354**
Newark, Notts., **465**
Newbald (*Neoweboldan*), Yorks., **112**, 11; **359**
Newbold-on-Stour (*Neoweboldan, Niowe-*), Worcs., **138**, 10, 16; **382**
Newington (*Niwantun*), Oxon., **182**, 21, 23; **430** f.
Newthorpe (*Niwanþorp*), Yorks., **166**, 2

Newton (*Niwentune*), Suffolk, **192**, 15; **440**
Newton St Cyres (*Niwantune*), Devon, **226**, 10; **475**
Nobottlegrove (*Neowbotlegraue*), Northants., **234**, 4; **483**
Norman Cross (*Normannescros*), Hunts., **74**, 2
Northampton (*Hamtone*), Northants., **76**, 19; Northamptonshire, sheriff of, **383**
Norðhealum, **90**, 15; **337**
Northumbria (*Norþhymbralande*), **112**, 7, 19; kings of, see Ælla, Ecgferth; earls of, see Eadulf, Ealdred, Morcar, Siweard, Tostig, Uhtred, Waltheof
Northwold (*Norðwold*), Norfolk, **100**, 15; **346**
Norton (*Norðtune*), Devon, **226**, 10; **475**
Norton (*Norðtun*), County Durham, **140**, 3; **384**
Norton (*Nortune*), Northants., **232**, 3
Norton (*Norðtune*), Worcs., **156**, 3; **404**
Norwich, transactions at, **331**
Nottingham (*Snotingaham*), **112**, 20 f.
Nunton (*Nunnetune*), Northants., **74**, 13; **329**
Nunwick (*Nunnewic*), Yorks., **166**, 28; **168**, 5; **416**
Nursling, Hants., **325**
Nynehead Flory (*Nigonhidon*), Somerset, **236**, 26; **238**, 7; **485**

Oake (*Acon*), Somerset, **238**, 1; **485**, **487**
Oakley (*Aclea*), Kent, **108**, 10
Oborne (*Womburnan*), Dorset, **104**, 20; **349**
Oddingley, Worcs., **363**
Offa's Dyke, **452**
Offham (*Offaham*), Kent, **108**, 17; **192**, 2; **354, 439**
Old Croft River, **328, 346**
Orleton (*Ealretune*), Worcs., **148**, 17
Orlingbury Hundred (*Ordlingbære*), Northants., **236**, 15
Orpington (*Orpedingtun*), Kent, **142**, 11; **170**, 21 f.; **182**, 13; **419**
Orsett (*Orseaþum*), Essex, **144**, 25 f.; **391**

538 INDEX LOCORUM

Orton, Hunts., boundary of (*Ofertuninga gemęre*), 56, 25; 314
Osmington (*Osmyntone*), Dorset, 46, 6
Otley (*Ottanle(a)ge*), Yorks., 110, 22; 166, 13, 17; 357
Otterbourne, Hants., 325
Oundle (*Undelum*), Northants., 72, 29; 78, 32; 82, 4ff.
Overhill (*Ufanhylle*), Kent, 108, 9; 353
Ovington, Hants., 325
Ower (*Ore*), Dorset, 46, 3; 302
Oxford (*Ox(a)naforde*), 176, 3; 246, 18; 423; Oxfordshire (*Oxenafordscire*), 182, 21; grant of estates in, 341
Oxney House (*Oxanege, -ige*), Northants., 80, 19f., 23, 26

Paddlesworth (*Peadleswyrþe, Pealles-*), Kent, 108, 26; 142, 17; 355, 385
Pakenham (*Paccenham, Paken-*), Suffolk, 196, 9, 33; 198, 21; 200, 1; 445
Palgrave (*Pallegrafe*), Suffolk, 194, 31; 200, 3; 443
Palster (*Palstre*), Kent, 170, 25; 419f.
Paston, Northants., 327
Patching (*Pæccingas*), Sussex, 182, 16; 429
Patney (*Peattanigge*), Wilts., 202, 17
Pebbewurðy (? Pebworth, Glos.), 164, 11; 413
Peckham (*Peccham*), Kent, 182, 15; 429; East and West (*þam twam Peccham*), 108, 15; 354
Penenden Heath, Kent, shire-meetings at, 439
Pepperness (*Pipernæsse*), Kent, 158, 19; 407
Perry Wood, Kent, 377
Pershore (*Presc(e)oran, Per-*), Worcs., abbey of, 172, 19; 208, 9; 210, 4; abbots of, *see* Ælfric, 421, 460; annals of, 457f.
Peterborough (*Burh*, earlier called *Medeshamstede*), Northants., 78, 22; abbey of St Peter at, 12, 1ff.; 68, 6; 72, 1ff.; 74, 3; 271; abbots of, *see* Ælfsige, Beonna, Ceolred, Ealdulf, Hedda, Leofric; list of abbots of, 271; community at, 274; cartulary of, 271, 455; restoration of, 323, 325; grants of land to, 323
Piddle Brook (*Pidelan*), Worcs., 66, 15
Pilsgate (*Pilesge(a)te*), Northants., 74, 16; 76, 15; 329
Pilton (*Pilletune*), Devon or Somerset, 246, 13
Pinden (*Pinindene*), Kent, 108, 6
Playford (*Playford*), Suffolk, 178, 13f.; 424
Plumesgate Hundred, Suffolk, 347
Polebrook Hundred (*Pocabroc*), Northants., 234, 1; 483
Poleshill (*Pauleshele*), Somerset, 238, 24; 490
Poole (*Pofle*), Yorks., 166, 22
Poppleton (*Popeltune*), Yorks., 112, 3
Portchester (*Portceastre*), Hants., 246, 4f.; 495
Potton (*Pottune*), Beds., 144, 11; 388
Powick, Worcs., 266f.
Prestbury (*Preosdabyrig*), Glos., 28, 26; 290
Preston (*Preostatun*), Kent, 182, 13; 428
Puddle, Little (*Litele Pudele*), Dorset, 46, 5

Ramsbury, Wilts., bishops of. *See* Ælfric, Ælfstan, Brihtwold, Hereman, Oda, Osulf, Sigeric
Ramsey, Cambs., abbey of St Benedict at, 271; foundation of, 319, 329, 361; will in favour of, 425; dean of, 374; *Historia Ramesiensis*, 306, 330, 374, 388, 397, 425, 467
Raunds (*Randan*), Northants., 82, 18
Reading, Berks., abbess of. *See* Leofrun
Reculver, Kent, 260, 407
Redfaresþorpe, 146, 4; 392
Redgrave (*Redgrafe*), Suffolk, 194, 31; 198, 32; 443
Redmarley d'Abitot, Worcs., 459
Ribbesford (*Ribbedforda*), Worcs., 148, 17f.; 396
Rickinghall (*Riking(e)hale, Ricyncga-*), Suffolk, 146, 2; 194, 32; 200, 8; 392
Ridgeway, the, 293

INDEX LOCORUM

Ripon (*Rypum*), Yorks., 112, 2; 166, 24; 168, 1; 358, 415
Ripple, Worcs., 264
Risborough (*Hrisbeorgan*), Bucks., 154, 13; 174, 8; 182, 20; 403
Risby (*Rysebi, Risby*), Suffolk, 196, 4; 200, 4; 444
Rochester (*Hrofe(s)ceastre*, etc.), Kent, 106, 24; 351; cathedral (St Andrew's) of, 84, 1f., 24; 86, 3; 122, 3; 130, 11; 140, 7; 204, 7; 260, 277, 279, 332; bishops of, see Ælfstan, Brihtsige, Burhric, Eardwulf, Godwine, 313, 353; cartulary of, 276
Rothwell Hundred (*Roðewelle*), Northants., 236, 7
Rougham (*Rucham, Ruh-*), Suffolk, 146, 3; 194, 34; 198, 32; 392, 444
Run(c)getune (? Runcton, Norfolk), 196, 5; 200, 7; 445
Rushwick, Worcs., 321

St Albans, Herts., abbots of. See Leofric, 374
St Cuthbert's, Chester-le-Street, then Durham, 48, 15; 124, 6; 140, 1, 4; 304, 368; gifts of King Æthelstan to, 304, 477, 480, 498; *Liber Vitae* of, 368, 475; MS. from, 480
St Mary Church (*Sce Maria circean*), Devon, 226, 6; 474
St Osyth (*Ticc* for *Cicc*), Essex, 144, 18; 389f.
Salcombe Regis (*Sealtcumbe*), Devon, 226, 5; 474
Saltwood (*Sealtwuda*), Kent, 128, 10; 142, 8, 15
Sandon (*Sandune*), Herts., 144, 23; 391
Sandwich (*Sandwic*), Kent, 158, 17, 27; 160, 2; 174, 14, 22; 176, 11ff.; 178, 4, 10; 182, 10; 270, 467
Sawley (*Sallege*), Yorks., 166, 30
Scarning, Norfolk, 432
Sceaftesige, 246, 20
Scirhylte, Worcs., 8, 8f.; 266f.
Sedgeberrow, Worcs., 261
Selby, Upper (*Seleby*), Yorks., 164, 24
Selsey, Sussex, bishops of. See Ælfmær, Æthelgar, Æthelric, Cynred, Eadhelm, Grimketel, Heca, Ordbriht, Wulfhun
Sempringham (*Sempingaham*), Lincs., 12, 2ff.; 271f.
Send (*Sendan*), Surrey, 92, 8, 13
Severn, River (*Sæferne*), 36, 10ff.; 204, 18ff.
Shaftesbury (*Sceaftesburi*), Dorset, abbey of, 24, 9; 284f.; register of, 281f., 284f.; body of Edward the Martyr removed to, 356
Shelve (*Scylfe*), Kent, 84, 22; 333
Shepreth, Cambs., 346
Sherborne (*Scireburnan*), Dorset, abbey of, 18, 3; 20, 4f.; 104, 22; 146, 9; 200, 13ff.; 202, 4; reconstruction of, 393; cartulary of, 278, 394; members of community at, 281; Lady Chapel at, 278, 349; bishops of, see Ælfmær, Ælfwold, Æthelheah, Æthelric, Æthelsige, Alfred, Asser, Brihtwine, Ealhstan, Heahmund, Wulfsige
Sherburn in Elmet (*Scireburnan*), Yorks., 112, 4ff.; 164, 23; 166, 7, 11; 248, 13; 358, 414f.
Sherrards Green, Worcs., 267
Shopland (*Seopinglande*), Essex, 144, 25; 391
Shrawley Brook, Worcs., 365
Sidbury (*Sydebirig*), Devon, 226, 10; 475
Sinton (*Suptune*), Worcs., 8, 8, 20; 266f.
Sinton Leigh, Worcs., 266f.
Skidby (*Scyteby*), Yorks., 112, 16; 359
Sleaford (*Slioforda*), Lincs., 12, 8f.; 272, 466
Sleningford (*Sleaningaforda*), Yorks., 168, 6; 416
Smeaton (*Smipatune*), Yorks., 124, 6
Snodland (*Snod(d)i(ng)lande*), Kent, 108, 25f.; 122, 2, 9; 140, 9, 25; 333, 355, 365
Soham (*Saham*), Suffolk, 194, 30; 200, 6; 443
Somerset, earls of. See Ean(w)ulf, 287
Southampton (*Hamtune*), Hants., 246, 5f.; 291

INDEX LOCORUM

Southchurch (*Suðcyrcean*), Essex, 182, 18; 430
Southminster (*Suðmynster*), Essex, 144, 27; 389, 391
Southwark (*Supriganaweorce*), Surrey, 246, 21
Southwell, Notts., 441
Southwick (*Suthwycan*), Northants., 76, 2
Southwood (*Supwuda*), Devon, 226, 16; 476
Sparkwell (*Spearcanwille*), Devon, 226, 7; 474
Sparsholt (*Spæresholte*), Hants., 202, 8; 449
Spelhoe Hundred (*Spelhoh*), Northants., 234, 14
Spellow Hundred (*Spelhoge*), Norfolk, 192, 24; 441
Spetchley, boundary of (*Spæchæme gemære*), Worcs., 126, 7 f.; 362, 458
Stainburn (*Stanburne*), Yorks., 110, 25
Stainley (*Stanleh*), Yorks., 112, 2; Nearer (*nyrran Stanlege*), 168, 4; North (*Norð Stanlege*), 166, 34; 168, 5
Stanground (*Stangrunde*), Hunts., 252, 19 f.; 254, 6, 13; 503
Stanton (*Stantune*), Suffolk, 200, 1
Staverton (*Stofordtune*), Devon, 226, 6; 474
Steeton (*Styfetun Styfing-*), Yorks., 166, 3, 9; 414
Stepney (*Stybbanhype*), London, 144, 24; 389, 391
Stockland, Devon, 303
Stoke, Glos., 264
Stoke (*Stoce*), Kent, 108, 2; 352
Stoke (*Stoce*), Northants., 74, 32; 76, 11; 82, 3, 14, 21; Stoke Hundred, 234, 29; 483
Stoke (*Stoca*), Suffolk, 194, 33; 443 f.
Stoke Canon (*Stoctune, Stoce*), Devon, 98, 2; 226, 9; 344, 475
Stoke Prior (*Stoce*), Herefordshire, 152, 2; 401
Stoke near Shalbourn (*Scealdeburnan Stoce*), Wilts., 94, 14
Stone (*Stane*), Kent, 108, 6; 352
Stoneham (*Stanham*), Hants., 54, 1; 309 f.

Stotfalde Hundred, Northants., 234, 25; 483
Stour, River, Kent, 278, 407; (*Sture*), Worcs., 44, 2, 5
Stow St Mary (*Sce Marian stowe*), Lincs., 212, 25; 216, 1; 465
Stowting (*Stuting*), Kent, 188, 17; 436 f.
Stræte, Kent, 150, 4; 398
Stratford, Warwicks., 264; Upper Stratford (*Uferan Strætforda*), 88, 6
Stretham (*Strætham*), Cambs., 254, 30; 256, 7, 9; 504
Stroat (*Stræt*), Glos., 204, 17; 452
Studley (*Stodlege*), Yorks., 166, 27; 416
Sunbury (*Sunnanbyrg*), Mdx., 90 4 ff.; 92, 8, 13; 339
Surrenden (*Swiðrædingdænne*), Kent, 148, 6; 395
Surrey (*Suðrie, -rian*), 168, 22; 182, 16; earl of, *see* Alfred
Sussex (*Supse(a)xan*), 46, 11; 86, 5; 130, 22; 150, 20; 168, 25; 182, 16; earl of, *see* Edwin
Sutton (*Suðtun*), Yorks., 164, 28; 166, 28; 168, 4; 416
Sutton-on-the-Forest (*Suptune*), Yorks., 124, 7; 368
Sutton Hundred (*Suttenes*), Northants., 230, 11; 481
Swanton (*Swanatune*), Kent, 108, 17; 354
Swanton Novers (*Swanetone*), Norfolk, 184, 4
Swiðrædingdænne. *See* Surrenden
Sydling (*Sidemyntone*), Dorset, 46, 11 f.

Talton (*Tætlin(c)tune*), Worcs., 138, 10 ff.; 382
Tarrant (*Terente*), Dorset, 24, 17; 284 f.
Taunton (*Tantune*), Somerset, 92, 19; 236, 25, 27; 339, 485
Tavistock (*Tæfingstoce*), Devon, 200, 21; 387; abbots of, *see* Sihtric, 423, 456
Tawsmead (*Tesan mede*), Wilts., 32, 28; 293
Teddington (*Teottingctun*), Worcs., 96, 4; 343, 377, 448

INDEX LOCORUM

Teme, River (*Temede, -an*), Worcs., 4, 5, 14; **64**, 20, 26; **261**
Teston (*Cærstane* for *Tær-*), Kent, **108**, 12; **353**
Tewkesbury, Glos., **266**
Thanet (*Tænet*), Kent, **182**, 10; **428**
Thetford (*Þiutforda*), Norfolk, **252**, 17; **331**
Tholthorpe (*Þurulfestun*), Yorks., **112**, 15; **359**
Thornbridge, Worcs., **4**, 10; **261**
Thorne (*Þorndune*), Worcs., **66**, 8 ff.; **322, 378**
Thorney (*Þornige*), Cambs., abbey of, **252**, 13; **254**, 10, 14; **324**, **467, 503**; foundation charter of, **323, 376**; Red Book of, **323**; gospel book from, **476**
Thornley (*Þornhlawa*), County Durham, **230**, 7; **481**
Thorpe (*Þorp*), Northants., **76**, 24, 27; **82**, 7
Thorpe (*Þorpa, -e*), Suffolk, **194**, 31; **200**, 3; **443**
Thorpe (*Þorp*), Yorks., **112**, 15; **359**
Thorpe Hall and Thorpe Willoughby (*twegen Þorpas*), Yorks., **164**, 27; **414**
Tibberton (*Tidbrihtingctune*), Worcs., **124**, 21; **370**
Tichborne (*Ticceburnan*), Hants., **38**, 17; **40**, 26; **296** f., **324**
Tickenhurst, Kent, **451**
Tiddington, Warwicks., **335, 343, 378**
Tidenham (*Dyddanhamme*), Glos., **204**, 16; **206**, 4; **216**, 24; **451**, **469**
Tillingham (*Tillingaham*), Essex, **144**, 18; **390**
Timble (*Timmel*), Yorks., **110**, 25; **166**, 15; **358**
Tisbury (*Tissanbyrig*), Wilts., **246**, 7
Tivetshall (*Tifteshale*), Suffolk, **200**, 8; **447**
Tolland (*Taalande*), Somerset, **238**, 2; **487**
Tollandune, **144**, 20; **390**
Tolleshunt (*Tollesfuntan*), Essex, **144**, 19
Topsham (*Toppeshamme*), Devon, **226**, 8; **475**
Tottenham (*Þottanheale*), Mdx., **144**, 21; **390**

Towcester, Northants., **404**; Towcester Hundred (*Uyceste*), **232**, 10; **482**
Traue, Berks. (?), **240**, 30; **492**
Trottiscliffe (*Trotescliue*), Kent, **108**, 5 f.; **352**
Twyford, Hants., **325**
Twywell, Northants., **383**

Uffington (*Uffentune*), Berks., **44**, 6; **300**
Uppprop. *See* Moreton
Upton, Glos., **318, 379**
Upton (*Uptune*), Northants., **76**, 15; **78**, 2; **80**, 34
Upton Green (*Uptunegrene*), Northants., double hundred of, **232**, 21; **482**
Uptuny, **164**, 13; **413**

Walbec, **194**, 1; **442**
Walkhampstead, Surrey, **323**
Wallingford (*Wælingforda*), Berks., **246**, 19; **496**
Walpole, Norfolk, **441**
Waltham, Essex, abbey at, **400**; charter of, **459**
Walton (*Waltune*), Northants., **76**, 13, 17
Walworth (*Wealawurð*), Surrey, **182**, 17; **429**
Wanborough (*Wænbeorgon*), Wilts., **14**, 4; **274**
Wansdyke, the, **292** f.
Wansford (*Wylmesforda*), Northants., **76**, 9; **80**, 31
Warden Hundred (*Werdunes*), Northants., **230**, 15; **482**
Wareham (*Werham*), Dorset, **246**, 9; **495**; Edward the Martyr buried at, **356**
Warehorne (*Werhornan, -as*), Kent, **170**, 16 f.; **182**, 12; **419**
Waresley, Worcs., **364**
Wargrave (*Weregrauæ*), Hants., **218**, 17; **470**
Warkton (*Werkentune*), Northants., **198**, 8; **446, 481**
Warmington (*Wyrmingtune, Werm-*), Northants., **74**, 31; **76**, 3, 5; **82**, 18 ff.
Warnford (*Wernæforda*), Hants., **212**, 18; **464**
Washbourne, Worcs., **361**

INDEX LOCORUM

Washington (*Hwessingatune*), Sussex, 68, 4; 323
Wassingwellan. *See* Westwell
Watchet (*Weced*), Somerset, 246, 14
Wateringbury (*Woþringabyran*), Kent, 108, 15; 354 f.
Water Newton (*Niwantune*), Hunts., 252, 15, 20; 254, 5; 503
Watlington (*Watlingetune*), Norfolk, 194, 1; 442
Wellan, 74, 1; 328
Welle, 184, 14; 432
Wellington (*Weolintun*), Herefordshire, 152, 5; 401
Wells, Somerset, bishops of. *See* Ælfheah, Brihthelm, Brihtwine, Duduc, Gisa, Lyfing, Sigegar, Wulfhelm
Wells, Norfolk, 432
Wenlock Abbey, Shropshire, 295
Wessex, kings of. *See* Æthelbald, Æthelbert, Æthelheard, Æthelwulf, Cynegils, Cynewalh, Ine; earl of, *see* Harold
Westbury on Trym, Glos., 264, 374
Westerham (*Westerham*), Kent, 108, 17
Westminster (*Westminstre*), 168, 26; abbots of, *see* Wulfnoth, Wulfsige
Weston-on-Avon, Glos., boundary of (*Westtunniga gemære*), 44, 3 f.; 299
West Row, Suffolk, 266
Westwell (*Wassingwellan*, *Wyll*), Kent, 16, 5, 8; 182, 12; 277 f., 428
Westwick (*Westwic*), Yorks., 166, 33
Weymouth (*Waimoupe*), Dorset, 46, 9
Whaddon, Cambs., 346
Whepstead (*Hwipstede*, *Hwep-*), Suffolk, 196, 2; 200, 5; 444
Whitchurch, Hants., 382
Whitchurch (*Hwitecyrcan*), Oxon., 138, 8; 382
Whitcombe (*Widecome*), Dorset, 46, 6
Whittington, Worcs., 362, 458
Whittlesey Mere (*Witlesmere*), Hunts., 72, 29; 252, 22, 24; 254, 6; 328, 503
Wichenford, Worcs., 261, 364
Wick Episcopi, Worcs., 261, 364

Wickham St Paul's (*Hinawicun*), Essex, 144, 20; 390
Wicklow (*Wichlawan*), Suffolk, 100, 24; 347
Wide Open (*Wibustan*), Yorks., 112, 15; 359
Wight, Isle of (*Wiht*), 184, 21; 200, 27
Wilford Hundred, Suffolk, 347
Willybrook Hundred (*Wilebroce*), Northants., 232, 17; 482
Wilsill (*Wifeleshealh*), Yorks., 166, 31
Wilton (*Wiltune*), Wilts., 246, 7; 275; abbey of, 202, 25; grant of land to, 350; abbess of, 348
Wiltshire, earl of, 275; grants of land in, 275, 287, 308, 337; harrying of, 297
Winchcombe (*Wincelcumbe*), Glos., abbey of, 148, 20; 180, 21; abbots of, *see* Godric, Godwine, 374; charter of, 268
Winchester (*Winta(n)ceastre*, *-cestræ*, *Winceastre*), Hants., 40, 10; 102, 10; 110, 9, 17; 246, 6; 495; bishops of, *see* Ælfheah, Ælfwine, Æthelwold, Beornstan, Brihthelm, Denewulf, Ealhferth, Ealhmund, Frithestan, Stigand, Swithhun, Tunbriht, Walchelin, Wigthegn
Cathedral, Old Minster (*ealdan mynstre*, *see Petre*, etc.), 14, 3; 26, 2; 28, 1; 30, 23; 38, 16 ff.; 48, 25 f.; 52, 29 ff.; 62, 1; 68, 16 ff.; 92, 19 ff.; 102, 17 ff.; 110, 1 ff.; 144, 6; 184, 19, 23; 186, 4; 202, 7, 10, 15 ff.; 212, 2 ff.; 218, 16; 274 f., 288, 291, 308, 324; dedication of, 305; expulsion of priests from, 325, 367; establishment of monks at, 317, 323, 325; cartulary of, 274
New Minster, afterwards Hyde Abbey (*niwan mynstre*, etc.), 52, 6; 54, 2 ff., 12 f., 18; 102, 18, 25; 104, 8; 110, 16, 19; 142, 24; 144, 6; 168, 27; 202, 11, 23; 212, 16, 21; foundation of, 274, 308; establishment of monks at, 317, 323; cartulary of (*Liber Monasterii de Hyda*), 307, 309 f.; *Liber Vitae* of, 309 f., 385, 421; abbots of, *see* Ælfsige, Ælfwine, Æthelgar

INDEX LOCORUM

Nunnery of St Mary (*nunnan mynstre*, etc.), **54**, 20; **102**, 23 f.; **110**, 16 f.; **144**, 6 f.; **311, 317**; abbess of, *see* Eadgifu
Wingate (*Windegatum*), County Durham, **230**, 10; **481**
Winsham (*Winesham*), Somerset or Devon, **200**, 25; **449**
Winterborne, Dorset, **380**
Wistow (*Wicstow*), Yorks., **164**, 24; **166**, 10
Witchley, West and East Hundreds (*Hwicc(l)eslea*), Northants., **234**, 19, 22; **331, 483**
Witley, Little (*Witlea*), Worcs., **120**, 1 ff.; **364**
Wittering (*Wiðeringa(e)ige, -ingige*), Northants., **78**, 4; **80**, 6, 25
Wittersham (*Wihtriceshamme*), Kent, **170**, 25
Wixoe, Suffolk, **432**
Woden's Barrow (*Wodnes beorge*), Wilts., **32**, 6; Woden's gate (*Woddes geat*), **32**, 13; **292** f.
Wolverley (*Wulfweardiglea*), Worcs., **210**, 21; **461**
Wolverton (*Wulfringctun*), Worcs., **114**, 1, 7; **360, 362, 458**
(?) Woodgate (*pudegate* for *wude-*), Somerset, **24**, 5; **283**
Woodgarston Farm, Hants., **310**
Woolland (*Wonlonde*), Dorset, **46**, 1; **302**
(?) Woolmer (*Wulfamere*), Hants., **136**, 2; **347, 380**
Woolpit (*Wlpet, Wulpet(tas)*), Suffolk, **146**, 3; **196**, 1; **200**, 2; **392**
Wootton (*Wudutun*), Sussex, **182**, 16; **429**
Worcester (*Weogornaceastre, Wigra-*, etc.), **30**, 8; **36**, 7; **88**, 14, etc.; (?) Worcester gate and road (*ceastergeate, -wege*), **116**, 22 ff.; **363**; fortifications at, **295**; meadowland at, **295**; shire-meeting at, **162**, 12; punitive expedition against, **400**; underking of, *see* Ealdred; bishops of, *see* Alhhun, Brihtheah, Cenwald, Deneberht, Ealdred, Ecgwine, Heahberht, Heathored, Leofsige, Lyfing, Milred, Oswald, Werfrith, Wilfrith, Wulfstan; diocese of, **260**

Cathedral and community at, **2**, 5 ff.; **8**, 19; **28**, 19; **34**, 4 ff.; **36**, 5; **38**, 14; **42**, 14; **62**, 15 ff.; **64**, 10, 15; **66**, 6, 13; **86**, 14, 19; **96**, 3 f.; **114**, 4, 10; **116**, 4, 8; **118**, 3 ff.; **120**, 4, 8; **124**, 13 ff.; **132**, 3 ff.; **134**, 3 f.; **138**, 12 f.; **154**, 2; **156**, 14 f.; **164**, 15; **172**, 11 ff.; **180**, 3, 20; **208**, 8, 24; **210**, 3 ff.; members of community at, **267, 296**; church built by Oswald, **413**; cartularies of, **259** (Hemming's), **263**; copies of charters from, **378**; fragments of charters from, **263, 266**; chirographs retained at, **318**; MSS. from, **498** f.
Worcestershire (*Wig(e)raceastrescire*), **180**, 22; **208**, 13 f.; **210**, 9; **260**; sheriff of, **404**; possible earl of, **456**
Wordwell (*Wridewellan*), Suffolk, **178**, 27; **426**
Worlingworth (*Wirlingaweorðe*), Suffolk, **194**, 30; **200**, 6; **443**
Wormleighton, Warwicks., **370**
Wouldham (*Wuldaham*), Kent, **84**, 1 ff.; **108**, 11; **332, 353**
Wrotham (*Wroteham*), Kent, **108**, 14
Wroxall (*Wroccesheale*), Hants., **184**, 21 f.; **433**
Wulfamere. See Woolmer
Wye (*Wii*), Kent, **192**, 5; **270, 439**
Wye, River (*Wæge*), **204**, 20 ff.
Wyllan, **100**, 22; **346**
Wymersley (*Wimereslea*), Northants., **236**, 20
Wyðreðe Cross, Northants., **78**, 18

Yaxley (*Geacesleа, Jaces-, Iaces-, Ieces-*), Hunts., **68**, 4 f.; **74**, 17, 25; **90**, 1; **252**, 20 f.; **254**, 9 ff.; **323, 329** f., **336**
York (*Euerwic*), **160**, 29; Minster (St Peter's), **112**, 20, 22; **360**; gospels in Dean and Chapter Library, **413**; *Liber Albus* of, **358**; archbishops of, *see* Ælfric, Cynesige, Ealdred, Egbert, Hrothward, Oscytel, Oswald, Wulfstan; earl of, *see* Oslac
Youlton (*Ioletun*), Yorks., **112**, 15; **359**

Zeal Monachorum, Devon, **448**

INDEX RERUM

Ad te levavi, **194**, 27f.; **228**, 5; **248**, 14; **250**, 17; **442**, **477**
Æcertyninge 'field-fencing', **206**, 11; **453**
Æht, -a 'property', 'possessions', **4**, 18f.; **30**, 22; **84**, 11; **98**, 24; **138**, 5; **150**, 18; **152**, 21; **158**, 10
Ælmespenegas 'alms pennies', **204**, 27; **452**
Ælmesse 'alms', 'charitable gift', **46**, 18; **188**, 14; **218**, 15, 23
Ærendraca, Erendwreoca 'messenger', 'negotiator', **6**, 5; **142**, 6
Ærfe lond 'heritable land', **10**, 2
Æscene, **242**, 3, 5; **493**
Agan 'to run out' (of a lease), **28**, 3 27f.; **30**, 3, 7; **289**
Agenland 'land held in absolute possession', **166**, 11ff.; **414**f.
Agreement. See *For(e)w(e)ard, Gerædnes*
Ahnung 'declaration, proof of ownership', **84**, 28; **122**, 28; **136**, 17; **334**, 366f.
Albs, **72**, 10; **194**, 19; linen for, **72**, 11
Alcuin, book by, **250**, 11; **500**
Ale, **58**, 25; **206**, 21; **252**, 3; clear, **12**, 11, 14; **38**, 24; mild, **12**, 15; Welsh, **12**, 12, 14; **38**, 23; **272**
Alendan 'to lease', **142**, 24
Alienation, cases of, **84**, 4; **142**, 5; **226**, 3; forbidden, **48**, 16ff.; **70**, 3ff.; **180**, 28; **210**, 22f.; curse invoked for, **182**, 4ff.; **210**, 25ff.; **216**, 4ff.
Almeslonde, **46**, 14; **303**
Altar, gift of, **226**, 24; **476**; altarcloths *'weofodsceatas'*, **72**, 14; **194**, 18f.; **226**, 27f.; **248**, 16f.; **326**, **477**; altar-covers *'oferbrædelsas'*, **226**, 28; **248**, 17
Amalarius: *Liber Officialis*, **228**, 27; **479**f.
Amber, **38**, 24; **148**, 9; **272**, 297
Anathema, **2**, 14ff.; **18**, 11ff.; **20**, 18ff.; **22**, 14ff.; **24**, 23f.; **36**, 28f.; **42**, 22ff.; **44**, 15ff.; **46**, 24ff.; **48**, 18ff.; **50**, 10ff.; **58**, 4ff.; **62**, 10ff.; **70**, 18ff.; **94**, 3ff.; **96**, 17ff.; **104**, 12ff.; **116**, 11ff.; **118**, 18ff.; **120**, 11ff.; **140**, 5f.; **142**, 18ff.; **146**, 6f.; **154**, 8ff.; **156**, 16ff.; **160**, 16ff.; **164**, 18ff.; **168**, 19ff.; **174**, 5f.; **180**, 12ff.; **182**, 4ff.; **188**, 31ff.; **200**, 27ff.; **210**, 25ff.; **216**, 4ff.; **218**, 10ff.; **222**, 15ff.; **230**, 3ff.; **240**, 23ff.; **427**, **480**
Anburge 'sureties', **98**, 1; **344**
Andaga 'appointed day', **90**, 5
Angield, **22**, 10; **282**
Anniversary, commemoration of, **10**, 9, 16; **42**, 18f.; **196**, 28, 32f.; **198**, 1ff.
Ar 'property', **14**, 9; **28**, 7; **46**, 20; **92**, 6, 8; **102**, 13ff.; **110**, 6; **122**, 14ff.; **130**, 1, 8; **190**, 10f.; **208** 8
Arable land, **10**, 20f.; **22**, 28; **36**, 15; **76**, 25; **78**, 3; **194**, 28
Arator, book by, **228**, 26; **479**
Aspiciens, **248**, 14; **496**
Auerian 'to furnish carrying service', **206**, 6; **452**
Augustine: *De Academicis*, **72**, 18

Badian 'to make distraint upon', **236**, 31
Banner *'merc'*, **228**, 1; **477**
Barontus, St, Vision of, **250**, 8; **499**
Barrels, *'bidenfate'*, **74**, 22
Basins *'læflas'*, **226**, 32
Beams (for a bridge) *'sylla'*, **106**, 27; **108**, 3ff.
Beanseed *'beansæd'*, **252**, 15, 21; **503**
Bear-skins, **226**, 28
Bed-covers, **72**, 13
Bede, books of, **100**, 7; *De Arte Metrica*, **250**, 10; *De Natura Rerum*, **250**, 9; *Expositio super Apocalipsin*, **228**, 23; **250**, 11; *Expositio super Evangelium Lucae*, **228**, 22; *Expositio super .VII. Epistolas Canonicas*, **228**, 23f.; *in Marcum*, **72**, 16; **479**

INDEX RERUM

Beer, 38, 23; 454
Bells, silver, 72, 6; hand-bells, 72, 12f.; 228, 3; 248, 17; hanging bells, 72, 12; 228, 2f.; 248, 17f.
Belucan, 84, 10; 332f.
Benedict, St, Rule of, 70, 12; 98, 18; in English, 250, 8; 325, 499
Benedictional 'bletsingboc', 228, 7; 478
Beodland, 12, 20; 48, 26; 50, 13, 15
Berewicks, 72, 26ff.; 327
Beweddian 'to give security', 8, 17
Bideripe 'reaping by request', 220, 3; 471
Bind (of eels) 'gebind', 170, 14; 420
Bishop, for archbishop, 92, 4, 9
Blakehad boc, 250, 18 f.; 501
Boc 'charter', 'title-deed', 10, 19; 14, 21; 16, 4f.; 60, 9; 62, 6; 86, 7; 90, 10, 27; 92, 2; 110, 12; 122, 6ff.; 144, 2; 160, 12, 21; 162, 9; 188, 13; 337; (ge)bocian 'grant by charter', 16, 7; 28, 21; 44, 6; 62, 23; 66, 21; 84, 2, 8; 88, 15; 90, 25; 110, 13; 112, 17; 132, 5; 134, 4; 138, 13; 180, 3; 188, 4
Bocland 'land held by title-deed', 278, 335
Boethius: De Consolatione Philosophiae, 228, 17; in English, 228, 10f.; 478
Book(s), 48, 14; 72, 15ff.; 194, 14ff.; 196, 7f.; 228, 3ff.; 250, 6ff.
Borh(hand) 'security', 'surety', 76, 14ff.; 82, 10; 150, 13; 164, 7; 398
Boundaries '(land)gemæra', 4, 5ff.; 22, 20ff.; 26, 23ff.; 32, 4ff.; 40, 26ff.; 44, 2ff.; 56, 21ff.; 64, 19ff.; 66, 14ff.; 116, 14ff.; 118, 9ff.; 120, 14ff.; 126, 3ff.; 134, 14ff.; 144, 1; 162, 16ff.; 261, 277f., 283, 287f., 292f., 298f., 314, 321f., 328, 343, 362f., 364f., 370f., 377
Bowl(s) 'hnæpf', 'hnæppas', 226, 30; 242, 6; 'bled', 250, 1, 3; 477
Boxes 'midreca', 228, 1
Bræde oððe beswice, butan 'without fraud or deceit', 16, 2
Bread, 252, 3, 6
Bridges, construction of, 18, 7; 26, 6; 50, 3; 56, 9; 86, 20f.; 96, 12f.; 106, 24; 114, 12; 134, 13; 138, 20; 180, 10; 210, 10; 222, 12; repair of, 126, 21f.
Brushwood 'græfe', 12, 5; 272
Bryce 'use', 'usufruct', 2, 26; 122, 21; 154, 4
Brytænwalda, 48, 24; 304f.
Bucks (for funeral feast), 252, 4, 7
Bullock(s) 'hriðer, -u', 38, 25; 58, 25; 198, 31; 200, 10; 226, 19; 240, 8; 252, 7; 491
Bur 'private room', 30, 8; 290
Burg 'manor-house', 6, 12; 265; 'town(-wall)', 36, 7, 21; 102, 23; 104, 12; 142, 18; 148, 13
Burhgerihtu 'borough dues', 236, 27; 238, 9, 13; 485f.
Burhhege 'manor-house hedge', 206, 12; 453
Burhwaru 'citizens', 110, 17; 142, 12; 204, 12; 214, 33
Burial fee. See Sawolsceatt
Byrig 7 butan, binnan, 148, 13f.; 188, 31; 204, 13f.; 216, 21
Byrigland 'borough-land', 234, 16; 483

Cæcilius Cyprianus, 72, 22f.; 327
Calendar 'gerim', 250, 13; 500
Calves, 256, 13
Candlesticks, 72, 5; 226, 31; 242, 7f.; 250, 2
Canon Law, book of, 228, 9
Cantor's copes 'cantercæppa', 194, 17f.; 226, 27; staffs 'canterstafas', 226, 27; 477
Capella, 228, 28; 480
Capitulary, 194, 16, 26; 228, 13; 250, 18
Caritas 'charitable gift', 196, 21, 26
Carpets, 226, 28
Casks 'tunnan', 12, 11
Cato, Dionysius, gloss on, 250, 12; 500
Cauldron 'lead', 74, 22; 250, 3
Ceap 'payment', 'purchase', 64, 19; 70, 5; 80, 5; 100, 27; 122, 29; 192, 3, 5; 439
Censers, 72, 5f.; 194, 21; 226, 32
Ceorlas 'peasants', 'commoners', 28, 24ff.; 150, 21; 206, 19; 290, 454

546 INDEX RERUM

Chalices, **72**, 7; **194**, 21, 24; **226**, 24; **248**, 15; **250**, 1, 4; **498**
Chasubles '*mæssehacelan*', **72**, 7f.; **194**, 17; **248**, 16
Cheese, **38**, 26; **60**, 1; **170**, 13; **192**, 19, 21; **196**, 19; **240**, 5; **248**, 22; **252**, 7
Chest '*cyste*', **228**, 2. See also Scrin
Chirographs, **104**, 14; **294**, 342, **348**ff., **403**, **411**, **421**, **427**, **436**, **438**f., **450**
Choral books '*sangbec*', **228**, 4
Chronicle '*cranc*', **250**, 16
Church dues '*ciricsceatt(as)*', '*ecclesiastici censi*', **26**, 7; **28**, 5; **30**, 11; **56**, 10; **62**, 22; **64**, 17; **66**, 10; **116**, 9; **118**, 16; **120**, 9; **132**, 13; **156**, 8; **206**, 9; **210**, 11; **236**, 27; **238**, 3ff.; **240**, 16ff.; **286**, **290**f., **321**, **404**, **453**, **485**, **487**
Church treasures and vestments, **72**, 1ff.; **194**, 17ff.; **226**, 21ff.; **242**, 3ff.; **248**, 13ff.; **250**, 1ff.
Cild (as title), **76**, 8; **106**, 20; **144**, 16; **148**, 13; **150**, 11; **200**, 23; **250**, 17; **323**, **369**, **395**
Circanlad 'carrying service for the church' (?), **86**, 21; **114**, 12; **334**f.
Ciricmitta 'church *mitta*', **206**, 21; **455**
Ciricsceatweorc 'work connected with church dues', **28**, 5; **289**
Clæne (of land) 'unburdened', '(granted) without reservation' (?), **76**, 20; **152**, 26; **162**, 14; **164**, 4f.; **331**, **402**
Cloaks '*pælles*', **72**, 10; **194**, 18; **326**, **442**
Clothing '*hrægl*', '*scrud*', grant of, **152**, 17; as treasure-trove, **160**, 2; grants in aid of '*to hregltalæ*', **48**, 26; '*to scrude*', **188**, 12; **214**, 6; **254**, 25; '*to scrudfultume*', **100**, 24. See also Scrudfeoh, Scrudland
Cniht, **96**, 5; **114**, 7; **116**, 5; **148**, 3; **150**, 12; **154**, 23; **164**, 14; **172**, 13; **174**, 8; **220**, 7; **394**
Coffin, **252**, 2; **501**f.
Collectareum, **228**, 4; **477**
Commemoration '*gemynd*', **30**, 26; **38**, 20; **40**, 4, 6; **42**, 17; '*gemynddæg*', **52**, 4; **292**

[*Commentum*] *Alchimi Aviti*, **72**, 22; **327**
Commentum Cantica Canticorum, **72**, 20f.; **327**
Commentum Martiani, **72**, 21f.; **327**
Community, members of, **6**, 5ff.; **8**, 11ff. and *passim*
Confraternity, admission to, **269**
Controversy '*(on)geantalu*', **178**, 18; **184**, 8; **186**, 20; **212**, 14; '*wiðercwide*', **30**, 4f.; **34**, 9f.; **210**, 1
Copes '*cæppan*', **72**, 8
Copse '*graf*', **28**, 25; **118**, 9f.
Corn, **74**, 21; **154**, 7f.; **156**, 13; **248**, 23; as church dues, **240**, 6ff.; cutting of, **220**, 5; as payment in kind, **148**, 9; purchase of, **256**, 7; as tithes, **74**, 6f.
Corporal '*corporale*', **72**, 9f.; **194**, 21; **226**, 25; **476**
Costnung 'persuasion', **122**, 20; **366**
Cows, **134**, 10; **150**, 6; **196**, 13; **230**, 9; pasture for, **202**, 18
Croft, **134**, 29
Crosier '*hæcce*', **242**, 8
Crosses, **72**, 4; **194**, 22; **242**, 4; **248**, 14
Cucu 7 dead, **236**, 25f.; **238**, 1; **485**
Cups, **72**, 14; **94**, 9; **242**, 5f.; **250**, 3
Cwide 'bequest', 'will', **16**, 4; **24**, 9; **58**, 19; **84**, 22ff.; **154**, 14, 20; **170**, 27; **182**, 7; **190**, 1; **333**
Cwideleas 'intestate', **84**, 17
Cyneham 'royal manor', **92**, 24
Cynerihta 'royal prerogatives', **90**, 21
Cytweras 'basket weirs', **204**, 18ff.; **452**

Dæg 'lifetime', *passim*; grants for life, **14**, 22f.; **28**, 2; **52**, 2ff.; **54**, 2; **58**, 21, 23; **60**, 6; **66**, 9; **84**, 13; **98**, 4; **146**, 20; **148**, 18; **154**, 16; **168**, 10 ('*his lyfes timan*'); **174**, 11; **178**, 14; **184**, 6, 22; **188**, 6; **200**, 16; **212**, 3ff.; **216**, 24; with right to appoint heir(s), **12**, 3f.; **62**, 19ff.; **64**, 13f.; **66**, 3f., 9, 11f.; **86**, 17f.; **88**, 11ff.; **114**, 8f.; **116**, 6f.; **118**, 6f.; **120**, 6f.; **124**, 17f.; **126**, 1f.; **180**, 7ff.; **202**, 19f.; **208**, 20f.; for two lives '*twegra manna dæg*' etc., **62**, 7; **132**, 12f.;

INDEX RERUM

138, 15; 186, 17ff.; 188, 8ff.; 202, 8; for three lives '*þreora manna dæg*' etc., 26, 3f.; 28, 22f.; 34, 7f.; 36, 23f.; 38, 18; 62, 24; 96, 7ff. (with restricted choice of heirs); 132, 5; 134, 6; 148, 19; 156, 3, 11; 172, 15; 208, 3f., 15; 319f.
Dæge 7 *æfter* (*dæge*), *ær, on*, 148, 7, 21; 162, 7; 164, 6; 192, 4
Dænn 'swine-pasture', 148, 6, 10
Dairymaid, 254, 21
Dalmæd 'partible meadow', 116, 21; 363
Dalmatics, 226, 26; 476
Danegeld, 493
Deadum oððe æt cwicum, æt, 230, 8; 481
Dean, 184, 10; 188, 26; 192, 6; 204, 7; 216, 12
De Duodecim Abusivis, 72, 20; 327
De Eucharistia, 72, 21; 327
De Grammatica Arte, treatise, 250, 12
De Litteris Grecorum, 72, 23
Descidia Parisiace polis, 72, 19; 327
Diadema Monachorum, 228, 27; 479
Dialogues (of Gregory), 250, 14; in English, 250, 6; 259, 498
Digging (as service), 206, 12; 453
Document '*gewrit*', 4, 24 and *passim*; preservation of, 10, 18ff.; 104, 14f.; 110, 18ff.; 148, 27ff.; 150, 21f.; 156, 14f.; 164, 14ff.; 170, 4ff.; 172, 7ff.; 178, 22f.; 184, 15ff.; 186, 4f., 20ff.; 190, 5ff., 23ff.; 192, 11ff.; 202, 4f., 12f., 24f.; 204, 14f.; 212, 20ff.; 216, 7ff.; 349; to be cast into fire or to mice, 160, 7f.
Donatus, 250, 20; *major* and *minor*, 250, 10f.; gloss on, 250, 14; 499
Dorsals '*rygcrægl*', '*ricghrægel*', 194, 20; 226, 29
Drowning, 68, 10; 92, 7
Duguð 'leading men', 124, 3; 140, 22

Ealdor 'superior' (of religious community), 100, 16; 102, 14; 146, 11
Ealdormann, 8, 17 and *passim*; 267
Earningaland, 194, 29; 443
Earthwork '*eorðburg*', 88, 9

Edmund, St, Life of, 194, 16f.; 442
Eels, 100, 21; 170, 14
Egþwirf, 74, 21; 329
Episcopal crosses, 226, 21f.
Episcopal estates '*bisceophamas*', 50, 16
Episcopal see '*bisc(e)opstol*', 92, 21; 140, 10; 226, 2
Epistle book '*pistelboc*', 194, 15; 228, 4, 14; 248, 14f.
Epistle vestments '*pistolclapas*', '*-roccas*', 72, 9; 226, 26; 476
Epistolar, 250, 17
Estate '*land*', *passim*; divided, 88, 4ff.
Ewes, 134, 9; 206, 28; 379
Exchange of estates, 16, 5ff.; 30, 29f.; 58, 9ff.; 68, 2ff.; 94, 15f.; 100, 11ff.; 110, 1ff.; 136, 5f.; 184, 19ff.
Expositio Hebreorum Nominum, 72, 17; 326
Ezekiel, book of the prophet, 228, 20

Fæge 'at the point of death' (?), 'dead' (?), 112, 10
Faldhriþer, -reþere, 74, 19; 248, 20; 329
Farm implements etc., 74, 21f.
Fearh 'young pig', 240, 4; 491
Fedelsswin 'fat pig', 74, 23; 329
Feld 'open country', 12, 18; 76, 14; 78, 25; 80, 20; 88, 7f. ('*feldland*'); 120, 15 ('*feldlond*'); 240, 10
Feldhryþer 'grazing bullock', 196, 13f.
Fen(s), 12, 18; 72, 31; 256, 14ff.; fenlands, 100, 23
Ferrying (rights) '*ouerfæreld*', 158, 25; 408
Feste 'security', 74, 30; 76, 6; 330
Festermen 'sureties', 74, 26, 29; 76, 7ff.; 78, 6ff.; 80, 4ff.; 82, 5ff.; 330
Fine '*wite*', 22, 9 ('*iwitradenne*'); 60, 2; 176, 22; 218, 18; 282, 316, 347
Fish, 38, 27; 196, 28, 34; 206, 1ff.; 252, 8
Fisheries, 42, 16
Flitches of bacon, 38, 26; 58, 25; 74, 20; 192, 16, 18; 196, 17; 248, 21; 252, 4; 256, 13

548 INDEX RERUM

Folcriht 'public law', 164, 23; 414
Folkland, 16, 9; 278
Food-rent *'feorm'*, 58, 24; 84, 20; 100, 31; 110, 8; 192, 19; 194, 30ff.; 196, 1ff.; 198, 30; 214, 7, 18; 316, 333, 465; to provide with *'(ge)feormian'*, 10, 9; 12, 13f.; 50, 7; 52, 3ff.; 110, 6; *fermfultum*, 192, 18; 440f.; *ferme land*, 230, 14, 24f.; 236, 3f.
Forespræc 'advocacy', 122, 20; 226, 4; 366
For(e)w(e)ard 'agreement', 'terms' etc., 142, 19; 148, 25ff.; 150, 1; 154, 1, 8, 11; 156, 1; 168, 9; 170, 12; 172, 1; 174, 9; 178, 12; 184, 1, 5, 18; 186, 14, 17; 188, 1ff.; 190, 8; 192, 14; 196, 28; 200, 11; 202, 14; 204, 4; 210, 19f.; 212, 9f., 23; 216, 10; 220, 1
Forfeiture, cases of, 68, 7; 92, 6; 122, 13ff.; 182, 24f.; 208, 7f.; 288, 338; forbidden, 358; grant invalidated by, 172, 17; impossible in case of an estate in which the holder has a life interest only, 62, 24f.; 66, 21f.; 88, 16; 168, 12; 178, 18
Forgieldan 'to pay compensation', 90, 6; 136, 29; 381
Forsegen ne forwerken, ne, 178, 18; 425
Forspekan ne forspillan, ne, 168, 12; 417
Forsteall 'obstruction', 24, 14; 236, 29; 238, 4ff.; 284, 486
Fortifications, construction of, *'festængewæorcæ'*, 50, 3; *'burhgeweorc'*, 222, 11f.; *'472'*; repair of *'burhbot'*, 56, 9; *'arcis restauratio'*, 126, 21f. *See also* Walls
Fostær 'food', 50, 15
Fosterland 'land to supply food', 46, 12; 70, 16; 170, 26; 180, 26; 182, 26. *See also* Sustenance
Fother, 12, 4ff.; 64, 18; 74, 6, 21; 154, 8; 206, 10, 25; 248, 23; 271
Freols '(charter of) freedom', 20, 3; 24, 4; 68, 16; 70, 19; 92, 19; 94, 2ff.; 220, 17; 222, 7, 29
Fuel (for funeral feast), 252, 5; 502

Full 7 *swa forð, swa,* 2, 26; 172, 14, 21; 176, 21; 186, 18; 218, 2f.
Funeral feast *'(h)ærflæ'*, 252, 5, 9; 502
Furlong, 246, 27ff.; 248, 1ff.
Fyrd. See Military service
Fyrdwite 'fine for neglect of military service', 236, 30; 486
Fyre oððe flode, to, 90, 12
Fyrþrung, grants for, 254, 10, 23, 26f.

Gafol 'rent', 16, 1; 28, 5; 58, 23; 60, 6; 176, 22; 188, 22; 204, 22
Gafolbere (gauolbærer) 'barley as rent', 206, 24; 455
Gafolland 'rent-paying land', 204, 17ff.
Gafolmæd (gauol-), 206, 24
Gafoltining (gauol-), 206, 27; 455
Gafolwudu (gauolwydu), 206, 26
Gara 'gore' (of land), 32, 10, 25; 292
Geagnian 'to claim or prove ownership', 86, 7; 92, 15; 136, 16; 339, 381
Gearwæstmas 'crops for the year', 52, 9f.
Gebotl 'dwelling-house', 80, 7
Gebugan into 'to commend oneself to', 128, 3ff.; 372; *under* 'to put oneself under', 90, 15
Gebur, services and dues rendered by, 206, 7ff.; 240, 17f.; 453f., 492
Gedale 'portions, strips of land', 80, 3; 331; *to gedale*, 124, 22; 370
Gedalland, 299
Geearnian 'earn (by means of services)', 16, 3; 30, 1f.; 66, 2; 84, 11; 134, 12; 138, 19; 156, 10; 170, 20; 180, 9; 182, 22f.; 208, 21; 277, 290, 333
Geese, 198, 31; 200, 10
Geferscipas 'associations', 60, 21; 316f.
Gegrynd, -grind 'plots of ground', 102, 18; 252, 17; 503
Gehadode ge læwede, ge, 'ecclesiastics and laymen', 128, 25; 148, 26; 154, 24; 170, 3; 174, 13; 186, 2f.; 188, 31; 190, 1
Geirfað 'stocked', 38, 18
Geneat, services and dues rendered by, 206, 5ff.; 240, 15f.; 452f.

INDEX RERUM

Geneatland, **240**, 13; **491** f.
Gerædnes 'agreement', 'terms', **12**, 3; **34**, 23; **36**, 29; **38**, 13; **58**, 8; **60**, 24; **180**, 11
Gerefland, **202**, 18; **450**
Gereflanges, **158**, 22; **408**
Gerihtu 'dues', **92**, 24; **158**, 18, 22; **206**, 19; **236**, 24; **238**, 2ff.; **240**, 1; **303**
Gerim. See Calendar
Gerisenum, to, **60**, 25f.; **317**
Gersuma 'treasure', 'money', **212**, 8f.; **226**, 4; **474**
(*Ge*)*sett* (of land) 'occupied (by tenants)', **204**, 17; **234**, 10, 15; **452**
(*Ge*)*swutelung* 'declaration' etc., **82**, 23; **104**, 15; **106**, 23; **110**, 18, 21; **128**, 6; **136**, 15; **140**, 12, 23; **142**, 4; **144**, 10; **384**
Gewerod 'stocked', 'furnished', **128**, 7; **142**, 26; **372**
Gierd 'rod', **206**, 11; 'rod, pole or perch', **104**, 6 (*metgyrd*); **106**, 27; **108**, 3ff.; **206**, 12, 27; **246**, 25ff.; **248**, 11; **351**; 'quarter-acre', **74**, 11ff.; **329**; 'yard-land', **118**, 4; **124**, 15; **202**, 16f.; **204**, 17ff.; **230**, 17f.; **234**, 6f., 27f.; **236**, 3, 6
Girdle, **250**, 2; **498**
Goats, **256**, 12
Gode ge for worulde, for, **56**, 1f.; **144**, 8f.; **312**
Gold, as grant, **152**, 17; as treasure-trove, **160**, 3
Goldsmith, **144**, 11; **388**
Gospel book '*Cristes boc*', **194**, 15; **248**, 13f.; English, **228**, 7; **478**; ornamented (with silver), **72**, 3f.; **226**, 23; **476**; entry of grants in, **104**, 20; **144**, 10; **152**, 29; **154**, 11; **174**, 7; **182**, 8; **226**, 1; **473**
Gospel exposition '*codspel traht*', **250**, 15
Grants in perpetuity '*a on ece*', '*ecelice*', '*to ecenesse*' etc., **2**, 26; **18**, 4ff.; **22**, 10; **48**, 25; **58**, 12; **104**, 9; **124**, 9; for as long as Christianity endures, **20**, 14ff.; **46**, 22ff. See also *Dæg*
Gretan 'to challenge' (an oath), **8**, 22; **267**

Gripbrice 'breach of the peace', **236**, 29; **238**, 4ff.; **486**
Hæcweras 'hackle weirs', **204**, 19f., 25; **452**
Halfpenny, payment of, **220**, 5
Haligdom 'holy things', 'relics', **140**, 6; **170**, 6; **419**
Ham, **20**, 4; 'manor', **50**, 16; **92**, 23; **100**, 12, 14; **114**, 6
Hamm 'river pasture' (?), **124**, 20; 'enclosed land', **134**, 28; **204**, 22; **452**
Hamsocn 'attacks on a man's house', **24**, 15; **236**, 29; **238**, 3ff.; **284**, **486**
Hamsteall 'homestead', **134**, 7; **216**, 14
Hana 'cock' (?), **250**, 2; **498**
Hand 'person', **36**, 22; *on þa spere hand* 'on the male side', **66**, 4; **322**
Handfangenþeof, **236**, 29; **238**, 4ff.; **486**
Harrows '*egeðan*', **252**, 19
Harvesting (as service), **28**, 6; **66**, 11; **206**, 13; **289**, **453**
Haven, grant of, **158**, 17ff.
Haymaking (as service), **66**, 11
Hens, **60**, 1; **198**, 32; **200**, 10; **454**
Heorðpenegas 'hearth pence', **236**, 27; **238**, 3ff.; **486**
Herds, driving of '*drafe drifan*' (as service), **206**, 7
Here '(Danish) host, population', **76**, 19f.; **330**f.; *hæres unæmetta* 'stress caused by a raid' (?), **40**, 1; **297**
Herrings, **206**, 2; **218**, 4; **252**, 14
Herring-season, **174**, 16; **423**
Hide, **2**, 24 and *passim*; divided, **88**, 6; **335**, **377**
Hidgeld, **242**, 2; **493**
Hiwisc 'hide', **32**, 1; **206**, 20; **292**, **455**
Hlafhwete 'wheat for bread', **206**, 21f.
Hogs, **254**, 30f.; **256**, 1ff.
Homilies, book of '*spellboc*', **194**, 16; **228**, 10; **250**, 18
Honey, **206**, 15; **248**, 22; **454**
Hordere 'cellarer', **220**, 1, 3
Horns, **72**, 13; **226**, 30; **242**, 7; **250**, 4; **498**

550 INDEX RERUM

Horses, **12**, 13; **134**, 10; **148**, 23; **150**, 6; to carry wood, **240**, 11f.; pasture for, **240**, 12f.
Hreddan (of land) 'to discharge the obligations upon', **208**, 14; **459**
Hregltalæ. See Clothing
Hrofleas (of land) 'roofless', 'uninhabited', **208**, 18f.; **460**
Hrygilebuc 'incense bowl', **242**, 4; **493**
Hundred (as territorial division), **74**, 1, 4; **76**, 8; **78**, 17, 26, 31; **82**, 5ff.; **100**, 23, 25; **192**, 23ff.; **230**, 11ff.; **232**, 1f.; **234**, 1ff.; **236**, 1ff.; **240**, 27
Hundredpenegas 'hundred pence', **236**, 28; **238**, 3ff.; **486**
Hunting (as service), **28**, 6
Huscarlan, **214**, 31
Husfast, **220**, 2; **471**
Husting, standard of, **170**, 24; **420**
Hymn books, **228**, 6; **248**, 15; **250**, 17
Hyringmannum, **256**, 10

Illicit union, **112**, 8, 13f.; **358**
Immunis (of land), **64**, 14; **320**
Incense spoon '*storsticca*', **226**, 32; **477**
Inheritance '*erfe*', '*yrfe*', **4**, 16; perpetual inheritance '*on ece yrfe*', **10**, 3ff.; **84**, 2ff.; **148**, 6; **188**, 5; '*on ece erfeweardnesse*', **42**, 14f.; '*to ecan yrfe*', **58**, 11
Inland, **34**, 8; **138**, 16; **166**, 7; **204**, 16, 22; **230**, 13ff.; **232**, 3ff.; **234**, 2ff.; **236**, 3ff.; **294**, 414, **482**
Innanbur(h)ware, **60**, 21; **316**f.
Innor ge utter, ge 'central and outlying', **132**, 8; **378**
Inventory '*erfgewrit*', **74**, 17
Inware, **156**, 4; **404**
Iron, **254**, 12; **504**; as treasure-trove, **160**, 3
Isaiah, book of the prophet, **228**, 20
Isidore: *De Miraculis Christi*, **228**, 25; *De Novo et Veteri Testamento*, **228**, 24; *Etymologiae*, **228**, 21; *Liber Differentiarum*, **72**, 22; *Synonyma*, **72**, 18f.; **327**, **479**

Jar '*cruce*', **242**, 6

Kettle, **250**, 4
King's companion '*cinges gefera*', **2**, 21; **260**
King's secretary '*writere*', **232**, 4; **482**
King's summons '*cinges bann*', **208**, 15; **459**
King's thegn '*cyninges ðegn*', **4**, 17; **130**, 4; meeting of king's thegns (?) '*cinges ðeningmanna gemot*', **122**, 8
Kitchen, payment to, **192**, 22

Lade lædan (as service), **206**, 6f.; **452**
Læn 'lease', 'land held on lease', **28**, 2; **84**, 14ff.; **166**, 11; *lænland*, **335**
Lændinge 'landing rights' (?), **158**, 17; **407**
Lætan 'to let, lease', **38**, 16, 19 (*tolætan*); **62**, 2; **184**, 25; **202**, 7, 16; **216**, 23
Lambs, **134**, 10; **206**, 28; **240**, 4
Landar 'estate', **6**, 11
Landboc 'land-charter', **122**, 3; **160**, 12, 21; **186**, 5; **188**, 13
Lande swa of lande, swa on, **206**, 5f.; **452**
Landgehwerf. See Exchange of estates
Landhlaford 'lord of the manor', **206**, 1
Lard, **196**, 25; **198**, 28
Lathe (Kentish), **108**, 9, 19; **124**, 4; **367**
Lease. See *Læn*, *Lætan*
Lectionary '*rædingboc*', **228**, 14; summer '*sumerrædingboc*', **228**, 8; winter '*winterrædingboc*', **194**, 23f.; **228**, 8
Legere, wið clænum, **92**, 10f.; **339**
Lepene, **200**, 9; **447**
Liber Bestiarum, **72**, 23; **327**
Liber Dialogorum, **228**, 16; **478**
Liber Machabeorum, **228**, 25f.; **479**
Liber Miraculorum, **72**, 16; **326**
Liber Pastoralis, **228**, 16; **478**
Life 7 *æfter life, on*, **14**, 11; **58**, 12; **144**, 11f.; **170**, 28; **204**, 5
Life 7 *for legere, for*, **90**, 26; **337**
Life, *on minon halan*, **174**, 3f.
Livestock '*yrfe*', **30**, 24; '*on cucan ceape*', **58**, 13; '*orfcynn*', **226**, 18

INDEX RERUM

Loaves, 12, 12; 38, 24f.; 58, 25; 192, 16, 18, 21
Loc 'settlement', 142, 6, 9

Mæsene sceala, 226, 29f.; 477
Mættan, 60, 22; 317
Mal, 230, 7, 9; 481
Malt, 192, 15, 18; 198, 30; 200, 9; 206, 15; 252, 5
Man, assessment of 1 man to 1 hide, 246, 24
Mancus, 80, 7, 23; 84, 6; 92, 14; 94, 9, 11; 104, 2f.; 106, 16f.; 112, 12; 122, 19; 148, 22; 254, 7ff.; 269, 332
Maniples 'handlin', 72, 9; subdeacon's, 226, 26
Manor (house). See Burg, Ham, Tun
Manslot 'a single holding' (?), 192, 23ff.; 441
Mantle, bequest of, 252, 10
Manual 'handboc', 194, 26
Marble stones 'marmarstan gesmiðede', 194, 22; 442
Mark, of gold, 184, 5; 186, 8; 192, 3; 216, 24; 218, 3; 242, 9; 435; of silver, 170, 23f.; 174, 2f.; 420; unspecified, 242, 5ff.; 252, 10f.
Marriage agreements, 148, 15ff.; 150, 1ff.
Marshes, 16, 10
Martyrology, 228, 9; 250, 16; 478; in English, 250, 7
Mass vestments 'mæssereaf', 194, 23ff.; 226, 25; 228, 15; 248, 16
Mast pasture, 8, 13f.; 206, 18; 454
Mead, 196, 34; 198, 23
Meadow 'medwe', 'mædland', 10, 21; 24, 2; 36, 10, 17; 42, 16; 46, 3; 78, 4; 80, 20; 88, 9f.; 124, 20; 202, 17; 204, 3; 295
Medicinalis, 72, 19; 327
Medicine, book on 'leceboc', 250, 18
Meeting, attendance at obligatory, 236, 30f.; 238, 5ff.; exemption from, by payment or petition, 238, 15; 487
Men, included on, or granted with, estates, 42, 15; 72, 28f.; 148, 22f.; 156, 12; 230, 9; included in inventories, 74, 17f.; 248, 19; for carrying wood, 240, 11f.

Messuage 'haga', 36, 7, 11; 126, 1; 142, 5; 188, 17; 210, 22
Met 'measure', 196, 35; 198, 30f.; 200, 9; 447
Mete 7 mid mannum, mid, 24, 11f.; 140, 3f.; 146, 5, 19, 21; 170, 15; 178, 16f., 26ff.; 184, 7f., 23; 188, 10; 200, 17f.; 212, 12f.; 218, 2
Military service 'fyrd', 18, 7; 22, 10; 26, 7; 50, 3; 'fyrding', 100, 21; 346; 'ferdfare', 86, 20; 96, 12; 114, 11; 'ferdnoð' (?), 56, 9; 312; 'ferdsocn', 134, 13; 138 20; 180, 10; 210, 11; 222, 11; 'contra hostes expeditio', 126, 22
Military wagon 'firdwæn', 228, 1
Milk (for funeral feast), 252, 8
Mills, 78, 14; 102, 19, 22; 104, 1; 254, 11, 20; 348; mill-oxen 'mylenoxan', 254, 7, 9; 504; millrent 'mylnegafel', 196, 21; millsite 'mylensteall', 26, 29; 88, 11
Missal 'mæsseboc', 194, 15ff.; 228, 3f.; 248, 15; 477
Mitta, 12, 12, 14; 30, 11; 272
Monastic life, adoption of, 102, 11
Monks, establishment of, 70, 9, 11; 72, 25f.; 98, 15; 100, 16; 317
Morgengifu 'marriage gift', 84, 18; 333
Morð 'deadly image' (?), 68, 9
Motlæðu, 238, 10f.
Mowing (as service), 206, 13; 453ff.
Mund 'guardian(ship)', mundian 'to act as guardian', 92, 3, 5; mund 7 (up)heald, 180, 27; 210, 31; 427
Mundbyrde 'protection', 10, 8
Mundebreche 'breach of protection', 24, 15; 284

Nets, 252, 16, 22; as treasure-trove, 160, 2; ball of net-yarn, 206, 16
Nocturnale 'nihtsang', 228, 5, 13
Nuns, 62, 5; establishment of, 98, 15

Oath, 8, 15ff.; 86, 7ff.; 136, 27; 138, 1, 4; 164, 1; 236, 29; 238, 4ff.; 486
Obstruction. See Forsteall
Odda's book, 250, 6f.; 499
Offertory cloths 'offrincsceatas', 'offringclaþas', 72, 10; 194, 21

Oftalu 'counterclaim', **140**, 18; **384**
(On)geantalu. See Controversy
Ontalu 'claim', **140**, 18; **384**
Ordeal, **236**, 29; **238**, 4ff.; **486**
Ore, **74**, 1; **80**, 7, 10; **186**, 9; **192**, 21; **196**, 22ff.; **252**, 1 ff.; **254**, 4ff.; **331**, **441**, **446**, **501**
Oserius, book of, **228**, 25; **479**
Outlawry, **68**, 11; **78**, 1, 34
Oxen, **74**, 18; **134**, 10; **150**, 6; **154**, 7; **156**, 12; **196**, 13; **230**, 9; **248**, 19; **256**, 12
Oxgang, **78**, 5, 7; **164**, 24, 28; **166**, 5ff.; **331**

Pall, **252**, 2
Passional, English, **250**, 6; **498**
Passionalis, **228**, 17f.
Passiones Apostolorum, **228**, 21f.; **479**
Pastorals, English, **250**, 8; **499**
Pasture '*læs*', '*leswe*', **8**, 9; **44**, 15; **78**, 25; **202**, 18f.
Patens, **72**, 7; **194**, 24; **248**, 16; **250**, 1, 4; **498**
Pence, **80**, 12ff. and *passim*
Penitential, English, '*scriftboc*', **228**, 9f.; **478**
Penny, final (in purchase of estates), **74**, 25; **78**, 21; third (of toll), **174**, 22; **176**, 25ff.; **178**, 10; fourth (of fines), **100**, 28f.; **347**; payment of one, **220**, 3
Persius, book of, **228**, 26; **250**, 10; **479**
Pier (of bridge) '*(land)per*', **106**, 27; **108**, 2ff.; **351**
Pilgrimage '*suðfor*', **6**, 2; **263**
Pinsticking magic, **68**, 8; **324**
Plogesland 'ploughland', **164**, 25f.; **166**, 1ff.; **331**
Plough (as unit of assessment), **74**, 6; **328**
Ploughing (as service), **206**, 8, 22; **453**, **455**
Ploughland. See *Plogesland*, *Sulung*
Porphyry: *Isagoge*, **228**, 17; **478**
Porpoises, **206**, 2; **218**, 4
Port 'town', **68**, 21; **188**, 18; **210**, 22
Portgerefa, **142**, 18; **192**, 10; **216**, 20
Portgerihtu 'market dues' (?), **92**, 26; **340**
Portman 'townsman' (?), **70**, 5
Portweall, **110**, 12

Pound, **78**, 14, 29 and *passim;* of gold, **150**, 3; of red gold and white silver, **162**, 5f.; **412**; of silver, **134**, 9; **186**, 8f.; **218**, 1; of pence, **190**, 18
Præfost 'prior', **146**, 12; **238**, 19 ('*mynsterprauost*'); **273**
Preostaland 'priests' land', **166**, 33
Previsio Futurarum Rerum, **72**, 17; **326**
Priest '*(mæsse)preost*', **4**, 16f. and *passim*; **364**; priest's dues, **26**, 7; **240**, 7ff.; **286**; payment to, **52**, 4f.; establishment of priests, **214**, 3; expulsion of, **70**, 10f.; **325**
Produce. See *Mete*
Property. See *Æht*, *Ar*
Prophets, books of the four, **228**, 16
Prosper, book of, **228**, 18; **478**f.
Prudentius: *De Martyribus*, **228**, 19; *Liber Hymnorum*, **228**, 18f.; *Psychomachia*, **228**, 18; **479**
Psalter(s), **194**, 16, 27; **228**, 5f.; **248**, 15; the great, **250**, 10; in English, **250**, 7, 16; **477**f.

Rædesmann 'steward' (?), **174**, 21; **423**
Reaflac, **48**, 17; **122**, 24; **128**, 16; **130**, 6; **136**, 28
Reeve '*gerefa*', **4**, 15; **34**, 6; **122**, 14; **240**, 13; **262**, **366**; king's, **138**, 7; **192**, 10; **440**
Refectory (of community) '*beoddern*', grants to, **30**, 24; **174**, 4f.; **210**, 18f., 22; to (refectory) table '*beod*', **10**, 13; **42**, 14. See also *Beodland*
Regl cęsternisce, **72**, 11; **326**
Regula Canonicorum, **228**, 8f.; **478**
Rent. See *Gafol*
Riding (as service), **206**, 6; **452**
Roc 'upper garment', 'vestment', **72**, 8; **194**, 14
Rod 'crucifix', oath sworn upon, **86**, 8
Rogation Days '*gangdagas*', **30**, 27; **206**, 31; **456**
Rymet 'space', **102**, 10ff.; **110**, 11

Sac 'quarrel', **102**, 12; **162**, 26; **413**
Sacan on 'bring a claim against', **162**, 10f.
Salthouse '*s(e)altern*', **16**, 11; **46**, 11; **278**

INDEX RERUM

Sammæle, 128, 3f.; 372, 398
Sanctuary, 316
Sawolsceatt, 26, 7f.; 56, 10; 286
Sceatt 'money', 'price', 106, 15; 148, 8; 180, 7; 188, 4; 202, 9, 21; 450
Sceatte ne wið ceape, wið nanan, 'neither for money nor for kind' (?), 70, 5
Sceppe 'bushel', 192, 15ff.; 440
Scipryne 'a channel for ships', 178, 3
Scipwealas 'Welsh sailors', 204, 22; 452
Scir 'exempt', 220, 6
Scir 'parish' (?), 240, 27; 492
Scriftæceras (at harvest), 240, 4; 491
Scrin 'chest', 'reliquary', 194, 22; 226, 24; 242, 6; 476
Scrudfeoh 'money for clothes', 254, 14
Scrudland 'land to provide clothing', 170, 23
Scufrægl 'movable curtains', 194, 20; 442
Sea-fish, 206, 2
Seal 'insegel', 136, 10; 140, 16; 380
Seamen 'scipmen', 144, 18; 389f.
Seat covers, 72, 12; 194, 20; 226, 29
Sedulius, book of, 228, 26; 250, 13; 479
Seed (as tithes), 74, 3ff.
Seht 'settlement', 'agreement', 162, 25, 27; 164, 4; 190, 14, 22; 413; seht (adj.) 'agreed', 212, 9
Seneschal 'discþegn', 136, 19; 148, 3; 394
Sermo super quosdam psalmos, 72, 20; 327
Service, of the church 'cericlic weorc', 62, 6; secular 'eorðlec ðeowdom', 50, 2; 'woruldweorc', 62, 6; 318; 'weoruldcund þeowet', 66, 9; royal and judicial services, 18, 5f.; 278f.; royal and official services, 22, 8f.; 222, 9f. See also Military service
Sester, 12, 15; 38, 23; 58, 25; 206, 15, 21; 240, 6ff.; 248, 22; 272
Sheaves (as tithes), 240, 15
Sheep, 74, 19; 154, 7; 156, 12; 192, 16; 196, 15; 248, 21; 256, 5, 12; pasture for, 202, 19; 240, 8ff.; washing and shearing of, 206, 29; two young sheep equivalent to a full-grown one, 206, 28f.

Shepherd, payment to, 256, 8
Sheriff 'scir(es)man', 'scirge. efa', 86, 3, 9; 140, 20; 142, 7, 13; 150, 10; 152, 1; 186, 12; 212, 17f.; 334
Ships, remission of dues on, 2, 3f., 11; 260; purchase of, 252, 16, 21; 254, 4f.; value of, 252, 23f.
Shire-moot, 136, 9; 150, 23; 152, 3ff.; 162, 12
Sibbe 7 to some, to 'for the sake of peace and concord', 102, 23
Silver, as treasure-trove, 160, 3
Sinodlic gemot, 8, 4; 266
Sker 7 sacleas, 240, 2; 491
Slæg(h)ryðer 'bullock for slaughtering', 192, 16; 440
Slaves, grant of, 150, 6; 154, 6f.; 254, 21
Slegneat 'cattle for slaughter', 12, 11; 272
Smean 'delicacies', 74, 20; 329
Smith, value of, 254, 18f.
Snæd, 28, 26; 290
Snasa 'sticks (of eels)', 256, 16ff.; 505
Socn, sac and soc 'jurisdiction', 'soke', 24, 14; 100, 23ff.; 112, 6, 15; 140, 4f.; 146, 5; 164, 23; 168, 14; 178, 26; 218, 17; 240, 2; 347, 384, 414
Socnland 'soke-lands', 166, 17; 168, 1
Sows, 254, 30; 256, 2ff.; 504
Spræc '(verbal) agreement', 4, 23; 263
Spreot 'pole', 158, 29; 408
Standards 'guðfana', 228, 1; 477
Statius, glosses of, 228, 27; 479
Sticca 'pieces of land', 80, 21; 331; 'sticks (of eels)', 256, 26
Stoles, 72, 8; 194, 18
Stottas 'inferior horses', 196, 15; 446
Strand 'shore-(dues)' (?), 176, 22
Stream 'water-(dues)' (?), 176, 22
Sturgeon, 206, 2
Subumbrale 'subucula', 72, 9; 326
Suit 'sp(r)æc', 8, 7; 92, 11, 24; 140, 15, 22; 150, 3; 162, 12; 164, 2; to sue 'sp(r)ecan æfter, on', 138, 2; 140, 13f.; 152, 4, 12; to owe suit to 'secan into', 74, 2

INDEX RERUM

Sulung 'ploughland', 6, 1; 16, 7f.; 84, 1; 190, 17; 269
Summer book '*sumerboc*', 194, 24
Superhumerals, 194, 19; 442
Sustenance of a religious community, grants for '*to bigleofan*', 98, 24; 174, 4; 226, 13; *to fodnoðe*, 214, 6. *See also Beodland, Fosterland,* Refectory
Swan 'swineherd', 254, 1, 3
Swangerefa, 8, 9, 20; 267
Swine, 38, 26; 74, 19; 196, 17, 25; 198, 27, 31; 200, 10; 206, 17f.; 240, 6; 248, 20; 252, 6; 254, 1ff.; 256, 1ff.; pasture for, 8, 12; 240, 10
Sword, 92, 7; 338
Swurrod 'neck-cross', 226, 23
Syflincge 'relish', 192, 21
Synod, 130, 7

Talu '(statement of a) claim', 122, 27; 140, 15; 152, 8, 12; 366, 384, 401
Taperæx, 158, 21; 408
Tax-gatherers '*nedbaderas*', 2, 12f.
Team 'vouching to warranty', 90, 4; 122, 27; 156, 9; 240, 3; 336, 366, 405
Te(a)mbyrste 'failure of *team*', 90, 8
Pegenland, 240, 19; 492
Thegns, grant of, 46, 10f.; as deputies from shire-moot, 152, 8f.; oath of, 164, 1; as witnesses, 44, 10; 106, 21; 150, 20; 216, 21; of Dorset, 148, 1f.; of East Kent and West Kent, 140, 17, 21; of Gloucestershire, 172, 11f.; of Hampshire, 202, 12, 23f.; 212, 19f.; of Herefordshire, 152, 2f.; 186, 12; of Worcestershire, both English and Danish, 180, 22f.; 208, 13f.; 210, 8f.
Peowdom. *See* Service
Thieves, arrest of '*ðeoffeng*', 18, 6; 222, 10; 279, 282
Thrave, 74, 7; 328
Timberlond, 46, 13
Tithes, 56, 10; 74, 2ff.; 156, 8; 236, 28; 240, 14ff.; 286, 404, 486
Toft 'homestead', 76, 17; 78, 3
Toll, 156, 9; 158, 25; 174, 22; 176, 28; 240, 2; 260, 405, 408

Trading dues (?) '*ciyping*' (for *ceaping*), 92, 26; 340
Treasure house '*madmhus*', 194, 17
Trivet, 74, 22
Tropere 'book of tropes', 228, 5; 250, 16, 19; 477
Troughs, 74, 22
Tube '*pipe*', 72, 7; 226, 25; 476
Tubs, 74, 22
Tun 'manor', 44, 11; 52, 9; 74, 5, 8; 96, 4; 110, 22; 112, 1; 166, 9; 208, 2, 22; 218, 17; 308; 'town', 62, 5; 92, 26
Tungan, on halre 'unequivocally', 24, 11; 84, 10; 92, 2; 284, 338
Twelfhynde men ge twyhynde, ægper ge, 92, 22; 340

Unagæn (of lease) 'not lapsed', 28, 27f.; 290
Uncontested '*unbecweden*', 92, 14; '*unbesacen*', 36, 21, 23; 40, 8; 138, 1; 142, 3; 154, 18; 162, 6, 14; 164, 6; 166, 16; 200, 18; *unbesprecen*, 60, 29
Uncræft 'evil practice', 104, 25
Undisputed '*unbefliten*', 6, 17; 14, 9; 28, 7; 200, 18; '*buton ælcum geflite*', 36, 25
Unopposed '*unforboden*', 92, 14; 162, 6, 14
Unwered (of land) 'which has not paid geld', 232, 20ff.; 236, 4ff.
Utanburhware, 60, 21f.; 316f.
Utware, 156, 4; 404

Vita Eustachii, 72, 19; 327
Vita Sancti Felicis, in verse, 72, 18; 326

Wagons, purchase of, 254, 3
Wall curtains, 72, 12; 194, 20; 226, 29; 477
Walls, construction of, 86, 20; 96, 12; 114, 11; 134, 13; 138, 20; 180, 10; 210, 10
Wapentake, 76, 29; 331
Watercourse '*weterscype*', 102, 25
Water dues, 158, 17f. *See also Stream*
Water vessel '*waterfet*', 72, 6
Wax, 252, 4
Weal(l)stillinge, 246, 23, 26; 248, 2ff.; 496
Weapons, as treasure-trove, 160, 2

INDEX RERUM

Wedd 'pledge', 'security', **82**, 27; **122**, 27; **330, 332**
Week-work, **206**, 8, 30; **453**f., **456**
Weir, **46**, 8ff.; **204**, 27; **256**, 10ff.; **504**; keeper of, **46**, 10; weir-building (as service), **206**, 10
Weorcland, **166**, 7f.; **415**
Weorcwyrðe (of men) 'able-bodied' (?), **72**, 28; **74**, 17f.; **248**, 19; **328, 497**
Wergeld '*wer*', **90**, 7, 11, 23; **92**, 9; **128**, 16ff.; **136**, 29; **337, 339**
Werian (of land) 'defend', 'discharge the obligations upon', 'pay geld', **70**, 1, 17; **208**, 19; **230**, 12ff.; **232**, 2ff.; **234**, 2ff.; **236**, 2ff.; **325, 460**
Wethers, **38**, 25; **58**, 25
Wey, **170**, 13; **240**, 5; **420, 455**
Wharf, **176**, 32
Wheat, **192**, 15; **196**, 35; **198**, 24, 31; **200**, 9; as church dues, **30**, 10f.; as tithes, **74**, 4

Wheat-growing land '*hwæteland*', **114**, 6
Winterstellas 'year-old stallions', **74**, 23; **329**
Witan 'council', 'councillors', **8**, 6ff. and *passim*
Woman, payment for, **256**, 9; theft of, **90**, 1; value of, **252**, 18; women included in inventory, **74**, 18
Wood(land) '*wudu*', **8**, 9, 13; **12**, 18; **16**, 11; **64**, 18; **76**, 13, 25; **78**, 24; **80**, 20, 22; **88**, 8; **116**, 21; **120**, 15; **134**, 7; **240**, 10ff.; right of cutting wood '*wuduræddenne*', **28**, 23f.; right of carting wood, **278**
Wood-pasture '*wuduleswe*', **8**, 8
Worðig 'homestead', **134**, 28

Yardland. *See* Gierd
Yoke (of land) '*gioc*', **10**, 20; **269**
Yokes, building of, **206**, 11; **453**